Eclipse

Building Comme

eclipse

SERIES EDITORS   Erich Gamma ▪ Lee Nackman ▪ John Wiegand

Eclipse is a universal tool platform, an open extensible integrated development environment (IDE) for anything and nothing in particular. Eclipse represents one of the most exciting initiatives hatched from the world of application development in a long time, and it has the considerable support of the leading companies and organizations in the technology sector. Eclipse is gaining widespread acceptance in both the commercial and academic arenas.

The Eclipse Series from Addison-Wesley is the definitive series of books dedicated to the Eclipse platform. Books in the series promise to bring you the key technical information you need to analyze Eclipse, high-quality insight into this powerful technology, and the practical advice you need to build tools to support this evolutionary Open Source platform. Leading experts Erich Gamma, Lee Nackman, and John Wiegand are the series editors.

Titles in the Eclipse Series

John Arthorne and Chris Laffra, *Official Eclipse 3.0 FAQs*, 0-321-26838-5

Kent Beck and Erich Gamma, *Contributing to Eclipse: Principles, Patterns, and Plug-Ins*, 0-321-20575-8

Frank Budinsky, David Steinberg, Ed Merks, Ray Ellersick, and Timothy J. Grose, *Eclipse Modeling Framework*, 0-131-42542-0

Eric Clayberg and Dan Rubel, *Eclipse: Building Commercial-Quality Plug-Ins*, 0-321-22847-2

Steve Northover and Mike Wilson, *SWT: The Standard Widget Toolkit, Volume 1*, 0-321-25663-8

Eclipse
Building Commercial-Quality Plug-ins

Eric Clayberg
Dan Rubel

⋏⋏Addison-Wesley

Boston • San Francisco • New York • Toronto • Montreal
London • Munich • Paris • Madrid
Capetown • Sydney • Tokyo • Singapore • Mexico City

Many of the designations used by manufacturers and sellers to distinguish their products are claimed as trademarks. Where those designations appear in this book, and Addison-Wesley was aware of a trademark claim, the designations have been printed with initial capital letters or in all capitals.

The authors and publisher have taken care in the preparation of this book, but make no expressed or implied warranty of any kind and assume no responsibility for errors or omissions. No liability is assumed for incidental or consequential damages in connection with or arising out of the use of the information or programs contained herein.

The publisher offers discounts on this book when ordered in quantity for bulk purchases and special sales. For more information, please contact:

U.S. Corporate and Government Sales
(800) 382-3419
corpsales@pearsontechgroup.com

For sales outside of the U.S., please contact:

International Sales
(317) 581-3793
international@pearsontechgroup.com

Visit Addison-Wesley on the Web: www.awprofessional.com

Library of Congress Cataloging-in-Publication Data

A CIP catalog record for this book can be obtained from the Library of Congress.

ISBN: 0-321-122847-2

Text printed on recycled paper

First printing

To our wives, Karen and Kathy,
and our children, Beth, Lauren, Lee, and David.

Contents

Chapter 2 A Simple Plug-in Example   83

Chapter 3 Eclipse Infrastructure   129

Chapter 4 The Standard Widget Toolkit   155

Foreword

To the millions of developers, engineers, and users all over the world, Eclipse is an extensible platform for tool integration. To the hundreds of thousands of commercial customers using Eclipse to develop plug-ins or complete tool platforms, Eclipse represents a proven, reliable, scaleable technology upon which commercial products can be quickly designed, developed, and deployed.

To the thousands of students and researchers, Eclipse represents a stable platform to innovation, freedom, and experimentation. To all these individuals, groups, and organizations, Eclipse is a vendor-neutral platform to tool integration supported by a diverse Eclipse Ecosystem.

The Eclipse vendor-neutral platform is built on industry standards, which support a wide range of tools, platforms, and languages. The Eclipse Technology is royalty-free and has worldwide redistribution rights. The Platform was designed from a clean slate to be extensible and to provide exemplarity tools. Eclipse development is based upon rules of open source engagements. This includes open, transparent, merit-based, and collaborative development. All individuals can participate and contribute. All plans are developed in the public. This platform and the open source development process creates an environment for creativity, originality, and freedom. Eclipse is unparalleled in the software-tool environment today.

The software-tool industry is undergoing massive changes from the commoditization of the technology to the company consolidation. New technology efforts are being redesigned, while a common set of tooling infrastructure is adopted as an industry standard. Successful developers and development paradigms are being challenged to adopt new skills and new, more efficient methods. Old business models are being challenged with free software. New business models are being developed.

The software-tool industry is deeply appreciative of Eric Clayberg and Dan Rubel for this authoritative book. This book provides the knowledge base so that developers, engineers, and users can learn and utilize the Eclipse Technology. This enables them to respond to these technology and industry change agents.

Eric and Dan leverage long careers of building software tooling. They each have extensive experience with using Smalltalk for 15 years, Java for eight years, and Eclipse for four years. They have developed extensive vendor and customer relationships that enable them to experience first-hand the necessary elements for building successful software. They are able to combine this direct knowledge of the technology with the experience from the users to create a book that provides an in-depth description of the process to build commercial quality Eclipse extensions.

This book provides an introduction and overview to the new developer of the entire process of plug-in development, including all of the best practices to achieve high quality results. This is a reference book to experienced Eclipse developers. It discusses the APIs and demonstrates many samples and examples. Detailed tutorials are provided for both the new and experienced developers. Eric and Dan leverage their broad knowledge of User Interface development and present the Eclipse SWT UI. This establishes the building blocks for all Eclipse user interface development. These authors articulate the development challenges of building tool software and establish proven in-depth solutions to these problems.

If you are a developer, engineer, or user wishing to build or use Eclipse, this book provides both a foundation and reference. This book provided the intellectual foundation to contribute to the open source Eclipse project and to develop commercial software.

—Skip McGaughey

Foreword

In the 1990s, when Java was in its infancy, learning the Java class libraries involved studying a handful of classes in four or five packages. The Java class libraries have grown in size and complexity, presenting a significant problem to developers wishing to learn Java today. Just like Java, the Eclipse platform has necessarily grown over the years, and therefore, considerably more time and effort is required to learn Eclipse 3.0 than its predecessors. One of the principles of the Eclipse platform is that a plug-in should integrate seamlessly with the workbench and with other plug-ins. To achieve seamless integration, it is necessary for plug-in developers to understand the best practices, conventions and strategies related to building software for Eclipse. *Eclipse: Building Commercial Quality Plug-ins* covers everything you need to know to develop Eclipse plug-ins of which you will be proud.

Through the development of a **Favorites** plug-in, the Eclipse Standard Widget Toolkit (SWT) and JFace frameworks are thoroughly discussed, teaching you how to build professional-looking user interfaces such as views, editors, preferences pages, and dialogs. In addition to stock-in-trade subjects, such as user interface design, lesser-understood Eclipse topics, such as building features and product branding, are extensively covered, as well as the best discussion I have seen on using Ant to build a product from a single source that targets multiple versions of Eclipse.

Java developers new to Eclipse often have difficulty understanding the extension point mechanism and the critical link between a plug-in's declarative manifest and the Java code necessary to implement a plug-in's functional behavior. *Eclipse: Building Commercial Quality Plug-ins* serves as a roadmap to using the Plug-in Development Environment (PDE) and the extension points defined by the Eclipse platform. This book provides the missing link that a developer needs to understand the aspects of a plug-in that should be described in the manifest, how to develop a plug-in using existing extension points, and how to contribute extension points of their own through which other developers may further contribute.

When I first saw CodePro Studio I was both impressed with the productivity gains it brought to Eclipse and the extent to which its plug-ins integrated with the Eclipse platform. Having used CodePro Studio for a while, it has become a part of my development toolkit that I cannot do without. By drawing on their extensive experience gained while developing CodePro Studio, Eric and Dan have done an excellent job at capturing in this book those aspects of plug-in development necessary to create a high-quality and professional-looking Eclipse product.

—Simon Archer

Preface

When we were first exposed to Eclipse back in late 1999, we were struck by the magnitude of the problem IBM was trying to solve. IBM wanted to unify all of its development environments on a single code base. At the time, the company was using a mix of technology composed of a hodgepodge of C/C++, Java, and Smalltalk.

Many of IBM's most important tools, including the award-winning Visual-Age for Java IDE, were actually written in Smalltalk—a wonderful language for building sophisticated tools, but one that was rapidly losing market share to languages like Java. While IBM had one of the world's largest collections of Smalltalk developers, there wasn't a great deal of industry support for it outside of IBM, and there were very few independent software vendors (ISVs) qualified to create Smalltalk-based add-ons.

Meanwhile, Java was winning the hearts and minds of developers worldwide with its promise of easy portability across a wide range of platforms, while providing the rich application programming interface (API) needed to build the latest generation of Web-based business applications. More importantly, Java was an object-oriented (OO) language, which meant that IBM could leverage the large body of highly skilled object-oriented developers it had built up over the years of creating Smalltalk-based tools. In fact, IBM took its premiere Object Technology International (OTI) group, which had been responsible for creating IBM's VisualAge Smalltalk and VisualAge Java environments (VisualAge Smalltalk was the first of the VisualAge brand family and VisualAge Java was built using it), and tasked it with creating a highly extensible integrated development environment (IDE) construction set based in Java. Eclipse was the happy result.

OTI was able to apply its highly evolved OO skills to produce an IDE unmatched in power, flexibility, and extensibility. The group was able to replicate most of the features that had made Smalltalk-based IDEs so popular the decade before, while simultaneously pushing the state-of-the-art in IDE development ahead by an order of magnitude.

The Java world had never seen anything as powerful or as compelling as Eclipse, and it now stands, with Microsoft's .NET, as one of the world's premier development environments. That alone makes Eclipse a perfect platform for developers wishing to get their tools out to as wide an audience as possible. The fact that Eclipse is completely free and open source is icing on the cake. An open, extensible IDE base that is available for free to anyone with a computer is a powerful motivator to the prospective tool developer.

It certainly was to us. At Instantiations and earlier at ObjectShare, we had spent the better part of a decade as entrepreneurs focused on building add-on tools for various IDEs. We had started with building add-ons to Digitalk's Smalltalk/V, migrated to developing tools for IBM's VisualAge Smalltalk, and eventually ended up creating tools for IBM's VisualAge Java (including our award-winning VA Assist product and our jFactor product, one of the world's first Java refactoring tools). Every one of these environments provided a means to extend the IDE, but they were generally not well-documented and certainly not standardized in any way. Small market shares (relative to tools such as VisualBasic) and an eclectic user base also afflicted these environments and, by extension, us.

As an Advanced IBM Business Partner, we were fortunate to have built a long and trusted relationship with the folks at IBM responsible for the creation of Eclipse. That relationship meant that we were in a unique position to be briefed on the technology and start using it on a daily basis nearly a year and half before the rest of the world even heard about it. When IBM finally announced Eclipse to the world in mid-2001, our team at Instantiations had built some of the first demo applications IBM had to show. Later that year when IBM released its first Eclipse-based commercial tool, WebSphere Studio Application Developer v4.0 (v4.0 so that it synchronized with its then current VisualAge for Java v4.0), our CodePro Studio product became the very first commercial add-on available for it (and for Eclipse in general) on the same day.

Our CodePro product currently adds hundreds of enhancements to Eclipse and any Eclipse-based IDE. Developing CodePro over the last several years has provided us with an opportunity to learn the details of Eclipse development at a level matched by very few others (with the obvious exception of the developers at IBM and OTI, who eat, sleep, and breathe this stuff on a daily basis). CodePro has also served as a testbed for many of the ideas and techniques presented in this book, providing us with a unique perspective from which to write.

Goals of the Book

This book provides an in-depth description of the process involved in building commercial-quality extensions for the Eclipse and WebSphere Studio Workbench (IBM's commercial version of Eclipse) development environments. To us, "commercial-quality" is synonymous with "commercial-grade" or "high–quality." Producing a "commercial-quality" plug-in means going above and beyond the minimal requirements needed to integrate with Eclipse. It means attending to all of those details contributing to the "fit and polish" of a commercial offering.

In the world of Eclipse plug-ins, very few people take the time to really go the extra mile, and most plug-ins fall into the open source, amateur category. For folks interested in producing high-quality plug-ins (which would certainly be the case for any software company wanting to develop Eclipse-based products), there are many additional steps to follow. Our book is meant to encompass the entire process of plug-in development, including all the extra things that need to be done to achieve high-quality results.

This book has several complementary goals:

- Provide a quick introduction to using Eclipse for new users
- Provide a reference for experienced Eclipse users wishing to expand their knowledge and improve the quality of their Eclipse-based products
- Provide a detailed tutorial on creating sophisticated Eclipse plug-ins suitable for new and experienced users alike

The first three chapters introduce the Eclipse development environment and outline the process of building a simple plug-in. The intention of these chapters is to help developers new to Eclipse quickly pull together a plug-in they can use to experiment with.

The first chapter, in particular, introduces the reader to the minimum set of Eclipse tools that he or she will need to build plug-ins. It is a fairly quick overview of the Eclipse IDE and relevant tools (one could write an entire book on that topic alone), and we would expect expert Eclipse users to skip that chapter entirely.

The second chapter introduces the example that we will use throughout most of the book and provides a very quick introduction to building a working plug-in from start to finish. The third chapter presents a high-level overview of the Eclipse architecture and the structure of plug-ins and extension points.

The fourth and fifth chapters of the book cover the Standard Widget Toolkit (SWT) and JFace, which are the building blocks for all Eclipse user interfaces (UIs). These chapters can act as a standalone reference; they are intended to provide just enough detail to get you going. Both of these topics are rich enough to warrant entire books and many no doubt are in the works.

The subsequent chapters, comprising the bulk of the book, are focused on describing each of the various aspects of plug-in development and providing the reader with in-depth knowledge of how to solve the various challenges involved. Each chapter focuses on a different aspect of the problem, and include an overview, a detailed description, a discussion of challenges and solutions, diagrams, screen shots, cookbook-style code examples, relevant API listings, and a summary.

We have structured the book so that the most important material required for every plug-in project appears in the first half of the book. Some of the packaging- and building-oriented material is placed at the end (like features and product build). This organizational scheme left several topics that, while not critical to every plug-in, were important to the creation of "commercial-quality" plug-ins. These topics were then placed in the second half of the book in an order based on the importance of the topic and how it related to earlier material. Internationalization, for example, is one of those topics. It isn't critical, and it isn't even all that complicated when you get right down to it. It is important to the premise of this book, so we felt it was a topic we needed to include. Since we aren't assuming that the reader is an Eclipse expert (or even a plug-in developer), we tried to take the reader through each of the important steps in as much detail as possible. While it is true that this is somewhat introductory, it is also an area that most plug-in developers totally ignore and have little or no experience with.

Sometimes a developer needs a quick solution, while at other times that same developer needs to gain in-depth knowledge on a particular aspect of development. The intent is to provide several different ways for the reader to absorb and use the information so that both needs can be addressed. Relevant APIs are included in several of the chapters so that the book may be used as a standalone reference during development without requiring the reader to look up those APIs in the IDE. Most API descriptions are copied or paraphrased from the Eclipse platform Javadoc.

As the originators of Eclipse and a major consumer of Eclipse-based technology, IBM is justifiably concerned that new plug-ins meet the same high-quality standards that IBM adheres to. To that end, IBM has established a rigorous "Ready for WebSphere Studio" (RFWS) certification program meant to insure the availability of high-quality add-ons to Eclipse and WebSphere Studio Workbench (WSW). RFWS certification should be one of the ultimate goals for anyone wishing to build and market Eclipse plug-ins. In each chapter, we will cover any relevant RFWS certification criteria and strategies.

The examples provided as part of each chapter describe building various aspects of a concrete Eclipse plug-in that you will see evolve over the course of the book. When this book is used as a reference rather than read cover-to-cover, you will typically start to look in one chapter for issues that are covered in another. To facilitate this type of searching, each chapter will contain numerous forward and backward references to related material that appears in other chapters.

Intended Audience

The audience for this book includes Java tool developers wishing to build products that integrate with Eclipse and other Eclipse-based products, relatively advanced Eclipse users wishing to customize their environments, or anyone who is curious about what makes Eclipse tick. You do not need to be an expert Eclipse user to make use of this book, as we introduce most of what you need to know to use Eclipse in Chapter 1, "Using Eclipse Tools." While we don't assume any preexisting Eclipse knowledge, we do expect the reader to be a fairly seasoned developer with a good grasp of Java and at least a cursory knowledge of extensible markup language (XML).

Conventions Used in this Book

The following formatting conventions are used throughout the book:

Bold—Used for the names of UI elements such as menus, buttons, field labels, tabs, and window titles.

Italic—Used for emphasizing new terms.

`Courier`—Used for code examples, references to class and method names, and filenames.

`Courier Bold`—Used to emphasize code elements.

"Quoted text"—Used for text to be entered by the user.

Acknowledgements

The authors would like to thank all of those who had a hand in putting this book together or who gave us their support and encouragement through the many months it took to create.

To our comrades at Instantiations, who gave us the time and encouragement to work on the book: Brent Caldwell, Paul Curtis, Mark Johnson, Warren Martin, Steve Messick, Tim O'Conner, Chuck Shawan, Julie Taylor, Mike Taylor, and Brian Wilkerson.

To our agent, Laura Lewin, and the staff at Studio B, who encouraged us from day one and worked tirelessly on our behalf.

To our editor, John Neidhart, our production editor, Kathleen Caren, our copy editor, Camie Goffi, and the staff at Pearson, for their encouragement and tremendous efforts in preparing this book for production.

To Simon Archer, who contributed an unparalleled number of changes and suggestions and helped us improve the book in almost every dimension.

To our technical reviewers, who helped us enhance the book in many ways: Joe Bowbeer, Brian Wilkerson, Joe Winchester, David Whiteman, Boris Pruesmann, and Raphael Enns.

To the series editors, Erich Gamma, Lee Nackman and John Weigand, for their thoughtful comments and for their on-going efforts to make Eclipse the best development environment in the world.

We would also like to thank our wives, Karen and Kathy, for their endless patience, and our children, Beth, Lauren, Lee, and David, for their endless inspiration.

About the Authors

Eric Clayberg is Senior Vice President for Product Development for Instantiations, Inc. Eric is a seasoned software technologist, product developer, entrepreneur, and manager with more than 15 years of commercial software development experience, including seven years of experience with Java and four years with Eclipse. He is the primary author and architect of more than a dozen commercial Java and Smalltalk add-on products, including the popular WindowBuilder Pro, CodePro Studio, and the award-winning VA Assist Enterprise product lines. He has a Bachelor of Science degree from MIT, an MBA from Harvard, and has co-founded two successful software companies.

Dan Rubel is Chief Technology Officer for Instantiations, Inc. He is an entrepreneur and an expert in the design and application of OO technologies with more than 15 years of commercial software development experience, including eight years of experience with Java and four years with Eclipse. He is the primary architect and product manager for several successful commercial products, including JFactor, jKit/GO, and jKit/Grid, and has played key design and leadership roles in other commercial products such as Window-Builder Pro, VA Assist, and CodePro Studio. He has a Bachelor of Science degree from Bucknell and has co-founded a successful company.

Instantiations is an Advanced IBM Business Partner and developer of many commercial add-ons for Eclipse and IBM's VisualAge and WebSphere product lines. Instantiations is a member of the Eclipse Foundation and a contributor to the Eclipse open source effort with responsibility for the Eclipse Collaboration Tools project known as Koi and joint responsibility for the Eclipse Visual Editor project.

How To Contact Us

While we have made every effort to make sure that the material in this book is timely and accurate, Eclipse is a rapidly moving target and it is quite possible that you may encounter differences between what we present in this book and what you experience using Eclipse. The Eclipse UI has evolved considerably over the years, and the latest 3.0 release is no exception. While we have targeted this book at Eclipse 3.0 and used it for all of our examples, this book was completed before Eclipse 3.0 was finally locked down. That means that you may encounter various views, dialogs, and wizards that are subtly different from the screen shots in the book.

- Questions about the book's technical content should be addressed to: *info@qualityeclipse.com*
- Sales questions should be addressed to Addison-Wesley at: *www.aw-bc.com/*
- Source code for the examples presented in the book can be found at: *www.qualityeclipse.com/examples*
- Errata can be found at: *www.qualityeclipse.com/errata*
- Tools used and described in the book may be found at: *www.qualityeclipse.com/tools*

CHAPTER 1

Using Eclipse Tools

This chapter discusses using the Eclipse development environment to create Java applications and, more to the point, to create enhancements for Eclipse itself. We start with an explanation of where to get Eclipse and how to set it up. This is followed by a quick introduction to the Eclipse user interface (UI) and how it can be customized. Next, this chapter introduces a number of important Eclipse tools and describes how they are used to create an initial Java project, navigate and search the environment, and create and edit Java code. Eclipse developers typically want to work as part of a team and share their code with other members of their team, so this chapter also includes the setup and use of the Concurrent Versions System (CVS), which ships as part of Eclipse. After creating an initial Java project and class, we follow up with details for executing, debugging, and testing the code that has been written.

1.1 Getting Started

Before using Eclipse, download it from the Web, install it, and set it up.

1.1.1 Getting Eclipse

The main Web site for Eclipse is *www.eclipse.org/* (see Figure 1–1). On that page, you can see the latest Eclipse news and links to a variety of online resources, including articles, newsgroups, bug tracking (see Section 20.2.2, "Bugzilla—Eclipse bug tracking system"), and mailing lists.

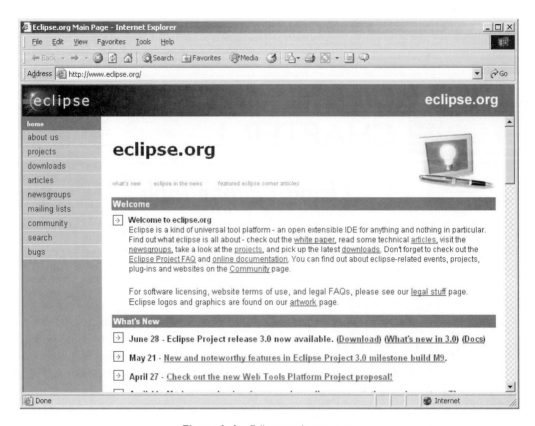

Figure 1–1   Eclipse.org home page.

The latest version of Eclipse can be downloaded from the main download page at *www.eclipse.org/downloads* (if the main download site is unavailable, a number of mirror sites around the world are available). Go ahead and download the latest release or stable build (also known as a *milestone*, as in Eclipse 3.0 M9). Typically, you should avoid the *integration* or *nightly* builds unless you are involved in the development of Eclipse itself.

The download page for each release includes various notes concerning that release as well as links to each platform version. Eclipse supports a large number of platforms, including Windows, Linux, Solaris, HP, Mac OSX, and others. Choose the **Eclipse SDK** download link corresponding to your platform and save the Eclipse zip file to your computer's hard drive. This will generally be a very large file (>85 MB), so be patient unless you have sufficient bandwidth available.

The download page includes a variety of other download links. You might also want to download the **Example plug-ins** file corresponding to your platform. Unless you have a specific need for one of the other downloads, you should ignore them.

> **Java Run-time Environment**   Eclipse is a Java program, but it does not include the Java Run-time Environment (JRE) necessary to make it run. Eclipse 3.0 can be used with any JRE newer than version 1.4, and most Java developers will already have a suitable JRE installed on their machines. If you don't have a JRE installed on your computer, you can download and install one from *java.sun.com*.

1.1.2   Installation

Once the Eclipse zip file has been successfully downloaded, unzip it to your hard drive. Eclipse does not modify the Windows registry, so it does not matter where it is installed. For the purposes of this book, we assume that it has been installed into `C:\eclipse`. If you also downloaded any Eclipse examples, unzip them into the same location.

1.2   The Eclipse Workbench

To start Eclipse, double-click on the `eclipse.exe` file in the `C:\eclipse` directory. The first time Eclipse is launched, it displays a dialog in which you can select the location for your workspace directory (typically a directory underneath the main Eclipse directory). To avoid seeing this dialog every time you start Eclipse, check the **Use this as the default and do not ask again** option.

> **Tip:** Creating a shortcut for launching Eclipse provides a way to specify an alternative workspace directory as well as increases the amount of memory allocated to the program. For example:

```
C:\eclipse\eclipse.exe -data C:\MyWorkspace -vmargs -Xms128M -Xmx256M
```

> In this example, the workspace has been set to `C:\MyWorkspace`, the starting amount of memory to 128 MB, and the maximum amount of memory to 256 MB. Setting the workspace location is essential if you plan to migrate to newer versions of Eclipse in the future. A complete list of these and other command-line switches such as -vm and -showlocation, can be found in the online help (see Chapter 15, "Implementing Help") under **Workbench User Guide > Tasks > Running Eclipse**. For more on memory usage, see *www.qualityeclipse.com/doc/memory.html*.

In a few moments, the main Eclipse workbench window appears (see Figure 1–2). Normally, it consists of a main menu bar and toolbar as well as a number of tiled panes known as views and editors (these will be discussed in great detail in Chapters 7, "Views," and 8, "Editors"). Initially, only a full-screen welcome page, known as the **Intro** view, is visible and fills the entire workbench window.

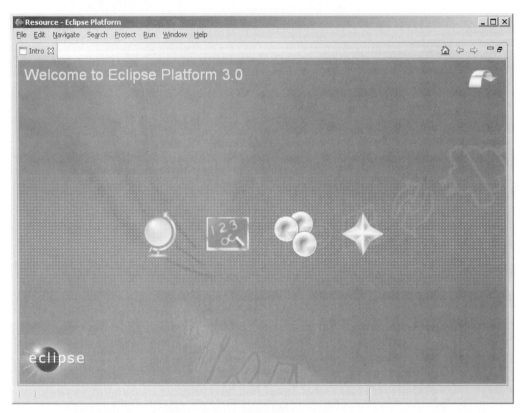

Figure 1–2 Eclipse workbench window.

The **Intro** view is opened automatically the first time Eclipse is launched (it can be reopened again at any time by using the **Help > Introduction** command). Take a moment to look it over as it provides links to other tools and resources to get you started with Eclipse such as an overview, tutorial, and list of sample applications. Closing the **Intro** view (by clicking the "x" button on its title tab) will reveal several additional views (see Figure 1–3).

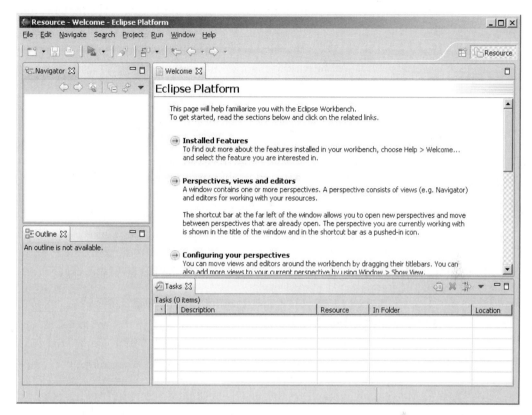

Figure 1–3   Workbench window with the Navigator view active.

1.2.1   Perspectives, views, and editors

Collectively, the various views (e.g., **Navigator, Outline,** and **Tasks**) and editors (used to work with various resources) visible within the Eclipse workbench are known as a *perspective*. A perspective can be thought of as one page within the Eclipse workbench. Multiple perspectives may be open at one time, and each has an icon (with or without a text description) visible in the perspective toolbar at the upper right corner of the workbench window. The perspective that is currently active has its name shown in the title bar of the window and its icon appears pressed.

Views are typically used to navigate resources and modify properties of a resource. Any changes made within a view are saved immediately. By contrast, editors are used to view or modify a specific resource and follow the common open-save-close model.

Each perspective has its own set of views, but open editors are shared by all open perspectives. Only a single instance of any one view may be open in a given perspective, while any number of editors of the same type may be open at one time.

The currently active view or editor has its title bar highlighted. This is the view or editor that will be the recipient of any global actions such as cut, copy, or paste. All the other panes are inactive and their title bars appear gray. For instance, when you click on the **Navigator** view, its title bar becomes highlighted, indicating that it is active (see Figure 1–3), and the title bar of the welcome page turns gray, indicating that it is now inactive.

Views and editors can be resized by dragging the sizing border that appears on each side of the pane. Since Eclipse uses a tiled display for each of its panes, making one larger makes its neighbors smaller, and vice versa.

Panes can be moved around by dragging their individual title bars. If you drag a view onto another view, the two views will stack up with tabs indicating each of the views. Selecting a tab brings that view to the top of that stack. If a view is dropped into the sizing area between views, the view grabs a portion of the available area and inserts itself next to the view that previously occupied that space. The views that originally occupied that space shrink in size to accommodate the new view.

Right-clicking on a view's tab and selecting the **Fast View** command caused the view to dock to the *fast view* bar at the bottom edge of the window (you can drag the fast view bar to the left or right side of the window as well). Fast views remain docked to the fast view bar as icons until clicked on, at which point they expand to overlap most of the window area. Fast views are ideal for views that don't need to be seen all the time, but require a great deal of screen area when they are visible.

Many different views are defined within Eclipse and only a few of them are initially visible when the workbench first opens. To add views to a perspective, select the **Window > Show View** command and choose the view you would like to see (or the **Other…** command to see a list of all views defined in the system).

1.2.1.1   *Resource perspective*

At this point, we should quickly review the various perspectives you are most likely to use while developing plug-ins. The initial perspective shown in the workbench window is the **Resource** perspective (see Figure 1–2).

The primary view with the **Resource** perspective is the **Navigator** view. The **Navigator** presents a hierarchical view of the resources (projects, folders, and files) loaded in the workbench. The **Navigator** has its own toolbar and view menu (see Figure 1–4) that provide various viewing and filtering options.

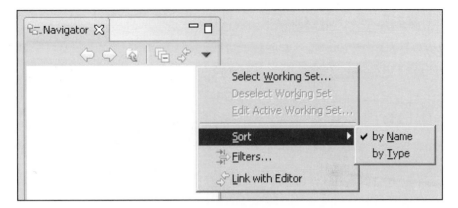

Figure 1–4   The Navigator view.

> **Tip:** Many third-party plug-ins are available, providing enhancements to the various Eclipse perspectives. For example, CodePro Studio (see Appendix A, "Eclipse Plug-ins and Resources") provides color-enhanced versions of the main Eclipse perspectives and views.

1.2.1.2   Java perspectives

While the **Resource** perspective provides a nice, general way to look at the resources in a system, it is not the ideal perspective to use for general Java development. Eclipse includes two different perspectives optimized for the development of Java code. Selecting the **Window > Open Perspective > Java** command (see Figure 1–5) opens the first, known as the **Java** perspective (see Figure 1–6).

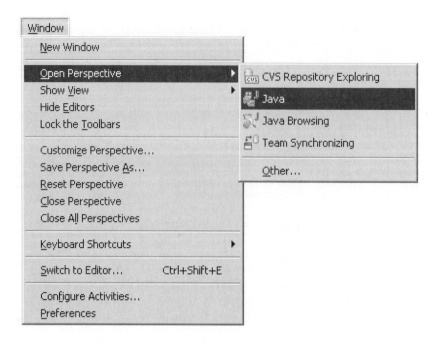

Figure 1–5   Opening the Java perspective.

The primary view within the Java perspective is the **Package Explorer**. The **Package Explorer** shows the hierarchy of Java files and resources within the Java projects loaded into your workbench, providing a very Java-centric view of resources rather than a file-centric view. For example, rather than showing Java packages as nested folders as in the **Navigator** view, the **Package Explorer** shows each package as a separate element in a flattened hierarchy. Any JAR file that is referenced within a project may also be browsed this way.

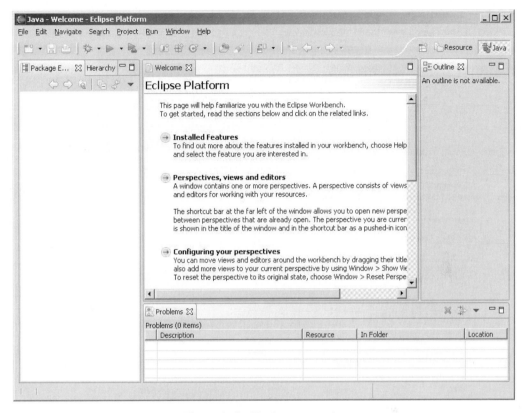

Figure 1–6   The Java perspective.

The second major Java perspective is the **Java Browsing** perspective. Selecting the **Window > Open Perspective > Java Browsing** command opens the Java Browsing perspective (see Figure 1–7).

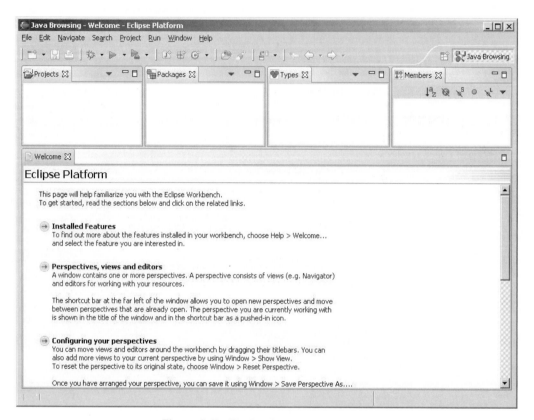

Figure 1–7   The Java Browsing perspective.

The **Java Browsing** perspective includes a series of linked views reminiscent of the browsers found in various Smalltalk integrated development environments (IDEs) or within IBM's VisualAge for Java IDE. The first view shows a list of loaded projects. Selecting a project shows its contained packages within the **Packages** view; selecting a package shows its types in the **Types** view; and selecting a type shows its members in the **Members** view.

> **Tip:** You can easily drag the individual views around to customize the layout to your individual taste. To get more vertical real estate associated with the editor area, consider stacking the four views vertically. Another common way to save some space in this perspective is to combine the **Projects** and **Packages** views into a single tabbed area, or drag the Projects view onto the fast view bar.

1.2.1.3   Debug perspective

Each perspective shown so far has been optimized for the purpose of writing code or editing resources. The next most common type of perspective that you will encounter is the **Debug** perspective, which you may access by selecting the **Window > Open Perspective > Debug** command (see Figure 1–8).

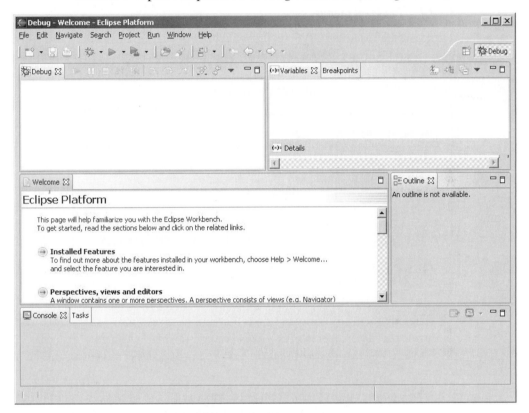

Figure 1–8   The Debug perspective.

As its name suggests, the **Debug** perspective is used to debug programs and easily find and correct run-time errors in Java code. You can step through individual statements within your code, set breakpoints, and inspect the values associated with individual variables. We will discuss this in more detail in Section 1.10.1, "Setting breakpoints."

1.2.2 Actions

In addition to the views and editors that make up the bulk of the display area, Eclipse includes a large number of menus and toolbar buttons that represent the various commands or actions available in the system.

1.2.2.1 Top-level menus

The basic Eclipse menu bar includes eight top-level menus: **File, Edit, Navigate, Search, Project, Run, Window,** and **Help** (see Figure 1–9). Additional menus may also be present depending on which add-on tools you have loaded or which perspectives and views you are using.

Figure 1–9 The Resource perspective menu bar and toolbar.

- The **File** menu provides actions to create new resources, save, close and print resources, refresh resources relative to their associated disk files, import and export resources, inspect the properties of resources, and exit the workbench.

- The **Edit** menu provides actions to work with the resources open in the editor area. It includes standard functions such as cut, copy, and paste as well as functions such as delete, select all, find, and replace.

- The **Navigate** menu provides actions to traverse the resources loaded in the workbench. It provides commands to drill down into resources and then navigate within them much like you would with a Web browser.

- The **Search** menu provides access to workbench-wide search tools such as global file search, help search, Java search, and plug-in search. We will discuss searching in more detail later.

- The **Project** menu provides actions to manipulate the projects loaded in the workbench. You can open any closed project, close any open projects, and manually build either an individual project or all the projects in the workbench.

- The **Run** menu contains perspective-specific items for running or debugging your Java applications. It also includes an **External Tools** option that allows you to run any arbitrary external tool on the resources in your workbench.

- The **Window** menu includes items to open additional workbench windows, open different perspectives, and add any view to the current perspective. It also allows you to customize the current perspective and access preferences for the entire workbench (more on this in the next section).

- The **Help** menu provides access to various tips and tricks, software updates, information about the current workbench configuration, and general help on the entire environment.

1.2.2.2 *Context menus*

Right-clicking on any view or editor (except on the title bar) will reveal a context-sensitive popup menu. The contents of the menu depend not only on the view or editor that was clicked on, but also on the resources that were selected at the time. For example, Figure 1–10 shows three sample context menus. The first sample is the context menu from the **Navigator** view when nothing is selected, the second example is the same context menu when a Java file is selected in the **Navigator**, and the third shows the context menu that appears when a Java file is selected in the **Package Explorer**. Note that some options, such as the **Refactor** submenu, only appear in certain views under the right circumstances.

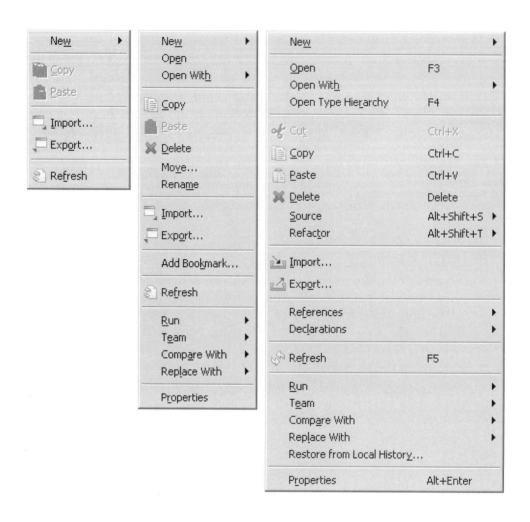

Figure 1–10   Context menus.

1.2.2.3   *Toolbars*

Much like the context menus that appear when right-clicking in a view, the toolbar items that appear are context-sensitive depending on which perspective is in use and which editor has focus. Standard, common items appear first on the toolbar and any editor-specific items at the end. When using the **Resource** perspective, the standard toolbar items that are visible by default include icons for creating new files, saving and printing resources, running external tools, accessing the search functions, and navigating recently accessed resources in browser style (see Figure 1–9).

Figure 1–11   The Java perspective menu bar and toolbar.

Switching to the **Java** perspective (see Figure 1–11) causes several new icons to appear for running or debugging your Java applications and for creating new Java projects, packages, and files.

1.2.2.4   Customizing available actions

You do have some limited control over which items appear on the toolbar and main menu bar. Many commands are part of *command groups* known as *action sets* that can be selectively enabled and disabled using the **Customize Perspective** dialog. To customize the current perspective, select the **Window > Customize Perspective** command, which opens the **Customize Perspective** dialog (see Figure 1–12). The toolbar and menu command groups are shown on the **Commands** page. Check the command groups that you want to keep and uncheck all others. Use the **Shortcuts** page of the dialog to customize the entries on the **New, Open Perspective,** and **Show View** menus.

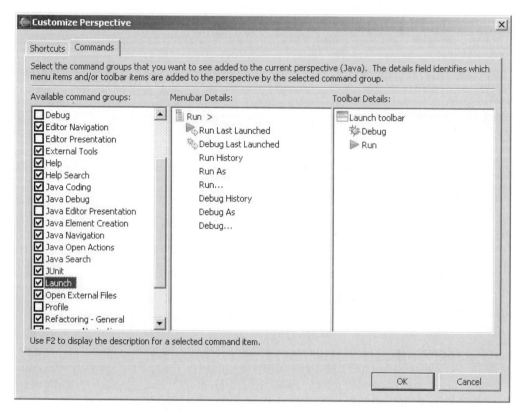

Figure 1–12   Customize Perspective dialog.

1.3   Setting up Your Environment

In the previous section, we briefly touched on customizing the current perspective, while in this section, we will go into more detail on how to customize your Eclipse environment by changing various Eclipse preferences. To customize Eclipse preferences, select the **Window > Preferences** command, which opens the **Preferences** dialog (see Figure 1–13). Dozens of individual preference pages are grouped together in the hierarchy pane on the left side of the dialog. General workbench preferences are in the **Workbench** group, while Java preferences are in the **Java** group.

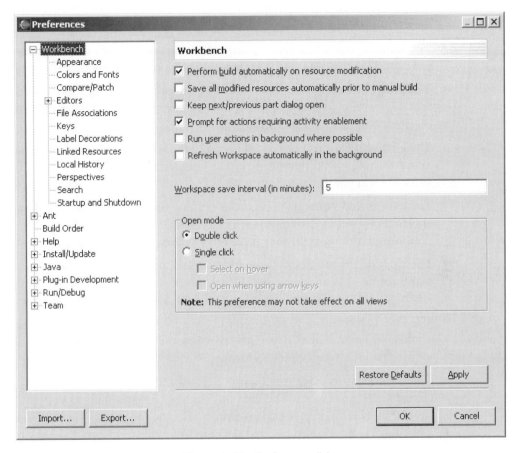

Figure 1–13   Preferences dialog.

Many hundreds of individual preferences can be accessed from the **Preferences** dialog. Changing a value and clicking the **Apply** button will lock in those changes and allow you to continue setting other preferences. Clicking the **OK** button will lock in the changes and close the dialog. The **Restore Defaults** button will reset the preferences on the current page to the system default values.

1.3.1   Workbench preferences

Most general Eclipse preferences can be found in the **Workbench** category. Some highlights include:

- The **Workbench** page provides various global build options and determines whether opening a resource requires single- or double-clicking.

- The **Appearance** page determines whether view and editor tabs appear on the top or bottom.

- The **Editors** page contains a variety of options controlling how editors are opened and closed and how many may be open at one time.

- The **Text Editor** page contains options controlling the appearance of editors such as the visibility of line numbers, current line highlighting, various item colors, and annotations.

- The **File Associations** page associates different editor types (both internal and external) with different file types. For example, if you wanted to associate Microsoft FrontPage with HTML files, you would do that here.

- The **Colors and Fonts** page provides options for customizing the colors and fonts for many different workspace elements such as the standard text font, dialog font, header font, error colors, and many others.

- The **Keys** page provides options for customizing the key bindings for many commands in the system. It includes a predefined standard set of key bindings as well as a set of Emacs key bindings.

- The **Label Decorators** page provides access to options that can enhance an item's icon and label. The **CVS** label decorator, for example, prepends a ">" character to all changed resources.

- The **Local History** page (see Figure 1–51) controls how many local changes are maintained. The default values are fairly small, so you should consider increasing them quite a bit. The more local history you keep, the more type and method versions you will be able to roll back to easily.

- The **Perspectives** page allows you to control which perspective is your default perspective and whether new perspectives are opened in the current window or in a new window.

- The **Startup** page shows a list of any plug-ins requiring early activation. Most plug-ins are activated on first use, but some need to be activated on startup. This page provides the option of preventing those plug-ins from starting up early.

1.3.2 *Java preferences*

Preferences specific to the Java development tools included in Eclipse can be found in the **Java** category of preferences. Some of the highlights include:

- The **Java** page provides options controlling the behavior of various Java views and editors.

- The **Appearance** page controls the appearance of Java elements in the various Java views.

- The **Build Path > Classpath Variables** page (see Figure 1–14) provides a place to define new classpath variables that can be added to a project's classpath.

- The **Code Style > Code Formatter** page (see Figure 1–39) controls the options that the Eclipse Java code formatter uses to format Java code. It includes options for controlling brace position, new lines, line length, and white space usage.

- The **Code Style > Code Templates** page defines the naming conventions and default comments used in generated code for types, methods, fields, variables and parameters.

- The **Compiler** page provides options for controlling the severity levels of various compilation and build path problems as well as various Java Development Kit (JDK) compliance options.

- The **Editor** page controls numerous options dealing with the appearance of elements within the Java editor (such as bracket matching, print margin, and current line highlighting), color highlighting of Java syntax (see Figure 1–38), the behavior and appearance of code assistance (see Figure 1–42), and problem annotations.

- The **Editor > Templates** page provides a place to define and edit various Javadoc and Java code templates (templates are common source code patterns that appear frequently in user-written code).

- The **Installed JREs** page provides options for specifying which JREs should be used with the workbench.

- The **Refactoring** page controls how the execution of various refactorings should be confirmed and whether modified resources should be automatically saved prior to refactoring.

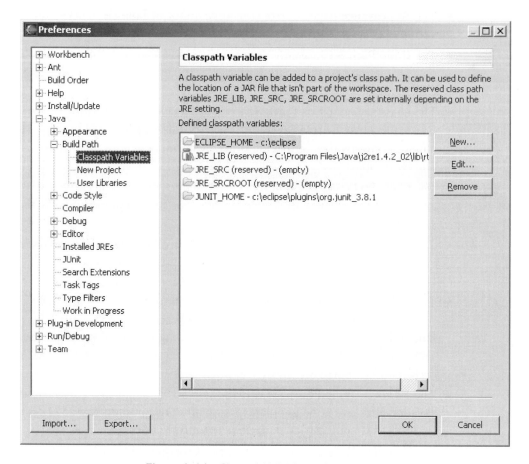

Figure 1–14   Classpath Variables preference page.

1.3.3   Importing and exporting preferences

Setting up multiple Eclipse workspaces or migrating from one Eclipse version to another can be inconvenient due to the difficulty of moving workspace preferences from one version to another. Likewise, configuring multiple users' workspaces with common settings (such as code formatting preferences and classpath variable settings) can also be very difficult.

The Eclipse **Preferences** dialog includes **Import** and **Export** buttons at the bottom of the dialog that are intended to help solve this problem. Clicking the **Export** button prompts for the name of a preference export file (an .epf file) and then records any non-default preference settings in that file. The **Import** button is then used to import a preference file. Options are provided to export your preferences at various levels of granularity. You can export all workspace

preferences, selected preferences or the preferences from the current preference page.

This mechanism for exporting and importing preferences is less than ideal,
however, because of problems handling various types of preferences, such as
classpath variables (which are exported using hard-coded paths rather than
workspace-relative paths) and code templates (which are not exported at all).

1.4   Creating a Project

Earlier sections of this chapter introduced the Eclipse workbench and showed
a number of ways to customize the environment. The next step is to actually
use Eclipse to get some work done. This section will take you through the
steps needed to create your first Eclipse project.

In the basic Eclipse environment, three different types of projects can be
created:

1. **Simple** projects, as their name implies, are the simplest type of Eclipse
   project. They can contain any type of arbitrary resource, including text
   files, HTML files, and so on.

2. **Java** projects are used to hold Java source code and resources needed to
   create a Java application. The next section will describe the process of
   creating a Java project.

3. **Plug-in development** projects are used to create Eclipse plug-ins. This is
   the type of project that this book will primarily concern itself with, and
   Chapter 2, "A Simple Plug-in Example," will go through a detailed
   example of creating a plug-in project.

1.4.1   Using the new java project wizard

To create a new Java project, select the **File > New > Project** command or click
the [icon] **New Java Project** toolbar button in the **Java** perspective to open the
New Project wizard (see Figure 1–15). On the first page of the wizard, select
Java Project from the list and click the **Next** button.

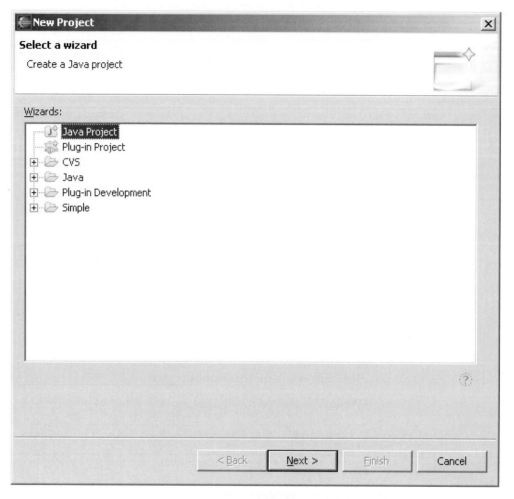

Figure 1–15   New Project wizard—selecting the project type.

On the second page of the wizard (see Figure 1–16), enter the name of the project (e.g., "First Project") and click the **Next** button. Note that this page also includes options for specifying the location of the project and its structure. By default, the project will be placed within the workspace directory and will use the project folder as the root for sources and class files.

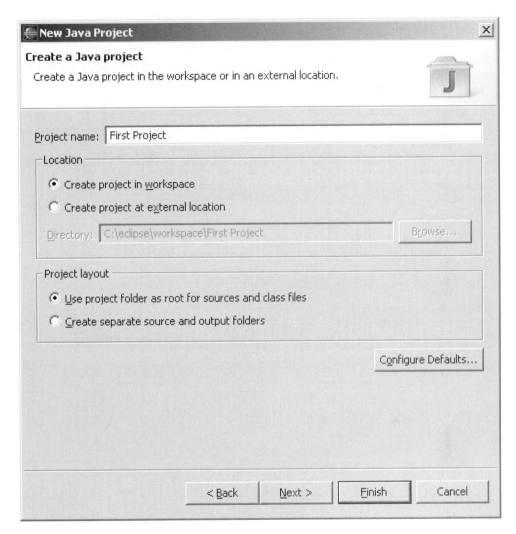

Figure 1–16   New Project wizard—naming the project.

   The next page of the wizard (see Figure 1–17) contains build path settings for the Java project. The **Source** tab provides a place to add source folders, which act as roots for packages containing Java files. The **Projects** tab allows you to set up project dependencies by selecting other projects in the workbench on which this project depends. The **Libraries** tab is the place to add JAR files (either stored in the workbench or out on the file system). The last tab, **Order and Export,** controls the order of build path elements and whether they are exported and visible to other projects that require this project. The **Default output folder** field, at the bottom the page, is used to specify the default location where compilation output will be stored. When the **Finish** button is clicked, the new project is created and appears in the **Package Explorer** view or the **Navigator** view, depending on which perspective is active.

> **Tip:** Traditionally, source files are placed in a separate source folder named **src** and the compiler output in a **bin** directory. Placing these types of files in separate directories results in an easier build process. Use the **Java > New Project** preference page to specify the default directory names used when creating new Java projects.

Figure 1–17   New Project wizard—specifying Java build settings.

1.4.2 .classpath and .project files

In addition to creating the project itself, two additional files are created. The
`.classpath` file stores the *Java build path* for the project. It should look
something like the following for the project you just created:

```
<?xml version="1.0" encoding="UTF-8"?>
<classpath>
    <classpathentry kind="src" path=""/>
    <classpathentry kind="con"
        path="org.eclipse.jdt.launching.JRE_CONTAINER"/>
    <classpathentry kind="output" path=""/>
</classpath>
```

Rather than editing the `.classpath` file directly, Eclipse provides a more
user-friendly approach. Right-click on the project and select **Properties**. In the
Properties dialog, selecting **Java Build Path** displays an interface similar to
Figure 1–17 for editing the project's classpath.

> **Java Build Path**   "Java classpath" is a generic term describing both the
> classpath used at compile-time and the classpath used at run-time. In Eclipse,
> the compile-time classpath is called the *Java build path*. When you are running
> or debugging Java application code, the run-time classpath is determined by
> the launch configuration (see Section 1.9.2, "Launch configurations"). When
> you are developing Eclipse plug-ins, the run-time classpath is determined by
> the dependency declaration in the plug-in manifest (see Section 2.3.1, "The
> plug-in manifest").

The .project file provides a complete description of the project suitable for
recreating the project in the workbench if it is exported and then imported.
Your new project should look like the following:

```
<?xml version="1.0" encoding="UTF-8"?>
<projectDescription>
    <name>First Project</name>
    <comment></comment>
    <projects>
    </projects>
    <buildSpec>
        <buildCommand>
            <name>org.eclipse.jdt.core.javabuilder</name>
        </buildCommand>
    </buildSpec>
    <natures>
        <nature>org.eclipse.jdt.core.javanature</nature>
    </natures>
</projectDescription>
```

The nature tag indicates what kind of project this is. The org.eclipse.jdt.core.javanature nature indicates that it is a Java project.

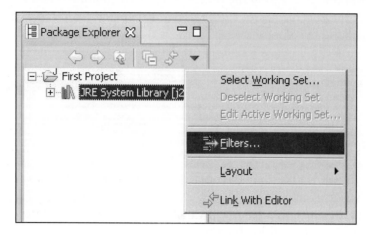

Figure 1–18   Filter menu.

By default, files beginning with "." are hidden from view via a filter. To show the files, select the **Filters** command from the drop-down view menu in the **Package Explorer** (see Figure 1–18), uncheck the **.*** **files** filter in the **Java Element Filters** dialog (see Figure 1–19) and click the **OK** button.

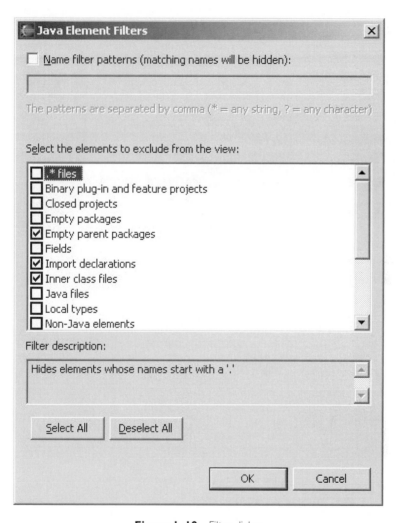

Figure 1–19   Filter dialog.

1.4.3   Using the java package wizard

To create a Java package, select **File > New > Package** or click the **New Java Package** toolbar button to open the **New Java Package** wizard (see Figure 1–20). Enter the name of the package (e.g., "com.qualityeclipse.sample") and click the **Finish** button.

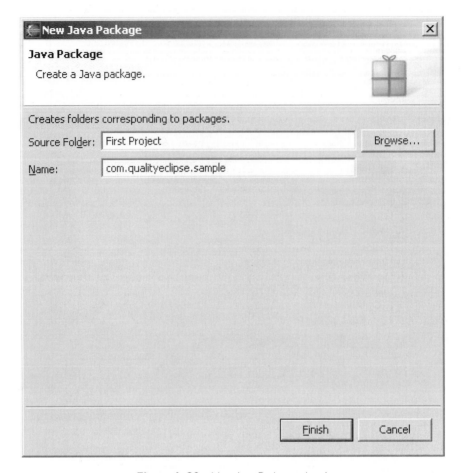

Figure 1–20   New Java Package wizard.

Note that the icon next to the new Java package name (see Figure 1–21) is hollow, indicating that it is empty. When one or more Java files are added to the package, the icon will appear in color.

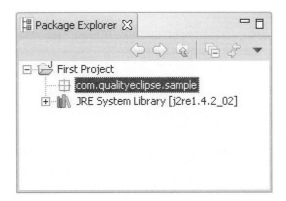

Figure 1–21 New Java package in the Package Explorer.

1.4.4 Using the java class wizard

To create a Java class, select **File > New > Class** or click the ⓒ **New Java Class** toolbar button to open the **New Java Class** wizard, as seen in Figure 1–22. Enter the name of the class (e.g., "HelloWorld"), check the **public static void main(String[] args)** checkbox, and click the **Finish** button. Note that the wizard presents numerous additional options for creating a new class, including its superclass, interfaces, and initial default methods.

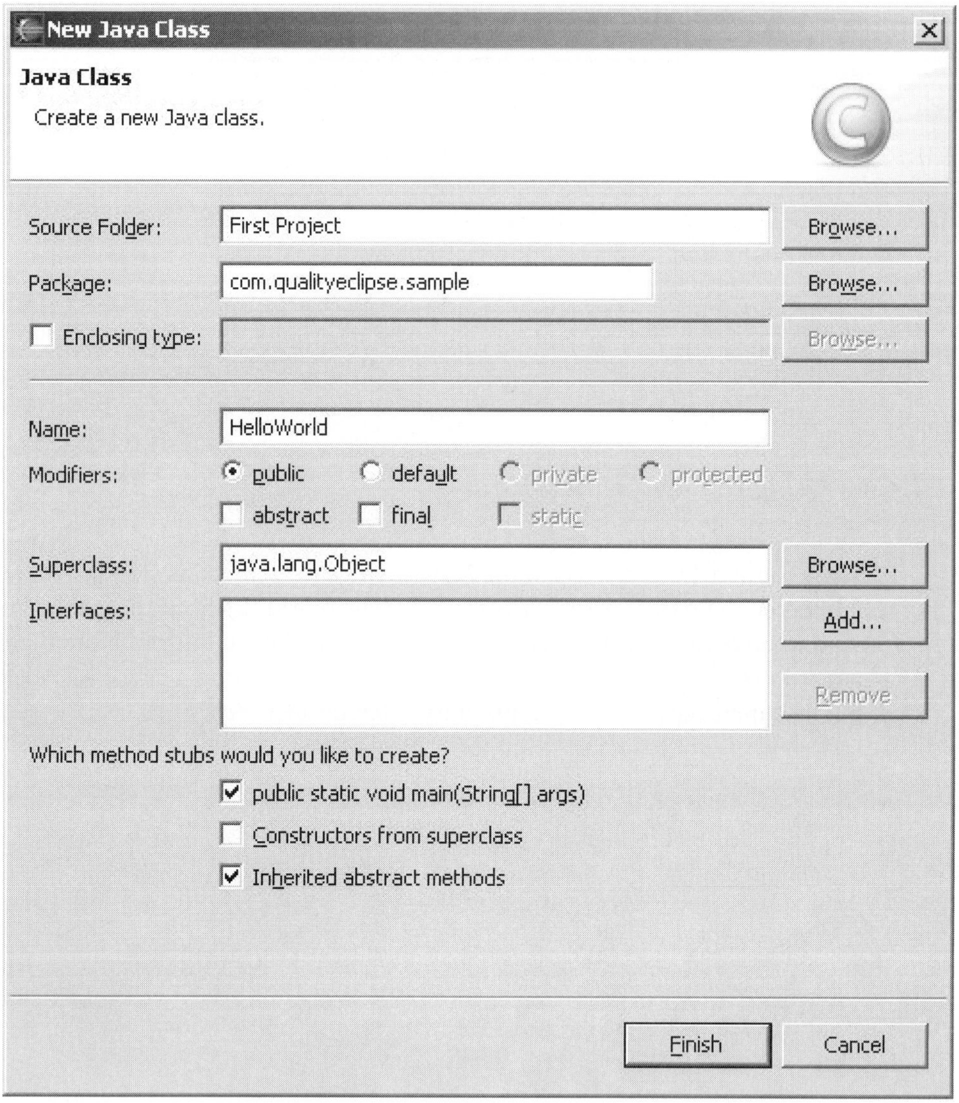

Figure 1–22   New Java Class wizard.

This process creates a new Java class (see Figure 1–23). The **Hello-World.java** entry represents the file itself. Expanding that item reveals elements representing the class and its single "main" method. Note that the icon next to the package name is now in color, indicating that it is no longer empty.

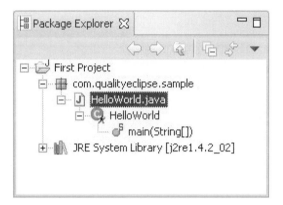

Figure 1–23   New Java class in the Package Explorer.

1.5   Navigating

Eclipse includes a number of tools designed to make it easy to navigate the system and find information. This section discusses some of the tools accessible from the Eclipse **Navigate** menu.

> **Tip:** Many third-party plug-ins are available that provide various navigational enhancements for Eclipse (see Appendix A). For example, CodePro Studio provides a Java History view that keeps track of any Java files you have accessed as well as Modified Type and Member views that track any types and members you have changed.

1.5.1   Open type dialog

The **Open Type** dialog is used to quickly jump to any Java class in the system. Select the **Navigate > Open Type** command to open the dialog (see Figure 1–24) or click the ▦ **Open Type** toolbar button, and then enter the name of the type that you want to find. The name field allows wildcards and will show a list of all types that match the entered pattern. Select the desired type from the list and click the **OK** button to open that type in an editor. If more than one type matches the name, the **Qualifier** list will display a list of packages that contain types by that name.

Figure 1–24 Open Type dialog.

1.5.2 Type hierarchy view

The **Type Hierarchy** view shows the superclasses and subclasses of a given type (see Figure 1–25). The view also has options for showing just the supertype hierarchy (both superclasses and implemented interfaces) or subtype hierarchy (subclasses and interface implementers) of a type.

The **Type Hierarchy** view can be accessed in several different ways. The easiest way is to select the name of the type in an editor and then select the **Navigate > Open Type Hierarchy** command (or use the **F3** keyboard shortcut). Alternatively, select the **Navigate > Open Type In Hierarchy** command to open the **Open Type** dialog, as shown in Figure 1–24.

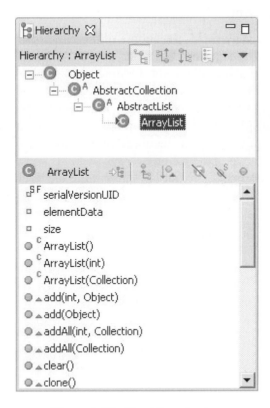

Figure 1–25 Type Hierarchy view.

1.5.3 Go to line

To jump to a specific line of code within a file, use the **Navigate > Go to Line** command. This opens a prompter for entering the desired line number (see Figure 1–26). Clicking the **OK** button jumps to that line in the editor.

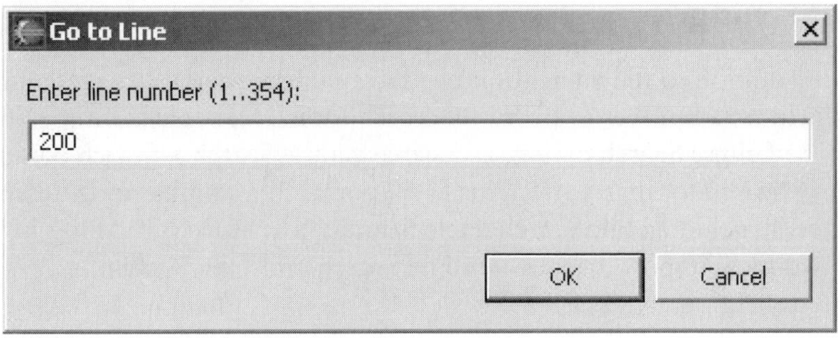

Figure 1–26 Line number prompter.

1.5.4 *Outline view*

The **Outline** view shows an outline of the structural elements of the selected editor. The contents vary depending on the type of editor in use. For example, when editing a Java class, the **Outline** view displays the classes, fields, and methods in the Java class being edited (see Figure 1–27).

The Java **Outline** view includes a number of options to control which elements are displayed within the outline. There are filters for hiding fields, static members, and non-public members. In addition, there are options for sorting members (shown in definition order by default) and drilling down to the top-level type (normally, the outline starts at the file level).

Figure 1–27 Outline view.

1.6 **Searching**

In addition to the navigation tools available from the **Navigate** menu, Eclipse includes a number of powerful search tools accessible from the **Search** menu. The Eclipse **Search** dialog, accessible via the **Search > Search** command or the 🔍 **Search** toolbar button, acts as a portal to a number of different searching tools, including **File Search, Help Search, Java Search,** and **Plug-in Search.** The two most important tools are **File Search** and **Java Search.**

1.6.1   File search

The **File Search** tab (see Figure 1–28) of the **Search** dialog provides a way to find arbitrary files in the workbench by name or by the text they contain. To search for files containing a certain expression, enter that expression into the **Containing text** field. Various wildcards are supported, such as "*" to match any set of characters and "?" to match any single character. By default, the search is case-sensitive. To make the search case-insensitive, uncheck the **Case sensitive** option. To perform complex text searches using regular expressions, turn on the **Regular expression** option. To search for files by name, leave the **Containing text** field blank. To restrict a search to certain types of files or files containing a certain naming pattern, enter the filename expression into the **File name patterns** field.

The **Scope** fields provide another way to further restrict a search. The **Workspace** scope encompasses the entire workspace while the **Working Set** scope limits a search to only those files contained in the selected working set. The **Selected Resources** scope limits a search to only those files that have been selected in the active view (for example, the **Navigator** view or **Package Explorer** view), while the **Enclosing Projects** scope limits a search to the projects containing the selected files.

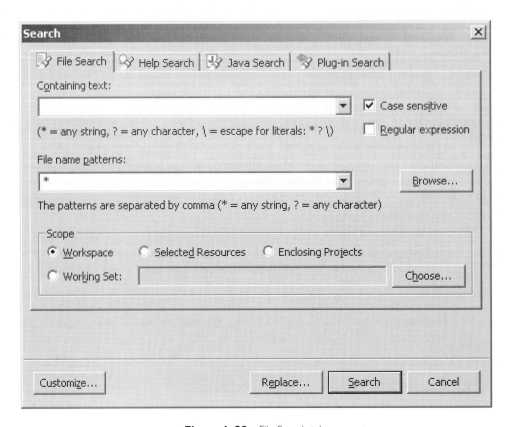

Figure 1–28   File Search tab.

For example, to search for all files containing the text "xml", enter that text into the **Containing text** field and leave the **File name patterns** field and Scope fields unchanged. When ready, click the **Search** button to find the matching files and display them in the **Search** view (see Figure 1–29). Clicking the **Replace** button rather than the **Search** button will perform the same search, but will open up a **Replace** dialog where you can enter replacement text.

Figure 1–29   File search results.

If your goal is to search for various Java elements like types, methods, fields, and so on, the **Java Search** option is much more powerful than the **File Search** option.

1.6.2   Java search

The **Java Search** tab (see Figure 1–30) locates Java elements such as types, methods, constructors, fields, and packages. You can use it to find declarations of a specific Java element, references to the element, or implementors of the element (in the case of a Java interface).

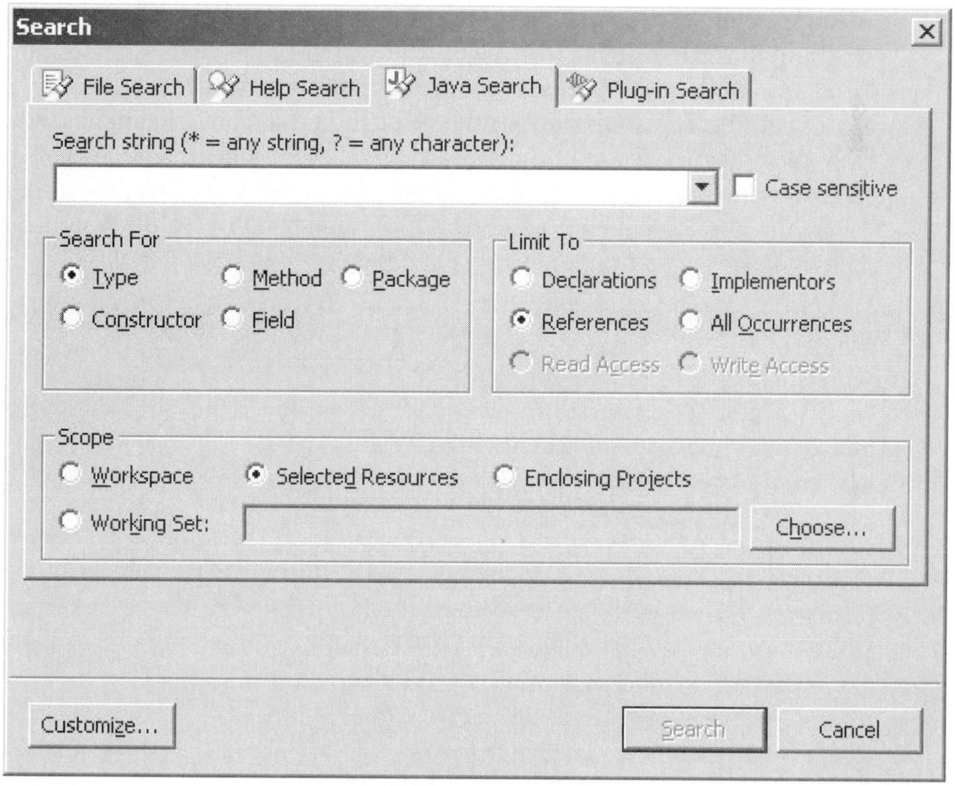

Figure 1–30   Java Search tab.

To search for elements with a specific name, enter the name in the **Search string** field (wildcards are supported). Depending on the kind of Java element you are interested in, select the **Type, Constructor, Method, Field,** or **Package** radio button. You can further limit search results to **Declarations, References,**

Implementors (of Java interfaces), **All Occurrences, Read Access** (for fields), or **Write Access** (for fields).

As in the **File Search** tab, the **Scope** fields provide another way to restrict a search. The **Workspace** scope includes the entire workspace, the **Working Set** scope limits the search to a specific working set, the **Selected Resources** scope limits the search to the selected files in the active view, and the **Enclosing Projects** scope limits the search to the projects containing the selected files.

> Tip: Consider building a reference project if you want to search the entire Eclipse plug-in source (see Section 20.1, "Advanced Search—Reference Projects").

For example, to search for all methods named "toLowerCase", enter that text into the **Search string** field, select the **Search For > Method** and **Limit To > Declarations** radio buttons, and leave the **Scope** fields unchanged. When ready, click the **Search** button to find the methods matching that name and display them hierarchically in the **Search** view. Several options are available on the view toolbar for grouping the results by project, package, file or class. Select the **Flat Layout** command from the view menu to see the results listed individually (see Figure 1–31).

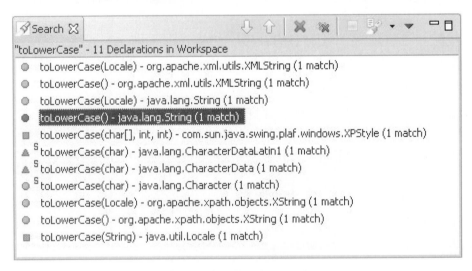

Figure 1–31   Java search results.

Double-clicking on any search result opens an editor on the file containing that result, highlights the search match in the text, and places a search marker in the left-hand gutter area (also known as the marker bar, or left-hand vertical ruler) of the editor (see Figure 1–32). Clicking the **Show Next Match** or

Show Previous Match buttons (the up and down arrows) in the **Search** view selects the next or previous match (opening a new editor on a different file if necessary). You can also continue to search ("drill-down") using the context menus in the **Search** view.

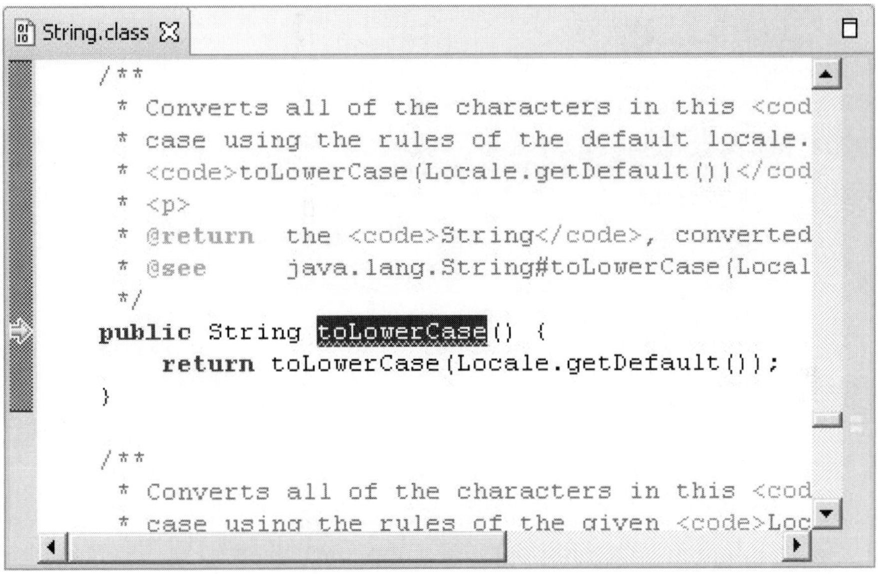

```
/**
 * Converts all of the characters in this <cod
 * case using the rules of the default locale.
 * <code>toLowerCase(Locale.getDefault())</cod
 * <p>
 * @return   the <code>String</code>, converted
 * @see      java.lang.String#toLowerCase(Local
 */
public String toLowerCase() {
    return toLowerCase(Locale.getDefault());
}


/**
 * Converts all of the characters in this <cod
 * case using the rules of the given <code>Loc
```

Figure 1–32   Editor showing search match and search marker.

1.6.3   Other search menu options

The **Search** menu contains a number of dedicated, easy-to-use Java search commands that replicate the options found on the **Java Search** page of the **Search** dialog (see Figure 1–33).

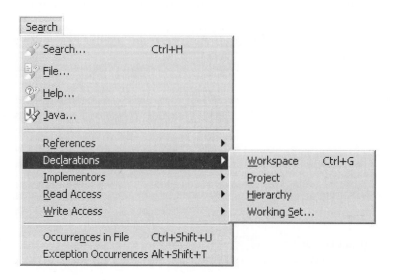

Figure 1–33   Dedicated Java search commands.

Selecting a Java element either in a view or in a Java editor and then selecting the **Search > Declarations** command finds all elements with matching declarations in the workspace, the current project, the current type hierarchy, or
a specific working set. Likewise, selecting the **Search > References** command
finds all the places where the element is used. The **Search > Implementors,
Search > Declarations**, and **Search > Write Access** commands work similarly.
Note that the same commands are also available from the context menu in the
Java editor and the **Search** view.

1.6.4   Working sets

Working sets have been mentioned a number of times so far. They are used to
create a group of elements to act either as a filter in various views (such as the
Navigator and **Package Explorer** views) or as search scopes in the **Search** dialog or any search menu. Working sets are extremely useful when you have a
large workspace containing many projects as they limit the scope of your code
and make many tasks easier.

To select a working set or create a new one, choose **Scope > Working Set**,
then click the **Choose** button in the **Search** dialog. This opens the **Select Working Sets** dialog (see Figure 1–34). To use an existing working set, select it from
the list and click the **OK** button. To edit a working set, click the **Edit** button
instead.

Figure 1–34 Select Working Sets dialog.

Click the **New...** button to create a new working set. This opens the **New Working Set** dialog (see Figure 1–35). Three different types of working sets may be created, including resource working sets, Java working sets, and help working sets. Select the type of working set you want to create and click the **Next** button.

Figure 1–35   New Working Set dialog.

The next page of the **New Working Set** dialog facilitates defining new working sets (see Figure 1–36). Enter the desired name into the **Working set name** field and select the contents from the **Working set content** list. Clicking the **Finish** button closes the **New Working Set** dialog and adds the new working set to the **Select Working Sets** dialog.

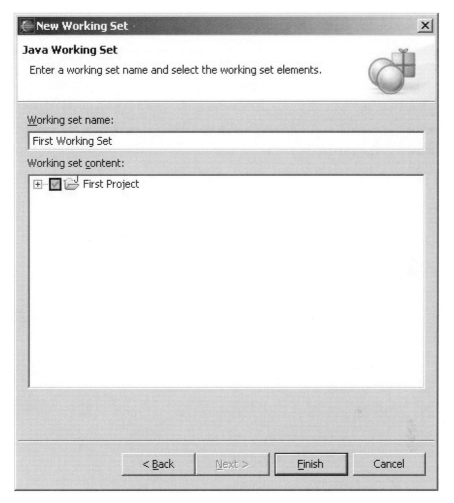

Figure 1–36 Define a new working set.

1.7 Writing Code

Now that we have created our first Java project and have explored different ways to navigate the system and find items we need, it is time to start using Eclipse tools to write new code. Eclipse supports a number of different editor types, both internal and external, for editing different types of resources. Double-clicking on a Java file, for example, opens the Java file editor (see Figure 1–37).

```
┌─────────────────────────────────────────────────────────────────────┐
│ J HelloWorld.java ⊠                                                 ▯ │
├─────────────────────────────────────────────────────────────────────┤
│   /*                                                              ▲   │
│    * Created on June 28, 2004                                     █   │
│    *                                                                  │
│ ✓⋮ * TODO To change the template for this generated file go to        │
│    * Window - Preferences - Java - Code Generation - Code and Cor █   │
│    */                                                                 │
│   package com.qualityeclipse.sample;                                  │
│                                                                      │
│   /**                                                                 │
│    * @author Administrator                                            │
│    *                                                                  │
│ ✓⋮ * TODO To change the template for this generated type comment     │
│    * Window - Preferences - Java - Code Generation - Code and Cor     │
│    */                                                                 │
│   public class HelloWorld {                                           │
│       public static void main(String[] args) {                       │
│       }                                                               │
│   }                                                              ▼   │
│ ◄                                                                ►   │
└─────────────────────────────────────────────────────────────────────┘
```

Figure 1–37   Java editor.

1.7.1   Java editor

The Java editor provides many features focused on the job of editing Java code such as:

- Colored syntax highlighting (see Figure 1–37)

- User-defined code formatting

- Import organization and correction

- Context-sensitive code assistance

- "Quick fix" automatic problem correction

Tip: Many former VisualAge for Java users loved the ability of that IDE to show only a single method at a time rather than the entire Java file. The Eclipse Java editor supports the same capability via the ▣ **Show Source of Selected Element Only** toolbar button. For this button to work, you must give focus to an editor since the button is not enabled until you're actually editing some code. This is one of those options in Eclipse that should really be a workspace preference rather than a button on the toolbar.

1.7.1.1   Colored syntax highlighting

The colored syntax highlighting feature controls how Java code will be
depicted. Independent control over color and font style (plain or bold) is provided for multi- and single-line comments, keywords, strings, characters, task
tags, and Javadoc elements via the **Java > Editor > Syntax** preference page (see
Figure 1–38).

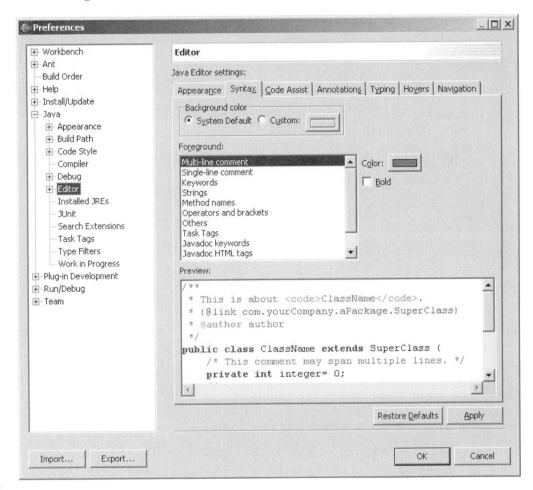

Figure 1–38   Syntax preference page.

1.7.1.2   User-defined code formatting

The code formatting feature controls how Java code will be formatted any
time the **Source > Format** command is issued. A variety of options are provided for controlling brace position, new lines, line length, and white space

usage via the **Java > Code Style > Code Formatter** preference page (see Figure 1–39).

> **Tip:** Alternate code formatters are available, including JIndent integration into Eclipse (*www.javadude.com/tools*).

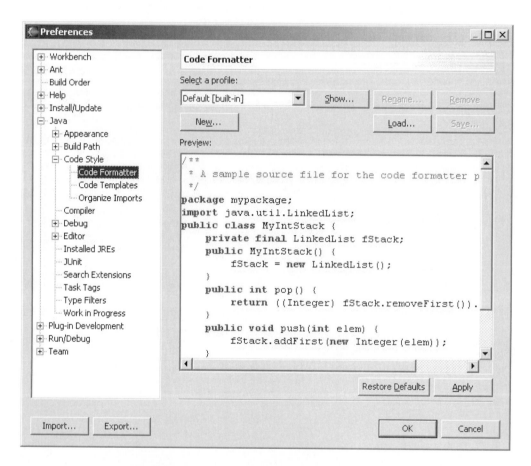

Figure 1–39   Code Formatter preference page.

1.7.1.3   *Organizing java import statements*

The import organization feature provides an easy way to clean up the import statements within a Java file. New imports may be added using the **Source > Add Import** command, and existing imports can be cleaned up using the **Source > Organize Imports** command. The **Java > Code Style > Organize Imports** preference page (see Figure 1–40) provides a means to set the default

order of import statements and the threshold above which wildcard imports
will be used.

Tip: Set the threshold to 1 to cause packages to be imported with ".*"
immediately, or keep the default value, 99, to always import each type
individually depending on your coding style.

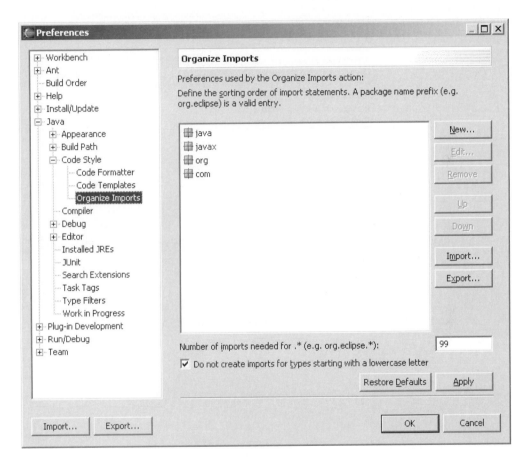

Figure 1–40   Organize Imports preference page.

1.7.1.4 *Context-sensitive code assist*

The context-sensitive code assist feature can help speed up the creation of Java
code quite dramatically. It can complete class names, method names, parameter names, and more. To use it, position the cursor at a location in your Java
code needing a suggestion and select either the **Edit > Content Assist** com-

mand or hold the **Ctrl** key down while pressing the **Space** key. This opens the popup code assist window (see Figure 1–41).

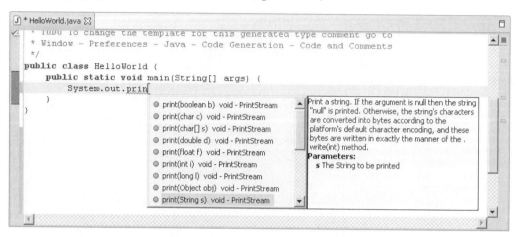

Figure 1–41   Code assistance in action.

> **Tip:** If the code assist window fails to open and the feature just beeps at you instead, check your Java build path and then check your code as it may have so many problems that the Java compiler cannot make sense of it. Remember, the Java compiler is always working in the background!

The **Java > Editor > Code Assist** preference page (see Figure 1–42) provides a number of options to control how the code assist feature acts when invoked.

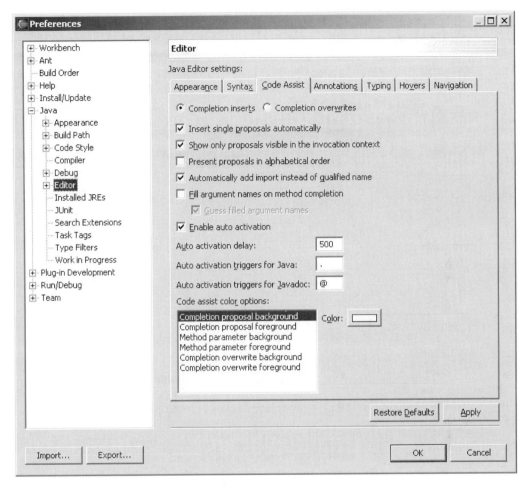

Figure 1–42   Code Assist preference page.

1.7.1.5   "Quick fix" automatic problem correction

The "quick fix" feature provides a way to easily fix common problems within the Java editor. Any time there is a problem detected that can be fixed, a light bulb icon is displayed in the marker bar (left-hand vertical ruler) of the editor. Clicking on the icon opens the popup quick fix window (see Figure 1–43). Selecting the appropriate fix from the list applies that fix to the Java source.

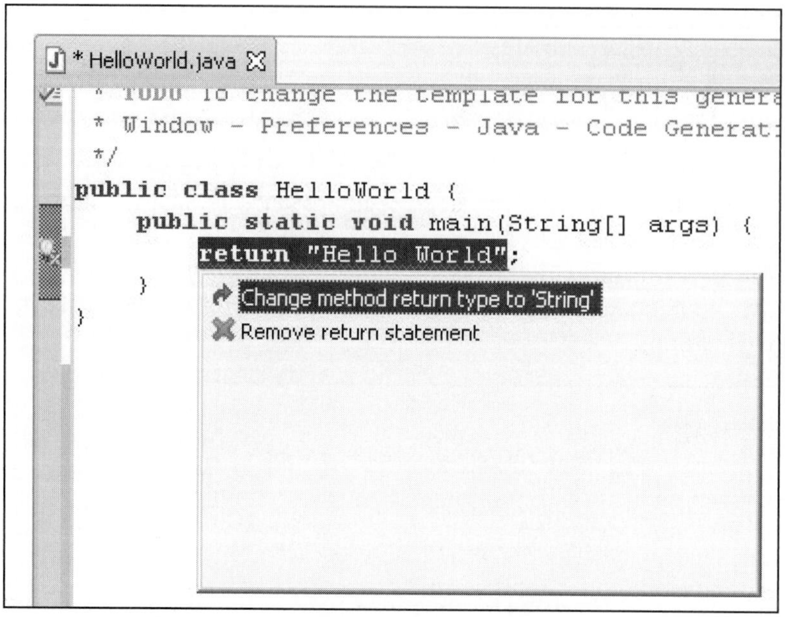

Figure 1-43   Quick fix in action.

There are dozens of built-in quick fixes available, including:

- Correcting missing or incorrect package declarations

- Removing unused and duplicate imports

- Changing the visibility of types, methods, and fields

- Renaming types, methods, and fields

- Removing unused private types, methods, and fields

- Creating new types, methods, and fields

- Fixing incorrect method arguments

- Adding or removing catch blocks

- Adding necessary cast operations

1.7.2   Templates

Templates are common source code patterns that appear frequently in user-written code. Eclipse has dozens of built-in templates and new ones are very easy to add.

To use a template, position the cursor at the desired position in your Java code, start to type the name of the template, and press **Ctrl+Space**. This opens the popup content assist window (see Figure 1–44). Note that some templates are parameterized with user-defined variables. Once a template has been expanded, use the **Tab** key to move between variables.

As an example, open the `HelloWorld` class we created in Section 1.4.4, "Using the java class wizard," type "sysout", and press **Ctrl+Space**. This expands the sysout template to `System.out.println();` with the cursor placed between the two parentheses. Type "Hello World" and press **Ctrl+S** to save your changes. We will run this application in Section 1.9, "Running Applications."

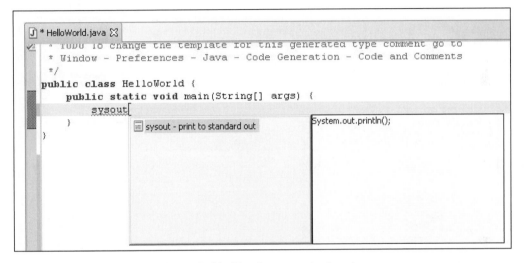

Figure 1–44 Template expansion in action.

The **Java > Editor > Templates** preference page (see Figure 1–45) provides a place to add new templates and edit existing ones.

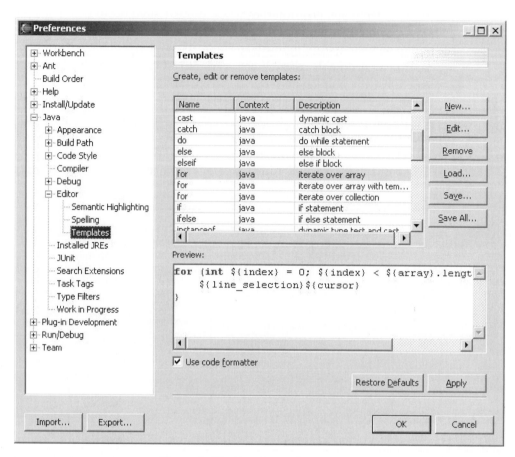

Figure 1–45 Template preference page.

To add a new template, click the **New** button to open the **Edit Template** dialog (see Figure 1–46). Enter the name for the pattern in the **Name** field, its description in the **Description** field, and the code pattern itself in the **Pattern** field (note that code assist is not case-sensitive). Eclipse supports two types of patterns, Java and Javadoc. Select the pattern type from the **Context** drop-down list. The **Insert Variable** button pops up a list of variables that can be inserted into the template. Click the **OK** button to add the template to the template list.

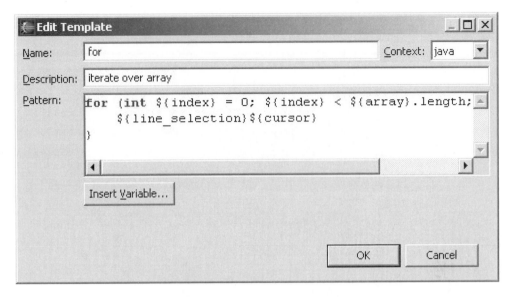

Figure 1–46 Edit Template dialog.

> **Tip:** Some third-party plug-ins provide enhanced templates known as patterns (see Appendix A).

1.7.3 Refactoring

Refactoring is the process of changing a software system to improve its internal structure and reusability, without altering the external behavior of the program. It is a disciplined way of cleaning up code that minimizes the chances of introducing bugs. In essence, when developers refactor, they are improving the design of the code. Eclipse provides a very powerful and comprehensive collection of refactoring tools that make refactoring operations quick, easy, and reliable.

The Eclipse refactoring commands are available either from the Java editor's context menu or from the **Refactor** menu that is available from the main menu bar anytime a Java editor is open. The **Refactor** menu (see Figure 1–47) includes more than a dozen different refactoring commands that modify some aspect of a Java element and then update any references to it elsewhere in the workspace.

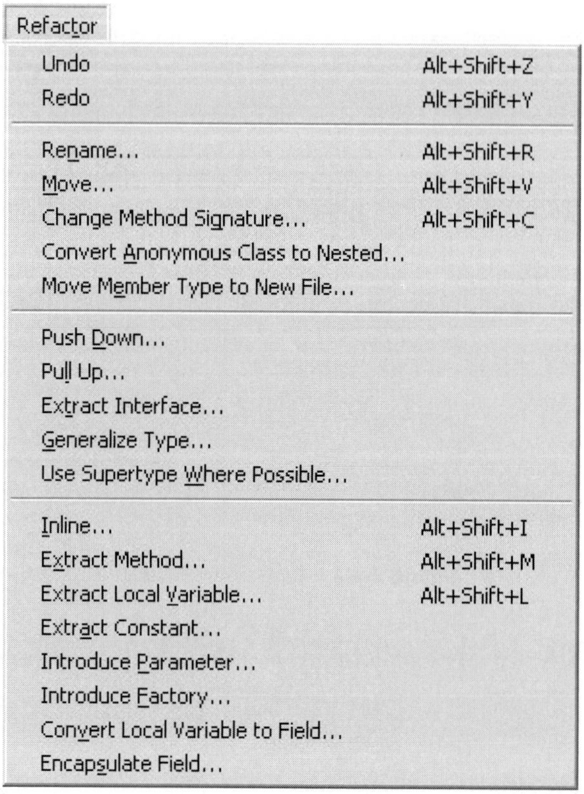

```
Refactor
    Undo                                      Alt+Shift+Z
    Redo                                      Alt+Shift+Y

    Rename...                                 Alt+Shift+R
    Move...                                   Alt+Shift+V
    Change Method Signature...                Alt+Shift+C
    Convert Anonymous Class to Nested...
    Move Member Type to New File...

    Push Down...
    Pull Up...
    Extract Interface...
    Generalize Type...
    Use Supertype Where Possible...

    Inline...                                 Alt+Shift+I
    Extract Method...                         Alt+Shift+M
    Extract Local Variable...                 Alt+Shift+L
    Extract Constant...
    Introduce Parameter...
    Introduce Factory...
    Convert Local Variable to Field...
    Encapsulate Field...
```

Figure 1–47   Refactor menu.

Supported refactoring commands include:

- **Rename**—Renames a Java element.

- **Move**—Moves a Java element.

- **Change Method Signature**—Changes method parameters (names, types, and order).

- **Convert Anonymous Class to Nested**—Converts an anonymous inner class to a named nested class.

- **Move Member Type to New File**—Converts a nested type into a top-level type.

- **Push Down**—Moves fields and methods from a class to one of its subclasses.

- **Pull Up**—Moves fields, methods, or member types from a class to one of its superclasses.

- **Extract Interface**—Creates a new interface from a collection of selected methods.

- **Generalize Type**—Generalizes the type of variable declarations, parameters, fields, and method return types.

- **Use Supertype Where Possible**—Replaces a type with one of its supertypes anywhere that transformation is possible.

- **Inline**—Inlines methods, constants, and local variables.

- **Extract Method**—Creates a new method based on the selected text in the current method and updates the current method to call the new method.

- **Extract Local Variable**—Creates a new local variable assigned to the selected expression and replaces the selection with a reference to the new variable.

- **Extract Constant**—Creates a static final field from the selected expression.

- **Introduce Parameter**—Replaces an expression with a parameter reference.

- **Introduce Factory**—Replaces a constructor invocation with a call to a new factory method.

- **Convert Local Variable to Field**—Converts a local variable into a field.

- **Encapsulate Field**—Replaces all direct references to a field with references to the field's getter and setter methods and creates those methods as necessary.

To use any refactoring command, select the Java element or expression that you would like to refactor and then select the refactoring command. Each refactoring dialog collects information appropriate to the task it needs to do. Once you have supplied that information (for example, the new method name as shown in Figure 1–48), click the **OK** button to complete the refactoring.

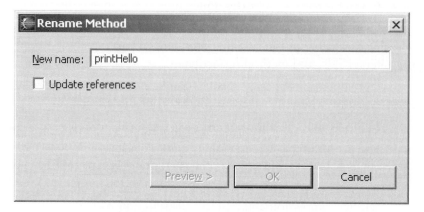

Figure 1–48   Rename Method dialog.

To preview the transformations that will be made by a refactoring method before they are committed, click the **Preview** button prior to clicking the **OK** button. The refactoring preview shows a hierarchy (a checkbox tree list) of the changes that will be made with text panes showing a before and after view of the affected code. If for some reason you want to exclude a particular change from the refactoring operation, uncheck it in the tree list.

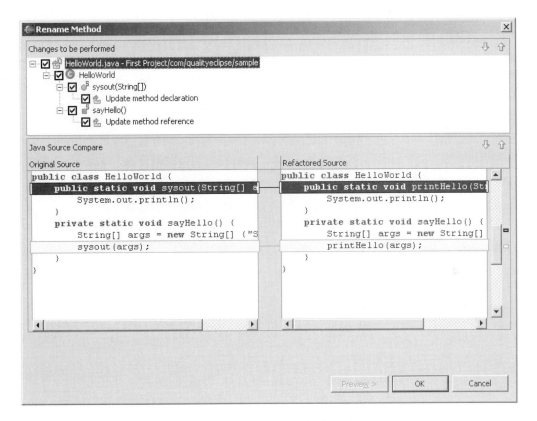

Figure 1–49   Rename Method preview.

1.7.4   Local history

Every time you make a change to a file and save it, a snapshot of that file at that moment in time is recorded to the Eclipse local history. This provides a way to revert back to an earlier version of a file or compare the current version with an earlier version to see the changes that have been made. Each entry in the local history is identified by the date and time it was created.

Note that "local history" is really local to the machine, and never stored in CVS or another source code repository. This means that the history is only available to you and not available to other users. This might be a surprise to VisualAge Java or ENVY users who expect "method editions" to be available in the repository.

To compare the current state of a file with an earlier version, right-click on the file and select the **Compare With > Local History** command from the context menu. This opens the **Compare with Local History** dialog (see Figure

1–50). Select any item in the history list to see a comparison relative to the current state of the file.

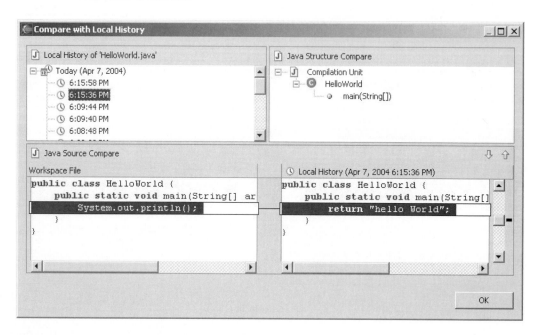

Figure 1–50   Compare with Local History dialog.

To replace the current version of a file with an earlier version, right-click on the file and select the **Replace With > Element from Local History** command from the context menu. This opens the **Replace from Local History** dialog, which is almost identical to the local history comparison dialog with the addition of **Replace** and **Cancel** buttons.

The **Workbench > Local History** preference page (see Figure 1–51) determines how much information is stored in the local history. You can control how many days worth of changes are maintained, how many unique changes per file are maintained, and how large the entire local history is allowed to grow.

Tip: Many former VisualAge for Java users loved the ability of that IDE to revert to any prior version of any method or class. The Eclipse local history feature provides a way to emulate that behavior on a local scale. There is no reason (other than disk space) to keep the Eclipse local history settings at the low values to which they default. Increasing the **Days to keep files** setting to 365, the **Entries per file** to 10,000, and the **Maximum file size (MB)** field to 1,000 will allow you to easily track an entire year of changes.

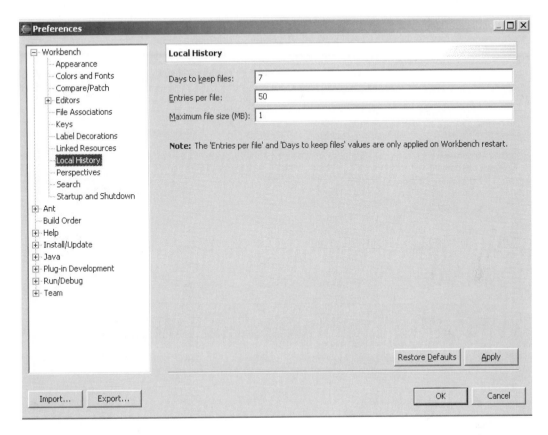

Figure 1-51   Local History preference page.

1.7.5 File extension associations

In addition to the built-in Java file editor, Eclipse includes built-in editors for text files, plug-in development files (such as plugin.xml, fragment.xml, and feature.xml), and others.

You can change which editor is assigned to a specific file type using the **Workbench > File Associations** preference page (see Figure 1–52). To change the editor, select the file type in the **File types** list, select the desired editor type in the **Associated editors** list, and click the **Default** button. If the desired editor type is not shown, use the **File types > Add** button to add it to the list.

To add an editor association for a file type not listed in the **File types** list, click the **File types > Add** button to reveal the **New File Type** dialog, as shown in Figure 1–53. For example, to add an editor for HTML files, enter ".html" into the **File type** field and click the **OK** button.

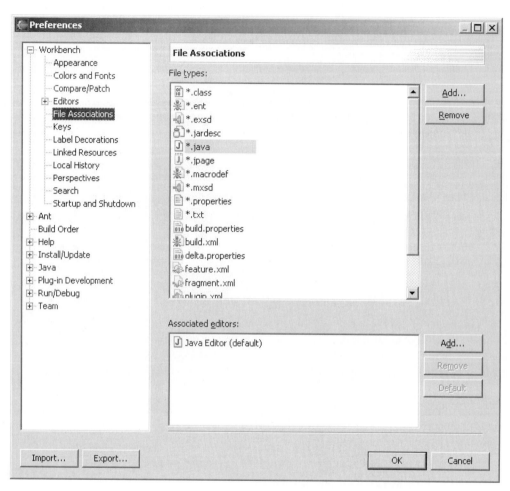

Figure 1–52 File Associations preference page.

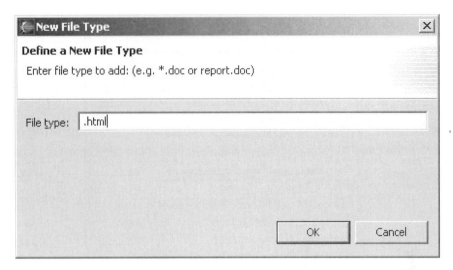

Figure 1–53   New File Type dialog.

Once the new file type has been added, an editor must be assigned to it. Click the **Associated editors > Add** button to open the **Editor Selection** dialog. By default, the various built-in editor types will be shown in the editor list. To see a list of available external editors, select the **External Programs** radio button (see Figure 1–54). If you have an HTML editor (such as Microsoft FrontPage) installed in your system, select it from the list and click the **OK** button. That editor will be added to the **Associated editors** list and automatically made the default (assuming that no other default was in place).

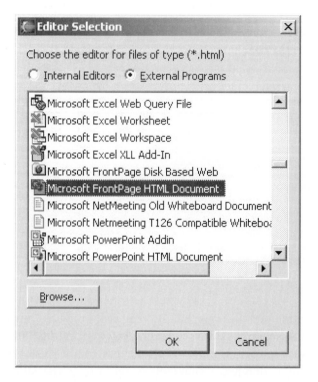

Figure 1–54   Editor Selection dialog.

> **Tip:** If you routinely edit XML files, the **XMLBuddy** plug-in, from
> www.xmlbuddy.com/, is one of several XML editors integrated into
> Eclipse (see Appendix A). The XMLBuddy editor provides user-
> configurable syntax highlighting, Document Type Definition- (DTD-)
> driven code assist, XML validation, and many other features.

1.8   Team Development Using CVS

Typically, you will want to work as part of a team and share your code with
other members of your team. This section shows how to set up and use CVS,
which ships as part of Eclipse.

As team members work on different aspects of a project, changes are
made locally to their own workspaces. When they are ready to share their
changes with other team members, they can commit those changes into the
shared CVS repository. Likewise, when they want to get any changes made by
other team members, they can update their workspaces with the contents of

the repository. In the event of conflicts (i.e., changes made to the same resource), Eclipse provides comparison and merge tools to resolve and integrate those changes.

CVS supports multiple streams of development known as *branches*. Each branch represents an independent set of changes made to the same set of resources. There may be multiple concurrent branches for various maintenance updates, bug fixes, experimental projects, and so on. The main branch, known as the "HEAD," represents the primary flow of work within a project.

Just as the Eclipse local history feature records changes made to various resources over time, the CVS repository maintains a history of every committed change made to every resource over time. A resource may be compared with or replaced with any prior revision using tools similar to those used with the local history feature.

1.8.1   Getting started with CVS

To start using CVS with Eclipse, you will need to connect your Eclipse workspace to your CVS repository (see *www.cvshome.org* for information on setting up the repository). Start by opening either the **CVS Repository Exploring** perspective using the **Window > Open Perspective > Other** command or the **CVS Repositories** view using the **Window > Show View > Other** command. Next, right-click within the **CVS Repositories** view and select the **New > Repository Location** command from the context menu (see Figure 1–55).

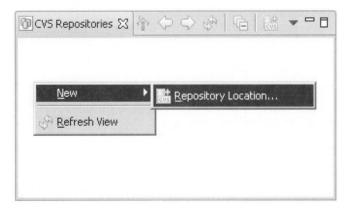

Figure 1–55   CVS Repositories view.

Within the **Add CVS Repository** dialog (see Figure 1–56), you need to specify the location of your repository and your login information. Enter the address of your CVS host into the **Host** field (e.g., "cvs.qualityeclipse.com") and the path of the repository relative to the host address into the **Repository**

path field. Next, enter your user name and password into the **User** and **Password** fields, respectively, or leave them blank for anonymous access. If you need to use a different connect type than the default, change that as well. When done, click the **Finish** button. Assuming that the CVS repository is found, it will show up in the **CVS Repositories** view.

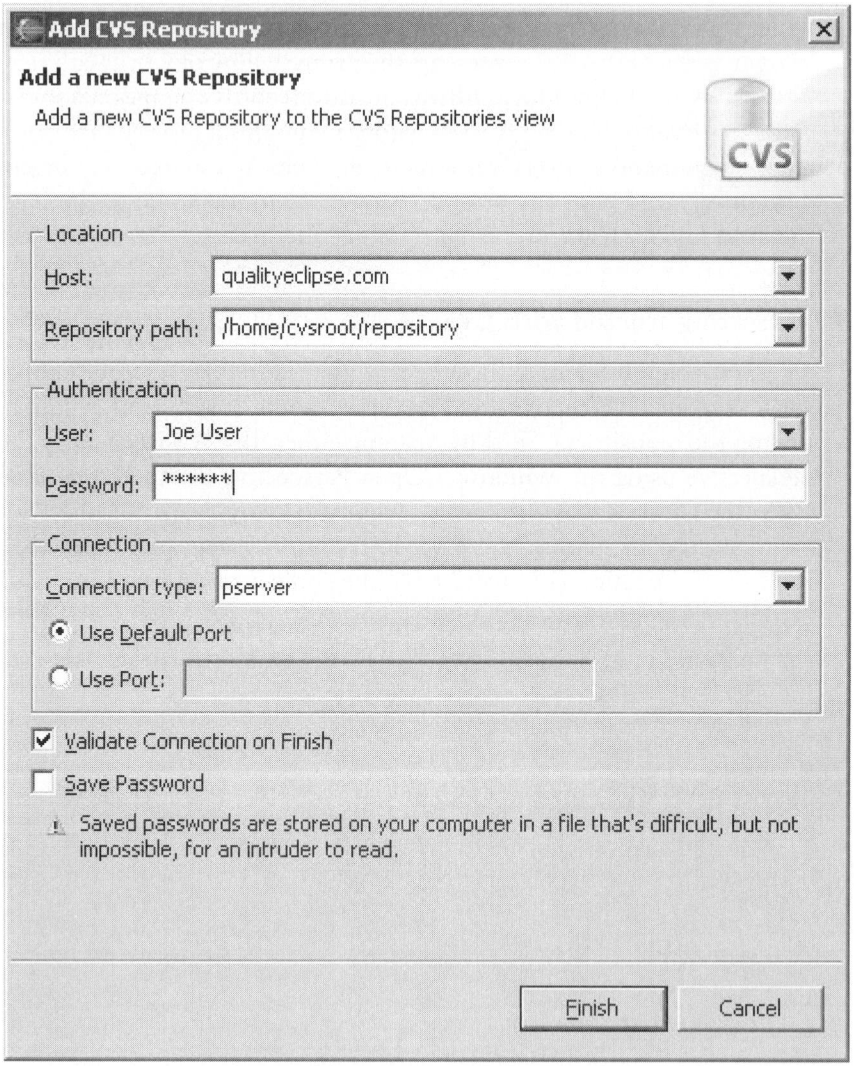

Figure 1–56   Add CVS Repository dialog.

1.8.2   *Checking out a project from CVS*

To check out a project from your CVS repository, expand the repository loca-tion and then the **HEAD** item until you see the project you want to load. Right-click on the project and select the **Check Out** command from the con-text menu (see Figure 1–57). This loads the project into your workspace. To load the project into a specially configured project (for example, a project out-side your workspace), use the **Check Out As...** command instead.

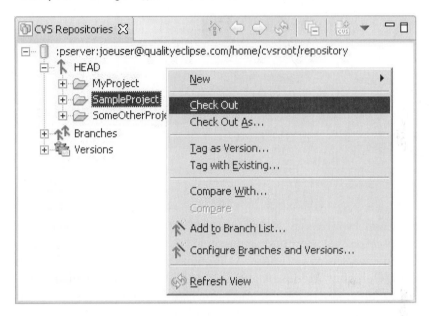

Figure 1–57   Checking out a project.

1.8.3   *Synchronizing with the repository*

Once changes have been made to the resources in the project, those changes should be committed back to the repository. Right-click on the resource (or the project containing the resource) and select the **Team > Synchronize with Repository** command (see Figure 1–58).

Figure 1–58   Team context menu.

After comparing the resources in the workspace to those in the repository, the **Synchronize** view opens (see Figure 1–59). The  **Incoming Mode** icon causes the view to only show incoming changes, while the **Outgoing Mode** icon causes it to only show outgoing changes (a third option is the **Incoming/Outgoing Mode**). Right-click on the outgoing changes and select the **Commit** command to commit those changes to the repository. Right-click on any incoming changes and select the **Update** command to load those changes into your workspace.

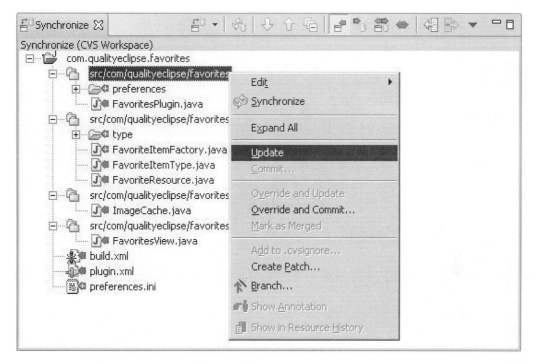

Figure 1–59 Synchronize view.

If any conflicts occur (e.g., changes made by you and another developer), you will need to use the merge tools provided in the **Synchronize** view to resolve the conflicts and then commit the merged version to the repository.

1.8.4 Comparing and replacing resources

To compare the current state of a file with an earlier revision stored in the repository, right-click on the file and select the **Compare With > Revision** command from the context menu. This opens the **Compare With Revision** dialog which shows earlier revisions of the file made to the HEAD stream (see Figure 1–60). Select any item in the revision list to see a comparison relative to the current state of the file.

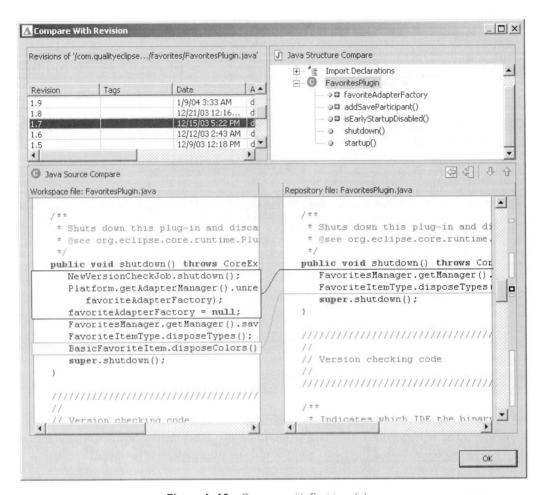

Figure 1–60   Compare with Revision dialog.

A number of other resource comparison commands are also available. The **Compare With > Latest from Head** command compares the current state of the resource with the most recent version committed to a repository, and the **Compare With > Another Branch or Version** command provides a way to compare a resource with a specific version or branch

To replace the current version of a file with an earlier revision, right-click on the file and select the **Replace With > Revision** command from the context menu. This opens the same comparison dialog as shown in Figure 1–60. Select on any revision and click the **Replace** button to load that version into the workspace.

1.8.5   CVS label decorators

To make it easier to see which resources are under repository control and which might have been changed but not committed, CVS provides a number of label decorations to augment the icons and labels of CVS-controlled resources. To turn on the CVS label decorators, use the **Workbench > Label Decorators** preference page (see Figure 1–61).

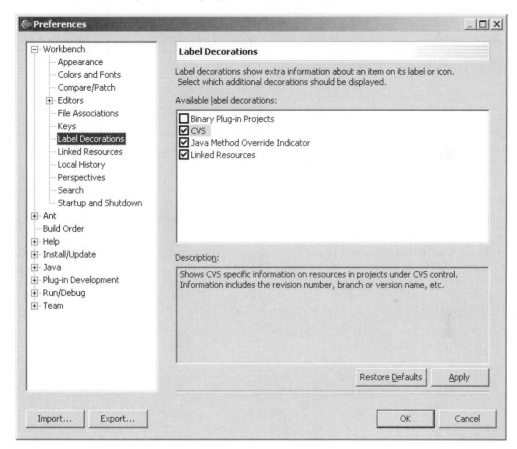

Figure 1–61   Label Decorations preference page.

The actual decorations added are controlled by the options on the **Team > CVS > Label Decorations** preference page. By default, outgoing changes are prefixed with ">".

> **Tip:** To make outgoing changes easier to see, CodePro includes a list colorization feature that changes the foreground or background color of any modified resource that is waiting to be committed to the repository. This and other third-party plug-ins are described in Appendix A.

1.9   Running Applications

Any Java application with a `main()` method, including the `.java` file created in Section 1.4.4 and enhanced in Section 1.7.2, "Templates," is marked with the "running man" icon decoration, indicating that it is runnable. This section shows the different ways to launch (run) a Java application.

1.9.1   *Launching java applications*

The easiest way to run a Java application is to select the class and then select the **Run As > Java Application** command from the **Run** menu or from the **Run** toolbar button (see Figure 1–62). This executes the `main()` method of the application and writes any output (in blue) and error text (in red) to the **Console** view (see Figure 1–63).

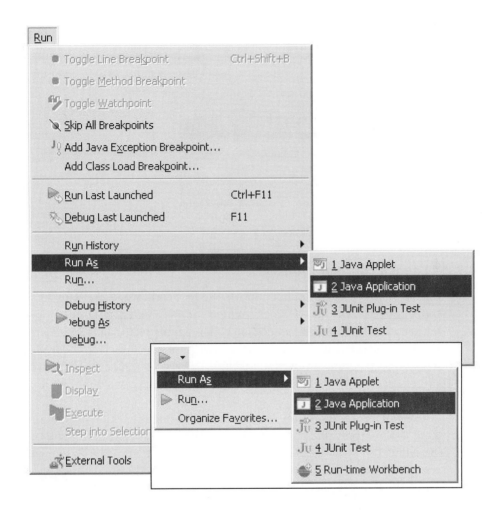

Figure 1–62   Run As > Java Application command.

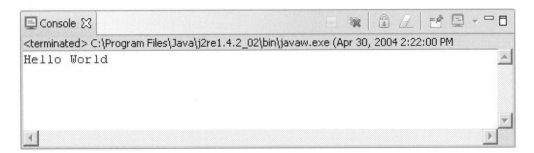

Figure 1–63   Console view.

Once an application has been run, it can be run again by selecting it from the **Run > Run History** menu or from the  **Run** toolbar button (see Figure 1–64). Clicking the **Run** toolbar button or pressing **Ctrl+F11** re-launches the last application you ran.

Figure 1–64   Run history.

1.9.2   *Launch configurations*

Whenever you run an application for the first time using the **Run As > Java Application** command, a *launch configuration* is created. A launch configuration records the information needed to launch a specific Java application. In addition to specifying the name of the Java class, the launch configuration can also specify program and virtual machine (VM) arguments, the JRE and classpath to use, and even the default perspectives to use when running or debugging the application.

A launch configuration may be edited using the launch configuration (**Run**) dialog accessible from the **Run > Run...** command (see Figure 1–65). The **Main** tab specifies the project and class to be run; the **Arguments** tab records the program parameters (as space-separated strings) and VM arguments; the **JRE** tab specifies the JRE to use (it defaults to the JRE specified in your **Java > Installed JREs** preferences); the **Classpath** tab is used to override or augment the default classpath used to find the class files needed run the application; the **Source** tab specifies the location of the source files used to display the source of an application while debugging; and the **Common** tab records information about where the launch configuration is stored and which perspectives to use when running or debugging the application.

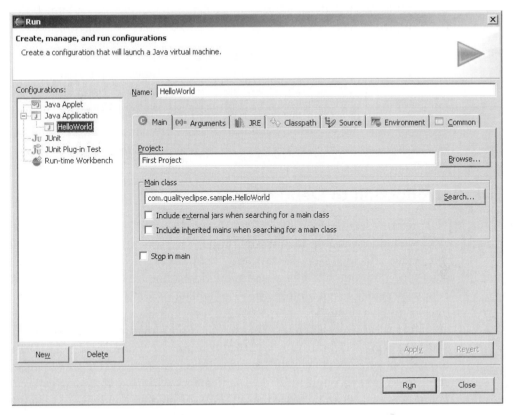

Figure 1–65   Launch configuration (Run) dialog.

The **Java Applet** configuration type is very similar to the **Java Application** type, but is specifically designed to be used with Java applets. In addition to the tabs available for Java applications, it adds a **Parameters** tab that specifies applet-specific information such as width, height, name, and applet parameters.

The **JUnit** configuration is used to run JUnit test cases. *JUnit test cases* are a special type of Java application, so many of the configuration options are the same as for Java applications and applets. It adds a **Test** tab for specifying settings unique to the test case that will be executed. We will discuss JUnit in more detail in Section 1.11, "Introduction to Testing."

The **Runtime Workbench** configuration is used specifically to test Eclipse plug-ins you are developing. It provides a mechanism for starting up another workbench with full control over which plug-ins are loaded, active, and debuggable. We will discuss this in more detail in Chapter 2, "A Simple Plug-in Example."

> **Tip:** Eclipse supports hot code replacement during debug operations when using JDK 1.4 to run an application. If JDK 1.4 isn't your default JRE, you can specify it as the one to use when running or debugging an application by selecting it from the drop-down list on the **JRE** tab of the launch configurations dialog (if it isn't in the list, you can add it via the **New** button).

1.10   Introduction to Debugging

The previous section showed how to run a Java application using the options available under the **Run** menu. Any output or errors are written to the **Console** view. Placing `System.out.printlin()` statements at appropriate places in your code will give you limited debugging capabilities. Fortunately, Eclipse provides a much more effective debugging solution in the form of its integrated Java debugger.

The easiest way to debug a Java application is to select the class and then select the **Run > Debug As > Java Application** command (or the 🐞 **Debug** toolbar button). This opens the **Debug** perspective (see Figure 1–8), which you can use to step through individual statements within your code, set breakpoints, and inspect and change the values associated with individual variables.

1.10.1   Setting breakpoints

To stop the debugger at a particular location in the code, set a breakpoint. At the location where you would like to set the breakpoint, right-click in the marker bar of the editor and select the **Toggle Breakpoint** command (see Figure 1–66). In addition to right-clicking, you can also double-click the marker bar to the left of the line at which you want to place the breakpoint. A breakpoint marker appears next to the appropriate source code line.

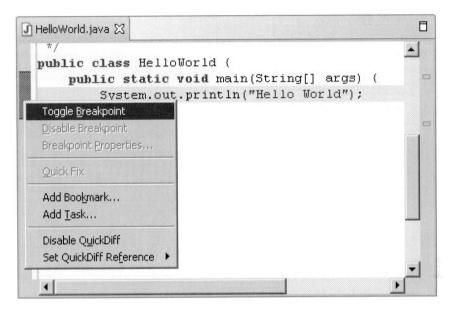

Figure 1–66   Adding a breakpoint.

Tip: If you are not hitting a breakpoint that you set, take a close look at how the breakpoint appears in the gutter. For an enabled breakpoint, you will see either a plain blue bullet or a blue bullet with a small checkmark. The checkmark icon only appears after launching the VM and the breakpoint exists in a loaded class.

With one or more breakpoints set, the application runs until it encounters a breakpoint and then stops before executing the line with the breakpoint. The debugger shows which program threads are running and which ones have been suspended. It also shows the line of code at which execution has stopped, and highlights that line of code in the editor (see Figure 1–67).

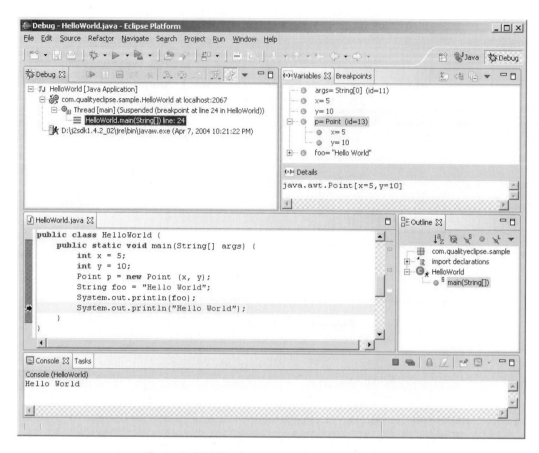

Figure 1–67   The debugger, stopping at a breakpoint.

Tip: Check the **Remove terminated launches when a new launch is created** checkbox on the **Run/Debug** preference page to automatically clean up old launches.

1.10.2   Using the debug view

Once execution has stopped on a breakpoint, the **Debug** view presents various options for resuming execution, stepping through the program statement-by-statement, or terminating it altogether.

The ⏵ **Resume** button (also the **F8** key) in the **Debug** view resumes the execution of a program until it either ends on its own or encounters another breakpoint, while the ⏹ **Terminate** button stops execution of a program entirely. The **Step Into** button (also the **F3** key) executes the next expression in the highlighted statement, while the 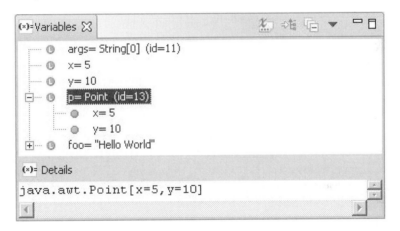 **Step Over** button (also the **F6** key) steps over the highlighted statement and stops on the next statement.

1.10.3   Using the variables view

The **Variables** view shows the state of the variables in the current stack frame (see Figure 1–68). Selecting a variable shows its value in the details pane at the bottom of the view. Primitive variable types show their values directly, while object types can be expanded to show their individual elements. You can change the value of a primitive in this view, but you can't change the value of object types unless you use the **Expressions** view (see Section 1.10.4, "Using the expressions view"). Note that the variables listed in the **Variables** view change as you step through your program.

Figure 1–68   Variables view.

1.10.4   Using the expressions view

The **Expressions** view (see Figure 1–69) provides a place to inspect values in the debugger and discover the results of various expressions entered into the editor, the detail pane of the **Variables** view, or the detail pane of the **Expressions** view.

To use the **Expressions** view, first select the expression to execute. This can be an existing expression or one that you enter. Next, select the **Display** or **Inspect** command from the popup menu in the editor, the **Variables** view, or the **Expressions** view.

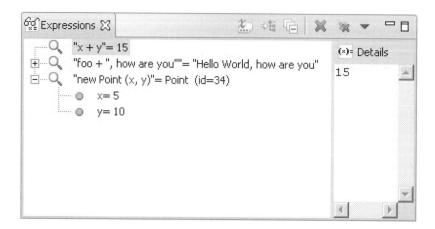

Figure 1–69   Expressions view.

If you select the **Display** command while an expression is selected in an editor, the results will be shown in the **Display** view. When an expression is selected in the **Variables** view or **Expressions** view, the results will be shown in the detail pane of that view.

If you select the **Inspect** command, a popup window will appear containing the results of the expression. Pressing **Ctrl+Shift+I** will move the results to the **Expressions** view. As with the **Variables** view, primitive variable types show their values directly while object types can be expanded to show their individual elements.

1.11   Introduction to Testing

In addition to manually testing an application by running or debugging it, Eclipse supports the JUnit framework (see *www.junit*.org) for creating and running repeatable test cases.

1.11.1   *Creating test cases*

To create a test case, you first need to add the junit.jar file (from the org.junit plug-in) to your project as an external JAR using the Java **Build Path > Libraries** project property page. Once this is done, select the class for which you want to create a test case, open the **New** wizard, and select the **Java > JUnit > JUnit Test Case** option. This invokes the **JUnit TestCase** wizard (see Figure 1–70), which creates a JUnit test case.

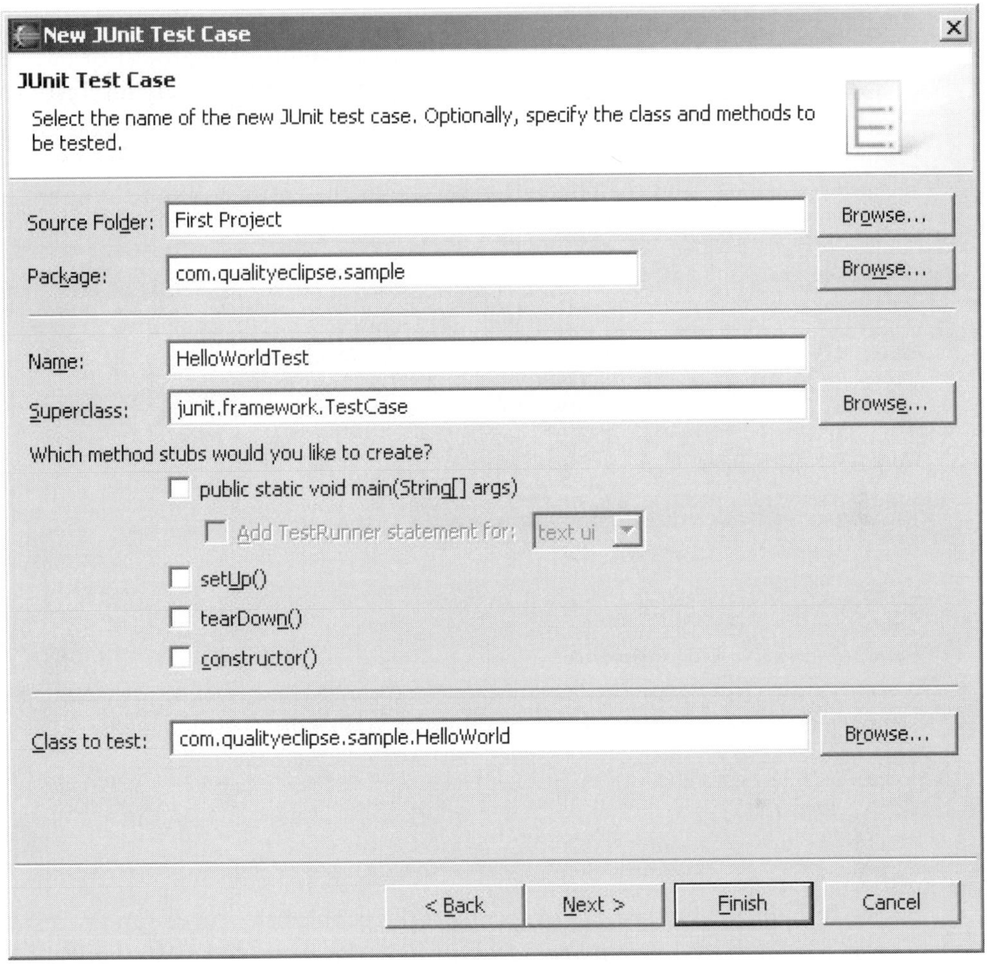

Figure 1–70   JUnit TestCase wizard.

By default, the name of the new test case is the name of the test class with the word "Test" added to the end. You can optionally have the wizard create `main()`, `setup()`, and `teardown()` methods as well as test methods for any public or protected method in the test class.

> **Tip:** CodePro includes a more advanced TestCase wizard that provides a number of enhancements over the Eclipse TestCase wizard, such as the ability to specify arbitrary test cases, generate better default code, and support the creation of test fixtures.

1.11.2   Running test cases

Once a test case is created, select the test case class (or the project or package containing the test case) and then select the **Run > Run As > JUnit Test** command. This opens the **JUnit** view (see Figure 1–71), which shows the results of the test run. The **Failures** tab shows a list of the failures that were recorded in the test case, and the **Hierarchy** tab shows the entire test suite as a tree.

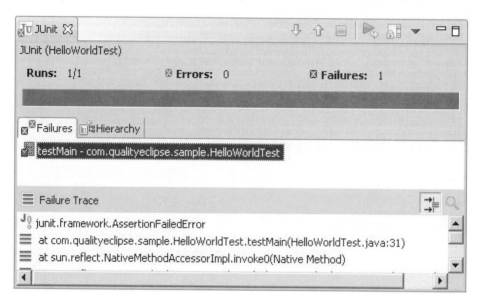

Figure 1–71   JUnit view.

If there are any test failures, correct the problem(s) and re-run the test by clicking on the ![Rerun icon] **Rerun last Test** button in the **JUnit** view. Alternatively, re-run the last test by selecting it from the **Run** menu or toolbar button. If you need to customize the test configuration, select the **Run > Run...** command to open the launch configuration dialog (see Figure 1–65).

1.12   Summary

In this chapter, we gave you a whirlwind tour of the major components of the Eclipse IDE that you will need to use to develop Eclipse plug-ins. At this point, you should be comfortable navigating the Eclipse UI and using the built-in Eclipse tools to create, edit, run, debug, and test your Java code.

In the next chapter, we will dive right in and get our hands dirty creating our first Eclipse plug-in. Over each succeeding chapter, we will introduce more and more layers of detail and slowly convert our plug-in from a simple example into a powerful tool that we can use on a daily basis while doing Eclipse development.

References

Eclipse-Overview.pdf (available on the *eclipse.org* Web site).

Shavor, Sherry, Jim D'Anjou, Scott Fairbrother, Dan Kehn, John Kellerman, and Pat McCarthy, *The Java Developer's Guide to Eclipse*, Addison-Wesley, Boston, MA, 2003.

Eclipse Wiki (*eclipsewiki.swiki.net*).

CVS (*www.cvshome.org*).

Fowler, Martin, *Refactoring: Improving the Design of Existing Code*, Addison-Wesley, Boston, MA, 1999 (*www.refactoring.com*).

JUnit (*www.junit.org*).

CHAPTER 2

A Simple Plug-in Example

Before covering each area of commercial plug-in construction in-depth, it is useful to create a simple plug-in on which discussion and examples will be based. This chapter takes a step-by-step approach to creating a simple but fully operational plug-in that will be enhanced bit-by-bit during the course of this book. This process provides valuable first-hand experience using the Eclipse IDE and touches on each aspect of building and maintaining a commercial plug-in.

2.1 The Favorites Plug-in

The **Favorites plug-in**, which you'll build over the course of this book, displays a list of resources, lets you add and remove resources from this list, easily opens an editor on a selected resource, updates the list automatically as a result of events elsewhere in the system, and more. Subsequent chapters discuss aspects of commercial plug-in development in terms of enhancements to the **Favorites** plug-in. This chapter starts the process by covering the creation of the **Favorites** plug-in in its simplest form using the following steps:

- Creating a plug-in project
- Reviewing the generated code
- Building a product
- Installing and running the product

2.2   Creating a Plug-in Project

The first step is to create a plug-in project using the Eclipse **New Project wizard**. In addition to creating a new project, this wizard has a number of different code generation options for creating sample plug-in code such as views, editors, and actions. To keep things simple and focus only on the essentials of plug-in creation, select the **Plug-in with a view** option as outlined in the next subsection.

2.2.1   New plug-in project wizard

From the **File** menu, select **New > Project** to launch the **New Project** wizard (see Figure 2–1). On this first page of the wizard, select **Plug-in Development > Plug-in Project** from the list, followed by the **Next** button.

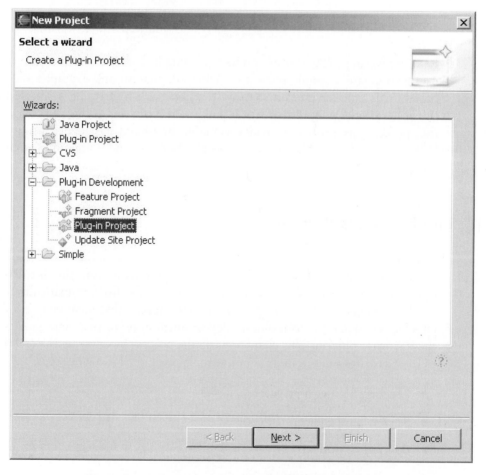

Figure 2–1   New Project wizard page 1—selecting a project type.

On the next page of the wizard (see Figure 2–2), enter the name of the project; in this case, it's `com.qualityeclipse.favorites`, which is the same as the Favorites plug-in identifier. Click the **Next** button. Chapter 3, "Eclipse Infrastructure," discusses plug-in identifiers and other aspects of plug-in architecture in more detail.

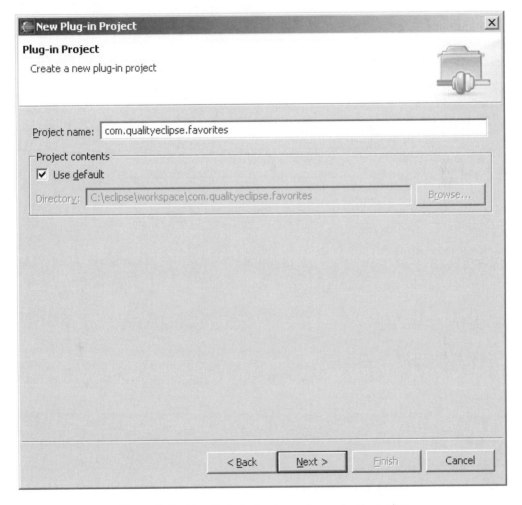

Figure 2–2   New Project wizard page 2—naming the project.

Tip: A project can be named anything, but it is easier to name it the same as the plug-in identifier. By convention, this is the plug-in project-naming scheme that the Eclipse organization uses for most of its work. Because of this, the New Project wizard assumes that the project name and the plug-in identifier are the same.

The next page of the wizard (see Figure 2–3) provides fields for specifying the Java project information. For the purposes of this example, all the default values provided by the **New Plug-in Project** wizard are correct, so click the **Next** button.

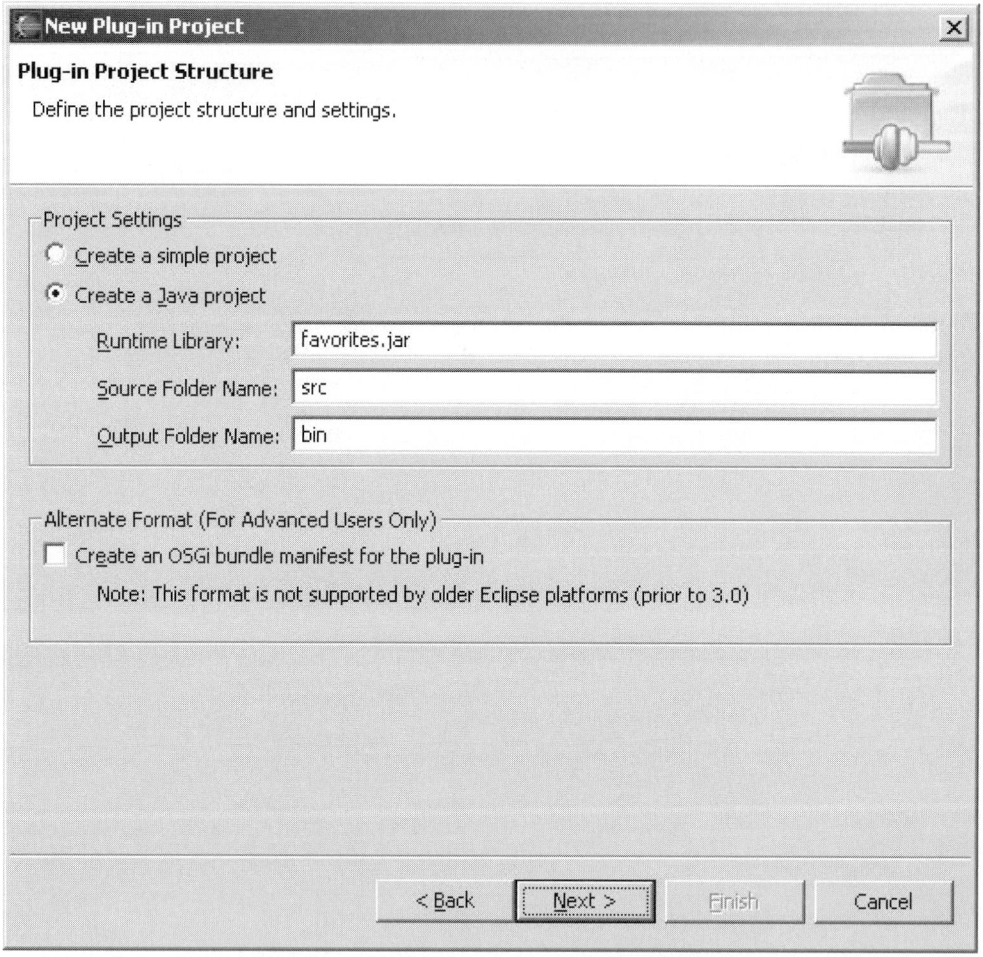

```
New Plug-in Project                                              [X]

Plug-in Project Structure
Define the project structure and settings.

┌─Project Settings──────────────────────────────────────────────┐
│  ○ Create a simple project                                     │
│  ● Create a Java project                                       │
│      Runtime Library:    │favorites.jar                      │ │
│      Source Folder Name: │src                                │ │
│      Output Folder Name: │bin                                │ │
└────────────────────────────────────────────────────────────────┘

┌─Alternate Format (For Advanced Users Only)────────────────────┐
│  ☐ Create an OSGi bundle manifest for the plug-in             │
│     Note: This format is not supported by older Eclipse platforms (prior to 3.0) │
└────────────────────────────────────────────────────────────────┘


                     < Back    Next >    Finish    Cancel
```

Figure 2–3 New Project wizard page 3—naming the plug-in.

2.2.2 Define the plug-in

Each plug-in has an XML manifest file named `plugin.xml` that defines the plug-in and how it relates to other plug-ins in the system, plus a Java class that represents the plug-in programmatically. The next wizard page (see Figure 2–4) displays options for generating both the plug-in manifest and plug-in Java class. Supply the **ID, Version, Name** and **Provider Name** for the plug-in.

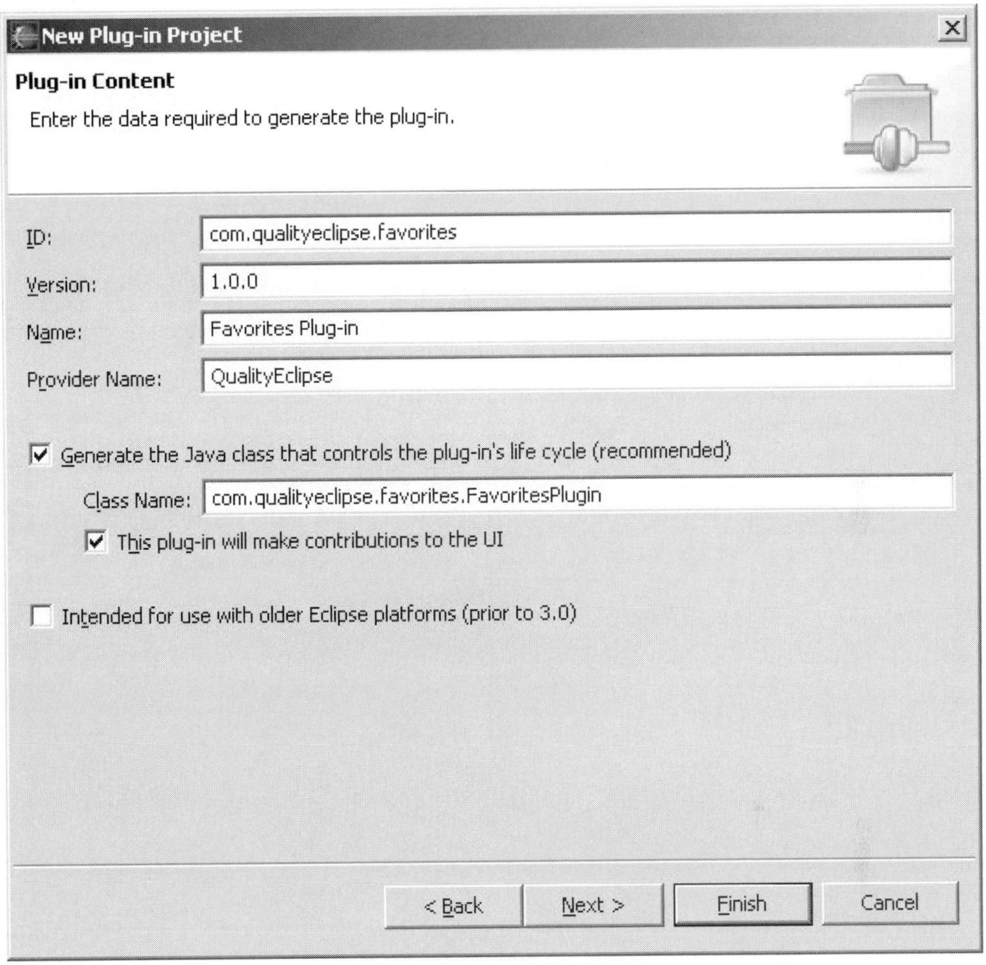

Figure 2–4   New Project wizard page 4—describing the plug-in.

The **New Project** wizard next displays the various plug-in pieces that can be automatically generated by the wizard (see Figure 2–5). There are many different options on this page for generating quite a bit of sample code. It is useful to try out each option and review the code that is generated, but for this example, select **Plug-in with a view** and click the **Next** button.

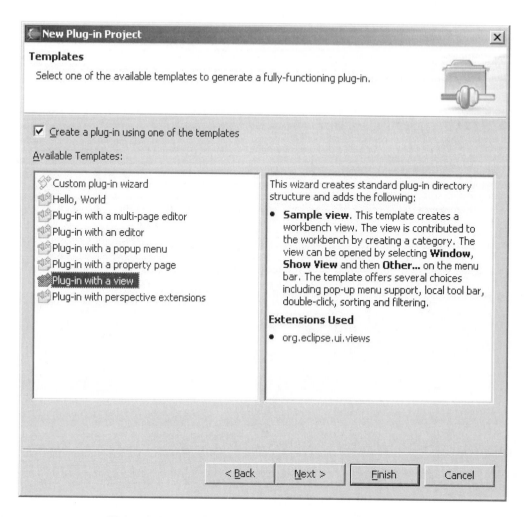

Figure 2–5   New Project wizard page 5—selecting a plug-in type.

2.2.3   Define the view

Selecting view code generation options is the next step in this process (see Figure 2–6). Most of the default values on this page are correct for this example. Change only the **View Category Name** field and uncheck the **Add the view to the resource perspective** checkbox to simplify the generated plug-in manifest file.

Finally, uncheck each of the code generation options on the last wizard page and click the **Finish** button (see Figure 2–7). Each of these checkboxes represents code that could be generated as part of the **Favorites** view. We'll cover these in subsequent chapters.

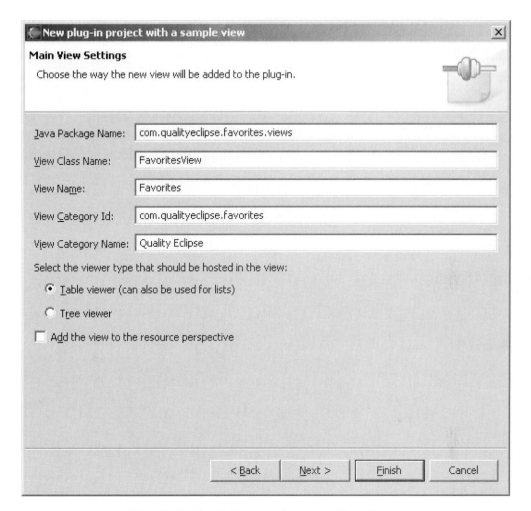

Figure 2–6   New Project wizard page 6—defining the view.

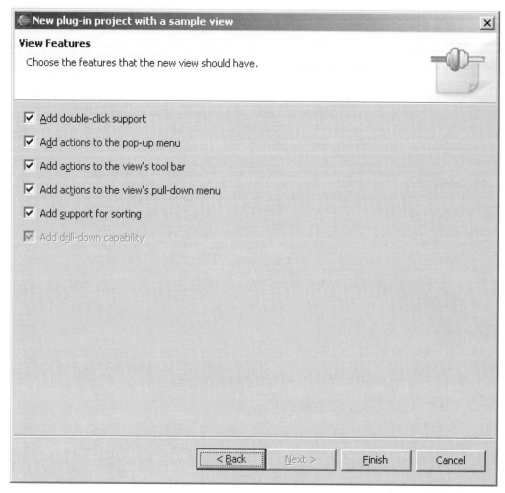

Figure 2–7 New Project wizard page 7—code generation options for the view.

2.2.4 Project welcome page

When you click the **Finish** button, the new plug-in project is created and the plug-in manifest editor is automatically opened (see Figure 2–8). The first page of this editor displays information about code the wizard generated and tips for working with the new plug-in project. Other aspects of the plug-in manifest editor are discussed in the "Plug-in manifest" section of this chapter.

> The information displayed on the project welcome page is stored in the `.template` file located in the project's root directory. The project's welcome page is distinct from the feature-level welcome page discussed in Section 18.2.3, "The welcome.xml page."

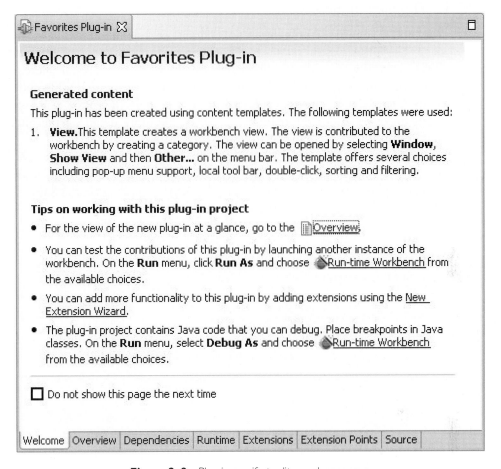

Figure 2–8   Plug-in manifest editor welcome page.

2.3   Reviewing the Generated Code

A review of the code generated by the **New Plug-in Project** wizard provides a brief look at the major parts comprising the sample plug-in:

- The plug-in manifest
- The plug-in class
- The **Favorites** view

2.3.1   The plug-in manifest

The plug-in manifest editor shows the contents of the plug-in manifest, which defines how this plug-in relates to all other plug-ins in the system. This editor is automatically opened to its first page (see Figure 2–8) as a result of creating a new plug-in project. If the plug-in manifest editor is closed, double-clicking on the plugin.xml file in the **Navigator** view reopens the editor. The following is an overview of the manifest editor, while more detail on the plug-in manifest itself can be found in Chapter 3.

Although the editor is a convenient way to modify the plug-in's description, it's still useful to peek at the XML behind the scenes to see how different parts of the editor relate to the underlying XML. Clicking on the **Source** tab of the editor displays the XML used to define the plug-in manifest:

```xml
<?xml version="1.0" encoding="UTF-8"?>

<?Eclipse version="3.0"?>
<plugin
   id="com.qualityeclipse.favorites"
   name="Favorites Plug-in"
   version="1.0.0"
   provider-name="QualityEclipse"
   class="com.qualityeclipse.favorites.FavoritesPlugin">

   <runtime>
      <library name="favorites.jar">
        <export name="*"/>
      </library>
   </runtime>
   <requires>
      <import plugin="org.eclipse.ui"/>
      <import plugin="org.eclipse.core.runtime.compatibility"/>
   </requires>

   <extension
        point="org.eclipse.ui.views">
      <category
          name="Quality Eclipse"
          id="com.qualityeclipse.favorites">
      </category>
      <view
          name="Favorites"
          icon="icons/sample.gif"
          category="com.qualityeclipse.favorites"
          class="com.qualityeclipse.favorites.views.FavoritesView"
          id="com.qualityeclipse.favorites.views.FavoritesView">
      </view>
   </extension>

</plugin>
```

The first line of this file declares the file to be an XML file, while the rest of the file can be divided into chunks of XML and associated with various pages in the manifest editor.

The **Overview** page of the manifest editor shows a summary of the plug-in manifest (see Figure 2–9). The section on this page describing general information such as the plug-in identification (ID), name, version, and provider corresponds to the first chunk of XML in the plug-in manifest:

```
<plugin
    id="com.qualityeclipse.favorites"
    name="Favorites Plug-in"
    version="1.0.0"
    provider-name="QualityEclipse"
    class="com.qualityeclipse.favorites.FavoritesPlugin">
```

You can edit the information on the **Overview** page or switch to the **Source** page and edit the XML directly.

> **Tip:** Making changes to any page other than the Source page of the manifest editor causes the manifest editor to reformat the XML. If you are particular about the formatting of this file, then either use only the Source page to perform editing or use another editor.

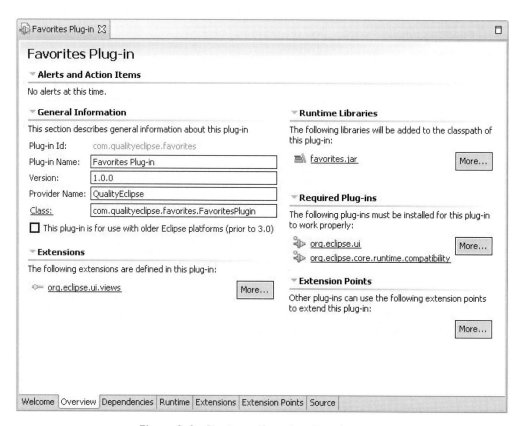

Figure 2–9   Plug-in manifest editor Overview page.

The reliance of this plug-in on other plug-ins in the system appears on the **Dependencies** page of the plug-in manifest editor (see Figure 2–10).

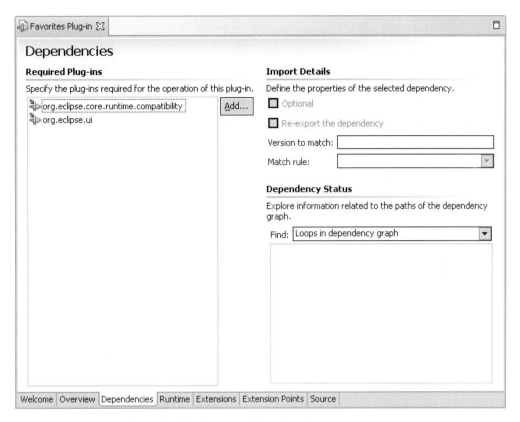

Figure 2–10   Plug-in manifest editor Dependencies page.

This corresponds to the `<requires>` chunk of XML in the plug-in manifest:

```
<requires>
  <import plugin="org.eclipse.ui"/>
  <import plugin="org.eclipse.core.runtime.compatibility"/>
</requires>
```

For the **Favorites** plug-in, this section indicates a dependency on the `org.eclipse.core.runtime.compatibity` and `org.eclipse.ui` plug-ins. This dependency declaration differs from the **Favorites** project's Java build path (also known as the compile-time classpath) because the Java build path is a compile-time artifact while the plug-in dependency declaration comes into play during plug-in execution. Because the project was created as a plug-in project and has the `org.eclipse.pde.PluginNature` nature (see Section 14.3, "Natures," for more on project natures), any changes to this dependency list will automatically be reflected in the Java build path, but not the reverse. If these two aspects of your plug-in get out of sync, then you can have a plug-in that compiles and builds, but does not execute properly.

> **Tip:** Edit this dependency list rather than the Java build path so that the two are automatically always in sync.

The **Run-time** page of the manifest editor (see Figure 2–11) corresponds to the `<runtime>` chunk of XML, which defines what libraries are delivered with the plug-in and used by the plug-in during execution, what package prefixes are used within each library (used to speed up plug-in loading time), and whether other plug-ins can reference the code in the library. For the **Favorites** plug-in, all the code is contained in a single JAR file named `favorites.jar`, which contains classes all using the "com.qualityeclipse.favorites" prefix:

```
<runtime>
   <library name="favorites.jar">
      <packages prefixes="com.qualityeclipse.favorites"/>
   </library>
</runtime>
```

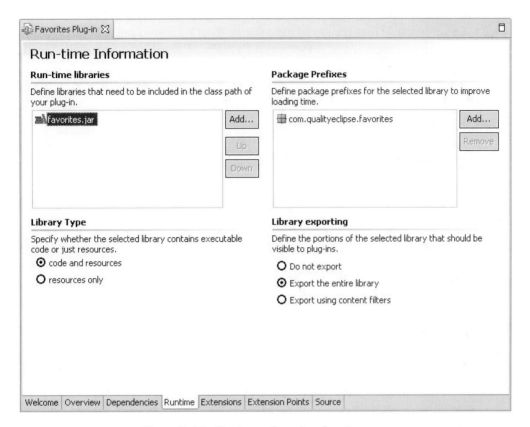

Figure 2–11 Plug-in manifest editor Run-time page.

The **Extensions** page (see Figure 2–12) displays how this plug-in augments functionality already provided by other plug-ins in the system, and corresponds to the `<extension point="org.eclipse.ui.views">` chunk of XML:

```
<extension
      point="org.eclipse.ui.views">
   <category
         name="Quality Eclipse"
         id="com.qualityeclipse.favorites">
   </category>
   <view
         name="Favorites"
         icon="icons/sample.gif"
         category="com.qualityeclipse.favorites"
         class="com.qualityeclipse.favorites.views.FavoritesView"
         id="com.qualityeclipse.favorites.views.FavoritesView">
   </view>
</extension>
```

The **Favorites** plug-in declares an extension to the `org.eclipse.ui` plug-in using the `org.eclipse.ui.views` extension point by providing an additional category of views named **Quality Eclipse** and a new view in that category named **Favorites**.

Figure 2–12   Plug-in manifest editor Extensions page.

Selecting an item in the tree on the **Extensions** page causes the **Properties** view to display the specifics for the selected element (see Figure 2–13). In this case, selecting **Favorites (view)** in the **Extensions** page displays the name, identifier, class, and more information about the **Favorites** view that is being declared. This corresponds to the XML attributes defined in the `<view>` chunk of XML shown previously.

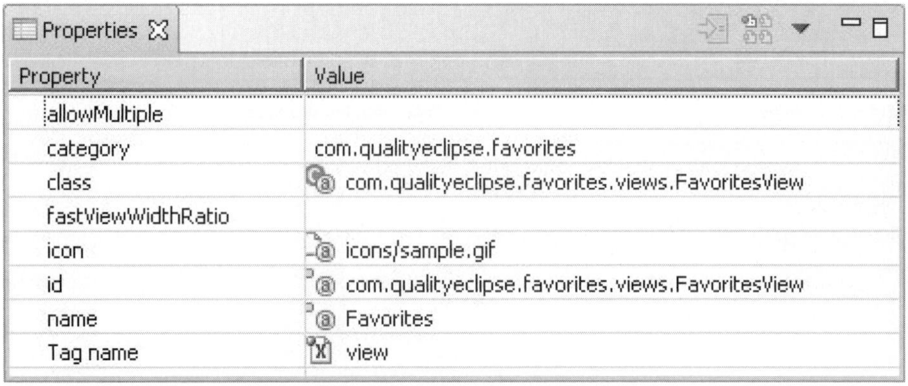

Properties ⊠	
Property	**Value**
allowMultiple	
category	com.qualityeclipse.favorites
class	🔳ⓐ com.qualityeclipse.favorites.views.FavoritesView
fastViewWidthRatio	
icon	⌐ⓐ icons/sample.gif
id	⁀ⓐ com.qualityeclipse.favorites.views.FavoritesView
name	⁀ⓐ Favorites
Tag name	🅇 view

Figure 2–13   Properties view showing extension information.

Finally, the **Extension Points** page of the manifest editor (see Figure 2–14) facilitates the definition of new extension points so that other plug-ins can augment functionality provided by this plug-in. At this time, the **Favorites** plug-in doesn't define any new functionality that can be augmented by other plug-ins, so no new extension points are declared on this page (see Section 17.2, "Defining an Extension Point").

Figure 2–14   Plug-in manifest editor Extension Points page.

2.3.2   The plug-in class

Each plug-in may optionally declare a class that represents the plug-in from a programmatic standpoint as displayed on the manifest editor's **Overview** page (see Figure 2–9). If the plug-in manifest does not declare a class for this purpose, the system automatically supplies a generic class to fill that role. In the **Favorites** plug-in, this class is named com.qualityeclipse.favorites .FavoritesPlugin.

```
package com.qualityeclipse.favorites;

import org.eclipse.ui.plugin.*;
import org.eclipse.core.runtime.*;

/**
 * The main plug-in class to be used in the desktop.
 */
public class FavoritesPlugin extends AbstractUIPlugin {
```

```
//The shared instance.
private static FavoritesPlugin plugin;

/**
 * The constructor.
 */
public FavoritesPlugin(IPluginDescriptor descriptor) {
    super(descriptor);
    plugin = this;
}

/**
 * Returns the shared instance.
 */
public static FavoritesPlugin getDefault() {
    return plugin;
}
}
```

When the plug-in is activated, the Eclipse system instantiates the plug-in class before loading any other classes in the plug-in. This single plug-in class instance is used by the Eclipse system throughout the life of the plug-in and no other instance is created.

Typically, plug-in classes declare a static field to reference this singleton so that it can be easily shared throughout the plug-in as needed. In our case, the **Favorites** plug-in defines a field named `plugin` that is assigned in the constructor and accessed using the `getDefault` method.

> **Tip:** The Eclipse system always instantiates exactly one instance of an active plug-in's `Plugin` class. You can add guard code to your `Plugin` class constructor to ensure that your own code does not create any new instances. For example:
>
> ```
> public FavoritesPlugin(IPluginDescriptor descriptor) {
>     super(descriptor);
>     if (plugin != null)
>         throw new IllegalStateException(
>             "Plug-in class already exists");
>     plugin = this;
> }
> ```

2.3.3   The favorites view

In addition to the plug-in manifest and plug-in class, the **New Plug-in Project** wizard generated code for a simple view (see below) called the **Favorites** view. At this point, the view creates and displays information from a sample model, but in subsequent chapters, this view will be hooked up to a favorites model and will display information from the favorites items contained within that model.

```
package com.qualityeclipse.favorites.views;

import org.eclipse.core.resources.*;
import org.eclipse.jface.dialogs.*;
import org.eclipse.jface.viewers.*;
import org.eclipse.swt.SWT;
import org.eclipse.swt.graphics.Image;
import org.eclipse.swt.widgets.Composite;
import org.eclipse.ui.ISharedImages;
import org.eclipse.ui.PlatformUI;
import org.eclipse.ui.part.ViewPart;

/**
 * This sample class demonstrates how to plug in a new
 * workbench view. The view shows data obtained from the
 * model. The sample creates a dummy model on-the-fly,
 * but a real implementation would connect to the model
 * available either in this or another plug-in (e.g.,
 * the workspace). The view is connected to the model
 * using a content provider.
 * <p>
 * The view uses a label provider to define how model
 * objects should be presented in the view. Each
 * view can present the same model objects using
 * different labels and icons, if needed. Alternatively,
 * a single label provider can be shared between views
 * to ensure that objects of the same type are
 * presented in the same way everywhere.
 * <p>
 */

public class FavoritesView extends ViewPart {
    private TableViewer viewer;

    /*
     * The content provider class is responsible for
     * providing objects to the view. It can wrap
     * existing objects in adapters or simply return
     * objects as-is. These objects may be sensitive
     * to the current input of the view, or ignore
     * it and always show the same content
     * (like the Task List, for example).
     */

    class ViewContentProvider
        implements IStructuredContentProvider {
```

```java
    public void inputChanged(Viewer v,
        Object oldInput,
        Object newInput) {
    }
    public void dispose() {
    }
    public Object[] getElements(Object parent) {
        return new String[] {"One","Two","Three"};
    }
}
class ViewLabelProvider extends LabelProvider
    implements ITableLabelProvider {
    public String getColumnText(Object obj, int index){
        return getText(obj);
    }
    public Image getColumnImage(Object obj, int index){
        return getImage(obj);
    }
    public Image getImage(Object obj) {
        return PlatformUI.getWorkbench().
            getSharedImages().getImage(
                ISharedImages.IMG_OBJ_ELEMENT);
    }
}

/**
 * The constructor.
 */
public FavoritesView() {
}

/**
 * This is a callback that will allow us
 * to create the viewer and initialize it.
 */
public void createPartControl(Composite parent) {
    viewer = new TableViewer(parent,
        SWT.MULTI | SWT.H_SCROLL | SWT.V_SCROLL);
    viewer.setContentProvider(new ViewContentProvider());
    viewer.setLabelProvider(new ViewLabelProvider());
    viewer.setInput(ResourcesPlugin.getWorkspace());
}

private void showMessage(String message) {
    MessageDialog.openInformation(
        viewer.getControl().getShell(),
        "Favorites",
        message);
}

/**
 * Passing the focus request to the viewer's control.
 */
public void setFocus() {
    viewer.getControl().setFocus();
}
```

```
/**
 * FOR TESTING: Answer the Favorites viewer.
 *
 * @return the Favorites viewer
 */
public TableViewer getFavoritesViewer() {
   return viewer;
}
}
```

2.4   Building a Product

Building a commercial product involves packaging up only those elements to
be delivered to the customer in a form that the customer can install into his or
her environment. You can build the product in several different ways, including manually or by using a Windows batch script, a UNIX shell script, or an
Apache Ant script. You can deliver the end-product as a single compressed file
or as a standalone executable. For our purposes, the **Favorites** plug-in will be
delivered with source code as a single compressed zip file.

2.4.1   Building manually

Building a product manually involves launching an Eclipse **Export** wizard, fill-
ing out a few fields, and clicking the **Finish** button. Select the **File > Export**
command to launch the desired export wizard. On the first wizard page (see
Figure 2–15), select **Deployable plug-ins and fragments** and click the **Next**
button.

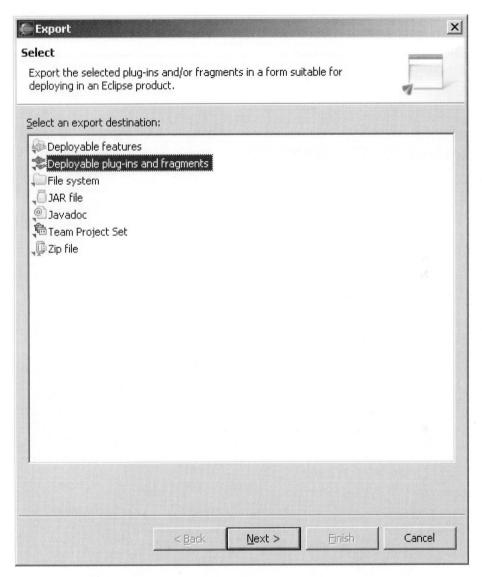

Figure 2–15 Export wizard page 1—choosing the type of export.

On the second page of the **Export** wizard (see Figure 2–16), select the plug-ins to be exported and enter the name of the zip file to contain the result.

Figure 2–16   Export wizard page 2—specifying the zip file's contents.

The created zip file contains the plug-in and its source code as specified in the **Export** wizard:

```
plugins/com.qualityeclipse.favorites_1.0.0/favorites.jar
plugins/com.qualityeclipse.favorites_1.0.0/favoritessrc.zip
plugins/com.qualityeclipse.favorites_1.0.0/plugin.xml
```

Unfortunately, this manual process is just that... manual, and therefore prone to errors. Manually building a product is fine once or twice, but what if a different person in the company needs to build the product? What happens as the product grows and encompasses more plug-ins? A commercial product needs a repeatable and reliable method for building the product.

2.4.2   Building with apache ant

An Apache Ant script provides a reliable, flexible, and repeatable process for building a commercial plug-in project. There is a little more up-front work to set up an Ant script, but it is much less error-prone over time than building a product manually. For more information about Ant and constructing more complex build scripts, see Chapter 19. For the **Favorites** plug-in, create a build.xml file in the com.qualityeclipse.favorites project and enter the following script:

```xml
<?xml version="1.0" encoding="UTF-8"?>
<project name="Favorites" basedir="." default="product">
   <target name="product">

      <!-- Temporary directory used to build
         the product... will be deleted. -->
      <property
         name="temp_dir"
         location="C:/QualityEclipseTemp"/>

      <!-- Product directory where final
         product will be placed. -->
      <property
         name="product_dir"
         location="C:/QualityEclipseProduct"/>

      <!-- Current product version number. -->
      <property
         name="product_version"
         value="1.0.0"/>

      <!-Plugin directory... subdirectory
         of temp directory. -->
      <property
         name="plugin_dir"
         location="${temp_dir}/plugins/
            com.qualityeclipse.favorites
            _${product_version}"/>
```

```
<!-- Clear out the temp directory. -->
    <delete dir="${temp_dir}"/>
    <mkdir dir="${plugin_dir}"/>
    <mkdir dir="${product_dir}"/>

    <!-- Assemble the product in the temp directory. -->
    <jar destfile="${plugin_dir}/favorites.jar">
       <fileset dir="bin"/>
    </jar>
    <copy todir="${plugin_dir}">
       <fileset dir="." includes="plugin.xml"/>
       <fileset dir="." includes="icons/*.gif"/>
    </copy>

    <!-- Build the product from the temp directory. -->
    <zip
       destfile="${product_dir}/
          QualityEclipseTools_v
          ${product_version}.zip">
       <fileset dir="${temp_dir}"/>
    </zip>

  </target>
</project>
```

To execute the Ant script, select the build.xml file in the **Navigator** view, and then from the popup context menu, select **Run Ant...** (see Figure 2–17). When the Ant wizard appears (see Figure 2–18), click the **Run** button to build the product.

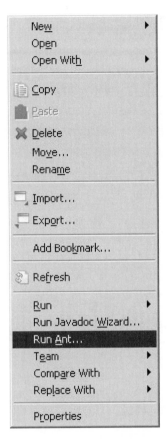

Figure 2–17   The build.xml popup context menu.

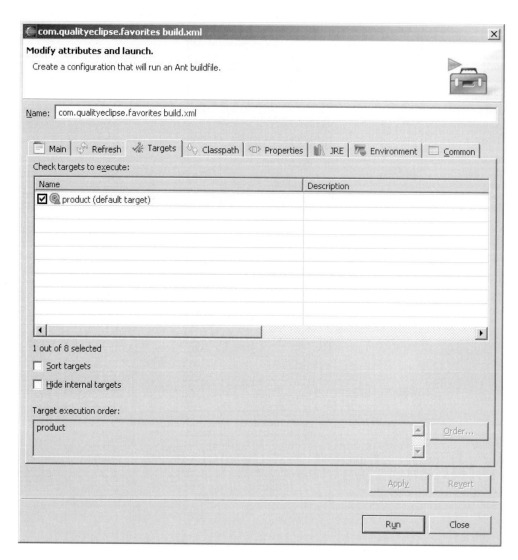

Figure 2–18   The Ant wizard.

2.5   Installing and Running the Product

To install the **Favorites** plug-in, shut down Eclipse, unzip the `QualityEclipseTools_v1.0.0.zip` file the Ant script generated, and restart Eclipse. After Eclipse has restarted, from the **Window** menu, select **Show View > Other...** (see Figure 2–19) to open the **Show View** dialog (see Figure 2–20). In the dialog, expand the **Quality Eclipse** category, select **Favorites,** and then click the **OK** button. This causes the **Favorites** view to open in the current page (see Figure 2–21).

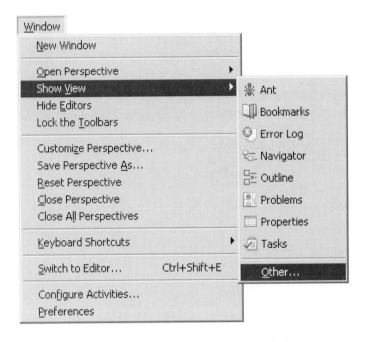

Figure 2–19   Show View > Other… from the Window menu.

Figure 2–20   Show View dialog.

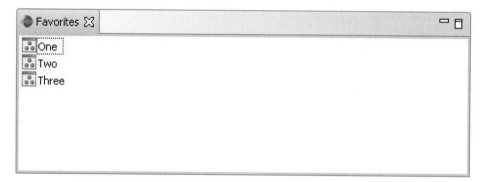

Figure 2–21   The Favorites view in its initial and simplest form.

2.6   Debugging the Product

Inevitably, during the course of producing a product, you'll need to debug a problem or you'll simply have to gain a better understanding of the code through a means more enlightening than just reviewing the source code. You can use the **Runtime Workbench** to determine exactly what happens during product execution so you can solve problems.

2.6.1   Creating a configuration

The first step in this process is to create a configuration in which the product can be debugged. Start by selecting **Debug...** in the **Debug** toolbar menu (see Figure 2–22).

Figure 2–22   Debug menu.

In the dialog that appears, select **Runtime Workbench,** and then click the **New** button (see Figure 2–23). Enter "Favorites" as the name of the configuration.

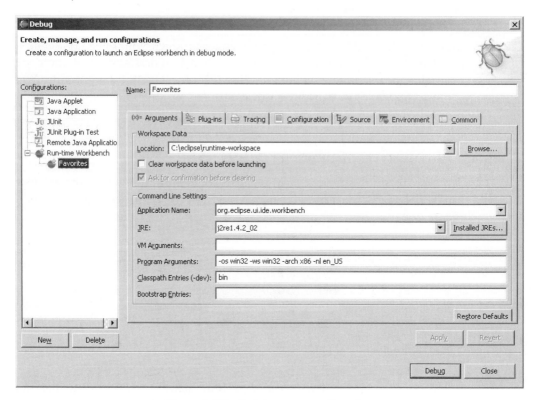

Figure 2–23 Defining a new configuration.

2.6.2 Selecting plug-ins and fragments

Next, select the **Plug-ins** tab and the radio button labeled **Choose plug-ins and fragments to launch from the list** (see Figure 2–24). In the list of plug-ins, make sure that the **Favorites** plug-in is selected in the **Workspace Plug-ins** category, but not in the **External Plug-ins** category.

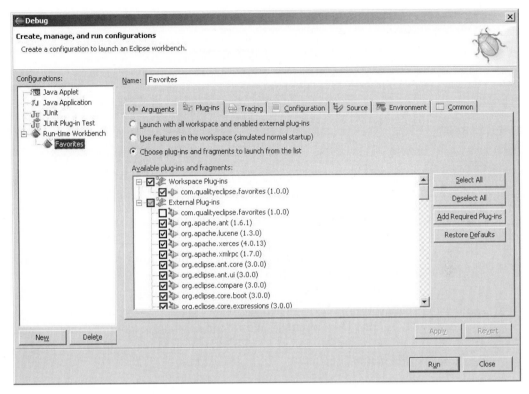

Figure 2–24   Selecting plug-ins in the configuration.

2.6.3   Launching the runtime workbench

Click the **Debug** button to launch the **Runtime Workbench** and debug the product. Now that you've defined the configuration and used it once, it appears in the **Debug** toolbar menu (see Figure 2–22). Selecting it from that menu launches the **Runtime Workbench** without opening the **Configuration** wizard. If the **Plug-in Conflict** dialog appears during this process (see Figure 2–25), open the **Configuration** wizard and review the plug-ins selected on the **Plug-ins and Fragments** page (see Figure 2–24).

Figure 2–25   The Plug-in Conflict dialog.

After clicking the **Debug** button in the **Configuration** wizard or selecting **Favorites** from the **Debug** toolbar menu, Eclipse opens a second workbench window (the **Runtime Workbench,** as opposed to the **Development Workbench**). This **Runtime Workbench** window executes the code in the projects contained by the **Development Workbench.** Making changes and setting breakpoints in the **Development Workbench** affects the execution of the **Runtime Workbench.**

2.7 PDE Views

The Plug-in Development Environment (PDE) provides several views for inspecting various aspects of plug-ins. To open the various PDE views, select **Window > Show View > Other...,** and in the **Show View** dialog, expand both the **PDE** and **PDE Run-time** categories.

2.7.1 The plug-in registry view

The **Plug-in Registry** view displays a tree view of all plug-ins discovered in the current workspace (see Figure 2–26). Expanding the plug-in in the tree shows its components such as extension points, extensions, prerequisites, and run-time libraries. Right-click and select **Properties** to display additional information about each element in the tree (see Figure 2–27).

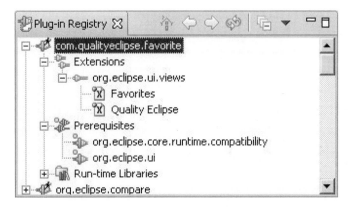

Figure 2–26 The Plug-in Registry view.

Property	Value
Activated	true
Install URL	platform:/plugin/com.qualityeclipse.favorites_1.0.0/
Name	Favorites Plug-in
Provider Name	QualityEclipse
Unique ID	com.qualityeclipse.favorites
Version	1.0.0

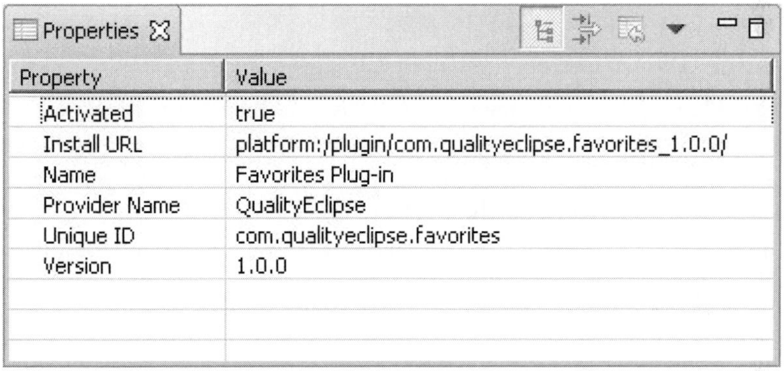

Figure 2–27 The Properties view showing plug-in properties.

2.7.2 The plug-ins view

The **Plug-ins** view shows a tree list of external plug-ins and plug-in projects in the current workspace and provides a quick way to review plug-ins that already exist (see Figure 2–28). You can expand each external plug-in in the tree to browse the files located in the plug-in directory. Similar to the **Plug-in Registry** view, selecting an element in the tree displays additional information about that element in the **Properties** view. Double-clicking on a file element opens that file in an editor for viewing.

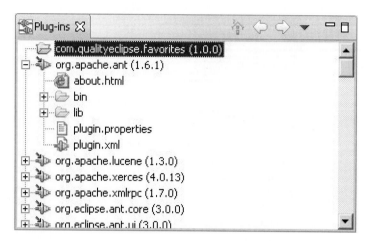

Figure 2–28   The Plug-ins view.

2.7.3   The plug-in dependencies view

The **Plug-in Dependencies** view shows a hierarchy of which plug-ins are
dependent on which other plug-ins, which in turn are dependent on other
plug-ins, and so on (see Figure 2–29). When the view opens, first right-click
and select **Focus On...**, then select the com.qualityeclipse.favorites
plug-in. Double-clicking on an element in the tree opens the plug-in manifest
editor for the corresponding plug-in.

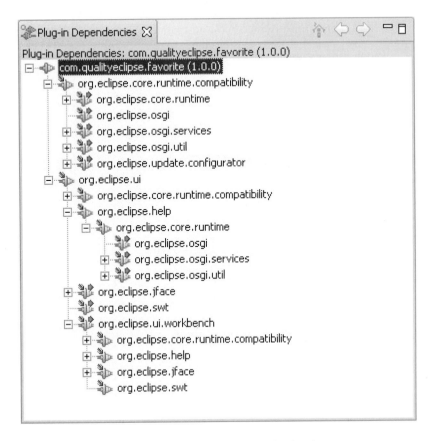

Figure 2–29   The Plug-in Dependencies view.

2.8   Writing Plug-in Tests

Eclipse is a continually moving target, and when building commercial plug-ins, tests are necessary to ensure that the product continues to function properly over multiple releases of Eclipse. If the goal was to develop and release a plug-in once, then manual testing would suffice, but automated tests are better at preventing regressions from creeping into the product over time.

2.8.1   Installing PDE JUnit

JUnit support is built into Eclipse and is excellent for testing normal Java code, but additional functionality is necessary to test plug-in code. The PDE JUnit plug-in provides this additional functionality and is part of the main

Eclipse 3.0 download. If you are using a version of Eclipse prior to Eclipse 3.0, it must be manually downloaded and installed using the following steps:

1. Open a browser on the JDT UI JUnit support page.

2. Go to *www.eclipse.org/*

3. Click on **projects** in the left column.

4. Click on **The Eclipse Project** in the main area.

5. Click on **JDT** in the left column.

6. Click on **UI** in the main area.

7. Click on **org.eclipse.jdt.junit**
   in the **Optional Plug-ins** section.

8. Download the appropriate version of the JUnit plug-in for the Eclipse development environment being used
   (e.g., **org.eclipse.pde.junit_2.1.5** for Eclipse 2.1).

9. Shut down Eclipse.

10. Unzip the downloaded file into the `Plugins` directory.

11. Restart Eclipse.

2.8.2 Creating a plug-in test project

Once PDE JUnit support is installed, use the same procedure as outlined in Section 2.2, "Creating a Plug-in Project," to create a new plug-in project with the following exceptions:

• Name the project **com.qualityeclipse.favorites.test**.

• Name the plug-in run-time library **favoritesTest.jar**.

• Select **Default Plug-in Structure** for code generation.

• Change the plug-in class name to
  com.qualityeclipse.favorites.test.FavoritesTestPlugin.

Once the project has been created, use the **Dependencies** page of the plug-in manifest editor to add the following required plug-ins, and then save the changes:

• **com.qualityeclipse.favorites** in the **Workspace Plug-ins** category (not from the **External Plug-ins** category)

• **org.junit** in the **External Plug-ins** category

2.8.3   Creating a plug-in test

When a project has been created and the plug-in manifest modified, it's time to create a simple test for the **Favorites** plug-in (see the following code example). The goal of the test is to show the **Favorites** view, validate its content, and then hide the view.

The `FavoritesViewTest` plug-in test class looks as follows:

```
package com.qualityeclipse.favorites.test;

import java.util.*;

import junit.framework.*;

import org.eclipse.core.internal.resources.*;
import org.eclipse.jface.dialogs.*;
import org.eclipse.jface.viewers.*;
import org.eclipse.swt.widgets.Display;
import org.eclipse.ui.PlatformUI;

import com.qualityeclipse.favorites.views.FavoritesView;

/**
 * The class <code>FavoritesViewTest</code> contains tests
 * for the class {@link
 *     com.qualityeclipse.favorites.views.FavoritesView}.
 *
 * @pattern JUnit Test Case
 * @generatedBy CodePro Studio
 */
public class FavoritesViewTest extends TestCase
{
    private static final String VIEW_ID =
        "com.qualityeclipse.favorites.views.FavoritesView";

    /**
     * The object that is being tested.
     *
     * @see com.qualityeclipse.favorites.views.FavoritesView
     */
    private FavoritesView testView;

    /**
    /**
     * Construct new test instance.
     *
     * @param name the test name
     */
    public FavoritesViewTest(String name) {
        super(name);
    }
```

```java
/**
 * Perform pre-test initialization.
 *
 * @throws Exception
 *
 * @see TestCase#setUp()
 */
protected void setUp() throws Exception {
    super.setUp();
    // Initialize the test fixture for each test
    // that is run.
    waitForJobs();
    testView = (FavoritesView)
        PlatformUI
            .getWorkbench()
            .getActiveWorkbenchWindow()
            .getActivePage()
            .showView(VIEW_ID);

    // Delay for 3 seconds so that
    // the Favorites view can be seen.
    waitForJobs();
    delay(3000);

    // Add additional setup code here.
}

/**
 * Perform post-test cleanup.
 *
 * @throws Exception
 *
 * @see TestCase#tearDown()
 */
protected void tearDown() throws Exception {
    super.tearDown();
    // Dispose of test fixture.
    waitForJobs();
    PlatformUI
        .getWorkbench()
        .getActiveWorkbenchWindow()
        .getActivePage()
        .hideView(testView);
    // Add additional teardown code here.
}

/**
 * Run the view test.
 */
public void testView() {
    TableViewer viewer = testView.getFavoritesViewer();

    Object[] expectedContent =
        new Object[] { "One", "Two", "Three" };
    Object[] expectedLabels =
        new String[] { "One", "Two", "Three" };
```

```
        // Assert valid content.
        IStructuredContentProvider contentProvider =
            (IStructuredContentProvider)
                viewer.getContentProvider();
        assertEquals(expectedContent,
            contentProvider.getElements(viewer.getInput()));

        // Assert valid labels.
        ILabelProvider labelProvider =
            (ILabelProvider) viewer.getLabelProvider();
        for (int i = 0; i < expectedLabels.length; i++)
            assertEquals(expectedLabels[i],
                labelProvider.getText(expectedContent[i]));
    }

    /**
     * Process UI input but do not return for the
     * specified time interval.
     *
     * @param waitTimeMillis the number of milliseconds
     */
    private void delay(long waitTimeMillis) {
        Display display = Display.getCurrent();

        // If this is the UI thread,
        // then process input.
        if (display != null) {
            long endTimeMillis =
                System.currentTimeMillis() + waitTimeMillis;
            while (System.currentTimeMillis() < endTimeMillis)
            {
                if (!display.readAndDispatch())
                    display.sleep();
            }
            display.update();
        }

        // Otherwise, perform a simple sleep.
        else {
            try {
                Thread.sleep(waitTimeMillis);
            }
            catch (InterruptedException e) {
                // Ignored.
            }
        }
    }

    /**
     * Wait until all background tasks are complete.
     */
    public void waitForJobs() {
        while (Platform.getJobManager().currentJob() != null)
            delay(1000);
    }
```

```
/**
 * Assert that the two arrays are equal.
 * Throw an AssertionException if they are not.
 *
 * @param expected first array
 * @param actual second array
 */
private void assertEquals(Object[] expected, Object[] actual) {
    if (expected == null) {
        if (actual == null)
            return;
        throw new AssertionFailedError(
            "expected is null, but actual is not");
    }
    else {
        if (actual == null)
            throw new AssertionFailedError(
                "actual is null, but expected is not");
    }
    assertEquals(
        "expected.length "
            + expected.length
            + ", but actual.length "
            + actual.length,
        expected.length,
        actual.length);
    for (int i = 0; i < actual.length; i++)
        assertEquals(
            "expected[" + i +
                "] is not equal to actual[" +
                i + "]",
            expected[i],
            actual[i]);
}
}
```

If you are running an older version of Eclipse, the Jobs API does not exist (see Section 20.8, "Background Tasks—Job API"). In this case, replace the waitForJobs method with the following:

```
/**
 * Wait for the Eclipse indexer to complete its work
 * by creating and executing a dummy search
 * so that operations such as the delete do not collide with it.
 */
public static void waitForIndexer() throws JavaModelException {
    new SearchEngine()
        .searchAllTypeNames(
            ResourcesPlugin.getWorkspace(),
            null,
            null,
            IJavaSearchConstants.EXACT_MATCH,
            IJavaSearchConstants.CASE_SENSITIVE,
            IJavaSearchConstants.CLASS,
```

```
      SearchEngine.createJavaSearchScope(new IJavaElement[0]),
      new ITypeNameRequestor() {
   public void acceptClass(
      char[] packageName,
      char[] simpleTypeName,
      char[][] enclosingTypeNames,
      String path) {
   }
   public void acceptInterface(
      char[] packageName,
      char[] simpleTypeName,
      char[][] enclosingTypeNames,
      String path) {
   }
 }, IJavaSearchConstants.WAIT_UNTIL_READY_TO_SEARCH, null);
}
```

2.8.4   Running a plug-in test

The next step after creating a test class is to configure and execute the test. Similar to creating a configuration described in Section 2.6.1, "Creating a configuration," creating a test configuration involves first selecting the **Run > Run As > JUnit Plug-in test** command. Once the **Configuration** wizard appears, name the configuration "**Favorites Test**" and select the com.quali-tyeclipse.favorites.test.FavoritesViewTest class as the **Test class** to be run (see Figure 2–30). To execute the test, click the **Run** button.

Did the test complete successfully? No? Checking the **Console** view turns up the following suspicious line: !MESSAGE Two plug-ins found with the same id: "com.qualityeclipse.favorites". Ignoring duplicate at "file:c:/eclipse/workspace/com.qualityeclipse .favorites/plugin.xml". It seems that the **Favorites** plug-in installed in the **Development Workspace** is interfering with the **Favorites** plug-in project that is being tested. To alleviate this problem, delete the **Favorites** plug-in from the **Development Workspace** as described in the next section.

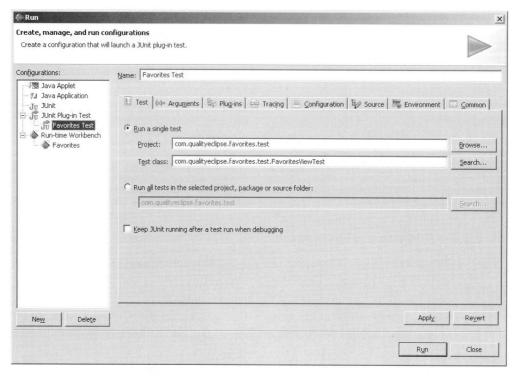

Figure 2–30   The test Configuration wizard.

2.8.5   Uninstalling the favorites plug-in

Use the following steps to delete the **Favorites** plug-in from the **Development Workspace**:

1. Close the **Favorites** view.

2. Shut down Eclipse.

3. Delete the `com.quality.favorites_1.0.0` directory in the Eclipse plug-ins directory.

4. Restart Eclipse. If you receive an error (see Figure 2–31) when restarting Eclipse, at least one of the **Favorites** views was not closed when Eclipse was shut down in Step 2.

5. Verify that the **Favorites** view is no longer available.

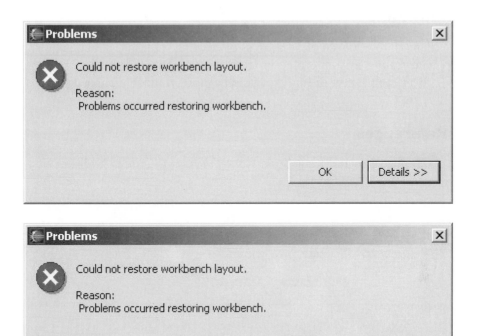

Figure 2–31   Error dialog when starting Eclipse.

To check that the **Favorites** view has been removed from Eclipse, open the **Show View** dialog (see Figures 2–19 and 2–20) and verify that the **Quality Eclipse** category is no longer present.

Now, when the test is executed, it completes successfully.

2.9   Summary

This chapter covered the process of creating, running, debugging, inspecting, and testing a simple plug-in from start to finish. Subsequent chapters will cover each aspect of this process plus more in much greater detail.

References

Gamma, Eric and Kent Beck, *Contributing to Eclipse*, Addison-Wesley, Boston, MA, 2003.

CHAPTER 3

Eclipse Infrastructure

This chapter discusses the architecture behind the code generated in the previous chapter. Before diving deeper into each aspect of Eclipse, it's time to step back and look at Eclipse as a whole. The simple example plug-in started in the previous chapter—the **Favorites** plug-in—provides a concrete basis on which to discuss the Eclipse architecture.

3.1 Overview

Eclipse isn't a single, monolithic program, but rather a small kernel called a plug-in loader surrounded by hundreds (and potentially thousands) of plug-ins (see Figure 3–1) of which the **Favorites** example plug-in is one. Each plug-in may rely on services provided by another plug-in, and may in turn provide services on which yet other plug-ins may rely. This modular design lends itself to discrete chunks of functionality that can be more readily reused to build applications not envisioned by the original developers.

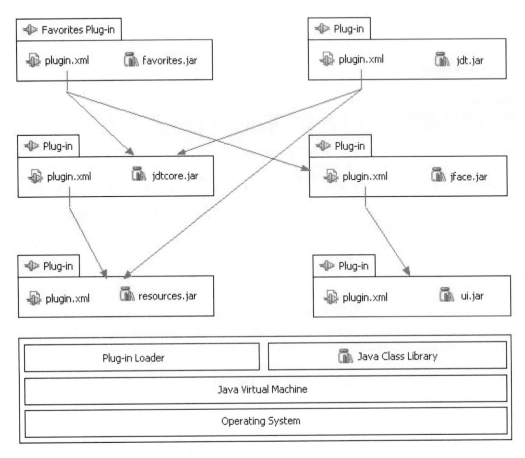

Figure 3–1   Eclipse plug-in structure. An example of how plug-ins depend on one another.

3.1.1   *Plug-in structure*

The behavior of each plug-in is in code, yet the dependencies and services of a plug-in are declared in a special XML file named plugin.xml (see Figure 3–2). This structure facilitates lazy-loading of plug-in code on an as-needed basis, thus reducing both the startup time and the memory footprint of Eclipse. On startup, the plug-in loader scans the plugin.xml file for each plug-in and builds a structure containing this information. This structure takes up some memory, but it allows the loader to find a required plug-in much more quickly and takes up a lot less space than loading all the code from all the plug-ins all the time.

Plug-ins are loaded but not unloaded   In Eclipse 2.1 and the current releases of 3.0, plug-ins are loaded lazily during a session, but not unloaded, causing the memory footprint to grow as the user requests more functionality. In future versions of Eclipse, this issue may be addressed by unloading plug-ins when they are no longer required (see *eclipse.org/equinox*, and more specifically deactivating plug-ins *dev.eclipse.org /viewcvs/index-tech.cgi/~checkout~/equinox-home/dynamicPlugins/deactivatingPlugins.html*).

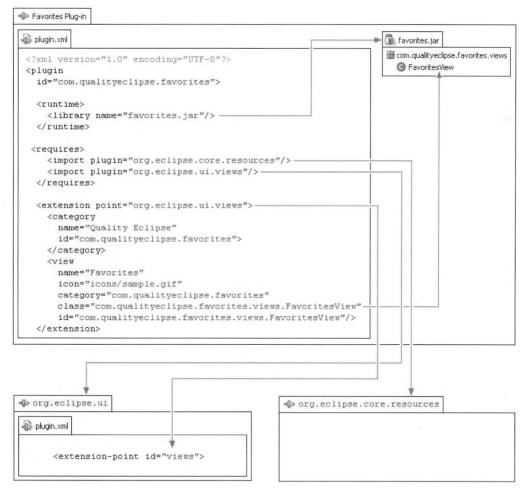

Figure 3–2   Declaring a new extension. This is an example of how a new extension is declared in the plug-in manifest with lines highlighting how the plug-in manifest references various plug-in artifacts.

3.1.2   Workspace

The Eclipse IDE displays and modifies files located in a ***workspace.*** The workspace is a directory hierarchy containing both user files such as projects, source code, and so on, and plug-in state information such as preferences. The plug-in state information located in the workspace directory hierarchy is associated only with that workspace, yet the Eclipse IDE, its plug-ins, and the static resources stored in the various plug-in directories are shared by multiple workspaces.

3.2   Plug-in Directory

The **Favorites** plug-in directory contains files similar to a typical plug-in, including *.jar files containing code, various images used by the plug-in, and the plug-in manifest.

> **favorites.jar**—A file containing the actual Java classes comprising the plug-in. Typically, the JAR file is named for the last segment in the plug-in's identifier, but it could have any name, so long as that name is declared in the `plugin.xml file`. In this case, since the **Favorites** plug-in identifier is `com.qualityeclipse.favorites`, the JAR file is named `favorites.jar`.

> **icons**—Image files are typically placed in an `icons` or `images` subdirectory and referenced in the `plugin.xml` and by the plug-in's various classes. Image files and other static resource files that ship as part of the plug-in can be accessed using methods in the plug-in class (see Section 3.4.3, "Static plug-in resources").

> **plugin.xml**—A file in XML format that describes the **Favorites** plug-in and how it integrates into Eclipse.

The plug-in directory must have a specific name and be placed inside a specific directory so that Eclipse can find and load it. The directory name must be a concatenation of the plug-in identifier, an underscore, and the plug-in version in dot-separated form, as in `com.qualityeclipse.favorites _1.0.0`. Additionally, the directory must be located in the plug-in's directory as a sibling to all the other Eclipse plug-ins, as is the case for the **Favorites** plug-in.

3.2.1   Link files

Alternately, plug-in directories comprising a product may be placed in a separate product specific directory, and then a link file can be provided for Eclipse so that Eclipse can find and load these plug-ins. Not only does this approach satisfy Ready for WebSphere Studio (RFWS) requirements, but it also allows for multiple installations of Eclipse to be linked to the same set of plug-ins. You must make several modifications to the **Favorites** example so that it can use this alternate approach.

To begin, remove the existing **Favorites** plug-in in its current form from the **Development Workbench** using the steps outlined in Section 2.8.5, "Uninstalling the favorites plug-in." Next, modify the Ant-based build.xml file so that the **Favorites** plug-in conforms to the new structure by inserting QualityEclipseTools/eclipse in the plugin_dir property value:

```xml
<?xml version="1.0" encoding="UTF-8"?>
<project name="Favorites" basedir="." default="product">
    <target name="product">
        <!-- Temporary directory used to build the
        product... will be deleted. -->
        <property
            name="temp_dir"
            location="C:/QualityEclipseTemp"/>

        <!-- Product directory where final product
        will be placed. -->
        <property
            name="product_dir"
            location="C:/QualityEclipseProduct"/>

        <!-- Current product version number. -->
        <property
            name="product_version"
            value="1.0.0"/>

        <!-- Plugin directory... subdirectory of temp
        directory. -->
        <property
            name="plugin_dir"
            location="${temp_dir}/QualityEclipseTools/eclipse/
            plugins/com.qualityeclipse.favorites
            ${product_version}"/>

        <!-- Clear out the temp directory. -->
        <delete dir="${temp_dir}"/>
        <mkdir dir="${plugin_dir}"/>
        <mkdir dir="${product_dir}"/>

        <!-- Assemble the product in the temp directory. -->
        <jar destfile="${plugin_dir}/favorites.jar">
            <fileset dir="bin"/>
        </jar>
        <copy todir="${plugin_dir}">
            <fileset dir="." includes="plugin.xml"/>
            <fileset dir="." includes="icons/*.gif"/>
        </copy>
```

```
      <!-- Build the product from the temp directory. -->
      <zip destfile="${product_dir}/QualityEclipseTools_
          v${product_version}.zip">
          <fileset dir="${temp_dir}"/>
      </zip>
   </target>
</project>
```

When the modified `build.xml` is executed, the resulting zip file contains files in the new directory structure:

```
QualityEclipseTools/plugins/
   com.qualityeclipse.favorites_1.0.0/favorites.jar
QualityEclipseTools/plugins/
   com.qualityeclipse.favorites_1.0.0/icons/sample.gif
QualityEclipseTools/plugins/
   com.qualityeclipse.favorites_1.0.0/plugin.xml
```

The zip file can be unzipped to any location, but for this example, we will assume the file is unzipped into the root directory of the C drive so that the plug-in directory is:

```
C:\QualityEclipseTools\eclipse\plugins\com.quality-
eclipse.favorites_1.0.0
```

The locations of both the Eclipse product directory and the Quality-EclipseTools product directory are determined by the user and thus not known at build time. Because of this, the link file that points to the QualityEclipseTools product directory must be manually created for now. Create the `links` subdirectory in the Eclipse product directory (e.g., `C:\eclipse\links`) and create a new file named com.qualityeclipse.link that contains the single line:

```
path=C:/QualityEclipseTools
```

To do this in Windows, you can use Notepad to create and save the file as a txt file, which you can then rename appropriately. Note that the path must use forward slashes rather than back slashes.

No relative paths in link files   Eclipse 2.1 does not allow link files to contain relative paths. This restriction may be changed in future versions of Eclipse (see Bugzilla entry 25941).

3.2.2 *Hybrid approach*

Some products use a hybrid approach, delivering the product in multiple forms. When installing into Eclipse, the installer places product plug-ins directly into the Eclipse plug-ins directory, whereas when installing into Web-Sphere Application Developer or any of the other WebSphere IDE family of products, the product plug-ins are placed in a separate product directory and a link file is created. In addition, these products are available in various zip file formats, each targeted at a specific type and version of Eclipse or WebSphere product. This hybrid approach facilitates a simpler and smaller zip-based installation for Eclipse where Ready for WebSphere certification is not required, and a cleaner and easier installer-based installation for the Web-Sphere IDE family of products.

After you install the QualityEclipseTools product and create the link file as described above, the QualityEclipseTools product is ready for use. Verify that you have correctly installed the QualityEclipseTools product in its new location by restarting Eclipse and opening the **Favorites** view. Once you have installed and verified the product, be sure to uninstall it by deleting the link file so that the JUnit tests described in Section 2.8, "Writing Plug-in Tests," will still run successfully.

3.3 Plug-in Manifest

As stated earlier, there is exactly one manifest per plug-in defining various high-level aspects so that the plug-in does not have to load until you require its functionality. The format and content for this file can be found in the Eclipse help facility accessed by **Help > Help Contents**; look under **Platform Plug-in Developer Guide > Reference > Other Reference Information > Plug-in manifest**. As with all plug-ins, the manifest for the **Favorites** plug-in is stored in a file named `plugin.xml` located in the plug-in directory.

OSGi and the 3.0 run-time   In 3.0, some of the information in the `plugin.xml` file can be moved to a manifest.mf file. This change is based on technology from the OSGi Alliance (www.osgi.org) and is being implemented by Eclipse.org as we write this book (see Section 20.10, "OSGi Bundles and the 3.0 Run-time").

3.3.1   Plug-in declaration

Within each plug-in manifest, there is exactly one plug-in declaration containing the name, identifier, version, provider, and plug-in class.

```
<plugin
    id="com.qualityeclipse.favorites"
    name="Favorites Plug-in"
    version="1.0.0"
    provider-name="QualityEclipse"
    class="com.qualityeclipse.favorites.FavoritesPlugin">
```

Strings in the plug-in manifest, such as the plug-in name, can be moved into a separate plugin.properties file. This process facilitates internationalization as discussed in Chapter 16, "Internationalization."

3.3.1.1   Plug-in identifier

The identifier is designed to uniquely identify the plug-in, and is typically constructed using Java naming conventions (e.g., com.<companyName>.<product OrProjectName>, or in our case, com.qualityeclipse.favorites). If several plug-ins are all part of the same product, then each plug-in name may have four or even five parts to it as in com.qualityeclipse.favorites.core and com.qualityeclipse.favorites.ui.

3.3.1.2   Plug-in version

Each plug-in specifies its version using three numbers separated by periods. The first number indicates the major version number, the second indicates the minor version number, and the third indicates the service level, as in 1.0.0. You can specify an optional qualifier that can include alphanumeric characters (no whitespace), as in 1.0.0.beta_1 or 1.0.0.2004-06-28. Eclipse does not use or interpret this optional qualifier in any way, so the product builder can use it to encode the build type, build date, or other useful information.

3.3.1.3   Plug-in name and provider

Both the name and provider are human-readable text, so they can be anything and are not required to be unique. To see the names, versions, and providers of the currently installed plug-ins, select **Help > About Eclipse Platform** to open the **About** dialog (see Figure 3–3), then click the **Plug-in Details** button to open the **Plug-ins** dialog (see Figure 3–4).

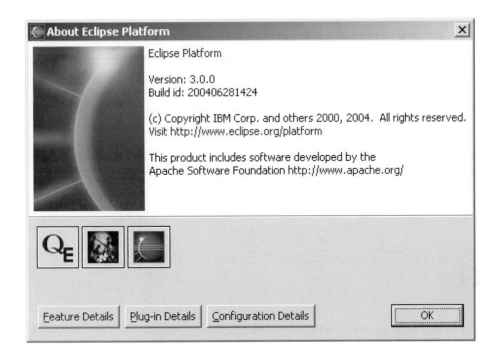

Figure 3–3   The About Eclipse dialog, showing information about the Eclipse platform.

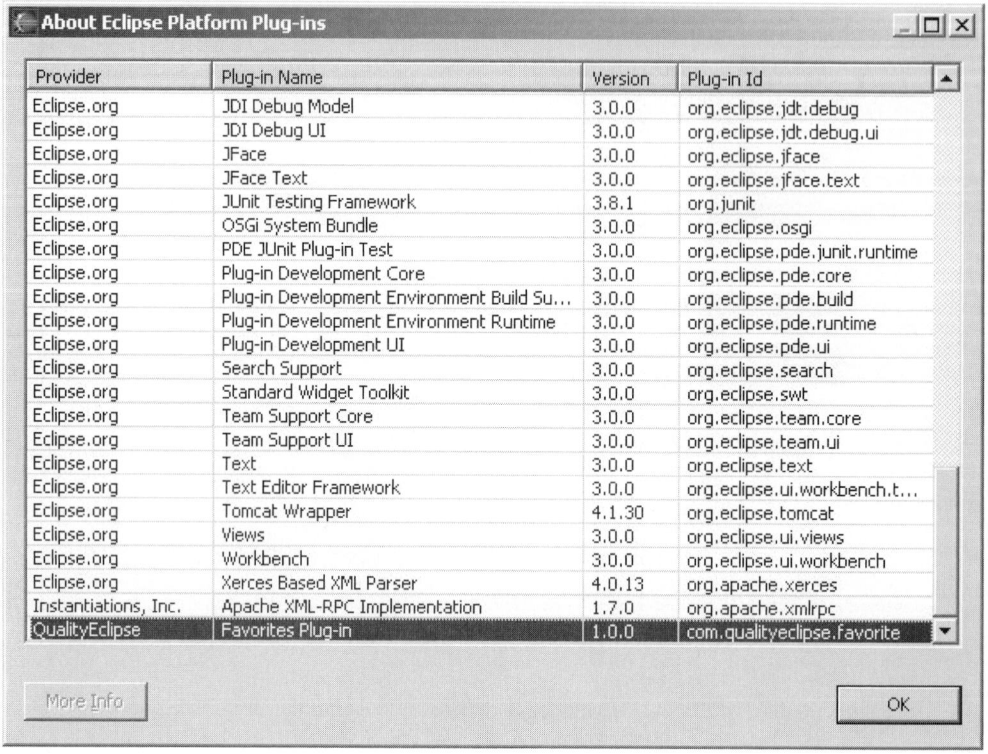

About Eclipse Platform Plug-ins

Provider	Plug-in Name	Version	Plug-in Id
Eclipse.org	JDI Debug Model	3.0.0	org.eclipse.jdt.debug
Eclipse.org	JDI Debug UI	3.0.0	org.eclipse.jdt.debug.ui
Eclipse.org	JFace	3.0.0	org.eclipse.jface
Eclipse.org	JFace Text	3.0.0	org.eclipse.jface.text
Eclipse.org	JUnit Testing Framework	3.8.1	org.junit
Eclipse.org	OSGi System Bundle	3.0.0	org.eclipse.osgi
Eclipse.org	PDE JUnit Plug-in Test	3.0.0	org.eclipse.pde.junit.runtime
Eclipse.org	Plug-in Development Core	3.0.0	org.eclipse.pde.core
Eclipse.org	Plug-in Development Environment Build Su...	3.0.0	org.eclipse.pde.build
Eclipse.org	Plug-in Development Environment Runtime	3.0.0	org.eclipse.pde.runtime
Eclipse.org	Plug-in Development UI	3.0.0	org.eclipse.pde.ui
Eclipse.org	Search Support	3.0.0	org.eclipse.search
Eclipse.org	Standard Widget Toolkit	3.0.0	org.eclipse.swt
Eclipse.org	Team Support Core	3.0.0	org.eclipse.team.core
Eclipse.org	Team Support UI	3.0.0	org.eclipse.team.ui
Eclipse.org	Text	3.0.0	org.eclipse.text
Eclipse.org	Text Editor Framework	3.0.0	org.eclipse.ui.workbench.t...
Eclipse.org	Tomcat Wrapper	4.1.30	org.eclipse.tomcat
Eclipse.org	Views	3.0.0	org.eclipse.ui.views
Eclipse.org	Workbench	3.0.0	org.eclipse.ui.workbench
Eclipse.org	Xerces Based XML Parser	4.0.13	org.apache.xerces
Instantiations, Inc.	Apache XML-RPC Implementation	1.7.0	org.apache.xmlrpc
QualityEclipse	Favorites Plug-in	1.0.0	com.qualityeclipse.favorite

More Info   OK

Figure 3–4 The Installed Plug-ins dialog, showing all the installed plug-ins with the Favorites plug-in highlighted at the bottom.

3.3.1.4 Plug-in class declaration

Each plug-in may optionally specify a plug-in class as the **Favorites** plug-in does (see Section 3.4, "Plug-in Class"). If a plug-in class is not specified, the plug-in loader automatically provides a generic plug-in class.

3.3.2 Plug-in run-time

The `runtime` section of each `plugin.xml` file describes which libraries (`*.jar` files) contain the plug-in code and which of those classes are accessible to other plug-ins.

```
<runtime>
   <library name="favorites.jar"/>
</runtime>
```

The library attribute specifies the file path of the library file relative to the plug-in directory. Typically, as in the **Favorites** plug-in, the library file is located in the plug-in directory itself, and is named the same as the last segment in the plug-in's unique identifier.

The `runtime` section of the plug-in manifest, as generated by the plug-in project wizard, does not define several aspects necessary for extensibility and performance. Open the plug-in manifest editor and switch to the **Runtime** page, to make the necessary changes (see Figure 3–5). In the section labeled **Library exporting**, select **Export the entire library**. Expand the section labeled **Package Prefixes**, click the **Add** button, select the `com.quality-eclipse.favorites` package, then click the **OK** button.

These changes result in modifications to the `runtime` section of the plug-in manifest:

```
<runtime>
   <library name="favorites.jar">
      <export name="*"/>
      <packages prefixes="com.qualityeclipse.favorites"/>
   </library>
</runtime>
```

The export declaration allows all other plug-ins to access any of the classes in the `favorites.jar` (see Section 20.2.4, "How eclipse is different"). For improved performance, the plug-in class loader uses the `packages` declaration to more efficiently locate classes to be loaded. In this case, since the `packages` declaration specifies the `com.qualityeclipse.favorites` prefix, the class loader knows not to look for classes without that package prefix in the `favorites.jar` file.

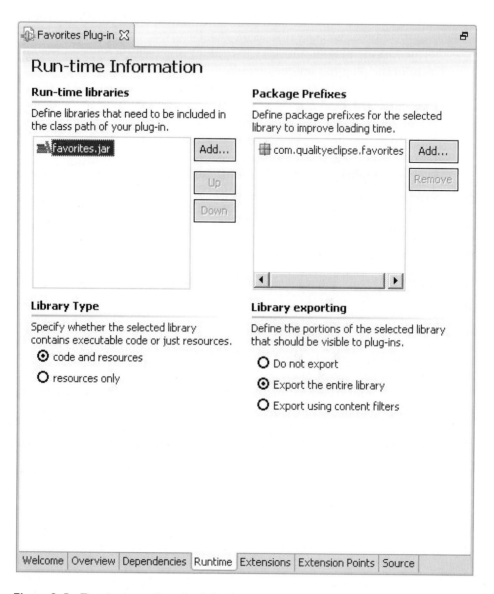

Figure 3–5 The plug-in manifest editor's Runtime page is used to define the run-time configuration for the plug-in, including the code location, package prefixes, and whether source should be included.

3.3.3 *Plug-in dependencies*

The plug-in loader instantiates a separate class loader for each loaded plug-in, and uses the `requires` section of the manifest to determine which other plug-ins—thus which classes—will be visible to that plug-in during execution (see

Section 20.9, "Plug-in Class Loaders," for information about loading classes not specified in the `requires` section).

```
<requires>
   <import plugin="org.eclipse.ui"/>
   <import plugin="org.eclipse.core.runtime.compatibility"/>
</requires>
```

If a plug-in has been successfully compiled and built, but throws a `NoClass-DefFoundError` during execution, it may indicate that the plug-in project's Java classpath is out of sync with the `requires` section declared in the plug-in manifest. As discussed in Chapter 2, "A Simple Plug-in Example," it is important to keep the classpath and `requires` section in sync.

When the plug-in loader is about to load a plug-in, it scans the `requires` section of a dependent plug-in and locates all the required plug-ins. If a required plug-in is not available, then the plug-in loader throws an exception, generating an entry in the log file (see Section 3.6, "Logging"), and does not load the dependent plug-in. When a plug-in gathers the list of plug-ins that extend an extension point it defines, it will not see any disabled plug-ins. In this circumstance, no exception or log entry will be generated for the disabled plug-ins.

Several attributes can be used in a dependent plug-in to indicate what version of another plug-in is required, and if the dependent plug-in can execute successfully without the required plug-in. For example, if a plug-in requires version 3.0.0 of the `org.eclipse.ui` plug-in, but can execute successfully without it, then you must modify the import statement to read as follows:

```
<import
   plugin="org.eclipse.ui" version="3.0.0"
   optional="true"/>
```

Here is the complete list of `import` attributes (as listed in the Eclipse documentation):

plugin—identifier of the required plug-in.

version—Optional version specification.

match—Version-matching rule. If the version attribute is specified, then this attribute determines how the version dependency is satisfied. There are four possible values:

- "perfect" —The actual version number must exactly match the expected version number.

- "equivalent" —The major and minor components must match exactly, but the actual version number's service or qualifier may be equal or greater than the expected version number's service or qualifier.

- "compatible" —The major component must match exactly, but the actual version number's minor component, service, or qualifier may be equal or greater than the expected version number's minor component, service or qualifier.

- "greaterOrEqual" —The actual version number must be greater than or equal to the expected version number.

export—Specifies whether the dependent plug-in classes are made visible (are (re)exported) to users of this plug-in. By default, dependent classes are not exported (i.e., they are not made visible).

optional—Specifies whether this dependency is strictly enforced. If set to <true> and this dependency cannot be satisfied, the dependency will be ignored.

3.3.4 *Extensions and extension points*

A plug-in declares extension points so other plug-ins can extend the functionality of the original plug-in in a controlled manner (see Section 17.1, "The Extension Point Mechanism"). This mechanism provides a layer of separation so that the original plug-in does not need to know about the existence of the extending plug-ins at the time you build the original plug-in. Plug-ins declare extension points as part of their plug-in manifest, as in the views extension point declared in the org.eclipse.ui plug-in:

```
<extension-point
    id="views"
    name="%ExtPoint.views"
    schema="schema/views.exsd"/>
```

You can find documentation for this extension point in the Eclipse help (select **Help > Help Contents**, then in the help dialog, select **Platform Plug-in Developer Guide > Reference > Extension Points Reference > Workbench > org.eclipse.ui.views**). It indicates that any plug-in using this extension point must provide the name of a class that implements the org.eclipse.ui.IViewPart interface (see Section 20.5, "Types Specified in an Extension Point").

Other plug-ins declare extensions to the original plug-in's functionality similar to the **Favorites** plug-in's view extensions. In this case, the **Favorites** plug-in declares a new category of views with the name **Quality Eclipse** and the class com.qualityeclipse.favorites.views.FavoritesView as a new type of view:

```
<extension
      point="org.eclipse.ui.views">
   <category
         name="Quality Eclipse"
         id="com.qualityeclipse.favorites">
   </category>
   <view
         name="Favorites"
         icon="icons/sample.gif"
         category="com.qualityeclipse.favorites"
         class="com.qualityeclipse
            .favorites.views.FavoritesView"
         id="com.qualityeclipse
            .favorites.views.FavoritesView">
   </view>
</extension>
```

Each type of extension point may require different attributes to define the extension. Typically, ID attributes take a form similar to the plug-in identifier. The category ID provides a way for the **Favorites** view to uniquely identify the category that contains it. The name attribute of both the category and view is human-readable text, while the icon attribute specifies a relative path from the plug-in directory to the image file associated with the view.

This approach allows Eclipse to load information about the extensions declared in various plug-ins without loading the plug-ins themselves, thus reducing the amount of time and memory required for an operation. For example, selecting the **Windows > Show View > Other...** menu opens a dialog showing all the views provided by all the plug-ins known to Eclipse (see Section 2.5, "Installing and Running the Product"). Because each type of view is declared in its plug-in's manifest, the Eclipse run-time can present a list of views to the user without actually loading each plug-in that contains the view.

3.4   Plug-in Class

By default, the plug-in class provides methods for accessing static resources associated with the plug-in, and for accessing and initializing plug-in-specific preferences and other state information. In addition, the plug-in class is the first class notified after the plug-in loads, and the last class notified when the plug-in is about to shut down.

```java
package com.qualityeclipse.favorites;

import org.eclipse.ui.plugin.*;
import org.eclipse.core.runtime.*;

/**
 * The main plug-in class to be used in the desktop.
 */
public class FavoritesPlugin extends AbstractUIPlugin {
    //The shared instance.
    private static FavoritesPlugin plugin;

    /**
     * The constructor.
     */
    public FavoritesPlugin(IPluginDescriptor descriptor) {
        super(descriptor);
        plugin = this;
    }

    /**
     * Returns the shared instance.
     */
    public static FavoritesPlugin getDefault() {
        return plugin;
    }

    /**
     * Starts up this plug-in.
     * @see org.eclipse.core.runtime.Plugin#startup()
     */
    public void startup() throws CoreException {
        super.startup();
        // TODO Any plug-in-specific startup code goes here.
    }

    /**
     * Shuts down this plug-in and discards all
     * plug-in states.
     * @see org.eclipse.core.runtime.Plugin#shutdown()
     */
    public void shutdown() throws CoreException {
        // TODO Any plug-in-specific shutdown code goes here.
        super.shutdown();
    }

}
```

3.4.1   Startup and shutdown

The plug-in loader notifies the plug-in class when the plug-in is loaded via the startup() method and when the plug-in shuts down via the shutdown() method. These methods allow the plug-in to save and restore any state information between Eclipse sessions. Be careful when overriding these methods;

always call the superclass implementation, and only take the minimum action necessary so you do not impact the speed or memory requirements during Eclipse startup or shutdown.

3.4.2   Early plug-in startup

Eclipse loads plug-ins lazily, so it may not call the `startup()` method when it launches. Eclipse can provide resource change information indicating the changes that occurred while the plug-in was inactive (see Section 9.5, "Delayed Changed Events"). If this is not enough and the plug-in *must* load and start when Eclipse launches, the plug-in can use the `org.eclipse.ui.startup` extension point by inserting the following into its plug-in manifest:

```
<extension point="org.eclipse.ui.startup"/>
```

Doing this also requires the plug-in class to implement the `org.eclipse.ui.IStartup` interface so that the workbench can call the `earlyStartup()` method immediately after the UI completes its startup. To specify a class other than the plug-in class that implements the `IStartup` interface, use an alternate form of this extension:

```
<extension point="org.eclipse.ui.startup">
   <startup class="myPackage.myClass"/>
</extension>
```

The user can disable early plug-in startup using the **Workbench > Startup and Shutdown** preference page. If you have added an early startup extension, then your plug-in will appear in this list, and the user can disable its startup. You can detect this situation and warn the user that some of your plug-in's functionality will be compromised:

```
public static boolean isEarlyStartupDisabled() {
   String plugins = PlatformUI
      .getWorkbench()
      .getPreferenceStore()
      .getString(
         IPreferenceConstants
            .PLUGINS_NOT_ACTIVATED_ON_STARTUP);
   String pluginId = FavoritesPlugin
      .getDefault()
      .getDescriptor()
      .getUniqueIdentifier();
   return plugins.indexOf(pluginId) != -1;
}
```

Like most plug-ins, the **Favorites** plug-in does not need to load and start when Eclipse launches, and so it does not use this extension point. If there is a need for early startup, then place only what is necessary for early startup into a separate plug-in and use the early startup extension point there so that the additional overhead of early startup has only a small impact on startup time and memory footprint.

3.4.3   *Static plug-in resources*

Plug-ins can include images and other file-based resources that are installed into the plug-in directory along with the plug-in manifest and library file. These files are static in nature and shared between multiple workbench incarnations. Declarations in the plug-in manifest such as actions, views, and editors can reference resources such as icons stored in the plug-in installation directory. Additionally, the plug-in class provides methods for locating and loading these resources:

> `find (IPath path)`—Returns a uniform resource locator (URL) for the given path or null if the URL could not be computed or created.

> `openStream (IPath file)`—Returns an input stream for the specified file. The file path must be specified relative to the plug-in's installation location (the plug-in directory).

3.4.4   *Plug-in preferences*

Plug-in preferences and other workspace-specific state information are stored in the workspace metadata directory hierarchy. For example, if Eclipse is installed at `C:\eclipse` and the default workspace location is being used, then the **Favorites** preferences would be stored in:

```
C:/eclipse/workspace/.metadata/.plugins/com.quality-
eclipse.favorites/
pref_store.ini
```

The plug-in class provides methods for accessing plug-in preferences and other state-related files as listed below:

> `getPluginPreferences ()`—Returns the preference store for this plug-in (see Section 12.3, "Preference APIs").

> `getStateLocation ()`—Returns the location in the local filesystem of the plug-in state area for this plug-in (see Section 7.5.2, "Saving global view information"). If the plug-in state area did not exist prior to this call, it is created.

`savePluginPreferences ()`—Saves preferences settings for this plug-in. Does nothing if the preference store does not need saving.

You can supply default preferences to a plug-in in several ways. To programmatically define default preference values, override the `initializeDefaultPluginPreferences ()` method. Alternately, you can specify default preferences in a preferences.ini file located in the plug-in directory (see Section 12.3.4, "Specifying default values in a file"). Using this second approach also lets you easily internationalize the plug-in using a `preferences.properties` file (see Section 16.1, "Externalizing the Plug-in Manifest").

3.4.5   Plugin and AbstractUIPlugin

All plug-in classes must be in the `Plugin` class hierarchy. Typically, UI-based plug-ins (plug-ins requiring the `org.eclipse.ui` plug-in) have a plug-in class that subclasses `AbstractUIPlugin`, while non-UI plug-ins subclass `Plugin`. Both of these classes provide basic plug-in services for the plug-in programmer, but there are important differences.

`AbstractUIPlugin` automatically saves plug-in preferences when the plug-in shuts down. When subclassing the `Plugin` class directly, modify the `shutdown()` method to always call the `savePluginPreferences()` method so that preferences will be persisted across sessions.

`AbstractUIPlugin` provides alternate preferences storage methods and classes that you should not use. These methods, such as `getPreferenceStore()` and the associated interface `IPreferenceStore`, predate Eclipse 2.0 and the `Plugin` class preference methods, such as `getPluginPreferences()` and the associated class `Preferences`. They exist only for backward compatibility. There is no advantage in using these older preference storage methods in `AbstractUIPlugin`, so we will use the `Preferences` interface and associated methods unless the Eclipse API specifically requires the older interface (see Chapter 12, "Preference Pages," for more on preferences).

Other methods provided by `AbstractUIPlugin` include:

`createImageRegistry()`—Returns a new image registry for this plug-in. You can use the registry to manage images that are frequently used by the plugin-in. The default implementation of this method creates an empty registry. Subclasses may override this method if needed.

`getDialogSettings()`—Returns the dialog settings for this UI plug-in (see Section 11.2.7, "Dialog settings"). The dialog settings hold persistent state data for the various wizards and dialogs of this plug-in in the context of a workbench.

`getImageRegistry()`—Returns the image registry for this UI plug-in (see Section 4.4.3, "Images," and 7.7, "Image Caching").

`initializeImageRegistry(ImageRegistry reg)`—Initializes an image registry with images that are frequently used by the plug-in.

`loadDialogSettings()`—Loads the dialog settings for this plug-in by looking first for a `dialog_settings.xml` file in the plug-in's metadata directory, then for a file with the same name in the plug-in directory; failing both of these, it creates an empty settings object. This method may be overridden, although this is typically unnecessary.

3.5   Plug-in Model

When Eclipse first launches, it scans each of the plug-in directories and builds an internal model representing each plug-ins it finds. This occurs by scanning each plug-in manifest and without loading the plug-ins. The methods in the next two sections are useful if you want to display information about plug-ins or perform operations based on specific plug-in characteristics without taking the time and memory usage hit associated with loading plug-ins.

3.5.1   *Plug-in registry*

You can access the plug-in registry using the `Plaform.getPluginRegistry()` method. It contains plug-in descriptors, each representing a plug-in. The registry provides several methods for extracting information about the various plug-ins without loading the plug-ins:

`getConfigurationElementsFor(String extensionPointId)`—Returns all configuration elements from all extensions configured into the identified extension point.

`getExtensionPoint(String extensionPointId)`—Returns the extension point with the given extension point identifier in this plug-in registry.

`getPluginDescriptor(String pluginId)`—Returns the plug-in descriptor with the given plug-in identifier in this plug-in registry.

`getPluginDescriptors()`—Returns all plug-in descriptors known to this plug-in registry.

3.5.2   *Plug-in descriptor*

Accessing a plug-in class requires the containing plug-in to be loaded whereas a plug-in descriptor does not carry such a penalty. The single instance of

`IPluginRegistry` contains instances of `IPluginDescriptor`, which in turn contain information about each plug-in. The plug-in descriptor contains several methods for obtaining information contained in the plug-in's manifest:

`find (IPath path)`—Returns a URL for the given path. Returns null if the URL could not be computed or created.

`getExtensionPoint (String extensionPointId)`—Returns the extension point with the given simple identifier declared in this plug-in, or null if there is no such extension point.

`getInstallURL()`—Returns the URL of this plug-in's install directory. This is the directory containing the plug-in manifest file, resource bundle, run-time libraries, and any other files supplied with this plug-in. This directory is usually read-only. Relative plug-in information should be written to the location provided by `Plugin.getStateLocation()`.

`getLabel()`—Returns a displayable label for this plug-in.

`getPlugin()`—Returns the plug-in run-time object corresponding to this plug-in descriptor. Unlike other methods on this object, invoking this method may activate the plug-in.

`getProviderName()`—Returns the name of the provider of this plug-in.

`getResourceBundle()`—Returns this plug-in's resource bundle for the current locale. The bundle is stored as the `plugin.properties` file in the plug-in install directory.

`getUniqueIdentifier()`—Returns the unique identifier of this plug-in.

`getVersionIdentifier()`—Returns the version identifier of this plug-in (see Section 19.2.1, "Version checking").

`isPluginActivated()`—Returns whether the plug-in described by this descriptor has been activated. Invoking this method will not cause the plug-in to be activated.

> **Tip:** For more on the plug-in registry, activation, and lifecycle, check out the equinox project at *www.eclipse.org/equinox*.

3.6 Logging

The RFWS requirements indicate that exceptions and other service-related information should be appended to a log file. To facilitate this, the plug-in class provides a method for accessing the plug-in logging mechanism via the `getLog()` method. For convenience, the `FavoritesLog` wraps the `ILog` interface returned by the `getLog()` method with several utility methods:

```
package com.qualityeclipse.favorites;
import org.eclipse.core.runtime.*;

/**
 * The logger of convenience for the Favorites plug-in.
 */
public class FavoritesLog {
    /**
     * Log the specified information.
     *
     * @param message, a human-readable message,
     * localized to the current locale.
     */
    public static void logInfo(String message) {
        log(IStatus.INFO, IStatus.OK, message, null);
    }

    /**
     * Log the specified error.
     *
     * @param exception, a low-level exception.
     */
    public static void logError(Throwable exception) {
        logError("Unexpected Exception", exception);
    }

    /**
     * Log the specified error.
     *
     * @param message, a human-readable message,
     * localized to the current locale.
     * @param exception, a low-level exception,
     * or <code>null</code> if not applicable.
     */
    public static void logError(
        String message, Throwable exception) {
        log(IStatus.ERROR, IStatus.OK, message, exception);
    }

    /**
     * Log the specified information.
     *
     * @param severity, the severity; one of the following:
     * <code>IStatus.OK</code>,
     *<code>IStatus.ERROR</code>,
     *<code>IStatus.INFO</code>,
     *or <code>IStatus.WARNING</code>.
     * @param pluginId. the unique identifier of the relevant
     * plug-in.
     * @param code, the plug-in-specific status code, or
     * <code>OK</code>.
     * @param message, a human-readable message,
     * localized to the current locale.
     * @param exception, a low-level exception,
     * or <code>null</code> if not applicable.
     */
```

```
public static void log(
   int severity,
   int code,
   String message,
   Throwable exception) {

   log(createStatus(severity, code, message, exception));
}

/**
 * Create a status object representing the
 * specified information.
 *
 * @param severity, the severity; one of the following:
 * <code>IStatus.OK</code>,
 *<code>IStatus.ERROR</code>,
 *<code>IStatus.INFO</code>,
 *or <code>IStatus.WARNING</code>.
 * @param pluginId, the unique identifier of the
 *              * relevant plug-in.
 * @param code, the plug-in-specific status code,
 * or <code>OK</code>.
 * @param message, a human-readable message,
 * localized to the current locale.
 * @param exception, a low-level exception,
 * or <code>null</code> if not applicable.
 * @return, the status object (not <code>null</code>).
 */
public static IStatus createStatus(
   int severity,
   int code,
   String message,
   Throwable exception) {

   return new Status(
      severity,
      FavoritesPlugin.getDefault()
         .getDescriptor().getUniqueIdentifier(),
      code,
      message,
      exception);
}

/**
 * Log the given status.
 *
 * @param status, the status to log.
 */
public static void log(IStatus status) {
   FavoritesPlugin.getDefault().getLog().log(status);
}

}
```

3.6.1   *Status objects*

The `IStatus` type hierarchy in the `org.eclipse.core.runtime` package provides a mechanism for wrapping, forwarding, and logging the result of an operation, including an exception if there is one. A single error is represented using an instance of `Status` (see method `createStatus` in the previous source code), while a `MultiStatus` object that contains zero or more child status objects represents multiple errors. When creating a framework plug-in that will be used by many other plug-ins, it is helpful to create status subtypes similar to `IResourceStatus` and `ResourceStatus`; but for the **Favorites** plug-in, the existing status types will do:

> `IStatus`—A status object that represents the outcome of an operation. All `CoreExceptions` carry a status object to indicate what went wrong. Status objects are also returned by methods needing to provide details of failures (e.g., validation methods).

> `IResourceStatus`—Represents status related to resources in the **Resources** plug-in and defines the relevant status code constants. Status objects created by the **Resources** plug-in bear its unique ID, `ResourcesPlugin.PI_RESOURCES`, and one of these status codes.

> `MultiStatus`—A concrete multistatus implementation, suitable either for instantiating or subclassing.

> `Status`—A concrete status implementation, suitable either for instantiating or subclassing.

3.6.2   *The error log view*

The PDE provides an **Error Log** view for inspecting the Eclipse log file. To open the **Error Log** view, select **Window > Show View > Other...**, and in the **Show View** dialog, expand the **PDE Runtime** category to find the **Error Log** view (see Figure 3–6). Double-clicking on any entry in the error log opens a dialog showing details for the error log entry. If Eclipse is installed in `C:\Eclipse` and the default workspace location is being used, you can find the Eclipse log file at `C:\Eclipse\workspace\.metadata\.log`.

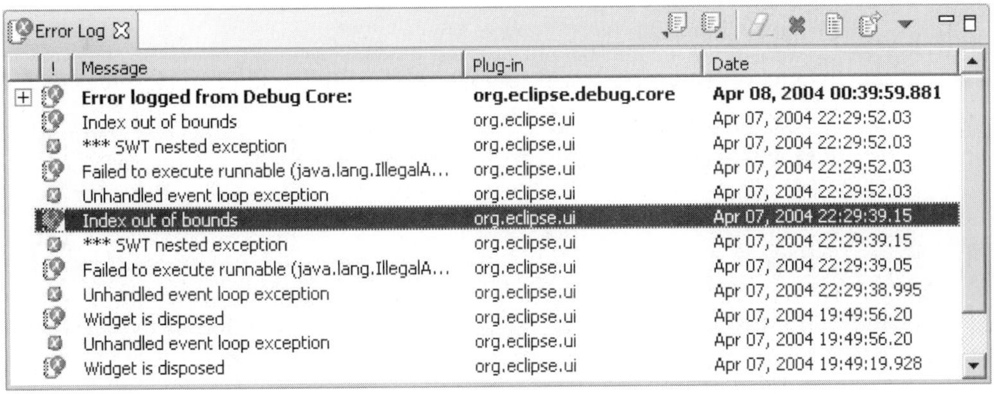

Figure 3–6   The Error Log view is provided by the Eclipse platform and displays information and exceptions generated while Eclipse is running.

3.7   Eclipse Plug-ins

Commercial plug-ins are built on one or more base plug-ins that ship as part of Eclipse. They are broken down into several groups, further separated into UI and Core, as listed below. UI plug-ins contain aspects of a user interface or rely on other plug-ins that do, while you can use Core plug-ins in a headless environment (an environment without a user interface).

Core—A general low-level group of non-UI plug-ins comprising basic services such as extension processing, resource tracking, and so on (see Chapters 9, 17, and 22).

SWT—The Standard Widget Toolkit, a general library of UI widgets tightly integrated with the underlying operating system (OS), but with an OS-independent API (see Chapters 4 and 19).

JFace—A general library of additional UI functionality built on top of SWT (see Chapters 5 and 11).

Workbench core—Plug-ins providing non-UI behavior specific to the Eclipse IDE itself, such as projects, project natures, and builders.

Workbench UI—Plug-ins providing UI behavior specific to the Eclipse IDE itself, such as editors, views, perspectives, actions, and preferences (see Chapters 6, 7, 8, 10, and 12).

Team—A group of plug-ins providing services for integrating different types of source code control management systems (e.g., CVS) into the Eclipse IDE.

Help—Plug-ins that provide documentation for the Eclipse IDE as part of the Eclipse IDE (see Chapter 15).

JDT core—Non-UI-based Java Development Tooling (JDT) plug-ins for the Eclipse IDE.

JDT UI—JDT UI plug-ins for the Eclipse IDE (see Chapter 18).

3.8   Summary

In this chapter, we tried to give you a deeper understanding of Eclipse and its structure as they relate to creating plug-ins. In the next two chapters, we will explore the user interface elements you will use to create you own plug-ins.

References

Eclipse-Overview.pdf (available on the *eclipse.org* Web site).

Notes on the Eclipse plug-in architecture (*www.bolour.com/papers/eclipse/plugin_architecture.html*).

Melhem, Wassim et. Al., "PDE Does Plug-ins", IBM, September 8, 2003 (*www.eclipse.org/articles/Article-PDE-does-plugins/PDE-intro.html*).

Bolour, Azad, "Notes on the Eclipse Plug-in Architecture," Bolour Computing, July 3, 2003 (*www.eclipse.org/articles/Article-Plug-in-architecture/plugin_architecture.html*).

Rufer, Russ, "Sample Code for Testing a Plug-in Into Existence," Yahoo Groups Message 1571, Silicon Valley Patterns Group (*groups.yahoo.com/group/siliconvalleypatterns/message/1571*).

Gamma, Erich, Richard Helm, Ralph Johnson, and John Vlissides, *Design Patterns, Elements of Reusable Object-Oriented Software*, Addition-Wesley, Boston, MA, 1995.

Buschmann, Frank et. al., *Pattern-Oriented Software Architecture*, John Wiley & Sons, Hoboken, NJ, 1996.

Estberg, Don, "How the Minimum Set of Platform Plugins Are Related," Wiki Page 2587, Eclipse Wiki (*eclipsewiki.swiki.net/2587*).

CHAPTER 4

The Standard Widget Toolkit

SWT is a thin compatibility layer on top of the platform's native controls. SWT provides the foundation for the entire Eclipse UI. We start this chapter with some history and philosophy of SWT, and then dive into using SWT to build applications. We will cover most of the widgets commonly encountered and the layout managers used to arrange them within a window. We will finish with a discussion of various resource management issues to be considered when using SWT.

4.1 SWT History and Goals

SWT has its roots going back more than a dozen years to work that Object Technology International, or OTI (then an independent pioneering OO software company and now a part of IBM) did in creating multiplatform, portable, native widget interfaces for Smalltalk (originally for OTI Smalltalk, which became IBM Smalltalk in 1993). IBM Smalltalk's "Common Widget" (CW) layer provided fast, native access to multiple platform widget sets while still providing a common API without suffering the "lowest common denominator" (LCD) problem typical of other portable graphical user interface (GUI) toolkits.

For many years, IBM had been using Smalltalk as its "secret weapon" when building development tools (IBM's first Java IDE, VisualAge for Java, was even written in Smalltalk), but Smalltalk had deployment and configuration problems that ultimately doomed its long-term use at IBM.

Java's promise of universal portability and ubiquitous VMs on every desktop was very appealing to the folks at IBM responsible for creating the next

155

generation of development tools. In Java, OTI also saw another language to which it could apply its many talents.

Sun's initial attempt at providing a portable widget API, the Abstract Windowing Toolkit (AWT), suffered from both an overly complex interface to the native widgets and the LCD problem. It provided access to a minimal set of widgets common across most platforms such as buttons, labels, and lists, but did not provide access to richer widgets such as tables, trees, and styled text. That, coupled with an anemic API, destined it to failure in the marketplace.

To solve the problems of AWT and provide Java with a more powerful, extensible GUI library, Sun decided to abandon native widget interfaces and developed its own portable, emulated widget library officially known as the Java Foundation Classes (JFC), but more commonly known as Swing. Interestingly enough, this paralleled the developments in the Smalltalk world many years earlier when ParcPlace brought the world's first, truly portable, multi-platform GUI environment to market in a product called VisualWorks (many of the ex-ParcPlace engineers responsible for the portable, emulated GUI library in VisualWorks ended up working at Sun).

While Swing solved the LCD problem by providing a rich set of widgets, the emulation of the platform widgets left much to be desired. Swing applications ended up feeling like Swing applications and not the platform native applications they were meant to replace. Swing applications also suffered from performance problems not present in their native counterparts.

While AWT was able to run on Java 2 Platform, Micro Edition (J2ME) devices, Swing was not because of the large run-time Java virtual machine (JVM) footprint and its reliance on fast native graphics to draw every emulated control. OTI was given the task within IBM of tooling for J2ME, and decided that AWT was not a good enough toolkit. It provided only a basic set of controls, and because it was architected around the JavaBeans component model, which allows null construction, it had a two-tiered object layer that used valuable JVM memory—something important to manage wisely on small devices.

Uncomfortable with the philosophy behind Swing and emulated widget libraries in general, and armed with deep knowledge about how to correctly build native, portable, multiplatform widget libraries, OTI set out to correct the faults of both AWT and Swing and produce the GUI library that AWT should have been. The result was SWT. OTI used the same developers who created CW for Smalltalk to create SWT for Java. SWT was designed to have as small a JVM footprint as possible. The CW had two layers, including an OS layer; however for SWT, it was felt that a single layer was better, where each platform's implementation would be a set of completely optimized Java classes that went straight to native as soon as possible. The public API was the same, but there was no indirection through an intermediate layer.

OTI used SWT to build VisualAge Micro Edition (VAME), their first IDE that was written in Java. When IBM decided to build a common tools platform (Eclipse) on which they could re-base their successful existing products, they initially built it using Swing. It was an early release of Swing in Java 1.2, and IBM was greatly disappointed with its performance and look-and-feel. There were memory leaks in Swing and other defects, which led to its eventual abandonment.

One of the reasons SWT was chosen was because IBM's tooling effort wanted to compete head-to-head with Microsoft, and it was felt that SWT would give a rich enough UI experience. It was a huge risk, because at the time, SWT had not been ported to many platforms, and also by adopting SWT there was the potential message to customers that "If Swing wasn't good enough for your toolkit, why should we use it?" Additionally, anyone writing plugins would have to use SWT instead of Swing, and there was fear that there would be a natural antagonism toward learning this new API. There was also the possibility that SWT versus Swing would fragment the Java community. All these fears came true.

However, SWT has found a lot of favor in people that are now using it to program applications outside of Eclipse because they like the high level of speed and platform integration, and arguably, Sun did take its eye off the ball with the 1.2 and 1.3 Swing releases. With JDK 1.4, Sun has much improved the performance of Swing and its look-and-feel classes so that Swing developers now have a greatly improved toolkit. Without SWT threatening to become the new standard, it's hard to know whether Sun would have done this work to try and catch up, so having the two toolkits is actually good for users of both. In the past, interoperability between the two toolkits was poor, although this has improved dramatically in Eclipse 3.0.

SWT is the foundation on which the entire Eclipse UI is based. It is fast, native, and multiplatform, but does not suffer the LCD problem present in AWT or the look-and-feel problem present in Swing. It does this by taking a best-of-both-worlds approach: It uses native widgets whenever possible on a platform and supplements them with emulated widgets on platforms where they don't exist (a good example of this is the tree widget that exists in native form under Windows, but is emulated under Linux). The result is a rich, portable API for building GUI applications that adhere very closely the look-and-feel of each platform they support.

> **Note:** While providing a consistent, high-level, public API, under the covers SWT is very different from one platform to the next. SWT has a unique implementation for each platform and low-level SWT APIs map one-to-one with their platform counterparts. For a detailed discussion on how SWT interfaces to the native platform, see *www.eclipse.org/articles/Article-SWT-Design-1/SWT-Design-1.html*

4.2   SWT Widgets

SWT provides a rich set of widgets that can be used to create either standalone Java applications or Eclipse plug-ins. Before we go into detail on each of the widgets you are likely to use, it is instructive to explore a simple standalone SWT example.

4.2.1   Simple Standalone Example

We will start by revisiting the simple Java project and `HelloWorld` application created in Chapter 1, "Using Eclipse Tools."

4.2.1.1   Adding the swt.jar file

Before we can start using the SWT classes, the swt.jar file needs to be added to the Java build path for the project. Right-click on the project and select the **Properties** command to open the **Properties** dialog. Next, select the **Java Build Path > Libraries** tab and click on the **Add Variable** button. Within the **New Variable Classpath Entry** dialog, select the `ECLIPSE_HOME` variable and then select the **Extend** button. Now find the `swt.jar` file and click **OK**. The `swt.jar` file can be found in the directory titled `plugins/org.eclipse.swt.<platform name & version number>.ws.<window system>`. Under Windows, for example, you would find it in the `plug-ins/org.eclipse.swt.win32_3.0.0/ws/win32` directory (see Figure 4–1).

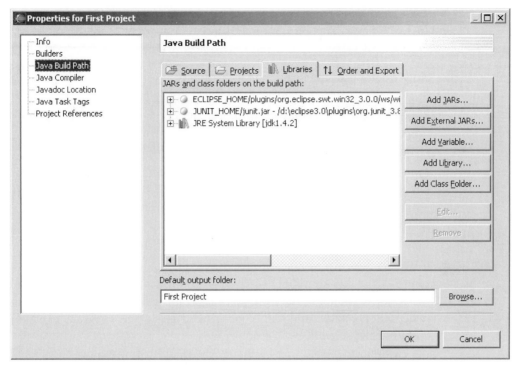

Figure 4–1   Java Build Path > Libraries properties.

4.2.1.2   Standalone swt code

Next, we will modify the `HelloWorld` class to convert it into a standalone SWT example. To do this, remove the contents of the `main()` method and replace it with the following:

```
1  public static void main(String[] args) {
2     Display display = new Display();
3     Shell shell = new Shell(display);
4     shell.setText("Hello World");
5     shell.setBounds(100, 100, 200, 50);
6     shell.setLayout(new FillLayout());
7     Label label = new Label(shell, SWT.CENTER);
8     label.setText("Hello World");
9     Color red = new Color(display, 255, 0, 0);
10    label.setForeground(red);
11    shell.open();
12    while (!shell.isDisposed()) {
13       if (!display.readAndDispatch()) display.sleep();
14    }
15    red.dispose();
16    display.dispose();
17 }
```

> **Note:** After entering the new method text, select the **Source > Organize Imports** command (or press **Ctrl+Shift+O**) to add imports for all the referenced SWT classes.

Now we will examine each line in detail:

Line 2—Each SWT-based application has one `Display` instance that represents the link between the underlying platform and SWT. In addition to managing the SWT event loop, it also provides access to platform resources SWT needs. It will be disposed in Line 14.

Line 3—Each window has a `Shell` representing the window frame with which the user interacts. It handles the familiar moving and sizing behavior common to all windows and acts as the parent for any widgets displayed within its bounds.

Line 4—The `setText()` method is used to set the title of the window frame.

Line 5—The `setBounds()` method is used to set the size and position of the window frame. In the example, the window frame will be 200 pixels wide, 50 pixels tall, and will be positioned 100 pixels from the top left corner of the screen.

Line 6—The `setLayout()` method sets the layout manager for the window frame. `FillLayout` is a simple layout that causes the single child widget to fill the entire bounds of its parent. SWT layout managers will be discussed in detail in Section 4.3, "Layout Management."

Line 7—This creates a simple label widget that has the shell as its parent and will display its text centered relative to itself.

Line 8—The `setText()` method is used to set the text of the label.

Line 9—This creates a `Color` instance with the color red.

Line 10—The `setForeground()` method sets the foreground color of the label.

Line 11—Up to this point, the window frame has not been visible. The `open()` method causes the window frame to appear.

Line 12—The `while` loop continually checks whether the window frame has been closed.

Line 13—The `display` manages the event loop. The `readAndDispatch()` method reads events from the platform's event queue and dispatches them to the appropriate receiver. The method returns `true` as long as there is more work to be done and `false` when the event queue is empty (thus allowing the UI thread to sleep until there is more work to be done).

Lines 15 and 16—When the loop detects that the window has been disposed, it is necessary to dispose of the color, display, and any associated platform resources.

4.2.1.3 Running the example

Normally, to launch a Java application, we would click on the **Run** toolbar button. Doing so at this point will cause an "UnsatisfiedLinkError" to be thrown, indicating that the SWT native library cannot be found. To correct the problem, select the **Run > Run** command to open the **launch configuration** dialog (see Section 1.9.2, "Launch configurations") and select the **Arguments** tab (see Figure 4–2). In the **VM arguments** field, add the following (for Windows):

```
-Djava.library.path=
c:\eclipse\plugins\org.eclipse.swt.win32_3.0.0\os\win32\x86
```

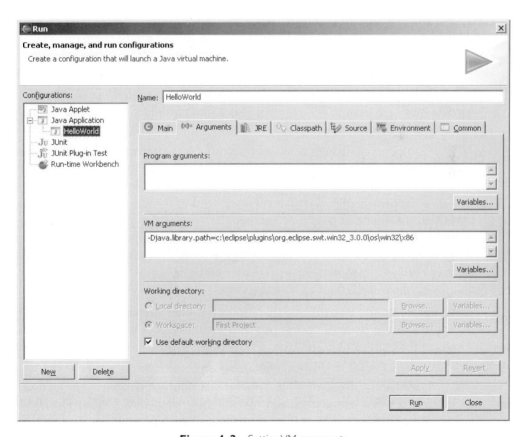

Figure 4–2 Setting VM arguments.

Click the dialog's **Run** button to launch the Java application (see Figure 4–3).

Figure 4–3   Running the standalone SWT application.

4.2.2 *Widget lifecycle*

One of SWT's goals is to be small and lean. To achieve this, a basic design decision was made that as much widget state as possible would be stored in the platform widget rather than in the SWT widget. This is in marked contrast to Swing, which maintains the entire widget state within the widget. By not duplicating the information maintained at the platform level, SWT widgets are very small with modest memory requirements.

One tradeoff to this approach is that SWT widgets cannot properly exist by themselves. When an SWT widget is created, its underlying platform counterpart is immediately created. Almost all requests for widget state information go to the platform widget.

Because most platforms require that widgets be created within the context of a specific parent, SWT requires that a parent widget be supplied as one of its constructor arguments.

Another requirement of many platforms is that certain style settings must be supplied at creation time (for example, buttons can be checkboxes, radio buttons, or simple buttons and text fields may be single- or multi-line). *Style bits* are represented by `int` constants defined in the `SWT` class. Styles are then OR'ed together and passed as another constructor argument to create the initial style of a widget. Note that all styles are not supported on all platforms, so in many cases, the requested styles are treated as suggestions that may or may not have any effect on a particular platform.

Another platform requirement imposed on SWT is that platform resources should be explicitly disposed when they are no longer needed. This applies to the widgets themselves and any resources (such as graphics and fonts) they have used. The basic rule is that, if you create a widget, you must destroy the widget using its `dispose()` method.

Fortunately, a widget that is a child of another widget is automatically destroyed when its parent is destroyed. This means that if you properly dispose of a shell, you do not need to dispose of each of its children as they will be disposed of automatically.

4.2.3 Widget events

An *event* is the mechanism that notifies an application when a user performs a mouse or keyboard action. The application can be notified about text entry, mouse clicks, mouse movements, focus changes, and so on. Events are handled by adding a listener to a widget. For example, a `SelectionListener` is used to inform the application that a `Button` has been pressed and released or an item has been selected from a list box. As another example, all widgets support a `Dispose` event that is invoked just before a widget is destroyed.

For each type of event, SWT defines a listener interface (e.g., `<Event-Name>Listener`), an event class, and if necessary, an adapter class (note that adapter classes are only provided in cases where the listener interface defines more than one method). Furthermore, for each widget that implements a specific event, there are corresponding `add<EventName>Listener` and `remove<EventName>Listener` methods.

Table 4–1 presents a list of the event types defined by SWT along with a description of when each event is generated and a list of the widgets that generate that event.

Table 4–1 Widget Events

Event Name	Generated When	Widgets
Arm	A menu item is armed (highlighted)	MenuItem
Control	A control is resized or moved	Control, TableColumn, Tracker
Dispose	A control is destroyed	Widget
Focus	A control gains or loses focus	Control
Help	The user requests help (e.g., by pressing the **F1** key)	Control, Menu, MenuItem
Key	A key is pressed or released	Control
Menu	A menu is hidden or shown	Menu
Modify	Text is modified	Combo, Text
Mouse	The mouse is pressed, released, or double-clicked	Control
MouseMove	The mouse moves over the control	Control

Table 4–1   Widget Events (continued)

Event Name	Generated When	Widgets
MouseTrack	The mouse enters, leaves, or hovers over the control	Control
Paint	A control needs to be repainted	Control
Selection	An item is selected in the control	Button, Combo, CoolItem, List, MenuItem, Sash, Scale, ScrollBar, Slider, StyledText, TabFolder, Table, TableColumn, TableTree, Text, ToolItem, Tree
Shell	The shell is minimized, maximized, activated, deactivated, or closed	Shell
Traverse	The control is traversed (tabbed)	Control
Tree	A tree item is collapsed or expanded	Tree, TableTree
Verify	Text is about to be modified	Text, StyledText

*This table was adapted from the *Platform Plug-In Developer Guide for Eclipse.*

4.2.4   *Abstract widget classes*

All the UI objects in the system are derived from the abstract classes `Widget` and `Control` (see Figure 4–4). In this section and the ones immediately following it, we will discuss the major widget types and their major APIs. API descriptions are taken from the Eclipse platform Javadoc.

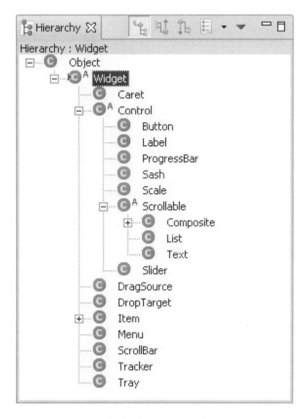

Figure 4–4   SWT widget hierarchy.

Note: For every event, there is an `add<EventName>Listener` method and a corresponding `remove<EventName>Listener` method. Likewise, for every widget property, there is a `get<PropertyName>` and `set<PropertyName>` method. In the interest of space, we will only list the `add<EventName>Listener` and `set<PropertyName>` methods. Each widget type has a constructor that requires the widget's parent as the first argument and the style (an `int`) as the second argument. Each method with a non-void return type will list its return type prior to its name.

4.2.4.1 Widget

The `Widget` class is the abstract superclass of the following classes: `Caret`, `Control` (discussed below), `DragSource`, `DropTarget`, `Item`, `Menu` (discussed below), `ScrollBar`, and `Tracker`. Useful APIs include:

> `addDisposeListener(DisposeListener)`—Adds the listener to the collection of listeners that will be notified when the widget is disposed.

`addListener(int, Listener)`—Adds the listener to the collection of listeners that will be notified when an event of the given type occurs.

`dispose()`—Disposes of the OS resources associated with the receiver and all its descendents.

`getData(String)`—Returns the application-defined property of the receiver with the specified name, or null if it has not been set.

`isDisposed()`—Returns `true` if the widget has been disposed, and `false` otherwise.

`notifyListeners(int, Event)`—Notifies all the receiver's listeners for events of the given type that one such event has occurred by invoking the `handleEvent()` method.

`setData(String, Object)`—Sets the application-defined property of the receiver with the specified name to the given value.

`toString()`—Returns a string containing a concise, human-readable description of the widget.

4.2.4.2 *Control*

The `Control` class is the abstract superclass of all the dialog and window component classes such as `Button`, `Label`, `ProgressBar`, `Sash`, `Scrollable`, and `Slider` (each of these is described below). Useful APIs include:

`addControlListener(ControlListener)`—Adds the listener to the collection of listeners that will be notified when the control is moved or resized by sending it one of the messages defined in the `ControlListener` interface.

`addFocusListener(FocusListener)`—Adds the listener to the collection of listeners that will be notified when the control gains or loses focus by sending it one of the messages defined in the `FocusListener` interface.

`addHelpListener(HelpListener)`—Adds the listener to the collection of listeners that will be notified when help events are generated for the control by sending it one of the messages defined in the `HelpListener` interface.

`addKeyListener(KeyListener)`—Adds the listener to the collection of listeners that will be notified when keys are pressed and released on the system keyboard by sending it one of the messages defined in the `KeyListener` interface.

`addMouseListener(MouseListener)`—Adds the listener to the collection of listeners that will be notified when mouse buttons are pressed and released by sending it one of the messages defined in the `MouseListener` interface.

`addMouseMoveListener(MouseMoveListener)`—Adds the listener to the collection of listeners that will be notified when the mouse moves by sending it one of the messages defined in the `MouseMoveListener` interface.

`addMouseTrackListener(MouseTrackListener)`—Adds the listener to the collection of listeners that will be notified when the mouse passes or hovers over controls by sending it one of the messages defined in the `MouseTrackListener` interface.

`addPaintListener(PaintListener)`—Adds the listener to the collection of listeners that will be notified when the receiver needs to be painted by sending it one of the messages defined in the `PaintListener` interface.

`addTraverseListener(TraverseListener)`—Adds the listener to the collection of listeners that will be notified when traversal events occur by sending it one of the messages defined in the `TraverseListener` interface.

`getDisplay()`—Returns the display on which the receiver was created.

`getParent()`—Returns the receiver's parent, which must be a `Composite` or null when the receiver is a shell that was created with null or a display for a parent.

`getShell()`—Returns the receiver's shell.

`isDisposed()`—Returns `true` if the widget has been disposed, and `false` otherwise.

`isEnabled()`—Returns `true` if the receiver is enabled and all the receiver's ancestors are enabled, and `false` otherwise.

`isVisible()`—Returns `true` if the receiver is visible and all the receiver's ancestors are visible, and `false` otherwise.

`pack()`—Causes the receiver to be resized to its preferred size.

`redraw()`—Causes the entire bounds of the receiver to be marked as needing to be redrawn.

`setBackground(Color)`—Sets the receiver's background color to the color specified by the argument, or to the default system color for the control if the argument is null.

`setBounds(Rectangle)`—Sets the receiver's size and location to the rectangular area specified by the argument.

`setEnabled(boolean)`—Enables the receiver if the argument is `true`, and disables it otherwise.

`boolean setFocus()`—Causes the receiver to have the keyboard focus such that all keyboard events will be delivered to it.

`setFont(Font)`—Sets the font that the receiver will use to paint textual information to the font specified by the argument, or to the default font for that kind of control if the argument is null.

`setForeground(Color)`—Sets the receiver's foreground color to the color specified by the argument, or to the default system color for the control if the argument is null.

`setLayoutData(Object)`—Sets the layout data associated with the receiver to the argument.

`setLocation(Point)`—Sets the receiver's location to the point specified by the argument that is relative to the receiver's parent (or its display if its parent is null).

`setRedraw(boolean)`—If the argument is `false`, causes subsequent drawing operations in the receiver to be ignored.

`setSize(Point)`—Sets the receiver's size to the point specified by the argument.

`setToolTipText(String)`—Sets the receiver's tool tip text to the argument, which may be null, indicating that no tool tip text should be shown.

`setVisible(boolean)`—Marks the receiver as visible if the argument is `true`, and marks it invisible otherwise.

`update()`—Forces all outstanding paint requests for the widget to be processed before this method returns.

4.2.4.3 *Scrollable*

The `Scrollable` class is the abstract superclass of all controls that can have scrollbars such as `Composite`, `List`, and `Text`. Useful APIs include:

`getClientArea()`—Returns a rectangle describing the area of the receiver that is capable of displaying data (that is, not covered by the "trimmings").

`getHorizontalBar()`—Returns the receiver's horizontal scrollbar if it has one, and null if it does not.

`getVerticalBar()`—Returns the receiver's vertical scrollbar if it has one, and null if it does not.

4.2.5   Top-level classes

As stated earlier, each SWT application needs a display and one or more shells (representing each window frame).

4.2.5.1   Display

The display represents the link between the underlying platform, the UI thread, and SWT. Although the `Display` constructors are public, under normal circumstances, you should not be constructing new instances (unless you are creating a standalone SWT application); instead, there are two static `Display` methods that return an instance:

> `getCurrent ()`—Returns the display associated with the currently running thread or null if the currently running thread is not a UI thread for any display.

> `getDefault ()`—Returns the default display. This is the instance that was first created by the system.

Calls to SWT methods that create widgets or modify currently visible widgets must be made from the UI thread, otherwise an `SWTException` is thrown indicating the call was made from a non-UI thread. A call to the `getCurrent()` method listed previously can be used to quickly determine whether or not the current thread is UI or non-UI. If the thread is non-UI, the following `Display` methods can be used to queue execution on the UI thread at the next available time:

> `asyncExec (Runnable)`—Causes the `run()` method of the runnable to be invoked by the UI thread at the next reasonable opportunity.

> `syncExec (Runnable)`—Causes the `run()` method of the runnable to be invoked by the UI thread at the next reasonable opportunity.

> `timerExec (int, Runnable)`—Causes the `run()` method of the runnable to be invoked by the UI thread after the specified number of milliseconds have elapsed.

These methods, combined with the methods listed previously, can be used to update visible widgets when responding to resource change events (see the end of Section 9.2, "Processing Change Events), displaying error messages (see Section 20.4.1, "OpenBrowserAction"), or simply deferring execution until the widgets have been initialized (see Section 8.2.5,"Label provider").

In addition to managing the UI event loop, it also provides access to platform resources that SWT needs. Useful APIs include:

> `addListener(int, Listener)`—Adds the listener to the collection of

listeners that will be notified when an event of the given type occurs.

`beep()`—Causes the system hardware to emit a short sound (if it supports this capability).

`close()`—Requests that the connection between SWT and the underlying OS be closed.

`disposeExec(Runnable)`—Causes the `run()` method of the runnable to be invoked by the UI thread just before the display is disposed.

`findWidget(int)`—Given the OS handle for a widget, returns the instance of the `Widget` subclass, which represents it in the currently running application, if such an instance exists, or null if no matching widget can be found.

`getActiveShell()`—Returns the currently active `Shell`, or null if no shell belonging to the currently running application is active.

`getBounds()`—Returns a rectangle describing the receiver's size and location.

`getClientArea()`—Returns a rectangle describing the area of the receiver that is capable of displaying data.

`getCursorControl()`—Returns the control that the on-screen pointer is currently over, or null if it is not currently over one of the controls built by the currently running application.

`getCursorLocation()`—Returns the location of the on-screen pointer relative to the top left corner of the screen.

`getData(String)`—Returns the application-defined property of the receiver with the specified name, or null if it has not been set.

`getDoubleClickTime()`—Returns the longest duration, in milliseconds, between two mouse button clicks that will be considered a double-click by the underlying OS.

`getFocusControl()`—Returns the control that currently has keyboard focus, or null if keyboard events are not currently going to any of the controls built by the currently running application.

`getShells()`—Returns an array containing all shells that have not been disposed and have the receiver as their display.

`getSystemColor(int)`—Returns the matching standard color for the given constant, which should be one of the color constants specified in the class SWT.

`getSystemFont()`—Returns a reasonable font for applications to use.

`readAndDispatch()`—Reads an event from the OS's event queue, dispatches it appropriately, and returns true if there is potentially more work to do, or `false` if the caller can sleep until another event is placed on the event queue.

`setCursorLocation(Point)`—Sets the location of the on-screen pointer relative to the top left corner of the screen.

`setData(String, Object)`—Sets the application-defined property of the receiver with the specified name to the given argument.

`sleep()`—Causes the UI thread to sleep (that is, to be put in a state where it does not consume central processing unit [CPU] cycles) until an event is received or it is otherwise awakened.

`update()`—Forces all outstanding paint requests for the display to be processed before this method returns.

4.2.5.2 *Shell*

Each window has a shell representing the window frame with which the user interacts. The shell handles the familiar moving and sizing behavior common to all windows and acts as the parent for widgets displayed within its bounds (see Section 11.1.10, "Opening a dialog—finding a parent shell"). Useful APIs include:

`addShellListener(ShellListener)`—Adds the listener to the collection of listeners that will be notified when operations are performed on the receiver by sending the listener one of the messages defined in the `ShellListener` interface.

`close()`—Requests that the window manager close the receiver in the same way it would be closed if the user clicked on the "close box" or performed some other platform-specific key or mouse combination that indicated the window should be removed.

`dispose()`—Disposes of the OS resources associated with the receiver and all its descendents.

`getDisplay()`—Returns the display on which the receiver was created.

`getShell()`—Returns the receiver's shell.

`getShells()`—Returns an array containing all shells that are descendents of the receiver.

`isEnabled()`—Returns `true` if the receiver is enabled and all the receiver's ancestors are enabled, and `false` otherwise.

`open()`—Moves the receiver to the top of the drawing order for the display on which it was created (so that all other shells on that display, which are not the receiver's children, will be drawn behind it), marks it visible, sets focus to its default button (if it has one), and asks the window manager to make the shell active.

`setActive()`—Moves the receiver to the top of the drawing order for the display on which it was created (so that all other shells on that display, which are not the receiver's children, will be drawn behind it), and asks the window manager to make the shell active.

`setEnabled(boolean enabled)`—Enables the receiver if the argument is `true`, and disables it otherwise.

`setVisible(boolean visible)`—Marks the receiver as visible if the argument is `true`, and marks it invisible otherwise.

4.2.6　Useful widgets

There are dozens of widgets defined within the SWT class hierarchy. In this section, we will discuss the widgets that are most commonly used in plug-in development such as labels, buttons, text fields, lists, tables, trees, containers, and tab folders. For each widget, we will provide a list of useful APIs and creation styles.

4.2.6.1　Label

Labels are static controls that display either strings or images as their contents. They do not generate any special events and do not support any user interaction. Useful APIs include:

`setAlignment(int)`—Controls how text and images will be displayed in the receiver. Valid arguments include `SWT.LEFT`, `SWT.RIGHT`, and `SWT.CENTER`.

`setImage(Image)`—Sets the receiver's image to the argument, which may be null, indicating that no image should be displayed.

`setText(String)`—Sets the receiver's text.

Useful creation styles include:

`SWT.SHADOW_IN`—Creates an inset shadow around the widget.

`SWT.SHADOW_OUT`—Creates an outset shadow around the widget.

`SWT.SHADOW_NONE`—Creates a widget with no shadow.

`SWT.WRAP`—Causes the text of the widget to wrap onto multiple lines, if necessary.

SWT.SEPARATOR—Creates a single vertical or horizontal line.

SWT.HORIZONTAL—Creates a horizontal line.

SWT.VERTICAL—Creates a vertical line.

SWT.LEFT—Left-justifies the widget within its bounding box.

SWT.RIGHT—Right-justifies the widget within its bounding box.

SWT.CENTER—Centers the widget within its bounding box.

4.2.6.2   Button

Buttons provide a mechanism to initiate an action when clicked. They generate a Selection event when pressed and released. Buttons can display either strings or images as their contents. Depending on their style settings, buttons can represent a number of common UI element types such as pushbuttons, checkboxes, radio buttons, toggle buttons, and arrow buttons. Useful APIs include:

addSelectionListener(SelectionListener)—Adds the listener to the collection of listeners that will be notified when the control is selected by sending it one of the messages defined in the Selection-Listener interface.

getSelection()—Returns true if the receiver is selected, and false otherwise.

setAlignment(int)–Controls how text, images, and arrows will be displayed in the receiver.

setImage(Image)—Sets the receiver's image to the argument, which may be null, indicating that no image should be displayed.

setSelection(boolean)—Sets the selection state of the receiver if it is of type SWT.CHECK, SWT.RADIO, or SWT.TOGGLE.

setText(String)—Sets the receiver's text.

Useful creation styles include:

SWT.ARROW—Creates an arrow button widget.

SWT.CHECK—Creates a checkbox widget.

SWT.PUSH—Creates a pushbutton widget.

SWT.RADIO—Creates a radio button widget.

SWT.TOGGLE—Creates a toggle button widget.

SWT.UP—Creates an upward-pointing arrow button.

SWT.DOWN—Creates a downward-pointing arrow button.

SWT.LEFT—Creates a leftward-pointing arrow button or left-justifies the widget within its bounding box.

SWT.RIGHT—Creates a rightward-pointing arrow button or right-justifies the widget within its bounding box.

SWT.CENTER—Centers the widget within its bounding box.

The following example (shown without import or package statements) creates a window with a single pushbutton. Clicking on the pushbutton will change the text of the button (see Figure 4–5).

Figure 4–5 Button example.

```
import org.eclipse.swt.*;
import org.eclipse.swt.events.*;
import org.eclipse.swt.layout.*;
import org.eclipse.swt.widgets.*;

public class ButtonExample {
   public static void main(String[] args) {
      Display display = new Display();
      Shell shell = new Shell(display);
      shell.setText("Button Example");
      shell.setBounds(100, 100, 200, 100);
      shell.setLayout(new FillLayout());
      final Button button = new Button(shell, SWT.PUSH);
      button.setText("Click Me Now");
      button.addSelectionListener(new SelectionAdapter() {
         public void widgetSelected(SelectionEvent event) {
            button.setText("I Was Clicked");
         }
      });
      shell.open();
```

```
          while (!shell.isDisposed()) {
             if (!display.readAndDispatch()) display.sleep();
          }
          display.dispose();
      }
}
```

Relative to the first example in this chapter, the interesting lines in the above example are highlighted in bold. After the creation of the button, a selection listener is added in which a `SelectionAdapter` is created that overrides the `widgetSelected()` method.

4.2.6.3 Text

Text widgets provide text viewing and editing capabilities. If the user types more text than can be accommodated within the widget, it will automatically scroll. Useful APIs include:

`addModifyListener(ModifyListener)`—Adds the listener to the collection of listeners that will be notified when the receiver's text is modified by sending it one of the messages defined in the `ModifyListener` interface.

`addSelectionListener(SelectionListener)`—Adds the listener to the collection of listeners that will be notified when the control is selected by sending it one of the messages defined in the `SelectionListener` interface.

`addVerifyListener(VerifyListener)`—Adds the listener to the collection of listeners that will be notified when the receiver's text is verified by sending it one of the messages defined in the `VerifyListener` interface.

`clearSelection()`—Clears the selection.

`copy()`—Copies the selected text.

`cut()`—Cuts the selected text.

`getSelectionText()`—Gets the selected text.

`getText()`—Gets the widget text.

`getText(int start, int end)`—Gets a range of text.

`insert(String)`—Inserts a string.

`paste()`—Pastes text from the clipboard.

`selectAll()`—Selects all the text in the receiver.

`setEchoChar(char echo)`—Sets the echo character.

`setEditable(boolean editable)`—Sets the editable state.

`setSelection(int start, int end)`—Sets the selection.

`setText(String)`—Sets the contents of the receiver to the given string.

`setTextLimit(int)`—Sets the maximum number of characters that the receiver is capable of holding to be the argument.

`setTopIndex(int)`—Sets the zero-relative index of the line that is currently at the top of the receiver.

Useful creation styles include:

`SWT.SINGLE`—Creates a single-line text widget.

`SWT.MULTI`—Creates a multi-line text widget.

`SWT.WRAP`—Causes the text of the widget to wrap onto multiple lines if necessary.

`SWT.READ_ONLY`—Creates a read-only text widget that cannot be edited.

`SWT.LEFT`—Creates a left-justified text widget.

`SWT.RIGHT`—Creates a right-justified text widget.

`SWT.CENTER`—Creates a center-justified text widget.

The following example creates a window frame with a single-line text field. The field will only allow digits (0-9) to be entered (see Figure 4–6).

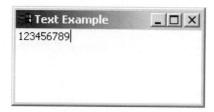

Figure 4–6   Text example.

```
import org.eclipse.swt.*;
import org.eclipse.swt.events.*;
import org.eclipse.swt.layout.*;
import org.eclipse.swt.widgets.*;

public class TextExample {
    public static void main(String[] args) {
        Display display = new Display();
        Shell shell = new Shell(display);
        shell.setText("Text Example");
        shell.setBounds(100, 100, 200, 100);
        shell.setLayout(new FillLayout());
```

```
        final Text text = new Text(shell, SWT.MULTI);
        text.addVerifyListener(new VerifyListener() {
           public void verifyText(VerifyEvent event) {
              event.doit = event.text.length() == 0
                   || Character.isDigit(event.text.charAt(0));
           }
        });
        shell.open();
        while (!shell.isDisposed()) {
           if (!display.readAndDispatch()) display.sleep();
        }
        display.dispose();
     }
}
```

As in the previous example, interesting lines are highlighted in bold. After the creation of the text widget, a verify listener is added in which a Veri-fyListener is created that overrides the verifyText() method to verify that the character entered is a digit. Note that, if the user deletes or backspaces over some text, the event.text will be empty.

4.2.6.4   List

List widgets present a list of items and allow the user to select one or more items from the list. Lists generate a Selection event when an item is selected. Useful APIs include:

add(String)—Adds the argument to the end of the receiver's list.

addSelectionListener(SelectionListener)—Adds the listener to the collection of listeners that will be notified when the receiver's selection changes by sending it one of the messages defined in the SelectionListener interface.

deselect(int)—Deselects the item at the given zero-relative index in the receiver.

deselectAll()—Deselects all selected items in the receiver.

getItem(int)—Returns the item at the given, zero-relative index in the receiver.

getItemCount()—Returns the number of items contained in the receiver.

getItems()—Returns an array of strings that are items in the receiver.

getSelection()—Returns an array of strings that are currently selected in the receiver.

getSelectionCount()—Returns the number of selected items contained in the receiver.

`getSelectionIndex()`—Returns the zero-relative index of the item that is currently selected in the receiver, or -1 if no item is selected.

`getSelectionIndices()`—Returns the zero-relative indices of the items which are currently selected in the receiver.

`indexOf(String)`—Gets the index of an item.

`remove(int)`—Removes the item from the receiver at the given zero-relative index.

`remove(String)`—Searches the receiver's list starting at the first item until an item is found that is equal to the argument and removes that item from the list.

`removeAll()`—Removes all the items from the receiver.

`select(int)`—Selects the item at the given zero-relative index in the receiver's list.

`selectAll()`—Selects all the items in the receiver.

`setItems(String[] items)`—Sets the receiver's items to be the given array of items.

`setSelection(int)`—Selects the item at the given zero-relative index in the receiver.

`setSelection(String[])`—Sets the receiver's selection to be the given array of items.

`setTopIndex(int)`—Sets the zero-relative index of the line that is currently at the top of the receiver.

Useful creation styles include:

`SWT.SINGLE`—Creates a single-selection list widget.

`SWT.MULTI`—Creates a multiple-selection list widget.

The following example creates a window frame with a single-selection list box. Clicking or double-clicking on an item will print the selection to the console (see Figure 4–7).

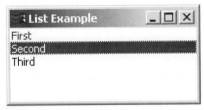

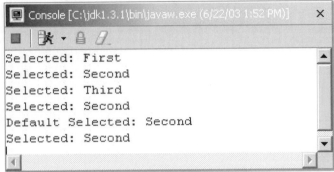

Figure 4–7   List example.

```
import org.eclipse.swt.*;
import org.eclipse.swt.events.*;
import org.eclipse.swt.layout.*;
import org.eclipse.swt.widgets.*;

public class ListExample {
    public static void main(String[] args) {
        Display display = new Display();
        Shell shell = new Shell(display);
        shell.setText("List Example");
        shell.setBounds(100, 100, 200, 100);
        shell.setLayout(new FillLayout());
        final List list = new List(shell, SWT.SINGLE);
        list.setItems(new String[]
           {"First", "Second", "Third"});
        list.addSelectionListener(new SelectionAdapter() {
            public void widgetSelected(SelectionEvent event) {
                String[] selected = list.getSelection();
                if (selected.length > 0)
                   System.out.println(
                       "Selected: " + selected[0]);
            }
            public void widgetDefaultSelected(
                SelectionEvent event) {
                String[] selected = list.getSelection();
                if (selected.length > 0)
                   System.out.println(
                       "Default Selected: " + selected[0]);
            }
        });
```

```
        shell.open();
        while (!shell.isDisposed()) {
           if (!display.readAndDispatch()) display.sleep();
        }
        display.dispose();
     }
}
```

After the creation of the list widget, its contents are set using the set-Items() method. Next, a selection listener is added in which a Selection-Adapter is created that overrides the widgetSelected() and widgetDefaultSelected() methods to print any items that are selected or double-clicked.

4.2.6.5 Combo

Similar to the list widget, the combo box widget enables the user to select a single item from a list of available items. Depending on how a combo is configured, it may also allow the user to type a new value into the text field. The last selected or entered item is displayed in the text box. Useful APIs include:

add(String)—Adds the argument to the end of the receiver's list.

addModifyListener(ModifyListener)—Adds the listener to the collection of listeners that will be notified when the receiver's text is modified by sending it one of the messages defined in the ModifyListener interface.

addSelectionListener(SelectionListener)—Adds the listener to the collection of listeners that will be notified when the receiver's selection changes by sending it one of the messages defined in the SelectionListener interface.

clearSelection()—Sets the selection in the receiver's text field to an empty selection starting just before the first character.

copy()—Copies the selected text.

cut()—Cuts the selected text.

deselect(int)—Deselects the item at the given zero-relative index in the receiver's list.

deselectAll()—Deselects all selected items in the receiver's list.

getItem(int)—Returns the item at the given, zero-relative index in the receiver's list.

getItemCount()—Returns the number of items contained in the receiver's list.

`getItems()`—Returns an array of strings that are items in the receiver's list.

`getSelectionIndex()`—Returns the zero-relative index of the item that is currently selected in the receiver's list, or -1 if no item is selected.

`getText()`—Returns a string containing a copy of the contents of the receiver's text field.

`indexOf(String)`—Searches the receiver's list starting at the first item (index 0) until an item is found that is equal to the argument and returns the index of that item.

`paste()`—Pastes text from the clipboard.

`remove(int)`—Removes the item from the receiver's list at the given zero-relative index.

`remove(String)`—Searches the receiver's list starting at the first item until an item is found that is equal to the argument and removes that item from the list.

`removeAll()`—Removes all the items from the receiver's list.

`select(int)`—Selects the item at the given zero-relative index in the receiver's list.

`setItems(String[] items)`—Sets the receiver's list to be the given array of items.

`setText(String)`—Sets the contents of the receiver's text field to the given string.

`setTextLimit(int)`—Sets the maximum number of characters that the receiver's text field is capable of holding to be the argument.

Useful creation styles include:

`SWT.DROP_DOWN`—Creates a drop-down list widget. Editable drop-down list widgets are also known as combo boxes.

`SWT.READ_ONLY`—Creates a read-only drop-down list widget.

`SWT.SIMPLE`—Creates a combo widget in which the list is always present.

The following example creates a window frame with two combo widgets and a list widget. Selecting an item from the first or second combo box or entering a new value into the second combo box will change the label's contents to reflect the selection (see Figure 4–8).

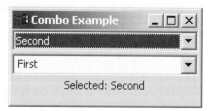

Figure 4–8　Combo box example.

```
import org.eclipse.swt.*;
import org.eclipse.swt.events.*;
import org.eclipse.swt.layout.*;
import org.eclipse.swt.widgets.*;

public class ComboExample {
    public static void main(String[] args) {
        Display display = new Display();
        Shell shell = new Shell(display);
        shell.setText("Combo Example");
        shell.setBounds(100, 100, 200, 100);
        shell.setLayout(new FillLayout(SWT.VERTICAL));
        final Combo combo1 = new Combo(shell,SWT.READ_ONLY);
        final Combo combo2 = new Combo(shell,SWT.DROP_DOWN);
        final Label label = new Label(shell, SWT.CENTER);
        combo1.setItems(new String[]
            {"First", "Second", "Third"});
        combo1.setText("First");
        combo1.addSelectionListener(new SelectionAdapter() {
            public void widgetSelected(SelectionEvent event) {
                label.setText("Selected: " + combo1.getText());
            }
        });
        combo2.setItems(new String[]
            {"First", "Second", "Third"});
        combo2.setText("First");
        combo2.addModifyListener(new ModifyListener() {
            public void modifyText(ModifyEvent event) {
                label.setText("Entered: " + combo2.getText());
            }
        });
        shell.open();
        while (!shell.isDisposed()) {
            if (!display.readAndDispatch()) display.sleep();
        }
        display.dispose();
    }
}
```

After the creation of the combo widgets and label widget, the contents of the combo widgets are set using the setItems() method and their initial selections (the contents of their text fields) with the setText() method. A selection listener is added to the first combo in which a SelectionAdapter is created that overrides the widgetSelected() method, and a modify listener is added to the second combo in which a `ModifyListener` is created that overrides the `modifyText()` method. Both methods update the contents of the label widget when their respective combo changes its selection.

4.2.6.6 Table

The table widget provides a vertical, multi-column list of items showing a row of cells for each item in the list. The columns of the table are defined by one or more `TableColumn` instances, each of which defines its own heading, width, and alignment. Useful APIs include:

`addSelectionListener(SelectionListener)`—Adds the listener to the collection of listeners that will be notified when the receiver's selection changes by sending it one of the messages defined in the `SelectionListener` interface.

`deselect(int)`—Deselects the item at the given zero-relative index in the receiver.

`deselectAll()`—Deselects all selected items in the receiver.

`getColumn(int)`—Returns the column at the given, zero-relative index in the receiver.

`getColumns()`—Returns an array of `TableColumns` that are columns in the receiver.

`getItem(int)`—Returns the item at the given, zero-relative index in the receiver.

`getSelection()`—Returns an array of `TableItems` that are currently selected in the receiver.

`getSelectionCount()`—Returns the number of selected items contained in the receiver.

`getSelectionIndex()`—Returns the zero-relative index of the item that is currently selected in the receiver, or -1 if no item is selected.

`getSelectionIndices()`—Returns the zero-relative indices of the items that are currently selected in the receiver.

`indexOf(TableColumn)`—Searches the receiver's list starting at the first column (index 0) until a column is found that is equal to the argument and returns the index of that column.

`indexOf(TableItem)`—Searches the receiver's list starting at the first item (index 0) until an item is found that is equal to the argument and returns the index of that item.

`remove(int)`—Removes the item from the receiver at the given zero-relative index.

`removeAll()`—Removes all the items from the receiver.

`select(int)`—Selects the item at the given zero-relative index in the receiver.

`selectAll()`—Selects all the items in the receiver.

`setHeaderVisible(boolean)`—Marks the receiver's header as visible if the argument is true, and marks it invisible otherwise.

`setLinesVisible(boolean)`—Marks the receiver's lines as visible if the argument is true, and marks it invisible otherwise.

`setSelection(int)`—Selects the item at the given zero-relative index in the receiver.

`setSelection(TableItem[])`—Sets the receiver's selection to be the given array of items.

`setTopIndex(int)`—Sets the zero-relative index of the item that is currently at the top of the receiver.

Useful creation styles include:

`SWT.SINGLE`—Creates a single-selection table widget.

`SWT.MULTI`—Creates a multiple-selection table widget.

`SWT.CHECK`—Creates a checkbox table widget.

`SWT.FULL_SELECTION`—Creates a table widget with row selection (rather than cell selection).

Useful `TableColumn` APIs include:

`addControlListener(ControlListener)`—Adds the listener to the collection of listeners that will be notified when the control is moved or resized by sending it one of the messages defined in the `ControlListener` interface.

`addSelectionListener(SelectionListener)`—Adds the listener to the collection of listeners that will be notified when the control is selected by sending it one of the messages defined in the `SelectionListener` interface.

`pack()`—Causes the receiver to be resized to its preferred size.

`setAlignment(int)`—Controls how text and images will be displayed in the receiver.

`setImage(Image)`—Sets the receiver's image to the argument, which may be null, indicating that no image should be displayed.

`setResizable(boolean)`—Sets the resizable attribute.

`setText(String)`—Sets the receiver's text.

`setWidth(int)`—Sets the width of the receiver.

Useful `TableItem` APIs include:

`getChecked()`—Returns `true` if the receiver is checked, and `false` otherwise.

`getText(int)`—Returns the text stored at the given column index in the receiver, or empty string if the text has not been set.

`setBackground(Color)`—Sets the receiver's background color to the color specified by the argument, or to the default system color for the item if the argument is null.

`setChecked(boolean)`—Sets the checked state of the checkbox for this item.

`setForeground(Color)`—Sets the receiver's foreground color to the color specified by the argument, or to the default system color for the item if the argument is null.

`setGrayed(boolean)`—Sets the grayed state of the checkbox for this item.

`setImage(Image)`—Sets the receiver's image to the argument, which may be null, indicating that no image should be displayed.

`setImage(Image[])`—Sets the image for multiple columns in the table.

`setImage(int, Image)`—Sets the receiver's image at a column.

`setImageIndent(int)`—Sets the image indent.

`setText(int, String)`—Sets the receiver's text at a column.

`setText(String)`—Sets the receiver's text.

`setText(String[])`—Sets the text for multiple columns in the table.

The following example creates a table with two columns and two items. Clicking on an item will print the cell's contents to the console (see Figure 4–9).

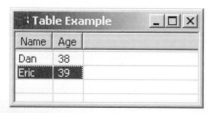

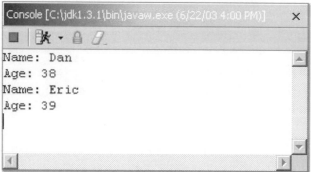

Figure 4–9   Table example.

```java
import org.eclipse.swt.*;
import org.eclipse.swt.events.*;
import org.eclipse.swt.layout.*;
import org.eclipse.swt.widgets.*;

public class TableExample {
    public static void main(String[] args) {
        Display display = new Display();
        Shell shell = new Shell(display);
        shell.setText("Table Example");
        shell.setBounds(100, 100, 200, 100);
        shell.setLayout(new FillLayout());
        final Table table = new Table(shell,
            SWT.SINGLE | SWT.BORDER | SWT.FULL_SELECTION);
        table.setHeaderVisible(true);
        table.setLinesVisible(true);
        TableColumn column1 =
            new TableColumn(table, SWT.NULL);
        column1.setText("Name");
        column1.pack();
        TableColumn column2 =
            new TableColumn(table, SWT.NULL);
        column2.setText("Age");
        column2.pack();
        TableItem item1 = new TableItem(table, SWT.NULL);
        item1.setText(new String[] {"Dan", "38"});
        TableItem item2 = new TableItem(table, SWT.NULL);
        item2.setText(new String[] {"Eric", "39"});
```

```
table.addSelectionListener(new SelectionAdapter() {
   public void widgetSelected(SelectionEvent event) {
      TableItem[] selected = table.getSelection();
      if (selected.length > 0) {
         System.out.println("Name: " +
            selected[0].getText(0));
         System.out.println("Age: " +
            selected[0].getText(1));
      }
   }
});
shell.open();
while (!shell.isDisposed()) {
   if (!display.readAndDispatch()) display.sleep();
}
display.dispose();
   }
}
```

The table widget is created with full selection behavior. Its headers are made visible with the setHeaderVisble() method and its lines are made visible with the setLinesVisible() method. Next, each column is created and it's a column header is set with the setText() method. The pack() method sets the size of each column to the maximum size of its contents. Each table row item is created next and cell contents are set with the setText() method (which expects an array of strings, one for each column). Finally, a selection listener is added to the table in which a SelectionAdapter is created that overrides the widgetSelected() method to print any items that are selected.

4.2.6.7 Tree

The tree widget is useful for displaying information in a hierarchical manner. A tree consists of a list of items composed of other items, which in turn can be composed of other items, and so on. A user navigates through a tree by expanding and collapsing items to view and hide their component items. Useful APIs include:

addSelectionListener(SelectionListener)—Adds the listener to the collection of listeners that will be notified when the receiver's selection changes by sending it one of the messages defined in the SelectionListener interface.

addTreeListener(TreeListener)—Adds the listener to the collection of listeners that will be notified when an item in the receiver is expanded or collapsed by sending it one of the messages defined in the TreeListener interface.

deselectAll()—Deselects all selected items in the receiver.

`getItemCount()`—Returns the number of items contained in the receiver that are direct item children of the receiver.

`getItems()`—Returns the number of items contained in the receiver that are direct item children of the receiver.

`getSelection()`—Returns an array of `TreeItems` that are currently selected in the receiver.

`getSelectionCount()`—Returns the number of selected items contained in the receiver.

`removeAll()`—Removes all the items from the receiver.

`selectAll()`—Selects all the items in the receiver.

`setSelection(TreeItem[])`—Sets the receiver's selection to be the given array of items.

`setTopItem(TreeItem)`—Sets the item that is currently at the top of the receiver.

Useful creation styles include:

`SWT.SINGLE`—Creates a single-selection tree widget.

`SWT.MULTI`—Creates a multiple-selection tree widget.

`SWT.CHECK`—Creates a checkbox tree widget.

Useful `TreeItem` APIs include:

`getChecked()`—Returns `true` if the receiver is checked, and `false` otherwise.

`getExpanded()`—Returns `true` if the receiver is expanded, and `false` otherwise.

`getItemCount()`—Returns the number of items contained in the receiver that are direct item children of the receiver.

`getItems()`—Returns an array of `TreeItems` that are the direct item children of the receiver.

`getParent()`—Returns the receiver's parent, which must be a `Tree`.

`getParentItem()`—Returns the receiver's parent item, which must be a `TreeItem` or null when the receiver is a root.

`setBackground(Color)`—Sets the receiver's background color to the color specified by the argument, or to the default system color for the item if the argument is null.

`setChecked(boolean)`—Sets the checked state of the receiver.

`setExpanded(boolean)`—Sets the expanded state of the receiver.

`setForeground(Color)`—Sets the receiver's foreground color to the color specified by the argument, or to the default system color for the item if the argument is null.

`setGrayed(boolean grayed)`—Sets the grayed state of the receiver.

`setImage(Image)`—Sets the receiver's image to the argument, which may be null, indicating that no image should be displayed.

`setText(String)`—Sets the receiver's text.

The following example creates a tree with three levels of items (see Figure 4–10). Clicking on an item will print its name to the console.

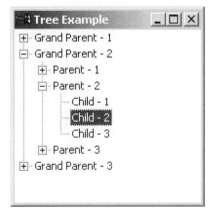

Figure 4–10   Tree example.

```
import org.eclipse.swt.*;
import org.eclipse.swt.events.*;
import org.eclipse.swt.layout.*;
import org.eclipse.swt.widgets.*;

public class TreeExample {
   public static void main(String[] args) {
      Display display = new Display();
      Shell shell = new Shell(display);
      shell.setText("Tree Example");
      shell.setBounds(100, 100, 200, 200);
      shell.setLayout(new FillLayout());
      final Tree tree = new Tree(shell, SWT.SINGLE);
      for (int i = 1; i < 4; i++) {
         TreeItem grandParent = new TreeItem(tree, 0);
         grandParent.setText("Grand Parent - " + i);
         for (int j = 1; j < 4; j++) {
            TreeItem parent = new TreeItem(grandParent,0);
            parent.setText("Parent - " + j);
            for (int k = 1; k < 4; k++) {
```

```
                    TreeItem child = new TreeItem(parent, 0);
                    child.setText("Child - " + k);
                }
            }
        }
        tree.addSelectionListener(new SelectionAdapter() {
            public void widgetSelected(SelectionEvent event) {
                TreeItem[] selected = tree.getSelection();
                if (selected.length > 0) {
                    System.out.println("Selected: " +
                        selected[0].getText());
                }
            }
        });
        shell.open();
        while (!shell.isDisposed()) {
            if (!display.readAndDispatch()) display.sleep();
        }
        display.dispose();
    }
}
```

After the creation of the tree widget, new items are created and their labels set with the setText() method. Many of the items have child items of their own. Finally, a selection listener is added in which a SelectionAdapter is created that overrides the widgetSelected() method to print a selected item.

4.2.6.8   Composite

The composite widget is used as a container for other widgets. The composite widget's children are widgets contained within the bounds of the composite and resize themselves relative to the composite. Useful APIs include:

getChildren()—Returns an array containing the receiver's children.

layout()—If the receiver has a layout, asks the layout to set the size and location of the receiver's children.

setLayout(Layout)—Sets the layout that is associated with the receiver to be the argument, which may be null.

setTabList(Control[])—Sets the tabbing order for the specified controls to match the order in which they occur in the argument list.

Useful creation styles include:

SWT.BORDER—Creates a composite widget with a border.

SWT.NO_RADIO_GROUP—Prevents child radio button behavior.

SWT.H_SCROLL—Creates a composite widget with a horizontal scroll-bar.

SWT.V_SCROLL—Creates a composite widget with a vertical scrollbar.

The following example expands on our earlier button example by inserting a composite widget between the shell and the button (see Figure 4–11).

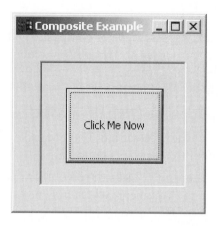

Figure 4–11   Composite example.

```
import org.eclipse.swt.*;
import org.eclipse.swt.events.*;
import org.eclipse.swt.widgets.*;

public class CompositeExample {
    public static void main(String[] args) {
        Display display = new Display();
        Shell shell = new Shell(display);
        shell.setText("Composite Example");
        shell.setBounds(100, 100, 200, 200);
        Composite composite = new Composite(
            shell,SWT.BORDER);
        composite.setBounds(25, 25, 150, 125);
        final Button button = new Button(composite,SWT.PUSH);
        button.setBounds(25, 25, 100, 75);
        button.setText("Click Me Now");
        button.addSelectionListener(new SelectionAdapter() {
            public void widgetSelected(SelectionEvent event) {
                button.setText("I Was Clicked");
            }
        });
        shell.open();
        while (!shell.isDisposed()) {
            if (!display.readAndDispatch()) display.sleep();
        }
        display.dispose();
    }
}
```

A composite widget is created as a child of the shell, and then the composite acts as the parent of the button widget. Note that the button is positioned relative to the composite, not the shell.

4.2.6.9 Group

Group widgets are a special type of composite widget that surrounds its children with an etched border and an optional label. Each child widget is contained within the bounds of the group and resizes itself relative to the group. Useful APIs include:

getChildren()—Returns an array containing the receiver's children.

layout()—If the receiver has a layout, asks the layout to set the size and location of the receiver's children.

setLayout(Layout)—Sets the layout that is associated with the receiver to be the argument, which may be null.

setTabList(Control[])—Sets the tabbing order for the specified controls to match the order in which they occur in the argument list.

setText(String)—Sets the receiver's text, which is the string that will be displayed as the receiver's title, to the argument, which may not be null.

Useful creation styles include:

SWT.BORDER—Creates a composite widget with a border.

SWT.NO_RADIO_GROUP—Prevents child radio button behavior.

The following example replaces the composite in the previous example with a group widget (see Figure 4–12).

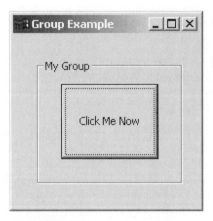

Figure 4–12 Group example.

```
import org.eclipse.swt.*;
import org.eclipse.swt.events.*;
import org.eclipse.swt.widgets.*;

public class GroupExample {
    public static void main(String[] args) {
        Display display = new Display();
        Shell shell = new Shell(display);
        shell.setText("Group Example");
        shell.setBounds(100, 100, 200, 200);
        Group group = new Group(shell, SWT.NULL);
        group.setText("My Group");
        group.setBounds(25, 25, 150, 125);
        final Button button = new Button(group, SWT.PUSH);
        button.setBounds(25, 25, 100, 75);
        button.setText("Click Me Now");
        button.addSelectionListener(new SelectionAdapter() {
            public void widgetSelected(SelectionEvent event) {
                button.setText("I Was Clicked");
            }
        });
        shell.open();
        while (!shell.isDisposed()) {
            if (!display.readAndDispatch()) display.sleep();
        }
        display.dispose();
    }
}
```

A group widget is created as a child of the shell and acts as the parent of
the button widget. In addition to the border, which is always present, the
group widget also has a label.

4.2.6.10   Tab folder

The tab folder widget is used to organize information within in a window
frame into multiple pages that appear as a set of notebook tabs. Clicking on
a tab brings that page to the front. Tabs may be labels with images and text.
Useful APIs include:

addSelectionListener(SelectionListener)—Adds the listener
to the collection of listeners that will be notified when the receiver's
selection changes by sending it one of the messages defined in the
SelectionListener interface.

TabItem getItem(int)—Returns the item at the given, zero-relative
index in the receiver.

getItemCount()—Returns the number of items contained in the
receiver.

getItems()—Returns an array of TabItems that are items in the
receiver.

`getSelection()`—Returns an array of `TabItems` that are currently selected in the receiver.

`getSelectionIndex()`—Returns the zero-relative index of the item that is currently selected in the receiver, or -1 if no item is selected.

`indexOf(TabItem item)`—Searches the receiver's list starting at the first item (index 0) until an item is found that is equal to the argument, and returns the index of that item.

`setSelection(int)`—Selects the item at the given zero-relative index in the receiver.

Useful tab folder APIs include:

`getControl()`—Returns the control that is used to fill the client area of the tab folder when the user selects the tab item.

`setControl(Control control)`—Sets the control that is used to fill the client area of the tab folder when the user selects the tab item.

`setImage(Image)`—Sets the receiver's image to the argument, which may be null, indicating that no image should be displayed.

`setText(String)`—Sets the receiver's text.

`setToolTipText(String)`—Sets the receiver's tool tip text to the argument, which may be null, indicating that no tool tip text should be shown.

The following example creates a tab folder with several tabs. Each tab contains a composite containing a single button (see Figure 4–13).

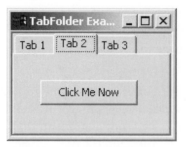

Figure 4–13   Tab folder example.

```
import org.eclipse.swt.*;
import org.eclipse.swt.events.*;
import org.eclipse.swt.layout.*;
import org.eclipse.swt.widgets.*;
```

```
public class TabFolderExample {
   public static void main(String[] args) {
      Display display = new Display();
      Shell shell = new Shell(display);
      shell.setText("TabFolder Example");
      shell.setBounds(100, 100, 175, 125);
      shell.setLayout(new FillLayout());
      final TabFolder tabFolder =
         new TabFolder(shell, SWT.BORDER);
      for (int i = 1; i < 4; i++) {
         TabItem tabItem =
            new TabItem(tabFolder, SWT.NULL);
         tabItem.setText("Tab " + i);
         Composite composite =
            new Composite(tabFolder, SWT.NULL);
         tabItem.setControl(composite);
         Button button = new Button(composite, SWT.PUSH);
         button.setBounds(25, 25, 100, 25);
         button.setText("Click Me Now");
         button.addSelectionListener(
            new SelectionAdapter(){
            public void widgetSelected(
               SelectionEvent event) {
               ((Button)event.widget)
                  .setText("I Was Clicked");
            }
         });
      }
      shell.open();
      while (!shell.isDisposed()) {
         if (!display.readAndDispatch()) display.sleep();
      }
      display.dispose();
   }
}
```

After the tab folder is created, several tab items are added. For each tab item, the `setControl()` method is used to fill its client area with a composite widget. A button widget is then added to each composite.

4.2.7   Menus

Menus provide an easy way for the user to trigger a variety of commands and actions. Top-level menus contain any number of menu item children. Useful menu APIs include:

`addHelpListener(HelpListener)`—Adds the listener to the collection of listeners that will be notified when help events are generated for the control by sending it one of the messages defined in the `HelpListener` interface.

`addMenuListener(MenuListener)`—Adds the listener to the collection of listeners that will be notified when menus are hidden or shown by sending it one of the messages defined in the `MenuListener` interface.

`getItem(int)`—Returns the item at the given, zero-relative index in the receiver.

`getItemCount()`—Returns the number of items contained in the receiver.

`getItems()`—Returns an array of menu items that are the items in the receiver.

`getParentItem()`—Returns the receiver's parent item, which must be a menu item or null when the receiver is a root.

`getParentMenu()`—Returns the receiver's parent item, which must be a menu or null when the receiver is a root.

`indexOf(MenuItem item)`—Searches the receiver's list starting at the first item (index 0) until an item is found that is equal to the argument and returns the index of that item.

`setEnabled(boolean enabled)`—Enables the receiver if the argument is `true`, and disables it otherwise.

`setVisible(boolean visible)`—Marks the receiver as visible if the argument is `true`, and marks it invisible otherwise.

Useful menu creation styles include:

`SWT.BAR`—Creates a menu bar.

`SWT.DROP_DOWN`—Creates a drop-down menu.

`SWT.POP_UP`—Creates a popup menu.

Useful menu item APIs include:

`addArmListener(ArmListener)`—Adds the listener to the collection of listeners that will be notified when the `Arm` events are generated for the control by sending it one of the messages defined in the `ArmListener` interface.

`addHelpListener(HelpListener)`—Adds the listener to the collection of listeners that will be notified when the help events are generated for the control by sending it one of the messages defined in the `HelpListener` interface.

`addSelectionListener(SelectionListener)`—Adds the listener to the collection of listeners that will be notified when the control is selected by sending it one of the messages defined in the `SelectionListener` interface.

`getParent()`—Returns the receiver's parent, which must be a menu.

`getSelection()`—Returns `true` if the receiver is selected, and `false` otherwise.

`isEnabled()`—Returns `true` if the receiver is enabled and all of the receiver's ancestors are enabled, and `false` otherwise.

`setAccelerator(int accelerator)`—Sets the widget accelerator.

`setEnabled(boolean enabled)`—Enables the receiver if the argument is `true`, and disables it otherwise.

`setImage(Image)`—Sets the image the receiver will display to the argument.

`setMenu(Menu)`—Sets the receiver's pull-down menu to the argument.

`setSelection(boolean)`—Sets the selection state of the receiver.

`setText(String)`—Sets the receiver's text.

Useful menu item creation styles include:

`SWT.CHECK`—Creates a check menu that toggles on and off.

`SWT.CASCADE`—Creates a cascade menu with a submenu.

`SWT.PUSH`—Creates a standard menu item.

`SWT.RADIO`—Creates a radio button menu.

`SWT.SEPARATOR`—Creates a menu item separator.

The following example creates a menu bar with a single menu containing two menu items and a separator (see Figure 4–14).

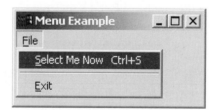

Figure 4–14   Menu example.

```
import org.eclipse.swt.*;
import org.eclipse.swt.events.*;
import org.eclipse.swt.widgets.*;

public class MenuExample {
   public static void main(String[] args) {
      Display display = new Display();
      final Shell shell = new Shell(display);
      shell.setText("Menu Example");
      shell.setBounds(100, 100, 200, 100);
```

```
Menu bar = new Menu(shell, SWT.BAR);
shell.setMenuBar(bar);
MenuItem fileMenu = new MenuItem(bar, SWT.CASCADE);
fileMenu.setText("&File");
Menu subMenu = new Menu(shell, SWT.DROP_DOWN);
fileMenu.setMenu(subMenu);
MenuItem selectItem = new MenuItem(
    subMenu, SWT.NULL);
selectItem.setText("&Select Me Now\tCtrl+S");
selectItem.setAccelerator(SWT.CTRL + 'S');
selectItem.addSelectionListener(
    new SelectionAdapter() {
    public void widgetSelected(SelectionEvent event) {
        System.out.println("I was selected!");
    }
});
MenuItem sep = new MenuItem(subMenu, SWT.SEPARATOR);
MenuItem exitItem = new MenuItem(subMenu, SWT.NULL);
exitItem.setText("&Exit");
exitItem.addSelectionListener(new SelectionAdapter(){
    public void widgetSelected(SelectionEvent event) {
        shell.dispose();
    }
});
shell.open();
while (!shell.isDisposed()) {
    if (!display.readAndDispatch()) display.sleep();
}
display.dispose();
    }
}
```

A menu widget is created as a child of the shell and set as the menu bar for the shell using the setMenuBar() method. Next, a cascade menu item is created as the parent for the **File** menu. A drop-down menu is then created as a child of the shell and associated with the **File** menu using the setMenu() method. Three menu items are then created as children of the drop-down menu (the second as a separator using the SWT.SEPARATOR creation style). The text of a menu item is set using the setText() method and the accelerator is set using the setAccelerator() method. To add behavior to the menu item, a selection listener is added in which a SelectionAdapter is created that overrides the widgetSelected() method.

4.3   Layout Management

In each of the examples presented in the previous section, the widget layouts are very simple. Widgets were either positioned relative to their parents using the setBounds() method (null layout) or they were designed to fill their parent entirely using a FillLayout. Eclipse provides several more powerful layout management algorithms that can be used to aesthetically place widgets under a variety of conditions.

Most layout managers in Eclipse trace their heritage to VisualAge for Smalltalk, and in particular, to the layout managers used to construct the wizards and dialogs in VisualAge for Java. As such, they were well-thought-out and thoroughly tested before ever being converted into Java as part of the Eclipse framework. Interestingly enough, the newest Eclipse layout manager, FormLayout, is based on the oldest and most powerful VisualAge for Smalltalk layout manager.

4.3.1   FillLayout

As we have seen, FillLayout provides an easy way for a widget (like a list or a table) to completely fill its parent (see Figure 4–5 or 4–6 for an example). FillLayout does more than this, however, as it provides a way to lay out a group of widgets in single row or column such that each widget is the same size as all the other widgets in the group (see Figure 4–8 for an example). The width and height of each widget matches the width and height of the widest and tallest widget in the group, and no options are provided to control the widget spacing, margins, or wrapping.

FillLayout defines only one significant attribute:

type—Determines the orientation of the layout. Valid values are SWT.HORIZONTAL (the default) and SWT.VERTICAL.

FillLayout is ideal for creating a uniform row or column of widgets like that found in a simple toolbar. The following example creates a row of buttons that are all the same size (see Figure 4–15).

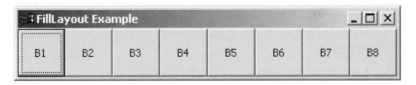

Figure 4–15   FillLayout example.

```
import org.eclipse.swt.*;
import org.eclipse.swt.events.*;
import org.eclipse.swt.layout.*;
import org.eclipse.swt.widgets.*;

public class FillLayoutExample {
    public static void main(String[] args) {
        Button button;
        Display display = new Display();
        Shell shell = new Shell(display);
        shell.setText("FillLayout Example");
        shell.setBounds(100, 100, 400, 75);
        shell.setLayout(new FillLayout());
        for (int i = 1; i <= 8; i++) {
            button = new Button(shell, SWT.PUSH);
            button.setText("B" + i);
            button.addSelectionListener(
                new SelectionAdapter() {
                public void widgetSelected(
                    SelectionEvent event) {
                    System.out.println(
                        ((Button)event.widget).getText() +
                        " was clicked!");
                }
            });
        }
        shell.open();
        while (!shell.isDisposed()) {
            if (!display.readAndDispatch()) display.sleep();
        }
        display.dispose();
    }
}
```

By default, `FillLayout` is oriented horizontally. When buttons are added to the shell, they line up left to right with uniform width and height.

4.3.2 *RowLayout*

RowLayout is very similar to FillLayout in that it lays out widgets in columns or rows, and has numerous additional options to control the layout. The spacing between widgets as well as the margins between the widgets and the parent container may be controlled. The widgets may be wrapped into multiple rows or columns or packed such that each widget will be the same size.

RowLayout defines several significant attributes:

justify—Specifies whether the controls in a row should be fully justified, with any extra space placed between the controls.

marginBottom—Specifies the number of pixels of vertical margin that will be placed along the bottom edge of the layout. The default value is 3.

marginLeft—Specifies the number of pixels of horizontal margin that will be placed along the left edge of the layout. The default value is 3.

marginRight—Specifies the number of pixels of horizontal margin that will be placed along the right edge of the layout. The default value is 3.

marginTop—Specifies the number of pixels of vertical margin that will be placed along the top edge of the layout. The default value is 3.

pack—Specifies whether all controls in the layout take their preferred size. If pack is false, all controls will have the same size, which is the size required to accommodate the largest preferred height and the largest preferred width of all controls in the layout.

spacing—Specifies the number of pixels between the edge of one cell and the edge of its neighboring cell. The default value is 3.

type—Determines the orientation of the layout. Valid values are SWT.HORIZONTAL (the default) and SWT.VERTICAL.

wrap—Specifies whether a control will be wrapped to the next row if there is insufficient space on the current row.

The width and height of each widget in the layout may be controlled using a RowLayout object that can be assigned to the widget using the setLayout-Data() method. RowLayout objects have two significant attributes:

width—Specifies the width of the cell in pixels.

height—Specifies the height of the cell in pixels.

The following example creates a row layout with 20 evenly spaced buttons inset from the edge of the window frame. Depending on the size and shape of the parent shell, the line of buttons wraps into one or more rows (see Figure 4–16).

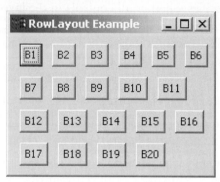

Figure 4-16   RowLayout example.

```
import org.eclipse.swt.*;
import org.eclipse.swt.events.*;
import org.eclipse.swt.layout.*;
import org.eclipse.swt.widgets.*;

public class RowLayoutExample {
    public static void main(String[] args) {
        Button button;
        Display display = new Display();
        Shell shell = new Shell(display);
        shell.setText("RowLayout Example");
        shell.setBounds(100, 100, 400, 100);
        RowLayout layout = new RowLayout();
        layout.marginLeft = 10;
        layout.marginRight = 10;
        layout.marginTop = 10;
        layout.marginBottom = 10;
        layout.spacing = 10;
        shell.setLayout(layout);
        for (int i = 1; i <= 20; i++) {
            button = new Button(shell, SWT.PUSH);
            button.setText("B" + i);
            button.addSelectionListener(
                new SelectionAdapter() {
                public void widgetSelected(
                    SelectionEvent event) {
                    System.out.println(
                        ((Button)event.widget).getText() +
                        " was clicked!");
```

```
            }
        });
    }
    shell.open();
    while (!shell.isDisposed()) {
        if (!display.readAndDispatch()) display.sleep();
    }
    display.dispose();
    }
}
```

By default, `RowLayout` is oriented horizontally. The margin spacing between the buttons and the parent shell is set using the four margin attributes: `marginLeft`, `marginRight`, `marginTop`, and `marginBottom`. The spacing between widgets is set using the `spacing` attribute. Once all of the layout attributes have been set, the layout is assigned to the shell using the `setLayout()` method.

4.3.3 *GridLayout*

Most dialogs, wizards, and preference pages are laid out using `GridLayout`. It is both one of Eclipse's most frequently used layout classes and one of the most complicated. `GridLayout` arranges its children in a highly configurable grid of rows and columns, where many options are provided to control the sizing behavior of each child element.

`GridLayout` defines several significant attributes:

`horizontalSpacing`—Specifies the number of pixels between the right edge of one cell and the left edge of its neighboring cell. The default value is 5.

`makeColumnsEqualWidth`—Specifies whether all columns should be forced to the same width. The default is `false`.

`marginWidth`—Specifies the number of pixels used for the margin on the right and the left edge of the grid. The default value is 5.

`marginHeight`—Specifies the number of pixels used for the margins on the top and bottom edge of the grid. The default value is 5.

`numColumns`—Specifies the number of columns that should be used to make the grid. The default value is 1.

`verticalSpacing`—Specifies the number of pixels between the bottom edge of one cell and the top edge of its neighboring cell. The default value is 5.

The layout characteristics of each widget in the layout may be controlled using a `GridData` object, which can be assigned to the widget using the `setLayoutData()` method. `GridData` objects have several significant attributes:

`grabExcessHorizontalSpace`—Specifies whether a cell should grow to consume extra horizontal space in the grid. After the cell sizes in the grid are calculated based on the widgets and their grid data, any extra space remaining in the composite will be allocated to those cells that grab excess space.

`grabExcessVerticalSpace`—Specifies whether a cell should grow to consume extra vertical space in the grid.

`heightHint`—Specifies a minimum height for the widget (and therefore for the row that contains it).

`horizontalAlignment`—Specifies the horizontal alignment of the widget within the cell. Valid values are `SWT.BEGINNING`, `SWT.CENTER`, `SWT.END`, and `SWT.FILL`. `SWT.FILL` means that the widget will be sized to consume the entire width of its grid cell.

`horizontalIndent`—Specifies the number of pixels between the widget and the left edge of its grid cell. The default value is `0`.

`horizontalSpan`—Specifies the number of columns in the grid that the widget should span. By default, a widget consumes one cell in the grid. It can take additional cells horizontally by increasing this value. The default value is `1`.

`verticalAlignment`—Specifies the vertical alignment of the widget within the cell. Valid values are `SWT.BEGINNING`, `SWT.CENTER`, `SWT.END`, and `SWT.FILL`. `SWT.FILL` means that the widget will be sized to consume the entire height of its grid cell.

`verticalSpan`—Specifies the number of rows in the grid the widget should span. By default, a widget takes up one cell in the grid. It can take additional cells vertically by increasing this value. The default value is `1`.

`widthHint`—Specifies a minimum width for the widget (and therefore the column that contains it).

The following example creates a two-column grid layout containing a two-column spanning label and two sets of labels and fields (see Figure 4–17).

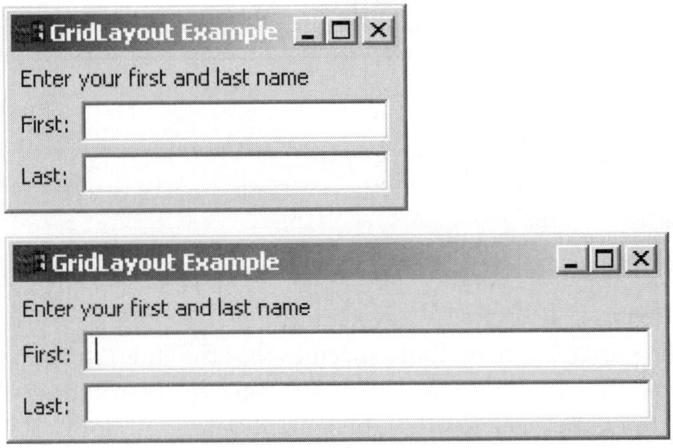

Figure 4–17 GridLayout example.

```java
import org.eclipse.swt.*;
import org.eclipse.swt.layout.*;
import org.eclipse.swt.widgets.*;

public class GridLayoutExample {
    public static void main(String[] args) {
        Label label;
        Text text;
        GridData gridData;
        Display display = new Display();
        Shell shell = new Shell(display);
        shell.setText("GridLayout Example");
        shell.setBounds(100, 100, 200, 100);
        GridLayout layout = new GridLayout();
        layout.numColumns = 2;
        shell.setLayout(layout);

        label = new Label(shell, SWT.LEFT);
        label.setText("Enter your first and last name");
        gridData = new GridData();
        gridData.horizontalSpan = 2;
        label.setLayoutData(gridData);

        label = new Label(shell, SWT.LEFT);
        label.setText("First:");
        text = new Text(shell, SWT.SINGLE | SWT.BORDER);
        gridData = new GridData();
        gridData.horizontalAlignment = GridData.FILL;
        gridData.grabExcessHorizontalSpace = true;
        text.setLayoutData(gridData);

        label = new Label(shell, SWT.LEFT);
        label.setText("Last:");
```

```
    text = new Text(shell, SWT.SINGLE | SWT.BORDER);
    gridData = new GridData();
    gridData.horizontalAlignment = GridData.FILL;
    gridData.grabExcessHorizontalSpace = true;
    text.setLayoutData(gridData);

    shell.open();
    while (!shell.isDisposed()) {
        if (!display.readAndDispatch()) display.sleep();
    }
    display.dispose();
  }
}
```

The `numColumn` attribute specifies that the `GridLayout` should have two columns. The `horizontalSpan` attribute of the `GridData` object created for the first label specifies that the label should span both columns. The `GridData` objects created for each text field have `horizontalAlignment` attributes that specify that each field should fill the entire cell and `grabExcessHorizontalSpace` attributes that specify that each field should grab any horizontal space that is left over.

4.3.4 FormLayout

Nowhere does Eclipse show its VisualAge for Smalltalk roots more than in the `FormLayout` class that implements an attachment-based layout manager. `FormLayout` is the most powerful Eclipse layout manager and is a close replica of the layout management system first used in VisualAge for Smalltalk more than a decade earlier.

With attachment-based layout, you have independent control over the sizing behavior of each of the four sides of a widget. The top, bottom, left, and right sides may be independently attached to the sides of the parent container or the sides of any sibling widget within the same container using either fixed or relative offsets. This proves to be surprisingly powerful and can be used to emulate any of the other layout managers.

The `FormLayout` class is very simple and only specifies the margins of the container. The real power is in the `FormData` object, which holds up to four different `FormAttachment` objects (one for each side). `FormLayout` defines two significant attributes:

`marginWidth`—Specifies the number of pixels of horizontal margin that will be placed along the left and right edges of the layout.

`marginHeight`—Specifies the number of pixels of vertical margin that will be placed along the top and bottom edges of the layout.

`FormData` specifies several significant attributes:

`top`—Specifies the attachment for the top side of the control.

`bottom`—Specifies the attachment for the bottom side of the control.

`left`—Specifies the attachment for the left side of the control.

`right`—Specifies the attachment for the right side of the control.

`width`—Specifies the preferred width in pixels of the control in the form.

`height`—Specifies the preferred height in pixels of the control in the form.

`FormAttachment` specifies several significant attributes:

`alignment`—Specifies the alignment of the control side that is attached to a control. `SWT.DEFAULT` indicates that the widget should be attached to the adjacent side of the specified control. For top and bottom attachments, `SWT.TOP`, `SWT.BOTTOM`, and `SWT.CENTER` are used to indicate attachment of the specified side of the widget to the specified side of the control. For left and right attachments, `SWT.LEFT`, `SWT.RIGHT`, and `SWT.CENTER` are used to indicate attachment of the specified side of the widget to the specified side of the control. (For example, using `SWT.TOP` indicates that the top side of the attachment's widget should be attached to the top side of the specified control.).

`control`—Specifies the target control to which the attachment's widget is attached.

`denominator`—Specifies the denominator of the "a" term in the equation $y=ax+b$, which defines the attachment.

`numerator`—Specifies the numerator of the "a" term in the equation $y=ax+b$, which defines the attachment.

`offset`—Specifies the offset in pixels of the control side from the attachment position. Can be positive or negative. This is the "b" term in the equation $y=ax+b$, which defines the attachment.

The following example creates a simple form layout with two buttons in the lower right corner and a text field that fills the remaining space. The **Cancel** button is attached to the lower right corner while the **OK** button is attached to the bottom side of the window and the left side of the **Cancel** button. The text field is attached to the top, left, and right sides of the window and to the top of the **Cancel** button.

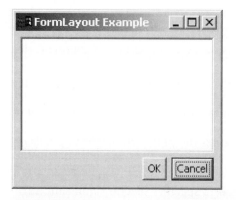

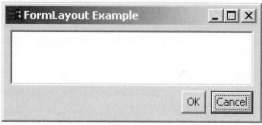

Figure 4–18   FormLayout example.

```
import org.eclipse.swt.*;
import org.eclipse.swt.layout.*;
import org.eclipse.swt.widgets.*;

public class FormLayoutExample {
    public static void main(String[] args) {
        FormData formData;
        Display display = new Display();
        final Shell shell = new Shell(display);
        shell.setText("FormLayout Example");
        shell.setBounds(100, 100, 220, 180);
        shell.setLayout(new FormLayout());

        Button cancelButton = new Button(shell, SWT.PUSH);
        cancelButton.setText("Cancel");
        formData = new FormData();
        formData.right = new FormAttachment(100,-5);
        formData.bottom = new FormAttachment(100,-5);
        cancelButton.setLayoutData(formData);

        Button okButton = new Button(shell, SWT.PUSH);
        okButton.setText("OK");
        formData = new FormData();
        formData.right = new FormAttachment(cancelButton,-5);
        formData.bottom = new FormAttachment(100,-5);
        okButton.setLayoutData(formData);
```

```
Text text = new Text(shell, SWT.MULTI | SWT.BORDER);
formData = new FormData();
formData.top = new FormAttachment(0,5);
formData.bottom = new FormAttachment(
   cancelButton,-5);
formData.left = new FormAttachment(0,5);
formData.right = new FormAttachment(100,-5);
text.setLayoutData(formData);

shell.open();
while (!shell.isDisposed()) {
   if (!display.readAndDispatch()) display.sleep();
}
display.dispose();
   }
}
```

The `FormData` assigned to the **Cancel** button has a `right` and `bottom` attachment to the lower right corner of the shell. The first argument to each `FormAttachment` object is the percentage of the shell to initially attach to (starting in the upper left corner with a zero percentage value). The value of 100 specifies the right and bottom sides, which are opposite the left and top sides. The second argument represents the fixed offset from the attachment point (with positive values pointing right and down). The value of -5 indicates that the widget should be offset 5 pixels from the bottom and right sides. Note that the left and top attachments are not specified. Leaving those blank will cause the widget to assume its preferred width and height.

The **OK** button is also attached to the bottom of the shell. Its right side is attached to the left side of the **Cancel** button rather than to the shell itself. This provides a way for the **OK** button to position itself relative to the preferred size of the **Cancel** button. This pattern can be particularly effective in internationalized applications where the text of the buttons (and thus their preferred sizes) is not known at design time.

Finally, the text field is attached with a fixed offset of 5 pixels from the left, right and top sides of the shell. The bottom of the text field is attached with a 5-pixel offset to the top of the **Cancel** button.

4.4   Resource Management

Consistent with the design of the rest of SWT, colors, fonts, and images are also thin wrappers around their platform counterparts that must be explicitly destroyed when no longer needed.

The basic rule is that, if you access a color, font, or image from somewhere else, you don't need to worry about it. If, on the other hand, you create the resource, then you must destroy it when you are done with it. For any resources that you anticipate routinely accessing within your application, consider creating a resource manager to manage those resources and then destroy them all when your application exits.

4.4.1   Colors

Colors are created for a specific device (which can be `null`, representing the default device) and are described by three integer values representing each color component (red, green, and blue) in the range of 0 to 255. For example, `new Color(null, 255, 0, 0)` creates the color red. The foreground and background colors of widgets can be set using the `setForeground()` and `setBackground()` methods, respectively.

To use one of the colors predefined by the platform, such as the window background color or the button background color, you can use the `Display.getSystemColor(int)` method, which takes the ID of the desired color as an argument. You don't need to dispose of any colors that you get this way.

4.4.2   Fonts

As with colors, fonts are also created for a specific device and are described by a font name ("Arial," "Times," etc.), a height in points, and a style (and combination of `SWT.NORMAL`, `SWT.BOLD`, or `SWT.ITALIC`). Fonts may be either created by specifying the name, height, and style directly or by referencing a `FontData` object that encodes those three values. For example, `new Font(null, "Arial", 10, SWT.BOLD)` creates a 10-point, bold Arial font. A widget's font can be set using the `setFont(...)` method.

4.4.3   Images

Images are frequently used in toolbars, buttons, labels, trees, and tables. Eclipse supports loading and saving images in a variety of common file formats such as GIF, JPEG, PNG, BMP (Windows bitmap), and ICO (Windows icon). Some formats, such as GIF, support transparency, which makes them ideal for use in toolbars and as item decorators in lists and tables.

Images are created for a specific device and are usually either loaded from a specific file or created from a device-independent `ImageData` object. For example, both of the following are equivalent:

```
Image img = new Image(null, "c:\\my_button.gif")
ImageData data = new ImageData( "c:\\my_button.gif");
Image img = new Image(null, data);
```

On widgets that support images as part of their content, such as labels and buttons, use the `setImage()` method to set the widget's image. For information on image caching and `ImageDescriptor`, see Section 7.7, "Image Caching."

4.5 Summary

SWT is a well-designed native UI library for Java that is based on a long history of similar work done by IBM and OTI over the years. It is the native UI library of Eclipse itself and will be used extensively in any Eclipse plug-in that you create. SWT is also more than powerful enough to be used for creating standalone Java applications that don't require any of the other Eclipse frameworks.

SWT includes a rich collection of built-in widgets that are mapped to native-platform widgets whenever possible and emulated when an appropriate widget is not present on a specific platform. SWT also includes a wide array of layout management classes ranging from the simple `FillLayout` to the more complex `GridLayout and FormLayout`. With these widgets and layout managers, you can create any UI that you desire for your plug-in.

References

Cornu, Christophe, "*A small cup of SWT*," IBM OTI Labs, September 19, 2003 (*www.eclipse.org/articles/Article-small-cup-of-swt/pocket-PC.html*).

Winchester, Joe, "*Taking a look at SWT Images*," IBM, September 10, 2003 (*www.eclipse.org/articles/Article-SWT-images/graphics-resources.html*).

Irvine, Veronika, "*Drag and Drop—Adding Drag and Drop to an SWT Application*," IBM, August 25, 2003 (*www.eclipse.org/articles/Article-SWT-DND/DND-in-SWT.html*).

Arthorne, John, "*Drag and Drop in the Eclipse UI*," IBM, August 25, 2003 (*www.eclipse.org/articles/Article-Workbench-DND/drag_drop.html*).

Bordeau, Eric, "*Using Native Drag and Drop with GEF*," IBM, August 25, 2003 (*www.eclipse.org/articles/Article-GEF-dnd/GEF-dnd.html*).

Savarese, Daniel F., "Eclipse vs. Swing," JavaPro, December 2002 (*www.ftponline.com/javapro/2002_12/magazine/columns/proshop/default_pf.aspx*).

CHAPTER 5

JFace Viewers

Because SWT provides a direct interface to the native platform widgets, it is limited to using simple data types—primarily strings, numbers, and images. This is fine for a large number of applications, but it represents a severe impedance mismatch when dealing with OO data that needs to be presented in lists, tables, trees, and text widgets. This is where JFace viewers step in to provide highly OO wrappers around their associated SWT widgets.

5.1 List-Oriented Viewers

JFace list viewers such as `ListViewer`, `TableViewer`, and `TreeViewer` allow you to directly use your domain model objects without needing to manually decompose them into their basic string, numerical, and image elements. They do this by providing adapter interfaces for things such as retrieving an item's label (both image and text), for accessing an item's children (in the case of a tree), for selecting an item from a list, for sorting items in the list, for filtering items in the list, and for converting an arbitrary input into a list suitable for the underlying SWT widget (see Figure 5–1).

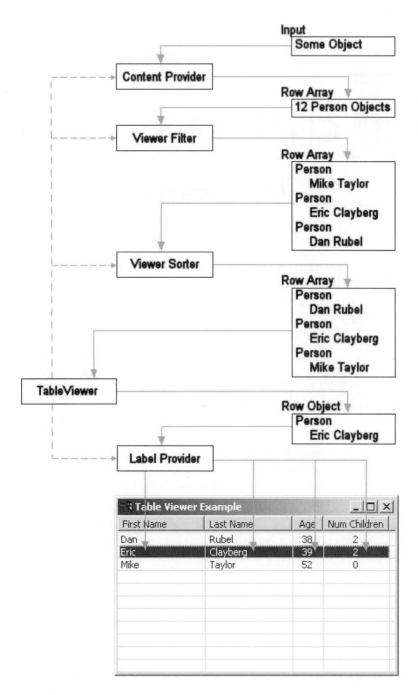

Figure 5–1   Relationship between viewers and adapters.

5.1.1 Label providers

A label provider is one of the most common adapter types that is used in list viewers. A label provider is used to map a domain model object into one or more images and text strings displayable in the viewer's widget. The two most common types of label providers are ILabelProvider (see Figure 5–2), used in lists and trees, and ITableLabelProvider (see Figure 5–3), used in tables. The former maps an item into a single image and text label while the latter maps into multiple images and text labels (one set for each column in the table). A label provider is associated with a viewer using the setLabel-Provider() method.

Useful APIs defined by ILabelProvider include:

getImage(Object)—Returns the image for the label of the given element.

getText(Object)—Returns the text for the label of the given element.

Figure 5–2   LabelProvider hierarchy.

Useful APIs defined by ITableLabelProvider include:

getColumnImage(Object, int)—Returns the label image for the given column of the given element.

getColumnText(Object, int)—Returns the label text for the given column of the given element.

Figure 5–3   TableLabelProvider hierarchy.

See Section 5.1.6, "ListViewer class," for an example of label providers.

5.1.2   Content providers

A content provider is another common adapter type used in list viewers. A content provider is used to map between a domain model object or a collection of domain model objects used as the input to the viewer and the internal list structure needed by the viewer itself. The two most common types of content providers are `IStructuredContentProvider`, used in lists and tables, and `ITreeContentProvider`, used in trees (see Figure 5–4). The former maps a domain model input into an array while the latter adds support for retrieving an item's parent or children within a tree. A content provider is associated with a viewer using the `setContentProvider()` method. A domain model input is associated with a viewer using the `setInput()` method.

Figure 5–4   ContentProvider hierarchy.

Useful APIs defined by `IStructuredContentProvider` include:

`getElements (Object)`—Returns the elements to display in the viewer when its input is set to the given element.

`inputChanged(Viewer, Object, Object)`—Notifies this content provider that the given viewer's input has been switched to a different element.

Useful APIs added by `ITreeContentProvider` include:

`Object[] getChildren(Object)`—Returns the child elements of the given parent element. The difference between this method and the `getElements(Object)` method listed above is that `getElements(Object)` is called to obtain the tree viewer's root elements, whereas `getChildren(Object)` is used to obtain the children of a given parent element in the tree (including a root).

`getParent(Object)`—Returns either the parent for the given element or null, indicating that the parent can't be computed.

hasChildren(Object)—Returns whether the given element has children.

See Section 5.1.6, "ListViewer class," for an example of content providers.

5.1.3   Viewer sorters

A viewer sorter (see Figure 5–5 for the ViewerSorter hierarchy) is used to sort the elements provided by the content provider (see Figure 5–1). If a viewer does not have a viewer sorter, the elements are shown in the order returned by the content provider. A viewer sorter is associated with a viewer using the setSorter() method.

The default sorting algorithm uses a two-step process. First, it groups elements into categories (ranked *0* through *n*), and second, it sorts each category based on the text labels returned by the label provider. By default, all items are in the same category, so all the items are sorted relative to their text labels. Your application can override the default categorization as well as the default comparison routine to use some criteria other than the item's text label.

Figure 5–5   ViewerSorter hierarchy.

Useful APIs defined by ViewerSorter include:

category(Object)—Returns the category of the given element.

compare(Viewer, Object, Object)—Returns a negative, zero, or positive number depending on whether the first element is less than, equal to, or greater than the second element.

getCollator()—Returns the collator used to sort strings.

isSorterProperty(Object, String)—Returns whether this viewer sorter would be affected by a change to the given property of the given element.

sort(Viewer viewer, Object[])—Sorts the given elements in place, modifying the given array.

See Section 5.1.6, "ListViewer Class," for an example of viewer sorters.

5.1.4 Viewer filters

A viewer filter (see Figure 5–6 for the `ViewerFilter` hierarchy) is used to display a subset of the elements provided by the content provider (see Figure 5–1). If a view does not have a viewer filter, all the elements are displayed. A viewer filter is associated with a viewer using the `setFilter()` method.

Figure 5–6   ViewerFilter hierarchy.

Useful APIs defined by `ViewFilter` are listed below. Simple viewer filters need only to override the `select(Viewer, Object, Object)` method to determine whether or not an object should be visible in the viewer.

`filter(Viewer, Object, Object[])`—Filters the given elements for the given viewer. The default implementation of this method calls the `select(Viewer, Object, Object)` method listed below.

`isFilterProperty(Object, String)`—Returns whether this viewer filter would be affected by a change to the given property of the given element. The default implementation of this method returns `false`.

`select(Viewer, Object, Object)`—Returns whether the given element makes it through this filter.

5.1.5 StructuredViewer class

The `StructuredViewer` class is the abstract superclass of list viewers, table viewers, and tree viewers (see Figure 5–7).

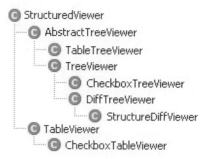

Figure 5–7   StructuredViewer hierarchy.

It defines a large number of useful APIs that are common to each class:

`addDoubleClickListener(IDoubleClickListener)`—Adds a listener for double-clicks in this viewer.

`addDragSupport(int, Transfer[], DragSourceListener)`—Adds support for dragging items out of this viewer via a user drag-and-drop operation.

`addDropSupport(int, Transfer[], DropTargetListener)`—Adds support for dropping items into this viewer via a user drag-and-drop operation.

`addFilter(ViewerFilter)`—Adds the given filter to this viewer and triggers refiltering and resorting of the elements.

`addHelpListener(HelpListener)`—Adds a listener for help requests in this viewer.

`addOpenListener(IOpenListener)`—Adds a listener for selection-open in this viewer.

`addSelectionChangedListener(ISelectionChangedListener)`—Adds a listener for selection changes in this selection provider.

`addPostSelectionChangedListener(ISelectionChangedListener)`—Adds a listener for post-selection in this viewer.

`getSelection()`—The `StructuredViewer` implementation of this method returns the result as an `IStructuredSelection`.

`refresh()`—Refreshes this viewer completely with information freshly obtained from this viewer's model.

`refresh(boolean)`—Refreshes this viewer with information freshly obtained from this viewer's model.

`refresh(Object)`—Refreshes this viewer starting with the given element.

`refresh(Object, boolean)`—Refreshes this viewer starting with the given element.

`resetFilters()`—Discards this viewer's filters and triggers refiltering and resorting of the elements.

`setComparer(IElementComparer)`—Sets the comparator to use for comparing elements, or null to use the default equals and `hashCode` methods on the elements themselves.

`setContentProvider(IContentProvider)`—The `StructuredViewer` implementation of this method checks to ensure that the content provider is an `IStructuredContentProvider`.

`setData(String, Object)`—Sets the value of the property with the given name to the given value, or to null if the property is to be removed.

`setInput(Object)`—The `ContentViewer` implementation of this viewer method invokes `inputChanged` on the content provider and then the `inputChanged` hook method. The content provider's `getElements(Object)` method is called later with this input object as its argument to determine the root-level elements in the viewer.

`setSelection(ISelection, boolean)`—The `StructuredViewer` implementation of this method updates the current viewer selection based on the specified selection.

`setSorter(ViewerSorter)`—Sets this viewer's sorter and triggers refiltering and resorting of this viewer's element.

`setUseHashlookup(boolean)`—Configures whether this structured viewer uses an internal hash table to speed up the mapping between elements and SWT items.

`update(Object[], String[])`—Updates the given element's presentation when one or more of its properties changes.

`update(Object, String[])`—Updates the given element's presentation when one or more of its properties changes.

5.1.6   *ListViewer class*

The `ListViewer` class wraps the `List` widget and is used to view a collection of objects rather than a flat collection of strings. A list viewer needs to be configured with a label provider and content provider. Useful APIs include:

`add(Object)`—Adds the given element to this list viewer.

`add(Object[])`—Adds the given elements to this list viewer.

`getControl()`—Returns the primary control associated with this viewer.

`getElementAt(int)`—Returns the element with the given index from this list viewer.

`getList()`—Returns this list viewer's list control.

`remove(Object)`—Removes the given element from this list viewer.

`remove(Object[])`—Removes the given elements from this list viewer.

`reveal(Object)`—Ensures that the given element is visible, scrolling the viewer if necessary.

`setLabelProvider(IBaseLabelProvider)`—The list viewer implementation of this `Viewer` framework method ensures that the given label provider is an instance of `ILabelProvider`.

The following example creates a list viewer with a label provider, content provider, and viewer sorter (see Figure 5–8).

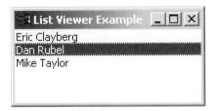

Figure 5–8   List viewer example.

```
import org.eclipse.jface.viewers.*;
import org.eclipse.swt.*;
import org.eclipse.swt.layout.*;
import org.eclipse.swt.widgets.*;

public class ListViewerExample {
    public static void main(String[] args) {
        Display display = new Display();
        Shell shell = new Shell(display);
        shell.setText("List Viewer Example");
        shell.setBounds(100, 100, 200, 100);
        shell.setLayout(new FillLayout());
        final ListViewer listViewer =
            new ListViewer(shell, SWT.SINGLE);
        listViewer.setLabelProvider(
            new PersonListLabelProvider());
        listViewer.setContentProvider(
            new ArrayContentProvider());
        listViewer.setInput(Person.example());
        listViewer.setSorter(new ViewerSorter() {
            public int compare(
                Viewer viewer, Object p1, Object p2) {
                return ((Person) p1).lastName
                    .compareToIgnoreCase(((Person) p2).lastName);
            }
        });
        listViewer.addSelectionChangedListener(
            new ISelectionChangedListener() {
            public void selectionChanged(
                SelectionChangedEvent event) {
                IStructuredSelection selection =
                    (IStructuredSelection) event.getSelection();
                System.out.println("Selected: "
                    + selection.getFirstElement());
            }
        });
        listViewer.addDoubleClickListener(
            new IDoubleClickListener() {
            public void doubleClick(DoubleClickEvent event)
            {
```

```
            IStructuredSelection selection =
                (IStructuredSelection) event.getSelection();
            System.out.println("Double Clicked: " +
                selection.getFirstElement());
        }
    });
    shell.open();
    while (!shell.isDisposed()) {
        if (!display.readAndDispatch()) display.sleep();
    }
    display.dispose();
    }
}
```

After creating the list viewer, the label provider is set using the setLa-belProvider() method and the content provider with the setContent-Provider() method. The label provider, PersonListLabelProvider, returns a text label composed of the person's first and last names and does not return an icon. The class looks like this:

```
public class PersonListLabelProvider extends LabelProvider {
    public Image getImage(Object) {
        return null;
    }
    public String getText(Object) {
        Person person = (Person) element;
        return person.firstName + " " + person.lastName;
    }
}
```

For the content provider, we use the built-in ArrayContentProvider class that maps an input collection to an array. The input object is set using the setInput() method. The viewer sorter defines a custom compare() method that sorts the elements based on a person's last name. Finally, a selectionChanged listener and doubleClick listener are added that override the selectionChanged() and doubleClick() methods, respectively.

The Person domain model class for this and the next few examples looks like this:

```
public class Person {
    public String firstName = "John";
    public String lastName = "Doe";
    public int age = 37;
    public Person[] children = new Person[0];
    public Person parent = null;

    public Person(String firstName, String lastName,
        int age) {
        this.firstName = firstName;
```

```
            this.lastName = lastName;
            this.age = age;
      }
      public Person(String firstName, String lastName,
            int age, Person[] children) {
            this(firstName, lastName, age);
            this.children = children;
            for (int i = 0; i < children.length; i++) {
                  children[i].parent = this;
            }
      }
      public static Person[] example() {
            return new Person[] {
                  new Person("Dan", "Rubel", 38, new Person[] {
                        new Person("Beth", "Rubel", 8),
                        new Person("David", "Rubel", 3)}),
                  new Person("Eric", "Clayberg", 39, new Person[] {
                        new Person("Lauren", "Clayberg", 6),
                        new Person("Lee", "Clayberg", 4)}),
                  new Person("Mike", "Taylor", 52)
            };
      }
      public String toString() {
            return firstName + " " + lastName;
      }
}
```

5.1.7   TableViewer class

The `TableViewer` class wraps the `Table` widget. A table viewer provides an editable, vertical, multicolumn list of items, showing a row of cells for each item in the list where each cell represents a different attribute of the item at that row. A table viewer needs to be configured with a label provider, a content provider, and a set of columns. The `CheckboxTableViewer` enhances this further by adding support for graying out individual items and toggling on and off an associated checkbox with each item. Useful APIs include:

add(Object)—Adds the given element to this table viewer. This method should be called (by the content provider) when a single element has been added to the model to cause the viewer to accurately reflect the model. This method only affects the viewer, not the model.

add(Object[])—Adds the given elements to this table viewer. This method should be called (by the content provider) when elements have been added to the model to cause the viewer to accurately reflect the model. This method only affects the viewer, not the model.

cancelEditing()—Cancels a currently active cell editor.

editElement(Object, int)—Starts editing the given element.

getElementAt(int)—Returns the element with the given index from this table viewer.

`getTable()`—Returns this table viewer's table control.

`insert(Object, int)`—Inserts the given element into this table viewer at the given position.

`isCellEditorActive()`—Returns whether there is an active cell editor.

`remove(Object)`—Removes the given element from this table viewer. This method should be called (by the content provider) when a single element has been removed from the model to cause the viewer to accurately reflect the model. This method only affects the viewer, not the model.

`remove(Object[])`—Removes the given elements from this table viewer. This method should be called (by the content provider) when elements have been removed from the model, in order to cause the viewer to accurately reflect the model. This method only affects the viewer, not the model.

`reveal(Object)`—Ensures that the given element is visible, scrolling the viewer if necessary.

`setCellEditors(CellEditor[])`—Sets the cell editors of this table viewer.

`setCellModifier(ICellModifier)`—Sets the cell modifier of this table viewer.

`setColumnProperties(String[])`—Sets the column properties of this table viewer.

`setLabelProvider(IBaseLabelProvider)`—The table viewer implementation of this `Viewer` framework method ensures that the given label provider is an instance of either `ITableLabelProvider` or `ILabelProvider`.

`CheckboxTableViewer` adds the following useful APIs:

`addCheckStateListener(ICheckStateListener)`—Adds a listener for changes to the checked state of elements in this viewer.

`getChecked(Object)`—Returns the checked state of the given element.

`getCheckedElements()`—Returns a list of elements corresponding to checked table items in this viewer.

`getGrayed(Object)`—Returns the grayed state of the given element.

`getGrayedElements()`—Returns a list of elements corresponding to grayed nodes in this viewer.

setAllChecked(boolean)—Sets to the given value the checked state for all elements in this viewer.

setAllGrayed(boolean)—Sets to the given value the grayed state for all elements in this viewer.

setChecked(Object, boolean)—Sets the checked state for the given element in this viewer.

setCheckedElements(Object[])—Sets which nodes are checked in this viewer.

setGrayed(Object, boolean)—Sets the grayed state for the given element in this viewer.

setGrayedElements(Object[])—Sets which nodes are grayed in this viewer.

The following example creates a table viewer with a label provider, content provider, and four columns (see Figure 5–9).

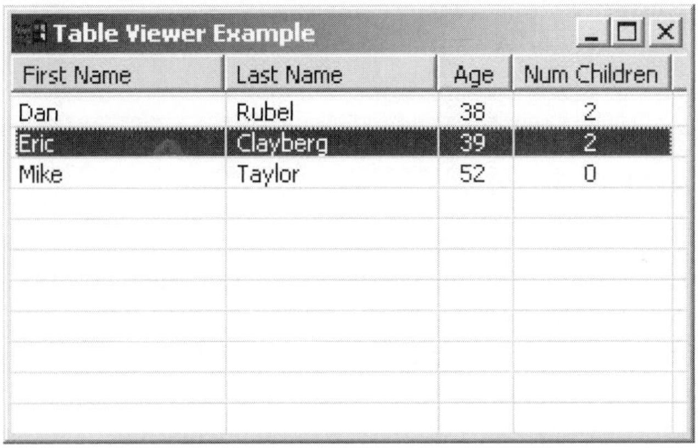

Figure 5–9   Table viewer example.

```
import org.eclipse.jface.viewers.*;
import org.eclipse.swt.*;
import org.eclipse.swt.layout.*;
import org.eclipse.swt.widgets.*;

public class TableViewerExample {
   public static void main(String[] args) {
      Display display = new Display();
      Shell shell = new Shell(display);
      shell.setText("Table Viewer Example");
      shell.setBounds(100, 100, 325, 200);
      shell.setLayout(new FillLayout());
```

```
final TableViewer tableViewer = new TableViewer(
    shell, SWT.SINGLE | SWT.FULL_SELECTION);
final Table table = tableViewer.getTable();
table.setHeaderVisible(true);
table.setLinesVisible(true);

String[] columnNames = new String[] {
    "First Name", "Last Name", "Age", "Num Children"};
int[] columnWidths = new int[] {
    100, 100, 35, 75};
int[] columnAlignments = new int[] {
    SWT.LEFT, SWT.LEFT, SWT.CENTER, SWT.CENTER};
for (int i = 0; i < columnNames.length; i++) {
    TableColumn tableColumn =
        new TableColumn(table, columnAlignments[i]);
    tableColumn.setText(columnNames[i]);
    tableColumn.setWidth(columnWidths[i]);
}

tableViewer.setLabelProvider(
    new PersonTableLabelProvider());
tableViewer.setContentProvider(
    new ArrayContentProvider());
tableViewer.setInput(Person.example());

shell.open();
while (!shell.isDisposed()) {
    if (!display.readAndDispatch()) display.sleep();
}
display.dispose();
    }
}
```

After creating the table viewer, the column headers and lines are made visible by calling the `setHeaderVisible()` and `setLinesVisible()` methods in the table viewer's underlying table. Four columns are then added to the table with different alignments. The header text and width of each column are set with the `setText()` and `setWidth()` methods (see Section 7.8, "Autosizing Table Columns").

The label provider is set using the `setLabelProvider()` method and the content provider with the `setContentProvider()` method. The label provider, `PersonTableLabelProvider`, returns a text label for each column in the table and does not return an icon. The class looks like this:

```
import org.eclipse.jface.viewers.*;
import org.eclipse.swt.graphics.*;

public class PersonTableLabelProvider
    extends LabelProvider
    implements ITableLabelProvider {
    public Image getColumnImage(
        Object element, int) {
        return null;
    }
```

```
    public String getColumnText(Object element, int index) {
        Person person = (Person) element;
        switch (index) {
            case 0 :
                return person.firstName;
            case 1 :
                return person.lastName;
            case 2 :
                return Integer.toString(person.age);
            case 3 :
                return Integer.toString(person.children.length);
            default :
                return "unknown " + index;
        }
    }
}
```

5.1.8   TreeViewer class

The TreeViewer class wraps the Tree widget. A tree viewer displays a hierarchical list of objects in a parent-child relationship. A tree viewer needs to be
configured with a label provider, a content provider, and a set of columns. The
CheckboxTreeViewer enhances this further by adding support for graying
out individual items and toggling on and off an associated checkbox with each
item. Useful APIs include:

add(Object, Object)—Adds the given child element to this viewer as
a child of the given parent element.

add(Object, Object[])—Adds the given child elements to this
viewer as children of the given parent element.

addTreeListener(ITreeViewerListener)—Adds a listener for
expanding and collapsing events in this viewer.

collapseAll()—Collapses all nodes of the viewer's tree, starting with
the root.

collapseToLevel(Object, int)—Collapses the subtree rooted at
the given element to the given level.

expandAll()—Expands all nodes of the viewer's tree, starting with the root.

expandToLevel(int)—Expands the root of the viewer's tree to the
given level.

expandToLevel(Object, int)—Expands all ancestors of the given
element so that the given element becomes visible in this viewer's tree
control, and then expands the subtree rooted at the given element to the
given level.

`getExpandedElements()`—Returns a list of elements corresponding to expanded nodes in this viewer's tree, including currently hidden ones that are marked as expanded but are under a collapsed ancestor.

`getExpandedState(Object)`—Returns whether the node corresponding to the given element is expanded or collapsed.

`Tree getTree()`—Returns this tree viewer's tree control.

`getVisibleExpandedElements()`—Gets the expanded elements that are visible to the user.

`isExpandable(Object)`—Returns whether the tree node representing the given element can be expanded.

`remove(Object)`—Removes the given element from the viewer.

`remove(Object[])`—Removes the given elements from this viewer.

`reveal(Object)`—Ensures that the given element is visible, scrolling the viewer if necessary.

`scrollDown(int, int)`—Scrolls the viewer's control down by one item from the given display-relative coordinates.

`scrollUp(int, int)`—Scrolls the viewer's control up by one item from the given display-relative coordinates.

`setAutoExpandLevel(int)`—Sets the auto-expand level.

`setContentProvider(IContentProvider)`—The `AbstractTreeViewer` implementation of this method checks to ensure that the content provider is an `ITreeContentProvider`.

`setExpandedElements(Object[])`—Sets which nodes are expanded in this viewer's tree.

`setExpandedState(Object, boolean)`—Sets whether the node corresponding to the given element is expanded or collapsed.

`setLabelProvider(IBaseLabelProvider)`—The tree viewer implementation of this `Viewer` framework method ensures that the given label provider is an instance of `ILabelProvider`.

`CheckboxTreeViewer` adds the following useful APIs:

`addCheckStateListener(ICheckStateListener)`—Adds a listener for changes to the checked state of elements in this viewer.

`getChecked(Object)`—Returns the checked state of the given element.

`getCheckedElements()`—Returns a list of checked elements in this viewer's tree, including currently hidden ones that are marked as checked but are under a collapsed ancestor.

getGrayed(Object)—Returns the grayed state of the given element.

getGrayedElements()—Returns a list of grayed elements in this viewer's tree, including currently hidden ones that are marked as grayed but are under a collapsed ancestor.

setChecked(Object, boolean)—Sets the checked state for the given element in this viewer.

setCheckedElements(Object[])—Sets which elements are checked in this viewer's tree.

setGrayChecked(Object, boolean)—Checks and grays the selection rather than calling both setGrayed and setChecked as an optimization.

setGrayed(Object, boolean)—Sets the grayed state for the given element in this viewer.

setGrayedElements(Object[])—Sets which elements are grayed in this viewer's tree.

setParentsGrayed(Object, boolean)—Sets the grayed state for the given element and its parents in this viewer.

setSubtreeChecked(Object, boolean)—Sets the checked state for the given element and its visible children in this viewer.

The following example creates a tree viewer with a label provider and content provider (see Figure 5–10).

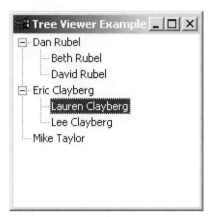

Figure 5–10   Tree viewer example.

```
import org.eclipse.jface.viewers.*;
import org.eclipse.swt.*;
import org.eclipse.swt.layout.*;
import org.eclipse.swt.widgets.*;

public class TreeViewerExample {
    public static void main(String[] args) {
        Display display = new Display();
        Shell shell = new Shell(display);
        shell.setText("Tree Viewer Example");
        shell.setBounds(100, 100, 200, 200);
        shell.setLayout(new FillLayout());

        final TreeViewer treeViewer =
            new TreeViewer(shell, SWT.SINGLE);
        treeViewer.setLabelProvider(
            new PersonListLabelProvider());
        treeViewer.setContentProvider(
            new PersonTreeContentProvider());
        treeViewer.setInput(Person.example());

        shell.open();
        while (!shell.isDisposed()) {
            if (!display.readAndDispatch()) display.sleep();
        }
        display.dispose();
    }
}
```

After creating the tree viewer, the label provider is set using the `setLabel-Provider()` method and the content provider with the `setContentPro-vider()` method. The content provider, `PersonTreeContent Provider`, returns the parent and children of each item. The class looks like this:

```
import org.eclipse.jface.viewers.*;

public class PersonTreeContentProvider
    extends ArrayContentProvider
    implements ITreeContentProvider {

    public Object[] getChildren(Object parentElement) {
        Person person = (Person) parentElement;
        return person.children;
    }

    public Object getParent(Object) {
        Person person = (Person) element;
        return person.parent;
    }

    public boolean hasChildren(Object) {
        Person person = (Person) element;
        return person.children.length > 0;
    }
}
```

5.2   Text Viewers

The TextViewer class wraps the StyledText widget (see Figure 5–11 for the TextViewer hierarchy). Individual runs of text may have different styles associated with them, including foreground color, background color, and bold.

Figure 5–11   TextViewer hierarchy.

Useful APIs include:

addTextListener(ITextListener)—Adds a text listener to this viewer.

appendVerifyKeyListener(VerifyKeyListener)—Appends a verify key listener to the viewer's list of verify key listeners.

canDoOperation(int)—Returns whether the operation specified by the given operation code can be performed.

changeTextPresentation(TextPresentation, boolean)— Applies the color information encoded in the given text presentation.

doOperation(int)—Performs the operation specified by the operation code on the target.

enableOperation(int, boolean)—Enables/disables the given text operation.

getSelectedRange()—Returns the range of the current selection in coordinates of this viewer's document.

getSelection()—Returns the current selection for this provider.

getTextWidget()—Returns the viewer's text widget.

isEditable()—Returns whether the shown text can be manipulated.

refresh()—Refreshes this viewer completely with information freshly obtained from the viewer's model.

setDocument(IDocument)—Sets the given document as the text viewer's model and updates the presentation accordingly.

setEditable(boolean)—Sets the editable mode.

setInput(Object)—Sets or clears the input for this viewer. The Text-Viewer implementation of this method calls setDocument(IDocument) with the input object if the input object is an instance of IDocument or with null if the input object is not.

setRedraw(boolean)—Enables/disables the redrawing of this text viewer.

setSelectedRange(int, int)—Sets the selection to the specified range.

setSelection(ISelection, boolean)—Sets a new selection for this viewer and optionally makes it visible.

setTextColor(Color)—Applies the given color to this viewer's selection.

setTextColor(Color, int, int, boolean)—Applies the given color to the specified section of this viewer.

setTextHover(ITextHover, String)—Sets this viewer's text hover for the given content type.

The following example creates a text viewer containing styled text (see Figure 5–12).

Figure 5–12   Text viewer example.

```
import org.eclipse.jface.text.*;
import org.eclipse.swt.*;
import org.eclipse.swt.custom.*;
import org.eclipse.swt.graphics.*;
import org.eclipse.swt.layout.*;
import org.eclipse.swt.widgets.*;

public class TextViewerExample {
   public static void main(String[] args) {
      Display display = new Display();
      Shell shell = new Shell(display);
      shell.setText("Text Viewer Example");
      shell.setBounds(100, 100, 225, 125);
      shell.setLayout(new FillLayout());

      final TextViewer textViewer =
         new TextViewer(shell, SWT.MULTI | SWT.VSCROLL);
```

```
String string = "This is plain text\n"
   + "This is bold text\n"
   + "This is red text";
Document document = new Document(string);
textViewer.setDocument(document);

TextPresentation style = new TextPresentation();
style.addStyleRange(
   new StyleRange(19, 17, null, null, SWT.BOLD));
Color red = new Color(null, 255, 0, 0);
style.addStyleRange(
   new StyleRange(37, 16, red, null));
textViewer.changeTextPresentation(style, true);

shell.open();
while (!shell.isDisposed()) {
   if (!display.readAndDispatch()) display.sleep();
}
display.dispose();
   }
}
```

After creating the text viewer, a Document object is created that holds a string of text and is then assigned to the viewer. Next, a TextPresentation object is created to hold the style ranges. Two style ranges are added: one that sets a range of text to bold and a second that sets a range of text to the color red. The first argument to the StyleRange constructor is the index of the first character in the string to which the style should apply. The second argument is the number of characters that should be affected by the style. Finally, the style object is assigned to the viewer.

5.3   Summary

JFace viewers are used extensively in Eclipse plug-in development. List viewers provide OO wrappers around the basic Eclipse widgets, making it easier to directly deal with high-level domain objects rather than simple strings, numbers, and images. Likewise, text viewers make it easier to deal with text documents that require more complex text styling.

CHAPTER 6

Actions

Actions, like everything else in Eclipse, are defined through various extension points so that new actions can be easily added at several different points throughout the Eclipse framework. Actions appear in several different places throughout the Eclipse IDE, including the menu bar, toolbars, and context menus. Filters control when an action is visible and enabled for selection by a user. In this chapter, we will cover all this with examples showing how to use actions and action sets in our example **Favorites** plug-in.

6.1 IAction versus IActionDelegate

An Eclipse *action* is composed of several parts, including the XML declaration of the action in the plug-in's manifest, the IAction object instantiated by the Eclipse UI to represent the action, and the IActionDelegate defined in the plug-in library containing the code to perform the action. This separation of the IAction object, defined and instantiated by the Eclipse UI based on the plug-in's manifest and the IActionDelegate defined in the plug-in's library, allows Eclipse to represent the action in a menu or toolbar without loading the plug-in that contains the operation until the user selects the menu item or clicks on the toolbar. This approach again represents one of the overarching themes of Eclipse: lazy plug-in initialization.

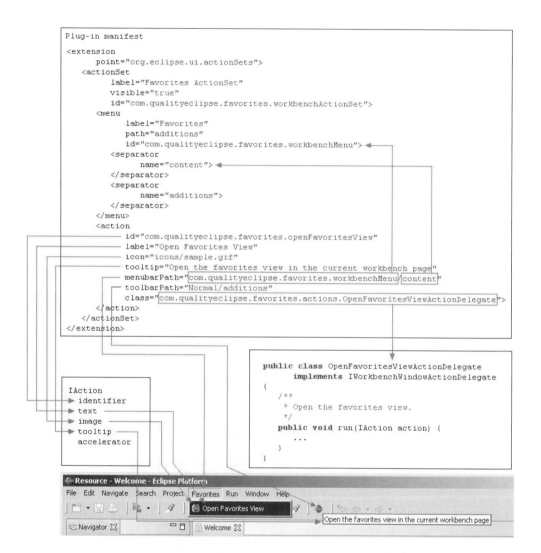

Figure 6–1   Action versus IActionDelegate.

There are several interesting subtypes of IActionDelegate:

IActionDelegate2—Provides lifecycle events to action delegates; if you are implementing IActionDelegate and need additional information such as when to clean up before the action delegate is disposed, then implement IActionDelegate2 instead.

IEditorActionDelegate—Provides lifecycle events to action delegates associated with an editor (see Section 6.5.3, "IEditorActionDelegate").

`IObjectActionDelegate`—Provides lifecycle events to action delegates associated with a context menu (see Section 6.3.3, "IObjectActionDelegate").

`IViewActionDelegate`—Provides lifecycle events to action delegates associated with a view (see Section 6.4.3, "IViewActionDelegate").

`IWorkbenchWindowActionDelegate`—Provides lifecycle events to action delegates associated with the workbench window menu bar or toolbar.

6.2   Workbench Window Actions

Where and when an action appears is dependent on the extension point and filter used to define the action. In this section, we'll add a new menu to the workbench menu bar and a new button to the workbench toolbar using the `org.eclipse.ui.actionSets` extension point (see Figure 6–1).

Both the menu item and toolbar button will open our **Favorites** view when selected by a user. The user can already open the `Favorites` view as outlined in Section 2.5, "Installing and Running the Product," but a top-level menu will really show off our new product by providing the user an easy way to find it.

> **Tip:** A top-level menu is a great way to show off a new product to a user, but be sure to read Section 6.2.9, "Discussion," concerning the pitfalls of this approach. Welcome pages are another great way to showcase a new product (see Section 18.2.3, "The welcome.xml file").

6.2.1   Defining a workbench window menu

To create a new menu to appear in the workbench menu bar, you have to create an **actionSet** extension in the **Favorites** plug-in manifest describing the new actions. That declaration must describe the location and content of the new menu and reference the action delegate class that performs the operation.

Open the **Favorites** plug-in manifest editor, select the **Extensions** tab, and click the **Add** button. You can also open the **New Extension** wizard by right-clicking to display the context menu, then select **New > Extension...** (see Figure 6–2).

Figure 6–2   The Extensions page of the Manifest editor.

Select **org.eclipse.ui.actionSets** from the list of all available extension points (see Figure 6–3). If you can't locate **org.eclipse.ui.actionSets** in the list, then uncheck the **Show only extension points from the required plug-ins** checkbox. Click the **Finish** button to add this extension to the plug-in manifest.

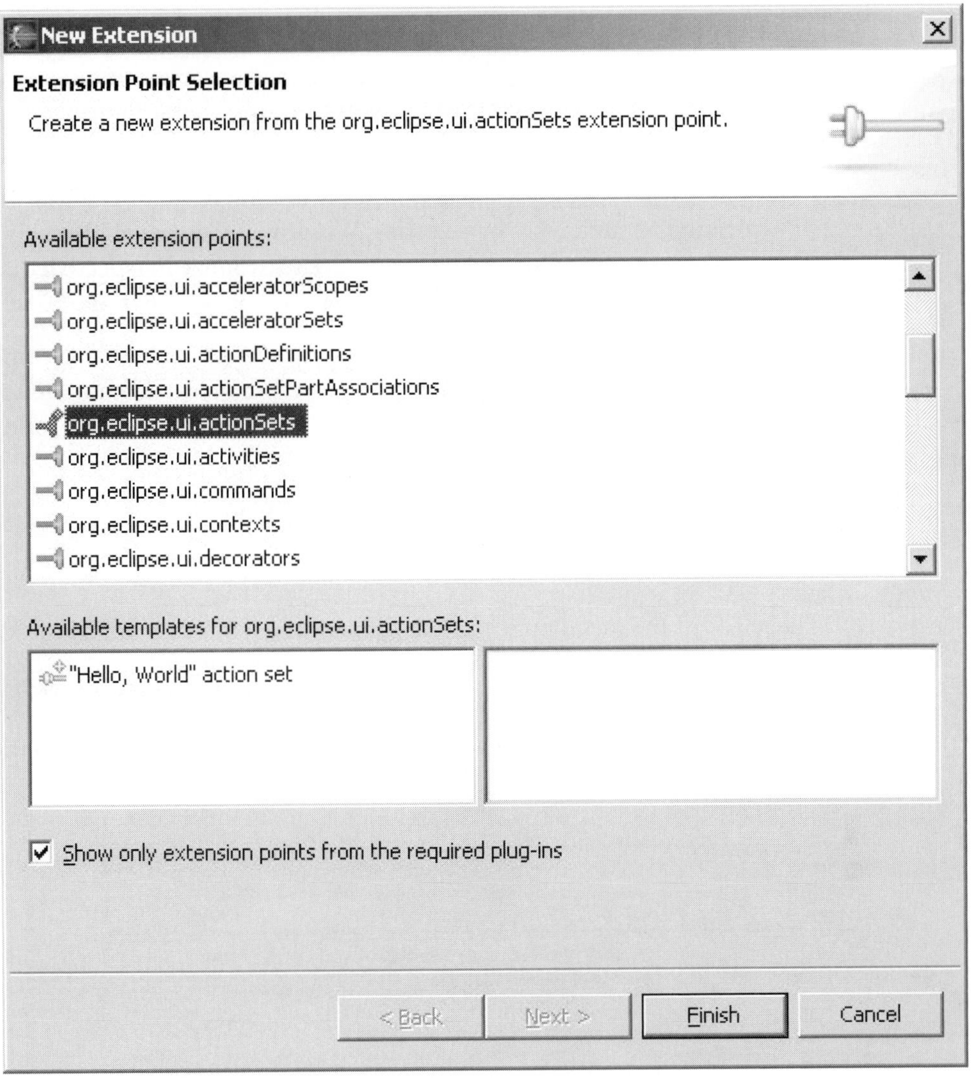

Figure 6–3   The New Extension wizard showing extension points.

Now, back in the **Extensions** page of the plug-in manifest editor, right-click on the **org.eclipse.ui.actionSets** extension and select **New > actionSet**. This immediately adds a new action set named **com.qualityeclipse.favor-ites.actionSet1** in the plug-in manifest. Double-clicking on this new action set opens the **Properties** view so that properties can be modified as follows:

id—"com.qualityeclipse.favorites.workbenchActionSet"
The unique identifier used to reference the action set.

label—"Favorites actionSet"
The text that appears in the **Customize Perspective** dialog.

visible—"true"
Determines whether or not the action set is initially visible. The user can show or hide an action set by selecting **Window > Customize Perspective...**, expanding the **Other** category in the **Customize Perspective** dialog, and checking or unchecking the various action sets that are listed.

Next, add a menu that will appear in the workbench menu bar by right-clicking on the new **Favorites actionSet** and selecting **New > menu**. Double-click on the new menu to set its attributes in the **Properties** view as follows (see Figure 6–4):

id—"com.qualityeclipse.favorites.workbenchMenu"
The unique identifier used to reference this menu.

label—"Fa&vorites"
The name of the menu appearing in the workbench menu bar. The "&" is for keyboard accessibility (see Section 6.6.5, "Keyboard accessibility").

path—"additions"
The insertion point indicating where the menu will be positioned in the menu bar (see Section 6.2.5, "Insertion points").

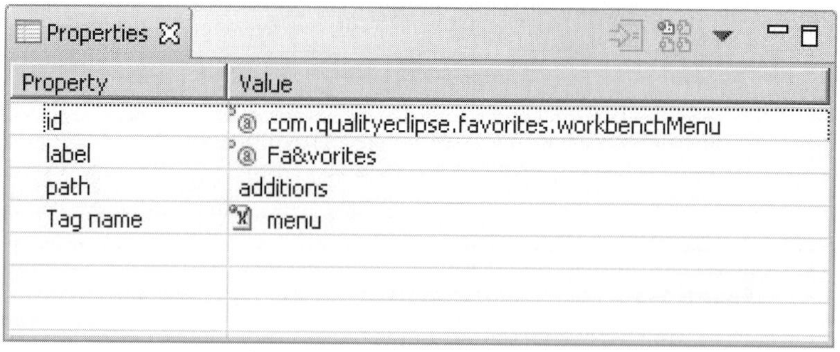

Property	Value
id	com.qualityeclipse.favorites.workbenchMenu
label	Fa&vorites
path	additions
Tag name	menu

Figure 6–4   The Properties view showing the Favorites menu's attributes.

6.2.2   Groups in a menu

Actions are added not to the menu itself, but to groups within the menu, so first we have to define some groups. Right-click on the new **Favorites** menu and select **New > groupMarker**. Double-click on the new *groupMarker* to

open the **Properties** view, and change the **name** to "content" to uniquely identify that group within the **Favorites** menu. Add a second group to the **Favorites** menu, but this time, select **New > separator** and give it the name
"additions". A *separator* group has a horizontal line above the first menu item
in the group, whereas a *groupMarker* does not have any horizontal line. We
will not use the additions group, but it exists as a matter of course in case
another other plug-in wants to contribute actions to our plug-in's menu.

6.2.3 *Defining a menu item and toolbar button*

Finally, we are ready to define the action that appears in both the **Favorites**
menu and the workbench toolbar. Right-click on the **Favorites actionSet** and
select **New > action**. Open the **Properties** view for this new action and enter
the following values:

> **id**—"com.qualityeclipse.favorites.openFavoritesView"
> The unique identifier used to reference the action.

> **label**—"Open Favo&rites View"
> The text appearing in the **Favorites** menu. The "&" is for keyboard
> accessibility (see Section 6.6.5).

> **menubarPath**—"com.qualityeclipse.favorites.workbenchMenu/content"
> The insertion point indicating where the action will appear in the menu
> (see Section 6.2.5).

> **toolbarPath**—"Normal/additions"
> The insertion point indicating where the button will appear in the tool-
> bar (see Section 6.2.5).

> **tooltip**—"Open the favorites view in the current workbench page"
> The text that appears when the mouse hovers over the action's icon in
> the workbench toolbar.

Other attributes discussed in subsequent sections include:

> **accelerator**—Deprecated; see `definitionId`.

> **allowLabelUpdate**—Optional attribute indicating whether the retarget
> action allows the handler to override its label and tooltip. Only applies if
> the retarget attribute is `true`.

> **class**—The `org.eclipse.ui.IWorkbenchWindowActionDelegate` dele-
> gate used to perform the operation is covered later (see Section 6.2.6,
> "Creating an action delegate"). If the pulldown style is specified, then
> the class must implement the `org.eclipse.ui.IWorkbenchWindowPull-`
> `downDelegate` interface. The class is instantiated using its no argument

constructor, but may be parameterized using the `IExecutableExtension` interface (see Section 20.5, "Types Specified in an Extension Point").

definitionId—The command identifier for the action, which allows a key sequence to be associated with the action. See Section 6.7, "RFWS Considerations," for more details.

disabledIcon—The image displayed when the action is disabled. See Section 6.2.4, "Action images," for more detail.

enablesFor—An expression indicating when the action will be enabled (covered in Section 6.3.2, "Action filtering and enablement"). If blank, then the action is always active unless overridden programmatically via the `IAction` interface.

helpContextId—The identifier for the help context associated with the action (covered in Chapter 15, "Implementing Help").

hoverIcon—An image displayed when the cursor *hovers* over the action without being clicked. See Section 6.2.4 for more detail.

icon—The associated image. See Section 6.2.4 for more detail.

pulldown—Deprecated; see `style`.

retarget—An optional attribute to retarget this action. When `true`, view and editor parts may supply a handler for this action using the standard mechanism for setting a global action handler (see Section 8.5.2.2, "Top-level menu") on their site using this action's identifier. If this attribute is true, the class attribute should not be supplied.

state—For an action with either the `radio` or `toggle` style, set the initial state to `true` or `false`.

style—An attribute defining the visual form of the action and having one of the following values:
push—A normal menu or toolbar item (the default style).
radio—A radio button-style menu or toolbar item where only one item at a time in a group of items all having the radio style can be active. See the state attribute.
toggle—A checked menu item or toggle tool item. See the state attribute.
pulldown—A submenu or drop-down toolbar menu. See the class attribute.

6.2.4   Action images

Next, associate an icon with the action that will appear in the workbench toolbar. Select the **icon** field in the **Properties** view and click the "..." button that appears to the right of the **icon** field. In the resulting dialog, expand the tree and select the **sample.gif** item from the **icons** folder (see Figure 6–5). Click the **OK** button and **icons/sample.gif** will appear in the **icon** field of the **Properties** view. The path appearing in the **Properties** view and in the plugin.xml is relative to the plug-in's installation directory. Other image-related attributes include **hoverIcon** and **disabledIcon** for specifying the image that will be used when the mouse is hovered over the toolbar button and when the action is disabled, respectively.

> **Creating Your Own Icons**   There are several programs available for creating and modifying images such as Jasc's Paint Shop Pro and Adobe's Photoshop Elements. Using one of these programs, you can create an icon from scratch or start with one of the many icons provided by Eclipse (see *plugins\org.eclipse.ui_3.0.0\icons\full* or *plugins\org.eclipse.jdt.ui_3.0.0\icons\full* for starters). Icons are typically *.gif files with a transparency color.

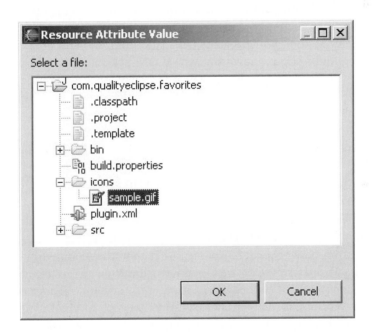

Figure 6–5   The Resource Selection dialog for selecting an icon.

6.2.5   *Insertion points*

Because Eclipse is composed of multiple plug-ins, each one capable of contributing actions but not necessarily knowing about one another at build-time, the absolute position of an action or submenu within its parent is not known until run-time. Even during the course of execution, the position might change due to a sibling action being added or removed as the user changes a selection. For this reason, Eclipse uses *identifiers* to reference a menu, group, or action, and a path, known as an *insertion point*, for specifying where a menu or action will appear.

Each insertion point is composed of one or two identifiers separated by a forward slash, indicating the parent (a menu in this case) and group where the action will be located. For example, the **Open Favorites View** action **menubar** attribute (see Section 6.2.3, "Defining a menu item and toolbar button," and Figure 6–1) is composed of two elements separated by a forward slash. The first element, com.qualityeclipse.favorites.workbenchMenu, identifies the **Favorites** menu, while the second element, content, identifies the group within the **Favorites** menu. In some cases, such as when the parent is the workbench menu bar or a view's context menu, the parent is implied and thus only the group is specified in the insertion point.

Typically, plug-ins make allowances for other plug-ins to add new actions to their own menus by defining an empty group labeled "**additions**" in which the new actions will appear. The "**additions**" identifier is fairly standard throughout Eclipse, indicating where new actions or menus will appear, and is included in Eclipse as the constant IWorkbenchActionConstants.MB_ADDITIONS. For example, the **Favorites** menu specifies a **path** attribute (see Section 6.2.1, "Defining a workbench window menu") having the value "**additions**" that causes the **Favorites** menu to appear to the left of the **Window** menu. Because the identifier for the **Window** menu is **window**, and if the **path** attribute of the **Favorites** menu is set to "**window/additions**", then the **Favorites** menu will appear as a submenu in the **Window** menu itself rather than in the workbench menu bar.

The **toolbarPath** attribute is also an insertion point and has a structure identical to the **menubarPath** attribute, but indicates where the action will appear in the workbench toolbar rather than the menu bar. For example, the **toolbarPath** attribute of the **Open Favorites View** action (see Section 6.2.3) is also composed of two elements separated by a forward slash: The first element, **Normal**, is the identifier of the workbench toolbar, while **additions**, the second element, is the group within that toolbar where the action will appear.

6.2.6   Creating an action delegate

The action is almost complete except for the action delegate, which contains the behavior associated with the action. In the **Properties** view, select the **class** field and click the "..." button that appears to the right of the **class** field to open the **Java Attribute Editor** for the action's class (see Figure 6–6). Since we have not already created a class for the action, we'll have Eclipse generate one for us that we can customize by selecting the **Generate a new Java class** radio button. Enter "com.qualityeclipse.favorites.actions" in the **Package Name** field and "OpenFavoritesViewActionDelegate" in the **Class Name** field. Click the **Finish** button to generate the new action delegate and open an editor on the new class.

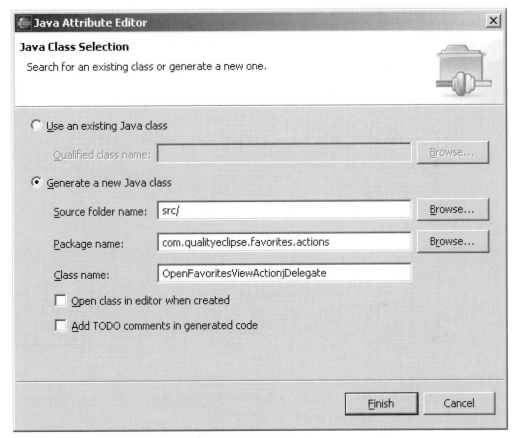

Figure 6–6   The Java Attribute Editor for an action's class.

Once the class has been created and the editor opened, modify the class as follows so that the **Favorites** view will open when a user selects the action:

```
package com.qualityeclipse.favorites.actions;

import org.eclipse.jface.action.*;
import org.eclipse.jface.viewers.*;
import org.eclipse.ui.*;
import com.qualityeclipse.favorites.*;
```

```
public class OpenFavoritesViewActionDelegate
   implements IWorkbenchWindowActionDelegate
{
   private static final String FAVORITES_VIEW_ID =
      "com.qualityeclipse.favorites.views.FavoritesView";

   private IWorkbenchWindow window;

   public void init(IWorkbenchWindow window) {
      this.window = window;
   }

   public void selectionChanged(
      IAction action,
      ISelection selection) {
   }

   public void run(IAction action) {

      // Get the active page.
      if (window == null)
         return;
      IWorkbenchPage page = window.getActivePage();
      if (page == null)
         return;

      // Open and activate the Favorites view.
      try {
         page.showView (FAVORITES_VIEW_ID);
      }
      catch (PartInitException e) {
         FavoritesLog.logError(
            "Failed to open the Favorites view",
            e);
      }
   }

   public void dispose() {
   }
}
```

6.2.6.1   selectionChanged method

While the action declaration in the plug-in manifest provides the initial state of the action, the selectionChanged(...) method in the action delegate provides an opportunity to dynamically adjust the state, enablement, or even the text of the action using the IAction interface. For example, the **enablesFor** attribute (see Section 6.3.2) is used to specify the number of objects to select for an action to be enabled, but further refinement of this enablement can be provided by implementing the selectionChanged(...) method. This method can interrogate the current selection and call the IAction.setEnabled(...) method as necessary to update the action enablement.

6.2.6.2   *run method*

The run(...) method is called when a user selects an action and expects an operation to be performed. Similar to the selectionChanged(...) method, the IAction interface can be used to change the state of an action dependent on the outcome of an operation. Be aware that if the plug-in is not loaded and the user selects a menu option causing the plug-in to be loaded, the selectionChanged(...) method *may not be called* before the run(...) method, so the run(...) method still needs the appropriate guard code.

6.2.7   *Manually testing the new action*

Testing the modifications we have just made involves launching the **Runtime Workbench** as discussed in Chapter 2, "A Simple Plug-in Example." If the **Favorites** menu does not appear in the **Runtime Workbench** menu bar or the **Favorites** icon cannot be found in the toolbar, try one of the following suggestions:

- Enable the action set by selecting **Window > Customize Perspective...** to open the **Customize Perspective** dialog. In the dialog, select the **Commands** tab, locate **Favorites actionSet,** and make sure it is checked (see Figure 6–7).

- Reinitialize the perspective using **Window > Reset Perspective.**

- Close and reopen the perspective.

- If nothing else works, then try clearing the workspace data before launching the **Runtime Workbench**. To do this, select **Run...** in the launch menu, select the **Favorites** launch configuration, and check the **Clear workspace data before launching** checkbox. Click the **Run** button to launch the **Runtime Workbench.**

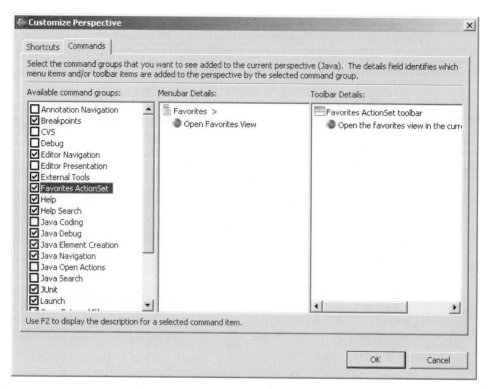

Figure 6–7   Customize Perspective dialog.

6.2.8   Adding a test for the new action

Before our work is complete, we need to devise a test for the new **Open Favorites View** action. From the FavoritesViewTest in Chapter 2, create a new abstract superclass for all our tests called AbstractFavoritesTest, and pull up the VIEW_ID constant, the delay(...) method, and the waitForJobs() method. Next, create a new test subclassing AbstractFavoritesTest that exercises the new OpenFavoritesViewActionDelegate class.

```
package com.qualityeclipse.favorites.test;

import org.eclipse.jface.action.*;
import org.eclipse.jface.viewers.*;
import org.eclipse.ui.*;
import com.qualityeclipse.favorites.actions.*;

public class OpenFavoritesViewTest
    extends AbstractFavoritesTest
{
```

```java
public OpenFavoritesViewTest(String name) {
    super(name);
}

protected void setUp() throws Exception {
    super.setUp();

    // Ensure that the view is not open.
    waitForJobs();
    IWorkbenchPage page =
        PlatformUI
            .getWorkbench()
            .getActiveWorkbenchWindow()
            .getActivePage();
    IViewPart view = page.findView(VIEW_ID);
    if (view != null)
        page.hideView(view);

    // Delay for 3 seconds so that
    // the Favorites view can be seen.
    waitForJobs();
    delay(3000);
}

public void testOpenFavoritesView() {

    // Execute the operation.
    (new Action("OpenFavoritesViewTest") {
        public void run() {
            IWorkbenchWindowActionDelegate delegate =
                new OpenFavoritesViewActionDelegate();
            delegate.init(
                PlatformUI
                    .getWorkbench()
                    .getActiveWorkbenchWindow());
            delegate.selectionChanged(
                this,
                StructuredSelection.EMPTY);
            delegate.run(this);
        }
    }).run();

    // Test that the operation completed successfully.
    waitForJobs();
    IWorkbenchPage page =
        PlatformUI
            .getWorkbench()
            .getActiveWorkbenchWindow()
            .getActivePage();
    assertTrue(page.findView(VIEW_ID) != null);
}
}
```

Rather than launching each test individually, the `FavoritesViewTest` and `OpenFavoritesViewTest` can be combined into a single test suite named `FavoritesTestSuite` that can be launched to execute both tests at once:

```
package com.qualityeclipse.favorites.test;

import junit.framework.*;

public class FavoritesTestSuite
{
   public static Test suite() {
      TestSuite suite =
         new TestSuite("Favorites test suite");
      //$JUnit-BEGIN$
      suite.addTest(new TestSuite(FavoritesViewTest.class));
      suite.addTest(
         new TestSuite(OpenFavoritesViewTest.class));
      //$JUnit-END$
      return suite;
   }
}
```

While individually launching tests is not a problem now with just two tests, in the future, as more tests are added for the **Favorites** plug-in, it can save time to have a single test suite. To launch the test suite, select **Run...** in the launch menu, select the **Favorites Test** launch configuration that was created in Chapter 2, and modify the target to be the new `FavoritesTestSuite` test suite.

6.2.9   *Discussion*

To define a top-level menu or not... that is the question. On the one hand, a top-level menu is a great way to promote a new product that has just been installed, providing a good way for a potential customer to become accustomed to new functionality. On the other hand, if every plug-in defined a top-level menu, then the menu bar would be cluttered and Eclipse would quickly become unusable. Additionally, the customer may become annoyed if he or she does not want to see the menu and continually have to use the multistep process outlined in Section 1.2.2.4, "Customizing available actions," to remove the menu. What to do?

Action sets are one answer to this question. They can be specified in the `plugin.xml` as visible everywhere in every perspective. Using the new `IActionSetDescriptor.setInitiallyVisible(...)` method, you can programmatically override the visibility specified in the `plugin.xml` so that the top-level menu no longer shows up in any newly opened perspectives. By using `setInitiallyVisible(...)` in conjunction with `IWorkbenchPage.hideAction-`

Set (…), you can create a new Action that removes your top-level menu from all current and future perspectives. Your product could contain a checkbox option in your Preference page (see Section 12.2, "Preference Page APIs") that uses this Action to show or hide your top-level menu.

> We submitted a feature request and patch to Eclipse (see Bugzilla entry #39455) for the new IActionSetDescriptor API discussed above, and it was accepted and integrated into Eclipse 3.0. This is a good example of how you and I as Eclipse users can contribute back to Eclipse (see Section 20.6.4, "Submitting the change to Eclipse"), making it a better platform for everyone.

Another option is to tie your top-level menu or action set to a particular perspective (see Section 10.2.3, "Adding action sets"). In this way, the menu and actions are only visible when that particular perspective is active. If there are one or more perspectives particularly suited for the functionality added by your plug-in, then this may be your best approach.

If an action is editor-related, Sections 6.5.4, "Defining an editor top-level menu," and 6.5.5, "Defining an editor top-level action," discuss adding menus and actions tied to a specific type of editor. With this approach, the top-level menu is only visible when an editor of that type is open.

The org.Eclipse.actionSetPartAssociations extension point provides yet another option, allowing an action set to be displayed whenever one or more specific types of views or editors are open, regardless of the perspective in which they are opened. This is an excellent way to ensure that specific actions appear in a wide range of perspectives without having to explicitly add the actions to those perspectives.

The remainder of this chapter focuses on providing actions in view-specific menus, or as operations directed at specific types of objects rather than top-level menus. In this way, the action will only be visible when it is needed and on the types of objects to which it applies. This approach avoids the top-level menu issue and prevents Eclipse from becoming cluttered. Various approaches for locally scoped actions are covered in subsequent sections.

6.3   Object Actions

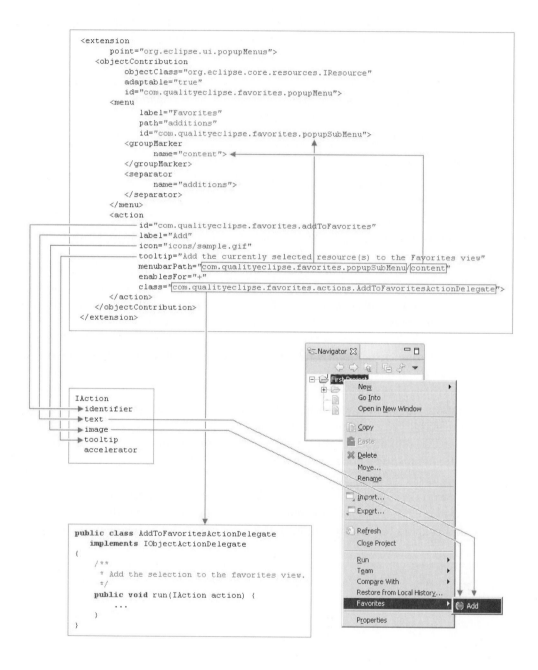

We want to make it easy for the user to add files and folders to the **Favorites** view. Object contributions are ideal for this because they appear in context menus only when the selection in the current view or editor contains an object compatible with that action (see Figure 6–8). In this manner, an object contribution is available to the user when he or she needs the action, yet not intrusive when the action does not apply.

6.3.1   *Defining an object-based action*

As in Sections 6.2.1, 6.2.2, and 6.2.3, use the **Extensions** page of the plug-in manifest editor to create the new object contribution. Click on the **Add** button to add an **org.eclipse.ui.popupMenus** extension, and then add an **objectContribution** with the following attributes:

> **adaptable**—"true"
> Indicates that objects that adapt to IResource are acceptable targets (see Section 20.3, "Adapters").
>
> **id**—"com.qualityeclipse.favorites.popupMenu"
> The unique identifier for this contribution.
>
> **nameFilter**—Leave blank.
> A wildcard filter specifying the names that are acceptable targets. For example, entering "*.java" would target only those files with names ending with ".java". More on this in Section 6.3.2.
>
> **objectClass**—"org.eclipse.core.resources.IResource"
> The type of object that is an acceptable target. Use the "..." button at the right of the **objectClass** field in the **Properties** editor to select the existing org.eclipse.core.resources.IResource class.

Next, add an action to the new objectContribution with the following attribute values. These attribute values are very similar to the action attributes covered in Section 6.2.3.

> **class**—"com.qualityeclipse.favorites.actions.AddToFavoritesActionDelegate"
> The action delegate for the action that implements the org.eclipse.ui. IObjectActionDelegate interface. See Section 6.3.3, "IObjectActionDelegate." The class is instantiated using its no argument constructor, but may be parameterized using the IExecutableExtension interface (see Section 20.5).
>
> **enablesFor**—"+"
> An expression indicating when the action will be enabled (see Section 6.3.2).

id—"com.qualityeclipse.favorites.addToFavorites"
The unique identifier for the action.

label—"Add to Favorites"
The text that appears in the context menu for the action.

menubarPath—"additions"
The insertion point for the action (see Section 6.2.5).

tooltip—"Add the selected resource(s) to the Favorites view"
The text that appears when the mouse hovers over the menu item in the context menu.

Other available action attributes not used in this example include:

helpContextId—The identifier for the help context associated with the action (see Chapter 15, "Implementing Help").

icon—The associated image (see Section 6.2.4).

overrideActionId—An optional attribute specifying the identifier for an action that the action overrides.

state—For an action with either the `radio` or `toggle` style, set the initial state to `true` or `false` (see Section 6.2.3).

style—An attribute defining the visual form of the action. This is covered in Section 6.2.3, with the exception that the `pulldown` style does not apply to object contributions.

6.3.2   Action filtering and enablement

In keeping with the lazy loading plug-in theme, Eclipse provides multiple declarative mechanisms for filtering actions based on the context, and enabling visible actions only when appropriate. Because they are declared in the plug-in manifest, these mechanisms have the advantage that they do not require the plug-in to be loaded for Eclipse to use them.

6.3.2.1   Basic filtering and enablement

In Section 6.2.3, the **nameFilter** and **objectClass** attributes are examples of filters, while the **enablesFor** attribute determines when an action will be enabled. When the context menu is activated, if a selection does not contain objects with names that match the wildcard **nameFilter** or are not of a type specified by the **objectClass** attribute, none of the actions defined in that object contribution will appear in the context menu. In addition, the **enablesFor** attribute uses the syntax in Table 6–1 to define exactly how many objects need to be selected for a particular action to be enabled:

Table 6–1   enabledFor attribute options

Syntax	Description
!	0 items selected.
?	0 or 1 items selected.
+	1 or more items selected.
multiple, 2+	2 or more items selected.
n	A precise number of items selected. For example, enablesFor=" 4" enables the action only when 4 items are selected.
*	Any number of items selected.

The techniques listed in this table represent those most commonly used for limiting visibility and enablement of actions; occasionally, a more refined approach is needed. The **visibility** and **filter** elements provide additional means to limit an action's visibility, while the **selection** and **enablement** elements provide a more flexible way to specify when an action is enabled. Still further refinement of action enablement can be provided via the selection-Changed(...) method in the action delegate, as discussed in Section 6.2.6.

6.3.2.2   The visibility element

The **visibility** element provides an alternate and more powerful way to specify when an object contribution's actions will be available to the user as compared with the object contribution's **nameFilter** and **objectClass**. For example, an alternate way to specify filtering for the object contribution described above would be:

```
<objectContribution …>
  <visibility>
     <objectClass
        name="org.eclipse.core.resources.IResource"/>
  </visibility>
  .. the other stuff here …
</objectContribution>
```

If the action is to be visible only for resources that are not read-only, then the visibility object contribution might look like this:

```
<objectContribution …>
  <visibility>
```

```
      <and>
         <objectClass
            name="org.eclipse.core.resources.IResource"/>
         <objectState name="readOnly" value="false"/>
      </and>
   </visibility>
   … the other stuff here …
</objectContribution>
```

As part of the `<visibility>` element declaration, you can use nested `<and>`, `<or>`, and `<not>` elements for logical expressions, plus the following Boolean expressions:

objectClass—Compares the class of the selected object against a name as shown above.

objectState—Compares the state of the selected object against a specified state as shown above (see Section 6.3.2.3, "The filter element").

pluginState—Compares the plug-in state, indicating whether it is `installed` or `activated`. For example, an expression such as `<pluginState id="org.eclipse.pde" value="installed"/>` would cause an object contribution to be visible only if the `org.eclipse.pde` plug-in is installed, and an expression such as `<pluginState id="org.eclipse.pde" value="activated"/>` would cause an object contribution to be visible only if the `org.eclipse.pde` plug-in has been activated in some other manner.

systemProperty—Compares the system property. For example, if an object contribution should only be visible when the language is English, then the expression would be `<systemProperty name="user.language" value="en"/>`

6.3.2.3   *The filter element*

The **filter** element is a simpler alternate form of the **objectState** element discussed previously. For example, if our object contribution was to be available for any non-read-only file, then the object contribution could be expressed like this:

```
<objectContribution …>
   <filter name="readOnly" value="false"/>
   … the other stuff here …
</objectContribution>
```

As with the **objectState** element, the **filter** element uses the `IActionFilter` interface to determine whether or not an object in the selection matches the criteria. Each selected object must either implement or adapt to the `IAction-`

`Filter` interface (more on adapters in Chapter 20, "Advanced Topics") and implement the appropriate behavior in the `testAttribute(...)` method to test the specified name/value pair against the state of the specified object. For resources, Eclipse provides the following built-in state comparisons as listed in the `org.eclipse.ui.IResourceActionFilter` class:

name—Comparison of the filename. "*" may be used at the start or end to represent "one or more characters."

extension—Comparison of the file extension.

path—Comparison against the file path. "*" may be used at the start or end to represent "one or more characters."

readOnly—Comparison of the read-only attribute of a file.

projectNature—Comparison of the project nature.

persistentProperty—Comparison of a persistent property on the selected resource. If the value is a simple string, then this tests for the existence of the property on the resource. If it has the format `propertyName=proper-tyValue`, this obtains the value of the property with the specified name and tests it for equality with the specified value.

projectPersistentProperty—Comparison of a persistent property on the selected resource's project with similar semantics to the `persistent-Property` listed above.

sessionProperty—Comparison of a session property on the selected resource with similar semantics to the `persistentProperty` listed above.

projectSessionProperty—Comparison of a session property on the selected resource's project with similar semantics to the `persistent-Property` listed above.

6.3.2.4   The selection element

The **selection** element is a technique for enabling an individual action based on its name and type, similar to the way that the **nameFilter** and **objectClass** attributes determine whether or not all actions in an object contribution are visible. For example, an alternate form for our object contribution using the **selection** element would be:

```
<objectContribution
      objectClass="java.lang.Object"
      id="com.qualityeclipse.favorites.popupMenu">
   <action
        label="Add to Favorites"
        tooltip="Add the selected resource(s) to the
                Favorites view"
```

```
        class="com.qualityeclipse.favorites.actions.
              AddToFavoritesActionDelegate"
        menubarPath="additions"
        enablesFor="+"
        id="com.qualityeclipse.favorites.addToFavorites">
    <selection
          class="org.eclipse.core.resources.IResource"
          name="*.java"/>
    </action>
</objectContribution>
```

With this declaration, the object contribution's actions would always be visible, but the **Add to Favorites** action would only be enabled if the selection contained only implementers of IResource that matched the name filter `*.java`.

6.3.2.5 *The enablement element*

The **enablement** element is a more powerful alternative to the **selection** element, supporting the same complex conditional logic expressions and comparisons as the **visibility** element. For example, an alternate object contribution declaration to the one outlined in the previous section but producing the same behavior would be:

```
<objectContribution
      objectClass="java.lang.Object"
      id="com.qualityeclipse.favorites.popupMenu">
    <action
        label="Add to Favorites"
        tooltip="Add the selected resource(s)
                to the Favorites view"
        class="com.qualityeclipse.favorites.actions.
              AddToFavoritesActionDelegate"
        menubarPath="additions"
        enablesFor="+"
        id="com.qualityeclipse.favorites.addToFavorites">
    <enablement>
        <and>
          <objectClass
            name="org.eclipse.core.resources.IResource"/>
          <objectState name="name" value="*.java"/>
        </and>
    </enablement>
    </action>
</objectContribution>
```

6.3.2.6   *Content-sensitive object contributions*

There is a new mechanism for filtering actions based on resource content. This filtering is specified in the plug-in manifest (does not load your plug-in) and determines whether or not an action should be visible or enabled by inspecting a file's content. For example, the **Run Ant...** command is associated with resources named `build.xml`, but no others; what if your Ant script is located in a file called `export.xml`? This new mechanism can determine whether or not the **Run Ant...** command should be visible based on the first XML tag or DTD specified in the file. This functionality is evolving, so for more information, navigate to **www.eclipse.org > projects > The Eclipse Project > Platform > UI > Development Resources > Content Sensitive Object Contributions,** or browse *dev.eclipse.org/viewcvs/index.cgi/~checkout~/platform-ui-home/object-aware-contributions/objCont.htm.*

6.3.3   *IObjectActionDelegate*

Getting back to our **Favorites** plug-in, the next task is to create an action delegate that implements the `IObjectActionDelegate` interface, which performs the operation behind the new **Add to Favorites** menu item. Create a new `AddToFavoritesActionDelegate` class as shown below. Since the **Favorites** view is not fully functional, the action displays a message rather than adding the selected items to the view (see Section 7.3.1, "Model actions," for more implementation details):

```
package com.qualityeclipse.favorites.actions;

import java.util.*;
import org.eclipse.jface.action.*;
import org.eclipse.jface.viewers.*;
import org.eclipse.ui.*;
import com.qualityeclipse.favorites.model.*;

public class AddToFavoritesActionDelegate
   implements IObjectActionDelegate
{
   private IWorkbenchPart targetPart;

   /**
    * Sets the active part for the delegate.
    * This method will be called every time
    * the action appears in a context menu.
    * The targetPart may change with each invocation.
    */
   public void setActivePart(IAction action,
      IWorkbenchPart targetPart) {

      this.targetPart = targetPart;
   }
```

```
public void selectionChanged(
   IAction action,
   ISelection selection) {
}

public void run(IAction action) {
   MessageDialog.openInformation(
      targetPart.getSite().getShell(),
      "Add to Favorites",
      "Triggered the "
         + getClass().getName()
         + " action");
   }
}
```

6.3.4 Creating an object-based submenu

Menus can be contributed to a context menu in a manner that is similar to
adding actions. If three or more similar actions are contributed, then think
about placing those actions in a submenu rather than in the context menu
itself. The **Favorites** plug-in only adds one action to the context menu, but let's
place the action in a submenu rather than in the context menu itself.

To create the **Favorites** menu, right-click on the **com.qualityeclipse.favor-
ites.popupMenu** object contribution in the **Extensions** page of the plug-in
manifest editor, and select **New > menu**. In the **Properties** view, enter the following values for this new menu:

id—"com.qualityeclipse.favorites.popupSubMenu"
The identifier for the submenu.

label—"Favorites"
The text appearing in the context menu as the name of the submenu.

path—"additions"
The insertion point that determines the location in the context menu
where the submenu will appear (see Section 6.2.5).

Next, add a **groupMarker** to the menu with the name "content" and a
separator with the name "additions" (see Section 6.2.2, "Groups in a menu").
Finally, modify the **Add to Favorites** action's attributes as follows so that the
action will now be part of the new **Favorites** submenu:

label—"Add"
The text appearing in the submenu as the name of the action.

menubarPath—"com.qualityeclipse.favorites.popupSubMenu/content"
The insertion point that determines where the **Favorites** submenu action
will appear (see Section 6.2.5).

6.3.5   Manually testing the new action

When the **Favorites Runtime Workbench** configuration is launched (see Chapter 2, Section 2.6, "Debugging the Product"), any context menu activated on a workbench resource will contain the **Favorites** menu with the **Add** submenu item. Selecting this submenu item displays a message box notifying you that the action was indeed triggered correctly.

6.3.6   Adding a test for the new action

The last task is to create an automated test that triggers the action and validates the result. Because this operation displays a message rather than adding a resource to the **Favorites** view, the code that validates the results of this test will have to wait until the next chapter, where the **Favorites** view will be more fully developed. For now, create the following new test case in the **Favorites** test project (see Section 2.8.2, "Creating a plug-in test project") and then modify the **Favorites** test suite to include this new test (see Section 6.2.8, "Adding a test for the new action"):

```
package com.qualityeclipse.favorites.test;

import org.eclipse.core.resources.*;
import org.eclipse.core.runtime.*;
import org.eclipse.jface.action.*;
import org.eclipse.jface.viewers.*;
import org.eclipse.ui.*;
import org.eclipse.ui.part.*;
import com.qualityeclipse.favorites.actions.*;

public class AddToFavoritesTest
extends AbstractFavoritesTest
{
    protected IProject project;

    public AddToFavoritesTest(String name) {
        super(name);
    }

    protected void setUp() throws Exception {
        super.setUp();
        IWorkspaceRoot root =
            ResourcesPlugin.getWorkspace().getRoot();
        project = root.getProject("TestProj");
        project.create(null);
        project.open(null);
    }

    protected void tearDown() throws Exception {
        super.tearDown();

        // Wait for a bit for the system to catch up
        // so that the delete operation does not collide
```

```
            // with any background tasks.
            delay(3000);
            waitForJobs();

            project.delete(true, true, null);
        }

        public void testAddToFavorites() throws CoreException {

            // Show the resource navigator and select the project.
            IViewPart navigator =
                PlatformUI.getWorkbench()
                    .getActiveWorkbenchWindow()
                    .getActivePage()
                    .showView(
                        "org.eclipse.ui.views.ResourceNavigator");
            StructuredSelection selection =
                new StructuredSelection(project);
            ((ISetSelectionTarget) navigator)
                .selectReveal(selection);

            // Execute the action.
            final IObjectActionDelegate delegate =
                new AddToFavoritesActionDelegate();
            IAction action = new Action("Test Add to Favorites") {
                public void run() {
                    delegate.run(this);
                }
            };
            delegate.setActivePart(action, navigator);
            delegate.selectionChanged(action, selection);
            action.run();

            // Add code here at a later time to verify that the
            // Add to Favorites action correctly added the
            // appropriate values to the Favorites view.
        }
    }
```

6.4   View Actions

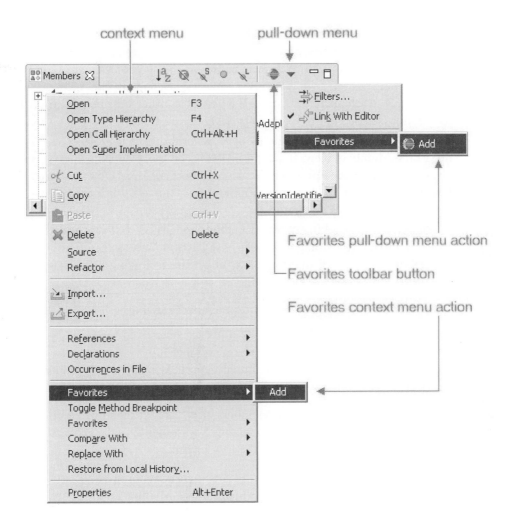

Figure 6–9   View actions.

There are several ways in which actions can be manifested as part of a view. For example, the **Members** view has toolbar buttons that appear in its title bar, a pull-down menu appearing at the right of the toolbar buttons, and a context menu containing yet more actions (see Figure 6–9). Actions are added to views using the extension point mechanism, similar to the discussions in the previous two sections. In addition, views can programmatically provide their own actions, bypassing the extension point mechanism (see Section 7.3, "View Actions").

6.4.1   *Defining a view context submenu*

Similar to an objectContribution, a viewerContribution is used to add a
menu item to a context menu. Whereas an objectContribution causes a
menu item to appear based on the selection in the viewer, a viewerContribution causes a menu item to appear based on the type of viewer. As with an
objectContribution, the viewerContribution element can have a single
visibility subelement that controls when all its other subelements are visible
to the user (see Section 6.3.2.2, "The visibility element").

The **Favorites** submenu shows up in several different types of views, but
not in the **Members** view. It would probably be more appropriate to use the
objectContribution approach discussed in Section 6.3, "Object Actions," to
target objects contained in the **Members** view, but we'll use the viewerContribution instead as an example.

Start by right-clicking on the popupMenu extension that was added as part
of Section 6.3.1, "Defining an object-based action," and select **New > viewer-
Contribution**. In the **Properties** view, fill in the following attributes for the
newly added viewerContribution:

> **id**—"com.qualityeclipse.favorites.membersViewPopup"
> The identifier for this view contribution.

> **targetID**—"org.eclipse.jdt.ui.MembersView"
> The identifier of the view's context menu to which the submenu will be
> added (see Section 20.6, "Modifying Eclipse to Find Part Identifiers").

Add the **Favorites** menu to the **Members** view context menu by right-clicking
on the viewerContribution and selecting **New > menu**. In the **Properties** view,
enter the following attributes for the new menu:

> **id**—"com.qualityeclipse.favorites.membersViewPopupSubMenu"
> The identifier for the **Favorites** menu in the **Members** view context
> menu.

> **label**—"Favorites"
> The text appearing in the **Members** view context menu as the name of
> the **Favorites** submenu.

> **path**—"additions"
> The insertion point that determines the location in the **Members** view
> context menu where the **Favorites** submenu will appear (see Section
> 6.2.5).

Next, add a **groupMarker** to the menu with the name "content" and a
separator with the name "additions" (see Section 6.2.2).

6.4.2   Defining a view context menu action

Finally, add an action to the **Favorites** submenu by right-clicking on the `viewerContribution`, selecting **New > action**, and entering the following attributes for the new action:

> **class**—"com.qualityeclipse.favorites.actions.AddToFavoritesActionDelegate"
> The fully qualified name of the class that implements the `org.eclipse.ui.IViewActionDelegate` interface and performs the action. In this case, the same action delegate used in the object contribution is used here as well, with a few modifications (see Section 6.4.3, "IViewActionDelegate"). The class is instantiated using its no argument constructor, but may be parameterized using the `IExecutableExtension` interface (see Section 20.5).

> **id**—"com.qualityeclipse.favorites.addToFavoritesInMembersView"
> The identifier for the action.

> **label**—"Add"
> The name of the action as it appears in the **Favorites** submenu.

> **menubarPath**—"com.qualityeclipse.favorites.membersViewPopupSubMenu/content"
> The insertion point that determines the location in the **Favorites** submenu where the action will appear (see Section 6.2.5). If the action is to appear directly in the **Members** view context menu rather than in the **Favorites** submenu, use the value "additions" instead.

> **tooltip**—"Add selected member's compilation unit to the Favorites view"
> The text describing the action.

Other action attributes applicable but not used here include:

> **enablesFor**—An expression indicating when the action will be enabled (see Section 6.3.2).

> **helpContextId**—The identifier for the help context associated with the action (see Chapter 15).

> **icon**—The associated image (see Section 6.2.4).

> **overrideActionId**—An optional attribute specifying the identifier for an action that the action overrides.

> **state**—For an action with either the `radio` or `toggle` style, set the initial state to `true` or `false` (see Section 6.2.3).

style—An attribute defining the visual form of the action. This is covered in Section 6.2.3, with the exception that the `pulldown` style does not apply to object contributions.

6.4.3   IViewActionDelegate

The action delegate for a view contribution must implement the `org.eclipse.ui.IViewActionDelegate` interface, so we must modify the `AddToFavoritesActionDelegate` class first introduced in Section 6.3.3. First, add the `IViewActionDelegate` interface to the implements clause, and then add the following method. All other aspects of the action delegate stay the same.

```
/**
 * Initializes this action delegate
 * with the view it will work in.
 *
 * @param view the view that provides
 * the context for this delegate
 * @see org.eclipse.ui.IViewActionDelegate
 * #init(org.eclipse.ui.IViewPart)
 */
public void init(IViewPart view) {
    targetPart = view;
}
```

6.4.4   Defining a view toolbar action

In addition to being in the **Favorites** submenu, we want our action to appear as a toolbar button in the **Members** view (see Section 7.3.3, "Toolbar buttons," to programmatically add a toolbar button to a view). As in Sections 6.2.1, 6.2.2, and 6.2.3, use the **Extensions** page of the plug-in manifest editor to create the new view contribution. Click the **Add** button to add an **org.eclipse.ui.viewActions** extension, then add a **viewContribution** to that with the following attributes:

> **id**—"com.qualityeclipse.favorites.membersViewActions"
> The identifier for the view contribution.
>
> **targeted**—"org.eclipse.jdt.ui.MembersView"
> The identifier of the view to which the actions are added.

Next, add an action to the **Members** view toolbar by right-clicking on the `viewContribution`, selecting **New > action**, and then entering the attributes shown below for the new action. All the `objectContribution` action attributes listed in Section 6.3.1 also apply to `viewContribution` actions.

> **class**—"com.qualityeclipse.favorites.actions.AddToFavoritesActionDelegate"

The fully qualified name of the class that implements the
org.eclipse.ui.IViewActionDelegate interface and performs the
action. In this case, the same action delegate used in the object contribution is used here as well, with a few modifications (see Section 6.4.3).

icon—"icons/sample.gif"
The icon displayed in the view's toolbar for the action.

id—"com.qualityeclipse.favorites.addToFavoritesInMembersView"
The identifier for the action.

toolbarPath—"additions"
The insertion point that determines the location in the **Members** view's
toolbar where the action will appear (see Section 6.2.5).

tooltip—"Add the selected items in the Members view to the Favorites
view"
The text describing the action appearing in the hover help when the cursor is positioned over the toolbar button associated with the action.

6.4.5   Defining a view pull-down submenu and action

The same viewContribution extension described in the previous section is
used to add a view pull-down submenu (see Section 7.3.2, "Context menu,"
for programmatically creating a view pull-down menu). Typically, a view pull-
down menu contains actions specific to that view, such as sorting and filtering
actions. To add our **Favorites** submenu and action to the **Members** view pull-
down menu (not that it really needs to be there in addition to everywhere else
we've added it), right-click on the viewContribution extension, select **New >
menu,** and set the attributes of the newly created menu as follows:

id—"com.qualityeclipse.favorites.membersViewPulldownSubMenu"
The identifier for the **Favorites** menu in the **Members** view.

label—"Favorites"
The text appearing in the **Members** view pull-down menu as the name of
the **Favorites** submenu.

path—"additions"
The insertion point that determines the location in the **Members** view
pull-down menu where the **Favorites** submenu will appear (see Section
6.2.5).

Next, add a **groupMarker** to the menu with the name "content" and a
separator with the name "additions" (see Section 6.2.2). Finally, the action
defined in Section 6.4.4, "Defining a view toolbar action," can be modified to

define a menu item in the menu we just created as well as the toolbar button it already described by modifying some of its attributes:

label—"Add"
The name of the action appearing in the **Favorites** submenu.

menubarPath—"com.qualityeclipse.favorites.membersViewPulldown-SubMenu/content"
The insertion point that determines the location in the **Favorites** submenu where the action will appear (see Section 6.2.5). If the action was to appear directly in the **Members** view pull-down menu rather than in the **Favorites** submenu, we would have to use a value of "additions" instead.

6.4.6 Manually testing the new actions

When the modifications to the plug-in manifest and the action delegate are complete, launching the **Runtime Workbench** and inspecting the **Members** view will show the new **Favorites** submenu and **Add to Favorites** toolbar button.

6.4.7 Adding tests for the new actions

There is no need for any additional test cases other than the ones created in Section 6.3.6, "Adding a test for the new action," because we are reusing the same action delegate. Once the **Favorites** view is fleshed out as part of Chapter 7, "Views," we'll add additional tests for new types of selections to the test case outlined in Section 6.3.6.

6.4.8 View context menu identifiers

Below are the context menu identifiers for some Eclipse views. For more information on how this table was generated, see Section 20.6.

Ant
```
id = org.eclipse.ant.ui.views.AntView
menuId = org.eclipse.ant.ui.views.AntView
```

Breakpoints
```
id = org.eclipse.debug.ui.BreakpointView
menuId = org.eclipse.debug.ui.BreakpointView
```

Console
```
id = org.eclipse.ui.console.ConsoleView
menuId = org.eclipse.ui.console.ConsoleView
```

Debug

```
id = org.eclipse.debug.ui.DebugView
menuId = org.eclipse.debug.ui.DebugView
```

Display

```
id = org.eclipse.jdt.debug.ui.DisplayView
menuId = org.eclipse.jdt.debug.ui.DisplayView
```

Expressions

```
id = org.eclipse.debug.ui.ExpressionView
menuId = org.eclipse.debug.ui.VariableView.detail
menuId = org.eclipse.debug.ui.ExpressionView
```

Members

```
id = org.eclipse.jdt.ui.MembersView
menuId = org.eclipse.jdt.ui.MembersView
```

Navigator

```
id = org.eclipse.ui.views.ResourceNavigator
menuId = org.eclipse.ui.views.ResourceNavigator
```

Package Explorer

```
id = org.eclipse.jdt.ui.PackageExplorer
menuId = org.eclipse.jdt.ui.PackageExplorer
```

Packages

```
id = org.eclipse.jdt.ui.PackagesView
menuId = org.eclipse.jdt.ui.PackagesView
```

Projects

```
id = org.eclipse.jdt.ui.ProjectsView
menuId = org.eclipse.jdt.ui.ProjectsView
```

Tasks

```
id = org.eclipse.ui.views.TaskList
menuId = org.eclipse.ui.views.TaskList
```

Threads and Monitors

```
id = org.eclipse.jdt.debug.ui.MonitorsView
menuId = org.eclipse.jdt.debug.ui.MonitorsView
menuId = org.eclipse.jdt.debug.ui.MonitorsView
menuId = org.eclipse.jdt.debug.ui.MonitorsView
```

Types

```
id = org.eclipse.jdt.ui.TypesView
menuId = org.eclipse.jdt.ui.TypesView
```

Variables

```
id = org.eclipse.debug.ui.VariableView
menuId = org.eclipse.debug.ui.VariableView.detail
menuId = org.eclipse.debug.ui.VariableView
```

6.5   Editor Actions

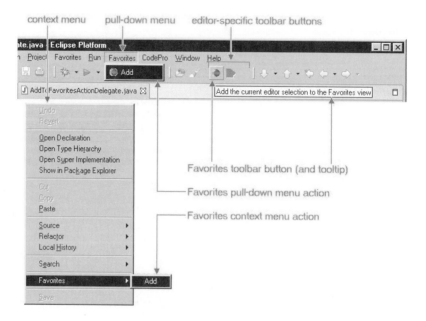

Figure 6–10   Editor actions.

Actions can be added to editors similar to the way they are added to views. For example, the Java editor has a context menu, so naturally we want our **Favorites** action to show up there, regardless of whether or not it's really needed. In addition, editors can add actions to themselves, bypassing the standard extension point mechanism. Some related sections include:

- Section 8.5, "Editor Actions," for more on editor actions

- Section 14.2.4, "Marker resolution—quick fix," for an example of manipulating text in an editor

- Chapter 17, "Creating New Extension Points," for more on extension points

6.5.1   Defining an editor context menu

To add our **Favorites** menu to the Java editor's context menu, revisit the **popupMenus** extension declared in Section 6.3.1, right-click, and select **New > viewerContribution**. Enter the following attributes in the **Properties** view for the new viewer contribution. As with object contributions, the visibility subelement can be used to control when the menu and actions appear in the editor's context menu (see Section 6.3.2.2).

id—"com.qualityeclipse.favorites.compilationUnitEditorPopup"
The identifier for the viewer contribution.

targetID—"#CompilationUnitEditorContext"
The identifier of the editor's context menu to which the actions will be added (see Section 20.6).

Next, create the **Favorites** submenu in the editor's context menu by right-clicking on the new viewer contribution extension and selecting **New > menu**. Enter the following attributes for the new menu declaration:

id—"com.qualityeclipse.favorites.compilationUnitEditorPopupSub-Menu"
The identifier for the **Favorites** menu in the editor's context menu.

label—"Favorites"
The text appearing in the editor's context menu as the name of the **Favorites** submenu.

path—"additions"
The insertion point that determines the location in the editor's context menu where the **Favorites** submenu will appear (see Section 6.2.5).

Next, add a **groupMarker** to the menu with the name "content" and a **separator** with the name "additions" (see Section 6.2.2).

6.5.2   *Defining an editor context action*

Add the **Add to Favorites** action to the **Favorites** submenu by right-clicking on the viewer contribution defined in Section 6.5.1 and selecting **New > action**. Enter the following action attributes:

class—"com.qualityeclipse.favorites.actions.AddToFavoritesActionDelegate"
The fully qualified name of the class that implements the org.eclipse.ui.IEditorActionDelegate interface and performs the action. In this case, the same action delegate used in the object contribution is used here as well, with a few modifications (see Section 6.5.4). The class is instantiated using its no argument constructor, but may be parameterized using the IExecutableExtension interface (see Section 20.5).

id—"com.qualityeclipse.favorites.addToFavoritesInCompilationUnitEditor"

The identifier for the action.

label—"Add"

The name of the action appearing in the **Favorites** submenu.

menubarPath—"com.qualityeclipse.favorites.compilationUnitEditor-PopupSubMenu/content"

The insertion point that determines the location in the **Favorites** submenu where the action will appear (see Section 6.2.5). To make the action appear directly in the editor's context menu rather than in the **Favorites** submenu, use a value of "additions" instead.

Other action attributes not listed here are the same as for viewer contributions outlined in Section 6.4.2, "Defining a view context menu action."

6.5.3   *EditorActionDelegate*

The action delegate for an editor contribution must implement the org.eclipse.ui.IEditorActionDelegate interface, so we must modify the AddToFavoritesActionDelegate class first introduced in Section 6.3.3, "IObjectActionDelegate." First add the IEditorActionDelegate interface to the implements clause, and then add the following method. All other aspects of the action delegate can stay the same.

```
/**
 * Sets the active editor for the delegate.
 * Implementors should disconnect from the old editor,
 * connect to the new editor, and update the action
 * to reflect the new editor.
 *
 * @param action the action proxy that handles
 * presentation portion of the action
 * @param targetEditor the new editor target
 * @see org.eclipse.ui.IEditorActionDelegate
 * #setActiveEditor(
 * org.eclipse.jface.action.IAction,
 * org.eclipse.ui.IEditorPart)
 */
public void setActiveEditor(
   IAction action,
   IEditorPart targetEditor) {
   targetPart = targetEditor;
}
```

6.5.4 *Defining an editor top-level menu*

Using the `org.eclipse.ui.editorActions` extension point, we can define a workbench window menu and toolbar button that are only visible when an editor of a particular type is open. As discussed in Section 6.2.9, think twice before adding menus or toolbar buttons to the workbench window itself. Our **Favorites** example doesn't really need this, but we'll take you through the process as a matter of course.

To start, click the **Add** button in the **Extensions** page of the plug-in manifest editor and add a new `org.eclipse.ui.editorActions` extension. Right-click on the new extension and select **New > editorContribution,** then enter the following `editorContribution` attributes:

> **id**—"com.qualityeclipse.favorites.compilationUnitEditorActions"
> The identifier for the editor contribution.

> **targetID**—"org.eclipse.jdt.ui.CompilationUnitEditor"
> The identifier of the type of editor that should be open for these menus and actions to be visible.

Add the **Favorites** menu by right-clicking on `editorContribution` and selecting **New > menu.** In the **Properties** view, enter the following attributes for the new menu:

> **id**—"com.qualityeclipse.favorites.compilationUnitEditorPopupSub-Menu"
> The identifier for the **Favorites** menu.

> **label**—"Favorites"
> The text appearing in the workbench window menu bar as the name of the **Favorites** submenu.

> **path**—"additions"
> The insertion point that determines the location in the workbench window menu bar where the **Favorites** submenu will appear (see Section 6.2.5).

Next, add a **groupMarker** to the menu with the name "content" and a **separator** with the name "additions" (see Section 6.2.2).

6.5.5 *Defining an editor top-level action*

Add an action to the **Favorites** menu by right-clicking on the `editorContribution`, selecting **New > action,** and entering the following attributes shown for the new action. Similar to object contributions, the `selection` and `enablement` elements can be used to limit the visibility and enablement of the action (see Sections 6.3.2.4, "The selection element," and 6.3.2.5, "The enablement element").

class—"com.qualityeclipse.favorites.actions.AddToFavoritesActionDelegate"
The fully qualified name of the class that implements the `org.eclipse.ui.IEditorActionDelegate` interface and performs the action. In this case, the same action delegate used in the object contribution is used here as well, with a few modifications (see Section 6.5.4).

id—"com.qualityeclipse.favorites.addToFavoritesInCompilationUnitEditor"
The identifier for the action.

label—"Add"
The text appearing in the **Favorites** menu for the action.

menubarPath—"com.qualityeclipse.favorites.compilationUnitEditorPopupSubMenu/content"
The insertion point indicating where the menu will be positioned in the menu bar (see Section 6.2.5).

Other available action attributes not used in this example include:

accelerator—Deprecated; see `definitionId`.

definitionId—The command identifier for the action, allowing a key sequence to be associated with the action. See Section 6.7 for more details.

enablesFor—An expression indicating when the action will be enabled (covered in Section 6.3.2). If blank, then the action is always active unless overridden programmatically via the `IAction` interface.

helpContextId—The identifier for the help context associated with the action (covered in Chapter 15).

hoverIcon—An image displayed when the mouse *hovers* over the action without being clicked (see Section 6.2.4 for more detail).

icon—The associated image (see Section 6.2.4 for more detail).

state—For an action with either the `radio` or `toggle` style, set the initial state to `true` or `false` (see Section 6.2.3).

style—An attribute that defines the visual form of the action, and having one of the following values:

    `push`—A normal menu or toolbar item (the default style).
    `radio`—A radio button-style menu or toolbar item where only one

item at a time in a group can be active (see the `state` attribute). `toggle`—A checked menu item or toggle tool item (see the `state` attribute).

toolbarPath—The insertion point indicating where the button will appear in the toolbar (see Section 6.2.5 for more detail).

tooltip—The text appearing when the mouse hovers over the action's icon in the workbench toolbar.

6.5.6   *Defining an editor toolbar action*

Similar to the way that workbench menu actions can be displayed as toolbar buttons, the editor action defined in Section 6.5.5 can be modified to show up in the workbench window toolbar by making the following modifications to its attributes:

`icon`—"icons/sample.gif"

`toolbarPath`—"Normal/additions"

`tooltip`—"Add the editor selection to the Favorites view"

6.5.7   *Adding tests for the new actions*

As stated in Section 6.4.7, "Adding tests for the new actions," we'll add tests in Chapter 7 for new types of selections to the same test case outlined in Section 6.3.6, "Adding a test for the new action."

6.5.8   *Editor context menu identifiers*

Below are the context menu identifiers for some Eclipse editors. For more information on how this table was generated, see Section 20.6.

Ant Editor (build.xml)
```
id = org.eclipse.ant.ui.internal.editor.AntEditor
menuId = #TextEditorContext
menuId = #TextRulerContext
```

Class File Editor (*.class)
```
id = org.eclipse.jdt.ui.ClassFileEditor
menuId = #ClassFileEditorContext
menuId = #ClassFileRulerContext
```

Compilation Unit Editor (*.java)
```
id = org.eclipse.jdt.ui.CompilationUnitEditor
menuId = #CompilationUnitEditorContext
menuId = #CompilationUnitRulerContext
```

Default Text Editor

```
id = org.eclipse.ui.DefaultTextEditor
menuId = #TextEditorContext
menuId = #TextRulerContext
```

Snippet Editor (*.jpage)

```
id = org.eclipse.jdt.debug.ui.SnippetEditor
menuId = #JavaSnippetEditorContext
menuId = #JavaSnippetRulerContext
```

6.6 Key Bindings

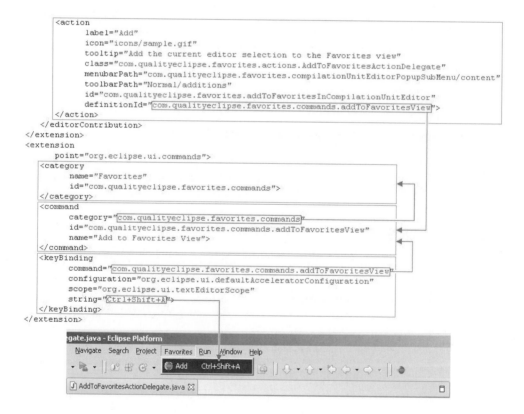

Figure 6–11   Key binding declaration.

Both workbench actions and editor actions can have accelerator keys associated with them (see Section 7.3.5, "Keyboard actions," for how to programmatically associate accelerator keys). Originally, the accelerator was specified as part of the action declaration, but that approach did not prevent multiple actions from declaring the same accelerator and did not allow the user to change key bindings. The new approach involves associating actions and key bindings with commands and grouping those commands into categories (see Figure 6–11). In addition, each command has a scope indicating when it will be available to the user, and is part of a configuration so that the user can select between different configurations to get different key bindings (e.g., Emacs key bindings vs. Eclipse key bindings).

6.6.1   Categories

Categories are used to group commands for presentation to the user. Categories appear in the **Workbench > Keys** preference page in the **Command / Category** drop-down list. To add a key binding for our **Add to Favorites** action, first we need to define a category. Create a new `org.eclipse.ui.commands` extension (see Section 6.2.1), then right-click and select **New > category**. Enter the following attributes for the new category:

> **description**—"Favorites Commands"
> A description of the commands contained in the category.

> **id**—"com.qualityeclipse.favorites.commands"
> The unique identifier for the category.

> **name**—"Favorites"
> The text displayed to the user as the category name.

6.6.2   Commands

Commands are contained in categories and have key bindings associated with them. Actions then reference commands to associate key bindings. To add a command for our **Add to Favorites** action, right-click on the `org.eclipse.ui.commands` extension and select **New > command**. Enter the following attributes for the new command:

> **category**—"com.qualityeclipse.favorites.commands"
> The identifier for the category that contains the command.

> **description**—"Add the selection to the Favorites"
> A description of the command.

> **icon**—"icons/sample.gif"
> The icon associated with the command.

> **id**—"com.qualityeclipse.favorites.commands.addToFavoritesView"
> The unique identifier for the command.

name—"Add to Favorites View"
The human-readable name for the command.

6.6.3 *Key bindings*

Commands do not reference key bindings; rather, key bindings are declared separately and reference commands. This allows for multiple key bindings to be associated with the same command. For example, the default accelerator for saving the contents of a file is **Ctrl+S**, but after switching to the Emacs configuration, the save accelerator becomes **Ctrl+X Ctrl+S**.

To add an accelerator for our **Add to Favorites** action, right-click on the `org.eclipse.ui.commands` extension and select **New > keyBinding**. Enter the following attributes for the new key binding:

command—"com.qualityeclipse.favorites.commands.addToFavorites-View"
The command triggered by the key binding.

configuration—"org.eclipse.ui.defaultAcceleratorConfiguration"
The configuration containing the key binding. Typically, key bindings are added to the default Eclipse configuration, but alternate key bindings can be added to other configurations such as "org.eclipse.ui.emacsAccelera-torConfiguration". New configurations can be defined by declaring a new `keyConfiguration`.

scope—"org.eclipse.ui.textEditorScope"
The context in which the key binding is available to the user. Global key bindings use the "org.eclipse.ui.globalScope" scope, while text editor-specific key bindings use the "org.eclipse.ui.textEditorScope" scope. New scopes can be defined by declaring a new `scope`.

string—"Ctrl+Shift+A"
The human-readable text appearing after the menu item that indicates to the user the key combination to use to trigger the action.

Other key binding attributes that are not used in the **Favorites** example include:

locale—An optional attribute indicating that the key binding is only defined for a specified locale. Locales are specified according to the format declared in `java.util.Locale`.

platform—An optional attribute indicating that the key binding is only defined for the specified platform. The possible values of the platform attribute are the set of the possible values returned by `org.eclipse.swt.SWT.getPlatform()`.

6.6.4   Associating commands with actions

The final step in defining an accelerator for our **Favorites** example involves modifying the editor action defined in Section 6.5.5, "Defining an editor top-level action," to reference the new command created in Section 6.7.2, "Action enablement delay." Select the editor action in the plug-in manifest and modify the **definitionId** attribute to have the value "com.qualityeclipse.favorites.commands.addToFavoritesView" so that the action now references the new command and associated key binding.

6.6.5   Keyboard accessibility

The keyboard can be used to select menu items in the workbench window. For example, if you press and release the **Alt** key and then press and release F (or press **Alt+F**), you will see the workbench window **File** menu pop down. If you look closely, you will see an underscore under at most one letter in each menu label and menu item label. When you are in this menu selection mode, pressing the letter with the underscore will activate that menu or menu command. Under some platforms such as Windows XP, these underscores are not visible unless you activate menu selection mode.

In your plug-in manifest, you can specify which character in a menu's or menu item's label should have an underscore by preceding that character with the "&" character. For example, in the following declaration, the "&" before the letter "r" in the word "Favorites" causes that letter to have an underscore when you activate the menu selection mode (see Figure 6–12).

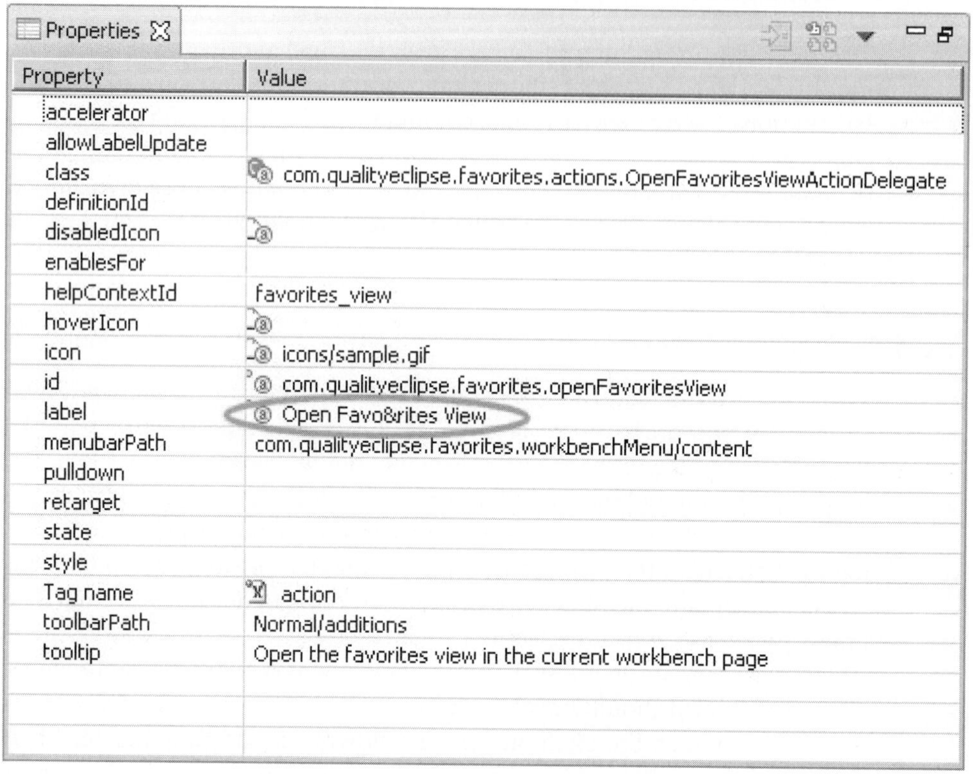

Figure 6–12   Properties view showing & for keyboard accessibility.

When viewing the XML for this same declaration, the "&" character appears as "&" because the "&" character has special meaning in XML.

```
<extension point="org.eclipse.ui.actionSets">
   <actionSet
      label="Favorites ActionSet"
      visible="true"
      id="com.qualityeclipse.favorites.workbenchActionSet">
      <action
         label="Open Favo&amp;rites View"
         icon="icons/sample.gif"
         helpContextId="favorites_view"
         class="com … OpenFavoritesViewActionDelegate"
         menubarPath="com … workbenchMenu/content"
         toolbarPath="Normal/additions"
         id="com … openFavoritesView"/>
```

If you use this same approach with the **Favorites** menu declaration (see Section 6.2.1), you can use a sequence of keystrokes to open the **Favorites** view without touching the mouse:

- Press and release the **Alt** key to enter menu selection mode.

- Press and release "v" to pop down the **Favorites** menu.

- Press and release "r" to activate the **Open Favorites View** action.

   or

- Press **Alt+V** to pop down the **Favorites** menu.

- Press and release "r" to activate the **Open Favorites View** action.

6.7   RFWS Considerations

Ready for WebSphere Studio Software   Starting with this chapter, we will list IBM's relevant RFWS certification requirements and briefly discuss what is required to pass each test. We will also endeavor to make sure that our ongoing Favorites example complies with any relevant requirements. The rule definitions themselves are quoted with permission from IBM's official *Ready for IBM WebSphere Studio Software Integration Requirements* document. To obtain more information about the RFWS program, see Appendix B, "The Ready for WebSphere Studio Validation Program," or visit the IBM Web site at *www.developer.ibm.com/Websphere/ready.html*.

The "User Interface" section of the *RFWS Requirements* includes two best practices dealing with actions. Both of them are derived from the Eclipse UI Guidelines.

6.7.1   Global action labels

User Interface Guideline #1 is a best practice that states:

*Adopt the labeling terminology of the workbench for **new**, **delete**, **add**, and **remove** actions. For consistency, any action that has a similar behavior to existing actions in the workbench should adopt the same terminology. When creating a resource, the term "**New**" should be used in an action or wizard. For instance, "**New File**", "**New Project**", and "**New Java Class**". The term "**Delete**" should be used when deleting an existing resource. When creating an object inside a resource (e.g., a tag in an XML file), the term "**Add**" should be used; the user is adding something to an existing resource. The term "**Remove**" should be used to remove an object from a resource.*

To pass this test, create a list of the actions defined by your application and demonstrate their use. Show that the terms "New," "Delete," "Add," and "Remove" are used properly and consistently with the workbench. In the case of the examples presented earlier in this chapter, we would show the **Favorites** editor actions (see Figure 6–10) and describe their use to the reviewers.

6.7.2   *Action enablement delay*

User Interface Guideline #2 is a best practice that states:

Action enablement should be quick. If action enablement cannot be quick, enable the action optimistically. If the action is invoked, it should calculate the real enablement and display an appropriate message if it cannot be completed.

In this case, *action enablement* is the process of determining whether or not a particular menu item should be enabled or disabled just before the menu that contains that item is displayed to the user. The time that it takes for each menu item to perform this calculation directly impacts how long the user has to wait between clicking the mouse and actually seeing the menu appear. If the determination of whether or not a menu item should be enabled involves a lengthy calculation such as accessing a remote machine over a network, then that menu item should be *optimistically enabled* rather than performing the lengthy calculation.

For this test, show any actions that are optimistically enabled to avoid unnecessary delays. If there are scenarios in which an action cannot be completed, show the error dialog that is displayed to the user.

6.8   Summary

An Eclipse user can trigger commands by using the workbench's pull-down menus or toolbar, or by using the context menus defined for various views. Each of these is an example of an action. In this chapter, we discussed how to create various actions and how to control their visibility and enablement state using filters.

References

Arsenault, Simon, "Contributing Actions to the Eclipse Workbench," 2003 (available on the *eclipse.org* Web site at *www.eclipse.org/articles*).

Shavor, Sherry, Jim D'Anjou, Scott Fairbrother, Dan Kehn, John Kellerman, and Pat McCarthy, *The Java Developer's Guide to Eclipse*, Addison Wesley, Boston, MA, 2003.

CHAPTER 7

Views

Many plug-ins either add a new Eclipse view or enhance an existing Eclipse view as a way to provide information to the user. This chapter covers creating a new view, modifying the view to respond to selections in the active editor or other views, and exporting the view's selection to the rest of Eclipse. In addition, we will briefly touch on the differences between editors and views, and when one should be used instead of the other.

Views must implement the `org.eclipse.ui.IViewPart` interface. Typically, views are subclasses of `org.eclipse.ui.part.ViewPart` and thus indirectly subclasses of `org.eclipse.ui.part.WorkbenchPart`, inheriting much of the behavior needed to implement the `IViewPart` interface (see Figure 7–1).

Views are contained in a *view site* (an instance of `org.eclipse.ui` `.IViewSite`), which in turn is contained in a *workbench page* (an instance of `org.eclipse.ui.IWorkbenchPage`). In the spirit of lazy initialization, the `IWorkbenchPage` holds on to instances of `org.eclipse.ui.IViewReference` rather than the view itself so that views can be enumerated and referenced without actually loading the plug-in defining the view.

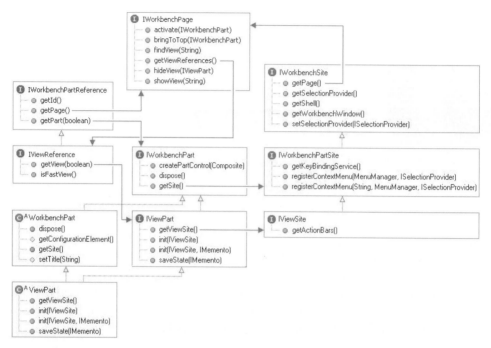

Figure 7–1   ViewPart classes.

Views share a common set of behaviors with editors via the
`org.eclipse.ui.part.WorkbenchPart` superclass and `org.eclipse.ui.`
`IWorkbenchPart` interface, but have some very important differences. Any
action performed in a view should immediately affect the state of the workspace and underlying resource(s), whereas editors follow the classic open-
modify-save paradigm. Editors appear in one area of Eclipse, while views are
arranged around the outside of the editor area (see Section 1.2.1, "Perspectives, views, and editors"). Editors are typically resource-based, while views
may show information about one resource, multiple resources, or even something totally unrelated to resources at all.

Because there are potentially hundreds of views in the workbench, views
are organized into categories. The **Show View** dialog presents a list of views
organized by category (see Section 2.5, "Installing and Running the Product")
so that a user can more easily find a desired view.

7.1   View Declaration

Three steps are involved in creating a new view:

- Define the view category in the plug-in manifest file.

- Define the view in the plug-in manifest file.

- Create the view part containing the code.

One way to do all this at once is to create the view when the plug-in itself is being created (see Section 2.2.3, "Define the view"). If the plug-in already exists, then this becomes a three-step process.

7.1.1 *Declaring a view category*

First, to define a new view category, edit the plug-in manifest and navigate to the **Extensions** page. Click the **Add...** button to add the org.eclipse .ui.views extension if it is not already present (see Figure 7–2). Right-click the org.eclipse.ui.views extension and select **New > category** to add a new category if one does not already exist.

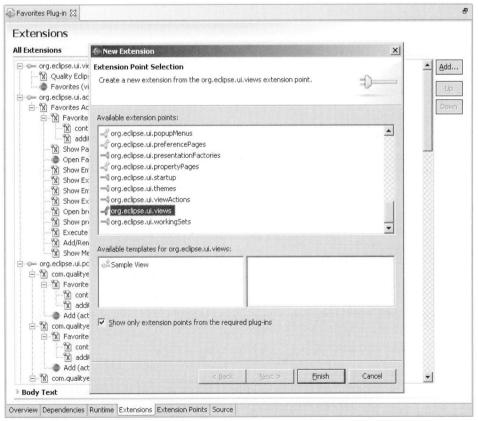

Figure 7–2 The New Extension wizard showing the org.eclipse.ui.views extension point selected.

The **Properties** view (see Figure 7–3) is used to modify the attributes of the category. For the category containing the **Favorites** view, the attributes would be as follows:

id—"com.qualityeclipse.favorites"
The unique identifier for the category.

name—"Quality Eclipse"
The human-readable name for the category that appears in the **Show View** dialog (see Figure 2–20 in Section 2.5).

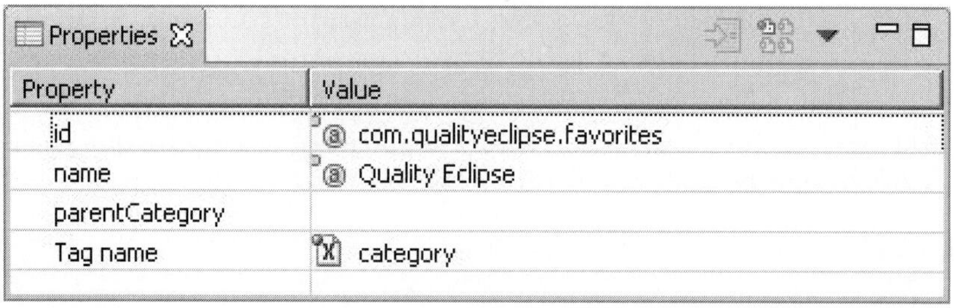

Figure 7–3   The Properties view showing the Quality Eclipse view category attributes.

7.1.2 Declaring a view

When the view category has been defined, right-click again on the `org.eclipse.ui.views` extension in the **Extensions** page and select **New > view** to define a new view. Use the **Properties** view (see Figure 7–4) to modify the attributes of the view. For the **Favorites** view, the attributes would be as follows:

category—"com.qualityeclipse.favorites"
The unique identifier for the view category that contains this view.

class—"com.qualityeclipse.favorites.views.FavoritesView"
The fully qualified name of the class defining the view and implementing the `org.eclipse.ui.IViewPart` interface. The class is instantiated using its no argument constructor, but may be parameterized using the `IExecutableExtension` interface (see Section 20.5, "Types Specified in an Extension Point").

icon—"icons/sample.gif"
The image displayed in the upper left corner of the view and in the **Show View** dialog (see Figure 2–20 in Section 2.5). Similar to an action image (see Section 6.2.4, "Action images"), this path is relative to the plug-in's installation directory.

id—"com.qualityeclipse.favorites.views.FavoritesView"
The unique identifier for this view.

name—"Favorites"
The human-readable name for the view displayed in the view's title bar
and the **Show View** dialog (see Figure 2–20 in Section 2.5).

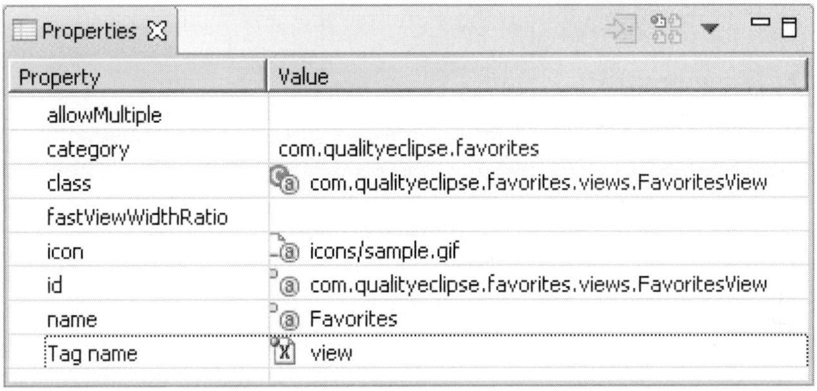

Figure 7–4   The Properties view showing the Favorites view attributes.

7.2   View Part

The code defining a view's behavior is found in a class implementing the
`org.eclipse.ui.IViewPart`   interface,   typically   by   subclassing   the
`org.eclipse.ui.part.ViewPart` abstract class.

Section 2.3.3, "The favorites view," reviewed the **Favorites** view in its simplest form.

7.2.1   View methods

`createPartControl(Composite)`—This method is *required* because it
creates the controls comprising the view. Typically, this method simply
calls more finely grained methods such as `createTable`, `createSortAc-
tions`, `createFilters`, and so on (see the next section).

`dispose()`—Cleans up any platform resources, such as images, clipboard, and so on, which were created by this class. This follows the *if
you create it, you destroy it* theme that runs throughout Eclipse.

`getAdapter(Class)`—Returns the adapter associated with the specified
interface so that the view can participate in various workbench actions.
Adapters returned by views include `IShowInSource`, `IShowInTarget`, and

IContributedContentsView, among others (see Section 20.3, "Adapters").

saveState(IMemento)—Saves the local state of this view, such as the current selection, current sorting, current filter, and so on (see Section 7.5.1, "Saving local view information").

setFocus()—This method is *required* because it sets focus to the appropriate control within the view (see the next section).

7.2.2 View controls

Views can contain any type and number of controls, but typically, a view such as the **Favorites** view contains a single table or tree control. The **Favorites** view could use the SWT table widget directly (org.eclipse.swt.widgets.Table [see Section 4.2.6.6, "Table"]), but the higher-level JFace table viewer (org.eclipse.jface.viewers.TableViewer [see Section 5.1.7, "TableViewer class"]) wraps the SWT table widget and is easier to use. It handles much of the underlying grunt work, allowing us to add, select, and remove our model objects directly rather than dealing with the underlying instances of Table-Item. With this in mind, we'll start by enhancing the createPartControl(...) method that was generated as part of building the Favorites plug-in (see Section 2.3.3) so that the table has three columns. The SWT.FULL_SELECTION style bit causes the entire row to be highlighted when the user makes a selection. Later, when we want to get more involved, we could auto-size the columns in the table (see Section 7.8, "Auto-sizing Table Columns") as follows:

```
viewer = new TableViewer(parent,
   SWT.H_SCROLL | SWT.V_SCROLL
   | SWT.MULTI | SWT.FULL_SELECTION);
final Table table = viewer.getTable();

TableColumn typeColumn =
   new TableColumn(table, SWT.LEFT);
typeColumn.setText("");
typeColumn.setWidth(18);

TableColumn nameColumn =
   new TableColumn(table, SWT.LEFT);
nameColumn.setText("Name");
nameColumn.setWidth(200);

TableColumn locationColumn =
   new TableColumn(table, SWT.LEFT);
locationColumn.setText("Location");
locationColumn.setWidth(450);

table.setHeaderVisible(true);
table.setLinesVisible(false);
```

7.2.3 View model

A view may have its own internal model such as the **Favorites** view, it may use existing model objects such as an IResource and its subtypes, or it may not have a model at all. In our case, we'll create:

- IFavoriteItem—An interface used to abstract the differences between different types of **Favorites** objects.

- FavoritesManager—Holds **Favorites** model objects.

- FavoriteResource—A class adapting a resource to the IFavoriteItem interface.

- FavoriteJavaElement—A class adapting a Java element to the IFavoriteItem interface.

The IFavoriteItem interface hides the differences between various types of Favorites objects. This enables the FavoritesManager and FavoritesView to deal with all Favorites items in a uniform manner. The naming convention we are following and which is used in many places throughout Eclipse is to prefix an interface with a capital "I" so that the interface name is IFavoriteItem rather than FavoriteItem, as one would expect.

```
package com.qualityeclipse.favorites.model;

public interface IFavoriteItem
{
    String getName();
    void setName(String newName);
    String getLocation();
    boolean isFavoriteFor(Object obj);
    FavoriteItemType getType();
    String getInfo();

    static IFavoriteItem[] NONE = new IFavoriteItem[] {};
}
```

The FavoriteItemType object returned by the getType() method is a type-safe enumeration that can be used for sorting and storing Favorites objects. It has a human-readable name associated with it for display purposes. Introducing the FavoriteItemType rather than a simple String or int allows the sort order to be separated from the human-readable name associated with a type of Favorites object. For now, these values are hard-coded, but in the future, these values will be defined by an extension point so that others can introduce new types of Favorites (see Section 17.3, "The Code behind an Extension Point").

Later, we will serialize **Favorites** items so they can be placed on the clip-board (see Section 7.3.7, "Clipboard actions") and saved to disk between Eclipse workbench sessions (see Section 7.5.2, "Saving global view informa-tion"). To this end, the getInfo() method for each item must return enough state so that the item can be correctly reconstructed later.

Since the workbench already provides images for various types of resources, the FavoriteItemType object simply returns the appropriate shared image. To return custom images for other types of Favorites objects, you could cache those images during the life of the plug-in and dispose of them when the plug-in is shut down (see Section 7.7, "Image Caching").

```
package com.qualityeclipse.favorites.model;

import org.eclipse.core.resources.*;
import org.eclipse.jdt.core.*;
import org.eclipse.swt.graphics.*;
import org.eclipse.ui.*;
import com.qualityeclipse.favorites.FavoritesLog;

public abstract class FavoriteItemType
   implements Comparable
{
   private static final ISharedImages PLATFORM_IMAGES =
      PlatformUI.getWorkbench().getSharedImages();

   ////////////// Constant Types //////////////

   public static final FavoriteItemType UNKNOWN =
      new FavoriteItemType("Unknown", "Unknown", 0) {
      public Image getImage() {
         return null;
      }
      public IFavoriteItem newFavorite(Object obj) {
         return null;
      }
      public IFavoriteItem loadFavorite(String info) {
         return null;
      }
   };

   public static final FavoriteItemType WORKBENCH_FILE =
      new FavoriteItemType(
         "WBFile", "Workbench File", 1) {
      public Image getImage() {
         return PLATFORM_IMAGES.getImage(
         org.eclipse.ui.ISharedImages.IMG_OBJ_FILE);
      }
      public IFavoriteItem newFavorite(Object obj) {
         if (!(obj instanceof IFile))
            return null;
         return new FavoriteResource(this, (IFile) obj);
      }
```

```
      public IFavoriteItem loadFavorite(String info) {
         return FavoriteResource.loadFavorite(this, info);
      }
};

public static final FavoriteItemType WORKBENCH_FOLDER =
   new FavoriteItemType(
      "WBFolder", "Workbench Folder", 2) {
      public Image getImage() {
         return PLATFORM_IMAGES.getImage(
         org.eclipse.ui.ISharedImages.IMG_OBJ_FOLDER);
      }
      public IFavoriteItem newFavorite(Object obj) {
         if (!(obj instanceof IFolder))
            return null;
         return new FavoriteResource(this, (IFolder) obj);
      }
      public IFavoriteItem loadFavorite(String info) {
         return FavoriteResource.loadFavorite(this, info);
      }
};

… more of the same …

//////////// Type Lookup /////////////////

private static final FavoriteItemType[] TYPES = {
   UNKNOWN,
   WORKBENCH_FILE,
   WORKBENCH_FOLDER,
   WORKBENCH_PROJECT,
   JAVA_PROJECT,
   JAVA_PACKAGE_ROOT,
   JAVA_PACKAGE,
   JAVA_CLASS_FILE,
   JAVA_COMP_UNIT,
   JAVA_INTERFACE,
   JAVA_CLASS,
};

public static FavoriteItemType[] getTypes() {
   return TYPES;
}

//////////// Instance Members /////////////

private final String id;
private final String printName;
private final int ordinal;

private FavoriteItemType(
   String id,
   String name,
   int position) {

   this.id = id;
```

```
         this.ordinal = position;
         this.printName = name;
      }

      public int compareTo(Object arg) {
         return this.ordinal
            -((FavoriteItemType) arg).ordinal;
      }

      public String getId() {
         return id;
      }

      public String getName() {
         return printName;
      }

      public abstract Image getImage();
      public abstract IFavoriteItem newFavorite(Object obj);
      public abstract IFavoriteItem loadFavorite(String info);
}
```

We want all **Favorites** views to show the same collection of **Favorites** objects, so the `FavoritesManager` is a singleton responsible for maintaining this global collection. Since more than one view will be accessing the information, the manager must be able to notify registered listeners when the information changes. The `FavoritesManager` will only be accessed from the UI thread, so we do not need to worry about thread safety (see Section 4.2.5.1, "Display," for more about the UI thread).

```
package com.qualityeclipse.favorites.model;

import java.util.*;
import org.eclipse.core.resources.*;

public class FavoritesManager {
   private static FavoritesManager manager;
   private Collection favorites;
   private List listeners = new ArrayList();

   private FavoritesManager() {}

   /////// IFavoriteItem Accessors ////////

   public static FavoritesManager getManager() {
      if (manager == null)
         manager = new FavoritesManager();
      return manager;
   }

   public IFavoriteItem[] getFavorites() {
      if (favorites == null)
         loadFavorites();
```

```
      return (IFavoriteItem[]) favorites.toArray(
         new IFavoriteItem[favorites.size()]);
   }

   public IFavoriteItem newFavoriteFor(Object obj) {
      FavoriteItemType[] types =
         FavoriteItemType.getTypes();
      for (int i = 0; i < types.length; i++) {
         IFavoriteItem item = types[i].newFavorite(obj);
         if (item != null)
            return item;
      }
      return null;
   }

   public IFavoriteItem[] newFavoritesFor(Iterator iter) {
      if (iter == null)
         return IFavoriteItem.NONE;
      Collection items = new HashSet(20);
      while (iter.hasNext()) {
         IFavoriteItem item =
            newFavoriteFor((Object) iter.next());
         if (item != null)
            items.add(item);
      }
      return (IFavoriteItem[]) items.toArray(
         new IFavoriteItem[items.size()]);
   }

   public IFavoriteItem[] newFavoritesFor(Object[] objects) {
      if (objects == null)
         return IFavoriteItem.NONE;
      return newFavoritesFor(
         Arrays.asList(objects).iterator());
   }

   public IFavoriteItem existingFavoriteFor(Object obj) {
      if (obj == null)
         return null;
      Object result;
      Iterator iter = favorites.iterator();
      while (iter.hasNext()) {
         IFavoriteItem item = (IFavoriteItem) iter.next();
         if (item.isFavoriteFor(obj))
            return item;
      }
      return null;
   }

   public IFavoriteItem[] existingFavoritesFor(Iterator iter)
   {
      List result = new ArrayList(10);
      while (iter.hasNext()) {
         IFavoriteItem item =
            existingFavoriteFor(iter.next());
```

```
        if (item != null)
            result.add(item);
    }
    return (IFavoriteItem[]) result.toArray(
        new IFavoriteItem[result.size()]);
}

public void addFavorites(IFavoriteItem[] items) {
    if (favorites == null)
        loadFavorites();
    if (favorites.addAll(Arrays.asList(items)))
        fireFavoritesChanged(items, IFavoriteItem.NONE);
}

public void removeFavorites(IFavoriteItem[] items) {
    if (favorites == null)
        loadFavorites();
    if (favorites.removeAll(Arrays.asList(items)))
        fireFavoritesChanged(IFavoriteItem.NONE, items);
}

private void loadFavorites() {
    // temporary implementation
    // to prepopulate list with projects
    IProject[] projects = ResourcesPlugin
        .getWorkspace().getRoot().getProjects();
    favorites = new HashSet(projects.length);
    for (int i = 0; i < projects.length; i++)
        favorites.add(new FavoriteResource(projects[i]));
}

/////// FavoriteManagerListener Methods ////////////
public void addFavoritesManagerListener(
    FavoritesManagerListener listener) {

    if (!listeners.contains(listener))
        listeners.add(listener);
}

public void removeFavoritesManagerListener(
    FavoritesManagerListener listener) {
    listeners.remove(listener);
}

private void fireFavoritesChanged(
    IFavoriteItem[] itemsAdded,
    IFavoriteItem[] itemsRemoved) {

    FavoritesManagerEvent event
        = new FavoritesManagerEvent(
            this, itemsAdded, itemsRemoved);
    for (Iterator iter = listeners.iterator();
        iter.hasNext();)
        ((FavoritesManagerListener) iter.next())
            .favoritesChanged(event);
}
}
```

In the future, the `FavoritesManager` will be enhanced to persist the list between Eclipse sessions (see Section 7.5.2), but for now, the list will be initialized with current workspace projects each time Eclipse starts. In addition, the current implementation will be extended in future chapters to include Favorites types added by other plug-ins (see Section 17.3).

The `FavoriteResource` wraps an `IResource` object, adapting it to the `IFavoriteItem` interface.

```java
package com.qualityeclipse.favorites.model;

import org.eclipse.core.resources.*;
import org.eclipse.core.runtime.*;

public class FavoriteResource
    implements IFavoriteItem
{
    private FavoriteItemType type;
    private IResource resource;
    private String name;

    FavoriteResource(
        FavoriteItemType type,
        IResource resource) {

        this.type = type;
        this.resource = resource;
    }

    public static FavoriteResource loadFavorite(
        FavoriteItemType type,
        String info) {

        IResource res = ResourcesPlugin
            .getWorkspace().getRoot()
            .findMember(new Path(info));
        if (res == null)
            return null;
        return new FavoriteResource(type, res);
    }

    public String getName() {
        if (name == null)
            name = resource.getName();
        return name;
    }

    public void setName(String newName) {
        name = newName;
    }

    public String getLocation() {
        IPath path =
            resource.getLocation().removeLastSegments(1);
```

```
      if (path.segmentCount() == 0)
         return "";
      return path.toString();
   }

   public boolean isFavoriteFor(Object obj) {
      return resource.equals(obj);
   }

   public FavoriteItemType getType() {
      return type;
   }

   public boolean equals(Object obj) {
      return this == obj
         || ((obj instanceof FavoriteResource)
            && resource.equals(
               ((FavoriteResource) obj).resource));
   }

   public int hashCode() {
      return resource.hashCode();
   }

   public Object getAdapter(Class adapter) {
      if (adapter.isInstance(resource))
         return resource;
      return Platform.getAdapterManager()
         .getAdapter(this, adapter);
   }

   public String getInfo() {
      return resource.getFullPath().toString();
   }
}
```

Similar to the `FavoriteResource`, the `FavoriteJavaElement` adapts an `IJavaElement` object to the `IFavoriteItem` interface. Before generating this class, you'll need to add the `org.eclipse.jdt.core` and `org.eclipse.jdt.ui` plug-ins to both the Favorites project's Java build path (see Section 1.4.2, ".classpath and .project files") and the Favorites plug-in's manifest (see Figure 7–5).

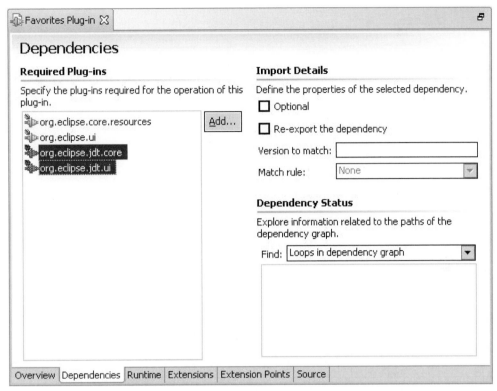

Figure 7–5 Plug-in manifest editor Dependencies page.

If the project is a plug-in project (see Section 2.2, "Creating a Plug-in Project"), modifying the plug-in's manifest causes the project's Java build path to be automatically updated.

```
package com.qualityeclipse.favorites.model;

import org.eclipse.core.resources.*;
import org.eclipse.core.runtime.*;
import org.eclipse.jdt.core.*;
import com.qualityeclipse.favorites.FavoritesLog;

public class FavoriteJavaElement
    implements IFavoriteItem
{
    private FavoriteItemType type;
    private IJavaElement element;
    private String name;

    public FavoriteJavaElement(
        FavoriteItemType type,
        IJavaElement element) {
```

```
      this.type = type;
      this.element = element;
   }

   public static FavoriteJavaElement loadFavorite(
      FavoriteItemType type,
      String info) {

      IResource res = ResourcesPlugin
         .getWorkspace().getRoot()
         .findMember(new Path(info));
      if (res == null)
         return null;
      IJavaElement elem = JavaCore.create(res);
      if (elem == null)
         return null;
      return new FavoriteJavaElement(type, elem);
   }

   public String getName() {
      if (name == null)
         name = element.getElementName();
      return name;
   }

   public void setName(String newName) {
      name = newName;
   }

   public String getLocation() {
      try {
         IResource res = element.getUnderlyingResource();
         if (res != null) {
            IPath path =
               res.getLocation().removeLastSegments(1);
            if (path.segmentCount() == 0)
               return "";
            return path.toString();
         }
      }
      catch (JavaModelException e) {
         FavoritesLog.logError(e);
      }
      return "";
   }

   public boolean isFavoriteFor(Object obj) {
      return element.equals(obj);
   }

   public FavoriteItemType getType() {
      return type;
   }
```

```
public boolean equals(Object obj) {
   return this == obj
      || ((obj instanceof FavoriteJavaElement)
         && element.equals(
            ((FavoriteJavaElement) obj).element));
}

public int hashCode() {
   return element.hashCode();
}

public Object getAdapter(Class adapter) {
   if (adapter.isInstance(element))
      return element;
   IResource resource = element.getResource();
   if (adapter.isInstance(resource))
      return resource;
   return Platform.getAdapterManager()
      .getAdapter(this, adapter);
}

public String getInfo() {
   try {
      return element.getUnderlyingResource()
         .getFullPath().toString();
   }
   catch (JavaModelException e) {
      FavoritesLog.logError(e);
      return null;
   }
}
}
```

7.2.4   Content provider

When the model objects have been created, they need to be linked into the view. A content provider is responsible for extracting objects from an input object, in this case, the FavoritesManager, and handing them to the table viewer for displaying, one object in each row of the table. Although the IStructuredContentProvider does not specify this, we will also make the content provider responsible for updating the viewer when the content of FavoritesManager changes.

After extracting the content provider that was automatically generated as part of the FavoritesView class (see Section 2.3.2, "The plug-in class") and reworking it to use the newly created FavoritesManager, it looks something like the following code:

```
package com.qualityeclipse.favorites.views;

import org.eclipse.jface.viewers.*;
import com.qualityeclipse.favorites.model.*;
```

```
class FavoritesViewContentProvider
   implements IStructuredContentProvider,
      FavoritesManagerListener
{
   private TableViewer viewer;
   private FavoritesManager manager;

   public void inputChanged(
      Viewer viewer,
      Object oldInput,
      Object newInput) {

      this.viewer = (TableViewer) viewer;
      if (manager != null)
         manager.removeFavoritesManagerListener(this);
      manager = (FavoritesManager) newInput;
      if (manager != null)
         manager.addFavoritesManagerListener(this);
   }

   public void dispose() {
   }

   public Object[] getElements(Object parent) {
      return manager.getFavorites();
   }

   public void favoritesChanged(FavoritesManagerEvent event)
   {
      viewer.getTable().setRedraw(false);
      try {
         viewer.remove(event.getItemsRemoved());
         viewer.add(event.getItemsAdded());
      }
      finally {
         viewer.getTable().setRedraw(true);
      }
   }
}
```

Tip: The method above uses the setRedraw method to reduce the flicker when adding and removing multiple items from the viewer.

Extracting and modifying the content provider means that the calls to setContentProvider and setInput in the createPartControl method have changed as follows:

```
viewer.setContentProvider(
   new FavoritesViewContentProvider());
viewer.setInput(FavoritesManager.getManager());
```

7.2.5   Label provider

The label provider takes a table row object returned by the content provider and extracts the value to be displayed in a column. After refactoring the FavoritesView.ViewLabelProvider inner class (see Section 2.3.3) into a top-level class and reworking it to extract values from the newly created model object, it looks something like the following code:

```
package com.qualityeclipse.favorites.views;

import java.util.*;
import org.eclipse.jface.viewers.*;
import org.eclipse.swt.graphics.*;
import com.qualityeclipse.favorites.model.IFavoriteItem;

class FavoritesViewLabelProvider extends LabelProvider
    implements ITableLabelProvider
{
    private HashMap imageMap;

    public String getColumnText(Object obj, int index) {
        switch (index) {
            case 0 : // Type column
                return "";
            case 1 : // Name column
                if (obj instanceof IFavoriteItem)
                    return ((IFavoriteItem) obj).getName();
                if (obj != null)
                    return obj.toString();
                return "";
            case 2 : // Location column
                if (obj instanceof IFavoriteItem)
                    return ((IFavoriteItem) obj).getLocation();
                return "";
            default :
                return "";
        }
    }

    public Image getColumnImage(Object obj, int index) {
        if ((index == 0) && (obj instanceof IFavoriteItem))
            return ((IFavoriteItem) obj).getType().getImage();
        return null;
    }
}
```

> **Tip:** If you are displaying workbench-related objects, WorkbenchLabelProvider and WorkbenchPartLabelProvider contain behavior for determining text and images for workbench resources implementing the IWorkbenchAdapter interface (see Section 20.3.4, "IWorkbenchAdapter").

7.2.6 Viewer sorter

While a content provider serves up row objects, it is the responsibility of the `ViewerSorter` to sort the row objects before they are displayed. In the Favorites view, there are currently three criteria by which items can be sorted in either ascending or descending order:

- Name
- Type
- Location

The `FavoritesViewSorter` delegates sorting to three comparators, one for each of the criteria listed above. In addition, the `FavoritesViewSorter` listens for mouse clicks in the column headers and resorts the table content based on the column that was selected. Clicking on a column a second time toggles the sort order.

```
package com.qualityeclipse.favorites.views;

import java.util.*;
import org.eclipse.jface.viewers.*;
import org.eclipse.swt.events.*;
import org.eclipse.swt.widgets.*;

public class FavoritesViewSorter extends ViewerSorter
{
   // Simple data structure for grouping
   // sort information by column.
   private class SortInfo {
      int columnIndex;
      Comparator comparator;
      boolean descending;
   }

   private TableViewer viewer;
   private SortInfo[] infos;

   public FavoritesViewSorter(
      TableViewer viewer,
      TableColumn[] columns,
      Comparator[] comparators) {

      this.viewer = viewer;
      infos = new SortInfo[columns.length];
      for (int i = 0; i < columns.length; i++) {
         infos[i] = new SortInfo();
         infos[i].columnIndex = i;
         infos[i].comparator = comparators[i];
         infos[i].descending = false;
```

```
            createSelectionListener(
                columns[i],
                infos[i]);
        }
    }

    public int compare(
        Viewer viewer,
        Object favorite1,
        Object favorite2) {

        for (int i = 0; i < infos.length; i++) {
            int result = infos[i].comparator
                .compare(favorite1, favorite2);
            if (result != 0) {
                if (infos[i].descending)
                    return -result;
                return result;
            }
        }
        return 0;
    }

    private void createSelectionListener(
        final TableColumn column,
        final SortInfo info) {
        column.addSelectionListener(new SelectionAdapter() {
            public void widgetSelected(SelectionEvent e) {
                sortUsing(info);
            }
        });
    }

    protected void sortUsing(SortInfo info) {
        if (info == infos[0])
            info.descending = !info.descending;
        else {
            for (int i = 0; i < infos.length; i++) {
                if (info == infos[i]) {
                    System.arraycopy(infos, 0, infos, 1, i);
                    infos[0] = info;
                    info.descending = false;
                    break;
                }
            }
        }
        viewer.refresh();
    }
}
```

We will introduce a new field to hold the sorter instance:

```
private FavoritesViewSorter sorter;
```

and the **Favorites** view createPartControl(Composite) method will be modified to call the new method shown below. Later, the current sort order, as chosen by the user, must be preserved between Eclipse sessions (see Section 7.5.1, "Saving local view information").

```
private void createTableSorter() {
    Comparator nameComparator = new Comparator() {
        public int compare(Object o1, Object o2) {
            return ((IFavoriteItem) o1)
                .getName()
                .compareTo(
                ((IFavoriteItem) o2).getName());
        }
    };
    Comparator locationComparator = new Comparator() {
        public int compare(Object o1, Object o2) {
            return ((IFavoriteItem) o1)
                .getLocation()
                .compareTo(
                ((IFavoriteItem) o2).getLocation());
        }
    };
    Comparator typeComparator = new Comparator() {
        public int compare(Object o1, Object o2) {
            return ((IFavoriteItem) o1)
                .getType()
                .compareTo(
                ((IFavoriteItem) o2).getType());
        }
    };
    sorter = new FavoritesViewSorter(
        viewer,
        new TableColumn[] {
            nameColumn, locationColumn, typeColumn },
        new Comparator[] {
            nameComparator, locationComparator, typeComparator
    });
    viewer.setSorter(sorter);
}
```

7.2.7 Viewer filters

ViewerFilter subclasses determine which of the row objects returned by a content provider will be displayed and which will not. While there can be only one content provider, only one label provider, and only one sorter, there can be any number of filters associated with a viewer. When there are multiple filters applied, only those items that satisfy all the applied filters will be displayed.

Similar to the sorting just discussed, the **Favorites** view can be filtered by:

• Name

• Type

• Location

Eclipse provides the type `org.eclipse.ui.internal.misc.String-Matcher`, which is ideal for wildcard filtering, but since the class is in an internal package, the first step is to copy the class into the `com` `.qualityeclipse.favorites.util` package. Although copying sounds horrid, there are already 10 copies of this particular class in various locations throughout Eclipse, all of them internal (see Section 20.2, "Accessing Internal Code," for more on internal packages and the issues that surround them).

Once that is complete, the `ViewerFilter` class for filtering the Favorites view by name looks like this:

```
package com.qualityeclipse.favorites.views;

import org.eclipse.jface.viewers.*;
import com.qualityeclipse.favorites.model.*;
import com.qualityeclipse.favorites.util.*;

public class FavoritesViewNameFilter extends ViewerFilter
{
    private final StructuredViewer viewer;
    private String pattern = "";
    private StringMatcher matcher;

    public FavoritesViewNameFilter(StructuredViewer viewer) {
        this.viewer = viewer;
    }

    public String getPattern() {
        return pattern;
    }

    public void setPattern(String newPattern) {
        boolean filtering = matcher != null;
        if (newPattern != null
            && newPattern.trim().length() > 0) {
            pattern = newPattern;
            matcher = new StringMatcher(pattern, true, false);
            if (!filtering)
                viewer.addFilter(this);
            else
                viewer.refresh();
        }
        else {
            pattern = "";
            matcher = null;
            if (filtering)
                viewer.removeFilter(this);
        }
    }

    public boolean select(
        Viewer viewer,
        Object parentElement,
        Object element) {
```

```
        return matcher.match(
            ((IFavoriteItem) element).getName());
    }
}
```

7.2.8   *View selection*

Now that the model objects and view controls are in place, other aspects of
the view, specifically actions, need a way to determine which **Favorites** items
are currently selected. Add the following method to the FavoritesView so that
actions can perform operations on the selected items:

```
public IFavoriteItem[] getSelectedFavorites() {
    IStructuredSelection selection =
        (IStructuredSelection) viewer.getSelection();
    IFavoriteItem[] items =
        new IFavoriteItem[selection.size()];
    Iterator iter = selection.iterator();
    int index = 0;
    while (iter.hasNext())
        items[index++] = (IFavoriteItem) iter.next();
    return items;
}
```

7.3   View Actions

A view action can appear as a menu item in a view's context menu, as a toolbar button on the right side of a view's title bar, and as a menu item in a view's
pull-down menu (see Figure 6–9). This section covers adding an action to a
view programmatically, whereas Section 6.4, "View Actions," discussed adding an action using declarations in the plug-in manifest.

7.3.1   *Model actions*

Now that the model objects are in place, the AddToFavoritesActionDelegate
class introduced in Section 6.3.3, "IObjectActionDelegate," can be completed. With the modifications outlined below, the action delegate adds the
selected items to the FavoritesManager, which then notifies the Favorites-
ViewContentProvider, which then refreshes the table to display the new information:

```
public void selectionChanged(
    IAction action,
    ISelection selection) {
```

```
         this.selection = selection;
         action.setEnabled(!selection.isEmpty());
      }

      public void run(IAction action) {
         if (selection instanceof IStructuredSelection) {
            FavoritesManager mgr =
               FavoritesManager.getManager();
            Iterator iter =
               ((IStructuredSelection) selection).iterator();
            mgr.addFavorites(mgr.newFavoritesFor(iter));
         }
      }
   }
```

7.3.2   Context menu

Typically, views have context menus populated by actions targeted at the view or selected objects within the view. There are several steps to creating a view's context menu and several more steps to register that view so that others can contribute actions (see Sections 6.3, "Object Actions," 6.4.1, "Defining a view context submenu," and 6.4.2, "Defining a view context menu action," for information concerning how actions are contributed to a view's context menus via the plug-in manifest).

7.3.2.1   Creating actions

The first step is to create the actions that will appear in the context menu. For the **Favorites** view, we need an action that will remove the selected elements from the view:

```
package com.qualityeclipse.favorites.actions;

import org.eclipse.jface.action.*;
import org.eclipse.jface.viewers.*;
import com.qualityeclipse.favorites.model.*;

public class RemoveFavoritesAction extends Action
{
   private FavoritesView view;

   public RemoveFavoritesAction(
      FavoritesView view,
      String text,
      ImageDescriptor imageDescriptor) {

      super(text, imageDescriptor);
      this.view = view;
   }
```

```
public void run() {
   FavoritesManager.getManager().removeFavorites(
      view.getSelectedFavorites());
   }
}
```

In the FavoritesView class, create a new action field as follows:

```
private RemoveFavoritesAction removeAction;
```

and call the following new method from createPartControl(Composite) to initialize the field:

```
private void createActions() {
   ImageDescriptor removeImage =
      PlatformUI
         .getWorkbench()
         .getSharedImages()
         .getImageDescriptor(
            ISharedImages.IMG_TOOL_DELETE);
   ImageDescriptor removeImageHover =
      PlatformUI
         .getWorkbench()
         .getSharedImages()
         .getImageDescriptor(
            ISharedImages.IMG_TOOL_DELETE_HOVER);
   removeAction =
      new RemoveFavoritesAction(
         this,
         "Remove",
         removeImage);
   removeAction.setHoverImageDescriptor(
      removeImageHover);
}
```

This same action is used later for keyboard-based actions (see Section 7.3.5, "Keyboard actions") and global actions (see Section 7.3.6, "Global actions").

7.3.2.2 Creating the context menu

The context menu must be created at the same time that the view is created, but because contributors add and remove menu items based on the current selection, its contents cannot be determined until just after the user clicks the right mouse button and just before the menu is displayed. To accomplish this, set the menu's RemoveAllWhenShown property to true so that the menu will be built from scratch each time, and add a menu listener to dynamically build the menu. In addition, the menu must be registered with the control so that it will be displayed, and with the view site so that other plug-ins can contribute actions to it (see Section 6.3, "Object Actions"). For the Favorites view, modify `createPartControl(...)` to call the new `createContextMenu()` method shown below:

```
private void createContextMenu() {
   MenuManager menuMgr = new MenuManager("#PopupMenu");
   menuMgr.setRemoveAllWhenShown(true);
   menuMgr.addMenuListener(new IMenuListener() {
      public void menuAboutToShow(IMenuManager m) {
         FavoritesView.this.fillContextMenu(m);
      }
   });
   Menu menu =
      menuMgr.createContextMenu(viewer.getControl());
   viewer.getControl().setMenu(menu);
   getSite().registerContextMenu(menuMgr, viewer);
}
```

7.3.2.3   Dynamically building the context menu

Each time the user clicks the right mouse button, the context menu's content must be rebuilt from scratch because contributors may add or remove actions based on the selected items. In addition, the context menu must contain a separator with the `IWorkbenchActionConstants.MB_ADDITIONS` constant indicating where contributed actions may appear in the menu. The `create ContextMenu()` method (see Section 7.3.2.2, "Creating the context menu") calls the new `fillContextMenu(IMenuManager)` method shown below:

```
private void fillContextMenu(IMenuManager menuMgr) {
   boolean isEmpty = viewer.getSelection().isEmpty();
   removeAction.setEnabled(!isEmpty);
   menuMgr.add(removeAction);
   menuMgr.add(
      new Separator(
         IWorkbenchActionConstants.MB_ADDITIONS));
}
```

7.3.2.4   Selection provider

When object-based actions are defined (see Section 6.3), they are targeted at the selected object rather than at the view. For object-based actions to appear in a view's context menu, the view must not only register the context menu (see Section 7.3.2.1, "Creating actions"), but it must also publish its selection for any other registered listeners (see Section 7.4.1, "Selection provider"). In addition, object-based actions are typically targeted at specific types of objects rather than all objects. This means that the selected object must implement the `IAdaptable` interface so that contributors can adapt the selected objects to any object they can interrogate and manipulate (see Section 7.4.2, "Adaptable objects").

7.3.2.5   Filtering unwanted actions

At this point, when the **Favorites** view context menu appears, it incorrectly contains the **Favorites** submenu with the **Add** menu item that was defined in Section 6.3.1. We want that **Favorites** submenu to appear everywhere else *except* in the **Favorites** view. To accomplish this, revisit the object contribution outlined in Section 6.3.1, "Defining an object-based action," and change the `adaptable` attribute to "false", then copy the entire object contribution into a new identical object contribution but change the `objectClass` attribute to be "org.eclipse.jdt.core.IJavaElement".

7.3.3   Toolbar buttons

Next, we'll programmatically add the remove action to the toolbar (see Section 6.4.4, "Defining a view toolbar action," for declaring a toolbar button using the plug-in manifest rather than programmatically). In addition, we would like the state of this toolbar button to change based on the selection in the **Favorites** view. In the `FavoritesView` class, call the following new method from the `createPartControl(Composite)` method:

```java
private void createToolbarButtons() {
   getViewSite()
      .getActionBars()
      .getToolBarManager()
      .add(removeAction);
   removeAction.setEnabled(false);
   viewer.addSelectionChangedListener(
      new ISelectionChangedListener() {
         public void selectionChanged(
            SelectionChangedEvent event) {
            removeAction.setEnabled(
               !event.getSelection().isEmpty());
         }
      });
}
```

7.3.4   Pull-down menu

In this section, we'll programmatically add an action to the **Favorites** view pull-down menu so that the name filter can be enabled and disabled (see Section 6.4.5, "Defining a view pull-down submenu and action," for defining a pull-down menu item in the plug-in manifest rather than programmatically). For now, the action will use a simple `InputDialog` to prompt for the name filter pattern, but this will be replaced with a specialized **Favorites** view filter dialog later in the book (see Section 11.1.2, "Common SWT dialogs").

```
package com.qualityeclipse.favorites.views;

import org.eclipse.jface.action.*;
import org.eclipse.jface.dialogs.*;
import org.eclipse.jface.viewers.*;
import org.eclipse.swt.widgets.*;

public class FavoritesViewFilterAction extends Action {
    private final Shell shell;
    private final FavoritesViewNameFilter nameFilter;

    public FavoritesViewFilterAction(
        StructuredViewer viewer,
        String text) {

        super(text);
        shell = viewer.getControl().getShell();
        nameFilter = new FavoritesViewNameFilter(viewer);
    }

    public void run() {
        InputDialog dialog =
            new InputDialog(
                shell,
                "Favorites View Filter",
                "Enter a name filter pattern"
                    + " (* = any string, ? = any character)"
                    + System.getProperty("line.separator")
                    + "or an empty string for no filtering:",
                nameFilter.getPattern(),
                null);
        if (dialog.open() == InputDialog.OK)
            nameFilter.setPattern(dialog.getValue().trim());
    }
}
```

The `createPartControl(...)` method is getting quite long and is in need of refactoring. After extracting the table columns as fields and extracting table creation and sorting into separate methods, the `createPartControl(...)` method is modified to call a new `createViewPulldownMenu()` method. This new method programmatically creates and initializes the **filter** field, and adds the new filter action to the **Favorites** view's pull-down menu (see Figure 7–6).

```
private FavoritesViewFilterAction filterAction;

private void createViewPulldownMenu() {
    IMenuManager menu =
        getViewSite().getActionBars().getMenuManager();
    filterAction =
        new FavoritesViewFilterAction(viewer, "Filter...");
    menu.add(filter);
}
```

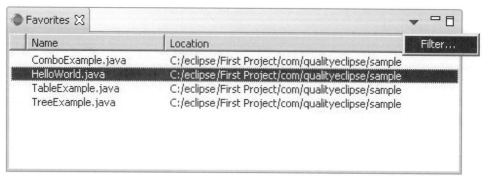

Figure 7–6   Favorites view showing the view's pull-down menu.

7.3.5   Keyboard actions

Rather than using the mouse to activate the context menu and then selecting the **Delete** command to remove an item from the **Favorites** view (see Section 7.3.2, "Context menu"), it would be quicker just to press the **Delete** key. This approach programmatically associates the **Delete** key with the RemoveFavoritesAction rather than defining the command via the plug-in manifest as in Section 6.7, "RFWS Considerations." For this to work, call the following new method from the createPartControl(...) method:

```
private void hookKeyboardActions() {
    viewer.getControl().addKeyListener(new KeyAdapter() {
        public void keyReleased(KeyEvent event) {
            handleKeyReleased(event);
        }
    });
}

protected void handleKeyReleased(KeyEvent event) {
    if (event.character == SWT.DEL
        && event.stateMask == 0) {
        removeAction.run();
    }
}
```

7.3.6   Global actions

Now that we have the RemoveFavoritesAction available both in the context menu (see Section 7.3.2.1) and by pressing the **Delete** key (see Section 7.3.5), we want that same action to be triggered when the user selects **Delete** from the **Edit** menu. The interface org.eclipse.ui.IWorkbenchActionConstants defines a number of constants for just this purpose, such as:

- Undo
- Redo
- Cut
- Copy
- Paste
- Delete

Calling the following new method from the `createPartControl(...)` method associates **Edit > Delete** with `RemoveFavoritesAction` when the **Favorites** view is active:

```
private void hookGlobalActions() {
   getViewSite().getActionBars().setGlobalActionHandler(
      IWorkbenchActionConstants.DELETE,
      removeAction);
}
```

7.3.7   Clipboard actions

The three clipboard-related actions are cut, copy, and paste. For the **Favorites** view, we want to provide the ability to cut selected items out of the view, copy selected items, and paste new items into the view using three separate actions. To support these three actions, we must lazily create a clipboard object:

```
private Clipboard clipboard;

public Clipboard getClipboard() {
   if (clipboard == null)
      clipboard = new Clipboard(
         getSite().getShell().getDisplay());
   return clipboard;
}
```

In addition, the clipboard, if it is defined, must be cleaned up when the view is closed by adding the following lines to the view's `dispose()` method:

```
if (clipboard != null)
   clipboard.dispose();
```

7.3.7.1   Copy

The copy action translates selected **Favorites** items into various formats such as resources and places that information into the clipboard. Transfer objects convert various formats such as resources into platform-specific byte streams and back so that information can be exchanged between different applications (see Section 7.3.8.3, "Custom transfer types," for more on transfer types). We'll add the following CopyFavoritesAction class to handle copying items from the **Favorites** view:

```java
package com.qualityeclipse.favorites.actions;

import java.util.*;
import org.eclipse.core.resources.*;
import org.eclipse.jface.action.*;
import org.eclipse.swt.*;
import org.eclipse.swt.dnd.*;
import org.eclipse.ui.part.*;
import com.qualityeclipse.favorites.model.*;
import com.qualityeclipse.favorites.views.*;

public class CopyFavoritesAction extends Action
{
   private FavoritesView view;

   public CopyFavoritesAction(
      FavoritesView view,
      String text) {

      super(text);
      this.view = view;
   }

   public void run() {
      IFavoriteItem[] items = view.getSelectedFavorites();
      if (items.length == 0)
         return;
      try {
         view.getClipboard().setContents(
            new Object[] {
               asResources(items),
               asText(items),
               },
            new Transfer[] {
               ResourceTransfer.getInstance(),
               TextTransfer.getInstance(),
               });
      }
      catch (SWTError error) {
         // Copy to clipboard failed.
         // This happens when another application
         // is accessing the clipboard while we copy.
         // Ignore the error.
      }
   }

   public static IResource[] asResources(
      IFavoriteItem[] items) {

      List resources = new ArrayList();
```

```
            for (int i = 0; i < items.length; i++) {
                IResource res =
                    (IResource) items[i].getAdapter(
                        IResource.class);
                if (res != null)
                    resources.add(res);
            }
            return (IResource[]) resources.toArray(
                new IResource[resources.size()]);
        }

        public static String asText(IFavoriteItem[] items) {
            StringBuffer buf = new StringBuffer();
            for (int i = 0; i < items.length; i++) {
                if (i > 0)
                    buf.append(
                        System.getProperty("line.separator"));
                buf.append(items[i].getName());
            }
            return buf.toString();
        }
    }
```

We'll create a field in FavoritesView to hold the copy action:

```
private CopyFavoritesAction copyAction;
```

initialize that field in the createActions() method:

```
copyAction = new CopyFavoritesAction(this, "Copy");
```

and hook the action to the global copy (see Section 7.3.6):

```
getViewSite().getActionBars().setGlobalActionHandler(
    IWorkbenchActionConstants.COPY,
    copyAction);
```

The copy action can also be added to the context menu by modifying the fillContextMenu(...) method (see Section 7.3.2.3, "Dynamically building the context menu") and to the view's toolbar (see Section 7.3.3, "Toolbar buttons").

7.3.7.2   Cut

The cut action is based on the copy and remove actions, first using the copy action to copy the selected **Favorites** items to the clipboard and then the remove action to remove the selected **Favorites** items from the **Favorites** view. It is initialized and used much like the copy operation described in the previous section.

```
package com.qualityeclipse.favorites.actions;

import org.eclipse.jface.action.*;

public class CutFavoritesAction extends Action
{
   private CopyFavoritesAction copyAction;
   private RemoveFavoritesAction removeAction;

   public CutFavoritesAction(
      CopyFavoritesAction copyAction,
      RemoveFavoritesAction removeAction,
      String text) {

      super(text);
      this.copyAction = copyAction;
      this.removeAction = removeAction;
   }

   public void run() {
      copyAction.run();
      removeAction.run();
   }
}
```

7.3.7.3 *Paste*

The paste operation takes information that was previously added to the clipboard by another operation and adds it to the **Favorites** view. As in the copy operation (see Section 7.3.7.1, "Copy"), transfer objects facilitate translation from platform-specific byte streams to objects, and the paste operation converts those objects into items that are added to the **Favorites** view. The initialization and use of the paste operation is much like the copy operation discussed in Section 7.3.7.1.

```
package com.qualityeclipse.favorites.actions;

import org.eclipse.core.resources.*;
import org.eclipse.jdt.core.*;
import org.eclipse.jdt.internal.corext.refactoring.reorg.*;
import org.eclipse.jface.action.*;
import org.eclipse.ui.part.*;
import com.qualityeclipse.favorites.model.*;
import com.qualityeclipse.favorites.views.*;

public class PasteFavoritesAction extends Action
{
   private FavoritesView view;

   public PasteFavoritesAction(
      FavoritesView view,
      String text) {

      super(text);
```

```
        this.view = view;
    }

    public void run() {
        if (pasteResources())
            return;
        if (pasteJavaElements())
            return;
        // Other transfer types here.
    }

    private boolean pasteResources() {
        ResourceTransfer transfer =
            ResourceTransfer.getInstance();
        IResource[] resources = (IResource[])
            view.getClipboard().getContents(transfer);
        if (resources == null || resources.length == 0)
            return false;
        FavoritesManager mgr = FavoritesManager.getManager();
        mgr.addFavorites(mgr.newFavoritesFor(resources));
        return true;
    }

    private boolean pasteJavaElements() {
        JavaElementTransfer transfer =
            JavaElementTransfer.getInstance();
        IJavaElement[] elements = (IJavaElement[])
            view.getClipboard().getContents(transfer);
        if (elements == null || elements.length == 0)
            return false;
        FavoritesManager mgr = FavoritesManager.getManager();
        mgr.addFavorites(mgr.newFavoritesFor(elements));
        return true;
    }
}
```

7.3.8   Drag-and-drop support

We have the ability to add objects to the **Favorites** view from another view
using the copy/paste actions, but it would be nice to allow objects to be
dragged into and out of the **Favorites** view. To accomplish this, we must add
drag source and *drop target* objects to the **Favorites** view by calling the following new method from the createPartControl(...) method. The FavoritesDragSource and FavoritesDropTarget types are defined in the next two
sections.

```
private void hookDragAndDrop() {
    new FavoritesDragSource(this, viewer);
    new FavoritesDropTarget(this, viewer);
}
```

7.3.8.1 Dragging objects out of the Favorites view

The FavoritesDragSource type initializes the drag source operation and handles conversions of **Favorites** items into resource objects and text. This allows the user to drag and drop selected **Favorites** items elsewhere within Eclipse or into another drag-and-drop-enabled application such as Microsoft Word (see Figure 7–7).

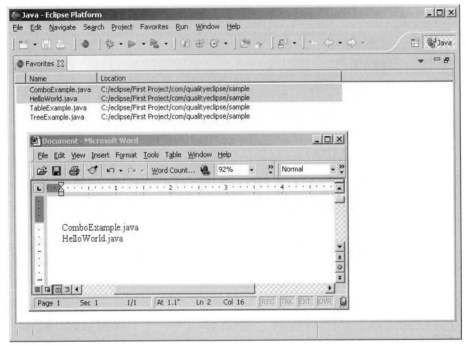

Figure 7–7   Drag-and-drop operation between Eclipse and Microsoft Word.

The constructor, called from the hookDragAndDrop() method (see Section 7.3.9, "Inline editing"), initializes the drag source by:

- Creating a drag source—new DragSource(...)

- Specifying available operations—DND.DROP_COPY
  Multiple operations can be specified as in DND.DROP_MOVE |
  DND.DROP_COPY if items can be both moved and copied.

- Specifying available data types—Resources and text
  (See Section 7.3.8.3 for more on transfer types.)

- Adding itself as a DragSourceListener to handle the data conversion
  from **Favorites** items to either resources or text.

When a user initiates a drag operation from the **Favorites** view, the drag-
Start (...) method is called to determine whether or not the drag operation can
be performed. In this case, we set the event.doit field to be true if there are
Favorites items selected, otherwise we set event.doit to false since the operation can only be performed when at least one **Favorites** item is selected.
When the user drops the objects, the dragSetData(...) method is called to convert the selected items before the transfer occurs, and then the dragFinish(...)
method is called after the transfer is complete.

```
package com.qualityeclipse.favorites.views;

import org.eclipse.jface.viewers.*;
import org.eclipse.swt.dnd.*;
import org.eclipse.ui.part.*;
import com.qualityeclipse.favorites.actions.*;

public class FavoritesDragSource
    implements DragSourceListener
{
    private FavoritesView view;

    public FavoritesDragSource(
        FavoritesView view,
        TableViewer viewer) {

        this.view = view;
        DragSource source =
            new DragSource(
                viewer.getControl(),
                DND.DROP_COPY);
        source.setTransfer(
            new Transfer[] {
                TextTransfer.getInstance(),
                ResourceTransfer.getInstance()});
        source.addDragListener(this);
    }

    public void dragStart(DragSourceEvent event) {
        event.doit = view.getSelectedFavorites().length > 0;
    }

    public void dragSetData(DragSourceEvent event) {
        if (TextTransfer.getInstance()
            .isSupportedType(event.dataType)) {
            event.data =
                CopyFavoritesAction.asText(
                    view.getSelectedFavorites());
        }
        else if (ResourceTransfer.getInstance()
            .isSupportedType(event.dataType)) {
            event.data =
                CopyFavoritesAction.asResources(
                    view.getSelectedFavorites());
        }
    }
}
```

```
        public void dragFinished(DragSourceEvent event) {
            // If this was a MOVE operation,
            // then remove the items that were moved.
        }
    }
}
```

7.3.8.2 Dragging objects into the Favorites view

The `FavoritesDropTarget` type allows items to be added to the **Favorites** view by dragging them from another view. This allows the user to drag resources or Java elements from the **Resource Navigator** view or the **Java Package** view into the **Favorites** view.

The constructor, called from the `hookDragAndDrop()` method (see Section 7.3.8, "Drag-and-drop support"), initializes the drop target by:

- Creating the drop target—`new DropTarget(...)`

- Specifying accepted operations—`DND.DROP_MOVE | DND.DROP_COPY`
  For convenience, we specify that a move operation is allowed, but when the actual operation is performed, we convert it to a copy operation.

- Specifying accepted data types—Resources and Java elements
  (See Section 7.3.8.3 for more on transfer types.)

- Adding itself as a `DropTargetListener` to handle data conversion from objects to **Favorites** items.

During the drag operation, there are several events that occur so that various drop targets can provide feedback to the user when the cursor enters, moves over, and exits a drag target. Since we want to add items to the **Favorites** view without removing them from their original location, and we want to make it convenient for the user so that he or she does not have to hold down the **Ctrl** key to perform the drag operation, we implement the `dragEnter(...)` method to convert a move operation into a copy operation. The conversion from a move operation to a copy operation is done in the `dragEnter(...)` method in addition to the `drop(...)` method so that the user gets visual feedback indicating that a copy will occur before the operation is performed.

When the user drops the objects on the **Favorites** view, the `drop(...)` method is called to perform the operation. It converts the objects into **Favorites** items and ensures that the operation is indeed a copy operation so that the objects are not removed from their original locations.

```
package com.qualityeclipse.favorites.views;

import org.eclipse.core.resources.*;
import org.eclipse.jdt.core.*;
import org.eclipse.jdt.internal.corext.refactoring.reorg.*;
import org.eclipse.jface.viewers.*;
import org.eclipse.swt.dnd.*;
import org.eclipse.ui.part.*;
```

```java
import com.qualityeclipse.favorites.model.FavoritesManager;

public class FavoritesDropTarget extends DropTargetAdapter
{
   private FavoritesView view;

   public FavoritesDropTarget(
      FavoritesView view,
      TableViewer viewer) {

      this.view = view;
      DropTarget target =
         new DropTarget(
            viewer.getControl(),
            DND.DROP_MOVE | DND.DROP_COPY);
      target.setTransfer(
         new Transfer[] {
            ResourceTransfer.getInstance(),
            JavaElementTransfer.getInstance()});
      target.addDropListener(this);
   }

   public void dragEnter(DropTargetEvent event) {
      if (event.detail == DND.DROP_MOVE
         || event.detail == DND.DROP_DEFAULT) {

         if ((event.operations & DND.DROP_COPY) != 0)
            event.detail = DND.DROP_COPY;
         else
            event.detail = DND.DROP_NONE;
      }
   }

   public void drop(DropTargetEvent event) {
      FavoritesManager mgr = FavoritesManager.getManager();
      if (ResourceTransfer.getInstance()
         .isSupportedType(event.currentDataType)
         && (event.data instanceof IResource[])) {

         mgr.addFavorites(
            mgr.newFavoritesFor((IResource[]) event.data));
         event.detail = DND.DROP_COPY;
      }
      else if (JavaElementTransfer.getInstance()
         .isSupportedType(event.currentDataType)
         && (event.data instanceof IJavaElement[])) {

         mgr.addFavorites(
            mgr.newFavoritesFor(
               (IJavaElement[]) event.data));
         event.detail = DND.DROP_COPY;
      }
      else
         event.detail = DND.DROP_NONE;
   }
}
```

7.3.8.3   Custom transfer types

Transfer objects convert various formats such as resources into platform-specific byte streams and back so that information can be exchanged between different applications. Eclipse provides several transfer types, including:

- ByteArrayTransfer
- EditorInputTransfer
- FileTransfer
- JavaElementTransfer
- MarkerTransfer
- PluginTransfer
- ResourceTransfer
- RTFTransfer
- TextTransfer

These transfer objects are useful for generic types of objects such as resources, but if you are dragging objects specific to your application from one view to another, these transfer objects may not completely capture the object's information being dragged. For example, if we were to drag a **Favorites** item from one **Favorites** view to another, and there was additional state information associated with the item, and we were using a `ResourceTransfer` object, then that additional state information would be lost.

To solve this problem requires building a custom transfer type such as the one shown below. A transfer type must be a subclass of the `org.eclipse.swt.dnd.Transfer` class, but subclassing `org.eclipse.swt.dnd.ByteArrayTransfer` is easier because of the additional behavior it provides. If we built a custom transfer type for **Favorites** items, then it would rely on functionality introduced in Section 7.5.2, "Saving global view information," and might be similar to the existing `ResourceTransfer` type.

```
package com.qualityeclipse.favorites.views;

import java.io.*;
import java.util.*;
import org.eclipse.swt.dnd.*;
import com.qualityeclipse.favorites.model.*;

/**
 * The <code>FavoritesTransfer</code> class is used
 * to transfer an array of <code>IFavoriteItem</code>s
 * from one part to another in a drag-and-drop operation
 * or a cut, copy, paste action.
 * <p>
```

```
 * In every drag-and-drop operation, there is
 * a <code>DragSource</code> and a <code>DropTarget</code>.
 * When a drag occurs, a <code>Transfer</code> is used
 * to marshall the drag data from the source
 * into a byte array. When a drop occurs,
 * another <code>Transfer</code> is used
 * to marshall the byte array into drop data for the target.
 * </p>
 * <p>
 * When a <code>CutAction</code> or a <code>CopyAction</code>
 * is performed, this transfer is used to place references
 * to the selected items on the <code>Clipboard</code>.
 * When a <code>PasteAction</code> is performed,
 * the references on the clipboard are used
 * to move or copy the items to the selected destination.
 * </p>
 */
public class FavoritesTransfer extends ByteArrayTransfer
{
   /**
    * Singleton instance.
    */
   private static final FavoritesTransfer INSTANCE =
      new FavoritesTransfer();

   /**
    * Create a unique ID to make sure that different
    * Eclipse applications use different "types"
    * of <code>FavoritesTransfer</code>.
    */
   private static final String TYPE_NAME =
      "favorites-transfer-format:"
         + System.currentTimeMillis()
         + ":"
         + INSTANCE.hashCode();

   /**
    * The registered identifier.
    */
   private static final int TYPEID =
      registerType(TYPE_NAME);

   /**
    * Singleton constructor.
    */
   private FavoritesTransfer() {
      super();
   }

   /**
    * Answer the single instance.
    */
   public static FavoritesTransfer getInstance() {
      return INSTANCE;
   }
```

```java
/**
 * Returns the platform-specfic IDs of the data types
 * that can be converted using this transfer agent.
 *
 * @return an array of data type identifiers
 */
protected int[] getTypeIds() {
   return new int[] { TYPEID };
}

/**
 * Returns the platform-specfic names of the data types
 * that can be converted using this transfer agent.
 *
 * @return an array of data type names
 * @see org.eclipse.swt.dnd.Transfer#getTypeNames()
 */
protected String[] getTypeNames() {
   return new String[] { TYPE_NAME };
}

/**
 * Converts a Java representation of data
 * to a platform-specific representation of the data.
 *
 * @param data a Java representation of the data
 * to be converted; the type of object that is passed
 * in is dependent on the <code>Transfer</code> subclass.
 *
 * @param transferData an empty TransferData object;
 * this object will be filled in on return with
 * the platform-specific representation of the data.
 * @see org.eclipse.swt.dnd.Transfer
 *     #javaToNative(
 *         java.lang.Object,
 *         org.eclipse.swt.dnd.TransferData)
 */
protected void javaToNative(
   Object data,
   TransferData transferData) {

   if (!(data instanceof IFavoriteItem[]))
       return;
   IFavoriteItem[] items = (IFavoriteItem[]) data;
   /**
    * The serialization format is:
    *  (int) number of items
    * Then, the following for each item:
    *  (String) the type of item
    *  (String) the item-specific info glob
    */
   try {
      ByteArrayOutputStream out =
         new ByteArrayOutputStream();
      DataOutputStream dataOut =
         new DataOutputStream(out);
```

```
            dataOut.writeInt(items.length);
            for (int i = 0; i < items.length; i++) {
                IFavoriteItem item = items[i];
                dataOut.writeUTF(item.getType().getId());
                dataOut.writeUTF(item.getInfo());
            }
            dataOut.close();
            out.close();
            super.javaToNative(
                out.toByteArray(),
                transferData);
        }
        catch (IOException e) {
            // Send nothing if there were problems.
        }
    }

    /**
     * Converts a platform-specific representation
     * of data to a Java representation.
     *
     * @param transferData the platform-specific
     * representation of the data to be converted
     * @return a java representation of the converted data
     * if the conversion was successful,
     * else <code>null</code>
     * @see org.eclipse.swt.dnd.Transfer
     *     #nativeToJava(org.eclipse.swt.dnd.TransferData)
     */
    protected Object nativeToJava(TransferData transferData) {
        /**
         * The serialization format is:
         *   (int) number of items
         * Then, the following for each item:
         *   (String) the type of item
         *   (String) the item-specific info glob
         */
        byte[] bytes =
            (byte[]) super.nativeToJava(transferData);
        if (bytes == null)
            return null;
        DataInputStream in =
            new DataInputStream(
                new ByteArrayInputStream(bytes));
        try {
            FavoritesManager mgr =
                FavoritesManager.getManager();
            int count = in.readInt();
            List items = new ArrayList(count);
            for (int i = 0; i < count; i++) {
                String typeId = in.readUTF();
                String info = in.readUTF();
                items.add(mgr.newFavoriteFor(typeId, info));
            }
            return (IFavoriteItem[]) items.toArray(
                new IFavoriteItem[items.size()]);
        }
```

```
    catch (IOException e) {
         return null;
      }
   }
}
```

> **Tip:** In input/output (I/O) code such as that above, consider using a
> `BufferedOutputStream` between the `ByteArrayOutputStream` and the
> `DataOutputStream`. While not always necessary, this can be a useful
> performance improvement.

7.3.9   Inline editing

Another feature we want to have is the ability to edit the name of the **Favorites**
items directly in the **Favorites** view quickly and easily. It is arguable that we
should trigger the rename action or refactoring so that the underlying resource
or Java element will be renamed rather than just editing the name of the item
itself, but we'll keep things simple for the purposes of demonstrating the inline
editing function.

To perform inline editing of a **Favorites** item's name, we need a new action
named `RenameFavoriteAction`. When the user selects the **Rename command** in
the context menu, a text field opens over the selected item's name in the **Favorites** view (see Figure 7–8). The user types the new name into the text field and
presses the **Return** key, which closes the editor and updates the item's name.

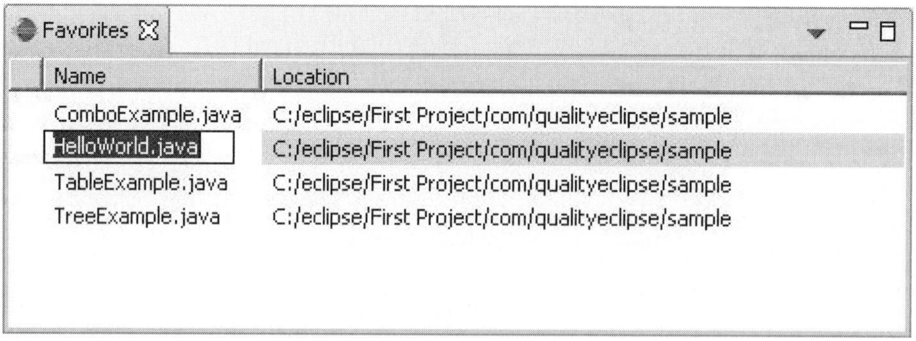

Figure 7–8   Favorites view showing the inline text field.

This new action is derived from `org.eclipse.ui.actions.RenameResourceAction` and uses two helper classes. The `TableEditor` is responsible
for positioning and sizing the text field over the item being renamed. The `TextActionHandler` temporarily redirects all global editing commands like cut,
copy, paste, clear, and select all to the text field rather than to the current

Eclipse editor. This class has very little code specific to the **Favorites** view, and
with a little refactoring, it could become a general-purpose inline edit action.

```java
package com.qualityeclipse.favorites.actions;

import org.eclipse.jface.action.*;
import org.eclipse.swt.*;
import org.eclipse.swt.custom.*;
import org.eclipse.swt.events.*;
import org.eclipse.swt.graphics.*;
import org.eclipse.swt.widgets.*;
import org.eclipse.ui.actions.*;
import com.qualityeclipse.favorites.model.*;
import com.qualityeclipse.favorites.views.*;

public class RenameFavoriteAction extends Action
{
    private static final int COLUMN_TO_EDIT = 1;

    private final FavoritesView view;
    private final Table table;
    private final TableEditor tableEditor;
    private final TextActionHandler textActionHandler;
    private Composite editorParent;
    private Text editor;
    private String originalText;

    public RenameFavoriteAction(
        FavoritesView view,
        Table table,
        String text) {

        super(text);
        this.view = view;
        this.table = table;
        tableEditor = new TableEditor(table);
        textActionHandler =
            new TextActionHandler(
                view.getViewSite().getActionBars());
    }

    public void run() {
        originalText = getTextToEdit();
        if (originalText == null)
            return;
        if (editor == null)
            createEditor();
        showEditor(originalText);
    }

    private void createEditor() {
        // Create the parent so that a simple border
        // can be painted around the text editor.
        editorParent = new Composite(table, SWT.NONE);
        TableItem[] tableItems = table.getSelection();
        tableEditor.horizontalAlignment = SWT.LEFT;
```

```java
tableEditor.grabHorizontal = true;
tableEditor.setEditor(
   editorParent, tableItems[0], COLUMN_TO_EDIT);
editorParent.setVisible(false);
editorParent.addListener(SWT.Paint, new Listener() {
   public void handleEvent(Event e) {
      // Paint a simple border around the text editor.
      Point textSize = editor.getSize();
      Point parentSize = editorParent.getSize();
      int w = Math.min(
         textSize.x + 4, parentSize.x—1);
      int h = parentSize.y—1;
      e.gc.drawRectangle(0, 0, w, h);
   }
});

// Create the editor itself.
editor = new Text(editorParent, SWT.NONE);
editorParent.setBackground(editor.getBackground());
editor.addListener(SWT.Modify, new Listener() {
   public void handleEvent(Event e) {
      Point textSize =
         editor.computeSize(SWT.DEFAULT, SWT.DEFAULT);
      textSize.x += textSize.y;
      // Add extra space for new characters.
      Point parentSize = editorParent.getSize();
      int w = Math.min(textSize.x, parentSize.x—4);
      int h = parentSize.y—2;
      editor.setBounds(2, 1, w, h);
      editorParent.redraw();
   }
});
editor.addListener(SWT.Traverse, new Listener() {
   public void handleEvent(Event event) {
      //Workaround for Bug 20214 due to extra
      //traverse events.
      switch (event.detail) {
         case SWT.TRAVERSE_ESCAPE :
            //Do nothing in this case.
            disposeEditor();
            event.doit = true;
            event.detail = SWT.TRAVERSE_NONE;
            break;
          case SWT.TRAVERSE_RETURN :
            saveChangesAndDisposeEditor();
            event.doit = true;
            event.detail = SWT.TRAVERSE_NONE;
            break;
      }
   }
});
editor.addFocusListener(new FocusAdapter() {
   public void focusLost(FocusEvent fe) {
      saveChangesAndDisposeEditor();
   }
});
```

```java
        // Add a handler to redirect global cut, copy, etc.
        textActionHandler.addText(editor);
    }

    private void showEditor(String name) {
        editor.setText(name);
        editorParent.setVisible(true);
        Point textSize =
            editor.computeSize(SWT.DEFAULT, SWT.DEFAULT);
        textSize.x += textSize.y;
        // Add extra space for new characters.
        Point parentSize = editorParent.getSize();
        int w = Math.min(textSize.x, parentSize.x-4);
        int h = parentSize.y-2;
        editor.setBounds(2, 1, w, h);
        editorParent.redraw();
        editor.selectAll();
        editor.setFocus();
    }

    protected void saveChangesAndDisposeEditor() {
        String newText = editor.getText();
        if (!originalText.equals(newText))
            saveChanges(newText);
        disposeEditor();
    }

    protected void disposeEditor() {
        textActionHandler.removeText(editor);
        if (editorParent != null) {
            editorParent.dispose();
            editorParent = null;
            editor = null;
            tableEditor.setEditor(null, null, COLUMN_TO_EDIT);
        }
    }

    protected String getTextToEdit() {
        String text = null;
        IFavoriteItem[] items = view.getSelectedFavorites();
        if (items.length == 1)
            text = items[0].getName();
        return text;
    }

    protected void saveChanges(String newText) {
        IFavoriteItem[] items = view.getSelectedFavorites();
        if (items.length == 1) {
            items[0].setName(newText);
            view.getFavoritesViewer().refresh(items[0]);
        }
    }
}
```

Next, we'll add a new field, a new line in `createActions()` to initialize the field, and a new line to the `fillContextMenu` (...) method so that the new **Rename** item appears in the **Favorites** view's popup menu:

```
private RenameFavoriteAction renameAction;

renameAction = new RenameFavoriteAction(
    this, viewer.getTable(), "Rename");

menuMgr.add(renameAction);
```

One alternate approach is to hook this up so that the user can press **F2** to directly edit the item name, similar to the way that we previously hooked the **Delete** key to the delete action (see Section 7.3.5). Another approach is to add a mouse listener so that **Alt+click** directly edits the item name.

```
private void hookMouse() {
    viewer.getTable().addMouseListener(new MouseAdapter() {
        public void mouseUp(MouseEvent e) {
            if ((e.stateMask & SWT.ALT) != 0)
                renameAction.run();
        }
    });
}
```

7.4   Linking the View

In many situations, the current selection in the active view may affect the selection in other views, cause an editor to open, change the selected editor, or change the selection within an already open editor. For example, in the Java browsing perspective (see Section 1.2.1.2, "Java perspectives"), changing the selection in the **Types** view changes the selection in both the **Projects** and the **Packages** views, changes the content displayed in the **Members** view, and changes the active editor. For a view to both publish its own selection and consume the selection of the active part, it must be both a *selection provider* and a *selection listener*.

7.4.1   Selection provider

For a view to be a selection provider, it must register itself as a selection provider with the view site. In addition, each of the objects contained in the view must be adaptable (see the next section) so that other objects can adapt the selected objects into objects they can understand. In the **Favorites** view, regis-

ter the view as a selection provider by adding the following to the `createTa-`
`ble(...)` method:

```
getSite().setSelectionProvider(viewer);
```

7.4.2   Adaptable objects

The `org.eclipse.core.runtime.IAdaptable` interface allows an object to
convert one type of object that it may not understand to another type of object
that it can interrogate and manipulate (more on adapters in Section 20.3). For
the **Favorites** view, this means that the `IFavoritesItem` interface must extend
the `IAdaptable` interface, and the following two `getAdapter(...)` methods
must be added to `FavoriteResource` and `FavoriteJavaElement`, respectively:

```
public Object getAdapter(Class adapter) {
    if (adapter.isInstance(resource))
        return resource;
    return Platform.getAdapterManager().getAdapter(
        this,
        adapter);
}

public Object getAdapter(Class adapter) {
    if (adapter.isInstance(element))
        return element;
    IResource resource = element.getResource();
    if (adapter.isInstance(resource))
        return resource;
    return Platform.getAdapterManager().getAdapter(
        this,
        adapter);
}
```

7.4.3   Selection listener

For a view to consume the selection of another part, it must add a selection
listener to the page so that when the active part changes or the selection in the
active part changes, it can react by altering its own selection appropriately.
For the **Favorites** view, if the selection contains objects that can be adapted to
the objects in the view, then the view should adjust its selection. To accomplish
this, add a call at the end of the `createPartControl(...)` method to the following new `hookPageSelection()` method:

```
private ISelectionListener pageSelectionListener;

private void hookPageSelection() {
    pageSelectionListener = new ISelectionListener() {
```

```
            public void selectionChanged(
                IWorkbenchPart part,
                ISelection selection) {
                    pageSelectionChanged(part, selection);
            }
        };
        getSite().getPage().addPostSelectionListener(
            pageSelectionListener);
    }

    protected void pageSelectionChanged(
        IWorkbenchPart part,
        ISelection selection) {
        if (part == this)
            return;
        if (!(selection instanceof IStructuredSelection))
            return;
        IStructuredSelection sel =
            (IStructuredSelection) selection;
        IFavoriteItem[] items =
            FavoritesManager
                .getManager()
                .existingFavoritesFor(sel.iterator());
        if (items.length > 0)
            viewer.setSelection(
                new StructuredSelection(items),
                true);
    }
```

and then override the `dispose()` method to clean up when the **Favorites** view is closed:

```
public void dispose() {
    if (pageSelectionListener != null)
        getSite().getPage().removePostSelectionListener(
            pageSelectionListener);
    super.dispose();
}
```

7.5 Saving View State

Up to this point, the **Favorites** view contains only the current list of projects when the Eclipse session starts up. Items can be added to the **Favorites** view during the course of the session, but as soon as Eclipse is shut down, the changes are lost. In addition, the view's sort and filter information should be saved so that the view will be returned to the same state when the session is restarted. To accomplish all this, we will use two different mechanisms.

7.5.1 Saving local view information

Eclipse provides a memento-based mechanism for saving view and editor state information. In our case, this mechanism is good for saving the sorting and filter state of a view because that information is specific to each individual view. It is not good for saving global information shared by multiple views, so we will tackle that in the next section.

To save the sorting state, we need to add two methods to the Favorites-ViewSorter. The first method saves the current sort state as an instance of IMemento by converting the sort order and ascending/descending state into an XML-like structure. The second method takes a very guarded approach to reading and resetting the sort order and ascending/descending state from IMemento so that the sort state will be valid even if IMemento is not what was expected.

```
private static final String TAG_DESCENDING = "descending";
private static final String TAG_COLUMN_INDEX = "columnIndex";
private static final String TAG_TYPE = "SortInfo";
private static final String TAG_TRUE = "true";

public void saveState(IMemento memento) {
    for (int i = 0; i < infos.length; i++) {
        SortInfo info = infos[i];
        IMemento mem = memento.createChild(TAG_TYPE);
        mem.putInteger(TAG_COLUMN_INDEX, info.columnIndex);
        if (info.descending)
            mem.putString(TAG_DESCENDING, TAG_TRUE);
    }
}

public void init(IMemento memento) {
    List newInfos = new ArrayList(infos.length);
    IMemento[] mems = memento.getChildren(TAG_TYPE);
    for (int i = 0; i < mems.length; i++) {
        IMemento mem = mems[i];
        Integer value = mem.getInteger(TAG_COLUMN_INDEX);
        if (value == null)
            continue;
        int index = value.intValue();
        if (index < 0 || index >= infos.length)
            continue;
        SortInfo info = infos[index];
        if (newInfos.contains(info))
            continue;
        info.descending =
            TAG_TRUE.equals(mem.getString(TAG_DESCENDING));
        newInfos.add(info);
    }
    for (int i = 0; i < infos.length; i++)
        if (!newInfos.contains(infos[i]))
            newInfos.add(infos[i]);
```

```
    infos = (SortInfo[]) newInfos.toArray(
        new SortInfo[newInfos.size()]);
}
```

In addition to saving the sort state, we need to save the filter state. This is accomplished by adding the following two methods to the FavoritesView-FilterAction type:

```
public void saveState(IMemento memento) {
    nameFilter.saveState(memento);
}

public void init(IMemento memento) {
    nameFilter.init(memento);
}
```

and then adding two new methods to FavoritesViewNameFilter:

```
private static final String TAG_PATTERN = "pattern";
private static final String TAG_TYPE = "NameFilterInfo";

public void saveState(IMemento memento) {
    if (pattern.length() == 0)
        return;
    IMemento mem = memento.createChild(TAG_TYPE);
    mem.putString(TAG_PATTERN, pattern);
}

public void init(IMemento memento) {
    IMemento mem = memento.getChild(TAG_TYPE);
    if (mem == null)
        return;
    setPattern(mem.getString(TAG_PATTERN));
}
```

These new methods are hooked to the view by adding the following field and methods to the FavoritesView:

```
private IMemento memento;


public void saveState(IMemento memento) {
    super.saveState(memento);
    sorter.saveState(memento);
    filterAction.saveState(memento);
}

public void init(IViewSite site, IMemento memento)
    throws PartInitException
{
    super.init(site, memento);
    this.memento = memento;
}
```

The sorting and filter state cannot be restored immediately in the init (…) method shown above because the part control has not been created. Instead, the method caches IMemento for use later during the initialization process. We must then modify both createTableSorter() and createViewPulldownMenu() as shown below to restore the sorting and filter state before we associate the sorter with the viewer and the filter action with the menu, respectively.

```
private void createTableSorter() {

   … same code as in Section 7.2.6…

   if (memento != null)
      sorter.init(memento);
   viewer.setSorter(sorter);
}

private void createViewPulldownMenu() {

   … same code as in a Section 7.3.4…

   if (memento != null)
      filterAction.init(memento);
   menu.add(filterAction);
}
```

7.5.2 Saving global view information

We now need to save the state of the FavoritesManager, which is shared by all **Favorites** views. For this, we need to augment the FavoritesPlugin, the FavoritesManager, and each **Favorites** item with the ability to save their information so that they can be recreated later. In the FavoritesPlugin, augment the shutdown() method to call a new saveFavorites() method in the FavoritesManager:

```
public void shutdown() throws CoreException {
   FavoritesManager.getManager().saveFavorites();
   super.shutdown();
}
```

The existing loadFavorites() method in the FavoritesManager must be revised as follows and new methods added so that the **Favorites** items will be lazily loaded when needed. Lazy initialization is the Eclipse theme, so the list will not be built until it is needed. In addition, a new saveFavorites() method must be added to store the **Favorites** items so that they can be restored when Eclipse is restarted.

```java
private static final String TAG_FAVORITES = "Favorites";
private static final String TAG_FAVORITE = "Favorite";
private static final String TAG_TYPEID = "TypeId";
private static final String TAG_INFO = "Info";

private void loadFavorites() {
   favorites = new HashSet(20);
   FileReader reader = null;
   try {
      reader = new FileReader (getFavoritesFile());
      loadFavorites(XMLMemento.createReadRoot(reader));
   }
   catch (FileNotFoundException e) {
      // Ignored... no Favorites items exist yet.
   }
   catch (Exception e) {
      // Log the exception and move on.
      FavoritesLog.logError(e);
   }
   finally {
      try {
         if (reader != null)
            reader.close();
      }
      catch (IOException e) {
         FavoritesLog.logError(e);
      }
   }
}

private void loadFavorites(XMLMemento memento) {
   IMemento [] children =
      memento.getChildren(TAG_FAVORITE);
   for (int i = 0; i < children.length; i++) {
      IFavoriteItem item =
         newFavoriteFor(
            children[i].getString(TAG_TYPEID),
            children[i].getString(TAG_INFO));
      if (item != null)
         favorites.add(item);
   }
}

private IFavoriteItem newFavoriteFor(String typeId, String info) {
   FavoriteItemType[] types = FavoriteItemType.getTypes();
   for (int i = 0; i < types.length; i++)
      if (types[i].getId().equals(typeId))
         return types[i].loadFavorite(info);
   return null;
}

public void saveFavorites() {
   if (favorites == null)
      return;
   XMLMemento memento =
      XMLMemento.createWriteRoot(TAG_FAVORITES);
```

```
         saveFavorites(memento);
         FileWriter writer = null;
         try {
             writer = new FileWriter(getFavoritesFile());
             memento.save(writer);
         }
         catch (IOException e) {
             FavoritesLog.logError(e);
         }
         finally {
             try {
                 if (writer != null)
                     writer.close();
             }
             catch (IOException e) {
                 FavoritesLog.logError(e);
             }
         }
     }

     private void saveFavorites(XMLMemento memento) {
         Iterator iter = favorites.iterator();
         while (iter.hasNext()) {
             IFavoriteItem item = (IFavoriteItem) iter.next();
             IMemento child = memento.createChild(TAG_FAVORITE);
             child.putString(TAG_TYPEID, item.getType().getId());
             child.putString(TAG_INFO, item.getInfo());
         }
     }

     private File getFavoritesFile() {
         return FavoritesPlugin
             .getDefault()
             .getStateLocation()
             .append("favorites.xml")
             .toFile();
     }
```

The load and save methods interact with a file named favorites.xml, which is located in the following workspace metadata subdirectory: <workspaceDir>\.metadata\.plugins\com.qualityeclipse.favorites. The file content is in XML format and might look something like this:

```
<?xml version="1.0" encoding="UTF-8"?>
<Favorites>
   <Favorite
       Info="/com.qualityeclipse.favorites/src"
       TypeId="WBFolder"/>
   <Favorite
       Info="/MyTest"
       TypeId="WBProj"/>
</Favorites>
```

> **Tip:** Eclipse can crash or lock up... not often, if ever, but it can. If it does, then the normal shutdown sequence is preempted and your plug-in will not get a chance to save its model state. To protect your data, you can register a save participant (`ISaveParticipant`) and store critical model states ("snapshots") at various times during the Eclipse session. The mechanism is the same as that used to receive resource change events when your plug-in is inactive (see Section 9.5, "Delayed Changed Events").

7.6 Testing

Now that we have modified the **Favorites** view, the JUnit tests for the **Favorites** view need to be updated to take the modifications into account. If the tests are run as they stand, you'll get the following failure:

```
testView(com.qualityeclipse.favorites.test.FavoritesViewTest)

junit.framework.AssertionFailedError: expected.length 3,
but actual.length 0 expected:<3> but was:<0>
at junit.framework.Assert.fail(Assert.java:47)
at junit.framework.Assert.failNotEquals(Assert.java:282)
at junit.framework.Assert.assertEquals(Assert.java:64)
at junit.framework.Assert.assertEquals(Assert.java:201)
at com.qualityeclipse.favorites.test.FavoritesViewTest
        .assertEquals(FavoritesViewTest.java:125)
at com.qualityeclipse.favorites.test.FavoritesViewTest
        .testView(FavoritesViewTest.java:93)
at sun.reflect.NativeMethodAccessorImpl
        .invoke0(Native Method)
... etc ...
```

On closer inspection, this test is looking for the default viewer content (see Section 2.8.3, "Creating a plug-in test"). Since we have removed this default content in favor of real content (see Section 7.2.4, "Content provider"), we need to modify the test as follows:

```
public void testView() {
    TableViewer viewer = testView.getFavoritesViewer();

    Object[] expectedContent = new Object[] { };
    Object[] expectedLabels = new String[] { };

    ... code for the rest of the test ...
}
```

7.7   **Image Caching**

`Image` is a Java construct that wraps a native resource and thus must be properly managed. As with all other native wrappers in Eclipse, the rule is that if you create it, you must dispose of it to prevent memory leaks. `ImageDescriptor`, on the other hand, is a pure Java type that identifies a particular image without its associated native resource. It does not need to be managed and removed properly; rather, it will be automatically managed and disposed by the Java garbage collector.

When a plug-in creates an instance of `Image`, it typically caches it in an object that maps the identifier for the image—typically an `ImageDescriptor`—to a particular image. Not only does the cache provide a way to remember which Image instances were created and thus need to be cleaned up, but it also keeps the same image from being loaded into memory more than once, preventing unnecessary usage of limited OS resources. Depending on where and when the image is used, the image cache may be disposed when the view closes, or it may be kept around for the life of the plug-in.

In our **Favorites** plug-in, if we need to load our own images (see Section 7.2.3), we would instantiate a class similar to the one below to cache loaded images. This class follows the Eclipse approach by lazily loading the images as they are requested rather than loading all images immediately when the plug-in starts or when the view is first opened. The plug-in's `shutdown()` method would be modified to call the `dispose()` method of this instance so that the images would be cleaned up when the plug-in is shut down.

```
package com.qualityeclipse.favorites.util;

import java.util.*;
import org.eclipse.jface.resource.*;
import org.eclipse.swt.graphics.*;

public class ImageCache {
   private final Map imageMap = new HashMap();

   public Image getImage(ImageDescriptor imageDescriptor) {
      if (imageDescriptor == null)
         return null;
      Image image = (Image) imageMap.get(imageDescriptor);
      if (image == null) {
         image = imageDescriptor.createImage();
         imageMap.put(imageDescriptor, image);
      }
      return image;
   }

   public void dispose() {
      Iterator iter = imageMap.values().iterator();
```

```
        while (iterator.hasNext())
            ((Image) iter.next()).dispose();
        imageMap.clear();
    }
}
```

Alternately, you can use the `org.eclipse.jface.resource.ImageRegistry` class or `Plugin.getImageRegistry()` method.

> **Tip:** SWT Designer (see Appendix A, "Eclipse Plug-ins and Resources") provides a `ResourceManager` that caches images, fonts, cursors, and so on.

7.8 Auto-sizing Table Columns

Another nice enhancement to the **Favorites** view is for the columns in the table to be automatically resized to fit the current space. To do this, we would replace the table layout:

```
table.setLayout(new AutoResizeTableLayout());
```

with an instance of this class:

```
package com.qualityeclipse.favorites.util;

import java.util.*;
import org.eclipse.jface.viewers.*;
import org.eclipse.swt.events.*;
import org.eclipse.swt.widgets.*;

public class AutoResizeTableLayout extends TableLayout
    implements ControlListener
{
    private final Table table;
    private List columns = new ArrayList();
    private boolean autosizing = false;

    public AutoResizeTableLayout(Table table) {
        this.table = table;
        table.addControlListener(this);
    }

    public void addColumnData(ColumnLayoutData data) {
        columns.add(data);
        super.addColumnData(data);
    }

    public void controlMoved(ControlEvent e) {
    }
```

```
public void controlResized(ControlEvent e) {
    if (autosizing)
        return;
    autosizing = true;
    try {
        autoSizeColumns();
    }
    finally {
        autosizing = false;
    }
}

private void autoSizeColumns() {
    int width = table.getClientArea().width;

    // XXX: Layout is being called with an invalid value
    // the first time it is being called on Linux.
    // This method resets the layout to null,
    // so we run it only when the value is OK.
    if (width <= 1)
        return;

    TableColumn[] tableColumns = table.getColumns();
    int size =
        Math.min(columns.size(), tableColumns.length);
    int[] widths = new int[size];
    int fixedWidth = 0;
    int numberOfWeightColumns = 0;
    int totalWeight = 0;

    // First calc space occupied by fixed columns.
    for (int i = 0; i < size; i++) {
        ColumnLayoutData col =
            (ColumnLayoutData) columns.get(i);
        if (col instanceof ColumnPixelData) {
            int pixels = ((ColumnPixelData) col).width;
            widths[i] = pixels;
            fixedWidth += pixels;
        }
        else if (col instanceof ColumnWeightData) {
            ColumnWeightData cw = (ColumnWeightData) col;
            numberOfWeightColumns++;
            int weight = cw.weight;
            totalWeight += weight;
        }
        else {
            throw new IllegalStateException(
                "Unknown column layout data");
        }
    }

    // Do we have columns that have a weight?
    if (numberOfWeightColumns > 0) {
        // Now, distribute the rest
        // to the columns with weight.
        int rest = width—fixedWidth;
        int totalDistributed = 0;
```

```
        for (int i = 0; i < size; i++) {
           ColumnLayoutData col =
              (ColumnLayoutData) columns.get(i);
           if (col instanceof ColumnWeightData) {
              ColumnWeightData cw = (ColumnWeightData) col;
              int weight = cw.weight;
              int pixels =
                 totalWeight == 0
                    ? 0
                    : weight * rest / totalWeight;
              if (pixels < cw.minimumWidth)
                 pixels = cw.minimumWidth;
              totalDistributed += pixels;
              widths[i] = pixels;
           }
        }

        // Distribute any remaining pixels
        // to columns with weight.
        int diff = rest-totalDistributed;
        for (int i = 0; diff > 0; i++) {
           if (i == size)
              i = 0;
           ColumnLayoutData col =
              (ColumnLayoutData) columns.get(i);
           if (col instanceof ColumnWeightData) {
              ++widths[i];
              --diff;
           }
        }
     }

     for (int i = 0; i < size; i++) {
        if (tableColumns[i].getWidth() != widths[i])
           tableColumns[i].setWidth(widths[i]);
     }
  }
}
```

7.9   RFWS Considerations

The "User Interface" section of the *RFWS Requirements* includes nine items—five requirements and four best practices—dealing with perspectives. All of them are derived from the Eclipse UI Guidelines.

7.9.1   *Views for navigation*

User Interface Guideline #26 is a requirement that states:

> Use a view to navigate a hierarchy of information, open an editor, or display the properties of an object.

To pass this test, create a list of the views defined by your application and demonstrate how they are used to navigate information, open editors, or display the properties of some object. In the case of the examples presented earlier in this chapter, we would show the **Favorites** view (see Figure 10-4) and describe its use to the reviewers. In particular, double-clicking on a file in the **Favorites** view will open the file in an editor.

7.9.2   Views save immediately

User Interface Guideline #27 is a requirement that states:

*Modifications made within a view must be saved immediately. For instance, if a file is modified in the **Navigator**, the changes must be committed to the workspace immediately. A change made in the **Outline** view must be committed to the edit model of the active editor immediately. For changes made in the **Properties** view, if the property is a property of an open edit model, it should be persisted to the edit model. If it is a property of a file, persist it to file. In the past, some views have tried to implement an editor-style lifecycle with a save action. This can cause confusion. The **File** menu within a workbench window contains a **Save** action, but it only applies to the active editor. It will not target the active view. This can lead to a situation where the **File > Save** action is in contradiction with the **Save** action within the view.*

For this test, show how changes made in your view are saved immediately. If your view updates an existing editor, make sure that the editor is immediately marked as dirty and shows the modification indicator (*). Further show that the **Save** menu does not need to be invoked for the view to save its changes.

7.9.3   One or more views?

User Interface Guideline #28 is a best practice that states:

If a view contains more than one control, it may be advisable to split it up into two or more views. In most cases, a view will contain a single control or viewer. However, it is possible to embed more than one viewer or control in the view. If these controls are linked such that selection in one control changes the input of another, it may be better to separate the view into two views. This makes it easier to reuse each control in other perspectives or scenarios.

Show that your views contain just a single control, or if they are composed of multiple controls, show that they would not be better represented as multiple linked views. The **Favorites** view easily satisfies this rule given that it is composed of only a single table control. An example of a multicontrol widget is the **Hierarchy** view provided in the base Eclipse platform.

7.9.4 View initialization

User Interface Guideline #29 is a requirement that states:

*When a view first opens, derive the view input from the state of the perspective. The view may consult the perspective input or selection, or the state of another view. For instance, if the **Outline** view is opened, it will determine the active editor, query the editor for an outline model, and display the outline model.*

To pass this test, show that your view reflects the input state of the perspective (if appropriate). If your view is meant to show some attribute of the selected editor, make sure that when your view is opened, it displays the appropriate information. For our **Favorites** view, this requirement probably does not apply. The **Favorites** view could be extended to update its own selection to reflect the currently active editor.

7.9.5 Selection-oriented actions

User Interface Guideline #30 is a best practice that states:

Fill the context menu with selection-oriented actions, not presentation actions. If an object is selected in a view and the context menu is opened, the context menu should only contain actions that are appropriate for the selection. Actions that affect the presentation of the view should not appear in the context menu.

Show that the items that appear in the view's context menu apply to the selected object rather than to the view as a whole. For the **Favorites** view, we would first select an item in the view, then select **Remove** to show that the action in the context menu applies to the selection rather than the entire view.

7.9.6 Register context menus

User Interface Guideline #31 is a best practice that states:

Register all context menus in the view with the platform. In the platform, the menu and toolbar for a view are automatically extended by the platform. By contrast, context menu extension is supported in collaboration between the view and the platform. To achieve this collaboration, a view must register each context menu it contains with the platform.

Show that the context menu of your view is extensible by the platform. If the platform defines commands that are appropriate for the objects contained in your view, those commands should appear in the context menu of your view. For the **Favorites** view, we would show that common Eclipse commands like "Replace With" and "Compare With" appear when we right-click on a **Favorites** item (see Figure 7–9).

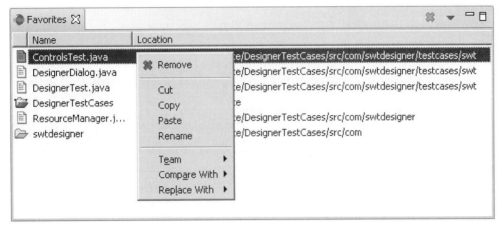

Figure 7–9 Favorites view showing platform contributions to the context menu.

7.9.7 Action filters for views

User Interface Guideline #32 is a best practice that states:

Implement an action filter for each object type in the view. An action filter makes it easier for one plug-in to add an action to objects in a view defined by another plug-in. An action target is described using object type and attributes.

As with the previous best practice, show that any commands contributed to your view's context menu are appropriate to the type of the selected object. Commands that don't apply should be filtered out. For the **Favorites** view, we would show that the platform commands contributed to the context menu are context-sensitive based on the type of object selected (see Figure 7–10).

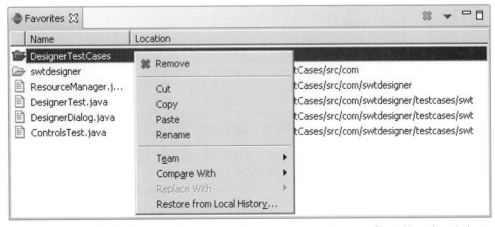

Figure 7–10 Favorites view showing that context menu items are filtered based on their type (projects show items other than files).

7.9.8 View global actions from menu bar

User Interface Guideline #33 is a requirement that states:

*If a view has support for **cut, copy, paste**, or any of the global actions, the same actions must be executable from the same actions in the window menu and toolbar. The window menu contains a number of global actions, such as **cut, copy**, and **paste** in the **Edit** menu. These actions target the active part, as indicated by a shaded title area. If these actions are supported within a view, the view should hook these window actions so that selection in the window menu or toolbar produces the same result as selection of the same action in the view. The following are the supported global actions: **undo, redo, cut, copy, paste, print, delete, find, select all**, and **bookmark**.*

For this requirement, if your view implements any of the items on the global action list, show that those commands may also be invoked from the window menus and toolbars. For the **Favorites** view, we would show that the **Cut, Copy, Paste**, and **Delete** (**Remove**) commands can be invoked from the platform **Edit** menu.

7.9.9 Persist view state

User Interface Guideline #34 is a requirement that states:

*Persist the state of each view between sessions. If a view is self-starting in the sense that its input is not derived from selection in other parts, the state of the view should be persisted between sessions. Within the workbench, the state of the **Navigator** view, including the input and expansion state, is saved between sessions.*

Show that your view persists its state between sessions. For the **Favorites** view, we would shut down and restart the workbench and show that the **Favorites** items appearing in the list are the same ones that were there when the workbench was shut down.

7.10 Summary

This chapter covered creating new views, modifying a view to respond to selections in the active editor or other views, and exporting a view's selection to the rest of Eclipse. The next chapter will discuss editors, which are used to edit the state of individual resources.

CHAPTER 8

Editors

Editors are the primary mechanism for users to create and modify resources (e.g., files). Eclipse provides some basic editors such as text and Java source editors, along with some more complex multipage editors such as the plug-in manifest editor. Products that need to present their own editors can use the same extension points used by the built-in Eclipse editors. In this chapter, we will create a new **Properties** editor, hook actions up to it, and link the editor to the **Outline** view.

Editors must implement the `org.eclipse.ui.IEditorPart` interface. Typically, views are subclasses of `org.eclipse.ui.part.EditorPart` and thus indirectly subclasses of `org.eclipse.ui.part.WorkbenchPart`, inheriting much of the behavior needed to implement the `IEditorPart` interface (see Figure 8–1).

Editors are contained in an `org.eclipse.ui.IEditorSite`, which in turn is contained in an `org.eclipse.ui.IWorkbenchPage`. In the spirit of lazy initialization, `IWorkbenchPage` holds on to instances of `org.eclipse.ui.IEditorReference` rather than the editor itself so that editors can be enumerated and referenced without actually loading the plug-in defining the editor.

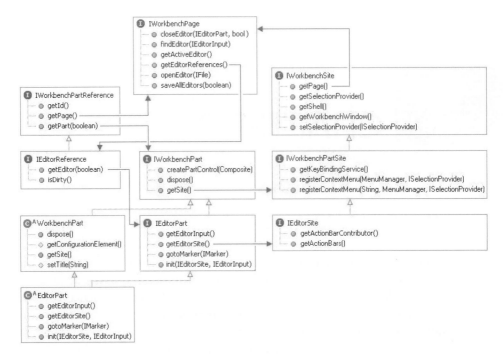

Figure 8–1   EditorPart classes.

Editors share a common set of behaviors with views via the `org.eclipse.ui.part.WorkbenchPart` superclass and `org.eclipse.ui .IWorkbenchPart` interface, but have some very important differences. Editors follow the classic open-modify-save paradigm, whereas any action performed in a view should immediately affect the state of the workspace and underlying resource(s). Editors appear in one area of Eclipse, while views are arranged around the outside of the editor area. Editors are typically resource-based, while views may show information about one resource, multiple resources, or even something totally unrelated to resources, such as available memory, network status, or builder errors.

8.1   Editor Declaration

There are two steps involved in creating a new editor:

• Define the editor in the plug-in manifest file.

• Create the editor part containing the code.

One way to do all this at once is to create the editor when the plug-in is being created, similar to the way that views can be created (see Section 2.2.3, "Define the view"). If the plug-in already exists, then this becomes a two-step process.

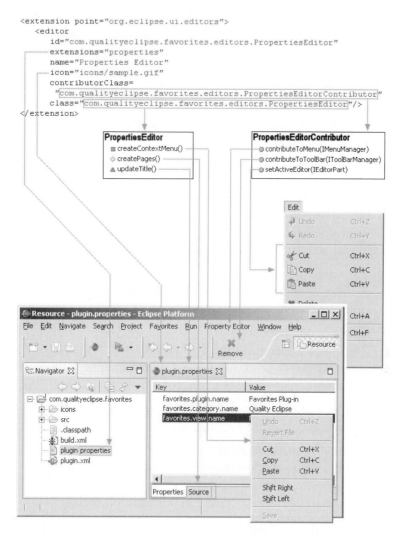

Figure 8–2   Editor declaration in plug-in manifest.

The first step in creating an editor is to define the editor in the plug-in manifest (see Figure 8–2). On the **Extensions** page of the plug-in manifest editor, click the **Add...** button in the upper right corner, select **org.eclipse.ui.editors**, and finally click **Finish**. Next, right-click on **org.eclipse.ui.editors** and select **New > editor** to add an editor extension. Double-click on the new editor extension to open the **Properties** view and then enter the following values:

class—"com.qualityeclipse.favorites.editors.PropertiesEditor"
The fully qualified name of the class defining the editor and implementing `org.eclipse.ui.IEditorPart`. Clicking on the "..." button at the right of the field opens a dialog for selecting an existing editor part or generating a new one. The attribute's class, command, and launcher are mutually exclusive. The class is instantiated using its no argument constructor, but may be parameterized using the `IExecutableExtension` interface (see Section 20.5, "Types Specified in an Extension Point").

contributorClass—"com.qualityeclipse.favorites.editors.PropertiesEditorContributor"
The fully qualified name of a class that implements `org.eclipse.ui.IEditorActionBarContributor` and adds new actions to the workbench menu and toolbar, reflecting the features of the editor type. This attribute should only be defined if the class attribute is defined. Clicking on the "..." button at the right of the field opens a dialog for selecting an existing editor contributor or generating a new one.

extensions—"properties"
A string of comma-separated file extensions indicating file types understood by the editor.

icon—"icons/sample.gif"
The image displayed at the upper left corner of the editor. Similar to action images (see Section 6.2.4, "Action images"), this path is relative to the plug-in's installation directory.

id—"com.qualityeclipse.favorites.editor.PropertiesEditor"
The unique identifier for this editor.

name—"Properties Editor"
The human-readable name for the editor.

Other attributes that are not used in this example include:

command—A command to run to launch an external editor. The executable command must be located on the system path or in the plug-in's directory. The attribute's class, command, and launcher are mutually exclusive.

default—"true" or "false" (blank = "false")
If `true`, this editor will be used as the default editor for the type. This is only relevant in the case where more than one editor is registered for the

same type. If an editor is not the default for the type, it can still be launched using the **Open with...** submenu for the selected resource.

filenames—A string containing comma-separated filenames indicating filenames understood by the editor. For instance, an editor that understands plug-in and fragment manifest files may register "plugin.xml, fragment.xml".

launcher—The name of a class that implements `org.eclipse.ui.IEditorLauncher` and opens an external editor. The attribute's class, command, and launcher are mutually exclusive.

8.2   Editor Part

The code defining the editor's behavior is found in a class implementing the `org.eclipse.ui.IEditorPart` interface, typically by subclassing either the `org.eclipse.ui.part.EditorPart` abstract class or `org.eclipse.ui.part.MultiPageEditorPart`. Our **Properties** editor will subclass `MultiPage-EditorPart` and provide two pages for the user to edit its content.

8.2.1   Editor methods

`EditorPart` methods:

> `createPartControl(Composite)`—Creates the controls comprising the editor. Typically, this method simply calls more finely grained methods such as `createTableTree`, `createTextEditor`, etc.

> `dispose()`—This method is automatically called when the editor is closed and marks the end of the editor's lifecycle. It cleans up any platform resources, such as images, clipboard, and so on, which were created by this class. This follows the *if you create it, you destroy it* theme that runs throughout Eclipse.

> `doSave(IProgressMonitor)`—Saves the contents of this editor. If the save is successful, the part should fire a property changed event (`PROP_DIRTY` property), reflecting the new dirty state. If the save is canceled via user action, or for any other reason, the part should invoke `setCanceled` on the `IProgressMonitor` to inform the caller (see Section 9.4, "Progress Monitor").

> `doSaveAs()`—This method is *optional*. It opens a **Save As** dialog and saves the content of the editor to a new location. If the save is successful, the part should fire a property changed event (`PROP_DIRTY` property), reflecting the new dirty state.

`gotoMarker(IMarker)`—Sets the cursor and selection state for this editor as specified by the given marker.

`init(IEditorSite, IEditorInput)`—Initializes this editor with the given editor site and input. This method is automatically called shortly after editor construction; it marks the start of the editor's lifecycle.

`isDirty()`—Returns whether the contents of this editor have changed since the last save operation.

`isSaveAsAllowed()`—Returns whether the "Save As" operation is supported by this part.

`setFocus()`—Asks this part to take focus within the workbench. Typically, this method simply calls `setFocus()` on one of its child controls.

`MultiPageEditorPart` provides the following additional methods:

`addPage(Control)`—Creates and adds a new page containing the given control to this multipage editor. The control may be `null`, allowing it to be created and set later using `setControl`.

`addPage(IEditorPart, IEditorInput)`—Creates and adds a new page containing the given editor to this multipage editor. This also hooks a property change listener on the nested editor.

`createPages()`—Creates the pages of this multipage editor. Typically, this method simply calls more finely grained methods such as `createTable-TreePage`, `createSourcePage`, and so on.

`getContainer()`—Returns the composite control containing this multipage editor's pages. This should be used as the parent when creating controls for individual pages. That is, when calling `addPage(Control)`, the passed control should be a child of this container.

`setPageImage(int, Image)`—Sets the image for the page with the given index.

`setPageText(int, String)`—Sets the text label for the page with the given index.

8.2.2   Editor controls

The new `PropertiesEditor` is a multipage editor containing a **Properties** page and a **Source** page. The **Properties** page contains a table tree displaying the property key/value pairs, while the **Source** page displays the text as it appears in the file itself. These two pages showcase building an editor out of individual controls (the **Properties** page) and nesting one type of editor inside another (the **Source** page).

```
package com.qualityeclipse.favorites.editors;

import org.eclipse.core.resources.*;
import org.eclipse.core.runtime.*;
import org.eclipse.jface.viewers.*;
import org.eclipse.swt.*;
import org.eclipse.ui.*;
import org.eclipse.ui.editors.text.*;
import org.eclipse.ui.part.*;

import com.qualityeclipse.favorites.FavoritesLog;

public class PropertiesEditor extends MultiPageEditorPart
{
   private TableTreeViewer tableTreeViewer;
   private TextEditor textEditor;

   public void init(
      IEditorSite site,
      IEditorInput editorInput)
      throws PartInitException {

      if (!(editorInput instanceof IFileEditorInput))
         throw new PartInitException(
            "Invalid Input: Must be IFileEditorInput");
      super.init(site, editorInput);
   }

   protected void createPages() {
      createTableTreePage();
      createSourcePage();
      updateTitle();
   }

   void createTableTreePage() {
      tableTreeViewer =
         new TableTreeViewer(
            getContainer(),
            SWT.MULTI | SWT.FULL_SELECTION);
      int index = addPage(tableTreeViewer.getControl());
      setPageText(index, "Properties");
   }

   void createSourcePage() {
      try {
         textEditor = new TextEditor();
         int index = addPage(textEditor, getEditorInput());
         setPageText(index, "Source");
      }
      catch (PartInitException e) {
         FavoritesLog.logError(
            "Error creating nested text editor",
            e);
      }
   }
```

```
void updateTitle() {
   IEditorInput input = getEditorInput();
   setTitle(input.getName());
   setTitleToolTip(input.getToolTipText());
}

public void setFocus() {
   switch (getActivePage()) {
      case 0:
         tableTreeViewer.getTableTree()
            .getTable().setFocus();
         break;
      case 1:
         textEditor.setFocus();
         break;
   }
}

public void gotoMarker(IMarker marker) {
   setActivePage(1);
   textEditor.gotoMarker(marker);
}

public boolean isSaveAsAllowed() {
   return true;
}

public void doSave(IProgressMonitor monitor) {
   textEditor.doSave(monitor);
}

public void doSaveAs() {
   textEditor.doSaveAs();
   setInput(textEditor.getEditorInput());
   updateTitle();
}
}
```

This code defines a very simple editor. When the editor is opened, the first page is an empty table tree (the content will be added in the next section), while the second page is an embedded text editor (see Figure 8–3). The editor handles all the normal text editing operations on the second page thanks to the embedded text editor, but the first page needs work.

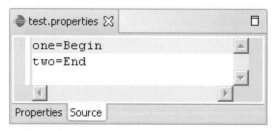

Figure 8–3 The Properties editor's Source page.

First, we need to add columns to the table tree by adding two new fields, refactoring the `createTableTreePage()` method, and adding the new `createTableTree()` method. Later, if we want the display to look more polished, we could auto-size the columns in the table tree (see Section 7.8, "Auto-sizing Table Columns").

```java
private TableColumn keyColumn;
private TableColumn valueColumn;

void createTableTreePage() {
   createTableTree();

   int index = addPage(tableTreeViewer.getControl());
   setPageText(index, "Properties");
}

void createTableTree() {
   tableTreeViewer =
      new TableTreeViewer(
         getContainer(),
         SWT.MULTI | SWT.FULL_SELECTION);
   TableTree tableTree = tableTreeViewer.getTableTree();
   Table table = tableTree.getTable();
   table.setHeaderVisible(true);

   keyColumn = new TableColumn(table, SWT.NONE);
   keyColumn.setText("Key");
   keyColumn.setWidth(150);

   valueColumn = new TableColumn(table, SWT.NONE);
   valueColumn.setText("Value");
   valueColumn.setWidth(150);
}
```

When run, the **Properties** editor now displays two empty columns on the **Properties** page (see Figure 8–4).

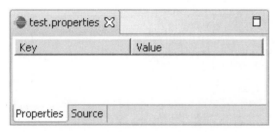

Figure 8–4   Properties editor's Properties page.

8.2.3 *Editor model*

The next step is to hook up the table tree so that content in the text editor appears in the table tree. To accomplish this, we need to build a model capable of parsing the text editor's content, and then attach that model, along with a label provider, to the table tree. Of course, there is lots of room for improvement in this model, such as splitting out the parsing and rebuilding code into a separate class and enhancing the parser to handle multiline values, but it will do for the purposes of our demonstration.

We start this process by introducing a new `PropertyElement` superclass for all property model objects:

```
package com.qualityeclipse.favorites.editors;

public abstract class PropertyElement
{
   public static final PropertyElement[] NO_CHILDREN = {};
   private PropertyElement parent;

   public PropertyElement(PropertyElement parent) {
      this.parent = parent;
   }

   public PropertyElement getParent() {
      return parent;
   }

   public abstract PropertyElement[] getChildren();

   public abstract void removeFromParent();
}
```

A `PropertyEntry` object represents a key/value pair in the property file:

```
package com.qualityeclipse.favorites.editors;

public class PropertyEntry extends PropertyElement
{
   String key;
   String value;

   public PropertyEntry(
      PropertyCategory parent,
      String key,
      String value) {

      super(parent);
      this.key = key;
      this.value = value;
   }
```

```java
   public String getKey() {
      return key;
   }

   public String getValue() {
      return value;
   }

   public PropertyElement[] getChildren() {
      return NO_CHILDREN;
   }

   public void setKey(String text) {
      if (key.equals(text))
         return;
      key = text;
      ((PropertyCategory) getParent()).keyChanged(this);
   }

   public void setValue(String text) {
      if (value.equals(text))
         return;
      value = text;
      ((PropertyCategory) getParent()).valueChanged(this);
   }

   public void removeFromParent() {
      ((PropertyCategory) getParent()).removeEntry(this);
   }
}
```

A PropertyCategory represents a group of related property entries with a comment preceding the group indicating the name. The category can extract its name and entries from a reader object.

```java
package com.qualityeclipse.favorites.editors;

import java.io.*;
import java.util.*;

public class PropertyCategory extends PropertyElement
{
   private String name;
   private List entries;

   public PropertyCategory(
      PropertyFile parent,
      LineNumberReader reader)
      throws IOException {

      super(parent);
```

```java
        // Determine the category name from comments.
        while (true) {
            reader.mark(1);
            int ch = reader.read();
            if (ch == -1)
                break;
            reader.reset();
            if (ch != '#')
                break;
            String line = reader.readLine();
            if (name == null) {
                line = line.replace('#', ' ').trim();
                if (line.length() > 0)
                    name = line;
            }
        }
        if (name == null)
            name = "";

        // Determine the properties in this category.
        entries = new ArrayList();
        while (true) {
            reader.mark(1);
            int ch = reader.read();
            if (ch == -1)
                break;
            reader.reset();
            if (ch == '#')
                break;
            String line = reader.readLine();
            int index = line.indexOf('=');
            if (index != -1) {
                String key = line.substring(0, index).trim();
                String value = line.substring(index + 1).trim();
                entries.add(new PropertyEntry(this, key, value));
            }
        }
    }

    public String getName() {
        return name;
    }

    public Collection getEntries() {
        return entries;
    }

    public PropertyElement[] getChildren() {
        return (PropertyElement[]) entries.toArray(
            new PropertyElement[entries.size()]);
    }

    public void setName(String text) {
        if (name.equals(text))
            return;
        name = text;
```

```
            ((PropertyFile) getParent()).nameChanged(this);
    }

    public void addEntry(PropertyEntry entry) {
        if (!entries.contains(entry)) {
            entries.add(entry);
            ((PropertyFile) getParent()).entryAdded(
                this, entry);
        }
    }

    public void removeEntry(PropertyEntry entry) {
        if (entries.remove(entry))
            ((PropertyFile) getParent()).entryRemoved(
                this, entry);
    }

    public void removeFromParent() {
        ((PropertyFile) getParent()).removeCategory(this);
    }

    public void keyChanged(PropertyEntry entry) {
        ((PropertyFile) getParent()).keyChanged(this, entry);
    }

    public void valueChanged(PropertyEntry entry) {
        ((PropertyFile) getParent()).valueChanged(this, entry);
    }
}
```

The PropertyFile object ties it all together:

```
package com.qualityeclipse.favorites.editors;

import java.io.*;
import java.util.*;

import com.qualityeclipse.favorites.FavoritesLog;

public class PropertyFile extends PropertyElement
{
    private PropertyCategory unnamedCategory;
    private List categories;
    private List listeners = new ArrayList();

    public PropertyFile(String content) {
        super(null);
        categories = new ArrayList();

        LineNumberReader reader =
            new LineNumberReader(new StringReader(content));
        try {
            unnamedCategory =
                new PropertyCategory(this, reader);
```

```
            while (true) {
                reader.mark(1);
                int ch = reader.read();
                if (ch == -1)
                    break;
                reader.reset();
                categories.add(
                    new PropertyCategory(this, reader));
            }
        }
        catch (IOException e) {
            FavoritesLog.logError(e);
        }
    }

    public PropertyElement[] getChildren() {
        List children = new ArrayList();
        children.addAll(unnamedCategory.getEntries());
        children.addAll(categories);
        return (PropertyElement[]) children.toArray(
            new PropertyElement[children.size()]);
    }

    public void addCategory(PropertyCategory category) {
        if (!categories.contains(category)) {
            categories.add(category);
            categoryAdded(category);
        }
    }

    public void removeCategory(PropertyCategory category) {
        if (categories.remove(category))
            categoryRemoved(category);
    }

    public void removeFromParent() {
        // Nothing to do.
    }

    void addPropertyFileListener(
      PropertyFileListener listener) {
        if (!listeners.contains(listener))
            listeners.add(listener);
    }

    void removePropertyFileListener(
        PropertyFileListener listener) {
        listeners.remove(listener);
    }

    void keyChanged(
        PropertyCategory category,
        PropertyEntry entry) {

        Iterator iter = listeners.iterator();
```

```
      while (iter.hasNext())
         ((PropertyFileListener) iter.next())
            .keyChanged(category, entry);
   }

   void valueChanged(
      PropertyCategory category,
      PropertyEntry entry) {

      Iterator iter = listeners.iterator();
      while (iter.hasNext())
         ((PropertyFileListener) iter.next())
            .valueChanged(category, entry);
   }

   void nameChanged(PropertyCategory category) {
      Iterator iter = listeners.iterator();
      while (iter.hasNext())
         ((PropertyFileListener) iter.next())
            .nameChanged(category);
   }

   void entryAdded(
      PropertyCategory category,
      PropertyEntry entry) {

      Iterator iter = listeners.iterator();
      while (iter.hasNext())
         ((PropertyFileListener) iter.next())
            .entryAdded(category, entry);
   }

   void entryRemoved(
      PropertyCategory category,
      PropertyEntry entry) {

      Iterator iter = listeners.iterator();
      while (iter.hasNext())
         ((PropertyFileListener) iter.next())
            .entryRemoved(category, entry);
   }

   void categoryAdded(PropertyCategory category) {
      Iterator iter = listeners.iterator();
      while (iter.hasNext())
         ((PropertyFileListener) iter.next())
            .categoryAdded(category);
   }

   void categoryRemoved(PropertyCategory category) {
      Iterator iter = listeners.iterator();
      while (iter.hasNext())
         ((PropertyFileListener) iter.next())
            .categoryRemoved(category);
   }
}
```

The `PropertyFileListener` interface is used by `ProperyFile` to notify registered listeners, such as `PropertiesEditor`, that changes have occurred in the model:

```
package com.qualityeclipse.favorites.editors;

public interface PropertyFileListener
{
   void keyChanged(
      PropertyCategory category,
      PropertyEntry entry);

   void valueChanged(
      PropertyCategory category,
      PropertyEntry entry);

   void nameChanged(
      PropertyCategory category);

   void entryAdded(
      PropertyCategory category,
      PropertyEntry entry);

   void entryRemoved(
      PropertyCategory category,
      PropertyEntry entry);

   void categoryAdded(
      PropertyCategory category);

   void categoryRemoved(
      PropertyCategory category);
}
```

8.2.4 *Content provider*

All these model objects are useless unless they can be properly displayed in the table tree. To accomplish this, we need to create a content provider and label provider. The content provider provides the rows appearing in the table tree along with parent/child relationships, but not the actual cell content.

```
package com.qualityeclipse.favorites.editors;

import org.eclipse.jface.viewers.*;

public class PropertiesEditorContentProvider
   implements ITreeContentProvider
{
   private PropertyFile input;

   public void inputChanged(
      Viewer viewer,
```

```
                   Object oldInput,
                   Object newInput) {

                input = (PropertyFile) newInput;
             }

             public Object[] getElements(Object element) {
                return getChildren(element);
             }

             public Object[] getChildren(Object element) {
                if (element instanceof PropertyElement)
                   return ((PropertyElement) element).getChildren();
                return null;
             }

             public Object getParent(Object element) {
                if (element instanceof PropertyElement)
                   return ((PropertyElement) element).getParent();
                return null;
             }

             public boolean hasChildren(Object element) {
                if (element instanceof PropertyElement)
                   return ((PropertyElement) element)
                      .getChildren()
                      .length
                      > 0;
                return false;
             }

             public void dispose() {
             }
          }
```

8.2.5   Label provider

The label provider converts the row element object as returned by the content provider into images and text that can be displayed in the table cells.

```
package com.qualityeclipse.favorites.editors;

import org.eclipse.jface.viewers.*;
import org.eclipse.swt.graphics.*;

public class PropertiesEditorLabelProvider
   extends LabelProvider
   implements ITableLabelProvider
{
   public Image getColumnImage(
      Object element,
      int columnIndex) {

      return null;
   }
```

```
public String getColumnText(
   Object element,
   int columnIndex) {

   if (element instanceof PropertyCategory) {
      PropertyCategory category =
         (PropertyCategory) element;
      switch (columnIndex) {
         case 0 :
            return category.getName();
         case 1 :
            return "";
      }
   }

   if (element instanceof PropertyEntry) {
      PropertyEntry entry = (PropertyEntry) element;
      switch (columnIndex) {
         case 0 :
            return entry.getKey();
         case 1 :
            return entry.getValue();
      }
   }

   if (element == null)
      return "<null>";
   return element.toString();
   }
}
```

Finally, we need to add a new `initTableTreeContent()` method called from the `createTableTreePage()` method, to associate the new content and label providers with the table tree. This method is followed by another new method to synchronize the text editor's content with the table tree's content. The call to `asyncExec(...)` ensures that the `updateTableTreeFromTextEditor` method is executed in the UI thread (see Section 4.2.5.1, "Display," for more on the UI thread).

```
private PropertiesEditorContentProvider
   tableTreeContentProvider;

void initTableTreeContent() {
   tableTreeContentProvider =
      new PropertiesEditorContentProvider();
   tableTreeViewer.setContentProvider(
      tableTreeContentProvider);
   tableTreeViewer.setLabelProvider(
      new PropertiesEditorLabelProvider());

   // Reset the input from the text editor's content
   // after the editor initialization has completed.
```

```
        tableTreeViewer.setInput(new PropertyFile(""));
        tableTreeViewer.getTableTree().getDisplay()
           .asyncExec(new Runnable() {
              public void run() {
                 updateTableTreeFromTextEditor();
              }
           });
        tableTreeViewer.setAutoExpandLevel(
           TableTreeViewer.ALL_LEVELS);
   }

   void updateTableTreeFromTextEditor() {
      propertyFile = new PropertyFile(
         textEditor
            .getDocumentProvider()
            .getDocument(textEditor.getEditorInput())
            .get());
      tableTreeViewer.setInput(propertyFile);
   }
```

When all this has been accomplished, the **Properties** editor's **Properties** page will have some content (see Figures 8–5 and 8–6).

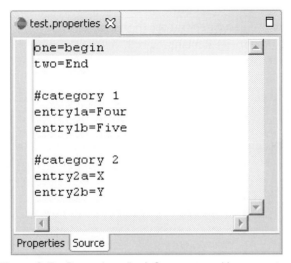

Figure 8–5   Properties editor's Source page with new content.

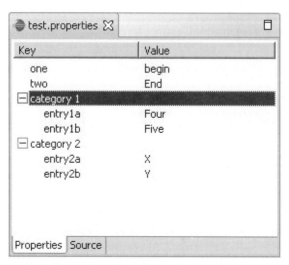

Figure 8–6   Properties editor's Properties page with new content.

8.3   Editing

When the **Properties** page displays the content in a table tree, we want to edit
the content without having to switch to the **Source** page (see Section 14.2.4,
"Marker resolution—quick fix," for an example of manipulating the content
in an existing text editor).

8.3.1   Cell editors

Cell editors use identifiers rather than a column index to identify what aspect
of a particular object is being edited. Before creating the cell editors, we first
create some constants used as identifiers:

```
public static final String VALUE_COLUMN_ID = "Value";
public static final String KEY_COLUMN_ID = "Key";
```

and then assign property identifiers to each column by adding a new init-
TableTreeEditors() method that is called from the createTableTreePage()
method:

```
tableTreeViewer.setColumnProperties(
    new String[] { KEY_COLUMN_ID, VALUE_COLUMN_ID });
```

The cell editors are created by adding code to the `initTableTreeEditors()` method:

```
final TextCellEditor keyEditor =
    new TextCellEditor(
        tableTreeViewer.getTableTree().getTable());
final TextCellEditor valueEditor =
    new TextCellEditor(
        tableTreeViewer.getTableTree().getTable());
tableTreeViewer.setCellEditors(
    new CellEditor[] { keyEditor, valueEditor });
```

8.3.2 Cell modifiers

Cell editors know nothing about the model being edited, which is where cell modifiers come in. Cell modifiers adapt the underlying model to an interface understood by cell editors so that the cell editors can present the correct value to the user and update the model with new values when a user has made modifications. We add new code to the `initTableTreeEditors()` method:

```
tableTreeViewer.setCellModifier(
    new PropertiesEditorCellModifier(this, tableTreeViewer));
```

and then create a new class to handle this editor/model interaction:

```
package com.qualityeclipse.favorites.editors;

import org.eclipse.jface.viewers.*;
import org.eclipse.swt.custom.*;

public class PropertiesEditorCellModifier
    implements ICellModifier
{
    private PropertiesEditor editor;
    private TableTreeViewer viewer;

    public PropertiesEditorCellModifier(
        PropertiesEditor editor,
        TableTreeViewer viewer) {

        this.editor = editor;
        this.viewer = viewer;
    }

    public boolean canModify(
        Object element,
        String property) {

        if (property == PropertiesEditor.KEY_COLUMN_ID) {
            if (element instanceof PropertyCategory)
                return true;
```

```
        if (element instanceof PropertyEntry)
            return true;
    }
    if (property == PropertiesEditor.VALUE_COLUMN_ID){
        if (element instanceof PropertyEntry)
            return true;
    }
    return false;
}

public Object getValue(
    Object element,
    String property) {

    if (property == PropertiesEditor.KEY_COLUMN_ID) {
        if (element instanceof PropertyCategory)
            return ((PropertyCategory) element).getName();
        if (element instanceof PropertyEntry)
            return ((PropertyEntry) element).getKey();
    }
    if (property == PropertiesEditor.VALUE_COLUMN_ID){
        if (element instanceof PropertyEntry)
            return ((PropertyEntry) element).getValue();
    }
    return null;
}

public void modify(
    Object item,
    String property,
    Object value) {

    // Null indicates that the validator rejected the value.
    if (value == null)
        return;

    Object element = item;
    if (element instanceof TableTreeItem)
        element = ((TableTreeItem) element).getData();

    String text = ((String) value).trim();
    if (property == PropertiesEditor.KEY_COLUMN_ID) {
        if (element instanceof PropertyCategory)
            ((PropertyCategory) element).setName(text);
        if (element instanceof PropertyEntry)
            ((PropertyEntry) element).setKey(text);
    }
    if (property == PropertiesEditor.VALUE_COLUMN_ID){
        if (element instanceof PropertyEntry)
            ((PropertyEntry) element).setValue(text);
    }
}
}
```

The `modify(Object, String, Object)` method calls a new `tableTree-Modified()` method in the `PropertiesEditor` class to notify any interested members that the editor's content has been modified.

```
public void tableTreeModified() {
   if (!isDirty())
      firePropertyChange(IEditorPart.PROP_DIRTY);
}
```

8.3.3 Change listeners

When a user edits a value, the model generates a change event to notify registered listeners. Our next step is to hook up a change listener in the `PropertiesEditor` class so that we can be notified of events and update the table tree appropriately.

```
private final PropertyFileListener propertyFileListener =
   new PropertyFileListener() {

   public void keyChanged(
      PropertyCategory category,
      PropertyEntry entry) {

      tableTreeViewer.update(
         entry,
         new String[] { KEY_COLUMN_ID });
      tableTreeModified();
   }
   public void valueChanged(
      PropertyCategory category,
      PropertyEntry entry) {

      tableTreeViewer.update(
         entry,
         new String[] { VALUE_COLUMN_ID });
      tableTreeModified();
   }
   public void nameChanged(
      PropertyCategory category) {

      tableTreeViewer.update(
         category,
         new String[] { KEY_COLUMN_ID });
      tableTreeModified();
   }
   public void entryAdded(
      PropertyCategory category,
      PropertyEntry entry) {

      tableTreeViewer.refresh();
      tableTreeModified();
   }
```

```
        public void entryRemoved(
            PropertyCategory category,
            PropertyEntry entry) {

            tableTreeViewer.refresh();
            tableTreeModified();
        }
        public void categoryAdded(
            PropertyCategory category) {

            tableTreeViewer.refresh();
            tableTreeModified();
        }
        public void categoryRemoved(
            PropertyCategory category) {

            tableTreeViewer.refresh();
            tableTreeModified();
        }
    };

    void updateTableTreeFromTextEditor() {
        PropertyFile propertyFile =
            (PropertyFile) tableTreeViewer.getInput();
        propertyFile.removePropertyFileListener(
            propertyFileListener);
        propertyFile = new PropertyFile(
            textEditor
                .getDocumentProvider()
                .getDocument(textEditor.getEditorInput())
                .get());
        tableTreeViewer.setInput(propertyFile);
        propertyFile.addPropertyFileListener(
            propertyFileListener);
    }
```

8.3.4 Cell validators

Cell editors have validators to prevent invalid input from reaching model
objects. Whenever a user modifies a cell editor's content, the isValid(Object)
method returns an error message if the object represents an invalid value, or
null if the value is valid. We assign each cell editor a validator in the init-
TableTreeEditors() method as follows:

```
keyEditor.setValidator(new ICellEditorValidator() {
    public String isValid(Object value) {
        if (((String) value).trim().length() == 0)
            return " Key must not be empty string";
        return null;
    }
});
```

```
valueEditor.setValidator(new ICellEditorValidator() {
   public String isValid(Object value) {
      return null;
   }
});
```

Whenever a user enters an invalid value, we have to decide how the user will be notified that the value is invalid. In our case, we will add an `ICellEditor-Listener` in the `initTableTreeEditors()` method so that the error message will appear in the window's status line (see Figure 8–7). For a more prominent error message, the editor's header area could be redesigned to allow an error image and message to be displayed just above the table tree rather than in the workbench's status line.

```
keyEditor.addListener(new ICellEditorListener() {
   public void applyEditorValue() {
      setErrorMessage(null);
   }
   public void cancelEditor() {
      setErrorMessage(null);
   }
   public void editorValueChanged(
      boolean oldValidState,
      boolean newValidState) {

      setErrorMessage(keyEditor.getErrorMessage());
   }
   void setErrorMessage(String errorMessage) {
      getEditorSite().getActionBars().getStatusLineManager()
         .setErrorMessage(errorMessage);
   }
});
```

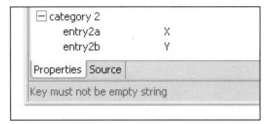

Figure 8–7   Error message in status line indicating invalid input.

8.3.5   *Editing versus selecting*

Before we added editing in the table tree, a user could easily select one or more rows, but now the cell editor is always opened. One possible solution is to only open the editor when the **Alt** key is held down, but select one or more rows when it is not. To accomplish this, we need to add some additional `Prop-`

ertiesEditor code to capture the state of the **Alt** key. This same approach could be used to capture the state of any modifier key.

```
private boolean isAltPressed;

private void addTableKeyListener() {
   tableTreeViewer.getTableTree().getTable()
      .addKeyListener(new KeyListener() {
      public void keyPressed(KeyEvent e) {
         if (e.keyCode == SWT.ALT)
            isAltPressed = true;
      }
      public void keyReleased(KeyEvent e) {
         if (e.keyCode == SWT.ALT)
            isAltPressed = false;
      }
   });
}

public boolean shouldEdit() {
   if (!isAltPressed)
      return false;
   // Must reset this value here because if an editor
   // is opened, we don't get the Alt key up event.
   isAltPressed = false;
   return true;
}
```

Next, we will modify the following method in PropertiesEditorCell-Modifier so that the cell editor will only be opened when the **Alt** key is held down:

```
public boolean canModify(
   Object element,
   String property) {

   if (property == PropertiesEditor.KEY_COLUMN_ID) {
      if (element instanceof PropertyCategory)
         return editor.shouldEdit();
      if (element instanceof PropertyEntry)
         return editor.shouldEdit();
   }
   if (property == PropertiesEditor.VALUE_COLUMN_ID){
      if (element instanceof PropertyEntry)
         return editor.shouldEdit();
   }
   return false;
}
```

8.4   Editor Lifecycle

Typical editors go through an open-modify-save-close lifecycle. When the editor is opened, the init(IEditorSite, IEditorInput) method is called to set the editor's initial content. When the user modifies the editor's content, the editor must notify others that its content is now "dirty" via the firePropertyChange(int) method. When a user saves the editor's content, the firePropertyChange(int) method must be used again to notify registered listeners that the editor's content is no longer dirty. Eclipse automatically registers listeners to perform various tasks based on the value returned by the isDirty() method, such as updating the editor's title, adding or removing an asterisk preceding the title, and enabling the **Save** menu. Finally, when the editor is closed, the editor's content is saved if the isDirty() method returns true.

8.4.1   Dirty editors

We need to ensure that the editor knows whether or not its content has been modified by the user since the last save operation. To do this, we introduce a new field to track whether or not the current page has been modified relative to the other pages:

```
private boolean isPageModified;
```

Whenever the current page's content has been modified, we need to set the new isPageModified field. Whenever the table tree is modified, the cell modifier calls the tableTreeModified() method (see Section 8.3.2, "Cell modifiers"), where we can set the new isPageModified field. In addition, whenever the text editor is modified, the MultiPageEditorPart's addPage(IEditorPart, IEditorInput) method uses the handlePropertyChange(int) method (see the createSourcePage method() in Section 8.2.2, "Editor controls") to notify others when the editor's content has changed. We can override this method to set the isPageModified field as appropriate:

```
public void tableTreeModified() {
   isPageModified = true;
   if (!super.isDirty())
      firePropertyChange(IEditorPart.PROP_DIRTY);
}

protected void handlePropertyChange (int propertyId) {
   if (propertyId == IEditorPart.PROP_DIRTY)
      isPageModified = isDirty();
   super.handlePropertyChange(propertyId);
}
```

Finally, we need to let other registered listeners know when the editor's content is dirty. The `MultiPageEditorPart`'s `isDirty()` method appropriately returns **true** for the nested text editor on the **Source** page, but knows nothing about modifications to the table tree. Overriding this method to add this knowledge causes the **Save** menu item to be enabled and the editor's title to be updated at the appropriate time.

```
public boolean isDirty() {
   return isPageModified || super.isDirty();
}
```

8.4.2   Switching pages

When switching between the **Properties** and **Source** pages, any edits made in the **Properties** page must automatically carry over to the **Source** page, and vice versa. To accomplish this, we override the `pageChange(int)` method to update the page content:

```
protected void pageChange(int newPageIndex) {
   switch (newPageIndex) {
      case 0 :
         if (isDirty())
            updateTableTreeFromTextEditor();
         break;
      case 1 :
         if (isPageModified)
            updateTextEditorFromTableTree();
         break;
   }
   isPageModified = false;
   super.pageChange(newPageIndex);
}
```

The `updateTableTreeFromTextEditor()` method has already been defined (see Section 8.2.3, "Editor model"), but the `updateTextEditorFromTableTree()` method has not, so we'll add it now:

```
void updateTextEditorFromTableTree() {
   textEditor
      .getDocumentProvider()
      .getDocument(textEditor.getEditorInput())
      .set(
         ((PropertyFile) tableTreeViewer.getInput())
            .asText());
}
```

The `updateTextEditorFromTableTree()` method calls a new `asText()` method in `PropertyFile`. The new `asText()` method reverses the parsing process in the `PropertyFile`'s constructor (see Section 8.2.3) by reassembling the model into a textual representation.

```
public String asText() {
    StringWriter stringWriter = new StringWriter(2000);
    PrintWriter writer = new PrintWriter(stringWriter);
    unnamedCategory.appendText(writer);
    Iterator iter = categories.iterator();
    while (iter.hasNext()) {
        writer.println();
        ((PropertyCategory) iter.next())
            .appendText(writer);
    }
    return stringWriter.toString();
}
```

The `asText()` method calls a new `appendText(PrintWriter)` method in PropertyCategory:

```
public void appendText(PrintWriter writer) {
    if (name.length() > 0) {
        writer.print("# ");
        writer.println(name);
    }
    Iterator iter = entries.iterator();
    while (iter.hasNext())
        ((PropertyEntry) iter.next()).appendText(writer);
}
```

which then calls a new `appendText(PrintWriter)` method in `PropertyEntry`:

```
public void appendText(PrintWriter writer) {
    writer.print(key);
    writer.print(" = ");
    writer.println(value);
}
```

8.4.3   Saving content

Because our current implementation uses the nested text editor to save content into the file being edited, changes on the **Properties** page will not be noticed unless the user switches to the **Source** page. We must modify the following methods to update the nested text editor before saving. Since save operations are typically long-running operations, the progress monitor is used to communicate progress to the user (see Section 9.4, "Progress Monitor").

```
public void doSave(IProgressMonitor monitor) {
    if (getActivePage() == 0 && isPageModified)
        updateTextEditorFromTableTree();
    isPageModified = false;
    textEditor.doSave(monitor);
}

public void doSaveAs() {
    if (getActivePage() == 0 && isPageModified)
        updateTextEditorFromTableTree();
    isPageModified = false;
    textEditor.doSaveAs();
    setInput(textEditor.getEditorInput());
    updateTitle();
}
```

8.5   Editor Actions

Editor actions can appear as menu items in the view's context menu, as toolbar buttons in the workbench's toolbar, and as menu items in the workbench's
menu (see Figure 6–10). This section covers adding actions to an editor programmatically, whereas Section 6.5, "Editor Actions," discussed adding
actions by using declarations in the plug-in manifest (see Section 14.2.4 for an
example of manipulating the content in an existing text editor).

8.5.1   Context menu

Typically, editors have context menus populated by actions targeted at the editor or at selected objects within the editor. There are several steps to creating
an editor's context menu and several more steps to register the editor so that
others can contribute actions (see Sections 6.3, "Object Actions," 6.5.1,
"Defining an editor context menu," and 6.5.2, "Defining an editor context
action," for information concerning how actions are contributed to an editor's context menus via the plug-in manifest).

8.5.1.1   Creating actions

The first step is to create the menu item actions that will appear in the context
menu. For the **Properties** editor, we need an action that will remove the
selected table tree elements from the editor. In addition, this action adds a
selection listener to facilitate keeping its enablement state in sync with the current table tree selection.

```
package com.qualityeclipse.favorites.editors;

import java.util.Iterator;
```

```
import org.eclipse.jface.action.*;
import org.eclipse.jface.resource.*;
import org.eclipse.jface.viewers.*;
import org.eclipse.swt.custom.*;

public class RemovePropertiesAction extends Action
{
    private final PropertiesEditor editor;
    private final TableTreeViewer viewer;

    private ISelectionChangedListener listener =
        new ISelectionChangedListener() {
        public void selectionChanged(SelectionChangedEvent e)
        {
            setEnabled(!e.getSelection().isEmpty());
        }
    };

    public RemovePropertiesAction(
        PropertiesEditor editor,
        TableTreeViewer viewer,
        String text,
        ImageDescriptor imageDescriptor) {

        super(text, imageDescriptor);
        this.editor = editor;
        this.viewer = viewer;
        setEnabled(false);
        viewer.addSelectionChangedListener(listener);
    }

    public void run() {
        ISelection sel = viewer.getSelection();
        TableTree tableTree = viewer.getTableTree();
        tableTree.setRedraw(false);
        try {
            Iterator iter =
                ((IStructuredSelection) sel).iterator();
            while (iter.hasNext())
                ((PropertyElement) ((Object) iter.next()))
                    .removeFromParent();
        }
        finally {
            tableTree.setRedraw(true);
        }
    }
}
```

Tip: As shown in the code above, use the table tree's `setRedraw(boolean)` method to reduce flashing when making more than one modification to a control or its model.

In `PropertiesEditor`, create a new field to hold the action and then call the following new method from `createPages()` method to initialize the field:

```
private RemovePropertiesAction removeAction;

private void createActions() {
   ImageDescriptor removeImage =
      PlatformUI
         .getWorkbench()
         .getSharedImages()
         .getImageDescriptor(
            ISharedImages.IMG_TOOL_DELETE);
   ImageDescriptor removeImageHover =
      PlatformUI
         .getWorkbench()
         .getSharedImages()
         .getImageDescriptor(
            ISharedImages.IMG_TOOL_DELETE_HOVER);
   removeAction =
      new RemovePropertiesAction(
         this,
         tableTreeViewer,
         "Remove",
         removeImage);
   removeAction.setHoverImageDescriptor(
      removeImageHover);
}
```

This same action is used later for keyboard-based actions (see Section 8.5.2.4, "Keyboard actions") and global actions (see Section 8.5.2.1, "Global actions").

8.5.1.2   Creating the context menu

The context menu must be created at the same time as the editor. However, because contributors can add and remove menu items based on the selection, its contents cannot be determined until just after the user clicks the right mouse button and just before the menu is displayed. To accomplish this, set the menu's `RemoveAllWhenShown` property to `true` so that the menu will be built from scratch each time, and add a menu listener to dynamically build the menu. In addition, the menu must be registered with the control so that it will be displayed, and with the editor site so that other plug-ins can contribute actions to it (see Section 6.4, "View Actions").

For the **Properties** editor, modify `createPages()` to call the new `create-ContextMenu()` method shown below:

```
private void createContextMenu() {
   MenuManager menuMgr = new MenuManager("#PopupMenu");
   menuMgr.setRemoveAllWhenShown(true);
   menuMgr.addMenuListener(new IMenuListener() {
```

```
        public void menuAboutToShow(IMenuManager m) {
            PropertiesEditor.this.fillContextMenu(m);
        }
    });
    Table table =
        tableTreeViewer.getTableTree().getTable();
    Menu menu = menuMgr.createContextMenu(table);
    table.setMenu(menu);
    getSite().registerContextMenu(
        menuMgr,
        tableTreeViewer);
}
```

8.5.1.3   Dynamically building the context menu

Each time a user clicks the right mouse button, the context menu's content must be rebuilt from scratch because contributors may add actions based on the editor's selection. In addition, the context menu must contain a separator with the IWorkbenchActionConstants.MB_ADDITIONS constant, indicating where those contributed actions will appear in the context menu. The create-ContextMenu() method (see the previous section) calls the new fillContext-Menu(IMenuManager) method shown below:

```
private void fillContextMenu(IMenuManager menuMgr) {
    boolean isEmpty =
        tableTreeViewer.getSelection().isEmpty();
    removeAction.setEnabled(!isEmpty);
    menuMgr.add(removeAction);
    menuMgr.add(
        new Separator(
            IWorkbenchActionConstants.MB_ADDITIONS));
}
```

When this functionality is in place, the context menu will appear containing only the **Remove** menu item (see Figure 8–8).

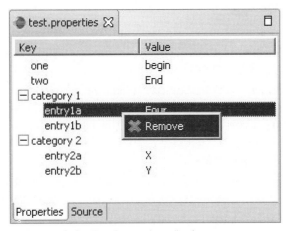

Figure 8–8   The Properties editor's context menu.

8.5.2   Editor contributor

An instance of `org.eclipse.ui.IEditorActionBarContributor` manages the installation and removal of global menus, menu items, and toolbar buttons for one or more editors. The plug-in manifest specifies which contributor, typically a subclass of `org.eclipse.ui.part.EditorActionBarContributor` or `org.eclipse.ui.part.MultiPageEditorActionBarContributor`, is associated with which editor type (see Section 8.1, "Editor Declaration"). The platform then sends the following events to the contributor, indicating when an editor has become active or inactive, so that the contributor can install or remove menus and buttons as appropriate:

> `dispose()`—This method is automatically called when the contributor is no longer needed. It cleans up any platform resources, such as images, clipboard, and so on, which were created by this class. This follows the *if you create it, you destroy it* theme that runs throughout Eclipse.
>
> `init(IActionBars, IWorkbenchPage)`—This method is called when the contributor is first created.
>
> `setActiveEditor(IEditorPart)`—This method is called when an associated editor becomes active or inactive. The contributor should insert and remove menus and toolbar buttons as appropriate.

The `EditorActionBarContributor` class implements the interface `IEditorActionBarContributor`, caches the action bar and workbench page, and provides two new accessor methods:

> `getActionBars()`—Returns the contributor's action bars provided to the contributor when it was initialized.
>
> `getPage()`—Returns the contributor's workbench page provided to the contributor when it was initialized.

The `MultiPageEditorActionBarContributor` class extends `EditorActionBarContributor`, providing a new method to override instead of the `setActiveEditor(IEditorPart)` method:

> `setActivePage(IEditorPart)`—Sets the active page of the multipage editor to the given editor. If there is no active page, or if the active page does not have a corresponding editor, the argument is null.

8.5.2.1   Global actions

Borrowing from `org.eclipse.ui.editors.text.TextEditorActionContributor` and `org.eclipse.ui.texteditor.BasicTextEditorActionContributor`, we will create our own contributor for the **Properties** editor. This contributor hooks up global actions (e.g., **cut, copy, paste,** etc. in the **Edit** menu) appropriate not only to the active editor, but also to the active page within the editor.

```
package com.qualityeclipse.favorites.editors;

import org.eclipse.jface.action.*;
import org.eclipse.jface.dialogs.*;
import org.eclipse.ui.*;
import org.eclipse.ui.part.*;
import org.eclipse.ui.texteditor.*;

public class PropertiesEditorContributor
    extends EditorActionBarContributor
{
    private static final String[] WORKBENCH_ACTION_IDS = {
        IWorkbenchActionConstants.DELETE,
        IWorkbenchActionConstants.UNDO,
        IWorkbenchActionConstants.REDO,
        IWorkbenchActionConstants.CUT,
        IWorkbenchActionConstants.COPY,
        IWorkbenchActionConstants.PASTE,
        IWorkbenchActionConstants.SELECT_ALL,
        IWorkbenchActionConstants.FIND,
        IWorkbenchActionConstants.BOOKMARK,
    };
    private static final String[] TEXTEDITOR_ACTION_IDS = {
        ITextEditorActionConstants.DELETE,
        ITextEditorActionConstants.UNDO,
        ITextEditorActionConstants.REDO,
        ITextEditorActionConstants.CUT,
        ITextEditorActionConstants.COPY,
        ITextEditorActionConstants.PASTE,
        ITextEditorActionConstants.SELECT_ALL,
        ITextEditorActionConstants.FIND,
        ITextEditorActionConstants.BOOKMARK,
    };

    public void setActiveEditor(IEditorPart part) {
        PropertiesEditor editor = (PropertiesEditor) part;
        setActivePage(editor, editor.getActivePage());
    }

    public void setActivePage(
        PropertiesEditor editor,
        int pageIndex) {

        IActionBars actionBars = getActionBars();
        if (actionBars != null) {
            switch (pageIndex) {
                case 0 :
                    hookGlobalTreeActions(editor, actionBars);
                    break;
                case 1 :
                    hookGlobalTextActions(editor, actionBars);
                    break;
            }
```

```
            actionBars.updateActionBars();
        }
    }

    private void hookGlobalTreeActions(
        PropertiesEditor editor,
        IActionBars actionBars) {

        for (int i = 0; i < WORKBENCH_ACTION_IDS.length; i++)
            actionBars.setGlobalActionHandler(
                WORKBENCH_ACTION_IDS[i],
                editor.getTableTreeAction(
                    WORKBENCH_ACTION_IDS[i]));
    }

    private void hookGlobalTextActions(
        PropertiesEditor editor,
        IActionBars actionBars) {

        ITextEditor textEditor = editor.getSourceEditor();
        for (int i = 0; i < WORKBENCH_ACTION_IDS.length; i++)
            actionBars.setGlobalActionHandler(
                WORKBENCH_ACTION_IDS[i],
                textEditor.getAction(TEXTEDITOR_ACTION_IDS[i]));
    }
}
```

Now we will modify the **Properties** editor to add accessor methods for the contributor, and to notify the contributor when the page has changed so that the contributor can update the menu items and toolbar buttons appropriately:

```
protected void pageChange(int newPageIndex) {

    … existing code …

    super.pageChange(newPageIndex);
    PropertiesEditorContributor contributor =
        (PropertiesEditorContributor) getEditorSite()
            .getActionBarContributor();
    if (contributor instanceof PropertiesEditorContributor)
        ((PropertiesEditorContributor) contributor)
            .setActivePage(this, newPageIndex);
}

public int getActivePage() {
    return super.getActivePage();
}

public ITextEditor getSourceEditor() {
    return textEditor;
}
```

```
public IAction getTableTreeAction(String workbenchActionId) {
   if (IWorkbenchActionConstants.DELETE
      .equals(workbenchActionId))
         return removeAction;
   return null;
}
```

8.5.2.2   Top-level menu

Next, we'll add the **remove** action to a top-level menu for the purpose of showing how it is accomplished. In this case, instead of referencing the action directly as we did with the context menu (see Section 8.5.1, "Context menu"), we'll use an instance of org.eclipse.ui.actions.RetargetAction, or more specifically, org.eclipse.ui.actions.LabelRetargetAction, which references the **remove** action indirectly via its identifier. We'll be using the IWorkbenchActionConstants.DELETE identifier, but you could use any identifier so long as setGlobalActionHandler(String, IAction) is used to associate the identifier with the action. To accomplish all this, we'll add the following to the PropertiesEditorContributor:

```
private LabelRetargetAction retargetRemoveAction;

public PropertiesEditorContributor() {
   retargetRemoveAction =
      new LabelRetargetAction(
         IWorkbenchActionConstants.DELETE,
         "Remove");
}

public void init(IActionBars bars, IWorkbenchPage page) {
   super.init(bars, page);
   page.addPartListener(retargetRemoveAction);
}

public void contributeToMenu(IMenuManager manager) {
   IMenuManager menu =
      new MenuManager("Property Editor");
   manager.prependToGroup(
      IWorkbenchActionConstants.MB_ADDITIONS,
      menu);
   menu.add(retargetRemoveAction);
}
```

Once in place, this code causes a new top-level menu to appear in the workbench's menu bar (see Figure 8–9).

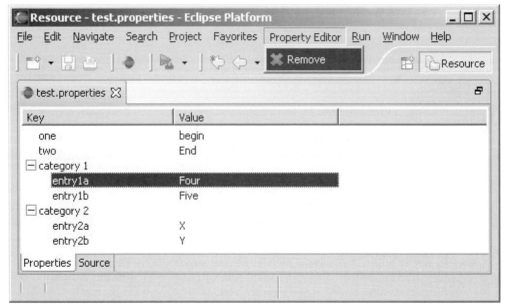

Figure 8–9   Property Editor menu.

8.5.2.3   Toolbar buttons

We can use the same retargeted action (see previous section) to add a button to the workbench's toolbar by including the following code in the PropertiesEditorContributor:

```
public void contributeToToolBar(IToolBarManager manager) {
   manager.add(new Separator());
   manager.add(retargetRemoveAction);
}
```

8.5.2.4   Keyboard actions

Using the **remove** action again (see Section 8.5.1.1, "Creating actions"), we can hook in the **Delete** key by modifying the addTableKeyListener() method introduced earlier (see Section 8.3.5, "Editing versus selecting") so that when a user presses it, the selected property key/value pairs in the table tree will be removed:

```
private void addTableKeyListener() {
   tableTreeViewer.getTableTree().getTable()
      .addKeyListener(new KeyListener() {
      public void keyPressed(KeyEvent e) {
         if (e.keyCode == SWT.ALT)
            isAltPressed = true;
```

```
            if (e.character == SWT.DEL)
                removeAction.run();
        }
        public void keyReleased(KeyEvent e) {
            if (e.keyCode == SWT.ALT)
                isAltPressed = false;
        }
    });
}
```

8.5.3   Undo/Redo

Adding the capability for a user to undo and redo actions involves building a manager to track changes. For expediency, we'll reuse the `javax.swing.undo.UndoManager` and related classes, but in reality, you'll want to consider reviewing other existing command frameworks or creating your own.

> **Tip:** Browse *www.qualityeclipse.com/undo* for more information about simple undo/redo frameworks for Eclipse.

For starters, we'll add an undo manager to the `PropertiesEditor`:

```
private UndoManager undoManager = new UndoManager();
```

and then add accessor methods for actions to register undoable edits (the `undoAction` and `redoAction` fields are declared later):

```
public void addUndoableEdit(UndoableEdit edit) {
    undoManager.addEdit(edit);
    updateUndoRedo();
}

public void updateUndoRedo() {
    undoAction.update();
    redoAction.update();
}
```

`RemovePropertiesAction` requires some refactoring to introduce an `Undo-ableEdit` inner class that can be registered with the **Properties** editor so that the remove operation can be undone and redone. Rather than performing the operation directly, the remove action constructs a new `RemovePropertiesEdit` to capture the state and perform the operation.

```
public void run() {
    List elemList =
        ((IStructuredSelection) viewer.getSelection())
            .toList();
    if (elemList.isEmpty())
        return;
```

```
      PropertyElement[] elemArray =
         (PropertyElement[]) elemList.toArray(
            new PropertyElement[elemList.size()]);
      UndoableEdit edit =
         new RemovePropertiesEdit(elemArray);
      edit.redo();
      editor.addUndoableEdit(edit);
   }

   private class RemovePropertiesEdit
      implements UndoableEdit
   {
      final PropertyElement[] elements;
      final PropertyElement[] parents;

      RemovePropertiesEdit(PropertyElement[] elements) {
         this.elements = elements;
         this.parents =
            new PropertyElement[elements.length];
      }

      public boolean canRedo() {
         return true;
      }

      public void redo() throws CannotRedoException {
         TableTree tableTree = viewer.getTableTree();
         tableTree.setRedraw(false);
         try {
            for (int i = 0; i < elements.length; i++) {
               parents[i] = elements[i].getParent();
               elements[i].removeFromParent();
            }
         }
         finally {
            tableTree.setRedraw(true);
         }
      }

      public boolean canUndo() {
         return true;
      }

      public void undo() throws CannotUndoException {
         TableTree tableTree = viewer.getTableTree();
         tableTree.setRedraw(false);
         try {
            for (int i = elements.length; --i >= 0;) {
               if (parents[i] instanceof PropertyCategory)
                  ((PropertyCategory) parents[i]).addEntry(
                     (PropertyEntry) elements[i]);
               else
                  ((PropertyFile) parents[i]).addCategory(
                     (PropertyCategory) elements[i]);
            }
         }
```

```
      finally {
         tableTree.setRedraw(true);
      }
   }

   public void die() {
   }
   public boolean addEdit(UndoableEdit anEdit) {
      return false;
   }
   public boolean replaceEdit(UndoableEdit anEdit) {
      return false;
   }
   public boolean isSignificant() {
      return true;
   }
   public String getPresentationName() {
      return "Remove";
   }
   public String getUndoPresentationName() {
      return "Undo " + getPresentationName();
   }
   public String getRedoPresentationName() {
      return "Redo " + getPresentationName();
   }
}
```

Next, we need to create the UndoPropertyEditAction (the RedoProper-tyEditAction is similar):

```
package com.qualityeclipse.favorites.editors;

import javax.swing.undo.*;
import org.eclipse.jface.action.*;

public class UndoPropertyEditAction extends Action
{
   private final PropertiesEditor editor;
   private final UndoManager undoManager;

   public UndoPropertyEditAction(
      PropertiesEditor editor,
      UndoManager undoManager) {

      super("Undo");
      setEnabled(false);
      this.editor = editor;
      this.undoManager = undoManager;
   }

   public void run() {
      if (undoManager.canUndo()) {
         undoManager.undo();
         editor.updateUndoRedo();
      }
   }
```

```
public void update() {
   setText(undoManager.getUndoPresentationName());
   setEnabled(undoManager.canUndo());
}
}
```

and then instantiate the new actions in the `PropertiesEditor`:

```
private UndoPropertyEditAction undoAction;
private RedoPropertyEditAction redoAction;

private void createActions() {

   … original code here …

   undoAction =
      new UndoPropertyEditAction(this, undoManager);
   redoAction =
      new RedoPropertyEditAction(this, undoManager);
}
```

Finally, the **Properties** editor must return these new actions via the `getTableTreeAction(...)` method so that the actions will be hooked up to the global **undo** and **redo** actions by the editor contributor (see Section 8.5.2.1).

```
public IAction getTableTreeAction(String workbenchActionId) {
   if (IWorkbenchActionConstants.DELETE
      .equals(workbenchActionId))
         return removeAction;
   if (IWorkbenchActionConstants.UNDO
      .equals(workbenchActionId))
         return undoAction;
   if (IWorkbenchActionConstants.REDO
      .equals(workbenchActionId))
         return redoAction;
   return null;
}
```

8.5.4   *Clipboard actions*

Clipboard-based actions for an editor are identical to their respective view-based operations (see Section 7.3.7, "Clipboard actions").

8.6   Linking the Editor

The selection in the active editor can be linked to the views that surround it in a technique similar to linking view selections (see Section 7.4, "Linking the View"). In addition, the editor can provide content for the **Outline** view by implementing the getAdapter(Class) method something like this (see Section 7.4.2, "Adaptable objects," for more about adapters):

```
public Object getAdapter(Class key) {
    if (key.equals(IContentOutlinePage.class)) {
        if (outlinePage == null)
            outlinePage = new PropertiesOutlinePage();
        return outlinePage;
    }
    return super.getAdapter(key);
}
```

The   PropertiesOutlinePage   class   would   implement   the org.eclipse.ui.views.contentoutline.IContentOutlinePage   interface, typically   by   extending   org.eclipse.ui.views.contentoutline.ContentOutlinePage and implementing a handful of methods. These methods are similar to the methods discussed earlier in this chapter and in the previous chapter; thus, they are not covered in detail here.

8.7   RFWS Considerations

The "User Interface" section of the *RFWS Requirements* includes 14 items—8 requirements and 6 best practices—dealing with editor. All of them are derived from the Eclipse UI Guidelines.

8.7.1   Using an editor to edit or browse

User Interface Guideline #13 is a requirement that states:

> *Use an editor to edit or browse a file, document, or other input object. This requirement tests that editors are used to edit files (or similar inputs) and views are used to aid navigation (e.g., Navigator) or handle simple modification tasks (e.g., Properties view). Editors must open on double- or single-click (depending on the workbench's single-click behavior preference) from the resource. While views may open simultaneously with the editor, it is improper to open only a view when the input follows an open-save-close lifecycle. Views must not retarget editor actions, contribute to the common toolbar, or otherwise substitute for proper editor behavior and appearance.*

For this test, demonstrate the editors provided by your plug-in. Show the file, document, or other input type that they are used to edit or browse. Based on the examples presented in this chapter, we would show how the **Property File** editor is used to edit property files.

8.7.2   Editor lifecycle

User Interface Guideline #14 is a requirement that states:

Modifications made in an editor must follow an open-save-close lifecycle model. When an editor first opens, the editor's contents should be unmodified (clean). If the contents are modified, the editor should communicate this change to the platform. In response, an asterisk should appear in the editor's tab. The modifications should be buffered within the edit model until such time as the user explicitly saves them. At that point, the modifications should be committed to the model storage.

To pass this test, open your editor on a file and show that the editor is initially unmodified. Then make a change using the editor and show that an asterisk appears in the editor's tab. Finally, save the editor and show that the changes have been committed to the file and that the editor has gone back to its unmodified state. See Section 8.4, "Editor Lifecycle," for more information about editor lifecycles.

8.7.3   Single editor instance per input

User Interface Guideline #15 is a requirement that states:

Only one instance of an editor may exist for each editor input within a perspective. An editor is document- or input-centric. Each editor has an input, and only one editor can exist for each editor input within a perspective. This policy has been designed to simplify part management.

Start by opening your editor on a specific file. Next, attempt to open the same file a second time and show that the existing editor comes to the top rather than a new editor being opened. If you implement your editor using the editor framework described in this chapter, the framework should automatically enforce this guideline.

8.7.4   Separate editors for each input

User Interface Guideline #16 is a requirement that states:

It must be possible to open a separate instance of an editor for each input.

For this test, open several different files and show that multiple instances of your editor may exist simultaneously with each editing or browsing its own file. If you implement your editor using the editor framework described in this chapter, the framework should automatically enforce this guideline.

8.7.5   Accessing global actions from the menu bar

User Interface Guideline #17 is a requirement that states:

*If an editor has support for **cut**, **copy**, **paste**, or any of the global actions, the same actions must be executable from the same actions in the window menu and toolbar. The window menu contains a number of global actions, such as **cut**, **copy**, and **paste** in the* **Edit** *menu. These actions target the active part, as indicated by a shaded title area. If these actions are supported within an editor, the editor should hook into these window actions so that selection in the window menu or toolbar produces the same result as selection of the same action in the editor. The editor should not ignore these actions and contribute duplicate actions to the window menu or toolbar. The following are the supported global actions:*

> *a. Undo*
>
> *b. Redo*
>
> *c. Cut*
>
> *d. Copy*
>
> *e. Paste*
>
> *f. Print*
>
> *g. Delete*
>
> *h. Find*
>
> *i. Select all*
>
> *j. Bookmark*

Show that your editor supports any relevant global actions such as **cut**, **copy**, and **paste**. Trigger those actions from within your editor and then show that they may also be triggered from the workbench's menu bar with the same effect. For our **Properties** editor, we would show that global actions such as **delete** can be accessed within both the **Properties** and **Source** pages of the editor. See Section 8.5.2.1 for more about hooking up global actions.

8.7.6   Registering editor menus

User Interface Guideline #18 is a best practice that states:

Register all context menus in the editor with the platform. In the platform, the menu and toolbar for an editor are automatically extended by the platform. By contrast, context menu extension is supported in collaboration between the editor and the platform. To achieve this collaboration, an editor must register each context menu it contains with the platform.

To pass this test, show that your editor's context menus have been registered with the platform. If they are properly registered, you should see the system contributing appropriate context menu items. See Section 8.5.1 for more about context menus.

8.7.7   Editor action filters

User Interface Guideline #19 is a best practice that states:

Implement an action filter for each object type in the editor. An action filter makes it easier for one plug-in to add an action to objects in an editor defined by another plug-in.

For this test, show that menu action filtering is in effect for the objects edited by your editor. See Section 6.3.2, "Action filtering and enablement," for more about using action filters and Section 8.5.1.2 for more about building context menus that can be extended by other plug-ins.

8.7.8   Closing the editor when the object is deleted

User Interface Guideline #20 is a requirement that states:

If the input to an editor is deleted and the editor contains no changes, the editor should be closed.

Show that your editor is closed automatically any time an input object to your editor (a specific resource, for example) is deleted. For our **Properties** editor, we would create a new properties file, open it with the **Properties** editor, and then delete the file in the **Navigator** view. If you implement your editor using the editor framework described in this chapter, the framework should automatically enforce this guideline.

8.7.9   Unsaved editor modifications

User Interface Guideline #21a is a requirement that states:

If the input to an editor is deleted and the editor contains changes, the editor should warn the user that there are unsaved editor changes.

User Interface Guideline #21b is a best practice that states:

If the input to an editor is deleted and the editor contains changes, the editor should give the user a chance to save the changes to another location, and then close.

Start by opening your editor on a file and then making a change. Next, select the file in the **Navigator** view and delete the file. Show that a warning message is displayed, informing the user that the editor contains unsaved changes. To pass the best practice component of this guideline, the user should be given the option to save the file to another location. If you implement your editor using the editor framework described in this chapter, the framework should automatically enforce this guideline.

8.7.10   Prefix dirty resources

User Interface Guideline #22 is a best practice that states:

If a resource is dirty, prefix the resource name presented in the editor tab with an asterisk.

This is essentially a subset of Guideline #14. Edit a file with your editor and show that the filename is prefixed with an asterisk. If you implement your editor using the editor framework described in this chapter, the framework should automatically enforce this guideline.

8.7.11   Editor outline view

User Interface Guideline #23 is a best practice that states:

*If the data within an editor is too extensive to see on a single screen, and will yield a structured outline, the editor should provide an outline model to the **Outline** view. In Eclipse, there is a special relationship between each editor and the **Outline** view. When an editor is opened, the **Outline** view will connect to the editor and ask it for an outline model. If the editor answers with an outline model, that model will be displayed in the **Outline** view whenever the editor is active. The outline is used to navigate through the edit data, or interact with the edit data at a higher level of abstraction.*

For this test, open your editor and show that it updates the contents of the **Outline** view and allows the data's structure to be navigated. If a different instance of your editor is selected, show that the **Outline** view's contents change appropriately. See Section 8.4 for information about linking an editor to the **Outline** view.

8.7.12   Synchronize with the outline view

User Interface Guideline #24 is a best practice that states:

*Notification about location between an editor and the **Outline** view should be two-way. Context menus should be available in the **Outline** view as appropriate.*

Select an item in the **Outline** view and show that it selects the corresponding item in the editor. Next, select an item in the editor and show that it selects the corresponding item in the **Outline** view.

8.7.13   *Synchronize with external changes*

User Interface Guideline #25 is a requirement that states:

*If modifications to a resource are made outside the workbench, users should be prompted to either override the changes made outside the workbench or back out of the **Save** operation when the save action is invoked in the editor.*

Open your editor on a file and make a change. Next, modify the file outside Eclipse. Finally, switch back to Eclipse and attempt to save the file. Show that you are prompted to override the external changes or cancel the save operation. If you implement your editor using the editor framework described in this chapter, the framework should automatically enforce this guideline.

8.8   Summary

In this chapter, we went into detail about how to create new editors for editing and browsing resources in the workbench. We showed how to set up a multi-page editor, handle the editor lifecycle, and create various editor actions.

CHAPTER 9

Resource Change Tracking

The Eclipse system generates resource change events indicating, for example, the files and folders that have been added, modified, and removed during the course of an operation. Interested objects can subscribe to these events and take whatever action is necessary to keep themselves synchronized with Eclipse. To demonstrate resource change tracking, we will modify our **Favorites** view (see Chapter 7, "Views") so that whenever a resource is deleted, we can remove the corresponding element from the **Favorites** view.

9.1 IResourceChangeListener

Eclipse uses the `org.eclipse.core.resources.IResourceChangeListener` interface to notify registered listeners when a resource has changed. The `FavoritesManager` (see Section 7.2.3, "View model") needs to keep its list of **Favorites** items synchronized with Eclipse. This is done by implementing the `org.eclipse.core.resources.IResourceChangeListener` interface and registering for resource change events. In addition, the `FavoritesPlugin` shutdown() method must be modified to call the new `FavoritesManager` shutdown() method so that the manager is no longer notified of resource changes once the plug-in has been shut down. Now, whenever a resource change occurs, Eclipse will call the `resourceChanged(...)` method.

```
public class FavoritesManager
    implements IResourceChangeListener
{
```

```
        private FavoritesManager() {
            ResourcesPlugin
                .getWorkspace()
                .addResourceChangeListener (
                    this,
                    IResourceChangeEvent.POST_CHANGE);
        }

        public static void shutdown() {
            if (manager != null) {
                ResourcesPlugin
                    .getWorkspace()
                    .removeResourceChangeListener  (
                    manager);
                manager = null;
            }
        }

        public void resourceChanged(IResourceChangeEvent e) {
            // Process events here.
        }

        … existing code from Section 7.2.3 here …
    }
```

9.1.1 IResourceChangeEvent

FavoritesManager is only interested in changes that have already occurred and therefore uses the IResourceChangeEvent.POST_CHANGE constant when subscribing to change events. Eclipse provides several IResourceChangeEvent constants that can be used in combination to specify when an interested object should be notified of resource changes. Below is the list of valid constants as they appear in the IResourceChangeEvent Javadoc:

POST_CHANGE–After-the-fact report of creations, deletions, and modifications to one or more resources expressed as a hierarchical resource delta as returned by getDelta().

PRE_CLOSE–Before-the-fact report of the impending closure of a single project as returned by getResource().

PRE_DELETE–Before-the-fact report of the impending deletion of a single project as returned by getResource().

PRE_AUTO_BUILD–Before-the-fact report of builder activity (see Section 14.1, "Builders").

POST_AUTO_BUILD–After-the-fact report of builder activity (see Section 14.1)

The IResourceChangeEvent class also defines several methods that can be used to query its state:

findMarkerDeltas(String, boolean)—Returns all marker deltas of the specified type that are associated with resource deltas for this event.

getDelta()—Returns a resource delta, rooted at the workspace, describing the set of changes that happened to resources in the workspace.

getResource()—Returns the resource in question.

getSource()—Returns an object identifying the source of this event.

getType()—Returns the type of event being reported.

9.1.2   IResourceDelta

Each individual change is encoded as an instance of a resource delta that is represented by the IResourceDelta interface. Eclipse provides several different constants that can be used in combination to identify the resource deltas handled by the system. Below is the list of valid constants as they appear in the IResourceDelta Javadoc:

ADDDED—Delta kind constant indicating that the resource has been added to its parent.

ADDED_PHANTOM—Delta kind constant indicating that a phantom resource has been added at the location of the delta node.

ALL_WITH_PHANTOMS—The bit mask that describes all possible delta kinds, including those involving phantoms.

CHANGED—Delta kind constant indicating that the resource has been changed.

CONTENT—Change constant indicating that the content of the resource has changed.

DESCRIPTION—Change constant indicating that a project's description has changed.

MARKERS—Change constant indicating that the resource's markers have changed.

MOVED_FROM—Change constant indicating that the resource was moved from another location.

MOVED_TO—Change constant indicating that the resource was moved to another location.

NO_CHANGE—Delta kind constant indicating that the resource has not been changed in any way.

OPEN—Change constant indicating that the resource was opened or closed.

REMOVED–Delta kind constant indicating that the resource has been removed from its parent.

REMOVED_PHANTOM–Delta kind constant indicating that a phantom resource has been removed from the location of the delta node.

REPLACED–Change constant indicating that the resource has been replaced by another at the same location (i.e., the resource has been deleted and then added).

SYNC–Change constant indicating that the resource's sync status has changed.

TYPE–Change constant indicating that the type of the resource has changed.

The IResourceDelta class also defines a large number of useful APIs such as:

findMember(IPath)–Finds and returns the descendent delta identified by the given path in this delta, or null if no such descendent exists.

getEditorArea()–Returns the special identifier for the editor area in this page layout.

getAffectedChildren()–Returns resource deltas for all children of this resource that were added, removed, or changed.

getAffectedChildren(int)–Returns resource deltas for all children of this resource whose kind is included in the given mask.

getFlags()–Returns flags that describe in more detail how a resource has been affected.

getFullPath()–Returns the full, absolute path of this resource delta.

getKind()–Returns the kind of this resource delta.

getMarkerDeltas()–Returns the changes to markers on the corresponding resource.

getMovedFromPath()–Returns the full path (in the "before" state) from which this resource (in the "after" state) was moved.

getMovedToPath()–Returns the full path (in the "after" state) to which this resource (in the "before" state) was moved.

getProjectRelativePath()–Returns the project-relative path of this resource delta.

getResource()–Returns a handle for the affected resource.

9.2   **Processing Change Events**

The POST_CHANGE resource change event is expressed not as a single change, but as a hierarchy describing one or more changes that have occurred. Events are batched in this manner for efficiency; reporting each change as it occurs to every interested object would dramatically slow down the system and reduce responsiveness to the user. To see this hierarchy of changes, add the following code to the FavoritesManager:

```
public void resourceChanged(IResourceChangeEvent e) {
   System.out.println(
      "FavoritesManager—resource change event");
   printResourcesChanged(e.getDelta(), 1);
}

private void printResourcesChanged(IResourceDelta delta, int
indent) {
   printOneResourceChanged(delta, indent);
   IResourceDelta[] children =
      delta.getAffectedChildren();
   for (int i = 0; i < children.length; i++)
      printResourcesChanged(children[i], indent + 1);
}

private void printOneResourceChanged(IResourceDelta delta, int
indent) {
   StringBuffer buf = new StringBuffer(80);
   for (int i = 0; i < indent; i++)
      buf.append("   ");
   switch (delta.getKind()) {
      case IResourceDelta.ADDED :
         buf.append("ADDED");
         break;
      case IResourceDelta.REMOVED :
         buf.append("REMOVED");
         break;
      case IResourceDelta.CHANGED :
         buf.append("CHANGED");
         break;
      default :
         buf.append("[");
         buf.append(delta.getKind());
         buf.append("]");
         break;
   }
   buf.append(" ");
   buf.append(delta.getResource());
   System.out.println(buf);
}
```

The code above will generate a textual representation of the hierarchical structure describing the resource changes in the system. To see this code in action, launch the **Runtime Workbench** (see Section 2.6, "Debugging the Product") and open the **Favorites** view. In the **Runtime Workbench**, create a simple project and then add folders and files as shown below (see Figure 9–1).

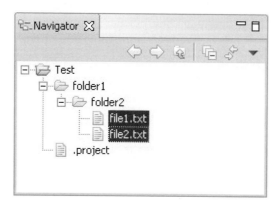

Figure 9–1   Navigator view.

During the creation process, you will see output generated to the **Console** view describing the resource change events that were sent by Eclipse. The FavoritesManager is specifically interested in the deletion of resources, and when you delete these two files, you'll see the following appear in the b view:

```
FavoritesManager—resource change event
  CHANGED R/
    CHANGED P/Test
      CHANGED F/Test/folder1
        CHANGED F/Test/folder1/folder2
          REMOVED L/Test/folder1/folder2/file1.txt
          REMOVED L/Test/folder1/folder2/file2.txt
```

This same type of thing can be accomplished using IResourceDeltaVisitor. To print the information above using a visitor pattern, the code might look something like this:

```
private void printResourcesChanged(IResourceDelta original) {
    IResourceDeltaVisitor visitor = new IResourceDeltaVisitor() {
        public boolean visit(IResourceDelta delta)
            throws CoreException
        {
            printOneResourceChanged(delta, 0);
            return true;
        }
    };
    try {
        original.accept(visitor);
    }
```

```
      catch (CoreException e) {
         FavoritesLog.logError(e);
      }
   }
}
```

The next step is to modify the FavoritesManager methods to do something with this information. These modifications will enable the Favorites-Manager to remove **Favorites** items that reference resources that have been removed from the system.

```
public void resourceChanged(IResourceChangeEvent e) {
   Collection itemsToRemove = new HashSet();
   resourceChanged(e.getDelta(), itemsToRemove);
   if (itemsToRemove.size() > 0)
      removeFavorites(
         (IFavoriteItem[]) itemsToRemove.toArray(
            new IFavoriteItem[itemsToRemove.size()]));
}

private void resourceChanged(
   IResourceDelta delta,
   Collection itemsToRemove) {

   if (delta.getKind() == IResourceDelta.REMOVED) {
      IFavoriteItem item =
         existingFavoriteFor(delta.getResource());
      if (item != null)
         itemsToRemove.add(item);
   }
   IResourceDelta[] children =
      delta.getAffectedChildren();
   for (int i = 0; i < children.length; i++)
      resourceChanged(children[i], itemsToRemove);
}
```

When the above code is in place, launch the **Runtime Workbench** to test this modification by creating a file in a project, adding that file as a **Favorites** item to the **Favorites** view, and then deleting the file from the project. The file is removed, but the **Favorites** item is not removed as it should be. Looking in the .log file (see Section 3.6.2, "The error log view") reveals the following exception:

```
org.eclipse.swt.SWTException: Invalid thread access
```

This indicates that an SWT component, such as the table in the **Favorites** view, is being accessed from a thread other than the UI thread (see Section 4.2.5.1, "Display," for more about Display.getDefault() and the UI thread). To alleviate this problem, modify the FavoritesViewContentManager favoritesChanged as shown below to ensure that the viewer is accessed on the UI thread:

```
public void favoritesChanged(
   final FavoritesManagerEvent event) {

   Display display = Display.getCurrent();
   if (display == null) {
      Display.getDefault().asyncExec(new Runnable() {
         public void run() {
            favoritesChanged(event);
         }
      });
   }
   … original code here …
}
```

9.3 Batching Change Events

Anytime a UI plug-in modifies resources, it should wrap the resource modification code by subclassing org.eclipse.ui.actions.WorkspaceModifyOper-
ation. The primary consequence of using this operation is that events that
typically occur as a result of workspace changes (such as the firing of resource
deltas, performance of autobuilds, etc.) are deferred until the outermost operation has successfully completed. In the **Favorites** view, if we wanted to implement a delete operation that removed the resources themselves rather than just
the **Favorites** items that referenced the resources, then it might be implemented as shown below. The run(…) method for the action would be called
by an Action or IActionDelegate. The run method would then call the exe-
cute(…) method, and then it would fire a single change event containing all of
the resources changed by the execute method.

```
package com.qualityeclipse.favorites.actions;

import java.lang.reflect.*;
import org.eclipse.core.resources.*;
import org.eclipse.core.runtime.*;
import org.eclipse.ui.actions.*;

public class DeleteResourcesAction
   extends WorkspaceModifyOperation
{
   private final IResource[] resources;

   public DeleteResourcesAction(IResource[] resources) {
      this.resources = resources;
   }

   protected void execute(IProgressMonitor monitor)
      throws
         CoreException,
         InvocationTargetException,
         InterruptedException
```

```
        {
            monitor.beginTask(
                "Deleting resources...",
                resources.length);
            for (int i = 0; i < resources.length; i++) {
                resources[i].delete(
                    true,
                    new SubProgressMonitor(monitor, 1));
            }
            monitor.done();
        }
    }
```

If you are modifying resources in a headless Eclipse environment or in a plug-in that does not rely on any UI plug-ins, the WorkspaceModifyOperation class is not accessible. In this case, use the IWorkspace.run(...) method to batch change events.

```
protected void execute(IProgressMonitor monitor)
    throws CoreException
{
    ResourcesPlugin.getWorkspace().run(
        new IWorkspaceRunnable() {
            public void run(IProgressMonitor monitor)
                throws CoreException
            {
                monitor.beginTask(
                    "Deleting resources...",
                    resources.length);
                for (int i = 0; i < resources.length; i++) {
                    resources[i].delete(
                        true,
                        new SubProgressMonitor(monitor, 1));
                }
                monitor.done();
            }
        }, monitor);
}
```

9.4 Progress Monitor

For long-running operations, the progress monitor indicates what the operation is doing and an estimate of how much more there is left to be done. In the code above, we used a progress monitor to communicate with the user, indicating that we were deleting resources and how many resources needed to be deleted before the operation completed.

9.4.1   IProgressMonitor

The `org.eclipse.core.runtime.IProgressMonitor` interface provides methods for indicating when an operation has started, how much has been done, and when it is complete.

`beginTask(String, int)`—Called once by the operation to indicate that the operation has started and approximately how much work must be done before it is complete. This method must be called exactly once per instance of a progress monitor.

`done()`—Called by the operation to indicate that the operation is complete.

`isCanceled()`—The operation should periodically poll this method to see if the user has requested that the operation be canceled.

`setCanceled(boolean)`—This method is typically called by UI code setting the canceled state to `false` when the user clicks on the **Cancel** button during an operation.

`setTaskName(String)`—Sets the task name displayed to the user. Usually, there is no need to call this method because the task name is set by `beginTask(String, int)`.

`worked(int)`—Called by the operation to indicate that the specified number of units of work has been completed.

9.4.2   Classes for displaying progress

Eclipse provides several classes that either implement the `IProgressMonitor` interface or provide a progress monitor via the `IRunnableWithProgress` interface. These classes are used under different circumstances to notify the user of the progress of long-running operations.

`SubProgressMonitor`—A progress monitor passed by a parent operation to a suboperation so that the suboperation can notify the user of progress as a portion of the parent operation (see Section 9.3, "Batching Change Events").

`WorkspaceModifyOperation`—An operation that batches resource change events and provides a progress monitor as part of its execution (see Section 9.3).

`ProgressMonitorDialog`—Opens a dialog that displays progress to the user and provides a progress monitor used by the operation to relate that information.

WizardDialog—When opened, optionally provides progress information as part of the wizard. The wizard implements the IRunnableContext, and thus the operation can call the run(boolean, boolean, IRunnable-WithProgress) and display progress in the wizard via the provided progress monitor (see Sections 11.2.3, "IWizardContainer," and 11.2.6, "Wizard example").

9.4.3 Workbench window status bar

The workbench window also provides a progress display area along the bottom edge of the window. Use the IWorkbenchWindow.run(...) method to execute the operation and the progress monitor passed to IRunnableWithProgress will be the progress monitor in the status bar. For example, the following snippet from an action delegate (see Section 6.2.6, "Creating an action delegate," for more on creating action delegates) shows simulated progress in the status bar:

```
private IWorkbenchWindow window;

public void init(IWorkbenchWindow window) {
   this.window = window;
}

public void run(IAction action) {
   try {
      window.run(true, true, new IRunnableWithProgress() {
         public void run(IProgressMonitor monitor)
            throws
               InvocationTargetException,
               InterruptedException {
            monitor.beginTask(
               "simulate progress in status bar:",
               20);
            for (int i = 20; i > 0; --i) {
               monitor.subTask("seconds left = " + i);
               try {
                  Thread.sleep(1000);
               }
               catch (InterruptedException e) {
                  // Ignored.
               }
               monitor.worked(1);
            }
            monitor.done();
         }
      });
   }
   catch (InvocationTargetException e) {
      FavoritesLog.logError(e);
   }
```

```
        catch (InterruptedException e) {
           // User canceled the operation... just ignore.
        }
    }
}
```

If you have a view or editor, you can obtain the containing `IWorkbench-Window` via `IworkbenchPart`, which both `IViewPart` and `IEditorPart` extend:

```
IWorkbenchWindow window
   = viewOrEditor.getWorkbenchSite().getWorkbenchWindow();
```

You can also obtain the progress monitor in the status bar directly via the `IStatusLineManager` interface:

```
viewPart.getViewSite().getActionBars()
   .getStatusLineManager().getProgressMonitor()
```

or:

```
editorPart.getEditorSite().getActionBars()
   .getStatusLineManager().getProgressMonitor()
```

9.5   Delayed Changed Events

Eclipse is based on lazy initialization: only load a plug-in when it is needed. This lazy initialization presents a problem for plug-ins that need to track changes. How does a plug-in track changes when it is not loaded?

Eclipse solves this problem by queuing change events for a plug-in that is not loaded. When the plug-in is loaded, it receives a single resource change event containing the union of the changes that have occurred during the time it was not active. To receive this event, your plug-in must register to be a save participant when it is started up as follows:

```
public static void addSaveParticipant() {
   ISaveParticipant saveParticipant = new ISaveParticipant(){
      public void saving(ISaveContext context)
         throws CoreException
      {
         // Save any model state here.
         context.needDelta();
      }
      public void doneSaving(ISaveContext context) {}
      public void prepareToSave(ISaveContext context)
         throws CoreException {}
      public void rollback(ISaveContext context) {}
   };
```

```
ISavedState savedState;
try {
   savedState = ResourcesPlugin
      .getWorkspace()
      .addSaveParticipant  (
         FavoritesPlugin.getDefault(),
         saveParticipant);
}
catch (CoreException e) {
   FavoritesLog.logError(e);
   // Recover if necessary.
   return;
}
if (savedState != null)
   savedState.processResourceChangeEvents(
      FavoritesManager.getManager());
}
```

> **Tip:** Even though Eclipse is based on lazy plug-in initialization, it does provide a mechanism for plug-ins to start when the workbench itself starts. To activate at startup, the plug-in must extend the `org.eclipse.ui.startup` extension point and implement the `org.eclipse.ui.IStartup` interface. Once the plug-in is started, the workbench will call the plug-in's `earlyStartup()` method (see Section 3.4.2, "Early plug-in startup"). A workbench preference option gives the user the ability to prevent a plug-in from starting early, so make sure that if your plug-in takes advantage of this extension point, it degrades gracefully in the event that it is not started early.

9.6   RFWS Considerations

The "Workspace Resource and Event Processing" section of the *RFWS Requirements* includes a single requirement for dealing with resource change events.

Requirement #1 states:

> *Add a IResourceChangeListener to the workspace if you need to be aware of or react to changes in resources. For example, you may use your plug-in's startup method to add custom workspace listeners to the run-time platform. The startup method is automatically invoked by the platform core the first time any code in the plug-in is executed.*

For this test, describe any scenarios where your plug-in reacts to workspace change events. For the **Favorites** view, we would show that deleting a resource from the workspace also deletes it from the **Favorites** view.

9.7 Summary

In this chapter, we demonstrated how to process resource change events propagated by the system. Anytime a resource is added, modified, or removed, a corresponding change event is generated. Responding to these events provides a way for your plug-in to stay synchronized with the Eclipse environment.

References

Arthorne, John, *"How You've Changed! Responding to resource changes in the Eclipse workspace,"* OTI, August 23, 2002 (*www.eclipse.org/articles/ Article-Resource-deltas/resource-deltas.html*).

CHAPTER 10

Perspectives

Perspectives are a way to group Eclipse views and actions for a particular task such as coding or debugging. Larger Eclipse enhancements that involve multiple plug-ins may provide their own perspectives. Smaller Eclipse enhancements that involve only one or two plug-ins and provide only one or two new Eclipse views typically enhance existing perspectives rather than provide entirely new perspectives. In this chapter, we will further extend the **Favorites** example by creating a new perspective for hosting the **Favorites** view and show how to add the **Favorites** view to existing perspectives.

10.1   Creating a Perspective

To create a new perspective, extend the `org.eclipse.ui.perspectives` extension point and then define the layout of the perspective by creating a perspective factory class implementing the `IPerspectiveFactory` interface (see Figure 10–1).

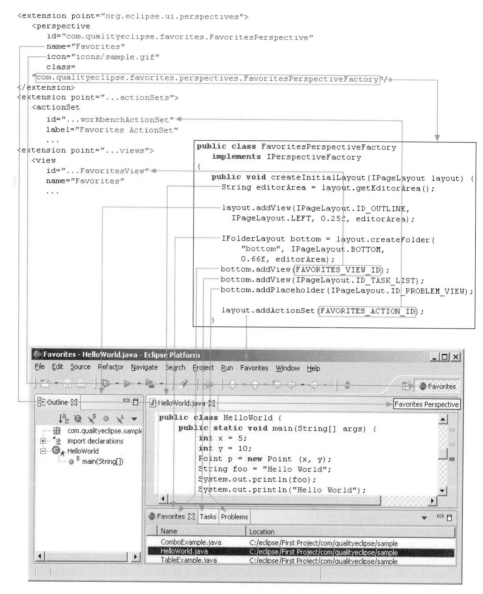

Figure 10–1   Perspective declaration and behavior.

10.1.1   Perspective Extension Point

Start by opening the **Favorites** plug-in manifest editor, selecting the **Extensions** tab, and clicking the **Add** button. When the **New Extension** wizard opens, select **org.eclipse.ui.perspectives** from the list of all available extension points (see Figure 10–2). Click the **Finish** button to add this extension to the plug-in manifest.

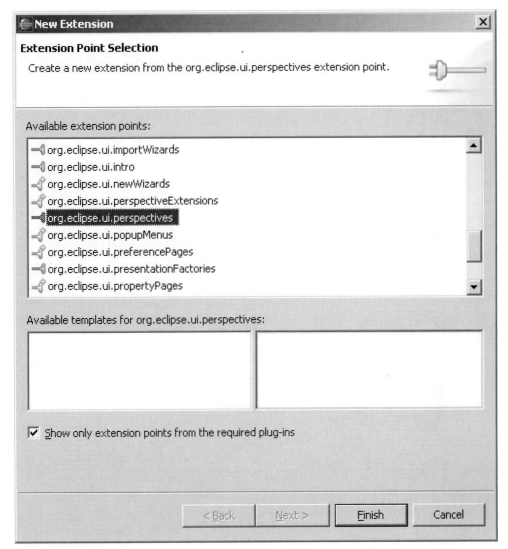

Figure 10–2 The New Extension wizard showing the org.eclipse.ui.perspectives extension point selected.

Now, back in the **Extensions** page of the plug-in manifest editor, right-click on the org.eclipse.ui.perspectives extension and select **New > perspective**. This immediately adds a perspective named com.quality-eclipse.favorites.perspective1 in the plug-in manifest. Double-clicking on this new perspective opens the **Properties** view so that the properties can be modified as follows (see Figure 10–3):

> **class**—"com.qualityeclipse.favorites.perspective.FavoritesPerspective-Factory"
> The class describing the layout of the perspective. The class is instantiated using its no argument constructor, but may be parameterized using the IExecutableExtension interface (see Section 20.5, "Types Specified in an Extension Point").
>
> **icon**—"icons/sample.gif"
> The icon associated with the perspective.
>
> **id**—"com.qualityeclipse.favorites.FavoritesPerspective"
> The unique identifier used to reference the perspective.
>
> **name**—"Favorites"
> The text label associated with the perspective.

Property	Value
class	com.qualityeclipse.favorites.perspectives.FavoritesPerspectiveFactory
fixed	
icon	icons/sample.gif
id	com.qualityeclipse.favorites.FavoritesPerspective
name	Favorites
Tag name	perspective

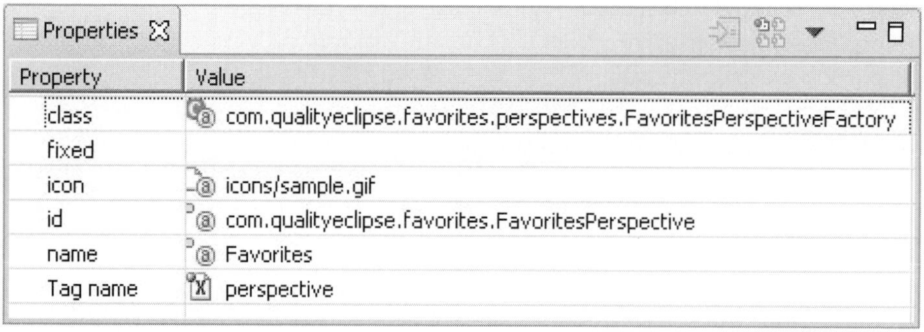

Figure 10–3   The Properties view showing the Favorites perspective's attributes.

If you switch to the **Source** page of the plug-in manifest editor, you will see the following new section of XML defining the new perspective:

```
<extension point="org.eclipse.ui.perspectives">
    <perspective
        name="Favorites"
        icon="icons/sample.gif"
        class="com.qualityeclipse.favorites.
              perspectives.FavoritesPerspectiveFactory"
        id="com.qualityeclipse.favorites.
            FavoritesPerspective"/>
</extension>
```

10.1.2 *Perspective factories*

When specifying the name of a perspective factory class, clicking on the
"..." button next to the **class** field in the **Properties** view will open a class
selection editor (see Figure 10–4), in which an existing class may be selected
or a new class (conforming to the IPerspectiveFactory interface) may be
created.

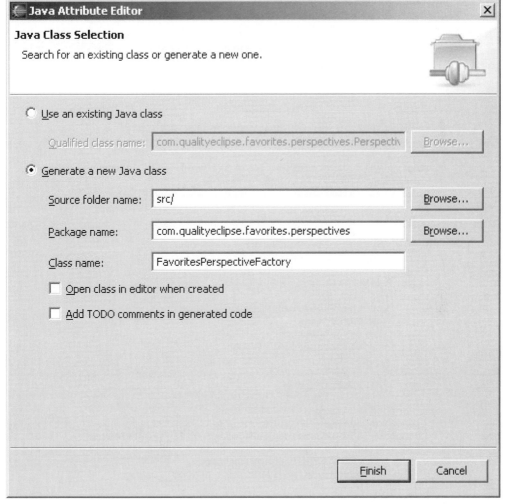

Figure 10–4 The Java Class Selection wizard.

The IPerspectiveFactory interface defines a single method, createIni-
tialLayout(), which specifies the initial page layout and visible action sets for
the perspective. The factory is only used to define the initial layout of the per-

spective and is then discarded. By default, the layout area contains space for the editors, but no views. The factory can add additional views, which are placed relative to the editor area or to another view.

Open the newly created FavoritesPerspectiveFactory class and modify it as follows so that the **Favorites** view will appear below the editor area and the standard **Outline** view will be shown to its left:

```
package com.qualityeclipse.favorites.perspectives;

import org.eclipse.ui.*;

public class FavoritesPerspectiveFactory
   implements IPerspectiveFactory
{
   private static final String FAVORITES_VIEW_ID =
      "com.qualityeclipse.favorites.views.FavoritesView";

   private static final String FAVORITES_ACTION_ID =
      "com.qualityeclipse.favorites.workbenchActionSet";

   public void createInitialLayout(IPageLayout layout) {
      // Get the editor area.
      String editorArea = layout.getEditorArea();

      // Put the Outline view on the left.
      layout.addView(
         IPageLayout.ID_OUTLINE,
         IPageLayout.LEFT,
         0.25f,
         editorArea);

      // Put the Favorites view on the bottom with
      // the Tasks view.
      IFolderLayout bottom =
         layout.createFolder(
            "bottom",
            IPageLayout.BOTTOM,
            0.66f,
            editorArea);
      bottom.addView(FAVORITES_VIEW_ID);
      bottom.addView(IPageLayout.ID_TASK_LIST);
      bottom.addPlaceholder(IPageLayout.ID_PROBLEM_VIEW);

      // Add the Favorites action set.
      layout.addActionSet(FAVORITES_ACTION_ID);
   }
}
```

Within the createInitialLayout() method, the addView() method is used to add the standard **Outline** view to the left of the editor area such that it takes up 25% of the horizontal area within the window. Using the create-Folder() method, a folder layout is created to occupy the bottom third of the layout below the editor area. The **Favorites** view and standard **Tasks** view are added to the folder layout so that each will appear stacked with a tab inside the folder. Next, a placeholder for the standard **Problems** view is added to the folder. If a user opened the **Problems** view, it would open in the location specified by the placeholder. Finally, the **Favorites** action set is made visible by default within the perspective.

When opened, the new **Favorites** perspective will look something like Figure 10–5.

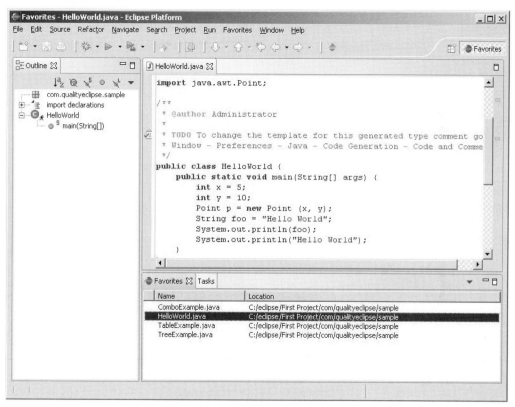

Figure 10–5 The Favorites perspective.

10.1.3 IPageLayout

As seen in the previous section, the IPageLayout interface defines the protocol necessary to support just about any possible perspective layout. It defines many useful APIs such as:

addActionSet(String)—Adds an action set with the given ID to the page layout.

`addFastView(String)`—Adds the view with the given ID to the page layout as a fast view.

`addFastView(String, float)`—Adds the view with the given ID to the page layout as a fast view with the given width ratio.

`addNewWizardShortcut(String)`—Adds a creation wizard to the **File New** menu.

`addPerspectiveShortcut(String)`—Adds a perspective shortcut to the **Perspective** menu.

`addPlaceholder(String, int, float, String)`—Adds a placeholder for a view with the given ID to the page layout.

`addShowInPart(String)`—Adds an item to the **Show In** prompter.

`addShowViewShortcut(String)`—Adds a view to the **Show View** menu.

`addView(String, int, float, String)`—Adds a view with the given ID to the page layout.

`createFolder(String, int, float, String)`—Creates and adds a folder with the given ID to the page layout.

`createPlaceholderFolder(String, int, float, String)`—Creates and adds a placeholder for a new folder with the given ID to the page layout.

`getEditorArea()`—Returns the special identifier for the editor area in the page layout.

`setEditorAreaVisible(boolean)`—Shows or hides the editor area for the page layout.

10.2   Enhancing an Existing Perspective

In addition to creating a new perspective, you can also extend an existing perspective by adding new views, placeholders, shortcuts, and action sets. To illustrate this, we will add several extensions to the standard **Resource** perspective.

To extend an existing perspective, open the **Favorites** plug-in manifest editor, select the **Extensions** tab, and click the **Add** button to open the **New Extension** wizard. Select the `org.eclipse.ui.perspectiveExtensions` extension point from the list of available extension points (see Figure 10–6).

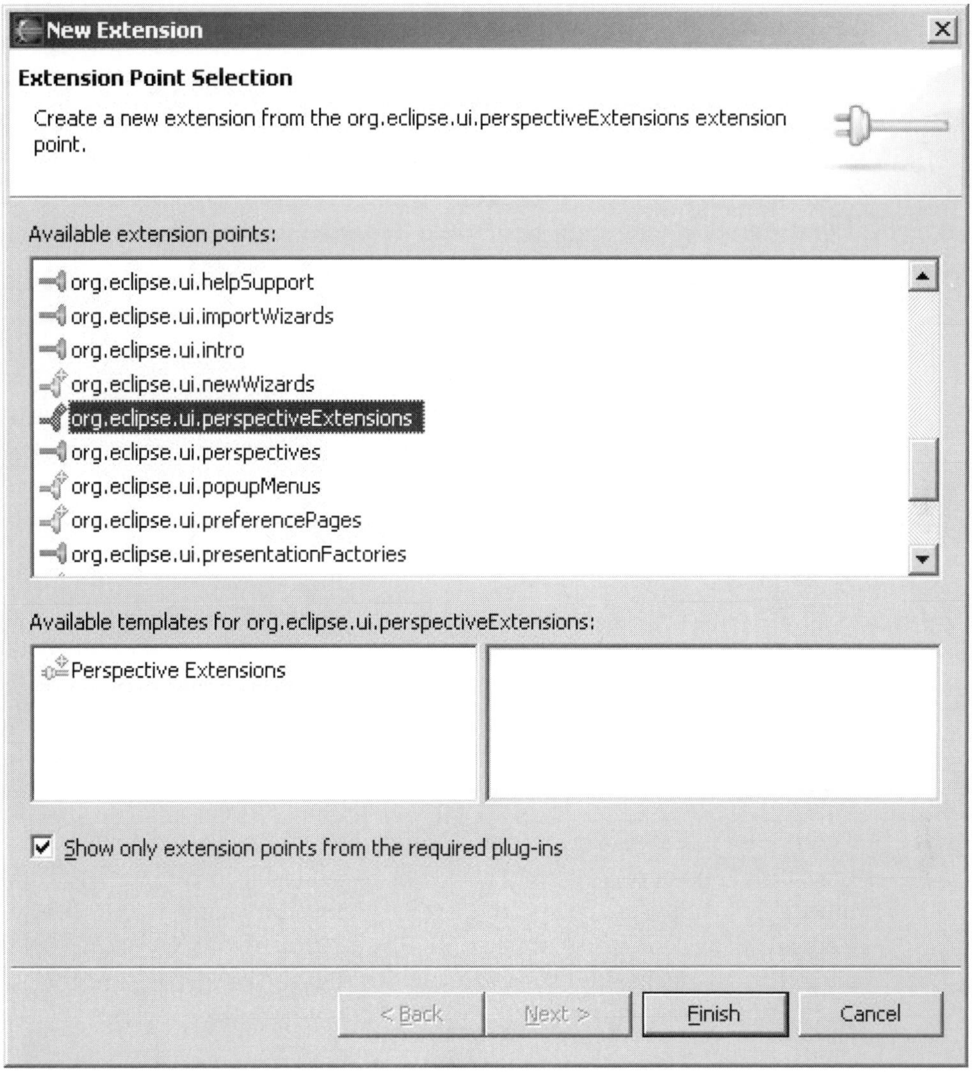

Figure 10–6   The New Extension wizard showing the org.eclipse.ui.perspectiveExtensions extension point selected.

On the **Extensions** page of the plug-in manifest editor, right-click on the `org.eclipse.ui.perspectiveExtensions` extension and select **New > per-spectiveExtension**. This immediately adds a perspective extension named `com.qualityeclipse.favorites.perspectiveExtension1` in the plug-in manifest. Double-click on this new perspective extension to open the **Proper-ties** view and change the **targetID** field to "`org.eclipse.ui.resourcePer-`

spective" (see Figure 10–7). This will change the name of the perspective extension as seen on the **Extensions** page.

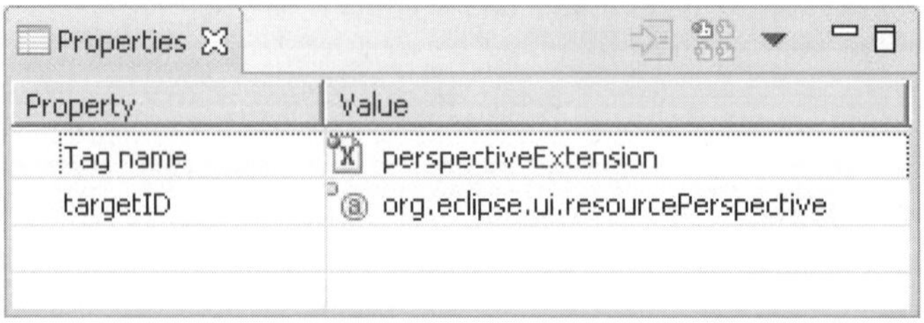

Figure 10–7   The properties view showing the perspective extension's attributes.

When the perspective extension has been created, a number of different extension types may be added, including views, placeholders, action sets, as well as shortcuts for views, perspectives, and the new wizards.

10.2.1   Adding views and placeholders

A view may be either directly added to an existing perspective or a placeholder may be added so that when the user opens the view, it appears in the correct place. As an example, we will add the **Favorites** view to the standard **Resource** perspective.

On the **Extensions** page, right-click on the newly created **org.eclipse.ui.resourcePerspective** extension and select **New > view**. This immediately adds a perspective view extension named com.quality-eclipse.favorites.view1 in the plug-in manifest. Double-clicking on this new extension opens the **Properties** view so that the properties can be modified as follows (see Figure 10–8):

id—"com.qualityeclipse.favorites.views.FavoritesView"
The unique identifier of the **Favorites** view.

relative—"org.eclipse.ui.views.TaskList"
The view relative to which the added view should be oriented.

relationship—"stack"
This specifies how the view should be oriented relative to the target view.

visible—"true"
The view should be initially visible.

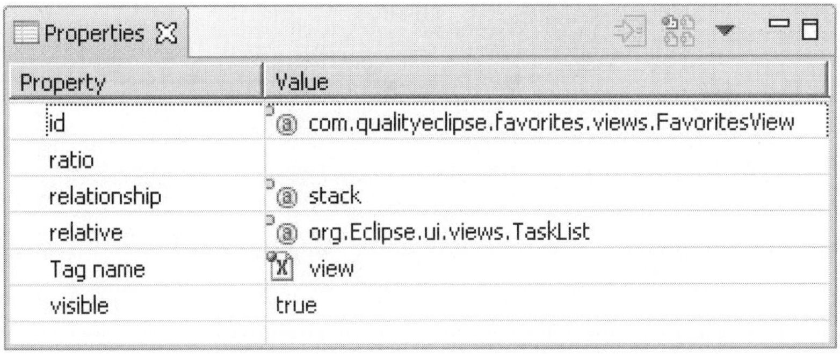

Property	Value
id	ⓐ com.qualityeclipse.favorites.views.FavoritesView
ratio	
relationship	ⓐ stack
relative	ⓐ org.Eclipse.ui.views.TaskList
Tag name	🗷 view
visible	true

Figure 10–8   The Properties view showing the perspective view extension's attributes.

The name of the perspective view extension as seen on the **Extensions** page will change to reflect the `id` entered.

In addition to being stacked in a folder relative to another view, the added view could also be placed at the left, right, above, or below the view specified in the **relative** field, or added as a fast view in the left-hand toolbar. If the new view is added at the left, right, above, or below, the **ratio** of space that the new view takes from the old view may also be specified.

If the **visible** field is specified as `true`, the new view will be opened when the perspective is opened. If it is set to `false`, the view will not be opened automatically. Rather, a placeholder will be established that defines the initial location of the view, if it is ever opened by a user.

Switching to the **Source** page of the plug-in manifest editor, you will see the following new section of XML defining the new perspective extension:

```
<extension point="org.eclipse.ui.perspectiveExtensions">
    <perspectiveExtension
        targetID="org.eclipse.ui.resourcePerspective">
        <view
            relative="org.eclipse.ui.views.TaskList"
            visible="true"
            relationship="stack"
            id="com.qualityeclipse.favorites.views.
                FavoritesView">
        </view>
    </perspectiveExtension>
</extension>
```

When the **Resource** perspective is opened, the **Favorites** view will appear stacked relative to the **Task** view (see Figure 10–9).

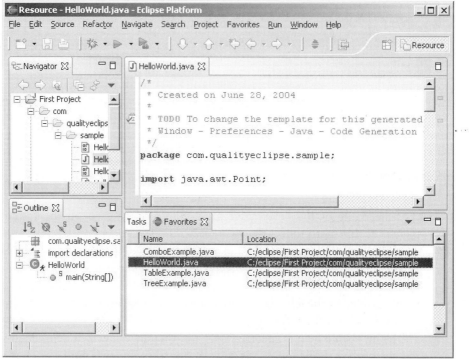

Figure 10–9   The Resource perspective showing the Favorites view.

10.2.2   Adding shortcuts

Shortcuts for quickly accessing related views, perspectives, and new wizards may also be added to a perspective. As an example, we will add shortcuts for accessing the **Favorites** view and perspective to the **Resources** perspective.

We will start by adding a view shortcut for accessing the **Favorites** view from the **Resource** perspective. On the **Extensions** page, right-click on the `org.eclipse.ui.resourcePerspective` extension and select **New > view-Shortcut**. This adds a view shortcut extension named `com.quality-eclipse.favorites.viewShortcut1` to the plug-in manifest. Double-click on it to open the **Properties** view and change the **id** field to "`com.quality-eclipse.favorites.views.FavoritesView`" (see Figure 10–10). This will change the name of the view shortcut extension as seen on the **Extensions** page.

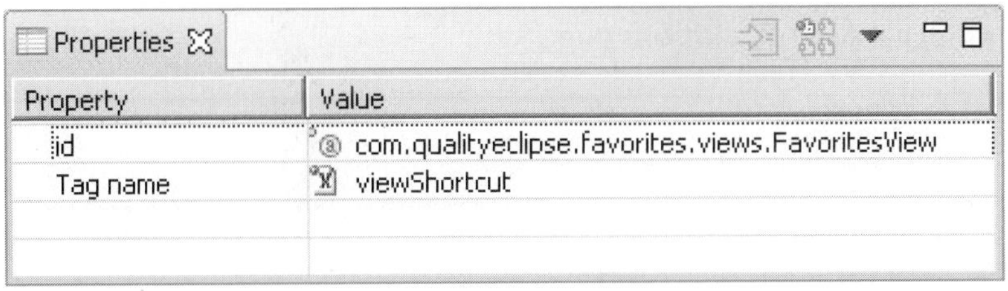

Figure 10–10   The Properties view showing the view shortcut extension's attributes.

When the **Resource** perspective is opened, this will add a shortcut to the **Favorites** view on the **Window > Show View** menu (see Figure 10–11).

Figure 10–11   The Show View menu showing the Favorites shortcut.

Next, we will add a perspective shortcut for accessing the **Favorites** perspective from the **Resource** perspective. On the **Extensions** page, right-click on the `org.eclipse.ui.resourcePerspective` extension and select **New > perspectiveShortcut**. This adds a perspective shortcut extension named `com.qualityeclipse.favorites.  perspectiveShortcut1` to the plug-in manifest. Double-click on it to open the **Properties** view and change the **id** field to "`com.qualityeclipse.favorites.FavoritesPerspective`" (see Figure 10–12). This will change the name of the perspective shortcut extension as seen on the **Extensions** page.

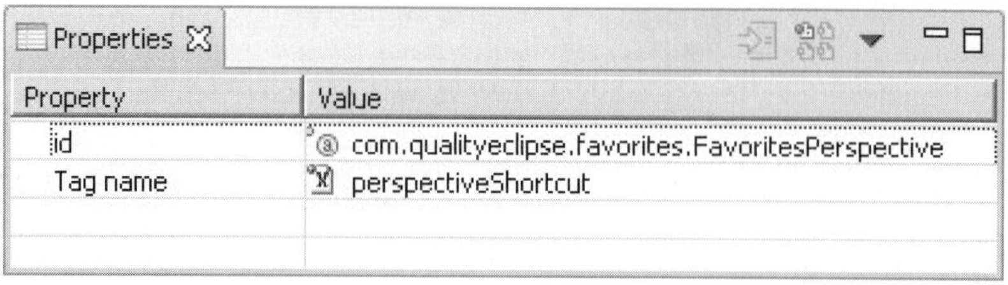

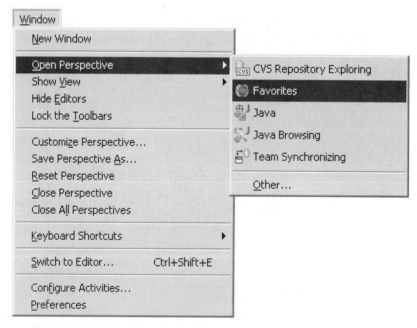

Figure 10–12   The Properties view showing the perspective shortcut extension's attributes.

When the **Resource** perspective is opened, this will add a shortcut to the **Favorites** view on the **Window > Open Perspective** menu (see Figure 10–13).

Figure 10–13   The Open Perspective menu showing the Favorites shortcut.

If you switch to the **Source** page of the plug-in manifest editor, you will see the following added section of XML defining the new view and perspective shortcuts:

```
<extension point="org.eclipse.ui.perspectiveExtensions">
   <perspectiveExtension
      targetID="org.eclipse.ui.resourcePerspective">
      <view
      . . .
```

```
      </view>
      <viewShortcut
         id="com.qualityeclipse.favorites.
            views.FavoritesView">
      </viewShortcut>
      <perspectiveShortcut
         id="com.qualityeclipse.favorites.
            FavoritesPerspective">
      </perspectiveShortcut>
   </perspectiveExtension>
</extension>
```

10.2.3 Adding action sets

Groups of commands (menu items and toolbar buttons) defined in action sets may also be added to a perspective (see Chapter 6, "Actions," for more about adding actions). As an example, we will add the **Favorites** action set to the **Resources** perspective.

On the **Extensions** page, right-click on the org.eclipse.ui.resource-Perspective extension and select **New > actionSet**. This adds an action set extension named com.qualityeclipse.favorites.actionSet1 to the plug-in manifest. Double-click on it to open the **Properties** view and change the **id** field to "com.qualityeclipse.favorites.workbenchActionSet" (see Figure 10–14). This will change the name of the action set extension as seen on the **Extensions** page.

Figure 10–14   The Properties view showing the action set extension's attributes.

If you switch to the **Source** page of the plug-in manifest editor, you will see the following added section of XML defining the new action set extension:

```
<extension point="org.eclipse.ui.perspectiveExtensions">
   <perspectiveExtension
      targetID="org.eclipse.ui.resourcePerspective">
      <view
      ...
      </view>
      ...
      <actionSet
         id="com.qualityeclipse.favorites.
            workbenchActionSet">
      </actionSet>
   </perspectiveExtension>
</extension>
```

With the above enhancements in place, the new perspective and perspective extensions will now be visible on the **Extensions** page (see Figure 10–15).

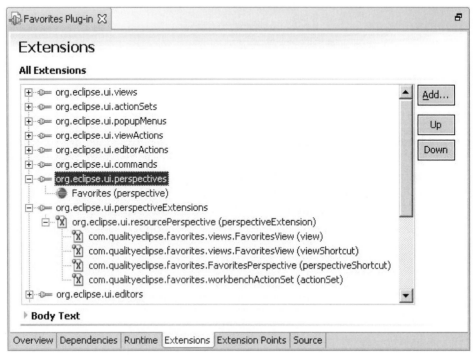

Figure 10–15   The Extensions page showing the new perspective and perspective extensions.

10.3   RFWS Considerations

The "User Interface" section of the *RFWS Requirements* includes five items— three requirements and two best practices—dealing with perspectives. All of them are derived from the Eclipse UI Guidelines.

10.3.1   Create perspective for long-lived tasks

User Interface Guideline #39 is a best practice that states:

Create a new perspective type for long-lived tasks that involve the performance of smaller, non-modal tasks. A new perspective type should be created when there is a group of related tasks that would benefit from a predefined configuration of actions and views, and these tasks are long-lived. A task-oriented approach is imperative

To pass this test, create a list of the perspectives defined by your application and demonstrate their use. For each perspective, describe the views, shortcuts, new wizard items, and action sets that are included. In the case of the examples presented earlier in this chapter, we would show the **Favorites** perspective (see Figure 10–5) and describe its use to the reviewers.

10.3.2   New view for existing perspectives

User Interface Guideline #40 is a best practice that states:

To expose a single view or two views, extend an existing perspective type. If a plug-in contributes a small number of views, and these augment an existing task, it is better to add those views to an existing perspective. For instance, if you create a view that augments the task of Java code creation, don't create a new perspective. Instead, add it to the existing Java perspective. This strategy provides better integration with the existing platform.

For this test, simply create a list of any views that your application adds to other existing perspectives. In the case of our earlier examples, we would show the **Favorites** view added to the **Resource** perspective (see Figure 10–9).

10.3.3   Perspectives without editors

User Interface Guideline #41 is a requirement that states:

If it is undesirable to have an editor area in a perspective; hide it. Do not resize the editor area to the point where it is no longer visible. In some scenarios, it may be undesirable to have an editor area within a perspective. In this case, the perspective factory should hide the editor area using existing Java methods. It is not acceptable to resize the editor area to a point where it is no longer visible. If a user does open an editor in the perspective, for whatever reason, he or she will be unable to see or resize it.

If any of your application perspectives don't require an editor area, show them to the reviewers (see `setEditorAreaVisible(boolean)` in Section 10.1.2, "Perspective factories," for information).

10.3.4   Adding perspective actions to window menu

User Interface Guideline #42 is a requirement that states:

Populate the window menu bar with actions and action sets that are appropriate to the task orientation of the perspective, and any larger workflow.

For this test, provide a list of any action sets that have been added to any perspectives. For the **Favorites** view, we would list things like the **Favorites** action set that was added to the **Resource** perspective in Section 10.2.3, "Adding action sets."

10.3.5 Newly opened perspectives

User Interface Guideline #43 is a requirement that states:

If a new perspective is opened, it should be opened as a page within the current window, or in a new window, depending on user preference. The user controls this option using the workbench preferences. If code within a plug-in opens a new perspective, the plug-in should honor the user's preferences.

If your product opens any perspectives on its own (as opposed to being opened manually by a user), demonstrate those scenarios to the reviewers and show that the new perspective opens either as a new page within the current window or in a new window depending on the user's settings. One example of this in Eclipse itself is the **Launch** command opening the **Debug** perspective (see Section 1.10, "Introduction to Debugging").

10.4 Summary

Perspectives provide a way to group views and actions together to support a specific task. In this chapter, we learned how to create a new perspective, define its default layout, and add various extensions to it.

CHAPTER 11

Dialogs and Wizards

Good UI guidelines suggest that developers construct modeless Eclipse editors and views, but there are times when a modal dialog or wizard is appropriate. This chapter lays out the Eclipse dialog and wizard framework, discusses when a dialog or wizard should be used instead of a view or editor, provides various examples, and discusses Eclipse's various built-in dialog classes.

11.1 Dialogs

Whenever information is requested from or presented to the user in a modeless fashion, it allows the user to freely interact with all the resources in the workbench. Windows, pages, editors, and views are all examples of modeless UI constructs that do not restrict the order in which the user interacts with them. Dialogs are typically modal, restricting the user to either entering the information requested or canceling the operation. The only time a modal UI construct should be used is when programming restrictions require a gathering or dissemination of information before any other processing can continue, and even then, for as short a time as possible.

In one case, the program could present two different versions of a file using a dialog. Unfortunately, this approach prevents the user from switching back and forth between the comparison and some other UI construct such as another editor or view. A better approach would be to present that same information in a comparison editor.

Creating a new project represents a different situation. In that case, the operation must gather all the necessary information sequentially before the operation can be performed. The user has requested the operation and typically does not need to interact with another aspect of the program until all the information is gathered and the operation is complete. In this case, a dialog or wizard is warranted.

11.1.1 SWT dialogs versus JFace dialogs

There are two distinct dialog hierarchies in Eclipse that should not be confused. SWT dialogs (`org.eclipse.swt.Dialog`) are Java representations of built-in platform dialogs such as a file dialog or font dialog; as such, they are not portable or extendable. JFace dialogs (`org.eclipse.jface.dialogs.Dialog`) are platform-independent dialogs on which wizards are built. SWT dialogs are only briefly discussed, while JFace dialogs are covered in detail.

11.1.2 Common SWT dialogs

Eclipse includes several SWT dialog classes that provide platform-independent interfaces to underlying platform-specific dialogs:

ColorDialog—Prompts the user to select a color from a predefined set of available colors.

DirectoryDialog—Prompts the user to navigate the filesystem and select a directory. Valid styles include SWT.OPEN for selecting an existing directory and SWT.SAVE for specifying a new directory.

FileDialog—Prompts the user to navigate the filesystem and select or enter a filename. Valid styles include SWT.OPEN for selecting an existing file and SWT.SAVE for specifying a new file.

FontDialog—Prompts the user to select a font from all available fonts in the system.

MessageBox—Displays a message to the user. Valid icon styles are shown in Table 11–1.

Table 11–1   Icon Styles

Constant	Icon
SWT.ICON_ERROR	
SWT.ICON_INFORMATION	
SWT.ICON_QUESTION	

Table 11-1 Icon Styles (continued)

SWT.ICON_WARNING	
SWT.ICON_WORKING	

Valid button styles include:

SWT.OK
SWT.OK | SWT.CANCEL
SWT.YES | SWT.NO
SWT.YES | SWT.NO | SWT.CANCEL
SWT.RETRY | SWT.CANCEL
SWT.ABORT | SWT.RETRY | SWT.IGNORE

`PrintDialog`–Prompts the user to select a printer and various print-related parameters prior to starting a print job.

With any of these SWT dialogs, one of the following modal styles can be specified:

`SWT.MODELESS`–Modeless dialog behavior.

`SWT.PRIMARY_MODAL`–Modal behavior with respect to the parent shell.

`SWT.APPLICATION_MODAL`–Modal behavior with respect to the application.

`SWT.SYSTEM_MODAL`–Modal behavior with respect to the entire system.

11.1.3   *Common JFace dialogs*

There are many JFace dialogs that can be either instantiated directly or reused via subclassing:

Abstract dialogs

`AbstractElementListSelectionDialog`–An abstract dialog to select elements from a list of elements.

`IconAndMessageDialog`–The abstract superclass of dialogs that have an icon and a message as the first two widgets.

`SelectionDialog`–An abstract dialog for displaying and returning a selection.

`SelectionStatusDialog`—An abstract base class for dialogs with a status bar and **OK/Cancel** buttons. The status message must be passed over as a `StatusInfo` object and can be an error, warning, or okay. The **OK** button is enabled or disabled depending on the status.

`TitleAreaDialog`–An abstract dialog having a title area for displaying a title and an image as well as a common area for displaying a description, a message, or an error message.

File dialogs

`FileSelectionDialog`–A standard file selection dialog that solicits a list of files from the user. The `getResult()` method returns the selected files.

`SaveAsDialog`–A standard "Save As" dialog that solicits a path from the user. The `getResult()` method returns the path. Note that the folder at the specified path might not exist and might need to be created.

Information dialogs

`ErrorDialog`—A dialog to display one or more errors to the user, as contained in an `IStatus` object. If an error contains additional detailed information, then a **Details** button is automatically supplied, which shows or hides an error details viewer when pressed by the user.

`MessageDialog`–A dialog for showing messages to the user.

Resource dialogs

`ContainerSelectionDialog`–A standard selection dialog that solicits a container resource from the user. The `getResult()` method returns the selected container resource.

`GotoResourceDialog`–Shows a list of resources to the user with a text entry field for a string pattern used to filter the list of resources.

`NewFolderDialog`–A dialog used to create a new folder. The folder can optionally be linked to a filesystem folder.

`ProjectLocationMoveDialog`–A dialog used to select the location of a project for moving.

`ProjectLocationSelectionDialog`–A dialog used to select the name and location of a project for copying.

`ResourceListSelectionDialog`–Shows a list of resources to the user with a text entry field for a string pattern used to filter the list of resources.

`ResourceSelectionDialog`–A standard resource selection dialog that solicits a list of resources from the user. The `getResult()` method returns the selected resources.

`TypeFilteringDialog`—A selection dialog that allows the user to select a file editor.

Selection dialogs

`CheckedTreeSelectionDialog`—A dialog to select elements out of a tree structure.

`ElementListSelectionDialog`—A dialog to select elements out of a list of elements.

`ElementTreeSelectionDialog`—A dialog to select elements out of a tree structure.

`ListDialog`—A dialog that prompts for one element from a list of elements. Uses `IStructuredContentProvider` to provide the elements and `ILabelProvider` to provide their labels.

`ListSelectionDialog`—A standard dialog that solicits a list of selections from the user. This class is configured with an arbitrary data model represented by content and label provider objects. The `getResult()` method returns the selected elements.

`TwoPaneElementSelector`—A list selection dialog with two panes. Duplicated entries will be folded together and are displayed in the lower pane (qualifier).

`YesNoCancelListSelectionDialog`—A list selection dialog that also allows the user to select "no" as a result.

Miscellaneous dialogs:

`InputDialog`—A simple input dialog for soliciting an input string from the user.

`ProgressMonitorDialog`—A modal dialog that displays progress during a long-running operation. (see Section 9.4, "Progress Monitor")

`TaskPropertiesDialog`—Shows the properties of a new or existing task, or a problem.

`WizardDialog`—A dialog displaying a wizard and implementing the `IWizardContainer` interface (see Section 11.2.3, "IWizardContainer")

11.1.4   Creating a JFace dialog

The default implementation of the `Dialog` class creates a dialog containing a content area for dialog-specific controls and a button bar below containing **OK** and **Cancel** buttons (see Figure 11–1).

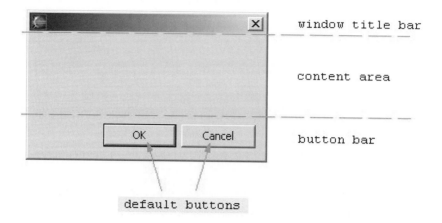

Figure 11–1 Default dialog structure.

Typically, new dialogs are created by subclassing `org.eclipse`
`.jface.dialogs.Dialog` and overriding a handful of methods to customize
the dialog for a particular purpose:

> `buttonPressed(int)`—Called when a button created by the `createBut-`
> `ton` method is clicked by the user. The default implementation calls
> `okPressed()` if the **OK** button is pressed and `cancelPressed()` if the
> **Cancel** button is pressed.

> `cancelPressed()`—Called when the user presses the **Cancel** button. The
> default implementation sets the return code to `Window.CANCEL` and closes
> the dialog.

> `close()`—Closes the dialog, disposes its shell, and removes the dialog
> from its window manager (if it has one).

> `createButton(Composite, int, String, boolean)`—Creates and
> returns a new button in the button bar with the given identifier and
> label. This method is typically called from the `createButtonsForBut-`
> `tonBar` method.

> `createButtonBar(Composite)`—Lays out a button bar and calls the `cre-`
> `ateButtonsForButtonBar` method to populate it. Subclasses may over-
> ride `createButtonBar` or `createButtonsForButtonBar` as necessary.

> `createButtonsForButtonBar(Composite)`—Creates buttons in the but-
> ton bar. The default implementation creates **OK** and **Cancel** buttons in
> the lower right corner. Subclasses may override this method to replace
> the default buttons, or extend this method to augment them using the
> `createButton` method.

createContents(Composite)—Creates and returns this dialog's contents. The default implementation calls createDialogArea and createButton-Bar to create the dialog area and button bar, respectively. Subclasses should override these methods rather than createContents.

createDialogArea(Composite)—Creates and returns the content area for the dialog above the button bar. Subclasses typically call the superclass method and then add controls to the returned composite.

okPressed()—Called when the user presses the **OK** button. The default implementation sets the return code to Window.OK and closes the dialog.

open()—Opens this dialog, creating it first if it has not yet been created. This method waits until the user closes the dialog, and then returns the dialog's return code. A dialog's return codes are dialog-specific, although two standard return codes are predefined: Window.OK and Window.CAN-CEL.

setShellStyle(int)—Sets the shell style bits for creating the dialog. This method has no effect after the shell is created. Valid style bits include:

```
SWT.MODELESS
SWT.PRIMARY_MODAL
SWT.APPLICATION_MODAL
SWT.SYSTEM_MODAL
SWT.SHELL_TRIM
SWT.DIALOG_TRIM
SWT.BORDER
SWT.CLOSE
SWT.MAX
SWT.MIN
SWT.RESIZE
SWT.TITLE
```

setReturnCode(int)—Sets the dialog's return code that is returned by the open() method.

11.1.5   Dialog units

If you are positioning controls in the dialog area based on absolute positioning (null layout) rather than using a layout manager such as GridLayout or FormLayout, then problems may arise when a different font is used. If the dialog is sized for a font with one pixel size and the user has his or her system set for a font in a different pixel size, then the controls will be either too big or too small for the font used. To alleviate this problem, you should position and size the controls based on the font's average character size or based on *dialog units* (see Figure 11–2).

Figure 11–2   Dialog units superimposed over the letter "T."

Dialog units are based on the current font and are independent of the display device; thus, they can be used to position controls within a dialog, independent of the font being used. They are defined as one-quarter of the average width of a character and one-eighth of the average height of a character.

```
dialog unit X = average character width / 4
dialog unit Y = average character height / 8
```

Therefore, to convert from dialog units to pixels:

```
pixelX = (dialog unit X * average character width) / 4
pixelY = (dialog unit Y * average character height) / 8
```

The Eclipse dialog framework provides several convenient methods for converting dialog units or character sizes into pixel sizes.

`convertHeightInCharsToPixels(int)`—Returns the number of pixels corresponding to the height of the given number of characters.

`convertHorizontalDLUsToPixels(int)`—Returns the number of pixels corresponding to the given number of horizontal dialog units.

`convertVerticalDLUsToPixels(int)`—Returns the number of pixels corresponding to the given number of vertical dialog units.

`convertWidthInCharsToPixels(int)`—Returns the number of pixels corresponding to the width of the given number of characters.

11.1.6   *Initial dialog location and size*

The default behavior for dialogs as implemented by the dialog framework is to initially position a dialog on top of its parent window specified in the dialog's constructor. To provide a different initial location or size for a dialog, you would override the following methods as necessary:

getInitialLocation(Point)—Returns the initial location to use for the dialog. The default implementation centers the dialog horizontally (half the difference to the left and half to the right) and vertically (one-third above and two-thirds below) relative to the parent shell or display bounds if there is no parent shell. The parameter is the initial size of the dialog, as returned by getInitialSize() method.

getInitialSize()—Returns the initial size to use for the dialog. The default implementation returns the preferred size of the dialog based on the dialog's layout and controls using the computeSize method.

11.1.7   *Resizable dialogs*

By default, subclasses of Dialog are not resizable, but there are examples of resizable dialogs within the Eclipse framework such as: org.eclipse .jdt.internal.ui.compare.ResizableDialog.

Unfortunately, this dialog is within an internal package, and thus should not be reused outside of its defining plug-in (see Section 20.2, "Accessing Internal Code"). The first step to making your wizard resizable is to include the SWT.RESIZE and SWT.MAX styles when the dialog is created to allow the user to resize the dialog and display the maximize window button, as follows:

```
public ResizableDialog(Shell parentShell) {
    super(parentShell);
    setShellStyle(getShellStyle() | SWT.RESIZE | SWT.MAX);
}
```

Next, to preserve the size and location of the dialog across invocations, subclasses of this new class must supply a location in which to store values. See Section 11.2.7, "Dialog settings," for more about IDialogSettings.

```
/**
 * Answer the dialog settings for this dialogs of this type
 */
protected abstract IDialogSettings getDialogSettings();
```

We need methods to load the bounds from the dialog settings and save the bounds into the dialog settings:

```
private static final String X = "x";
private static final String Y = "y";
private static final String WIDTH = "width";
private static final String HEIGHT = "height";

private Rectangle loadBounds() {
   IDialogSettings settings = getDialogSettings();
   try {
      return new Rectangle(
         settings.getInt(X),
         settings.getInt(Y),
         settings.getInt(WIDTH),
         settings.getInt(HEIGHT));
   }
   catch (NumberFormatException e) {
      return null;
   }
}

private void saveBounds(Rectangle bounds) {
   IDialogSettings settings = getDialogSettings();
   settings.put(X, bounds.x);
   settings.put(Y, bounds.y);
   settings.put(WIDTH, bounds.width);
   settings.put(HEIGHT, bounds.height);
}
```

We override the getInitialLocation(...) and getInitialSize() methods so that when the dialog is first opened, its prior location and size are restored:

```
protected Rectangle cachedBounds;

protected Point getInitialSize() {

   // Track the current dialog bounds.
   getShell().addControlListener(new ControlListener() {
      public void controlMoved(ControlEvent arg0) {
         cachedBounds = getShell().getBounds();
      }
      public void controlResized(ControlEvent arg0) {
         cachedBounds = getShell().getBounds();
      }
   });

   // Answer the size from the previous incarnation.
   Rectangle b1 = getShell().getDisplay().getBounds();
   Rectangle b2 = loadBounds();
   if (b2 != null)
      return new Point(
         b1.width < b2.width ? b1.width : b2.width,
         b1.height < b1.height ? b2.height : b2.height);

   return super.getInitialSize();
}
```

```
protected Point getInitialLocation(Point initialSize) {

    // Answer the location from the previous incarnation.
    Rectangle displayBounds =
        getShell().getDisplay().getBounds();
    Rectangle bounds = loadBounds();
    if (bounds != null) {
        int x = bounds.x;
        int y = bounds.y;
        int maxX =
            displayBounds.x
                + displayBounds.width
              -initialSize.x;
        int maxY =
            displayBounds.y
                + displayBounds.height
              -initialSize.y;
        if (x > maxX)
            x = maxX;
        if (y > maxY)
            y = maxY;
        if (x < displayBounds.x)
            x = displayBounds.x;
        if (y < displayBounds.y)
            y = displayBounds.y;
        return new Point(x, y);
    }

    return super.getInitialLocation(initialSize);
}
```

Finally, we override the `close` method to save the dialog bounds for future incarnations:

```
public boolean close() {
    boolean closed = super.close();
    if (closed && cachedBounds != null)
        saveBounds(cachedBounds);
    return closed;
}
```

11.1.8   Favorites view filter dialog

As an example, we will create a specialized filter dialog for the **Favorites** view that presents the user the option of filtering content based on name, type, or location (see Sections 7.2.7, "Viewer filters," and 7.3.4, "Pull-down menu"). The dialog restricts itself to presenting and gathering information from the user and providing accessor methods for the filter action.

```java
package com.qualityeclipse.favorites.dialogs;

import java.util.*;
import org.eclipse.jface.dialogs.*;
import org.eclipse.swt.SWT;
import org.eclipse.swt.events.*;
import org.eclipse.swt.layout.*;
import org.eclipse.swt.widgets.*;
import com.qualityeclipse.favorites.model.*;

public class FavoritesFilterDialog extends Dialog
{
    private String namePattern;
    private String locationPattern;
    private Collection selectedTypes;

    private Text namePatternField;
    private Text locationPatternField;
    private Map typeFields;

    public FavoritesFilterDialog(
        Shell parentShell,
        String namePattern,
        String locationPattern,
        FavoriteItemType[] selectedTypes) {

        super(parentShell);
        this.namePattern = namePattern;
        this.locationPattern = locationPattern;
        this.selectedTypes = new HashSet();
        for (int i = 0; i < selectedTypes.length; i++)
            this.selectedTypes.add(selectedTypes[i]);
    }

    protected Control createDialogArea(Composite parent) {
        // $begin code generated by SWT-Designer$
        Composite area =
            (Composite) super.createDialogArea(parent);
        area.setLayout(new FormLayout());

        final Label label = new Label(area, SWT.NONE);
        final FormData formData = new FormData();
        formData.top = new FormAttachment(0, 5);
        formData.left = new FormAttachment(0, 5);
        label.setLayoutData(formData);
        label.setText(
            "Enter a filter (* = any number of "
                + "characters, ? = any single character)"
                + "\nor an empty string for no filtering:");

        final Composite composite =
            new Composite(area, SWT.NONE);
        final GridLayout gridLayout = new GridLayout();
        gridLayout.numColumns = 2;
        composite.setLayout(gridLayout);
        final FormData formData_1 = new FormData();
```

```
formData_1.right = new FormAttachment(100, -5);
formData_1.top =
   new FormAttachment(label, 5, SWT.BOTTOM);
formData_1.left = new FormAttachment(0, 20);
composite.setLayoutData(formData_1);

final Label label_1 = new Label(composite, SWT.NONE);
label_1.setLayoutData(
   new GridData(GridData.HORIZONTAL_ALIGN_END));
label_1.setText("Name:");

namePatternField = new Text(composite, SWT.BORDER);
namePatternField.setLayoutData(
   new GridData(GridData.FILL_HORIZONTAL));
namePatternField.addModifyListener(
   new ModifyListener() {
      public void modifyText(ModifyEvent e) {
         namePattern = namePatternField.getText();
      }});

final Label label_2 = new Label(composite, SWT.NONE);
label_2.setLayoutData(
   new GridData(GridData.HORIZONTAL_ALIGN_END));
label_2.setText("Location:");

locationPatternField = new Text(composite, SWT.BORDER);
locationPatternField.setLayoutData(
   new GridData(GridData.HORIZONTAL_ALIGN_FILL));
locationPatternField.addModifyListener(
   new ModifyListener() {
      public void modifyText(ModifyEvent e) {
         locationPattern =
            locationPatternField.getText();
      }});

final Label label_3 = new Label(area, SWT.NONE);
final FormData formData_2 = new FormData();
formData_2.top =
   new FormAttachment(composite, 5, SWT.BOTTOM);
formData_2.left =
   new FormAttachment(label, 0, SWT.LEFT);
label_3.setLayoutData(formData_2);
label_3.setText(
   "Select the types of favorites to be shown:");

final Composite composite_1 =
   new Composite(area, SWT.NONE);
final GridLayout gridLayout_1 = new GridLayout();
gridLayout_1.numColumns = 2;
composite_1.setLayout(gridLayout_1);
final FormData formData_3 = new FormData();
formData_3.bottom = new FormAttachment(100, -5);
formData_3.right =
   new FormAttachment(composite, 0, SWT.RIGHT);
formData_3.top =
   new FormAttachment(label_3, 5, SWT.BOTTOM);
```

```
          formData_3.left =
             new FormAttachment(composite, 0, SWT.LEFT);
          composite_1.setLayoutData(formData_3);
          // $end code generated by SWT-Designer$

          createTypeCheckboxes(composite_1);
          initContent();

          return area;
       }

    private void createTypeCheckboxes(Composite parent) {
       typeFields = new HashMap();
       FavoriteItemType[] allTypes =
          FavoriteItemType.getTypes();
       for (int i = 0; i < allTypes.length; i++) {
          final FavoriteItemType eachType = allTypes[i];
          if (eachType == FavoriteItemType.UNKNOWN)
             continue;
          final Button button =
             new Button(parent, SWT.CHECK);
          button.setText(eachType.getName());
          typeFields.put(eachType, button);
          button
             .addSelectionListener(new SelectionAdapter() {
             public void widgetSelected(SelectionEvent e) {
                if (button.getSelection())
                   selectedTypes.add(eachType);
                else
                   selectedTypes.remove(eachType);
             }
          });
       }
    }

    private void initContent() {
       namePatternField.setText(
          namePattern != null ? namePattern : "");
       locationPatternField.setText(
          locationPattern != null ? locationPattern : "");
       FavoriteItemType[] allTypes =
          FavoriteItemType.getTypes();
       for (int i = 0; i < allTypes.length; i++) {
          FavoriteItemType eachType = allTypes[i];
          if (eachType == FavoriteItemType.UNKNOWN)
             continue;
          Button button = (Button) typeFields.get(eachType);
          button.setSelection(
             selectedTypes.contains(eachType));
       }
    }

    protected void configureShell(Shell newShell) {
       super.configureShell(newShell);
       newShell.setText("Favorites View Filter Options");
    }
```

```
      public String getNamePattern() {
         return namePattern;
      }

      public String getLocationPattern() {
         return locationPattern;
      }

      public FavoriteItemType[] getSelectedTypes() {
         return (FavoriteItemType[]) selectedTypes.toArray(
            new FavoriteItemType[selectedTypes.size()]);
      }
   }
```

The filter action (see `FavoritesViewFilterAction` in Section 7.3.4) must be modified to fill the dialog with the current filter settings, open the dialog, and process the specified filter settings if the user closes the dialog using the **OK** button. If the dialog is closed using the **Cancel** button or any other way besides the **OK** button, the changes are discarded as per standard dialog operation guidelines. The type and location view filters referenced in the following code are left as an exercise for the reader:

```
public void run() {
   FavoritesFilterDialog dialog =
      new FavoritesFilterDialog(
         shell,
         nameFilter.getPattern(),
         typeFilter.getTypes(),
         locationFilter.getPattern());
   if (dialog.open() != InputDialog.OK)
      return;
   nameFilter.setPattern(dialog.getNamePattern());
   typeFilter.setPattern(dialog.getSelectedTypes());
   locationFilter.setPattern(dialog.getLocationPattern());
}
```

When these changes are complete, the filter dialog presents the filter settings to the user when the **Filter...** menu item is selected (see Figure 11–3).

Figure 11-3 image:

Favorites View Filter Options

Enter a filter (* = any number of characters, ? = any single character) or an empty string for no filtering:

Name: [   ]

Location: [   ]

Select the types of favorites to be shown:

☑ Workbench File   ☑ Workbench Folder
☑ WorkbenchProject   ☑ Java Project
☑ Java Package Root   ☑ Java Package
☑ Java Class File   ☑ Java Compilation Unit
☑ Java Interface   ☑ Java Class

[OK]   [Cancel]

Figure 11-3 New Favorites View Filter Options dialog.

11.1.9 Details dialog

One of the RFWS criteria includes identifying the plug-in and plug-in creator when reporting problems to the user. In other words, whenever the application needs to report an error message or exception to the user, the plug-in's unique identifier, version, and creator must be visible in the dialog. The `org.eclipse.jface.dialogs.ErrorDialog` can display exception information in a details section that is shown or hidden using a **Details** button, but it does not display the necessary product information as required by RFWS standards. To satisfy this requirement, we created `ExceptionDetailsDialog` (see Figure 11–4).

RuntimeException

❌ This is a test

[OK]   [Details >>]

Figure 11-4 Details dialog with details hidden.

When the **Details** button is pressed, the dialog resizes itself to show additional information (see Figure 11–5).

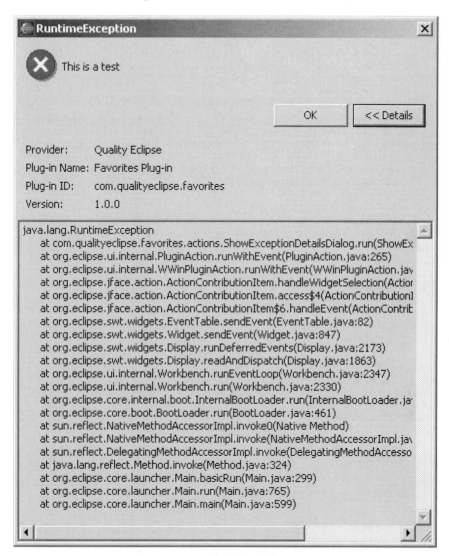

Figure 11–5 Details dialog with details showing.

The ExceptionDetailsDialog class implements this expanding details behavior.

```java
package com.qualityeclipse.favorites.dialogs;

import java.io.*;
import java.lang.reflect.*;
import java.text.*;
import org.eclipse.core.runtime.*;
import org.eclipse.jface.dialogs.*;
import org.eclipse.jface.dialogs.Dialog;
import org.eclipse.jface.resource.*;
import org.eclipse.swt.*;
import org.eclipse.swt.graphics.Image;
import org.eclipse.swt.layout.*;
import org.eclipse.swt.widgets.*;
import com.qualityeclipse.favorites.*;

public class ExceptionDetailsDialog
    extends AbstractDetailsDialog
{
    /**
     * The details to be shown ({@link Exception},
     * {@link IStatus}, or <code>null</code> if no details).
     */
    private final Object details;

    public ExceptionDetailsDialog(
        Shell parentShell,
        String title,
        Image image,
        String message,
        Object details) {

        super(
            parentShell,
            getTitle(title, details),
            getImage(image, details),
            getMessage(message, details));

        this.details = details;
    }

    protected Control createDetailsArea(Composite parent) {

        // Create the details area.
        Composite panel = new Composite(parent, SWT.NONE);
        panel.setLayoutData(new GridData(GridData.FILL_BOTH));
        GridLayout layout = new GridLayout();
        layout.marginHeight = 0;
        layout.marginWidth = 0;
        panel.setLayout(layout);

        // Create the details content.
        createProductInfoArea(panel);
        createDetailsViewer(panel);

        return panel;
    }
```

```
protected Composite createProductInfoArea(
   Composite parent) {

   Composite composite = new Composite(parent, SWT.NULL);
   composite.setLayoutData(new GridData());
   GridLayout layout = new GridLayout();
   layout.numColumns = 2;
   layout.marginWidth =
      convertHorizontalDLUsToPixels(
         IDialogConstants.HORIZONTAL_MARGIN);
   composite.setLayout(layout);

   new Label(composite, SWT.NONE).setText("Provider:");
   new Label(composite, SWT.NONE).setText("Quality Eclipse");
   new Label(composite, SWT.NONE).setText("Plug-in Name:");
   new Label(composite, SWT.NONE).setText(
      FavoritesPlugin
         .getDefault()
         .getDescriptor()
         .getLabel());
   new Label(composite, SWT.NONE).setText("Plug-in ID:");
   new Label(composite, SWT.NONE).setText(
      FavoritesPlugin
         .getDefault()
         .getDescriptor()
         .getUniqueIdentifier());
   new Label(composite, SWT.NONE).setText("Version:");
   new Label(composite, SWT.NONE).setText(
      FavoritesPlugin
         .getDefault()
         .getDescriptor()
         .getVersionIdentifier()
         .toString());

   return composite;
}

protected Control createDetailsViewer(Composite parent) {
   if (details == null)
      return null;

   Text text =
      new Text(
         parent,
         SWT.MULTI
            | SWT.READ_ONLY
            | SWT.BORDER
            | SWT.H_SCROLL
            | SWT.V_SCROLL);
   text.setLayoutData(new GridData(GridData.FILL_BOTH));

   // Create the content.
```

```
StringWriter writer = new StringWriter(1000);
if (details instanceof Throwable)
   appendException(
      new PrintWriter(writer),


 (Throwable) details);
else if (details instanceof IStatus)
   appendStatus(
      new PrintWriter(writer),
      (IStatus) details,
      0);
text.setText(writer.toString());

return text;
}

/**
 * Answer the title based on the provided title and
 * details object.
 */
public static String getTitle(
   String title,
   Object details) {

   if (title != null)
      return title;
   if (details instanceof Throwable) {
      Throwable e = (Throwable) details;
      while (e instanceof InvocationTargetException)
         e =
            ((InvocationTargetException) e)
               .getTargetException();
      String name = e.getClass().getName();
      return name.substring(name.lastIndexOf('.') + 1);
   }
   return "Exception";
}

/**
 * Answer the image based on the provided image and
 * details object.
 */
public static Image getImage(
   Image image,
   Object details) {

   if (image != null)
      return image;
   ImageRegistry imageRegistry =
      JFaceResources.getImageRegistry();
   if (details instanceof IStatus) {
      switch (((IStatus) details).getSeverity()) {
         case IStatus.ERROR :
            return imageRegistry.get(
               Dialog.DLG_IMG_ERROR);
```

```
                case IStatus.WARNING :
                    return imageRegistry.get(
                        Dialog.DLG_IMG_WARNING);
                case IStatus.INFO :
                    return imageRegistry.get(
                        Dialog.DLG_IMG_INFO);
                case IStatus.OK :
                    return null;
            }
        }
        return imageRegistry.get(Dialog.DLG_IMG_ERROR);
    }

    /**
     * Answer the message based on the provided message
     * and details object.
     */
    public static String getMessage(
        String message,
        Object details) {

        if (details instanceof Throwable) {
            Throwable e = (Throwable) details;
            while (e instanceof InvocationTargetException)
                e = ((InvocationTargetException) e)
                        .getTargetException();
            if (message == null)
                return e.toString();
            return MessageFormat.format(
                message,
                new Object[] { e.toString()});
        }
        if (details instanceof IStatus) {
            String statusMessage =
                ((IStatus) details).getMessage();
            if (message == null)
                return statusMessage;
            return MessageFormat.format(
                message,
                new Object[] { statusMessage });
        }
        if (message != null)
            return message;
        return "An Exception occurred.";
    }

    public static void appendException(
        PrintWriter writer,
        Throwable ex) {
        if (ex instanceof CoreException) {
            appendStatus(
                writer,
                ((CoreException) ex).getStatus(),
                0);
            writer.println();
        }
        appendStackTrace(writer, ex);
        if (ex instanceof InvocationTargetException)
```

```
                appendException(
                    writer,
                    ((InvocationTargetException) ex)
                        .getTargetException());
        }

        public static void appendStatus(
            PrintWriter writer,
            IStatus status,
            int nesting) {
            for (int i = 0; i < nesting; i++)
                writer.print("  ");
            writer.println(status.getMessage());
            IStatus[] children = status.getChildren();
            for (int i = 0; i < children.length; i++)
                appendStatus(writer, children[i], nesting + 1);
        }

        public static void appendStackTrace(
            PrintWriter writer,
            Throwable ex) {
            ex.printStackTrace(writer);
        }
    }
```

The ExceptionDetailsDialog class is built on top of the more generic AbstractDetailsDialog class.

```
package com.qualityeclipse.favorites.dialogs;

import org.eclipse.jface.dialogs.*;
import org.eclipse.swt.*;
import org.eclipse.swt.graphics.*;
import org.eclipse.swt.layout.*;
import org.eclipse.swt.widgets.*;

public abstract class AbstractDetailsDialog
    extends Dialog
{
    private final String title;
    private final String message;
    private final Image image;

    private Button detailsButton;
    private Control detailsArea;
    private Point cachedWindowSize;

    public AbstractDetailsDialog(
        Shell parentShell,
        String title,
        Image image,
        String message) {

        super(parentShell);
```

```
        this.title = title;
        this.image = image;
        this.message = message;


   setShellStyle(
        SWT.DIALOG_TRIM
            | SWT.RESIZE
            | SWT.APPLICATION_MODAL);
}

protected void buttonPressed(int id) {
   if (id == IDialogConstants.DETAILS_ID)
      toggleDetailsArea();
   else
      super.buttonPressed(id);
}

protected void configureShell(Shell shell) {
   super.configureShell(shell);
   if (title != null)
      shell.setText(title);
}

protected void createButtonsForButtonBar(
   Composite parent) {

   createButton(
      parent,
      IDialogConstants.OK_ID,
      IDialogConstants.OK_LABEL,
      false);
   detailsButton =
      createButton(
         parent,
         IDialogConstants.DETAILS_ID,
         IDialogConstants.SHOW_DETAILS_LABEL,
         false);
}

protected Control createDialogArea(Composite parent) {
   Composite composite =
      (Composite) super.createDialogArea(parent);
   composite.setLayoutData(
      new GridData(GridData.FILL_HORIZONTAL));

   if (image != null) {
      ((GridLayout) composite.getLayout())
         .numColumns = 2;
      Label label = new Label(composite, 0);
      image.setBackground(label.getBackground());
      label.setImage(image);
      label.setLayoutData(
         new GridData(
            GridData.HORIZONTAL_ALIGN_CENTER
```

```
                         | GridData.VERTICAL_ALIGN_BEGINNING));
        }

        Label label = new Label(composite, SWT.WRAP);
        if (message != null)
            label.setText(message);
        GridData data =
            new GridData(
                GridData.FILL_HORIZONTAL
                    | GridData.VERTICAL_ALIGN_CENTER);
        data.widthHint =
            convertHorizontalDLUsToPixels(
                IDialogConstants.MINIMUM_MESSAGE_AREA_WIDTH);
        label.setLayoutData(data);
        label.setFont(parent.getFont());

        return composite;
    }

    /**
     * Toggles the unfolding of the details area. This is
     * triggered by the user pressing the Details button.
     */
    protected void toggleDetailsArea() {
        Point oldWindowSize = getShell().getSize();
        Point newWindowSize = cachedWindowSize;
        cachedWindowSize = oldWindowSize;

        // Show the details area.
        if (detailsArea == null) {
            detailsArea =
                createDetailsArea((Composite) getContents());
            detailsButton.setText(
                IDialogConstants.HIDE_DETAILS_LABEL);
        }

        // Hide the details area.
        else {
            detailsArea.dispose();
            detailsArea = null;
            detailsButton.setText(
                IDialogConstants.SHOW_DETAILS_LABEL);
        }

        /*
         * Must be sure to call
         * getContents().computeSize(SWT.DEFAULT,
         * SWT.DEFAULT) before calling
         * getShell().setSize(newWindowSize);
         * since controls have been added or removed.
         */

        // Compute the new window size.
        Point oldSize = getContents().getSize();
        Point newSize =
            getContents().computeSize(
                SWT.DEFAULT,
                SWT.DEFAULT);
```

```
            if (newWindowSize == null)
               newWindowSize =
                  new Point(
                     oldWindowSize.x,
                     oldWindowSize.y + (newSize.y—oldSize.y));

            // Crop new window size to screen.
            Point windowLoc = getShell().getLocation();
            Rectangle screenArea =
               getContents().getDisplay().getClientArea();
            if (newWindowSize.y
               > screenArea.height—(windowLoc.y—screenArea.y))
               newWindowSize.y =
                  screenArea.height
                    —(windowLoc.y—screenArea.y);

            getShell().setSize(newWindowSize);
            ((Composite) getContents()).layout();
         }

      protected abstract Control createDetailsArea(
         Composite parent);
   }
```

11.1.10   Opening a dialog—finding a parent shell

When constructing a new dialog, you need to know about the parent shell. You can specify null for the parent shell, but this will prevent proper association of the dialog with its parent; if the dialog is modal as many dialogs are, then specifying the correct parent shell will prevent the user from being able to activate the parent window before closing the dialog. So the question becomes: How do we obtain the parent shell?

IWorkbenchWindowActionDelegate (see example code in Section 6.2.6, "Creating an action delegate")—If you have an action delegate, then Eclipse provides the workbench window from which a shell can be obtained. Immediately after the action delegate is instantiated, Eclipse calls the init(...) method with the workbench window as the argument. Cache this window and pass the window's shell as an argument when constructing your dialog:

```
private IWorkbenchWindow window;

public void init(IWorkbenchWindow window) {
   this.window = window;
}

public void run(IAction action) {
   Shell parentShell = window.getShell();
   MyDialog dialog = new MyDialog(parentShell, …);
   … etc …
}
```

IObjectActionDelegate (see Section 6.3.3, "IObjectActionDelegate")—If you have an action in a context menu, the Eclipse provides the target part from which a shell can be obtained. Before the `run(...)` method is called, Eclipse calls `setActivePart(...)` with the target part. Cache this part and pass the shell containing the part as an argument when constructing your dialog:

```
private IWorkbenchPart targetPart;

public void setActivePart(IAction action,
    IWorkbenchPart targetPart) {
    this.targetPart = targetPart;
}

public void run(IAction action) {
    Shell parentShell = targetPart.getSite().getShell();
    MyDialog dialog = new MyDialog(parentShell, …);
    … etc …
}
```

IViewPart or **IEditorPart** (see Section 7.2, "View Part," or 8.2, "Editor Part")—If you have a view or editor, then you can obtain the workbench window containing that part, and from that obtain the shell as follows:

```
Shell parentShell = viewOrEditor.getSite().getShell();
```

PlatformUI—The platform UI provides the workbench window from which a shell can be obtained:

```
Shell parentShell =
    PlatformUI.getWorkbench()
        .getActiveWorkbenchWindow ().getShell();
```

Display (see Section 4.2.5.1, "Display")—If all else fails, you can obtain the shell of the active window from `Display`:

```
Shell parentShell = Display.getDefault().getActiveShell();
```

11.2 Wizards

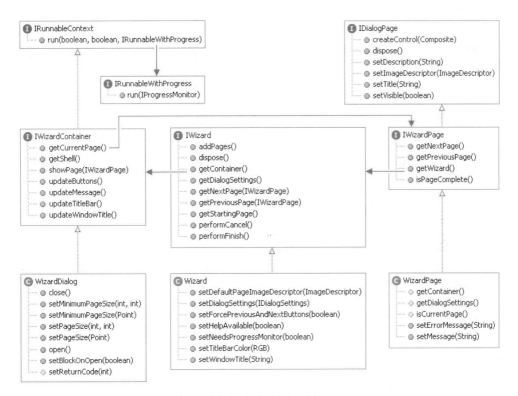

Figure 11–6 Wizard class hierarchy.

org.eclipse.jface.wizard.WizardDialog is a specialized subclass of Dialog (see Figure 11–6), used when a modal operation requires a particular sequence for its information collection or when a single screen has too many fields. Wizards have a title area along the top, a content area in the middle showing the wizard pages, a progress bar as needed, and **Help, Next, Back, Finish,** and **Cancel** buttons (or some subset) along the bottom (see Figure 11–7). The title area contains the wizard's title, description, an optional image, and an error, warning, or informational message as required.

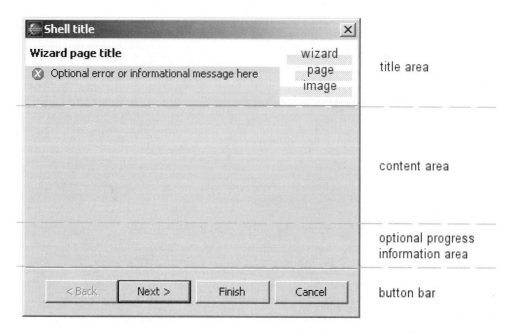

Figure 11–7   Default wizard dialog structure.

11.2.1   IWizard

Rather than subclass WizardDialog, you should subclass org.eclipse
.jface.wizard.Wizard, which implements the org.eclipse.jface.wizard
.IWizard interface for use with WizardDialog. The WizardDialog uses the
IWizard interface to obtain the pages to be displayed and notify the wizard of
user interaction. The concrete wizard class provides much of the IWizard
behavior for you, allowing you to focus on a subset of the IWizard interface.
The wizard's task is to create and initialize the pages it contains, handle any
special customized flow and information between pages, and execute the
operation when the **Finish** button is pressed.

> addPages()–Subclasses should override this method to add the appropri-
> ate pages by calling addPage(...).

> dispose()—Cleans up any native resources, such as images, clipboard,
> and so on, which were created by this class. This follows the *if you create
> it, you destroy it* theme that runs throughout Eclipse.

> getContainer()–Returns the wizard container in which this wizard is
> being displayed.

> getDialogSettings()–Returns the dialog settings for this wizard page.

`getNextPage(IWizardPage)`—Returns the wizard page to be shown after the specified wizard page, or `null` if none. The default implementation shows pages in the order in which the pages were added to the wizard, so subclasses need only to override this method to implement a custom page flow.

`getPreviousPage(IWizardPage)`—Returns the wizard page to be shown before the specified wizard page, or `null` if none. The default implementation shows pages in the order in which the pages were added to the wizard, so subclasses need only to override this method to implement a custom page flow.

`getStartingPage()`—Answers the first page to be displayed in the wizard. The default implementation answers the first wizard page added to the wizard, so subclasses need only to override this method if the starting page is not the first page added.

`performCancel()`—Called by the wizard container if the wizard is canceled. Subclasses need only to override this method to provide any custom cancel processing. Return `true` if the wizard container can be closed, or `false` if it should remain open.

`performFinish()`—Called by the wizard container when the **Finish** button is pressed. Subclasses should override this method to perform the wizard operation and return `true` to indicate that the wizard container should be closed, or `false` if it should remain open.

`setDefaultPageImageDescriptor(ImageDescriptor)`—Sets the image displayed in the wizard's title area if the current wizard page does not specify an image.

`setHelpAvailable(boolean)`—Sets whether help is available and whether the **Help** button is visible.

`setNeedsProgressMonitor(boolean)`—Sets whether this wizard needs a progress monitor. If `true`, then space is reserved below the page area and above the buttons for a progress bar and progress message to be displayed (see Section 9.4, "Progress Monitor").

`setTitleBarColor(RGB)`—Sets the color of the title area.

`setWindowTitle(String)`—Sets the window title.

11.2.2   IWizardPage

Wizards use the `org.eclipse.jface.wizard.IWizardPage` interface to communicate with the pages they contain. Typically, you will subclass the `org.eclipse.jface.wizard.WizardPage` class, accessing and overriding the methods listed below, rather than implement the `IWizardPage` interface. The wizard page's task is to present a page of information to the user, validate any information entered by the user on that page, and provide accessors for the wizard to gather the information entered.

`createControl(Composite)`—Creates the controls comprising this wizard page.

`dispose()`—Cleans up any native resources, such as images, clipboard, and so on, which were created by this class. This follows the *if you create it, you destroy it* theme that runs throughout Eclipse.

`getContainer()`—Returns the wizard container for this wizard page.

`getDialogSettings()`—Returns the dialog settings for this wizard page.

`getWizard()`—Returns the wizard that hosts this wizard page.

`setDescription(String)`—Sets the descriptive text appearing in the wizard's title area.

`setErrorMessage(String)`—Sets or clears the error message for this page.

`setImageDescriptor(ImageDescriptor)`—Sets the image that appears in the wizard's title area.

`setMessage(String)`—Sets or clears the message for this page.

`setPageComplete(boolean)`—Sets whether this page is complete. This forms the basis for determining whether or not the **Next** and **Finish** buttons are enabled.

`setTitle(String)`—Sets the title that appears in the title area of the wizard, not the title on the shell.

`setVisible(boolean)`—Sets the visibility of this dialog page. Subclasses can extend this method (being sure to call the superclass method) to detect when a page becomes the active page.

One approach for validating information entered by a user on a wizard page is for each field to have a listener that calls an `updatePageComplete()` method in the wizard page (snipped from Section 11.2.8, "Page content based on selection"):

```
sourceFileField = new Text(container, SWT.BORDER);
sourceFileField.addModifyListener(new ModifyListener()  {
   public void modifyText(ModifyEvent e) {
      updatePageComplete();
   }
});
```

This `updatePageComplete()` method would be responsible for checking the content in each field, displaying an error message as appropriate, and calling the `setPageComplete(...)` method (see Section 11.2.8 for an example). The pageComplete attribute is used by the wizard container to determine whether or not the **Next** and **Finish** buttons should be enabled.

11.2.3 IWizardContainer

The wizard uses the `org.eclipse.jface.wizard.IWizardContainer` interface to communicate with the context in which it is being displayed.

`getCurrentPage()`–Returns the current page being displayed.

`getShell()`–Returns the shell for this wizard container.

`run(boolean, boolean, IRunnableWithProgress)`–Runs the given runnable in the context of the wizard dialog. The first argument "fork" indicates whether or not the runnable should be executed in a separate thread. The second argument "cancelable" indicates whether the user should be allowed to cancel the operation while it is in progress (see Section 4.2.5.1, "Display," for more on the UI thread).

`showPage(IWizardPage)`–Shows the specified wizard page. This should not be used for normal next/back page flow, but exists for custom page flow such as double-clicking in a list.

`updateButtons()`–Adjusts the enable state of the **Back, Next,** and **Finish** buttons to reflect the state of the active page in this container.

`updateMessage()`–Updates the message shown in the message line to reflect the state of the currently active page in this container.

`updateTitleBar()`–Updates the title bar (title, description, and image) to reflect the state of the active page in this container.

`updateWindowTitle()`–Updates the window title to reflect the state of the wizard.

11.2.4 Nested wizards

One wizard can contain one or more nested wizards such as the **Import** and **Export** wizards. The `org.eclipse.jface.wizard.WizardSelectionPage` class provides behavior for managing one or more nested wizards. When a nested wizard can be determined, a `WizardSelectionPage` subclass calls the `setSelectedNode(...)` method. When a user clicks the **Next** button, the `WizardSelectionPage` class uses that information via the org.eclipse.jface.wizard.IWizardNode interface to create and manage the nested wizard.

11.2.5   *Launching a wizard*

You can hook a wizard into the Eclipse framework using one of the predefined wizard extension points, or you can manually launch a wizard as a result of a user action.

11.2.5.1   *Wizard extension points*

If you want Eclipse to automatically provide an action delegate and display your wizard in a predefined location, you can extend one of the following wizard extension points:

> `org.eclipse.ui.exportWizards`–Adds a nested wizard in the **Export** wizard, which is displayed by selecting **File > Export...**. Wizard classes associated with this extension point must implement the `org.eclipse.ui.IExportWizard` interface.
>
> `org.eclipse.ui.importWizards`–Adds a nested wizard in the **Import** wizard, which is displayed by selecting **File > Import...**. Wizard classes associated with this extension point must implement the `org.eclipse.ui.IImportWizard` interface.
>
> `org.eclipse.ui.newWizards`–Adds a nested wizard in the **New** wizard, which is displayed by selecting **File > New > Other...**. Wizard classes associated with this extension point must implement the `org.eclipse.ui.INewWizard` interface.

These three extension points share several common attributes:

> `class`–The wizard class to be launched by the parent wizard. This wizard must implement the appropriate interface for the extension point as outlined earlier. The class is instantiated using its no argument constructor, but may be parameterized using the `IExecutableExtension` interface (see Section 20.5).
>
> `icon`–The icon associated with this wizard, similar to action images (see Section 6.2.4, "Action images")
>
> `id`–The unique identifier for the wizard.
>
> `name`–The human-readable name for the wizard.

The `org.eclipse.ui.newWizards` extension point requires an additional `category` attribute to identify how wizards are to be hierarchically organized. This `category` is declared using the same extension point with the following attributes:

> `id`–The unique identifier for the category.

name–The human-readable name for the category.

parentCategory–The unique identifier for the category in which the category will appear, if there is one.

If a wizard declared using one of the aforementioned extension points implements the IExecutableExtension interface, then Eclipse will communicate additional initialization information encoded in the declaration to the wizard using that interface (see Section 20.5).

You can use the plug-in manifest editor to quickly create a wizard class with stub methods that is hooked into one of the wizard extension points. In the plug-in manifest editor, navigate to the **Extensions** page and click the **Add...** button to add, for example, an org.eclipse.ui.newWizards extension (see Section 6.2.1, "Defining a workbench window menu," for an example of adding extensions). Then, right-click on the org.eclipse.ui.newWizards extension in the plug-in manifest editor and select **New > wizard**. Double-click on the wizard extension that was added to open the **Properties** view (see Figure 11–8).

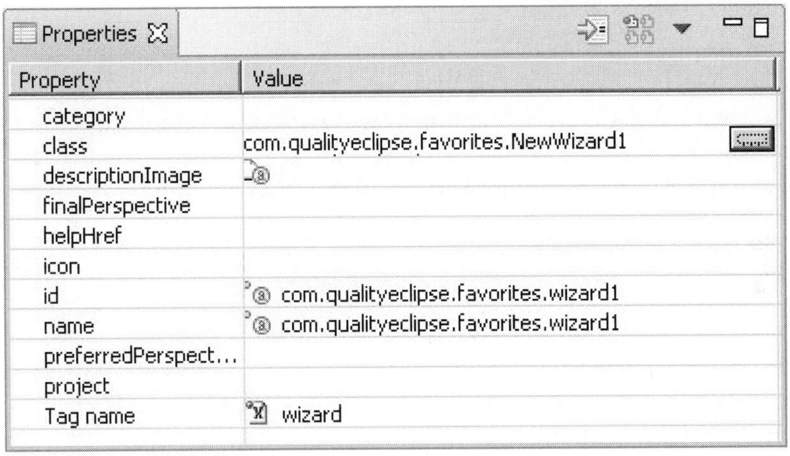

Properties ⊠	
Property	Value
category	
class	com.qualityeclipse.favorites.NewWizard1
descriptionImage	
finalPerspective	
helpHref	
icon	
id	com.qualityeclipse.favorites.wizard1
name	com.qualityeclipse.favorites.wizard1
preferredPerspect...	
project	
Tag name	wizard

Figure 11–8 Properties view showing newWizard extension.

In the **Properties** view, select the class attribute to make the "..." button appear to the right of the class attribute's value. Clicking this button opens a dialog for selecting an existing Java class or creating a new one (see Figure 11–9).

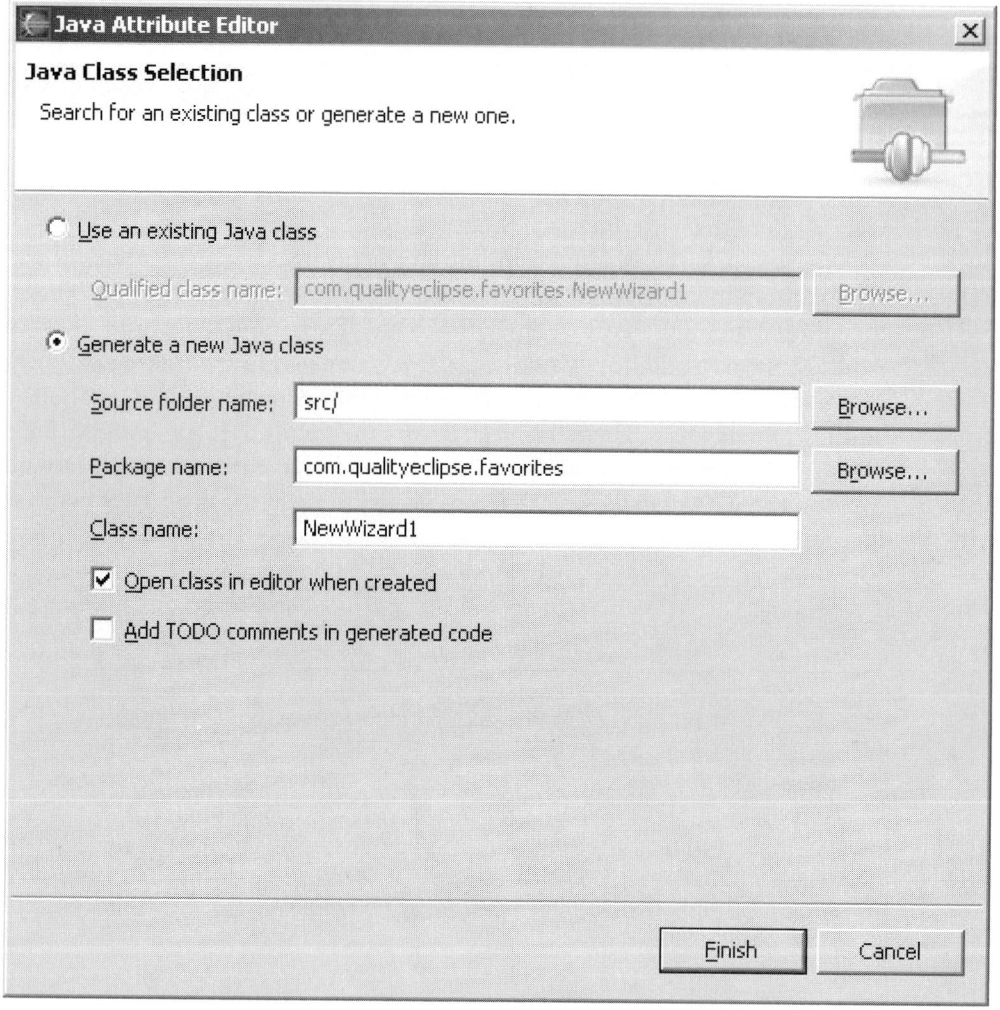

Figure 11–9   Java Attribute Editor dialog showing class creation.

Selecting the **Generate a new Java class** radio button and completing the required fields generates a new Java class and hooks that class into the plug-in manifest. The generated plug-in manifest entry and stub Java wizard class are:

```
<extension
     point="org.eclipse.ui.newWizards">
   <wizard
       name="com.qualityeclipse.favorites.wizard1"
       class="com.qualityeclipse.favorites.NewWizard1"
```

```
                    id="com.qualityeclipse.favorites.wizard1">
      </wizard>
</extension>
```

```
package com.qualityeclipse.favorites;

import org.eclipse.ui.*;
import org.eclipse.jface.viewers.*;
import org.eclipse.jface.wizard.*;
import org.eclipse.ui.*;

public class NewWizard1 extends Wizard
   implements INewWizard
{
   public void init(
      IWorkbench workbench,
      IStructuredSelection selection
   ) {
      // Initialization code here.
   }

   public boolean performFinish() {
      // Perform operation here.
      return false;
   }
}
```

11.2.5.2   Manually launching a wizard

Alternatively, you can launch a wizard from an action delegate. In our case, we will implement an action delegate with a run() method that launches our **Extract Strings** wizard (see next section):

```
public void init(IWorkbenchWindow window) {
   this.window = window;
}

public void selectionChanged(
   IAction action,
   ISelection selection) {

   this.selection =
      selection instanceof IStructuredSelection
         ? (IStructuredSelection) selection
         : null;
}

public void run(IAction action) {
   ExtractStringsWizard wizard = new ExtractStringsWizard();
   wizard.init(
      window.getWorkbench(),
      (IStructuredSelection) selection);
```

```
WizardDialog dialog =
   new WizardDialog(window.getShell(), wizard);
dialog.open();
}
```

11.2.6 Wizard example

For our example, we will create a two-page wizard for extracting strings from a `plugin.xml` file and placing those strings into a separate `plugin.properties` file as specified by the RFWS requirements. The wizard is responsible for instantiating the two pages, facilitating communication from the first page to the second, and gathering information from the two pages and performing the operation when the user presses the **Finish** button. The operation is performed in a separate thread so that the user can cancel the operation (see Section 9.4 for more about progress monitors and Section 4.2.5.1 for more about the UI thread).

In the following code example, the `init(...)` method is called directly by our action delegate, while the `addPages()` method is called indirectly by the dialog framework when the wizard dialog is created and opened. This approach parallels the `INewWizard` interface so that this wizard can easily implement that interface and thus be launched by **File > New > Other....**

```
package com.qualityeclipse.favorites.wizards;

import java.lang.reflect.*;
import org.eclipse.core.runtime.*;
import org.eclipse.jface.dialogs.*;
import org.eclipse.jface.operation.*;
import org.eclipse.jface.viewers.*;
import org.eclipse.jface.wizard.*;
import org.eclipse.ui.*;
import com.qualityeclipse.favorites.*;

public class ExtractStringsWizard extends Wizard
{
   private SelectFilesWizardPage selectFilesPage;
   private SelectStringsWizardPage selectStringsPage;
   private IStructuredSelection initialSelection;

   public void init(
      IWorkbench workbench,
      IStructuredSelection selection) {

      initialSelection = selection;
   }

   public void addPages() {
      setWindowTitle("Extract");

      selectFilesPage = new SelectFilesWizardPage();
```

```java
        addPage(selectFilesPage);
        selectStringsPage = new SelectStringsWizardPage();
        addPage(selectStringsPage);

        selectFilesPage.init(initialSelection);
    }

    /**
     * This method is called by the wizard framework when
     * the user presses the Finish button.
     */
    public boolean performFinish() {

        // Perform the operation in a separate thread
        // so that the operation can be canceled.
        try {
            getContainer()
                .run(true, true, new IRunnableWithProgress() {
                    public void run(IProgressMonitor monitor)
                        throws
                            InvocationTargetException,
                            InterruptedException {

                        performOperation(monitor);
                    }
                });
        }
        catch (InvocationTargetException e) {
            // Log and report the exception.
            e.printStackTrace();
            return false;
        }
        catch (InterruptedException e) {
            // User canceled, so stop but don't close wizard.
            return false;
        }
        return true;
    }

    /**
     * Called by the performFinish method on a separate thread
     * to extract strings from the source file.
     *
     * @param monitor the progress monitor
     */
    private void performOperation(IProgressMonitor monitor) {
        ExtractedString[] extracted =
            selectStringsPage.getSelection();
        // Perform the operation here.
    }
}
```

11.2.7   Dialog settings

Dialog settings can be used to store current values for a wizard or dialog to use the next time the wizard or dialog is opened. In our case, we instantiate and cache the dialog settings object in the wizard's constructor for use by the various wizard pages. The getSection(...) call is used to isolate settings for this wizard from settings for other wizards. Each page can then use the various IDialogSetting get(...) and put(...) methods to load and save values across sessions.

```
public ExtractStringsWizard() {
   IDialogSettings favoritesSettings =
      FavoritesPlugin.getDefault().getDialogSettings();
   IDialogSettings wizardSettings =
      favoritesSettings.getSection("ExtractStringsWizard");
   if (wizardSettings == null)
      wizardSettings =
         favoritesSettings.addNewSection("ExtractStringsWizard");
   setDialogSettings(favoritesSettings);
}
```

11.2.8 Page content based on selection

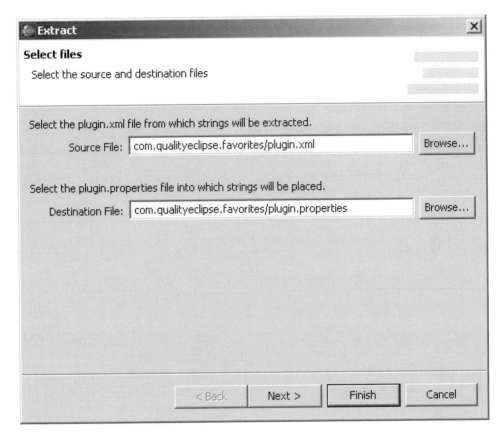

Figure 11–10 The Extract Strings wizard.

The first page of our **Extract Strings** wizard displays **Source File** and **Destination File** text fields, each with a browse button to the right (see Figure 11–10). The createControl(...) method creates and aligns each of the wizard page controls:

```
package com.qualityeclipse.favorites.wizards;

import java.util.*;
import org.eclipse.core.resources.*;
import org.eclipse.core.runtime.*;
import org.eclipse.jdt.core.*;
import org.eclipse.jface.viewers.*;
import org.eclipse.jface.wizard.*;
import org.eclipse.swt.*;
import org.eclipse.swt.events.*;
import org.eclipse.swt.layout.*;
import org.eclipse.swt.widgets.*;
```

```java
public class SelectFilesWizardPage
    extends WizardPage
{
    private Text sourceFileField;
    private Text destinationFileField;
    private IPath initialSourcePath;

    public SelectFilesWizardPage() {
        super("selectFiles");
        setTitle("Select files");
        setDescription(
            "Select the source and destination files");
    }

    public void createControl(Composite parent) {
        // $begin code generated by SWT-Designer$
        Composite container = new Composite(parent, SWT.NULL);
        final GridLayout gridLayout = new GridLayout();
        gridLayout.numColumns = 3;
        container.setLayout(gridLayout);
        setControl(container);

        final Label label = new Label(container, SWT.NONE);
        final GridData gridData = new GridData();
        gridData.horizontalSpan = 3;
        label.setLayoutData(gridData);
        label.setText(
            "Select the plugin.xml file " +
            "from which strings will be extracted.");

        final Label label_1 = new Label(container, SWT.NONE);
        final GridData gridData_1 =
            new GridData(GridData.HORIZONTAL_ALIGN_END);
        label_1.setLayoutData(gridData_1);
        label_1.setText("Source File:");

        sourceFileField = new Text(container, SWT.BORDER);
        sourceFileField.addModifyListener(new ModifyListener()
        {
            public void modifyText(ModifyEvent e) {
                updatePageComplete();
            }
        });
        sourceFileField.setLayoutData(
            new GridData(GridData.FILL_HORIZONTAL));

        final Button button = new Button(container, SWT.NONE);
        button.addSelectionListener(new SelectionAdapter() {
            public void widgetSelected(SelectionEvent e) {
                browseForSourceFile();
            }
        });
        button.setText("Browse...");

        final Label label_2 = new Label(container, SWT.NONE);
```

```
        final GridData gridData_2 = new GridData();
        gridData_2.horizontalSpan = 3;
        label_2.setLayoutData(gridData_2);

        final Label label_3 = new Label(container, SWT.NONE);
        final GridData gridData_3 = new GridData();
        gridData_3.horizontalSpan = 3;
        label_3.setLayoutData(gridData_3);
        label_3.setText(
            "Select the plugin.properties file " +
            "into which strings will be placed.");

        final Label label_4 = new Label(container, SWT.NONE);
        final GridData gridData_4 = new GridData();
        gridData_4.horizontalIndent = 20;
        label_4.setLayoutData(gridData_4);
        label_4.setText("Destination File:");

        destinationFileField =
            new Text(container, SWT.BORDER);
        destinationFileField.addModifyListener(
            new ModifyListener() {
                public void modifyText(ModifyEvent e) {
                    updatePageComplete();
                }
            });
        destinationFileField.setLayoutData(
            new GridData(GridData.HORIZONTAL_ALIGN_FILL));

        final Button button_1 =
            new Button(container, SWT.NONE);
        button_1
            .addSelectionListener(new SelectionAdapter() {
            public void widgetSelected(SelectionEvent e) {
                browseForDestinationFile();
            }
        });
        button_1.setText("Browse...");
        // $end code generated by SWT-Designer$

        initContents();
    }
}
```

As always, our goal is to save time for the user. If the user has already selected something in the workbench, we want to populate the wizard page based on that information. For this wizard page, the init (...) method analyzes the current selection and caches the result, while the initContents() method initializes the field content based on that cached result.

```
public void init(ISelection selection) {
    if (!(selection instanceof IStructuredSelection))
        return;
```

```java
// Find the first plugin.xml file.
Iterator iter =
   ((IStructuredSelection) selection).iterator();
while (iter.hasNext()) {
   Object item = (Object) iter.next();
   if (item instanceof IJavaElement) {
      IJavaElement javaElem = (IJavaElement) item;
      try {
         item = javaElem.getUnderlyingResource();
      }
      catch (JavaModelException e) {
         // Log and report the exception.
         e.printStackTrace();
         continue;
      }
   }
   if (item instanceof IFile) {
      IFile file = (IFile) item;
      if (file.getName().equals("plugin.xml")) {
         initialSourcePath = file.getLocation();
         break;
      }
      item = file.getProject();
   }
   if (item instanceof IProject) {
      IFile file =
      ((IProject) item).getFile("plugin.xml");
      if (file.exists()) {
         initialSourcePath = file.getLocation();
         break;
      }
   }
}
}

private void initContents() {
   if (initialSourcePath == null)
      return;
   IPath rootLoc = ResourcesPlugin.getWorkspace()
      .getRoot().getLocation();
   IPath path = initialSourcePath;
   if (rootLoc.isPrefixOf(path))
      path = path
         .setDevice(null)
         .removeFirstSegments(rootLoc.segmentCount());
   sourceFileField.setText(path.toString());
   destinationFileField.setText(
      path
         .removeLastSegments(1)
         .append("plugin.properties")
         .toString());
   updatePageComplete();
   setMessage(null);
   setErrorMessage(null);
}
```

Wizards provide a message area just below the title in which feedback can be provided. Generally this area is used to indicate to the user the additional information needs to be entered before proceeding to the next wizard page or performing the operation. In our case, the updatePageComplete() method is called once after initial contents are determined and again by various text field listeners anytime the content changes. This method then inspects the current text field contents, displays an error or warning message, and enables or disables the **Next** and **Finish** buttons as appropriate.

```
/**
 * Update the current page complete state
 * based on the field content.
 */
private void updatePageComplete() {
   setPageComplete(false);
   IPath rootLoc =
      ResourcesPlugin.getWorkspace()
         .getRoot().getLocation();

   IPath sourceLoc = getSourceLocation();
   if (sourceLoc == null
      || !sourceLoc.toFile().exists()) {
      setMessage(null);
      setErrorMessage("Please select an existing plugin.xml file");
      return;
   }

   IPath destinationLoc = getDestinationLocation();
   if (destinationLoc == null) {
      setMessage(null);
      setErrorMessage(
         "Please specify a plugin.properties file"
            + " to contain the extracted strings");
      return;
   }

   setPageComplete(true);

   IPath sourceDirPath = sourceLoc.removeLastSegments(1);
   IPath destinationDirPath =
      destinationLoc.removeLastSegments(1);
   if (!sourceDirPath.equals(destinationDirPath)) {
      setErrorMessage(null);
      setMessage(
         "The plugin.properties file is typically"
            + " located in the same directory"
            + " as the plugin.xml file",
         WARNING);
      return;
   }
```

```
if (!destinationLoc
   .lastSegment()
   .equals("plugin.properties")) {
   setErrorMessage(null);
   setMessage(
       "The destination file is typically"
           + " named plugin.properties",
       WARNING);
   return;
}

setMessage(null);
setErrorMessage(null);
}
```

11.2.9 Page content based on previous page

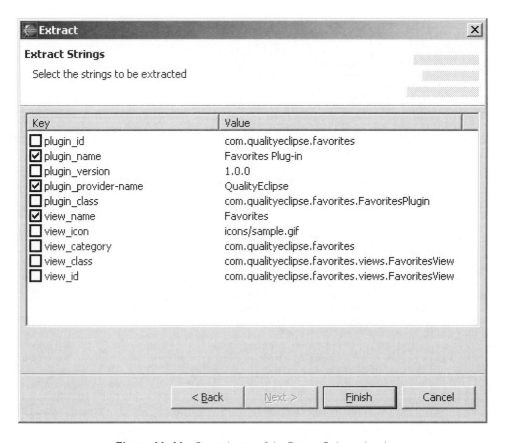

Figure 11–11   Second page of the Extract Strings wizard.

The second page of the wizard contains a checkbox list of key/value pairs that can be extracted from the source file (see Figure 11–11). Rather than initializing its contents when first created, this page updates its contents whenever it becomes visible by overriding the setVisible(...) method.

```
package com.qualityeclipse.favorites.wizards;

import org.eclipse.core.runtime.*;
import org.eclipse.jface.viewers.*;
import org.eclipse.jface.wizard.*;
import org.eclipse.swt.*;
import org.eclipse.swt.layout.*;
import org.eclipse.swt.widgets.*;

public class SelectStringsWizardPage extends WizardPage
{
    private CheckboxTableViewer checkboxTableViewer;
    private IPath sourceLocation;
    private ExtractedStringsModel stringModel;

    public SelectStringsWizardPage() {
        super("selectStrings");
        setTitle("Extract Strings");
        setDescription("Select the strings to be extracted");
    }

    public void createControl(Composite parent) {
        // $begin code generated by SWT-Designer$
        Composite container = new Composite(parent, SWT.NULL);
        container.setLayout(new FormLayout());
        setControl(container);

        checkboxTableViewer =
            CheckboxTableViewer.newCheckList(
                container,
                SWT.BORDER);
        checkboxTableViewer.setContentProvider(
            new ExtractedStringsContentProvider());
        checkboxTableViewer.setLabelProvider(
            new ExtractedStringsLabelProvider());
        final Table table = checkboxTableViewer.getTable();
        final FormData formData = new FormData();
        formData.bottom = new FormAttachment(100, 0);
        formData.right = new FormAttachment(100, 0);
        formData.top = new FormAttachment(0, 0);
        formData.left = new FormAttachment(0, 0);
        table.setLayoutData(formData);
        table.setHeaderVisible(true);

        final TableColumn tableColumn =
            new TableColumn(table, SWT.NONE);
        tableColumn.setWidth(200);
        tableColumn.setText("Key");
```

```
    final TableColumn tableColumn_1 =
        new TableColumn(table, SWT.NONE);
    tableColumn_1.setWidth(250);
    tableColumn_1.setText("Value");
    // $end code generated by SWT-Designer$
}

/**
 * Update the content before becoming visible.
 */
public void setVisible(boolean visible) {
    if (visible) {
        IPath location =
            ((ExtractStringsWizard) getWizard())
                .getSourceLocation();
        if (!location.equals(sourceLocation)) {
            sourceLocation = location;
            stringModel =
                new ExtractedStringsModel(sourceLocation);
            checkboxTableViewer.setInput(stringModel);
        }
    }
    super.setVisible(visible);
}

/**
 * Return the currently selected strings.
 */
public ExtractedString[] getSelection() {
    Object[] checked =
        checkboxTableViewer.getCheckedElements();
    int count = checked.length;
    ExtractedString[] extracted =
        new ExtractedString[count];
    System.arraycopy(checked, 0, extracted, 0, count);
    return extracted;
}
}
```

11.3   RFWS Considerations

The "User Interface" section of the *RFWS Requirements* includes 10 items—
8 requirements and 2 best practices—dealing with dialogs and wizards. All of
them are derived from the Eclipse UI Guidelines.

11.3.1   *Initial dialog focus*

User Interface Guideline #3 is a requirement that states:
   *When a dialog opens, set the initial focus to one of the controls in the con-
tainer.*

   For this test, open one of your dialogs and demonstrate that the initial
focus is set to one of the widgets in the dialog.

11.3.2   Slush bucket widget usage

User Interface Guideline #4 is a best practice that states:

The slush bucket widget (or twin box) should flow from left to right with the source objects on the left-hand side. It should have the >, <, >>, and << control buttons in this order. Figure 11–12 is an example of a slush bucket widget.

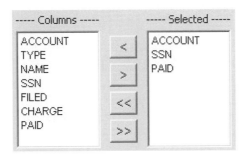

Figure 11–12   Slush bucket widget.

If your plug-in happens to use a slush bucket, show that it flows from left to right with the selectable objects on the left and the results of the selection on the right.

11.3.3   Use wizards for multistep tasks

User Interface Guideline #5 is a best practice that states:

Use a wizard for tasks consisting of many steps that must be performed in a specific order.

For this test, show that your wizard is used to complete a multistep task.

11.3.4   Wizard look and feel

User Interface Guideline #6 is a requirement that states:

*Each wizard must contain a header with a banner graphic and a text area for user feedback. It must also contain **Back**, **Next**, **Finish**, and **Cancel** buttons in the footer. A one-page wizard does not need to have the **Back** and **Next** buttons.*

Show that your wizards conform to the standard wizard look and feel. Make sure that they contain the proper buttons in the correct order as well as an appropriate banner graphic.

11.3.5   Wizard field initialization

User Interface Guideline #7 is a requirement that states:

*Seed the fields within a wizard using the current workbench state. The initial state of a wizard should be derived from the context where it is opened. For instance, in the **New File** wizard, the current workbench selection should be examined. If it points to a valid project or folder, the wizard should pre-populate the parent field with the parent project or folder name, and put the cursor focus in the next field requiring user input. If the user's selection does not point to a valid parent project or folder, the wizard should not pre-populate the folder name. Instead, it should leave the field blank and put the cursor focus in the field. When the user's selection is on a file, a wizard may also go through these calculations using the parent folder or project of the file.*

Show that your wizard's fields are populated whenever possible based on the workbench state. For the **Extract Strings** wizard presented in this chapter, we would show that the **Source File** field is populated based on the project selected in the workbench (see Section 11.2.8).

11.3.6   Wizard data validation

User Interface Guideline #8 is a requirement that states:

Validate the wizard data in tab order. Display a prompt when information is absent, and an error when information is invalid. If the first required field is empty, an informative prompt should be shown in the text area, directing the user to fill in the field. If the first required field is in error, an error message should be shown in the text area. If the first required field is valid, check the next field, and so on. The text area should not be used to display more than one prompt or error at a time.

Show that your wizard validates the fields in the data in tab order. Show that the wizard prompts the user when any required information is absent and displays an error when any information is incorrect. When the required information is provided or the error corrected, show that the message is removed. For the **Extract Strings** wizard, we would show that the **Source File** and **Destination File** fields are validated for correctness (see Section 11.2.8).

11.3.7   Wizard browse button

User Interface Guideline #9 is a requirement that states:

Use a browse button whenever an existing object is referenced in a wizard. The browse button should be used in combination with an edit field. The edit field is used for direct input of the existing object, and the browse button is used to browse and select the object from a list of all possible choices.

Show that your wizard provides a browse button anywhere the user might need to select an existing object or file. In the **Extract Strings** wizard, we would show that both the **Source File** and **Destination File** fields have associated browse buttons used to select files (see Section 11.2.8).

11.3.8 Open new file in editor

User Interface Guideline #10 is a requirement that states:

If a new file is created, open the file in an editor. If a group of files is created, open the most important, or central file, in an editor.

If your wizard creates a file, show that it automatically opens in an editor when the wizard is finished. For the **Extract Strings** wizard, we would show that the `plugin.properties` file is opened after the wizard creates it.

11.3.9 New project switches perspective

User Interface Guideline #11 is a requirement that states:

If a new project is created, change the active perspective to suit the project type.

If your plug-in provides a new project wizard and an associated perspective, show that the system automatically switches to your perspective when your wizard is used to create a new project.

11.3.10 Show new object

User Interface Guideline #12 is a requirement that states:

If a single new object is created, select and reveal the new object in the appropriate view. In cases where the creation of a resource results in the creation of project or folder resources, the wizard should propose reasonable default locations.

If your wizard creates a file, show that it is automatically selected in the appropriate view. For the **Extract Strings** wizard, we would show that the `plugin.properties` file is selected in the **Navigator** view after the wizard creates it.

11.4 Summary

In this chapter, we introduced a number of the common SWT and JFace dialog classes that you will encounter when developing Eclipse plug-ins. When a built-in dialog or wizard isn't available that meets your needs, you can create your own using the techniques described in this chapter.

CHAPTER 12

Preference Pages

Most Eclipse plug-ins provide user-configurable preferences for controlling how they will execute and display information. The Eclipse *preference framework* provides a mechanism for displaying these options to the user and saving these values across multiple Eclipse sessions. In this chapter, we will discuss how to create an Eclipse preference page and the techniques for recording and restoring a plug-in's preferences.

12.1   Creating a Preference Page

We want to contribute a preference page that will allow the user to select the columns that will be visible to the **Favorites** product. To accomplish this, we need to create an `org.eclipse.ui.preferencePages` extension in our plug-in manifest. Fortunately, Eclipse provides a wizard for creating preference pages.

Open the **Favorites** `plugin.xml` file and switch to the **Extensions** page. Click the **Add...** button to open the **New Extension** wizard, select `org.eclipse.ui.preferencePages` from the extension point list and **Preference Page** in the template list, and then click **Next** (see Figure 12–1). On the following page, modify the **Page Class Name** and **Page Name** to "FavoritesPreferencePage" and "Favorites," respectively (see Figure 12–2) and click **Finish**.

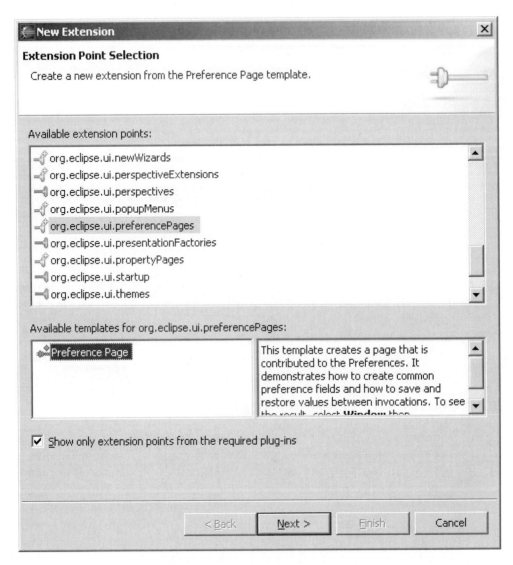

Figure 12–1   New Extension wizard.

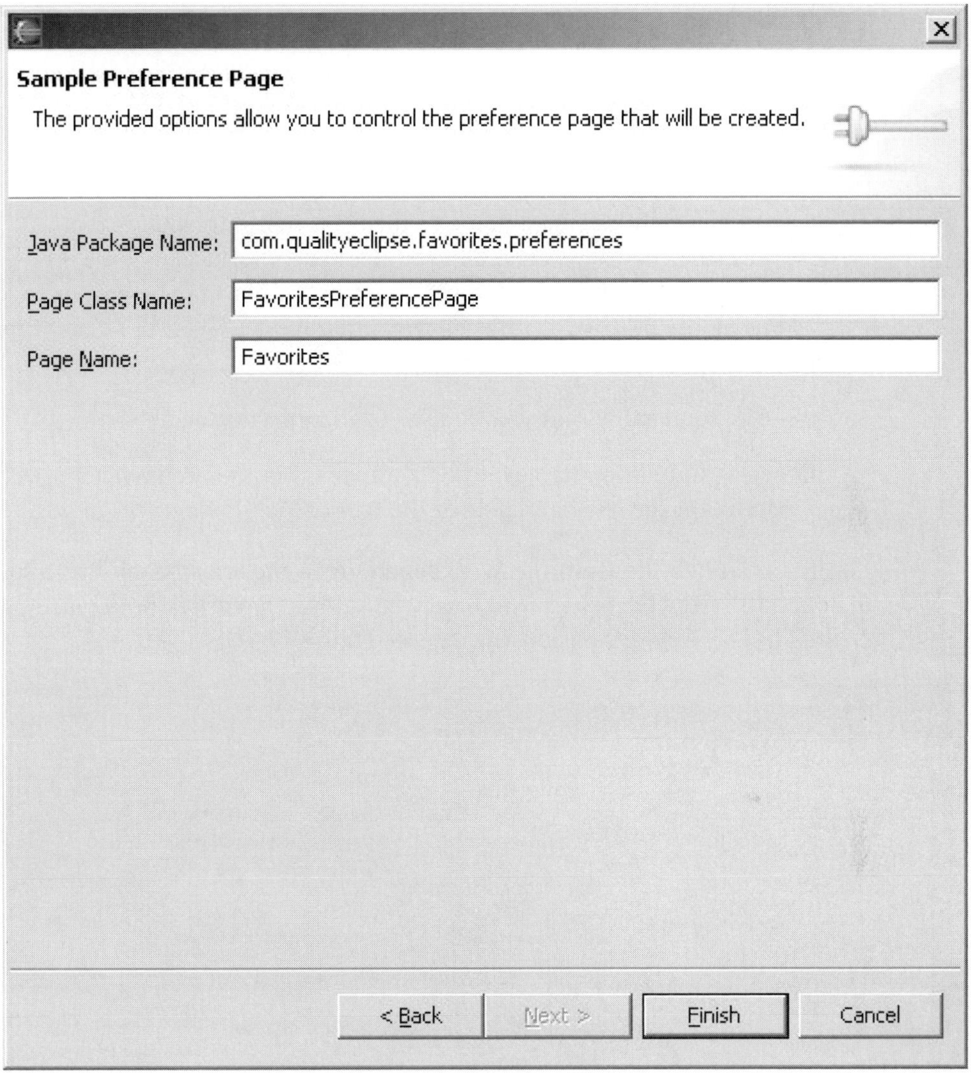

Figure 12–2 Sample Preference Page wizard.

Double-click on the new **Favorites (page)** extension under the `org.eclipse.ui.preferencePages` extension on the **Extensions** page to open the **Properties** view. In the **Properties** view, you'll see the following attributes as described in the Eclipse online help. Change the `id` attribute to "com.qualityeclipse.favorites.prefs.view".

category —The **Preferences** dialog box provides for a hierarchical grouping of the pages. For this reason, a page can optionally specify a `category` attribute. This attribute represents a path composed of parent page IDs separated by '/'. If this attribute is omitted or if any of the parent nodes in the path cannot be found, the page will be added at the root level (see Section 12.2.6, "Nested preference pages").

class —The fully qualified name of the class that implements the `org.eclipse.ui.IWorkbenchPreferencePage` interface. The class is instantiated using its no argument constructor, but may be parameterized using the `IExecutableExtension` interface (see Section 20.5, "Types Specified in an Extension Point").

id—A unique name that will be used to identify this page.

name—A human-readable name that appears in the preference page hierarchy on the left-hand side of the workbench **Preferences** dialog.

If you launch the **Runtime Workbench,** open the workbench **Preferences** dialog, and select **Favorites,** you'll see the sample **Favorites** preference page created by the **New Extension** wizard (see Figure 12–3).

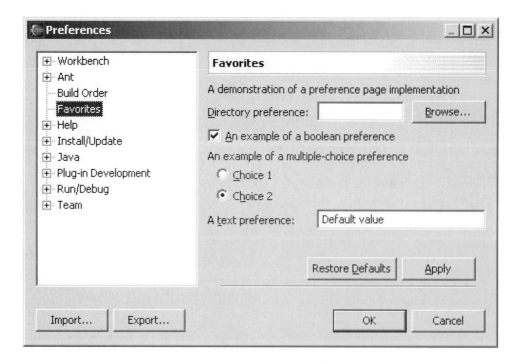

Figure 12–3   Sample Favorites preference page.

12.2   Preference Page APIs

Before we modify the preference page to suit our purposes, let's examine what was generated by the wizard (see Figure 12–4). The plug-in manifest contains the name, identifier, and fully qualified name of the class defining the page content and behavior, as listed in the previous section. Preference pages must implement the `org.eclipse.ui.IWorkbenchPreferencePage` interface, and the abstract classes, `org.eclipse.jface.preference.PreferencePage` and `org.eclipse.jface.preference.FieldEditorPreferencePage`,   provide much of the infrastructure for that purpose.

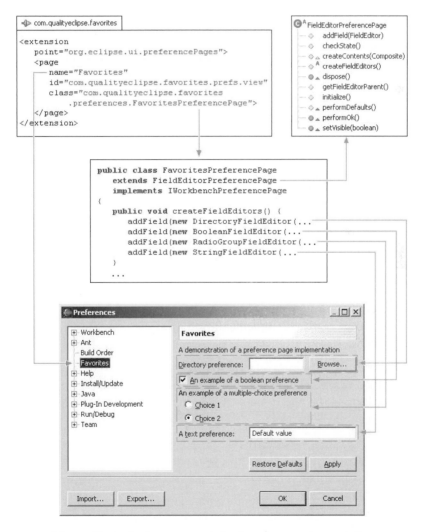

Figure 12–4   Preference page declaration, classes, and presentation.

12.2.1 FieldEditorPreferencePage

Our preference page extends `FieldEditorPreferencePage`, which, along with the various editor classes in the `org.eclipse.jface.preference.*` package, provide a quick and easy way to present and capture simple preferences. Subclasses of `FieldEditorPreferencePage` need only to implement the `createFieldEditors()` and `init(...)` methods to display a simple preference page, but there are several other methods of which you need to be aware for more involved preference pages:

> `addField(FieldEditor)`—Called from the `createFieldEditors()` method to add a field to the page.

> `checkState()`–Called by `FieldEditorPreferencePage` to validate the page content. The `FieldEditorPreferencePage` implementation of this method asks each field to validate its content and calls `setValid(...)` with the result. Override this method to perform additional page validation.

> `createContents(Composite)`–Creates the composite in which field editors appear. Typically, subclasses override the `createFieldEditors()` method instead.

> `createFieldEditors()`–Creates the field editors that appear in the preference page. Subclasses should call `getFieldEditorParent()` and `addField(...)` once for each field created. The parent returned by `getFieldEditorParent()` should not be used for more than one editor as the parent may change for each field editor depending on the layout style of the page.

> `dispose()`–Cleans up any native resources allocated by this page. Typically, there is no need to override this method because the `FieldEditorPreferencePage` implementation of `dispose()` handles cleanup for all fields.

> `getFieldEditorParent()`–Returns the parent to be used when creating a field editor. The parent returned should not be used for more than one editor as the parent may change for each field editor depending on the page's layout style.

> `initialize()`–Called by `createContents(...)` after the fields have been created to initialize the field contents. Typically, there is no need to override this method because `FieldEditorPreferencePage` asks each field to initialize itself.

> `isValid()`–Returns whether the contents of this preference page are currently valid.

performDefaults()—Loads all fields with their default values. Typically, there is no need to override this method because FieldEditorPreferencePage asks each field to reset its content to its default value.

performOK()—Saves the field editor values in the preferences store. Typically, there is no need to override this method because FieldEditorPreferencePage asks each field to save its contents.

setValid(boolean)—Sets whether the contents of this preference page are currently valid.

setVisible(boolean)—Called to show or hide the page. Subclasses may extend this method.

12.2.2   Field editors

A field editor is designed to load, display, edit, and save a particular preference setting. The org.eclipse.jface.preference package provides many different field editors, some of which we've already seen. Some editors contain a single control, while others contain several. Each editor has FieldEditor as its common superclass, providing FieldEditorPreferencePage with a common way to access each editor. Table 12–1 is a list of the field editors in the org.eclipse.jface.preference package, plus others available as public APIs elsewhere throughout Eclipse.

Table 12–1   PreferencePage Field Editors

Field Editor	Description
BooleanFieldEditor	A checkbox representation of a Boolean.
☐ Boolean	
ColorFieldEditor	A label and button where the button displays the color preference and opens a color chooser when clicked.
Color: [ ]	
DirectoryFieldEditor	A label, text field, and button for choosing a directory. The button opens a directory chooser when clicked.
Directory: [ ] Browse...	

Table 12–1   PreferencePage Field Editors (continued)

FileFieldEditor	A label, text field, and button for selecting a file preference. The button opens a file chooser when clicked. The editor can optionally enforce an absolute file path and filter against specific file extensions.

File: [_____]   Browse...

FontFieldEditor	A label, font name, and button for selecting a font. The button opens a font chooser when clicked.

Font: Tahoma-regular-8   Change...

IntegerFieldEditor	A label and text field for selecting an integer. This editor can optionally enforce a value within a range.

Integer: [0_____]

PathEditor	A label, list, and group of buttons for selecting zero or more paths. The **New...** button opens a directory chooser, while the other buttons manipulate paths already in the list.

Path:
C:\Program Files\Eclipse\eclipse_202
C:\Program Files\Eclipse\eclipse_211
C:\Program Files\Eclipse\eclipse_300

New...
Remove
Up
Down

RadioGroupFieldEditor	A label and series of radio buttons for selecting one of several properties. Optionally, the radio buttons can be grouped and displayed in multiple columns.

Radio Group
  ● Choice 1
  ○ Choice 2

ScaleFieldEditor	A label and slider for selecting a range of integer values.

Scale:

StringFieldEditor	A label and text field for entering a string value.

String: [_____]

Field editors are designed around the concept of *"create them and forget them."* In other words, you create a field editor with all that it needs to know about the preferences it is to represent, and then the field editor, in combination with the `FieldEditorPreferencePage`, handles the rest.

Field editors excel at presenting and manipulating simple types of preferences such as strings, integers, colors, and so on. If your preferences lend themselves to simple values such as these, then field editors will save you the hassle of writing code to load, display, validate, and store these simple preferences. If the data you wish to present is more structured and complex, then you may need to build your preference page without field editors, subclassing `PreferencePage` rather than `FieldEditorPreferencePage`. If you need to interact with a field editor directly or create a new type of field editor, here are some of the field editor methods you might need to know:

`adjustForNumColumns(int)`–Adjusts the horizontal span of the field editor's basic controls.

`dispose()`–Cleans up any native resources allocated by this editor.

`doFillIntoGrid(Composite, int)`–Creates the controls comprising the editor.

`doLoad()`–Initializes the editor content with the current value from the preferences store.

`doLoadDefault()`–Initializes the editor content with the default value.

`doStore()`–Saves the current editor value into the preferences store.

`fireStateChanged(String, boolean, boolean)`–Informs the field editor's listener, if it has one, about a change to Boolean-valued properties. Does nothing if the old and new values are the same.

`fireValueChanged(String, Object, Object)`–Informs the field editor's listener, if it has one, about a change to a property.

`getLabelControl()`—Returns the label that is part of the editor or **null** if none.

`getLabelControl(Composite)`–Returns the label that is part of the editor. Creates the label if label text has been specified either in the constructor or the `setLabelText(...)` method.

`getLabelText()`–Returns the label text specified either in the constructor or the `setLabelText(...)` method.

`getNumberOfControls()`—Returns the number of controls comprising the editor. This value is passed to the `doFillIntoGrid(Composite, int)` method.

`getPreferenceName()`—Returns the name/key of the preference displayed by the editor.

`getPreferenceStore()`—Returns the preferences store containing the preference being edited.

`isValid()`—Returns whether the editor's contents are valid. Subclasses should override this method along with the `presentsDefaultValue()` method.

`load()`—Loads the current value from the preferences store into the editor. Subclasses should override the `doLoad()` method rather than this method.

`loadDefault()`—Loads the default value into the editor. Subclasses should override the `doLoadDefault()` method rather than this method.

`presentsDefaultValue()`—Returns whether the editor is currently displaying the default value.

`refreshValidState()`—Determines if the editor's content is valid. Subclasses should override this method to perform the validation and the `isValid()` method to return the state.

`setFocus()`—Sets focus to the editor. Subclasses may override this method to set focus to a particular control within the editor.

`setLabelText(String)`—Sets the text to appear in the label associated with the editor.

`setPreferenceName(String)`—Sets the name of the preference being displayed by the editor.

`setPreferenceStore(IPreferenceStore)`—Sets the preferences store in which the editor's value is saved.

`setPresentsDefaultValue(boolean)`—Sets whether or not the editor is displaying the default value.

`setPropertyChangeListener(IPropertyChangeListener)`—Sets the property change listener that should be notified via the `fireState-Changed(...)` or `fireValueChanged(...)` methods when the editor's content has changed.

`showErrorMessage(String)`—Convenient method for displaying an error message at the top of the preference page.

`showMessage(String)`—Convenient method for displaying a message at the top of the preference page.

`store()`—Saves the editor's current value into the preferences store. Subclasses should override `doStore()` rather than this method.

12.2.3   PreferencePage

`FieldEditorPreferencePage` assumes that all the preferences on the page are field editors and handles most of the work involved in loading, validating, and saving field editor content. For more complex preference pages, you can use `PreferencePage` instead, which is the superclass of `FieldEditorPreference-Page`. The downside is that you must do more of the work yourself.

`createContents(Composite)`—Creates the controls for the preference page.

`doGetPreferenceStore()`—Answers a page-specific preferences store or null to use the container's preferences store. Subclasses may override this method as necessary.

`getPreferenceStore()`—Answers the preferences store for this preference page.

`isValid()`—Returns whether the contents of the preference page are currently valid.

`performDefaults()`—Loads all fields with their default values.

`performOk()`—Saves all field values in the preferences store.

`setErrorMessage(String)`—Used to display an error message at the top of the preference page when a field's value is invalid.

`setMessage(String, int)`—Used to display a message at the top of the preference page.

`setValid(boolean)`—Sets whether the contents of the preference page are currently valid.

If you use `PreferencePage`, you can still use the various types of field editors, but you must do more of the work yourself loading, validating, and saving values. The extra work involves adding some method calls when the field editors are constructed; for example:

```
protected Control createContents(Composite parent) {
   ...
   editor = new BooleanFieldEditor(
      "boolean", "Boolean", parent);
   editor.setPreferencePage(this);
   editor.setPreferenceStore(getPreferenceStore());
   editor.load();
   ...
}
```

and when the user resets the values to their defaults:

```
protected void performDefaults() {
   editor.loadDefault();
   ...
   super.performDefaults();
}
```

and when the user decides to save the current preference value:

```
public boolean performOk() {
   ...
   editor.store();
   return true;
}
```

and to perform any additional validation other than that which is enforced by the field.

12.2.4   *Favorites preference page*

For the **Favorites** view, we need one Boolean preference for each column, indicating whether or not that column is to be visible in the **Favorites** view. First, we create an interface containing preference constants that can be shared by various classes in the **Favorites** product:

```
public interface IFavoritesPreferences
{
   public static final String
      FAVORITES_VIEW_NAME_COLUMN_VISIBLE_PREF =
         "favorites.view.name.column.visible";
   public static final String
      FAVORITES_VIEW_LOCATION_COLUMN_VISIBLE_PREF =
         "favorites.view.location.column.visible";
}
```

The FavoritesPreferencePage is then modified to display these two preferences using Boolean preference field editors:

```
public class FavoritesPreferencePage
   extends FieldEditorPreferencePage
   implements IWorkbenchPreferencePage, IFavoritesPreferences
{
   private BooleanFieldEditor namePrefEditor;
   private BooleanFieldEditor locationPrefEditor;

   public FavoritesPreferencePage() {
      super(GRID);
      setPreferenceStore(
         FavoritesPlugin.getDefault().getPreferenceStore());
      setDescription("Favorites view column visibility:");
   }
```

```
public void init(IWorkbench workbench) {
}

public void createFieldEditors() {
   namePrefEditor =
      new BooleanFieldEditor(
         FAVORITES_VIEW_NAME_COLUMN_VISIBLE_PREF,
         "Show name column",
         getFieldEditorParent());
   addField(namePrefEditor);
   locationPrefEditor =
      new BooleanFieldEditor(
         FAVORITES_VIEW_LOCATION_COLUMN_VISIBLE_PREF,
         "Show location column",
         getFieldEditorParent());
   addField(locationPrefEditor);
   }
}
```

Now, when the **Favorites** preference page is displayed, it shows our two-column visibility preferences (see Figure 12–5).

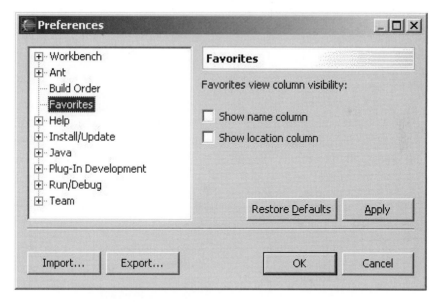

Figure 12–5 Favorites preference page with column visibility.

12.2.5 Validation

Our preference page looks good (see Figure 12–5), but there are two problems. First, the visibility for the name and location columns should default to true; that problem is addressed in Sections 12.3.3, "Specifying default values programmatically," and 12.3.4, "Specifying default values in a file." Second, we want at least one column visible at all times. Field editors enforce local validation of their own contents based on the type of editor and the parameters specified during creation. If we want validation between various editors, then we must enforce it ourselves in the PreferencePage class by overriding the FieldEditorPreferencePage checkState() method:

```
protected void checkState() {
   super.checkState();
   if (!isValid())
      return;
   if (!namePrefEditor.getBooleanValue()
      && !locationPrefEditor.getBooleanValue()) {
      setErrorMessage(
         "Must have at least one column visible");
      setValid(false);
   }
   else {
      setErrorMessage(null);
      setValid(true);
   }
}
```

The FieldEditorPropertyPage listens for FieldEditor.IS_VALID property change events and then calls checkState() and setValid(...) as necessary. The Boolean field editors are never in an invalid state and thus do not issue FieldEditor.IS_VALID property change events, only FieldEditor.VALUE property change events. We must override the FieldEditorPreferencePage propertyChange(...) method to call checkState() method when the FieldEditor.VALUE property change event is received:

```
public void propertyChange(PropertyChangeEvent event) {
   super.propertyChange(event);
   if (event.getProperty().equals(FieldEditor.VALUE)) {
      if (event.getSource() == namePrefEditor
         || event.getSource() == locationPrefEditor)
         checkState();
   }
}
```

Now, when both preferences are unchecked, an error message is displayed across the top of the preference page and the **Apply** and **OK** buttons are disabled (see Figure 12–6).

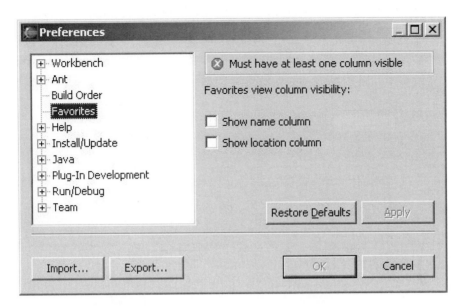

Figure 12–6   Favorites preference page with error message.

12.2.6   Nested preference pages

Nested preference pages provide a mechanism for hierarchically organizing related preference pages when a single page is not enough. Typically, the parent page contains root-level preferences or even just information, while the child preference pages focus on specific aspects. To create a nested preference page in the **Favorites** product (see Figure 12–7), we would add a new declaration in the plug-in manifest where the category attribute specifies the parent preference page (see the category attribute in Section 12.1, "Creating a Preference Page"). If Eclipse cannot find a parent page with the specified identifier, the preference page appears at the root level.

```
<page
   name="Nested Prefs"
   category="com.qualityeclipse.favorites.prefs.view"
   class="com.qualityeclipse.favorites
      .preferences.NestedPreferencePage"
   id="com.qualityeclipse.favorites.prefs.nested">
```

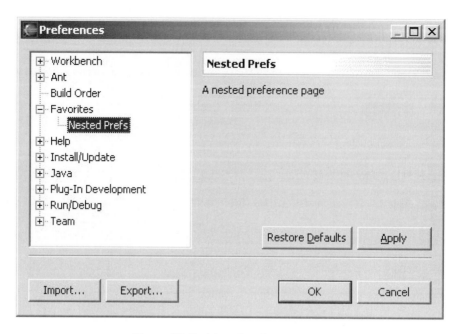

Figure 12–7   Nested preference pages.

Preference pages can be nested any number of levels deep by specifying the identifier for the parent preference page, prefixed by the identifier for the grandparent preference page, prefixed by the identifier for the great-grandparent preference page, and so on, each separated by the '/' character. For instance, to add a **Favorites** preference page nested two levels deep, the declaration might look like this:

```
<page
   name="Nested Prefs 2"
   category="com.qualityeclipse.favorites.prefs.view
      /com.qualityeclipse.favorites.prefs.nested"
   class="com.qualityeclipse.favorites
      .preferences.NestedPreferencePage2"
   id="com.qualityeclipse.favorites.prefs.nested2">
```

> **Tip:** The root preference page can contain basic information about the product, while the child preference pages contain the actual preferences. For example, the root preference page in Figure 12–8 contains information about the product, including version and build date, where the product is installed, information about the company producing the product, and buttons for generating email.

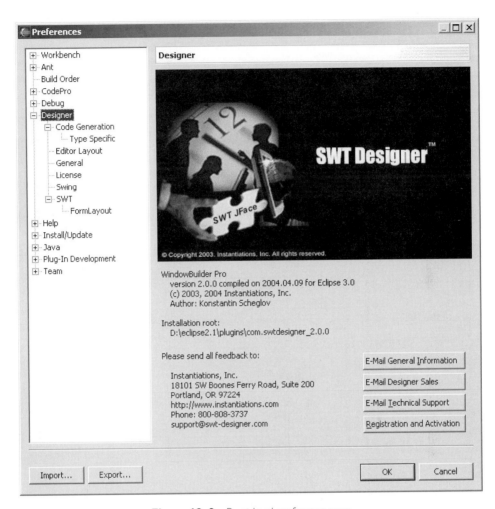

Figure 12–8   Root-level preference page.

12.2.7   Tabbed preference pages

Tabbed preference pages are another approach for organizing more preferences than will fit on a page (see Figure 12–9). In this case, tabs across the top of the preference page (see Section 4.2.6.10, "Tab folder") provide separation between groups of related preferences. The advantage is that tabbed preference pages are located on a single page, and thus one page can handle any inter-related field validation. The disadvantage is that the FieldEditorPreferencePage cannot be used for this purpose, so you must do more of the work yourself, basing your preference page on the PreferencePage class instead (see Section 12.2.3, "PreferencePage"). Of course, both nested pages and tabbed pages can be used in the same product as needed.

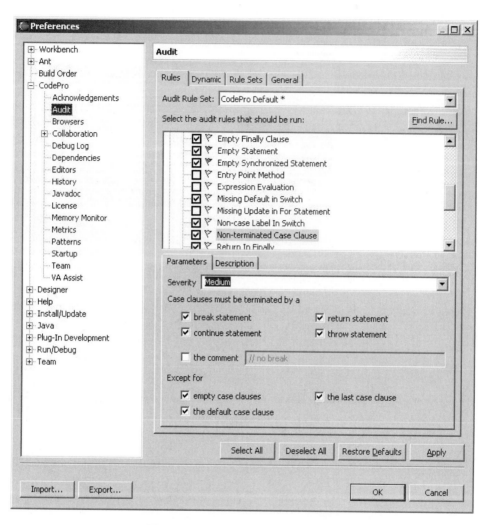

Figure 12–9   Tabbed preference page.

12.3   Preference APIs

The Preference API included in Eclipse provides simple string-based key/value pair storage in a flat structure. The plug-in infrastructure provides each plug-in its own preference storage file named pref_store.ini, located in the workspace metadata area. For example, if you use the **Favorites** preference page created in the previous sections to change column visibility, then examining the pref_store.ini file in <workspace>\.metadata\.plugins\ com.qualityeclipse.favorites directory reveals:

```
#Thu Jun 28 13:09:08 EST 2004
favorites.view.name.column.visible=true
favorites.view.location.column.visible=true
```

> **Tip:** If you have highly structured preference data that does not lend itself to simple, independent key/value pairs, then you might consider storing those preference elements in an XML-formatted preference file located in the plug-in's metadata area, similar to the way that the `FavoritesManager` stores its information (see Section 7.5.2, "Saving global view information").

12.3.1 Default Preferences

Each preference has three values associated with it:

> **current value**—Each preference has a current value, which is the same as the default value if the current value has not been specified.

> **default value**—Each preference has a default value, which is the same as the default-default value if the default value has not been specified. The default value can be programmatically specified (see Section 12.3.3) or specified in a special file located in the plug-in's installation directory (see Section 12.3.4).

> **default-default value**—The default-default value is hard-coded into the Eclipse preference system and is used if no current value and no default value is specified for the preference in question.

The default-default values hard-coded into the Eclipse system depend on the API being used to access the preference. In Table 12–2, the default-default value on the right is returned by a method with the return type shown on the left if no current value and no default value have been specified for a preference.

Table 12–2 Default Preference Values

Preference Method Return Type	Default-Default Value
Boolean	false
double	0.0
float	0.0f
int	0
long	0L
String	" "

The contents of the preference file represent only those preferences whose values are *different* from the preference's default value. If the preference's current value is the same as the preference's default value, then that value is *not* written into the preference file.

12.3.2 *Accessing preferences*

There are two APIs for accessing preferences in Eclipse:

- org.eclipse.core.runtime.Preferences
- org.eclipse.jface.preference.IPreferenceStore

As covered in Section 3.4.5, "Plugin and abstractUIPlugin," there is no advantage to using the older IPreferenceStore interface, so we will concentrate on the newer Preferences interface and related API.

The preferences for a particular plug-in can be accessed using the getPluginPreferences() method in the plug-in class itself. The Preferences object returned by that method has many convenient methods for accessing the underlying string-based preference values in a variety of formats, including Boolean, int, long, and so on:

getBoolean(String)—Returns the preference value as a Boolean. A value other than true is interpreted as false.

getDefaultBoolean(String)—Returns the default preference value as a Boolean. A value other than true is interpreted as false.

getDefaultDouble(String)—Returns the default preference value as a double. A value that does not represent a double is interpreted as 0.0.

getDefaultFloat(String)—Returns the default preference value as a float. A value that does not represent a float is interpreted as 0.0f.

getDefaultInt(String)—Returns the default preference value as an int. A value that does not represent an int is interpreted as 0.

getDefaultLong(String)—Returns the default preference value as a long. A value that does not represent a long is interpreted as 0L.

getDefaultString(String)—Returns the default preference value as a string.

getDouble(String)—Returns the preference value as a double. A value that does not represent a double is interpreted as 0.0.

getFloat(String)—Returns the preference value as a float. A value that does not represent a float is interpreted as 0.0f.

getInt(String)—Returns the preference value as an int. A value that does not represent an int is interpreted as 0.

getLong(String)—Returns the preference value as a long. A value that does not represent a long is interpreted as 0L.

getString(String)—Returns the preference value as a string.

isDefault(String)—Returns true if the current value of the specified preference is the same as its default value.

setDefault(String, boolean)—Sets the default value of the specified preference to a Boolean.

setDefault(String, double)—Sets the default value of the specified preference to a double.

setDefault(String, float)—Sets the default value of the specified preference to a float.

setDefault(String, int)—Sets the default value of the specified preference to an int.

setDefault(String, String)—Sets the default value of the specified preference to a string.

setDefault(String, long)—Sets the default value of the specified preference to a long.

setToDefault(String)—Sets the current value of the specified preference to its default value.

setValue(String, boolean)—Sets the value of the specified preference to a Boolean.

setValue(String, double)—Sets the value of the specified preference to a double.

setValue(String, float)—Sets the value of the specified preference to a float.

setValue(String, int)—Sets the value of the specified preference to an int.

setValue(String, String)—Sets the value of the specified preference to a string.

setValue(String, long)—Sets the value of the specified preference to a long.

In addition, there are various methods for loading, saving, and checking the state of a preference object:

contains(String)—Returns whether the given preference has a value that is not the default value or a default value that is not the default-default value.

`defaultPropertyNames()`—Returns a list containing the names of all preferences that have default values other than their default-default value.

`load(InputStream)`—Loads the non-default-valued preferences for the preference object from the specified `InputStream` using `java.util.Properties.load(...)`. Default preference values are not affected.

`needsSaving()`—Returns whether at least one preference value has changed since the last time preferences were saved (see `store(...)`).

`propertyNames()`—Returns a list containing the names of all preferences that have current values other than their default value.

`store(OutputStream, String)`—Saves the non-default-valued preferences to the specified `OutputStream` using `Properties.store(...)`, and resets the `dirty` flag so that `needsSaving()` will return `false` until a preference value is modified.

> As covered in Section 3.4.5, if your plug-in class is a subclass of `org.eclipse.core.runtime.Plugin` rather than `org.eclipse.ui.plugin.AbstractUIPlugin`, you must modify the `shutdown()` method to always call the `savePluginPreferences()` method so that preferences will be persisted across sessions.

12.3.3   Specifying default values programmatically

Default values can be specified programmatically using the `Preferences` API when a plug-in is first started. Extend the `initializeDefaultPluginPreferences()` method of your plug-in class and call the various `setDefault*` methods. For the **Favorites** product, we'll modify the `FavoritesPlugin` class to implement the `IFavoritesPreferences` interface and extend the `initializeDefaultPluginPreferences()` method to set the default value for the name column visibility preference. Now, when the **Favorites** preference page is displayed for the first time, the **Show name column** preference will already be checked.

```
protected void initializeDefaultPluginPreferences() {
    super.initializeDefaultPluginPreferences();
    getPluginPreferences().setDefault(
        FAVORITES_VIEW_NAME_COLUMN_VISIBLE_PREF,
        true);
}
```

Now that we have programmatically specified `true` as the default value for the name column visibility preference, the only time it will appear in the `pref_store.ini` file is when the preference is *not* `true`.

12.3.4 Specifying default values in a file

Default preferences can also be specified in a special `preferences.ini` file located in the plug-in's installation directory. This file has an identical format to the `pref_store.ini` file (see Section 12.3, "Preference APIs") and can be installed when the plug-in is installed. The advantage to placing default values in a file is that it extracts them from the code, making them more easily changeable without modifying code. The disadvantage is that default values specified in this way cannot be dynamically adjusted as they can if they are specified programmatically, but typically, a default preference specification does not need that type of flexibility. For the **Favorites** product, we will add a new `preferences.ini` file in the project root containing a single line specifying a default value for the location column visibility:

```
favorites.view.location.column.visible=true
```

> **Tip:** You can use the **Workbench > File Associations** page in the workbench Preferences dialog (see Section 1.3.1, "Workbench preferences") to associate the internal text editor with any *.ini file so that double-clicking on the `preferences.ini` file will open a text editor on the file within Eclipse.

To complete the process, the build script must be modified to include this new `preferences.ini` file as part of the product (see Chapter 19, "Building a Product," for more on building the product). Now that we have specified `true` as the default value for the location column visibility preference, the only time it will appear in the `pref_store.ini` file is when the preference is *not* `true`.

12.3.5 Hooking up the favorites view

Now that we have the **Favorites** preference page in place, we can hook up these preferences to the **Favorites** view. First, we'll extract the initial column widths into constants using **Extract Constant** refactoring:

```
private static final int LOCATION_COLUMN_INITIAL_WIDTH = 450;
private static final int NAME_COLUMN_INITIAL_WIDTH = 200;
```

Next, we'll implement the `IFavoritesPreferences` interface so that we can easily use the constants defined there. Then we'll create a new `updateColumn-`

Width() method that is called from the createPartControl(Composite) method right after the table is created:

```
private void updateColumnWidths() {
   Preferences prefs = FavoritesPlugin
      .getDefault().getPluginPreferences();

   boolean showNameColumn = prefs.getBoolean(
      FAVORITES_VIEW_NAME_COLUMN_VISIBLE_PREF);
   nameColumn.setWidth(
      showNameColumn
         ? NAME_COLUMN_INITIAL_WIDTH
         : 0);

   boolean showLocationColumn = prefs.getBoolean(
      FAVORITES_VIEW_LOCATION_COLUMN_VISIBLE_PREF);
   locationColumn.setWidth(
      showLocationColumn
         ? LOCATION_COLUMN_INITIAL_WIDTH
         : 0);
}
```

When these two changes are in place, the **Favorites** view will show the name and location columns as specified in the **Favorites** preference page.

12.3.6   *Listening for preference changes*

When the **Favorites** view is first opened, the columns conform to the settings specified on the **Favorites** preference page, but what if the preferences are changed while the **Favorites** view is already opened? For the **Favorites** view to stay synchronized with the preferences specified on the **Favorites** preference page, we need to add listeners to the object containing the preferences. Back in the FavoritesView, we can add a new propertyChangeListener field that listens for property change events and calls updateColumnWidths() as appropriate:

```
private final IPropertyChangeListener propertyChangeListener
   = new IPropertyChangeListener() {
   public void propertyChange(PropertyChangeEvent event) {
      if (event.getProperty().equals(
            FAVORITES_VIEW_NAME_COLUMN_VISIBLE_PREF)
         || event.getProperty().equals(
            FAVORITES_VIEW_LOCATION_COLUMN_VISIBLE_PREF))
         updateColumnWidths();
   }
};
```

This new propertyChangeListener must be added as a listener when the view is created at the end of the createPartControl(...) method:

```
FavoritesPlugin
   .getDefault()
   .getPluginPreferences()
   .addPropertyChangeListener(propertyChangeListener);
```

The listener must be removed in the dispose () method when the view is closed:

```
FavoritesPlugin
   .getDefault()
   .getPluginPreferences()
   .removePropertyChangeListener(propertyChangeListener);
```

12.3.7   Preference levels

As we are writing this book, the Eclipse team is busy adding different levels of preferences (See Bugzilla entry #36965), as shown in Table 12–3.

Table 12–3 Preference Levels

Level	Description
User	Settings that apply to all Eclipse-based products for the same user.
Config	Settings that apply to all instances of a particular Eclipse-based product for a particular user.
Instance	Settings that apply to a single instance; an instance is equivalent to the Eclipse IDE's concept of a workspace.
Project	Settings that apply to a single project; a project is a discrete piece of an instance. Project settings can be local (applying only to the instance in which they were created) or shared (via CVS, for example).

The majority of the current set of preferences will be moved to the "config" level (seamlessly). Preferences with absolute paths will remain in the "instance" level. Plug-ins storing absolute paths in preferences will be expected to modify their code so that their reading/writing of absolute paths goes to the "instance" level.

12.4   RFWS Considerations

The "User Interface" section of the *RFWS Requirements* includes two requirements dealing with preferences. Both of them are derived from the Eclipse UI Guidelines.

12.4.1   Preferences dialog use

User Interface Guideline #49 is a requirement that states:

*Global options will be exposed within the **Preferences** dialog. A new preference page must be created when you need to expose global options to the user. For instance, the global preferences for Java compilation are exposed as a group of preference pages in the **Preferences** dialog. If these preferences are changed, they affect the entire Java plug-in.*

To pass this test, show a sample of your product's preference pages and demonstrate that the preference settings control global options in your product. Change a preference and then shut down and restart Eclipse to show that the preference's value properly persists. For the **Favorites** preferences, we would show that the column visibility options globally affect the columns shown in all **Favorites** views open in any perspective.

12.4.2   Preferences dialog misuse

User Interface Guideline #50 is a requirement that states:

*Expose the local options for a particular view, editor, or window in the view itself, via a menu or tool item. A preference page must not be used to expose the local options for a particular instance of a view, editor, or window. In this situation, the user will look to the menu and toolbar of the control itself to customize it. If these options are exposed in the **Preferences** dialog, it will blur the location of customization and confuse the user.*

This requirement is essentially the opposite of the previous one. Here you need to show you are not misusing your preference pages to host local options for your editors and views. For the **Favorites** view, we would show that local options (like the view filter) are presented locally through the **View** menu.

12.5   Summary

Almost any significant plug-in will contain global options controlling its execution and interaction with the user. In this chapter, we explored the Eclipse preference page API and discussed the choices open to the developer for creating both simple and complex preference pages. We also demonstrated how to persist preference settings across workspace sessions.

References

Creasey, Tod, "Preferences in the Eclipse Workbench UI," August 15, 2002 (*www.eclipse.org/articles/Article-Preferences/preferences.htm*).

Cooper, Ryan, "Simplifying Preference Pages with Field Editors,"August 21, 2002 (*www.eclipse.org/articles/Article-Field-Editors/field_editors.html*).

CHAPTER 13

Properties

Whereas preferences apply to plug-ins or chunks of functionality, properties apply to resources or other objects that appear in the Eclipse environment. One typical way to access an object's properties is to select the **Properties** command from its context menu, opening the **Properties** dialog. Another way is to open the **Properties** view, which displays properties for the selected object. This chapter covers the creation of a property on a particular object and the display of that property in both the object's **Properties** dialog and the **Properties** view.

13.1 Creating Properties

We want to add properties for color and comments to our **Favorites** product. The color property will determine the color used to display an item in the **Favorites** view, while the comment property will be displayed as an item's hover help.

Since properties are associated with objects, we must decide which type of object will contain our properties. We'll add the color property to **Favorites** items; when an item is removed from the **Favorites** view, the color property will be discarded. Conversely, we want the comment property associated with the resource behind the **Favorites** items so that when the resource is removed and then added to the **Favorites** view, the comment property will be preserved.

13.1.1 *FavoriteItem properties*

A property can be associated with an object in many different ways, but typically, a property value is accessed through *get* and *set* methods on the object

itself. For **Favorites** items, we need to add accessor methods to the IFavoriteItem interface for the new Color property:

```
Color getColor();
void setColor(Color color);
```

Because this property is to be implemented identically across all **Favorites**
items, we will place this behavior into a new abstract superclass called Basic-
FavoriteItem, which all our other item types will extend.

```
package com.qualityeclipse.favorites.model;

import java.util.*;
import org.eclipse.core.runtime.*;
import org.eclipse.swt.graphics.*;
import org.eclipse.swt.widgets.*;
import com.qualityeclipse.favorites.*;

public class BasicFavoriteItem
{
    private Color color;

    public Color getColor() {
        if (color == null)
            return getDefaultColor();
        return color;
    }

    public void setColor(Color color) {
        this.color = color;
    }

    public static Color getDefaultColor() {
        if (defaultColor == null)
            defaultColor = getColor(new RGB(0, 0, 0));
        return defaultColor;
    }

    public static void setDefaultColor(Color color) {
        defaultColor = color;
    }
}
```

There are two types of properties: persistent properties and session properties. Persistent properties are preserved across multiple workbench sessions,
while session property values are discarded when Eclipse exits. To persist the
Color property across multiple sessions, we would need to modify the loading
and saving methods outlined in Section 7.5.2, "Saving global view information." This is left as an exercise for the reader, and for now, the Color property
will not be preserved across sessions.

A `Color` object has an underlying OS resource and must be managed properly. Add `BasicFavoriteItem` utility methods to cache, reuse, and dispose of colors:

```
private static final Map colorCache = new HashMap();
private static Color defaultColor;

public static Color getColor(RGB rgb) {
   Color color = (Color) colorCache.get(rgb);
   if (color == null) {
      Display display = Display.getCurrent();
      color = new Color(display, rgb);
      colorCache.put(rgb, color);
   }
   return color;
}

public static void disposeColors() {
   Iterator iter = colorCache.values().iterator();
   while (iter.hasNext())
      ((Color) iter.next()).dispose();
   colorCache.clear();
}
```

When the **Favorites** plug-in shuts down, we must clean up any `Color` objects that we have been managing. Add the following line to the `FavoritesPlugin.shutdown()` method:

```
BasicFavoriteItem.disposeColors();
```

13.1.2 *Resource properties*

Eclipse has a generic mechanism for associating properties with resources that we can use to store our resource comments. Methods in `IResource` provide both session properties, which are discarded when Eclipse exits, and persistent properties, which are preserved across multiple workspace sessions. Both types of properties can be used to determine whether or not an action should be visible (see Section 6.3.2.3, "The filter element"):

> `getPersistentProperty(QualifiedName)`—Returns the value of the persistent property of the resource identified by the given key, or `null` if this resource has no such property. These properties are preserved across different sessions.

> `getSessionProperty(QualifiedName)`—Returns the value of the session property of the resource identified by the given key, or `null` if this resource has no such property. These properties are discarded when Eclipse exits.

setPersistentProperty(QualifiedName, String)—Sets the value of the persistent property of the resource identified by the given key. If the supplied value is null, the persistent property is removed from the resource. These properties are preserved across different sessions.

setSessionProperty(QualifiedName, Object)—Sets the value of the session property of the resource identified by the given key. If the supplied value is null, the session property is removed from the resource.

The QualifiedName argument in these methods is the key used to store and retrieve a property value. By convention, a key is composed of the plug-in identifier and a string identifying a property within the plug-in. For the **Favorites** product, we'll define a constant key for the comment property in the BasicFavoriteItem class:

```
public static final QualifiedName COMMENT_PROPKEY =
   new QualifiedName(
      FavoritesPlugin
         .getDefault()
         .getDescriptor()
         .getUniqueIdentifier(),
      "comment");
```

As discussed earlier, there are two types of properties: persistent properties and session properties. Persistent properties are preserved across multiple workbench sessions, while session property values are discarded when Eclipse exits. We want the comment property to be persisted across multiple workbench sessions, so we will use the getPersistentProperty(…) and setPersistentProperty(…) methods like this:

```
String comment =
   resource.getPersistentProperty(
      BasicFavoriteItem.COMMENT_PROPKEY);

resource.setPersistentProperty(
   BasicFavoriteItem.COMMENT_PROPKEY,
   comment);
```

If a resource object does not have a **Favorites** comment associated with it, then we want to display a default comment. Add BasicFavoriteItem utility methods to access the default comment.

```
public static final String COMMENT_PREFKEY = "defaultComment";

public static String getDefaultComment() {
   return FavoritesPlugin
      .getDefault()
      .getPluginPreferences()
      .getString(COMMENT_PREFKEY);
}

public static void setDefaultComment(String comment) {
   FavoritesPlugin
      .getDefault()
      .getPluginPreferences()
      .setValue(COMMENT_PREFKEY, comment);
}
```

13.2   Displaying Properties in the Properties Dialog

Now that we have defined the properties, we want to display and edit those properties in a **Properties** dialog. First, we will add a page to the existing resource **Properties** dialog to display and edit the comment property. Second, we will open a **Properties** dialog on **Favorites** items selected in the **Favorites** view to display and edit both the color and comment properties.

13.2.1   Declaring a property page

To create a new **Property** page appearing in a resource's **Properties** dialog, we need to declare the page in the **Favorites** plug-in manifest. The declaration references the new `FavoriteResourcePropertyPage` class, which handles creation and user interaction in the new page (see Figure 13–1).

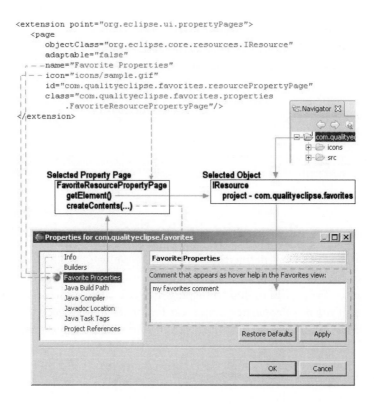

Figure 13–1   Property page declaration.

To create the **Property** page declaration in the plug-in manifest, edit the **Favorites** `plugin.xml`, switch to the **Extensions** page, and click **Add....** In the **New Extensions** dialog, select `org.eclipse.ui.propertyPages` and click **Finish.**

In the **Extensions** page of the plug-in manifest editor, right-click on `org.eclipse.ui.propertyPages` and select **New > page.** Double-click on the new `com.qualityeclipse.favorites.page1` page declaration to open the **Properties** view, and enter the following attributes:

id—"com.qualityeclipse.favorites.resourcePropertyPage"
A unique name used to identify the **Property** page.

name—"Favorite Properties"
A human-readable name for the **Property** page.

icon—"icons/sample.gif"
A relative path to an icon displayed in the UI along with the name

attribute. Use the "…" button at the right of the icon attribute value to select the `sample.gif` file in the **Favorites** project.

objectClass—"org.eclipse.core.resources.IResource"
A fully qualified name of the class for which the page is registered. We want the **Favorites** properties to appear for all resources.

class—"com.qualityeclipse.favorites.properties
.FavoriteResourcePropertyPage"
A fully qualified name of the class that implements
`org.eclipse.ui.IWorkbenchPropertyPage`. Use the "…" button at the right of the class attribute value to automatically generate the `Favor-iteResourcePropertyPage` class.

nameFilter—" "
An optional attribute that allows conditional registration on a wildcard match applied to the target object name. We don't want to use a filter for the **Favorites** properties, but if we wanted to limit it to only Java source files, we would enter "*.java".

adaptable—"false"
A flag that indicates whether types that adapt to `IResource` should use the **Property** page. This flag is used if **objectClass** adapts to `IResource`. The default value is `false`.

If we set the **adaptable** attribute to `true`, then the selected object is adapted to an `IResource` using the `IAdaptable` interface. The advantage of this is that one **Property** page declaration would cause the **Favorites Property** page to appear for any object that adapted to a resource such as `IJavaEle-ment`; we would not need to add a separate **Property** page declaration for `IJa-vaElement` or `IFavoriteItem`. The downside is that the framework automatically adapts the selected object from its original type to a resource object before the page gets the selection. Because `IFavoriteItem` is itself adaptable to `IResource`, the `getElement()` method would return a resource rather than the currently selected instance of `IFavoriteItem`, preventing the **Property** page from accessing information specific to the selected `IFavor-iteItem`. To work around this problem, we have to set the **adaptable** attribute to `false` and create two additional **Property** page declarations.

Add a new **Property** page declaration containing the same information as the original except for the `objectClass` attribute:

objectClass = "org.eclipse.jdt.core.IJavaElement"

Add another **Property** page declaration containing the same information as the previous declarations except for the following attributes. The `Favor-`

iteItemPropertyPage is a refinement of the FavoriteResourcePropertyPage page containing an additional property field.

> **class** = "com.qualityeclipse.favorites.properties .FavoriteItemPropertyPage"

> **objectClass** = "com.qualityeclipse.favorites.model.IFavoriteItem"

> > **Tip:** Most **Property** pages do **not** have an associated icon. If you associate an icon with your **Property** page, then the list of **Property** pages looks funny with all the blank space in front of all the other **Property** page names. To illustrate our point, we have an icon associated with the **Favorites Property** page (see Figure 13–2), but we recommend that you do not do this.

One way to narrow down the resources to which our **Property** page applies is to add the nameFilter attribute as just described. Another way is to add a filter subelement by right-clicking on the **Favorites Property** page declaration in the **Extensions** page of the plug-in manifest editor and selecting **New > filter.** The filter subelement specifies an attribute name and value:

> **name**—The name of an object attribute.

> **value**—The value of an object attribute. In combination with the **name** attribute, the name/value pair is used to define the target object for a **Property** page.

The selected object for which properties are being displayed must have the specified value for that attribute before the **Property** page is displayed. For example, to display a **Property** page for read-only files, you would specify a filter subelement with name="readOnly" and value="true". To use the filter subelement, the selected object must implement the org.eclipse.ui .IActionFilter interface. Eclipse workbench resource types such as IFile and IFolder currently implement this interface.

13.2.2   Creating a resource property page

When the **Property** page declaration is complete, we fill in the FavoriteResourcePropertyPage class stub generated by the Java attribute editor, starting with some fields and the createContents(...) method. Since FavoriteResourcePropertyPage extends PropertyPage and inherits behavior from the **Preference** page framework (see PreferencePage in Chapter 12, "Preference Pages"), the createContents(...) method is called to create and initialize the page controls (see Figure 13–2).

```
private Text textField;

protected Control createContents(Composite parent) {
   Composite panel = new Composite(parent, SWT.NONE);
   GridLayout layout = new GridLayout();
   layout.marginHeight = 0;
   layout.marginWidth = 0;
   panel.setLayout(layout);

   Label label = new Label(panel, SWT.NONE);
   label.setLayoutData(new GridData());
   label.setText(
      "Comment that appears as hover help"
         + " in the Favorites view:");

   textField =
      new Text(panel, SWT.BORDER | SWT.MULTI | SWT.WRAP);
   textField.setLayoutData(
      new GridData(GridData.FILL_BOTH));
   textField.setText(getCommentPropertyValue());

   return panel;
}
```

The `PropertyPage` class contains a `getElement()` accessor method for retrieving the object whose properties are being edited. Create accessor methods for getting and setting the comment associated with the current element:

```
protected String getCommentPropertyValue() {
   IResource resource =
      (IResource) getElement().getAdapter(
         IResource.class);
   try {
      String value =
         resource.getPersistentProperty(
            BasicFavoriteItem.COMMENT_PROPKEY);
      if (value == null)
         return BasicFavoriteItem.getDefaultComment();
      return value;
   }
   catch (CoreException e) {
      FavoritesLog.logError(e);
      return e.getMessage();
   }
}

protected void setCommentPropertyValue(String comment) {
   IResource resource =
      (IResource) getElement().getAdapter(
         IResource.class);
   String value = comment;
   if (value.equals(BasicFavoriteItem.getDefaultComment()))
      value = null;
```

```
   try {
      resource.setPersistentProperty(
         BasicFavoriteItem.COMMENT_PROPKEY,
         value);
   }
   catch (CoreException e) {
      FavoritesLog.logError(e);
   }
}
```

Because `FavoriteResourcePropertyPage` extends `PropertyPage` and inherits behavior from the **Preference** page framework (see `PreferencePage` in Chapter 12), the `performOk()` method is called when the **OK** button is clicked, giving the **Property** page an opportunity to save its values.

```
public boolean performOk() {
   setCommentPropertyValue(textField.getText());
   return super.performOk();
}
```

When all of this is in place, opening the **Properties** dialog for the **Favorites** project displays the **Favorites Property** page (see Figure 13–2).

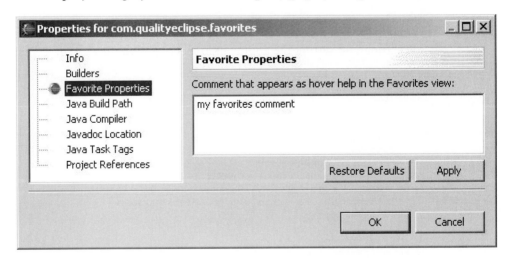

Figure 13–2   Favorites resource Property page for Favorites project.

13.2.3   Creating a favorites item resource page

We have successfully added a **Property** page to the resource **Properties** dialog, and now we want to display a similar **Property** page with an additional field for instances of `IFavoriteItem`. Whereas the resource **Property** page described in the previous section only displayed a comment property, this new `FavoriteItemPropertyPage` will extend `FavoriteResourcePropertyPage` to add a field for displaying the `Color` property. Begin by creating the new class and adding the `createContents(...)` method:

```
protected Control createContents(Composite parent) {
   Composite panel = new Composite(parent, SWT.NONE);
   GridLayout layout = new GridLayout();
   layout.numColumns = 2;
   layout.marginHeight = 0;
   layout.marginWidth = 0;
   panel.setLayout(layout);

   Label label = new Label(panel, SWT.NONE);
   label.setLayoutData(new GridData());
   label.setText(
      "Color of item in Favorites View:");

   colorEditor = new ColorEditor(panel);
   colorEditor.setColorValue(getColorPropertyValue());
   colorEditor.getButton().setLayoutData(
      new GridData(100, SWT.DEFAULT));

   Composite subpanel =
      (Composite) super.createContents(panel);
   GridData gridData = new GridData(GridData.FILL_BOTH);
   gridData.horizontalSpan = 2;
   subpanel.setLayoutData(gridData);

   return panel;
}
```

Create accessor methods for getting and setting the color of the selected **Favorites** item:

```
protected RGB getColorPropertyValue() {
   IFavoriteItem item = (IFavoriteItem) getElement();
   Color color = item.getColor();
   return color.getRGB();
}

protected void setColorPropertyValue(RGB rgb) {
   IFavoriteItem item = (IFavoriteItem) getElement();
   Color color = BasicFavoriteItem.getColor(rgb);
   if (color.equals(BasicFavoriteItem.getDefaultColor()))
      color = null;
   item.setColor(color);
}
```

Create a `performOk()` method to store the color value back into the selected **Favorites** item:

```
public boolean performOk() {
   setColorPropertyValue(colorEditor.getColorValue());
   return super.performOk();
}
```

This **Property** page relies on `ColorEditor` to display and edit the color property. There are at least four copies of the `ColorEditor` class in Eclipse, but they all reside in internal packages, so we will not use them (see Section 20.2, "Accessing Internal Code," for more on internal APIs). Instead, copy the `org.eclipse.ui.internal.editors.text.ColorEditor` into the `com.qualityeclipse.favorites.properties` package so we can use it.

> **Tip:** If you see something like this in an internal package that you think should be a public API, then let your voice be heard by entering a feature request in Bugzilla (see Section 20.2). Be sure to vote for the bugs that you want fixed so that the Eclipse team can get a better feel for which changes are important and which are not.

13.2.4 Opening the properties dialog

We have created a new, refined `FavoriteItemPropertyPage` for displaying **Favorites** item properties, but that page will only appear in a **Properties** dialog opened on an instance of `IFavoriteItem`. To open the **Properties** dialog on an instance of `IFavoriteItem`, we need to add a **Properties** command to the end of the **Favorites** view context menu. Eclipse already provides an action for opening the **Properties** dialog, so add the following lines to the end of the `FavoritesView.fillContextMenu(...)` method:

```
menuMgr.add(new Separator());
menuMgr.add(
   new PropertyDialogAction(getSite().getShell(), viewer));
```

Now, selecting **Properties** in the **Favorites** view context menu displays the **Properties** dialog for the selected **Favorites** item (see Figure 13–3).

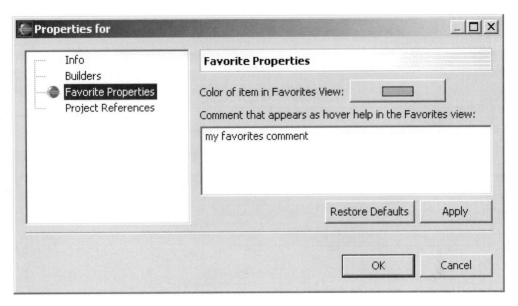

Figure 13–3   Favorites item Property page for Favorites project.

13.3   Displaying Properties in the Properties View

Another place that properties can be displayed and edited is in the **Properties**
view. The **Properties** view examines the workbench selection to determine if
the selected objects support the org.eclipse.ui.views.properties.IProp-
ertySource interface. An object can support the IPropertySource interface
by either directly implementing IPropertySource or by implementing the
getAdapter(...) method to return an object that implements the IProperty-
Source interface (see Figure 13–4).

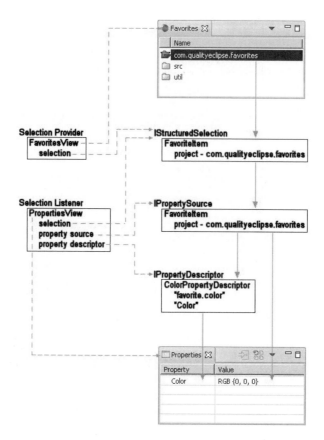

Figure 13–4   From selection to the Properties view.

13.3.1   Properties view API

The `IPropertySource` interface provides a descriptor for each property to be displayed in the **Properties** view, as well as methods for getting and setting property values. The `id` argument in the methods below is the identifier associated with the descriptor for that property.

> `getPropertyDescriptors()`—Returns an array of descriptors, one for each property to be displayed in the **Properties** view.
>
> `getPropertyValue(Object)`–Returns the value of the property that has the specified identifier.
>
> `isPropertySet(Object)`—Returns `true` if the property specified by the identifier has a value different than its default value.
>
> `resetPropertyValue(Object)`—Sets the value of the property specified by the identifier to its default value.

`setPropertyValue(Object, Object)`—Sets the value of the property specified by the identifier to the specified value.

Property descriptors, objects that implement the `IPropertyDescriptor` interface, contain a property identifier and create a property editor as necessary for the **Properties** view. Eclipse provides some implementations of the `IPropertyDescriptor` interface (see Figure 13–5).

Figure 13–5   IPropertyDescriptor hierarchy.

Instances of `PropertyDescriptor` are constructed with a property identifier and a display name for the property. If an object has many properties, then it's useful to group similar properties visually by calling `setCategory(...)` on each descriptor in the group. Other useful methods include:

`setAlwaysIncompatible(boolean)`—Sets a flag indicating whether the property descriptor is to be considered always incompatible with any other property descriptor. Setting this flag prevents a property from displaying during multiple selections.

`setCategory(String)`—Sets the name of the category to which the property belongs. Properties belonging to the same category are grouped together visually. This localized string is shown to the user. If the category is not set on any of the descriptors, the property will appear ungrouped at the top level in the **Properties** view. If the category is set on at least one descriptor, then any descriptors with an unset category will appear in a miscellaneous category.

`setDescription(String)`—Sets a brief description of the property. This localized string is shown to the user when the property is selected.

`setFilterFlags(String[])`—Sets a list of filter types to which the property belongs. The user is able to toggle the filters to show/hide properties belonging to a filter type. Currently, the only valid value for these flags is `IPropertySheetEntry.FILTER_ID_EXPERT`.

`setHelpContextIds(Object)`—Sets the help context ID for the property. Even though the method name is plural, only a string can be specified, indicating the singular associated help context (see Section 15.3.1, "Associating context IDs with items").

`setLabelProvider(ILabelProvider)`—Sets the label provider for the property. The label provider is used to obtain the text (and possible image) for displaying the value of this property.

`setValidator(ICellEditorValidator)`—Sets the input validator for the cell editor for this property descriptor.

13.3.2   *Favorite properties in the properties view*

For the **Favorites** product, we want to display the **Color** property and a **Hash Code** property. Using `setAlwaysIncompatible(true)`, we specify that the **Hash Code** property should appear in the **Properties** view only when the **Show Advanced Properties** option is turned on. The **Favorites** view is already a workbench selection provider (see Section 7.4.1, "Selection provider"), so the **Properties** view is already examining the selected **Favorites** items. All that's left is for `BasicFavoriteItem` to implement the `IPropertySource` interface.

```
private static final String COLOR_ID = "favorite.color";
private static final ColorPropertyDescriptor
COLOR_PROPERTY_DESCRIPTOR =
   new ColorPropertyDescriptor(COLOR_ID, "Color");

private static final String HASH_ID = "favorite.hash";
private static final TextPropertyDescriptor HASH_PROPERTY_DESCRIPTOR
   = new TextPropertyDescriptor(HASH_ID, "Hash Code");
static {
   HASH_PROPERTY_DESCRIPTOR.setCategory("Other");
   HASH_PROPERTY_DESCRIPTOR.setFilterFlags(
      new String[] {
         IPropertySheetEntry.FILTER_ID_EXPERT });
   HASH_PROPERTY_DESCRIPTOR.setAlwaysIncompatible(true);
}

private static final IPropertyDescriptor[] DESCRIPTORS =
   { COLOR_PROPERTY_DESCRIPTOR, HASH_PROPERTY_DESCRIPTOR };

public Object getEditableValue() {
   return this;
}

public IPropertyDescriptor[] getPropertyDescriptors() {
   return DESCRIPTORS;
}

public Object getPropertyValue(Object id) {
   if (COLOR_ID.equals(id))
      return getColor().getRGB();
```

```
      if (HASH_ID.equals(id))
         return new Integer(hashCode());
      return null;
   }

   public boolean isPropertySet(Object id) {
      if (COLOR_ID.equals(id))
         return getColor() != getDefaultColor();
      return false;
   }

   public void resetPropertyValue(Object id) {
      if (COLOR_ID.equals(id))
         setColor(null);
   }

   public void setPropertyValue(Object id, Object value) {
      if (COLOR_ID.equals(id))
         setColor(getColor((RGB) value));
   }
```

Now, when an item is selected in the **Favorites** view, the **Properties** view displays the **Color** property for that item. When the **Show Advanced Properties** option is turned on, the **Hash Code** property appears (see Figure 13–6).

Figure 13–6   Properties view showing expert properties.

13.4   **Property Pages Reused as Preference Pages**

Since `PropertyPage` inherits from `PreferencePage`, with a little work you can reuse a **Property** page as a **Preference** page. In our case, we want to reuse the `FavoriteItemPropertyPage` as a **Preference** page for specifying the `Color` and `comment` properties' default values. To accomplish this, create a new `FavoriteDefaultsPreferencePage` as a subclass of `FavoriteItemPropertyPage` that implements `org.eclipse.ui.IWorkbenchPreferencePage` and overrides the property accessor methods:

```
package com.qualityeclipse.favorites.properties;

import org.eclipse.swt.graphics.*;
import org.eclipse.ui.*;
import com.qualityeclipse.favorites.model.*;
```

```
public class FavoriteDefaultsPreferencePage
   extends FavoriteItemPropertyPage
   implements IWorkbenchPreferencePage
{

   public void init(IWorkbench workbench) {
   }

   protected RGB getColorPropertyValue() {
      return BasicFavoriteItem.getDefaultColor().getRGB();
   }

   protected void setColorPropertyValue(RGB rgb) {
      BasicFavoriteItem.setDefaultColor(
         BasicFavoriteItem.getColor(rgb));
   }

   protected String getCommentPropertyValue() {
      return BasicFavoriteItem.getDefaultComment();
   }

   protected void setCommentPropertyValue(String comment) {
      BasicFavoriteItem.setDefaultComment(comment);
   }
}
```

Then, create a new **Preference** page declaration in the **Favorites** plug-in manifest (see Section 12.1, "Creating a Preference Page") with the following attributes:

category = "com.qualityeclipse.favorites.prefs.view"

class = "com.qualityeclipse.favorites.properties
.FavoriteDefaultsPreferencePage"

id = "com.qualityeclipse.favorites.prefs.defaults"

name = "Defaults"

When complete, the **Defaults** preference page appears in the workbench **Preferences** dialog as a child of the **Favorites** preference page (see Figure 13–7).

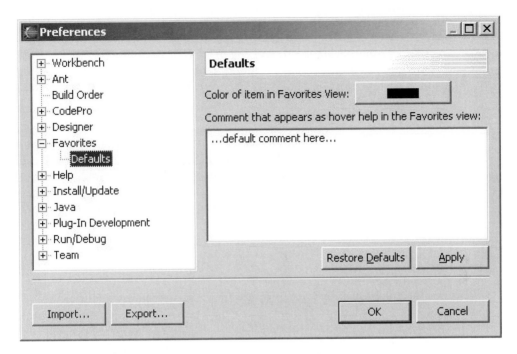

Figure 13–7 Favorite Defaults preference page.

13.5 RFWS Considerations

The "User Interface" section of the *RFWS Requirements* includes one requirement and three best practices dealing with properties. Each of them is derived
from the Eclipse UI Guidelines.

13.5.1 Properties views for quick access

User Interface Guideline #42 is a requirement that states:

*Use the Properties view to edit the properties of an object when quick
access is important, and you will switch quickly from object to object.*

To pass this test, show which objects in your plug-in have properties that
are editable using the **Properties** view. For our **Favorites** view, we would show
that each **Favorites** item shows its color and hash code within the **Properties**
view (see Figure 13–6).

13.5.2   Properties dialog for expensive calculations

User Interface Guideline #43 is a best practice that states:

Use a Properties dialog to edit the properties of an object that are expensive to calculate. If it is too expensive to calculate the properties for an object, the quick access to properties offered by the Properties view becomes worthless. In this situation, where quick access is not possible, a Properties dialog should be used.

For this test, show which objects in your plug-in have properties that are editable using the **Properties** dialog. Show that any properties that are calculation-intensive are relegated to the **Properties** dialog and do not appear in the **Properties** view. For our **Favorites** view, we would show that opening the **Properties** dialog on a **Favorites** item will display its color and comment (see Figure 13–3).

13.5.3   Properties dialog for complex relationships

User Interface Guideline #44 is a best practice that states:

Use a Properties dialog to edit the properties of an object that have complex relationships to one another. In some cases, the properties for an object are dependent on one another such that a change in one will affect another, or even enable/disable the option to change another. In this situation, a Properties dialog should be used to represent the semantic link between these properties.

In addition to using the **Properties** dialog to show properties that are expensive to calculate, you should also use the **Properties** dialog to show any properties that exhibit complex interrelationships, which could not be properly represented in the **Properties** view.

13.5.4   Properties dialog contains superset of items

User Interface Guideline #45 is a best practice that states:

Properties dialogs should contain the superset of items shown in the Properties view.

For this test, show that any properties available in the **Properties** view are also available in the **Properties** dialog. For the **Favorites** view, we would show that the color property is available in both locations.

13.6   Summary

Many plug-ins will need to create and manage their own plug-in-specific resources. While preferences are global settings applicable to entire plug-ins and chunks of functionality, properties are local settings applicable to a single resource. In this chapter, we explored the Eclipse property API and discussed the various choices open to the developer for accessing properties using the **Properties** view or the **Properties** dialog. We also demonstrated how to persist properties across workspace sessions.

References

Daum, Berthold, "Mutatis mutandis—Using Preference Pages as Property Pages," October 24, 2003 (*www.eclipse.org/articles/Article-Mutatis-mutandis/overlay-pages.html*).

Johan, Dicky, "Take control of your properties," May 20, 2003 (*www.eclipse.org/articles/Article-Properties-View/properties-view.html*).

CHAPTER 14

Builders, Markers, and Natures

Incremental project builders, also knows as *builders*, automatically execute whenever a resource in an associated project changes. For example, when a Java source file is created or revised, Eclipse's incremental Java compiler annotates the source file and generates a class file. Because Java class files can be entirely regenerated by the compiler from the Java source files, they are known as *derived resources*.

Markers are used to annotate locations within a resource. For example, the Eclipse Java compiler annotates source files by adding markers to indicate compilation errors, deprecated member usage, bookmarks, and so on. These markers show up along the left margin, which is sometimes referred to as the *gutter*, when editing a Java file, and in the **Problems** view or **Task** view as appropriate.

Project *natures* are used to associate projects and builders (see Figure 14–1). The Java nature of a project makes it a Java project and associates the Eclipse incremental Java compiler.

Our goal in this chapter is to discuss builders, markers, and natures in the context of a new `plugin.properties` file auditor in our **Favorites** product. The properties auditor is implemented as a builder and cross-references property keys in the `plugin.xml` with entries in the `plugin.properties` file. Markers are used to report problems that the auditor finds; keys in the `plugin.xml` that are not declared in the `plugin.properties` file are marked as missing, while keys in the `plugin.properties` file that are not referenced in the `plugin.xml` file are marked as unused. A new project nature is created to associate our auditor with a project.

```
<extension point="org.eclipse.core.resources.natures"
    id="propertiesAuditor"
    name="Favorites Properties Auditor">
    <builder id="com ... propertiesFileAuditor"/>
    <requires-nature id="org.eclipse.jdt.core.javanature"/>
    <requires-nature id="org.eclipse.pde.PluginNature"/>
    <one-of-nature id="pluginAuditors"/>
    <runtime>
        <run class="com ... PropertiesAuditorNature"/>
    </runtime>
</extension>
                        <extension point="org.eclipse.core.resources.builders"
                            id="propertiesFileAuditor">
                            <builder hasNature="true">
                                <run class="com ... PropertiesFileAuditor"/>
                            </builder>
                        </extension>

public class PropertiesAuditorNature
    implements IProjectNature
{
    public void configure() throws CoreException {
        PropertiesFileAuditor.addBuilderToProject(project);
        new Job("Properties File Audit") {
            protected IStatus run(IProgressMonitor monitor) {
                try {
                    project.build(
                        PropertiesFileAuditor.FULL_BUILD,
                        PropertiesFileAuditor.BUILDER_ID,
                        null, monitor);
                }
                catch (CoreEx     public class PropertiesFileAuditor
                    FavoritesL         extends IncrementalProjectBuilder
                }                  {
                return Status          protected IProject[] build(
            }                              int kind,
        }.schedule();                      Map args,
    }                                      IProgressMonitor monitor)
                                           throws CoreException
    public void deconfigur         {
        removeBuilderFromPr            if (shouldAudit(kind)) {
        deleteAuditMarkers(                ResourcesPlugin.getWorkspace().run(
    }                                          new IWorkspaceRunnable() {
                                                   public void run(IProgressMonitor monitor)
                                                       throws CoreException
                                                   {
                                                       auditPluginManifest(monitor);
                                                   }
                                           }, monitor);
                                       }
                                       return null;
                                   }
```

Figure 14–1   Builders and natures.

14.1   Builders

A builder is scoped to a project. When one or more resources in a project change, the builders associated with the project are notified. If these changes have been batched (see Section 9.3, "Batching Change Events"), the builder receives a single notification containing a list of all the changed resources rather than individual notifications for each changed resource.

> **Tip:** If you want a global builder not associated with any specific project, hook into the early startup extension point (see Section 3.4.2, "Early plug-in startup") and add a workspace resource change listener (see Section 9.1, "IresourceChangeListener"). The downside of this approach is that the builder will consume memory and execution cycles regardless of whether it is really needed.

Builders process the list of changes and update their *build state* by regenerating the necessary derived resources (see Section 14.1.3, "Derived resources"), annotating source resources, and so on. Builders are notified when a resource changes, such as when a user saves a modified Java source file, and thus are executed quite frequently. Because of this, a builder must execute incrementally, meaning that it must rebuild only those derived resources that have changed. If the Eclipse Java compiler rebuilt all the Java source files in the project every time a single Java source file was saved, it would bring Eclipse to its knees.

14.1.1 *Declaring a builder*

The first step in creating our `plugin.properties` auditor involves adding a builder declaration to the **Favorites** plug-in manifest. Open the plug-in manifest editor on the **Favorites** `plugin.xml` file, switch to the **Extensions** page, and add an `org.eclipse.core.resources.builders` extension (see Figure 14–2).

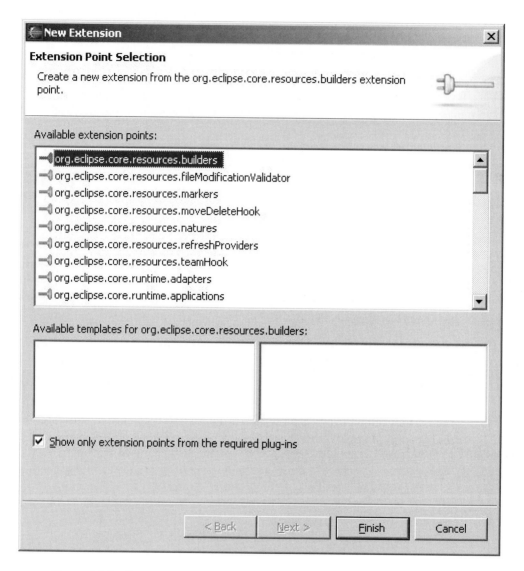

Figure 14–2　The New Extension wizard showing the org.eclipse.core.resources.builders extension point selected.

Double-click on the `org.eclipse.core.resources.builders` extension to open the **Properties** view to set the `id` attribute for the extension (see Figure 14–3):

> id—"propertiesFileAuditor"
> The last segment of the builder's unique identifier. If the declaration

appears in the com.qualityeclipse.favorites plug-in, then the
builder's fully qualified identifier is com.qualityeclipse.favor-
ites.propertiesFileAuditor.

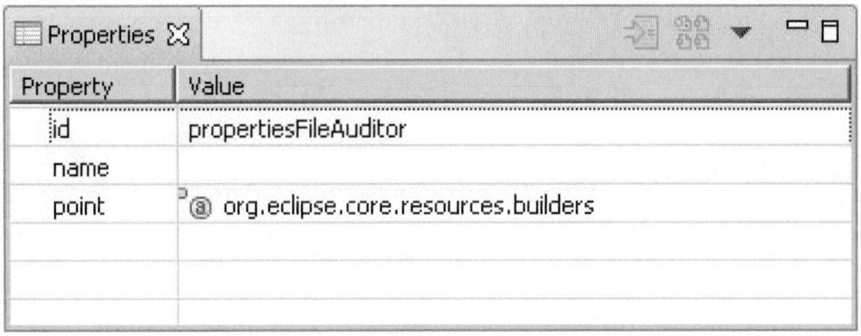

Figure 14–3 The Properties view showing the builder's extension.

Right-click on the extension and select **New > builder** in the context
menu. The builder element has only one attribute (see Figure 14–4):

hasNature—"true"
A Boolean indicating whether the builder is owned by a project nature. If
true and no corresponding nature is found, this builder will not run, but
will remain in the project's build spec. If the attribute is not specified, it is
assumed to be false.

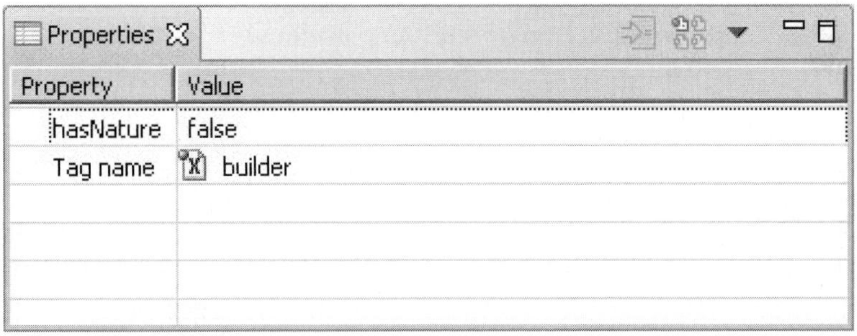

Figure 14–4 The Properties view showing the builder's attributes.

Right-click on the builder element and selecting **New > run** in the context
menu to associate a Java class with the builder. The Java class will provide
behavior for the builder. The run element has only one attribute (see Figure
14–5), class, specifying the Java class to be executed. Click the "…" button
at the right of the **class** field and use the **Java Attribute Editor** to create a new
class in the **Favorites** project with the specified package and class name:

class—"com.qualityeclipse.favorites.builder.PropertiesFileAuditor"
The fully qualified name of a subclass of
`org.eclipse.core.resources.IncrementalProjectBuilder`. The class
is instantiated using its no argument constructor, but may be parameter-
ized using the `IExecutableExtension` interface (see Section 20.5.1,
"Parameterized types").

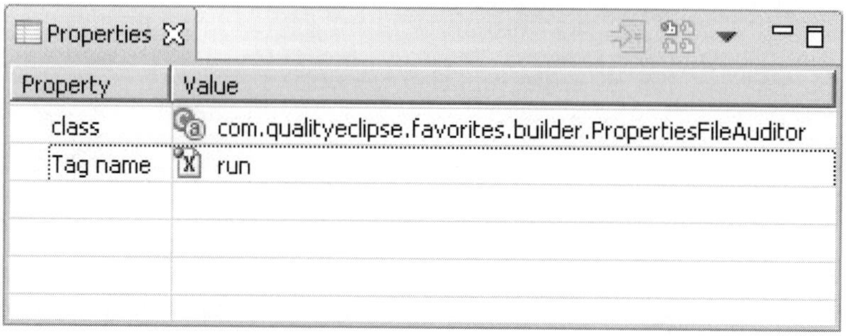

Property	Value
class	com.qualityeclipse.favorites.builder.PropertiesFileAuditor
Tag name	run

Figure 14–5   The Properties view showing run attributes.

The complete declaration in the **Favorites** plug-in manifest should look
like this:

```
<extension
    id="propertiesFileAuditor"
    point="org.eclipse.core.resources.builders">
    <builder hasNature="false">
        <run
            class="com.qualityeclipse.favorites.builder
                .PropertiesFileAuditor"/>
    </builder>
</extension>
```

14.1.2   *IncrementalProjectBuilder*

The class specified in the declaration of the previous section must be a subclass
of `IncrementalProjectBuilder`, and at the very least, implement the
`build(...)` method. This method has several arguments providing build information and a mechanism for displaying progress to the user:

`kind`–The kind of build being requested. Valid values include:
`FULL_BUILD`, `INCREMENTAL_BUILD`, and `AUTO_BUILD`.

`args`–A map of builder-specific arguments keyed by argument name (key
type: `String`, value type: `String`) or `null`, indicating an empty map.

`monitor`–A progress monitor, or `null` if progress reporting and cancella-
tion are not desired.

The `kind` argument can have one of three values:

`FULL_BUILD`–The builder should rebuild all derived resources and perform its work as if it has not been executed before.

`INCREMENTAL_BUILD`–The builder should only rebuild those derived resources that need to be updated and only perform the work that is necessary based on its prior build state.

`AUTO_BUILD`–Same as `INCREMENTAL_BUILD`, except that the build was an automatically triggered incremental build (auto-building ON).

The are several interesting methods in `IncrementalProjectBuilder`:

`build(int, Map, IProgressMonitor)`–Overridden by subclasses to perform the build operation. See the description earlier in this section and implementation example later in this section.

`forgetLastBuiltState()`–Requests that this builder forget any state it may be caching regarding previously built states. This may need to be called by a subclass if the build process is interrupted or canceled (see `checkCancel()` method later in this section).

`getDelta(IProject)`–Returns the resource delta recording the changes in the given project since the last time the builder was run, or `null` if no such delta is available. See Section 9.2, "Processing Change Events," for details on processing resource change events, and the `shouldAudit()` method later on in this section.

`getProject()`–Returns the project with which this builder is associated.

`isInterrupted()`–Returns whether an interrupt request has been made for this build. Background autobuild is interrupted when another thread tries to modify the workspace concurrently with the build thread. See `shouldAudit()` method later on in this section.

`setInitializationData(IConfigurationElement, String, Object)`– Called immediately after the builder is instantiated with configuration information specified in the builder's declaration (see Section 20.5.1).

After declaring our builder in the previous section, we must implement `PropertiesFileAuditor`, a subclass of `org.eclipse.core.resources.IncrementalProjectBuilder`, to perform the operation. When the `build(...)` method is called, our `PropertiesFileAuditor` builder delegates to `shouldAudit(...)` to see if an audit should be performed, and if necessary, to `auditPluginManifest()` to perform the audit.

```
package com.qualityeclipse.favorites.builder;

import java.util.*;
import org.eclipse.core.resources.*;
import org.eclipse.core.runtime.*;
import com.qualityeclipse.favorites.*;

public class PropertiesFileAuditor
    extends IncrementalProjectBuilder
{
    protected IProject[] build(
        int kind,
        Map args,
        IProgressMonitor monitor)
        throws CoreException {

        if (shouldAudit(kind))
            auditPluginManifest(monitor);
        return null;
    }
    … other methods discussed later inserted here …
}
```

The shouldAudit(...) method checks for FULL_BUILD, or if the plugin.xml or plugin.properties files of a project have changed (see Section 9.2). If a builder has never been invoked before, then getDelta(...) returns null.

```
private boolean shouldAudit(int kind) {
    if (kind == FULL_BUILD)
        return true;
    IResourceDelta delta = getDelta(getProject());
    if (delta == null)
        return false;
    IResourceDelta[] children =
        delta.getAffectedChildren();
    for (int i = 0; i < children.length; i++) {
        IResourceDelta child = children[i];
        String fileName =
            child.getProjectRelativePath().lastSegment();
        if (fileName.equals("plugin.xml")
            || fileName.equals("plugin.properties"))
            return true;
    }
    return false;
}
```

If the shouldAudit(...) method determines that the manifest and properties files should be audited, then the auditPluginManifest() method is called to scan the plugin.xml and plugin.properties files and correlate the key/value pairs; any keys appearing in plugin.xml should have a corresponding key/value pair in plugin.properties. Before each lengthy operation, we check to see if the build has been interrupted or canceled. After each lengthy operation, we report progress to the user (see Section 9.4, "Progress Monitor"); while this is not strictly necessary, it is certainly polite. If you do prematurely exit your build process, you may need to call `forgetLastBuildState()` before exiting so that a full rebuild will be performed the next time.

```
private void auditPluginManifest(IProgressMonitor monitor) {
   monitor.beginTask("Audit plugin manifest", 4);

   if (checkCancel(monitor))
      return;
   Map pluginKeys = scanPlugin(
      getProject().getFile("plugin.xml"));
   monitor.worked(1);

   if (checkCancel(monitor))
      return;
   Map propertyKeys = scanProperties(
      getProject().getFile("plugin.properties"));
   monitor.worked(1);

   if (checkCancel(monitor))
      return;
   Iterator iter = pluginKeys.entrySet().iterator();
   while (iter.hasNext()) {
      Map.Entry entry = (Map.Entry) iter.next();
      if (!propertyKeys.containsKey(entry.getKey()))
         reportProblem(
            "Missing property key",
            ((Location) entry.getValue()),
            1,
            true);
   }
   monitor.worked(1);

   if (checkCancel(monitor))
      return;
   iter = propertyKeys.entrySet().iterator();
   while (iter.hasNext()) {
      Map.Entry entry = (Map.Entry) iter.next();
      if (!pluginKeys.containsKey(entry.getKey()))
         reportProblem(
            "Unused property key",
            ((Location) entry.getValue()),
            2,
            false);
   }
   monitor.done();
}

private boolean checkCancel(IProgressMonitor monitor) {
   if (monitor.isCanceled()) {
      // Discard build state if necessary.
      throw new OperationCanceledException();
   }
```

```
    if (isInterrupted()) {
        // Discard build state if necessary.
        return true;
    }
    return false;
}
```

The auditPluginManifest(...) method delegates scanning the plugin.xml and plugin.properties to two separate scan methods:

```
private Map scanPlugin(IFile file) {
    Map keys = new HashMap();
    String content = readFile(file);
    int start = 0;
    while (true) {
        start = content.indexOf("\"%", start);
        if (start < 0)
            break;
        int end = content.indexOf('"', start + 2);
        if (end < 0)
            break;
        Location loc = new Location();
        loc.file = file;
        loc.key = content.substring(start + 2, end);
        loc.charStart = start + 1;
        loc.charEnd = end;
        keys.put(loc.key, loc);
        start = end + 1;
    }
    return keys;
}

private Map scanProperties(IFile file) {
    Map keys = new HashMap();
    String content = readFile(file);
    int end = 0;
    while (true) {
        end = content.indexOf('=', end);
        if (end < 0)
            break;
        int start = end-1;
        while (start >= 0) {
            char ch = content.charAt(start);
            if (ch == '\r' || ch == '\n')
                break;
            start--;
        }
        start++;
        String found =
            content.substring(start, end).trim();
        if (found.length() == 0
            || found.charAt(0) == '#'
            || found.indexOf('=') != -1)
            continue;
        Location loc = new Location();
```

```
            loc.file = file;
            loc.key = found;
            loc.charStart = start;
            loc.charEnd = end;
            keys.put(loc.key, loc);
            end++;
        }
        return keys;
    }
```

The two scan methods read the file content into memory using the read-File(...) method:

```
private String readFile(IFile file) {
    if (!file.exists())
        return "";
    InputStream stream = null;
    try {
        stream = file.getContents();
        Reader reader =
            new BufferedReader(
                new InputStreamReader(stream));
        StringBuffer result = new StringBuffer(2048);
        char[] buf = new char[2048];
        while (true) {
            int count = reader.read(buf);
            if (count < 0)
                break;
            result.append(buf, 0, count);
        }
        return result.toString();
    }
    catch (Exception e) {
        FavoritesLog.logError(e);
        return "";
    }
    finally {
        try {
            if (stream != null)
                stream.close();
        }
        catch (IOException e) {
            FavoritesLog.logError(e);
            return "";
        }
    }
}
```

The reportProblem(...) method appends a message to standard output. In subsequent sections, we'll enhance this method to generate markers instead (see Section 14.2.2, "Creating and deleting markers").

```
private void reportProblem(
    String msg,
```

```
Location loc,
int violation,
boolean isError) {

System.out.println(
    (isError ? "ERROR: " : "WARNING: ")
        + msg + " \""
        + loc.key + "\" in "
        + loc.file.getFullPath());
}
```

The `Location` inner class is defined as an internal data holder with no associated behavior.

```
private class Location
{
    IFile file;
    String key;
    int charStart;
    int charEnd;
}
```

When hooked up to a project (see Section 14.1.4, "Associating a builder with a project," and Section 14.3.7, "Associating a nature with a project"), the builder will append problems similar to the following to standard output:

```
ERROR: Missing property key "favorites.category.name"
    in /Test/plugin.xml
ERROR: Missing property key "favorites.view.name"
    in /Test/plugin.xml
WARNING: Unused property key "two"
    in /Test/plugin.properties
WARNING: Unused property key "three"
    in /Test/plugin.properties
```

14.1.3 Derived resources

Derived resources are resources that can be fully regenerated by a builder. Java class files are derived resources because the Java compiler can fully regenerate them from the associated Java source file. When a builder creates a derived resource, it should mark that file as derived using the `IResource.set-Derived(...)` method. A team provider can then assume that the file does not need to be under version control by default.

> `setDerived(boolean)`—Sets whether this resource subtree is marked as derived. This operation does not result in a resource change event, and does not trigger autobuilds.

14.1.4   Associating a builder with a project

Using a nature to associate a builder with a project is the preferred approach
(see Section 14.3, "Natures"), but you can associate builders with projects
without using a nature. We could create an action in a workbench window
(see Section 6.2.6, "Creating an action delegate") that calls the following add-
BuilderToProject(...) method to associate our auditor with the currently
selected projects. Alternately, we could, on startup, cycle through all the
projects in the workbench and call the following addBuilderToProject(...)
method. There are no advantages or disadvantages with associating a builder
with a project using an action delegate as opposed to using a project nature,
but in our case, we will create a project nature to make the association (see
Section 14.3).

```
public static final String BUILDER_ID =
   FavoritesPlugin.getDefault().getDescriptor()
      .getUniqueIdentifier() + ".propertiesFileAuditor";

public static void addBuilderToProject(IProject project) {

   // Cannot modify closed projects.
   if (!project.isOpen())
      return;

   // Get the description.
   IProjectDescription description;
   try {
      description = project.getDescription();
   }
   catch (CoreException e) {
      FavoritesLog.logError(e);
      return;
   }

   // Look for builder already associated.
   ICommand[] cmds = description.getBuildSpec();
   for (int j = 0; j < cmds.length; j++)
      if (cmds[j].getBuilderName().equals(BUILDER_ID))
         return;

   // Associate builder with project.
   ICommand newCmd = description.newCommand();
   newCmd.setBuilderName(BUILDER_ID);
   List newCmds = new ArrayList();
   newCmds.addAll(Arrays.asList(cmds));
   newCmds.add(newCmd);
   description.setBuildSpec(
      (ICommand[]) newCmds.toArray(
         new ICommand[newCmds.size()]));
   try {
      project.setDescription(description, null);
   }
```

```
      catch (CoreException e) {
         FavoritesLog.logError(e);
      }
}
```

Each workbench project contains a .project file (see Section 1.4.2, ".classpath and .project files") that contains build commands. Executing this method causes the following to appear in the buildSpec section of the project's .project file:

```
<buildCommand>
   <name>
      com.qualityeclipse.favorites.propertiesFileAuditor
   </name>
   <arguments>
</arguments>
</buildCommand>
```

In addition to the addBuilderToProject (...) method, we would need a corresponding removeBuilderFromProject (...) method:

```
public static void removeBuilderFromProject(IProject project) {
   // Cannot modify closed projects.
   if (!project.isOpen())
      return;

   // Get the description.
   IProjectDescription description;
   try {
      description = project.getDescription();
   }
   catch (CoreException e) {
      FavoritesLog.logError(e);
      return;
   }

   // Look for builder.
   int index = -1;
   ICommand[] cmds = description.getBuildSpec();
   for (int j = 0; j < cmds.length; j++) {
      if (cmds[j].getBuilderName().equals(BUILDER_ID)) {
         index = j;
         break;
      }
   }
   if (index == -1)
      return;

   // Remove builder from project.
   List newCmds = new ArrayList();
   newCmds.addAll(Arrays.asList(cmds));
   newCmds.remove(index);
   description.setBuildSpec(
```

```
        (ICommand[]) newCmds.toArray(
           new ICommand[newCmds.size()])]);
    try {
       project.setDescription(description, null);
    }
    catch (CoreException e) {
       FavoritesLog.logError(e);
    }
}
```

14.1.5 Invoking builders

Normally, the build process for a project is triggered either by the user selecting a build action or by the workbench during an autobuild in response to a resource change. If need be, you can trigger the build process programmatically using one of the following methods:

IProject

> build(int, IProgressMonitor)—Runs the build processing on the project, causing *all* associated builders to be run. The first argument indicates the kind of build, FULL_BUILD or INCREMENTAL_BUILD (see Section 14.1.2, "IncrementalProjectBuilder").

> build(int, String, Map, IProgressMonitor)—Triggers a single builder to be run on the project. The first argument indicates the kind of build, FULL_BUILD or INCREMENTAL_BUILD (see Section 14.1.2), while the second specifies which builder is to be run.

IWorkspace

> build(int, IProgressMonitor)—Runs the build processing on all open projects in the workspace. The first argument indicates the kind of build, FULL_BUILD or INCREMENTAL_BUILD (see Section 14.1.2).

14.2 Markers

Markers are used to annotate specific locations within a resource. For example, the Eclipse Java compiler not only produces class files from source files, but it also annotates the source files by adding markers to indicate compilation errors, deprecated code usage, and so on. Markers do not modify the resources they annotate, but instead are stored in the workspace metadata area. Markers are automatically updated by editors so that when a user edits a file, the markers are repositioned or deleted appropriately. Rather than sending messages to the **console**, we want our PropertiesFileAuditor to create a marker indicating where a problem exists (see Figure 14–6).

Figure 14–6 Marker declaration and data structures.

14.2.1 Marker types

Markers are grouped by marker type. Each marker type has an identifier and zero or more supermarker types but no behavior. New marker types are declared in terms of existing marker types. Marker types added by the `org.eclipse.core.resources` plug-in appear as constants in `IMarker` and include:

> `org.eclipse.core.resources.bookmark` – `IMarker.BOOKMARK`—The super type of marker that appears in the **Bookmarks** view.

> `org.eclipse.core.resources.marker`–`IMarker.MARKER`—The root super type of all markers.

> `org.eclipse.core.resources.problemmarker` – `IMarker.PROBLEM`—The super type of marker that appears in the **Problems** view.

org.eclipse.core.resources.taskmarker - IMarker.TASK—The super type of marker that appears in the **Tasks** view.

org.eclipse.core.resources.textmarker - IMarker.TEXT—The super type of all text-based markers.

For our purposes, we want to introduce a new marker type for our plug-in manifest audit results. Switch to the **Extensions** page of the plug-in manifest editor and click the **Add...** button to add an org.eclipse.core.resources .markers extension (see Figure 14–7).

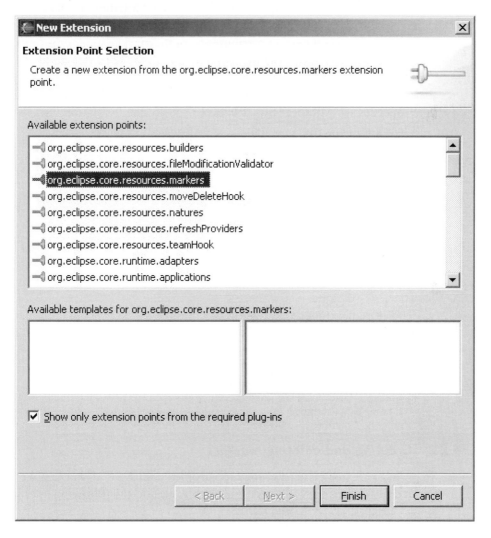

Figure 14–7   The New Extension wizard showing the org.eclipse.core.resources.markers extension point selected.

We want our markers to appear in the **Problems** view, so specify `org.eclipse.core.resources.problemmarker` as a super type by right-clicking on the markers' extension and selecting **New > super**. Double-click on the new super element and enter "org.eclipse.core.resources.problemmarker" for the type attribute in the **Properties** view. Our markers relate to a range of sources in the plug-in manifest or plug-in properties files, so we specify `org.eclipse.core.resources.textmarker` as well as use the same procedure.

We want our markers to persist across multiple sessions, so right-click on the `markers` declaration and select **New > persistent**. Double-click on the new `persistent` element and enter "true" for the value attribute in the **Properties** view.

We inherit several marker attributes from the marker super types specified earlier, but we want to associate two new attributes with our audit marker. Right-click on the `markers` declaration and select **New > attribute**. Double-click on the new `attribute` element and enter "key" for the value attribute in the **Properties** view. Repeat this process to specify the "violation" attribute.

Once complete, our new marker type declaration looks like this:

```
<extension
   id="auditmarker"
   point="org.eclipse.core.resources.markers"
   name="Properties Auditor Marker">
   <super type="org.eclipse.core.resources.problemmarker"/>
   <super type="org.eclipse.core.resources.textmarker"/>
   <attribute name="key"/>
   <attribute name="violation"/>
   <persistent value="true"/>
</extension>
```

The aforementioned declaration specifies the marker's local identifier; the full identifier is the plug-in identifier plus the local identifier that we add as a constant in `PropertiesFileAuditor`.

```
private static final String MARKER_ID =
   FavoritesPlugin.getDefault().getDescriptor()
      .getUniqueIdentifier() + ".auditmarker";
```

14.2.2   *Creating and deleting markers*

We want to create one marker for each problem that we find, but first we must remove any old markers. To accomplish this, we add the following lines in the `auditPluginManifest(...)` method:

```
private void auditPluginManifest(IProgressMonitor monitor) {
   monitor.beginTask("Audit plugin manifest", 4);
```

```
   if (!deleteAuditMarkers(getProject()))
      return;

   if (checkCancel(monitor))
      return;

   … etc …
}
```

which calls the following new method to delete all existing markers in the specified project:

```
public static boolean deleteAuditMarkers(IProject project) {
   try {
      project.deleteMarkers(
         MARKER_ID,
         false,
         IResource.DEPTH_INFINITE);
      return true;
   }
   catch (CoreException e) {
      FavoritesLog.logError(e);
      return false;
   }
}
```

Next, add two constants and rework the reportProblem(…) method (see Section 14.1.2) to create a marker and set marker attributes (see the next section) to indicate problems. The revised method not only creates a marker, but sets various marker attributes that are discussed in the next section:

```
public static final String KEY = "key";
public static final String VIOLATION = "violation";

private void reportProblem(
   String msg,
   Location loc,
   int violation,
   boolean isError) {

   try {
      IMarker marker = loc.file.createMarker(MARKER_ID);
      marker.setAttribute(
         IMarker.MESSAGE,
         msg + ": " + loc.key);
      marker.setAttribute(
         IMarker.CHAR_START,
         loc.charStart);
      marker.setAttribute(
         IMarker.CHAR_END,
         loc.charEnd);
```

```
      marker.setAttribute(
         IMarker.SEVERITY,
         isError
            ? IMarker.SEVERITY_ERROR
            : IMarker.SEVERITY_WARNING);
      marker.setAttribute(KEY, loc.key);
      marker.setAttribute(VIOLATION, violation);
   }
   catch (CoreException e) {
      FavoritesLog.logError(e);
      return;
   }
}
```

Finally, creating, setting attributes, and deleting markers generates resource change events. For efficiency, modify the build(...) method to wrap the call to auditPluginManifest(...) in a IWorkspaceRunnable so that events will be batched and sent when the operation has completed (see Section 9.3):

```
protected IProject[] build(
   int kind,
   Map args,
   IProgressMonitor monitor)
   throws CoreException {

   if (shouldAudit(kind)) {
      ResourcesPlugin.getWorkspace().run(
         new IWorkspaceRunnable() {
            public void run(IProgressMonitor monitor)
               throws CoreException
            {
               auditPluginManifest(monitor);
            }
         },
         monitor
      );
   }
   return null;
}
```

When this is in place, the problems reported by the PropertiesFileAuditor appear in the **Problems** view rather than the **Console** view (see Figure 14–8). In addition, the markers appear as small warning and error icons along the left-hand side of the plugin.xml and plugin.properties editors.

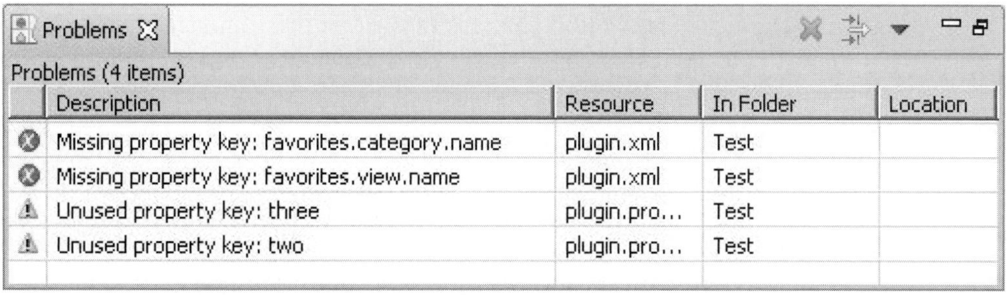

	Description	Resource	In Folder	Location
⊗	Missing property key: favorites.category.name	plugin.xml	Test	
⊗	Missing property key: favorites.view.name	plugin.xml	Test	
⚠	Unused property key: three	plugin.pro...	Test	
⚠	Unused property key: two	plugin.pro...	Test	

Problems ⊠

Problems (4 items)

Figure 14–8 Problems view containing problems found by the auditor.

14.2.3 Marker attributes

Marker attributes take the form of key/value pairs, where the key is a string and the value can be a string, an integer, or a Boolean. `IMarker` methods for accessing attributes include:

getAttribute(String)—Returns the attribute with the given name. The result is an instance of a `string`, an `integer`, or a `Boolean`. Returns `null` if the attribute is undefined.

getAttribute(String, boolean)—Returns the Boolean-valued attribute with the given name. Returns the given default value if the attribute is undefined, the marker does not exist, or it is not a Boolean value.

getAttribute(String, int)—Returns the integer-valued attribute with the given name. Returns the given default value if the attribute is undefined, the marker does not exist, or it is not an integer value.

getAttribute(String, String)—Returns the string-valued attribute with the given name. Returns the given default value if the attribute is undefined, the marker does not exist, or it is not a string value.

getAttributes()—Returns a map of the attributes for the marker. The map has String keys and values that are `string`, `integer`, `Boolean`, or `null`. If the marker has no attributes, then `null` is returned.

getAttributes(String[])—Returns the attributes with the given names. The result is an array whose elements correspond to the elements of the given attribute name array. Each element is a `string`, `integer`, `Boolean`, or `null`.

setAttribute(String, boolean)—Sets the Boolean-valued attribute with the given name. This method changes resources; these changes will be reported in a subsequent resource change event, including an indication that this marker has been modified.

setAttribute(String, int)—Sets the integer-valued attribute with the given name. This method changes resources; these changes will be reported in a subsequent resource change event, including an indication that this marker has been modified.

setAttribute(String, Object)—Sets the attribute with the given name. The value must be a string, integer, Boolean, or null. If the value is null, the attribute is considered to be undefined. This method changes resources; these changes will be reported in a subsequent resource change event, including an indication that this marker has been modified.

setAttributes(String[], Object[])—Sets the given attribute key/value pairs on this marker. The values must be string, integer, Boolean, or null. If a value is null, the new value of the attribute is considered to be undefined. This method changes resources; these changes will be reported in a subsequent resource change event, including an indication that this marker has been modified.

setAttributes(Map)—Sets the attributes for this marker to be the ones contained in the given map. The values must be instances of a string, integer, or Boolean. Attributes previously set on the marker but not included in the given map are considered to be removals. Passing a null parameter is equivalent to removing all marker attributes. This method changes resources; these changes will be reported in a subsequent resource change event, including an indication that this marker has been modified.

Marker attributes are declared in the plug-in manifest for documentation purposes, but are not used during compilation or execution. For example, in our marker type declaration, we declared two new attributes for the marker type named key and violation. Alternately, they could be documented using XML <!-- --> comments, but we recommend using the attribute declaration below because future versions of Eclipse might utilize those declarations:

```
<extension
   id="auditmarker"
   point="org.eclipse.core.resources.markers"
   name="Properties Auditor Marker">
   <super type="org.eclipse.core.resources.problemmarker"/>
   <super type="org.eclipse.core.resources.textmarker"/>
   <attribute name="key"/>
   <attribute name="violation"/>
   <persistent value="true"/>
</extension>
```

The `org.eclipse.core.resources` plug-in introduces several attributes used commonly throughout Eclipse. The following attribute keys are defined in `IMarker`:

CHAR_END—Character end marker attribute. An integer value indicating where a text marker ends. This attribute is zero-relative and exclusive.

CHAR_START—Character start marker attribute. An integer value indicating where a text marker starts. This attribute is zero-relative and inclusive.

DONE—Done marker attribute. A Boolean value indicating whether a marker (e.g., a task) is considered done.

LINE_NUMBER—Line number marker attribute. An integer value indicating the line number for a text marker. This attribute is 1-relative.

LOCATION—Location marker attribute. The location is a human-readable (localized) string that can be used to distinguish between markers on a resource. As such, it should be concise and aimed at users. The content and form of this attribute is not specified or interpreted by the platform.

MESSAGE—Message marker attribute. A localized string describing the nature of the marker (e.g., a name for a bookmark or task). The content and form of this attribute is not specified or interpreted by the platform.

PRIORITY—Priority marker attribute. A number from the set of constants defined in `IMarker`: `PRIORITY_HIGH`, `PRIORITY_LOW`, and `PRIORITY_NORMAL`.

SEVERITY—Severity marker attribute. A number from the set of constants defined in `IMarker`: `SEVERITY_ERROR`, `SEVERITY_WARNING`, `SEVERITY_INFO`.

TRANSIENT—Transient marker attribute. A Boolean value indicating whether the marker (e. g., a task) is considered transient even if its type is declared as persistent.

USER_EDITABLE—User-editable marker attribute. A Boolean value indicating whether a user should be able to manually change the marker (e.g., a task). The default is `true`.

In the revised `reportProblem(...)` method (see Section 14.2.2), we set several marker attributes that are later interpreted by Eclipse. The **Problems** view uses the `IMarker.MESSAGE` and `IMarker.LOCATION` attributes to populate the **Description** and **Location** columns. Editors use the `IMarker.CHAR_START` and `IMarker.CHAR_END` attributes to determine what range of text should be highlighted.

14.2.4   Marker resolution—quick fix

Now that we can generate markers, the user can quickly jump to the location of a problem by double-clicking on the corresponding entry in the **Problems** view, but we provide no help with fixing the problem. Using marker resolution, we can provide an automated mechanism for fixing the problems that our builder identifies.

Create a new `org.eclipse.ui.ide.markerResolution` extension (see Figure 14–9), add a `markerResolutionGenerator` nested element (see Figure 14–10), and specify the marker type as "`com.qualityeclipse.favorites.audit-marker`".

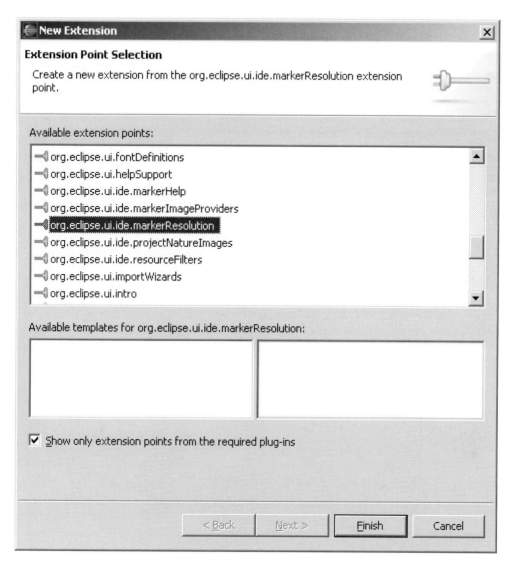

Figure 14–9   The New Extension wizard showing the org.eclipse.ui.ide.markerResolution extension point selected.

Use the **Java Attribute Editor** to generate a marker resolution class named `ViolationResolutionGenerator` in the package `com.qualityeclipse.favorites.build`. When complete, the declaration should look something like this:

```
<extension point="org.eclipse.ui.ide.markerResolution">
   <markerResolutionGenerator
      markerType=
         "com.qualityeclipse.favorites.auditmarker"
```

```
      class="com.qualityeclipse.favorites.builder
         .ViolationResolutionGenerator">
   </markerResolutionGenerator>
</extension>
```

Properties ⊠	
Property	Value
class	com.qualityeclipse.favorites.builder.ViolationResolutionGenerator
markerType	com.qualityeclipse.favorites.auditmarker
Tag name	markerResolutionGenerator

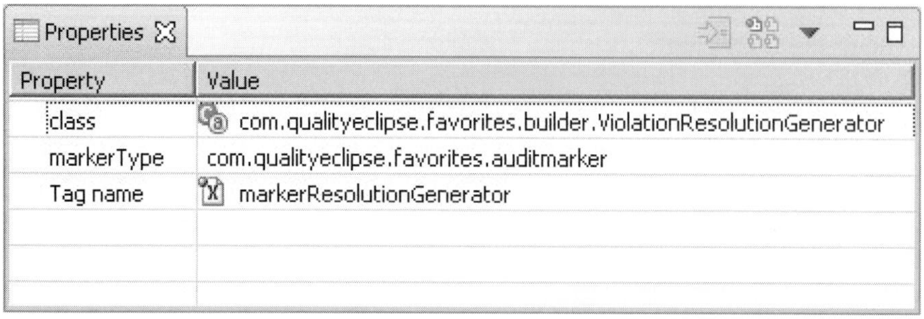

Figure 14–10   The Properties view showing markerResolutionGenerator attributes.

The ViolationResolutionGenerator class provides possible resolution for the user for any com.qualityeclipse.favorites.auditmarker marker via the org.eclipse.ui.IMarkerResolutionGenerator2 interface (IMarkerResolutionGenerator2 was introduced in Eclipse 3.0, providing additional functionality and replacing the now deprecated IMarkerResolutionGenerator).

```
package com.qualityeclipse.favorites.builder;

import java.util.*;
import org.eclipse.core.resources.*;
import org.eclipse.ui.*;

public class ViolationResolutionGenerator
   implements IMarkerResolutionGenerator2
{
   public boolean hasResolutions(IMarker marker) {
      switch (getViolation(marker)) {
         case 1 :
            return true;
         case 2 :
            return true;
         default :
            return false;
      }
   }

   public IMarkerResolution[] getResolutions(IMarker marker){
      List resolutions = new ArrayList();
      switch (getViolation(marker)) {
         case 1 :
            resolutions.add(
               new CreatePropertyKeyResolution());
            break;
```

```
            case 2 :
               resolutions.add(
                  new DeletePropertyKeyResolution());
               resolutions.add(
                  new CommentPropertyKeyResolution());
               break;
            default :
               break;
         }
      return (IMarkerResolution[]) resolutions.toArray(
         new IMarkerResolution[resolutions.size()]);
   }

   private int getViolation(IMarker marker) {
      return marker.getAttribute(
         PropertiesFileAuditor.VIOLATION,
         0);
   }
}
```

The `ViolationResolutionGenerator` class returns one or more instances of `org.eclipse.ui.IMarkerResolution2` (similar to `IMarkerResolution Generator2`, `IMarkerResolution2` was introduced in Eclipse 3.0, replacing the now deprecated `IMarkerResolution`), indicating the possible resolutions for a violation. For example, an instance of `CreatePropertyKeyResolution` is returned for missing property key violations. If the user selects this resolution, the `run(...)` method is executed, opening or activating the properties editor and appending a new property key/value pair:

```
package com.qualityeclipse.favorites.builder;

import java.io.*;
import org.eclipse.core.resources.*;
import org.eclipse.core.runtime.*;
import org.eclipse.jface.text.*;
import org.eclipse.swt.graphics.*;
import org.eclipse.ui.*;
import org.eclipse.ui.ide.*;
import org.eclipse.ui.part.*;
import org.eclipse.ui.texteditor.*;
import com.qualityeclipse.favorites.*;

public class CreatePropertyKeyResolution
   implements IMarkerResolution2
{
   public String getDescription() {
      return "Append a new property key/value pair"
         + " to the plugin.properties file";
   }

   public Image getImage() {
      return null;
   }
```

```java
public String getLabel() {
   return "Create a new property key";
}

public void run(IMarker marker) {

   // Get the corresponding plugin.properties.
   IFile file =
      marker.getResource().getParent().getFile(
         new Path("plugin.properties"));
   if (!file.exists()) {
      ByteArrayInputStream stream =
         new ByteArrayInputStream(new byte[] {});
      try {
         file.create(stream, false, null);
      }
      catch (CoreException e) {
         FavoritesLog.logError(e);
         return;
      }
   }

   // Open or activate the editor.
   IWorkbenchPage page =
      PlatformUI
         .getWorkbench()
         .getActiveWorkbenchWindow()
         .getActivePage();
   IEditorPart part;
   try {
      part = IDE.openEditor(page, file, true);
   }
   catch (PartInitException e) {
      FavoritesLog.logError(e);
      return;
   }

   // Get the editor's document.
   if (!(part instanceof ITextEditor))
      return;
   ITextEditor editor = (ITextEditor) part;
   IDocument doc =
      editor.getDocumentProvider().getDocument(
         new FileEditorInput(file));

   // Determine the text to be added.
   String key;
   try {
      key = (String) marker.getAttribute(
         PropertiesFileAuditor.KEY);
   }
   catch (CoreException e) {
      FavoritesLog.logError(e);
      return;
   }
```

```
String text = key + "=Value for " + key;

// If necessary, add a newline.
int index = doc.getLength();
if (index > 0) {
   char ch;
   try {
      ch = doc.getChar(index-1);
   }
   catch (BadLocationException e) {
      FavoritesLog.logError(e);
      return;
   }
   if (ch != '\r' || ch != '\n')
      text = System.getProperty("line.separator")
         + text;
}

// Append the new text.
try {
   doc.replace(index, 0, text);
}
catch (BadLocationException e) {
   FavoritesLog.logError(e);
   return;
}

// Select the value so the user can type.
index += text.indexOf('=') + 1;
editor.selectAndReveal(
   index,
   doc.getLength()-index);
   }
}
```

14.2.5 Finding markers

You can query a resource for all its markers or all its markers of a given type. If the resource is a container such as folder, project, or the workspace root, you can request all markers for that container's children as well. The depth can be zero (just that container), one (the container and its direct children), or infinite (the resource and all direct and indirect children). For example, to retrieve all markers associated with a folder and its children to an infinite depth, you might use an expression like this:

```
IMarker[] markers;
try {
   markers = myFolder.findMarkers(
      IMarker.PROBLEM, true, IResource.DEPTH_INFINITE);
}
catch (CoreException e) {
   // Log the exception and bail out.
}
```

14.3   Natures

A nature is used to associate a project with functionality such as a builder, a tool, or a process. A nature can also be used to determine whether or not an action should be visible (see Section 6.3.2.3, "The filter element"). Whereas a marker has only limited functionality but can be applied to any resource, a nature is designed to contain additional functionality but can only be applied to projects. A marker applies only to a resource in a single workspace, while a nature is part of a project and thus is shared by multiple developers.

The Java nature is what makes a project a Java project, distinguishing it from all other types of projects. When a nature such as the Java nature is added to a project, the project's .project file (see Section 1.4.2) is modified to include the nature's identifier (see Section 14.1.4) and the nature has the opportunity to configure the project. For example, the Java nature configures a project by adding the Java compiler as a build command. A nature also causes a project to be treated differently by the workbench; for example, only projects that possess the Java nature are displayed by the **Package Explorer** view. When a nature is removed, it has the opportunity to deconfigure or remove aspects of itself from the project. There are several natures defined within Eclipse providing various types of behavior:

org.eclipse.jdt.core.javanature–Associates the Eclipse incremental Java compiler with a project and causes the project to appear in Java-related views such as the **Package Explorer** view.

org.eclipse.pde.PluginNature–Associates the plug-in manifest and extension-point schema builders with a project, validating the content of the plugin.xml file and updating the project's Java build path based on its plug-in dependency declaration (see Section 2.3.1, "The plug-in manifest").

org.eclipse.pde.FeatureNature–Associates the feature builder with a project, validating the content of the feature.xml file (see Section 18.1.2, "Feature manifest files").

org.eclipse.pde.UpdateSiteNature–Associates the site builder with a project, validating the content of the site.xml file (see Section 18.3.2, "The site.xml file").

14.3.1   Declaring a nature

For our **Favorites** product, we want a new propertiesAuditor nature to associate our property file audit builder with a project. We begin creating a new org.eclipse.core.resources.natures extension in our **Favorites** plug-

in manifest. Switch to the **Extensions** page, click the **Add...** button, select
org.eclipse.core.resources.natures, and then click **Finish** (see Figure
14–11).

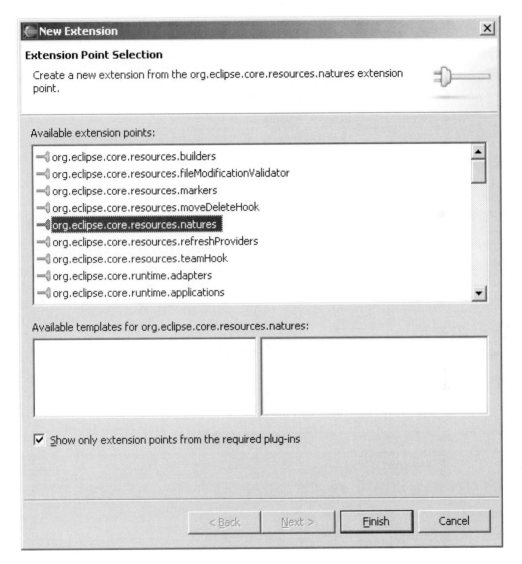

Figure 14–11 The New Extension wizard showing the org.eclipse.core.resources.natures
extension point selected.

Double-click on the new extension to open the properties file, change the
id to "propertiesAuditor", and change the name to "Favorites Properties
Auditor" (see Figure 14–12). The nature declaration should look like this:

```
<extension
    id="propertiesAuditor"
    name="Favorites Properties Auditor"
    point="org.eclipse.core.resources.natures">
</extension>
```

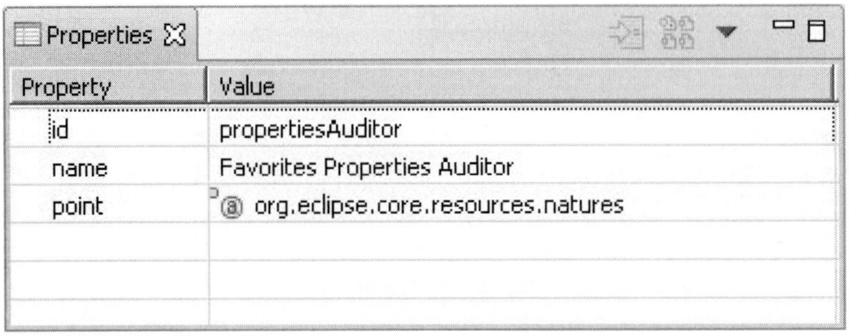

Figure 14–12   The Properties view showing the nature's attributes.

Similar to build declarations, the nature declaration contains the nature's local identifier. The nature's full identifier is the plug-in identifier containing the nature concatenated with the nature's local identifier, or in our case, com.qualityeclipse.favorites.propertiesAuditor.

14.3.2   Associating builders and natures

Now we want to associate our builder with our nature. Right-click on the org.eclipse.core.resources.natures extension point and select **New > builder.** In the **Properties** view, enter the builder id, which in our case is "com.qualityeclipse.favorites.propertiesFileAuditor" (see Figure 14–13).

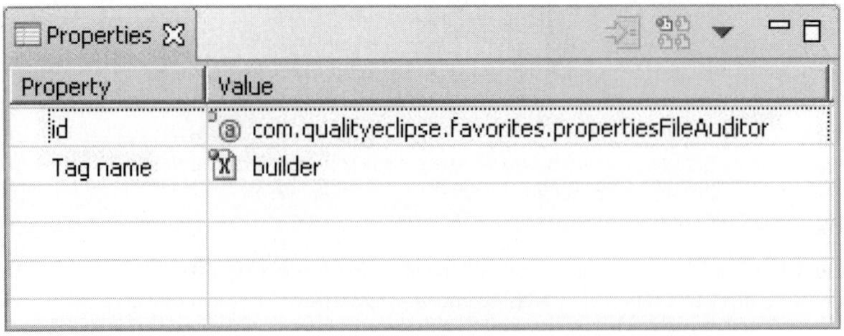

Figure 14–13   The Properties view showing the builder's attributes.

In addition, return to the builder declaration (see Section 14.1.1) and modify the `hasNature` attribute to be "true". Once this has been accomplished, the nature declaration should look like this:

```
<extension
   id="propertiesAuditor"
   name="Favorites Properties Auditor"
   point="org.eclipse.core.resources.natures">
   <builder id="com.qualityeclipse.favorites
      .propertiesFileAuditor"/>
</extension>
```

These changes ensure that our builder will be omitted from a project's build process if our nature is not associated with the project. If you want your builder to work regardless of whether or not your nature is present, then omit this from your nature's declaration.

14.3.3   IProjectNature

Natures can have behavior to configure and deconfigure a project. Similar to the Java nature, we want our nature to add our builder to the project's build spec. Right-click on the `org.eclipse.core.resources.natures` extension point and select **New > runtime**, then right-click on the `(runtime)` nested element and select **New > run**. In the **Properties** view, click on the "..." button at the right of the **class** field, then use the **Java Attribute Editor** to generate a new class named `PropertiesAuditorNature` in the package `com.qualityeclipse.favorites.builder`. When this is complete, the nature declaration should look like this:

```
<extension
   id="propertiesAuditor"
   name="Favorites Properties Auditor"
   point="org.eclipse.core.resources.natures">
   <builder id="com.qualityeclipse.favorites
      .propertiesFileAuditor"/>
   <runtime>
      <run class="com.qualityeclipse.favorites.builder
         .PropertiesAuditorNature"/>
   </runtime>
</extension>
```

The class specified in the nature declaration must implement `org.eclipse.core.resources.IProjectNature`. When the nature is added to a project, this class is instantiated and the `setProject(...)` method is called, followed by the `configure()` method; the `deconfigure()` method is called when the nature is removed from a project.

Similar to the Java nature, we want our nature to add our builder to the project's build spec via the `addBuilderToProject(...)` method (see Section 14.1.4) and trigger a build in the background (see Section 20.8, "Jobs API") when the project is configured. When the nature is removed from the project, the build spec is modified and all audit markers are removed.

```java
package com.qualityeclipse.favorites.builder;

import org.eclipse.core.resources.*;
import org.eclipse.core.runtime.*;

public class PropertiesAuditorNature
    implements IProjectNature
{
    private IProject project;

    public IProject getProject() {
        return project;
    }

    public void setProject(IProject project) {
        this.project = project;
    }

    public void configure() throws CoreException {
        PropertiesFileAuditor.addBuilderToProject(project);
        new Job("Properties File Audit") {
            protected IStatus run(IProgressMonitor monitor) {
                try {
                    project.build(
                        PropertiesFileAuditor.FULL_BUILD,
                        PropertiesFileAuditor.BUILDER_ID,
                        null,
                        monitor);
                }
                catch (CoreException e) {
                    FavoritesLog.logError(e);
                }
                return Status.OK_STATUS;
            }
        }.schedule();
    }

    public void deconfigure() throws CoreException {
        PropertiesFileAuditor
            .removeBuilderFromProject(project);
        PropertiesFileAuditor.deleteAuditMarkers(project);
    }
}
```

14.3.4 Required natures

A dependency of one nature on another nature can be expressed in the nature's declaration (see Section 14.3.1, "Declaring a nature"). When the required nature is not present or not enabled, Eclipse disables the nature having the requirement. For example, our `propertiesAuditor` nature depends on the Java nature and PDE nature. If we were to express this in our nature's declaration, it would look like this:

```
<extension
    id="propertiesAuditor"
    name="Favorites Properties Auditor"
    point="org.eclipse.core.resources.natures">
    <builder id="com.qualityeclipse.favorites
        .propertiesFileAuditor">
    </builder>
    <runtime>
        <run class="com.qualityeclipse.favorites.builder
            .PropertiesAuditorNature"/>
    </runtime>
    <requires-nature id="org.eclipse.jdt.core.javanature"/>
    <requires-nature id="org.eclipse.pde.PluginNature"/>
</extension>
```

14.3.5 Conflicting natures

The conflict of one nature with one or more other natures can also be expressed in the nature's declaration. In our nature's declaration, we add a one-of-nature nested element specifying the name of a set of natures. If any other nature specifies the same string in a one-of-nature nested element and is added to the same project as our nature, then Eclipse will disable both natures.

```
<extension
    id="propertiesAuditor"
    name="Favorites Properties Auditor"
    point="org.eclipse.core.resources.natures">
    <builder id="com.qualityeclipse.favorites
        .propertiesFileAuditor">
    </builder>
    <runtime>
        <run class="com.qualityeclipse.favorites.builder
            .PropertiesAuditorNature"/>
    </runtime>
    <requires-nature id="org.eclipse.jdt.core.javanature"/>
    <requires-nature id="org.eclipse.pde.PluginNature"/>
    <one-of-nature id="pluginAuditors">
</extension>
```

14.3.6 Nature image

A project nature can have an image associated with it using the org.eclipse.ui.ide.projectNatureImages extension point. The specified image is displayed over the top right corner of the standard project image. For example, the org.eclipse.jdt.ui plug-in associates an image of a "J" with the Java nature so that the icon for all Java projects has a small blue "J" in the top right corner.

```
<extension point="org.eclipse.ui.ide.projectNatureImages">
   <image
      icon="icons/full/ovr16/java_ovr.gif"
      natureId="org.eclipse.jdt.core.javanature"
      id="org.eclipse.ui.javaProjectNatureImage"/>
</extension>
```

Our nature does not define the type of project so much as associate our properties audit tool with the project, so it is not appropriate for us to supply a project nature image.

14.3.7 Associating a nature with a project

Similar to associating a builder with a project (see Section 14.1.4), you can associate a nature with a project by modifying the project's description. To demonstrate this, we'll build an action delegate that toggles the properties-Auditor nature for a project. First, create an action declaration to add a new command in the top-level **Favorites** menu (see Section 6.2.1, "Defining a workbench window menu"):

```
<extension point="org.eclipse.ui.actionSets">
   <actionSet
      label="Favorites ActionSet"
      visible="true"
      id="com.qualityeclipse.favorites.workbenchActionSet">
      ...
      <action
         label="Add/Remove propertiesAuditor
            project nature"
         class="com.qualityeclipse.favorites.actions
            .ToggleProjectNatureActionDelegate"
         menubarPath="com.qualityeclipse.favorites
            .workbenchMenu/content"
         id="com.qualityeclipse.favorites
            .toggleProjectNature"\>
   </actionSet>
</extension>
```

Next, create an action delegate (see Section 6.2.6) that checks the natures associated with each selected project and adds the `propertiesAuditor` nature to each selected project that does not have that nature associated with it and removes that nature from all other selected projects. Typically, a nature is added to or removed from a project as part of a larger process such as creating a Java project, but this action delegate suffices to show the mechanics of how it is accomplished.

```java
package com.qualityeclipse.favorites.actions;

import java.util.*;
import org.eclipse.core.resources.*;
import org.eclipse.core.runtime.*;
import org.eclipse.jface.action.*;
import org.eclipse.jface.viewers.*;
import org.eclipse.ui.*;
import com.qualityeclipse.favorites.*;

public class ToggleProjectNatureActionDelegate
    implements IWorkbenchWindowActionDelegate
{
    private static final String NATURE_ID =
        FavoritesPlugin.getDefault().getDescriptor()
            .getUniqueIdentifier() + ".propertiesAuditor";

    private ISelection selection;

    public void init(IWorkbenchWindow window) {
        // Ignored.
    }

    public void selectionChanged(
        IAction action,
        ISelection selection)
    {
        this.selection = selection;
    }

    public void run(IAction action) {
        if (!(selection instanceof IStructuredSelection))
            return;
        Iterator iter =
            ((IStructuredSelection) selection).iterator();
        while (iter.hasNext()) {
            Object element = iter.next();
            if (!(element instanceof IProject))
                continue;
            IProject project = (IProject) element;

            // Cannot modify closed projects.
            if (!project.isOpen())
                continue;
```

```
        // Get the description.
        IProjectDescription description;
        try {
            description = project.getDescription();
        }
        catch (CoreException e) {
            FavoritesLog.logError(e);
            continue;
        }

        // Toggle the nature.
        List newIds = new ArrayList();
        newIds.addAll(
            Arrays.asList(description.getNatureIds()));
        int index = newIds.indexOf(NATURE_ID);
        if (index == -1)
            newIds.add(NATURE_ID);
        else
            newIds.remove(index);
        description.setNatureIds(
            (String[]) newIds.toArray(
                new String[newIds.size()]));

        // Save the description.
        try {
            project.setDescription(description, null);
        }
        catch (CoreException e) {
            FavoritesLog.logError(e);
        }
    }
}

public void dispose() {
}
}
```

14.4   RFWS Considerations

The "Build" section of the *RFWS Requirements* includes six items—three requirements and three best practices—dealing with builders.

14.4.1   *Use builders to convert resources*

Requirement #1 states:

> *Any product that converts resources from one format into another where the resources are synchronized, such as compilers, must use the build APIs and* org.eclipse.core.resources.builders *extension point.*

To pass this requirement, start by showing your builder in action. Describe how it is invoked and what resources it transforms. Turn off the

Workbench > Perform build automatically on resource modification preference and show that your builder does not run. Invoke the **Project > Rebuild Project** command to show that your builder correctly processes any accumulated changes.

14.4.2   Builders must be added by natures

Requirement #2 states:

A builder must be added to a project by a nature. The nature implementation, as identified in the `org.eclipse.core.resources.natures` *extension, will add any builders required as part of the configure() method.*

For this test, show your nature definition in the `plugin.xml` file. Create a project with your nature and demonstrate that the builder is automatically configured. Add your nature to an existing project's `.project` file and show that your builder is invoked as soon as the file is saved.

14.4.3   Do not replace existing builders

Requirement #3 states:

Plug-ins cannot replace the builders associated with project natures provided by the workbench, or by other vendors.

Start by configuring a project to use your builder. Open the project's `.project` file to show that your builder has been added and that none of the existing builders (such as `org.eclipse.jdt.core.javabuilder`) have been removed.

14.4.4   Do not misuse the term "build"

Best Practice #4 states:

The term "build" should not be overloaded to have a meaning other than build processing triggered using the workbench build APIs. That is, do not use the term "build" in your product implementation or documentation to describe a process that is not implemented as a builder in the workbench.

Show any places in your product documentation where the term "build" is used and confirm that any such uses are related to your plug-in's builders.

14.4.5   Mark builder-created resources as "derived"

Best Practice #5 states:

Resources created by builders should be identified as derived when they are not source (as in `.java`*), or some other type of artifact that can be or will* *be modified by the user, or are required for deployment to a run-time platform.*

For this test, demonstrate that any resources created by your builder are marked as derived. In the case of a `.class` file created by the Java compiler, we would open the **Properties** dialog and show that the **Derived** option has been checked (see Figure 14–14).

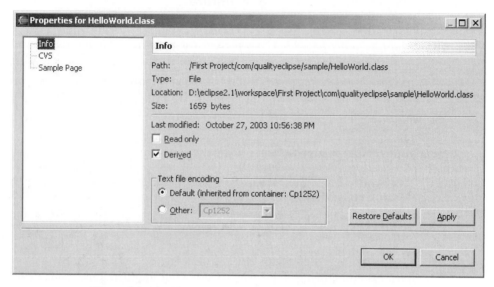

Figure 14–14   The Properties dialog for the HelloWorld.class file.

14.4.6   *Use IResourceProxy objects when possible*

Best Practice #6 states:

Builders often need to process all the resources in a project when an `IncrementalProjectBuilder.FULL_BUILD` *has been requested. There is an improved technique available starting with Eclipse 2.1. An* `IResourceProxyVisitor` *should be used in place of an* `IResourceVisitor`. *The proxy visitor provides access to lightweight* `IResourceProxy` *objects. These can return a real* `IResource` *object when required, but when not required, they result in improved overall builder performance for full builds.*

To pass this test, you should avoid using `IResourceVisitor` objects and use `IResourceProxyVistor` objects instead. Search your plug-in source code for references to `IResourceVisitor` and explain why `IResourceProxyVistor` could not be used instead.

14.5 Summary

In this chapter, we went into detail about how to create builders, markers, and natures. Builders execute in response to resource changes within a project. Builders can create new, derived resources or tag existing resources with markers. Markers are used to tag locations within a resource, while natures are used to tag entire projects and configure any associated builders.

References

Arthorne, John, "Project Builders and Natures," IBM OTI Labs, 2003 (*www.eclipse.org/articles/Article-Builders/builders.html*).

Glozic, Dejan and Jeff McAffer, "Mark My Words," IBM OTI Labs, 2001 (*www.eclipse.org/articles/Article-Mark%20My%20Words/Mark%20My%20Words.html*).

CHAPTER 15

Implementing Help

No matter how wonderful and easy-to-use your plug-in might be, eventually, your users will have questions about how some feature works or they might want further detail on some operation or setting. Fortunately, Eclipse provides a comprehensive framework for including online help within your applications.

In this chapter, we will begin with an overview of how to access the Eclipse help system and then follow up with a discussion of how to implement help for your application. After that, we will discuss how to add context-sensitive (F1) help and finish up with a discussion of how to programmatically access the help system.

15.1 Using Help

Users can access your full product documentation via the **Help > Help Contents** menu (see Figure 15–1).

Figure 15–1   The Eclipse Help menu.

This will open the Eclipse **Help** window (see Figure 15–2). The Eclipse **Help** window is separate from the Eclipse workbench window, which makes it easy to switch back and forth between the two. In early versions of Eclipse, the **Help** window was originally implemented as its own perspective. This made it difficult to access the help system while working with various workbench facilities (especially modal dialogs or wizards).

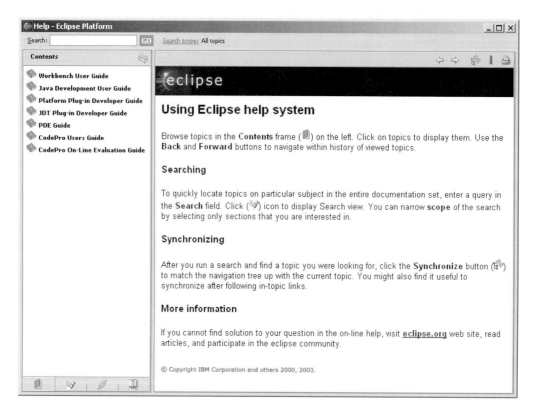

Figure 15–2   The Eclipse Help window.

The **Help** window has several major components. At the upper left is a **Search** field. Entering a search term and clicking the **Go** button will cause the help system to search all the help topics in the system. Quoting the search term causes an "exact match" search rather than the default "stemmed search." A *stemmed search* uses word roots and will yield more hits than an exact match search, but it is not as helpful when searching for an exact word or phrase.

At the right of the **Search** field is a link used to set the search scope. Clicking on the **Search scope** link will open the **Select Search Scope** dialog (see Figure 15–3).

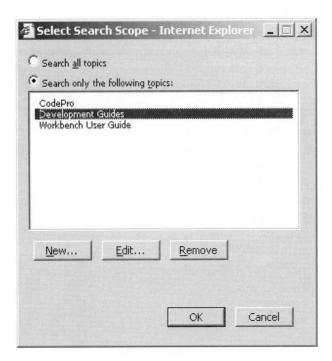

Figure 15–3 The Select Search Scope dialog.

Within this dialog, you can choose to search all available topics or select a set of topics defined as a working set. Clicking the **New** button in the dialog will allow you to create a new working set composed of top-level help topics (see Figure 15–4).

Figure 15–4   The Edit Search List dialog.

Below the search fields, you will find a list of top-level help books available in the system. Here you will find built-in help books such as the Eclipse **Workbench User Guide** and **Platform Plug-in Developer Guide**, as well as books contributed by other plug-ins. Each book can be expanded to show its individual help topics. Selecting a help topic will display that help page in the content area to the right of the topic list (see Figure 15–5).

Figure 15–5   The Help window showing a selected help topic.

15.2   Implementing Help

Eclipse provides the infrastructure necessary to plug your own help documentation into the environment. Eclipse doesn't care how the help files are created
and will happily use content created in HTML or PDF format (you can even
create dynamic, "active," help if you want to). Your help can either be integrated into your main plug-in or it can be placed into its own standalone plug-
in (this is the common practice in the base Eclipse plug-ins).

After you have your help content created, assuming simple Hypertext
Markup Language (HTML) files for the moment, integrating them into
Eclipse involves four simple steps:

1. Create a new plug-in project to contain your help plug-in.

2. Set up your help file directory structure within the project.

3. Update the table of contents (toc) files to reference your help files.

4. Update the plug-in manifest to reference the toc files.

15.2.1   *Creating a new help project*

Due to the power of the Eclipse project creation wizards, most of the files needed to set up your help project can be generated automatically. We will begin by using the **New Project** wizard to create a new **Plug-in Project** (see Figure 15–6). There are quite a few steps in creating a project, but they are worth the time given how much of the project structure will be created automatically.

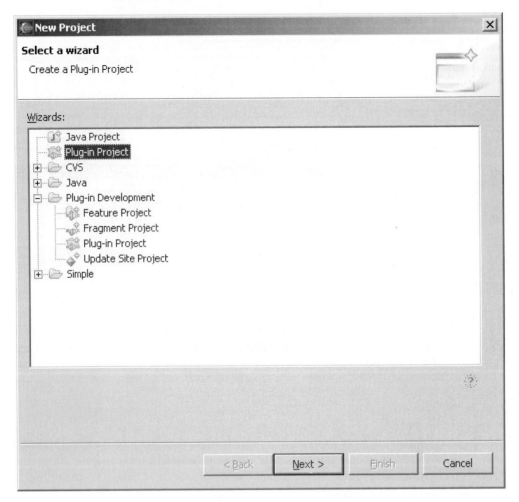

Figure 15–6   The New Project wizard.

On the first page of the **New Plug-in Project** wizard (see Figure 15–7), enter "com.qualityeclipse.favorites.help" as the project name. We will leave the **Use default** checkbox checked so that the project is created within our default workspace.

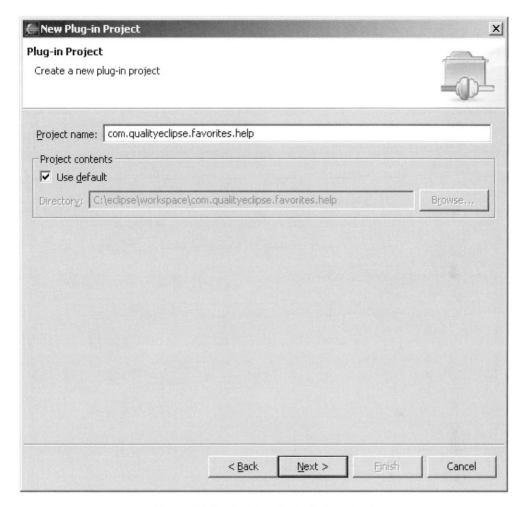

Figure 15–7   The New Plug-in Project wizard.

On the second page of the wizard (see Figure 15–8), select the **Create a simple project** option. Since we don't want any Java files to be created, this is the correct choice.

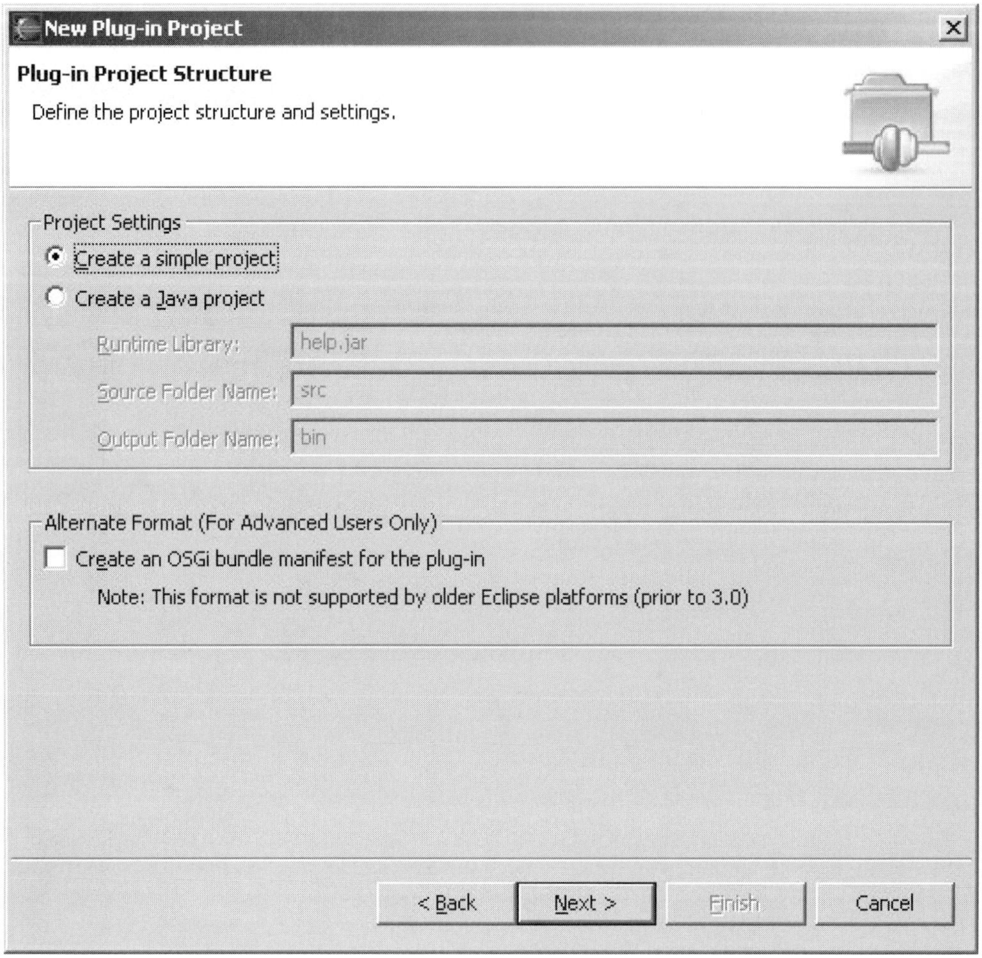

Figure 15–8   The Plug-in Project Structure page.

On the third page of the wizard (see Figure 15–9), leave the plug-in ID as "com.qualityeclipse.favorites.help", and change the name to "Favorites Help." Since we selected the simple project option and don't plan to execute any Java code, there is no need for a plug-in startup class.

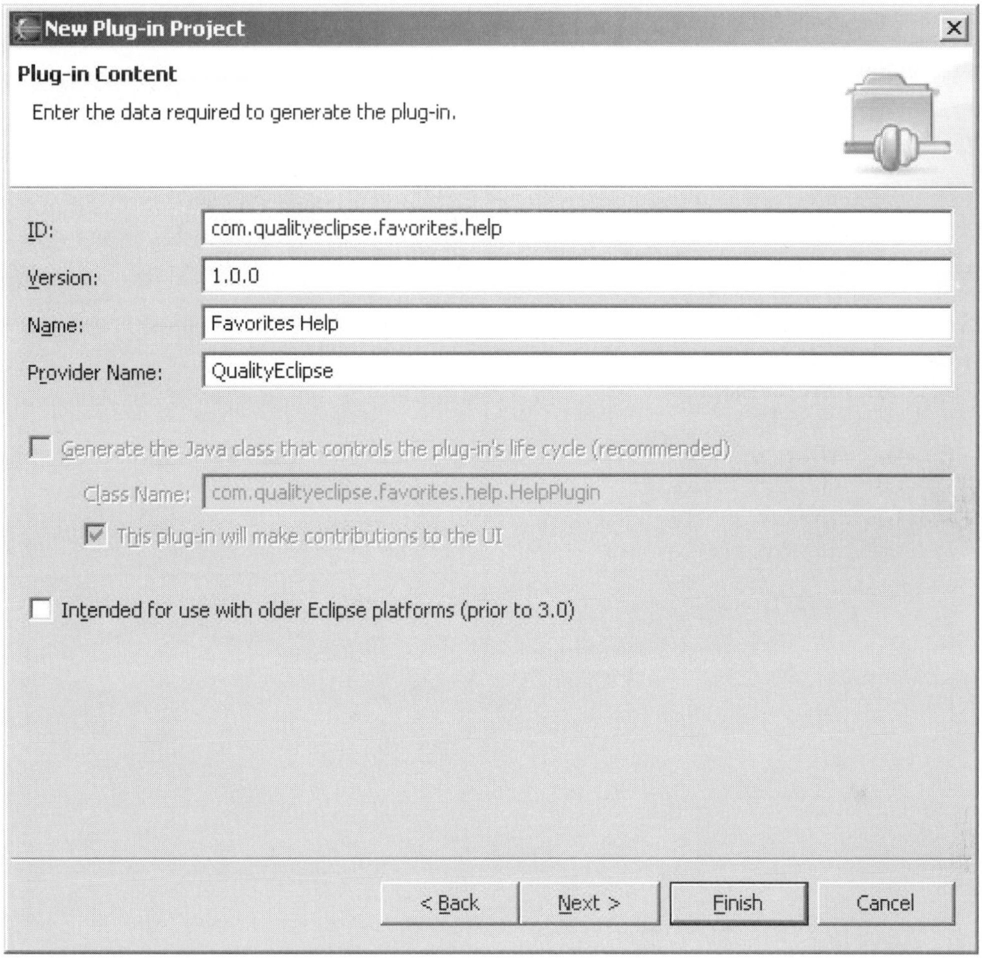

Figure 15–9   The Plug-in Content page.

On the next page of the wizard (see Figure 15–10), select the **Create a plug-in project using a code generation wizard** option. In the list of **Available code generation wizards**, select the **Custom plug-in wizard** option. This will take us to a page that will allow us to create many of the needed project files.

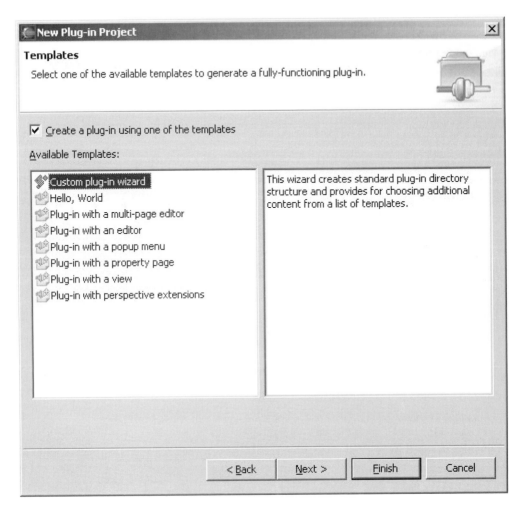

Figure 15–10   The Templates page.

On the **Template Selection** page of the wizard (see Figure 15–11), select
the **Help Table of Contents** option. This will create a default table of contents
(toc) file, as well as any needed secondary toc files.

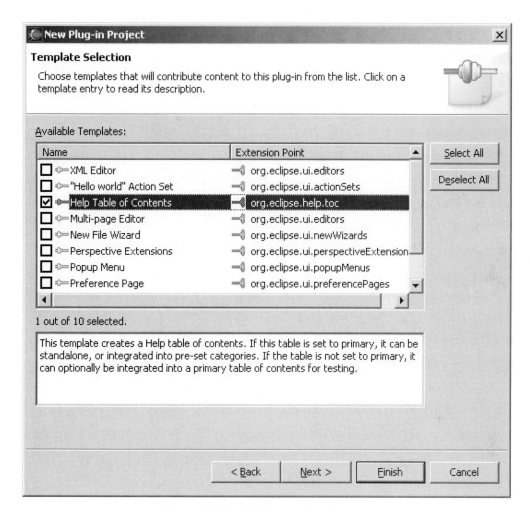

Figure 15–11   The Template Selection page.

On the next and final (whew!) page of the wizard (see Figure 15–12), set the **Label for table of contents** field to "Favorites Guide". This is the name of the book that will show up as a top-level item in the **Help** window's contents pane. Next, select the **Primary** option. This will create a primary toc file. Primary toc files represent the top-level items in the **Help** window. Any number of toc files may exist in the project, but they will all be subordinate to one or more primary toc files.

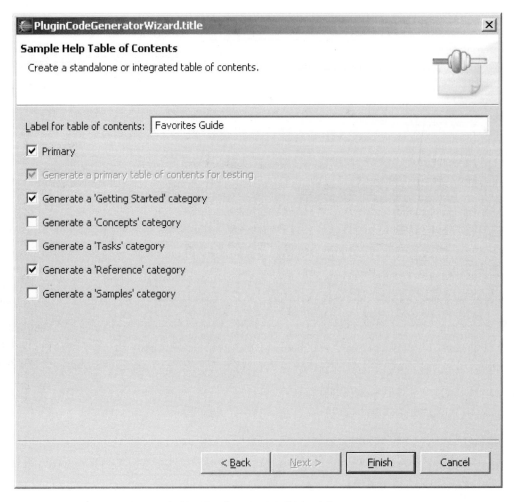

Figure 15–12   The Sample Help Table of Contents page.

Finally, we are given the choice of creating one or more of several pre-defined secondary toc files covering major topic areas within our help documentation. Creating secondary toc files is optional. All your help files may be easily referenced from your main toc file. Partitioning your help using multiple secondary toc files provides more granularity and makes it easier for multiple people to update different parts of the documentation without colliding. We'll select the options for creating "Getting Started" and "Reference" categories to illustrate how the various files are structured. Click **Finish** to complete the process and generate all the files (finally!).

15.2.2   *Plug-in manifest files*

Given the options selected earlier, a variety of files will be created, including several dummy HTML files and four XML files: `plugin.xml`, `toc.xml`, `tocgettingstarted.xml`, and `tocreference.xml`. The plug-in manifest file will look like this:

```
<?xml version="1.0" encoding="UTF-8"?>
<?eclipse version="3.0"?>
<plugin
   id="com.qualityeclipse.favorites.help"
   name="Favorites Help"
   version="1.0.0"
   provider-name="QualityEclipse">

   <requires>
      <import plugin="org.eclipse.help"/>
   </requires>

   <extension
       point="org.eclipse.help.toc">
      <toc
          file="toc.xml"
          primary="true">
      </toc>
      <toc
          file="tocgettingstarted.xml">
      </toc>
      <toc
          file="tocreference.xml">
      </toc>
   </extension>
</plugin>
```

The most important thing here is the extension of the **org.eclipse.help.toc** extension point. This extension point is used to specify the primary and secondary toc files. The `file` attribute is used to specify the names of the toc files that will be used, while the `primary` attribute indicates whether an individual toc file should appear as a top-level book in the help topics list in the **Help** window. Any toc files without the `primary` attribute set to `true` will not show up unless they are linked to from one or more of the primary toc files.

The **org.eclipse.help.toc** extension point also defines an additional, rarely used `extradir` attribute that specifies the name of a directory that contains additional documentation files. Unless they are referenced by a specific topic element in one of the toc files, these files won't be accessible via the topics list, but they will be indexed and accessible via the help search facility.

15.2.3   *Table of contents (toc) files*

Next, we will take a look at a couple of the generated toc files. The `toc.xml` file represents the primary help topic entry for the plug-in and looks like this:

```xml
<?xml version="1.0" encoding="UTF-8"?>
<?NLS TYPE="org.eclipse.help.toc"?>

<toc label="Favorites Guide" topic="html/toc.html">
   <topic label="Getting Started">
      <anchor id="gettingstarted"/>
   </topic>
   <topic label="Reference">
      <anchor id="reference"/>
   </topic>
</toc>
```

Within the toc file, the `label` attributes specify the text that is displayed in the topic list, while the `topic` attribute specifies a link to a single documentation page that should be displayed when that topic is selected.

The structure of this toc file illustrates how the help topic tree can be built out of multiple, nested toc files. Eclipse supports two different approaches to building the help topic tree: top-down nesting and bottom-up composition. The aforementioned toc file illustrates the latter. In bottom-up composition, the toc file will define various *anchor points* to which other toc files can contribute additional topics.

Here, we have defined two subtopics for our documentation, "Getting Started" and "Reference," each of which defines an anchor point (essentially an empty container for other toc files to fill). Note that each of these subtopics could have also defined its own hard-coded documentation links (we will see an example of this in the next toc file we examine).

Next, we will examine one of the two remaining toc files (both follow the same pattern, so we only need to look at one of them). The `tocgettingstarted.xml` file looks like this:

```xml
<?xml version="1.0" encoding="UTF-8"?>
<?NLS TYPE="org.eclipse.help.toc"?>

<toc label="Getting Started"
   link_to="toc.xml#gettingstarted">
   <topic label="Main Topic"
      href="html/gettingstarted/maintopic.html">
      <topic label="Sub Topic"
         href="html/gettingstarted/subtopic.html" />
   </topic>
   <topic label="Main Topic 2">
      <topic label="Sub Topic 2"
         href="html/gettingstarted/subtopic2.html" />
   </topic>
</toc>
```

This toc file provides topic links to the actual HTML files representing the plug-in's documentation using the `href` attributes (we will replace the default boilerplate generated by the wizard with links to our documentation files later). The most interesting aspect of this toc file is the use of the `link_to` attribute to link this file to the `gettingstarted` anchor in the main toc file.

> **Tip:** Note that your plug-in help pages are not limited to only linking in to your own anchor points. The core Eclipse documentation provides numerous anchor points to which you can attach your help files. If your plug-in augments one of the basic Eclipse functions, linking your help pages to the appropriate section of the Eclipse docs is a nice touch.

Both of the toc files we have just reviewed provide an example of bottom-up composition with the secondary toc files linking to the primary toc file while the primary toc file has no knowledge of the secondary toc files. This approach closely mirrors the extension point concept used within Eclipse. The opposite approach of top-down nesting switches this around such that the main toc file will directly link to the secondary toc files.

Converting these two toc files to use the top-down approach is simple. First, we replace the `anchor` attributes in the primary toc file with `link` attributes pointing to the secondary toc files. The `toc.xml` file will now look like this:

```
<?xml version="1.0" encoding="UTF-8"?>
<?NLS TYPE="org.eclipse.help.toc"?>

<toc label="Favorites Guide" topic="html/toc.html">
   <topic label="Getting Started">
      <link toc="tocgettingstarted.xml"/>
   </topic>
   <topic label="Reference">
      <link toc="tocreference.xml"/>
   </topic>
</toc>
```

Next, we can remove the `link_to` attribute from the secondary toc files as it is no longer needed.

The top-down approach provides better control over and visibility of which files are included in the help documentation and does not provide any opportunities for other entities to augment the help provided by the plug-in. Conversely, the bottom-up approach provides a great deal of flexibility in structuring the help documentation and organically growing it over time with additional contributions both from within and outside the plug-in.

Internationalization   If your application needs to support multiple languages, your toc files and documentation files may be translated into multiple languages and placed into specially named subdirectories of your plug-in's root directory (for more information, see Chapter 16, "Internationalization").

The translated files should be placed into the nl/<language> or nl/<language>/<country> directory, where <language> and <country> represent the two-letter codes used to signify the target language and country. For example, Brazilian translations would be placed into the nl/pt/br directory, while standard Portuguese translations would be placed into the nl/pt directory.

The help system will first look in the nl/<language>/<country> directory. If nothing is found there, the nl/<language> will be used instead. If no translation for the target language is found, it will default to using the files found in the root of the plug-in directory.

15.2.4   Creating HTML content

In addition to the XML files, the wizard creates several dummy HTML files:

```
html/
    gettingstarted/
       maintopic.html
       subtopic.html
       subtopic2.html
    reference/
       maintopic.html
       subtopic.html
       subtopic2.html
    toc.html
```

Assuming that we create our own documentation files for the **Favorites** view with the following structure:

```
html/
    gettingstarted/
       installation.html
       favorites_view.html
       adding_favorites.html
       removing_favorites.html
    reference/
       view.html
       actions.html
       preferences.html
    toc.html
```

we would need to update the two secondary toc files. The `tocgetting-started.xml` file, for example, would end up looking like this:

```xml
<?xml version="1.0" encoding="UTF-8"?>
<?NLS TYPE="org.eclipse.help.toc"?>

<toc label="Getting Started">
  <topic label="Installation"
    href="html/gettingstarted/installation.html"/>
<topic label="Favorites View"
    href="html/gettingstarted/favorites_view.html"/>
    <topic label="Adding Favorites"
      href="html/gettingstarted/adding_favorites.html" />
    <topic label="Removing Favorites"
      href="html/gettingstarted/removing_favorites.html" />
  </topic>
</toc>
```

> **Tip:** If your application needs more than a handful of help files, you might consider placing all of them into a single ZIP file. If you package your help files into a file called `doc.zip` (preserving the same directory structure), Eclipse will be able to find them. Eclipse will look for help files in the `doc.zip` file before looking for them in the plug-in directory.

With these changes, our help plug-in is functionally complete! Launching Eclipse with this new help plug-in in place will add our "Favorites Guide" to the list of books in the **Help** window (see Figure 15–13).

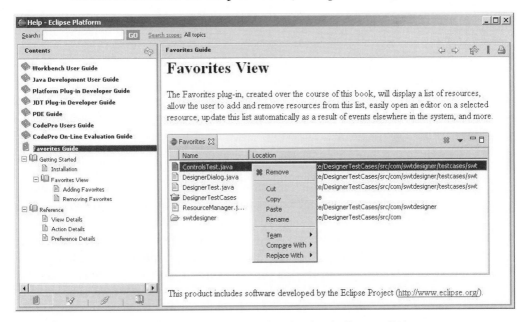

Figure 15–13   The Help window showing the *Favorites Guide*.

15.3 Context-Sensitive "Infopop" Help (F1)

Eclipse provides support for context-sensitive "infopop" help for widgets, windows, actions, and menus using the **F1** key. The infopop window that appears may contain a small amount of context-sensitive help for the selected item as well as links to more detailed documentation. For example, opening the Eclipse **Hierarchy** view and pressing **F1** will open an infopop window (see Figure 15–14) containing links relevant to the **Hierarchy** view as well as views in general.

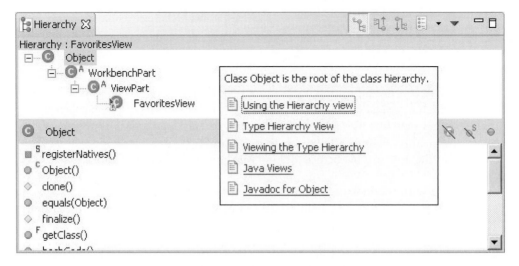

Figure 15–14   The Hierarchy view showing its associated infopop window.

In general, to add infopop help to an item, you need to associate a context ID with the item, provide a short description of the item, and create a list of links relevant to the item.

15.3.1 Associating context IDs with items

Whenever a user opens the **Favorites** view and presses **F1**, we would like an infopop window to appear. First, we need to associate a context ID with the view using the `setHelp()` method from `org.eclipse.ui.help.WorkbenchHelp`.

The context ID is a string with the form `<plug-in_id>.<local_context_id>`, where `<plug-in_id>` is the unique plug-in identifier for the plug-in defining the workbench view or editor and `<local_context_id>` is an identifier unique within that plug-in identifying the context. The `<local_context_id>` can be composed of any alphanumeric characters and underscore ("_"), but must not contain any whitespace or periods ("."). In our case,

the <plug-in_id> is "com.qualityeclipse.favorites" and we have chosen a
<local_context_id> of "favorites_view" for our **Favorites** view, so our context ID is "com.qualityeclipse.favorites.favorites_view".

Since the **Favorites** view consists of a single table widget, we will associate
the help context ID with the table widget itself. Begin by creating a setHelp-
ContextIDs() method in the FavoritesView class that looks like this:

```
// FavoritesView.java
private void setHelpContextIDs() {
   WorkbenchHelp.setHelp(
      viewer.getControl(),
      "com.qualityeclipse.favorites.favorites_view");
}
```

We can then call this method from the existing createPartControl()
method in the FavoritesView class.

Help contexts are inherited by child controls. In our case, we assigned a help
context to the **Favorites** viewer control, which has no children. If you assign a
help context to a composite, then its children inherit the same help context
unless you specifically override it by calling setHelp() on a child control.

The **Favorites** view also defines several different actions with which we
would like to associate help context IDs. We will do this by enhancing the
setHelpContextIDs() method as follows:

```
private void setHelpContextIDs() {
   // Assign a comtext ID to the view
   WorkbenchHelp.setHelp(viewer.getControl(),
      "com.qualityeclipse.favorites.favorites_view");
   // Assign context IDs to the actions.
   WorkbenchHelp.setHelp(copyAction,
      "com.qualityeclipse.favorites.copyAction");
   WorkbenchHelp.setHelp(cutAction,
      "com.qualityeclipse.favorites.cutAction");
   WorkbenchHelp.setHelp(pasteAction,
      "com.qualityeclipse.favorites.pasteAction");
   WorkbenchHelp.setHelp(removeAction,
      "com.qualityeclipse.favorites.removeAction");
   WorkbenchHelp.setHelp(renameAction,
      "com.qualityeclipse.favorites.renameAction");
}
```

Help context IDs may also be assigned to actions defined within the plug-
in manifest file by defining a helpContextId attribute. For example, we can
enhance the definition of the "Open Favorites View" action like this:

```
<action
   label="Open Favorites View"
   icon="icons/sample.gif"
```

```
tooltip="Open the favorites view in
        the current workbench page"
class="com.qualityeclipse.favorites.actions.
        OpenFavoritesViewActionDelegate"
menubarPath="com.qualityeclipse.favorites.
            workbenchMenu/content"
toolbarPath="Normal/additions"
helpContextId="favorites_view"
id="com.qualityeclipse.favorites.openFavoritesView">
</action>
```

Note that if local context identifiers are used in the plug-in manifest, then the unique identifier for the declaring plug-in is prepended to make the full context identifier.

15.3.2   *WorkbenchHelp API*

The `WorkbenchHelp` class defines a number of useful static APIs for assigning help context IDs and programmatically displaying help, such as:

`createHelpListener(ICommand command)`—Creates a new help listener for the given command.

`displayContext(IContext context, int x, int y)`—Displays context-sensitive help for the given context.

`displayHelp()`—Displays the entire help bookshelf.

`displayHelp(IContext context)`—Displays context-sensitive help for the given context.

`displayHelp(String contextId)`—Calls the help support system to display the given help context ID.

`displayHelpResource(String href)`—Displays the help content for the help resource with the given uniform resource locator (URL).

`isContextHelpDisplayed()`—Returns whether the context-sensitive help window is currently being displayed.

`setHelp(Control control, String contextId)`—Sets the given help context ID on the given control.

`setHelp(IAction action, String contextId)`—Sets the given help context ID on the given action.

`setHelp(MenuItem item, String contextId)`—Sets the given help context ID on the given menu item.

`setHelp(Menu menu, String contextId)`—Sets the given help context ID on the given menu.

15.3.3   Creating infopop content

When context IDs have been assigned to views, we need to create the content for each infopop, which consists of a description and a set of links. This content is described in one or more context manifest files in XML format. For the items we assigned context IDs to in the previous section, the `contexts.xml` file might look like this:

```
<contexts>
   <context
      id="favorites_view">
      <description>This is the Favorites view.</description>
      <topic href="html/gettingstarted/favorites_view.html"
         label="Using the Favorites View"/>
      <topic href="html/gettingstarted/installation.html"
         label="Installing the Favorites View"/>
      <topic href="html/reference/preferences.html"
         label="Favorites View Preferences"/>
   </context>
   <context id="copyAction">
      <description>
         This command copies a Favorites item from the view.
      </description>
      <topic href="html/gettingstarted/actions.html"
         label="Favorites View Actions"/>
   </context>
   <context id="cutAction">
      <description>
         This command cuts a Favorites item from the view.
      </description>
      <topic href="html/gettingstarted/actions.html"
         label="Favorites View Actions"/>
   </context>
   <context id="pasteAction">
      <description>
         This command pastes a Favorites item to the view.
      </description>
      <topic href="html/gettingstarted/actions.html"
         label="Favorites View Actions"/>
   </context>
   <context id="removeAction">
      <description>
         This command removes a Favorites item.
      </description>
      <topic href="html/gettingstarted/actions.html"
         label="Favorites View Actions"/>
   </context>
   <context id="renameAction">
      <description>
         This command renames a Favorites item.
      </description>
      <topic href="html/gettingstarted/actions.html"
         label="Favorites View Actions"/>
   </context>
</contexts>
```

Within the `contexts.xml` file, each context ID is described by its own *context element*. Each context element has a *description element* and zero or more *topic elements* that link to the actual documentation. Each topic element has an `href` attribute providing the link and a `label` attribute describing the text of the link, as it will appear in the infopop.

15.3.4 *Context Extension Point*

Now that context IDs have been associated with our view and actions, and context for each infopop has been defined, we need to update our `plugin.xml` file to point to our `contexts.xml` file and associate it with our main plug-in. The built-in Eclipse wizards make this easy.

Start by opening the `plugin.xml` file in our help project and switching to the **Extensions** page (see Figure 15–15). Next, click the **Add** button.

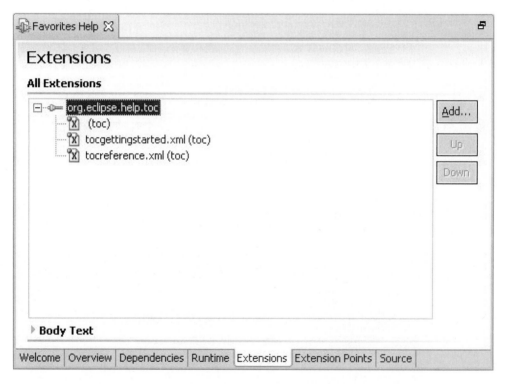

Figure 15–15 The Favorites Help manifest file showing the Extensions page.

When the **New Extension** wizard opens, select `org.eclipse.help.contexts` from the list of all available extension points (see Figure 15–16). If you don't see `org.eclipse.help.contexts` in the list, uncheck the **Show only**

extension points from the required plug-ins checkbox. Click the **Finish** button to add this extension to the plug-in manifest.

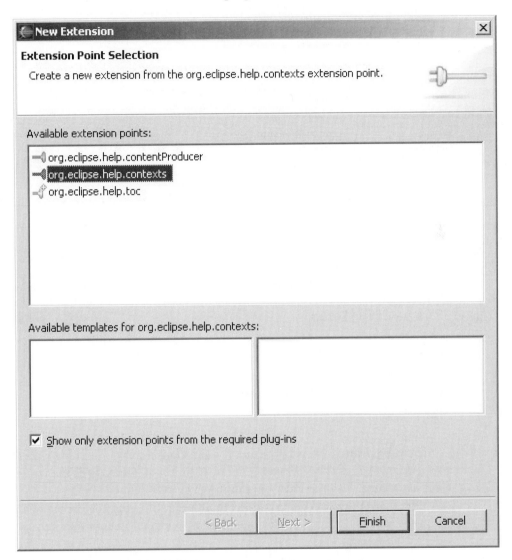

Figure 15–16   The New Extension wizard showing the org.eclipse.help.contexts extension point selected.

Now, back in the **Extensions** page of the plug-in manifest editor, right-click on the **org.eclipse.help.contexts** extension and select **New > contexts**. This immediately adds a context item to the plug-in manifest. Double-clicking on this new context item opens the **Properties** view so that the properties can be modified as follows (see Figure 15–17):

File—"contexts.xml"
The name of the context's XML file.

plug-in—"com.qualityeclipse.favorites"
The text label associated with the perspective.

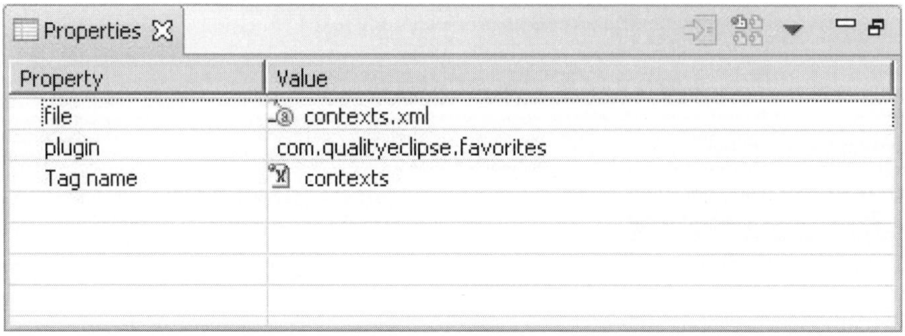

Figure 15–17   The Properties view showing Favorites context file attributes.

If you switch to the **Source** page of the plug-in manifest editor, you will see the following new section of XML defining the new context file:

```
<extension
    point="org.eclipse.help.contexts">
    <contexts
        file="contexts.xml"
        plugin="com.qualityeclipse.favorites">
    </contexts>
</extension>
```

The `plugin` attribute is important for associating this context file with the `com.qualityeclipse.favorites` plug-in. If that is not specified, the context file is associated with the local plug-in in which it is defined.

Note that multiple context files from different plug-ins may be associated with the context ID. This allows one plug-in to extend the context help provided by another.

Now that we have completed the definition of our context-sensitive infopop help, we can test it by opening the **Favorites** view and pressing **F1**. The infopop content for the "favorites_view" context ID should appear (see Figure 15–18).

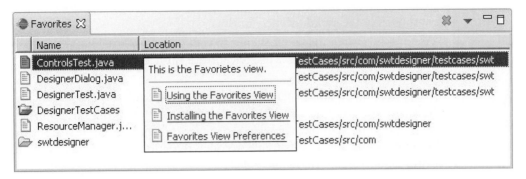

Figure 15–18   The Favorites view showing the context-sensitive infopop help.

15.3.5 Marker help

The `org.eclipse.ui.ide.markerHelp` extension point allows plug-ins to associate a help context ID with a particular marker type. In Chapter 14, "Builders, Markers, and Natures," we had one marker type representing two different violations, so we needed to further qualify the help declaration, creating one declaration for each type of violation. The expression `<attribute name="violation" value="1"/>` indicates that the help context should only be applied to markers having a "violation" attribute with a value of "`1`".

```
<extension point="org.eclipse.ui.ide.markerHelp">
   <markerHelp
      markerType="com.qualityeclipse.favorites.auditmarker"
      helpContextId="com.qualityeclipse.favorites
         .violationHelp1">
      <attribute name="violation" value="1"/>
   </markerHelp>
   <markerHelp
      markerType="com.qualityeclipse.favorites.auditmarker"
      helpContextId="com.qualityeclipse.favorites
         .violationHelp2">
      <attribute name="violation" value="2"/>
   </markerHelp>
</extension>
```

The help content for the violation markers is defined as part of the `contexts.xml` file (see Section 15.3.3, "Creating infopop content").

15.4 Accessing Help Programmatically

So far, we have seen how to integrate help into the Eclipse **Help** window and access it using standard Eclipse mechanisms such as the **Help > Help Contents** menu and the **F1** key. There may be times when you want to provide help in ways other than the standard mechanisms.

As we saw earlier, the `WorkbenchHelp` class defines a large number of useful APIs. In this section, we will concentrate on a couple of the "display" methods.

To programmatically open the **Help** window, call the `displayHelp()` method without an argument. To programmatically open the infopop for a specific context ID, call the `displayHelp()` method with the context ID string as the single argument. For example, to open the infopop associated with the **Favorites** view, use the following code:

```
WorkbenchHelp.displayHelp(
    "com.qualityeclipse.favorites.favorites_view");
```

15.4.1   *Opening a specific help page*

The most interesting API, however, is the `displayHelpResource()` method that takes a single string argument representing the path to the help page to be displayed. For example, to open the main help page for the **Favorites** plug-in, use the following code:

```
WorkbenchHelp.displayHelpResource(
    "/com.qualityeclipse.favorites.help/html/toc.html");
```

The path argument is composed of the ID of the plug-in containing the help file and the path to the resource relative to the plug-in root directory. Based on this last example, we can easily add a custom help button to the toolbar of the **Favorites** view (see Figure 15–19) by creating the following method in the `FavoritesView` class and calling it from the `createPartControl()` method:

```
private void addHelpButtonToToolBar() {
    Action helpAction = new Action() {
        public void run() {
            WorkbenchHelp.displayHelpResource(
                "/com.qualityeclipse.favorites.help" +
                "/html/toc.html");
        }
    };
    helpAction.setToolTipText(
        "Open the Favorites view help");
    helpAction.setImageDescriptor(
        ImageDescriptor.createFromFile(
            FavoritesView.class, "help.gif"));
```

```
getViewSite()
   .getActionBars()
      .getToolBarManager()
      .add(helpAction);
}
```

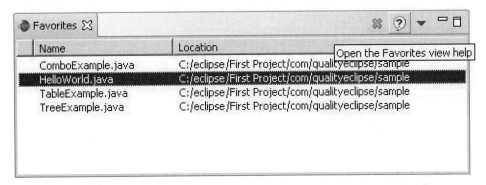

Figure 15–19   The Favorites view with the new help button showing.

15.4.2   Opening a web page

In addition to opening a specific help page in the Eclipse **Help** window, you might want to open a Web browser on a specific Web page. Eclipse includes a class, `org.eclipse.swt.program.Program`, which is used to launch external programs, including the system Web browser. In particular, we are interested in the `launch()` method, which takes a string encoding the path to the program to be launched or the URL of the Web page to be accessed.

We can now add a button to the **Favorites** view's toolbar (see Figure 15–20) that will open a specific Web page (we'll use the Web page for this book as an example). We will do this by adding the following method to the `Favorites View` class and calling it from the `createPartControl()` method (see Section 20.4, "Opening a Browser or Creating an Email," for more):

```
private void addWebButtonToToolBar() {
   Action webAction = new Action() {
      public void run() {
         Program.launch("http://www.qualityeclipse.com");
      }
   };
   webAction.setToolTipText("Open a web page");
   webAction.setImageDescriptor(
      ImageDescriptor.createFromFile(
         FavoritesView.class, "web.gif"));
   getViewSite()
      .getActionBars()
      .getToolBarManager()
      .add(webAction);
}
```

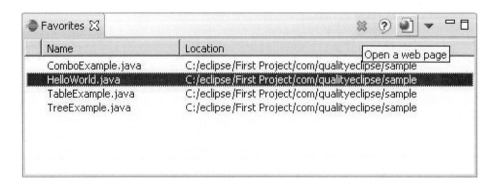

Figure 15–20   The Favorites view with the new Web button showing.

> **Tip:** You can use this technique to generate an email message from your application back to your sales or support group. For example, executing the following:
>
> ```
> Program.launch(
>     "mailto:info@qualityeclipse.com" +
>     "?Subject=Information Request")
> ```
>
> will generate an email message with the subject "Information Request." Embedding a "?Body=" tag gives you the ability to pre-populate the body of the message with information such as the user's Eclipse configuration.

15.5   RFWS Considerations

The "Help" section of the *RFWS Requirements* includes nine items—three requirements and six best practices—dealing with help.

15.5.1   *Existing documentation is not modified*

Requirement #1 states:

Do not delete or replace existing documentation during the installation of your product component into an existing workbench install.

This is an easy requirement to pass by demonstrating that your plug-in does not replace any of the existing documentation. Open the Eclipse **Help** window and show all the help books available.

15.5.2   Provide help through the workbench help system

Requirement #2 states:

Help for the plug-in's workbench UI should be provided through the workbench help system integrated to the workbench. This includes the interface (menu items, toolbar entries, etc.) used to launch externally integrated vendor tools. Help for portions of your tool that are not tightly integrated to the workbench may be provided through any existing help system it may use.

To pass this requirement, open the plug-in manifest for your help plug-in and point out the use of the `org.eclipse.help.toc` extension point. For the **Favorites** view, we would point to the following lines from the `plugin.xml` file:

```
<extension point="org.eclipse.help.toc">
   <toc file="toc.xml" primary="true"/>
   <toc file="tocgettingstarted.xml"/>
   <toc file="tocreference.xml"/>
</extension>
```

Next, open up the Eclipse **Help** window and show that your plug-in's help book appears in the main topic list. For the **Favorites** view, we would show that *Favorites Guide* appears in the list (see Figure 15–13).

If your plug-in includes online help that is not provided through the Eclipse help system, show it here.

15.5.3   Include proper Eclipse acknowledgement

Requirement #3 states:

All online end-user documentation must include the following acknowledgement: "This product includes software developed by the Eclipse Project (http://www.eclipse.org/)."

This is also an easy requirement to pass. Simply make sure to include the specified acknowledgement line within your product help pages (at the bottom of the first help page is generally sufficient). For the **Favorites** view, we would show that the acknowledgement appears at the bottom of the first help page (see Figure 15–21).

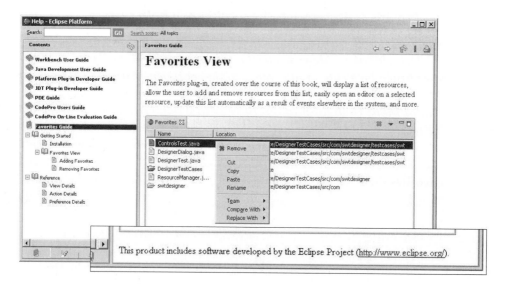

Figure 15–21   The Favorites view help page showing the Eclipse acknowledgement.

15.5.4   Provide all help via the workbench help system

Best Practice #4 states:

Provide all help for your plug-in through the workbench help system integrated to the workbench.

As with *Requirement #2*, open the plug-in manifest for your help plug-in and point out the use of the `org.eclipse.help.toc` extension point. Open the Eclipse **Help** window and show that your help book is available. This best practice is actually a refinement of *Requirement #2*, where the only difference is that, to pass this test, your plug-in should provide all its online help through the Eclipse help system.

15.5.5   Context help activated using F1

Best Practice #5 states:

Context help, if available, should be activated through F1. For products that are tightly integrated, this requires that help be associated with one or more of the SWT or JFace widgets used to construct the UI.

To pass this test, provide scenarios where pressing **F1** will show context-sensitive infopops for your plug-in. For the **Favorites** view, we would show the infopop associated with that view (see Figure 15–18).

15.5.6   Implement active help

Best Practice #6 states:

> *Implement active helps for topics that are best illustrated by using workbench actions. For example, consider a topic called "Importing external plug-ins." Instead of telling the user to go to the workbench and select* **File > Import**, *and then select* **External Plug-ins and Fragments** *and click* **Next**, *the topic could simply say "Click here to open the Import External Fragments wizard." The link would call a class you have defined, which in turn would open the wizard on that page.*

Passing this test is much more difficult as it requires implementing one or more active help elements. Show how your active help elements call back into your plug-in to launch various wizards or other commands. For more information on creating active help, see the "Active Help" topic in the *Platform Plug-in Developer Guide* included in the online Eclipse documentation.

15.5.7   Use of standalone help

Best Practice #7 states:

> *If help is not tightly integrated to the workbench, then use standalone help or a Web server-based information center.*

This test is basically the reverse of *Best Practice #4*, so only one or the other may be passed (good thing they are not both listed as requirements!). For this test, demonstrate any non-workbench-based help provided with your application. For the **Favorites** view, the Web page access button we added earlier might qualify.

15.5.8   Use of additional documentation

Best Practice #8 states:

> *If additional documentation is provided (beyond readme files), it should be included in one of the plug-in directories used to implement the product or provide integrated help. This might be in a \doc subdirectory or a plug-in directory with a name such as co.tool.doc.*
>
> *Last-minute additions to the documentation or other product guidance that did not make it into the integrated documentation should be included in a readme file in the plug-in directory.*

To pass this test, show any additional documentation provided with your plug-in such as any readme files or evaluation guides.

15.5.9   Pre-build help indexes

Best Practice #9 states:

Products should pre-build, package, install, and deliver the documentation indexes of their help documents.

When a user searches the help contents of a product, the search is performed within a documentation index. By default, this index is created on the first invocation of a help search, but can be pre-built and delivered to the user with a product. This avoids indexing from occurring on the user machine and lets the user obtain first search results faster.

This test applies to standalone Eclipse-based products rather than simple plug-ins. For this test, show that one or more `doc_index.zip` files have been provided with your product (one for each language supported by your help files). For more information on this topic, see the Eclipse help page titled "Pre-built documentation index."

15.6   Summary

After introducing the Eclipse help system, we illustrated how to create and integrate your own online help. We showed how to make your help available from within the Eclipse **Help** window as well as by using the context-sensitive **F1** key.

References

Adams, Greg and Dorian Birsan, "Help Part 1, Contributing a little help," August 9, 2002 (*www.eclipse.org/articles/Article-Online%20Help%20for%202_0/help1.htm*)

Eclipse Help: **Platform Plug-in Developer Guide > Programmer's Guide > Plugging in help**

CHAPTER 16

Internationalization

If a plug-in developer's audience is to be wider than a single country such as the United States, then internationalization becomes an important aspect of development. Both Eclipse and the underlying Java run-time environments provide APIs for separating language and UI-related issues from the code. In this chapter, we will cover the techniques involved and provide examples of internationalizing our example plug-in.

Every application—and an Eclipse plug-in is no exception—includes dozens of human-readable strings that present themselves to the user in windows, dialogs, and menus. Isolating those strings so that they can be localized (translated) for different countries and languages is the most important step in internationalizing your plug-in.

The strings that present themselves to the user of a plug-in come from different types of files. The plug-in manifest file contains the names for views and perspectives and labels for menus and actions. The plug-in's about.ini file (discussed in more detail in Chapter 18, "Features and Branding") contains the text shown in the Eclipse **About** dialog. Other strings visible in the plug-in's interface, such as widget labels and error message text, come from the Java classes implementing the plug-in. Different techniques and tools exist for externalizing the strings found in these various files.

16.1 Externalizing the Plug-in Manifest

The plug-in manifest file contains a variety of strings for identifying elements of the plug-in. Some strings, such as plug-in identifiers and the unique IDs associated with extensions, do not need to be translated, as they are never shown to the user. In fact, translating identifiers and unique IDs will likely break your plug-in. Other strings, such as the name of the plug-in itself, the names of views, and the labels of actions, need to be translated as they are seen by the user.

Externalizing the human-readable strings from the plug-in manifest file is straightforward. The file plugin.properties (a standard Java resource bundle file) contains the extracted strings. As an example, we will start with the following fragment from the **Favorites** plug-in manifest:

```
<plugin
    id="com.qualityeclipse.favorites"
    name="Favorites Plug-in"
    version="1.0.0"
    provider-name="QualityEclipse"
    class="com.qualityeclipse.favorites.FavoritesPlugin">
    ...
    <extension point="org.eclipse.ui.views">
        <category
            name="Quality Eclipse"
            id="com.qualityeclipse.favorites">
        </category>
        <view
            name="Favorites"
            icon="icons/sample.gif"
            category="com.qualityeclipse.favorites"
            class="com.qualityeclipse.favorites.
                views.FavoritesView"
            id="com.qualityeclipse.favorites.
                views.FavoritesView">
        </view>
    </extension>
    ...
</plugin>
```

The lines shown in **bold** are the ones containing strings that need to be extracted. The other lines contain text that does not need to be extracted, such as class names, identifiers, filenames, and version numbers.

Each string is replaced with a descriptive key that starts with a percent ("%") sign. These are the same keys that will be used in the associated plug-in.properties file. The only rule is that the keys need to be unique within the plug-in. You should also endeavor to give the keys descriptive names so that they are easily identifiable within the plugin.xml and plugin.properties files.

After extraction, the fragment will look like this:

```
<plugin
    id="com.qualityeclipse.favorites"
    name="%favorites.plugin.name"
    version="1.0.0"
    provider-name="QualityEclipse"
    class="com.qualityeclipse.favorites.FavoritesPlugin">
```

```
...
<extension point="org.eclipse.ui.views">
   <category
         name="%favorites.category.name"
         id="com.qualityeclipse.favorites">
   </category>
   <view
         name="%favorites.view.name"
         icon="icons/sample.gif"
         category="com.qualityeclipse.favorites"
         class="com.qualityeclipse.favorites.
               views.FavoritesView"
         id="com.qualityeclipse.favorites.
            views.FavoritesView">
   </view>
</extension>
...
</plugin>
```

The `plugin.properties` file would then look like this:

```
# Contains translated strings for the Favorites plug-in
favorites.plugin.name=Favorites Plug-in
favorites.category.name=Quality Eclipse
favorites.view.name=Favorites
```

When the strings have been extracted to the `plugin.properties` file, they may be translated. The translated files for each targeted language should be named `plugin_<language>_<country>.properties`, where `<language>` and `<country>` represent the two-letter codes (ISO 639 and ISO 3166) used to signify the language and country (the country component is optional). For example, the standard German translation would be named `plugin_de.properties` and would look something like this:

```
# Enthält übersetzten Text für die steckbaren Lieblingeh
favorites.plugin.name=Lieblinge Steckbar
favorites.category.name= Qualitätseklipse
favorites.view.name=Lieblinge
```

Likewise, the standard French translation would be named `plugin_fr.properties` and would look something like this:

```
# Contient le texte traduit pour les favoris plugin
favorites.plugin.name=Favoris plugin
favorites.category.name= Éclipse De Qualité
favorites.view.name=Favoris
```

> **Tip:** A list of ISO 639 language codes may be found at:
> *www.unicode.org/onlinedat/languages.html*
> A list of ISO 3166 country codes may be found at:
> *www.unicode.org/onlinedat/countries.html*

16.2   Externalizing Plug-in Strings

When the plug-in manifest has been externalized, the other major source of human-readable strings is the Java source for the plug-in. Within our **Favorites** example, there are dozens of strings that are presented to the user in the form of UI elements and messages.

To show the process for externalizing the strings in your Java source files, we will take you through the process of extracting the strings from the `FavoritesView` class. The **Favorites** view contains several hard-coded strings that are used for UI elements such as menu labels and table column headers (see Figure 16–1).

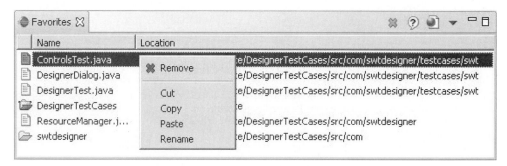

Figure 16–1   The Favorites view showing various strings.

Within the `FavoritesView` class, we will focus on the following hard-coded string definitions:

```
private static final String CUT = "Cut";
private static final String COPY = "Copy";
private static final String PASTE = "Paste";
private static final String RENAME = "Rename";
private static final String REMOVE = "Remove";
private static final String NAME = "Name";
private static final String LOCATION = "Location";
```

Eclipse includes a powerful string externalization tool that will do most of the work for us. Start by selecting the `FavoritesView` class. Next, select the **Source > Externalize Strings...** command to open the **Externalize Strings** wizard (see Figure 16–2).

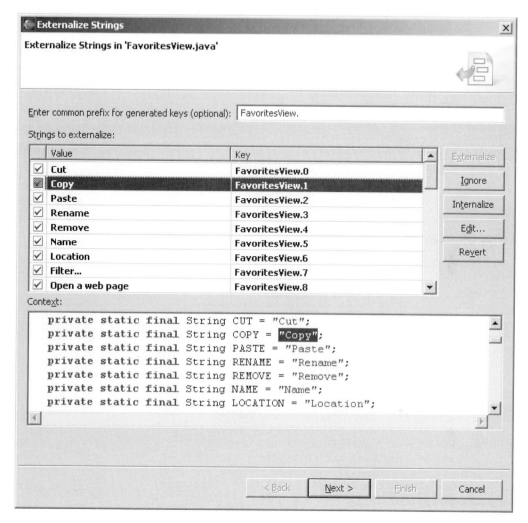

Figure 16–2 The Externalize Strings wizard.

The wizard scans the class for any string literals and presents them in the **Strings to externalize** list. The first column of the table is used to determine whether the string is translated, never translated, or skipped (until the next time the wizard is run on this class). The key column contains the wizard's first attempt at generating a unique key for the string (initially numbered 1 through *n*). The value column contains the strings that were found. Selecting an entry in the table will highlight it in context in the text pane below the table.

At the top of the wizard, the **common prefix** field has been pre-populated with the name of the class in which the strings were found. This value will be prefixed to the keys in the table to create the final keys that will be associated with each string.

Because the generated keys are not very meaningful, the first thing we will do is edit them to represent the strings they will replace. Since the strings we want to replace are simple, we will have the keys duplicate the values (see Figure 16–3).

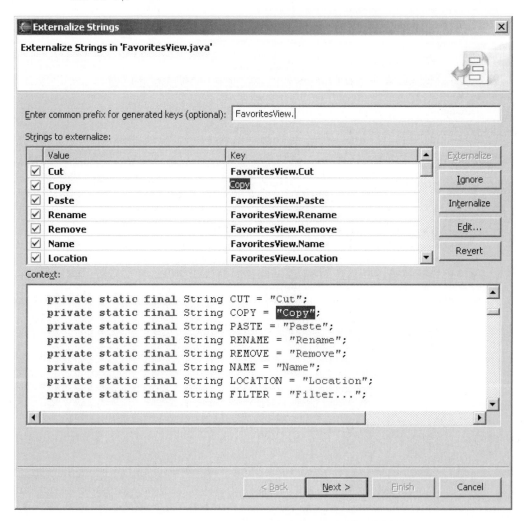

Figure 16–3   Externalize Strings wizard with better key names.

After providing better keys for the strings we want to extract, we need to go through the list and identify which strings we want to be extracted and which ones should never be translated (see Figure 16–4).

By default, all the strings will be extracted. This means that each string with its key will be added to the properties file. Within the Java source file, the string will be replaced by code used to programmatically access the string from the properties file using its key. The key string will then be marked with an end-of-line comment (e.g., `//$NON-NLS-1$`), indicating that it should be ignored in the future. The number at the end of the comment indicates which string should be ignored when there is more than one string on the same line. If more than one string should be ignored on the line, each string will have its own end-of-line comment in that exact same format (including the leading double slashes). If you know that a string should not be extracted, you should manually add these end-of-line comments during development to make the string extraction process easier later on.

Tip: Think carefully about how you write your code, since it can cause more strings that need externalization than is strictly necessary. Replace single-character strings with single characters, look for opportunities to reuse keys rather than creating new ones, and use message binding to reduce the number of strings that need to be externalized. For example, assuming that "Count" has already been externalized, we might encounter the following three scenarios:

```
// Bad, we don't want to externalize "Count ("
label.setText("Count (" + count + ")");
// Good, we already have "Count" externalized.
label.setText("Count" + " (" + count + ')'); //$NON-NLS-2$
// Better, use binding patterns where possible.
label.setText(
    MessageFormat.format("Count (%1)",
    new String[] {count})
```

In the second scenario, we can reuse the key assigned to "Count" and reduce the number of keys needed. In the third scenario, we can create a single new key that encodes a dynamic argument in a translation relative position (in other languages, the %1 argument might appear elsewhere in the string).

Selecting a string and clicking the **Internalize** button will tell the wizard to mark the string as non-translatable using the same end-of-line comment used earlier. Clicking the **Ignore** button will cause the wizard to take no action. Alternatively, you can click on the checkbox image in the first column of the table. The image will cycle through the three options: ☑ **Externalize**, ☒ **Internalize**, and ⬆ **Ignore**.

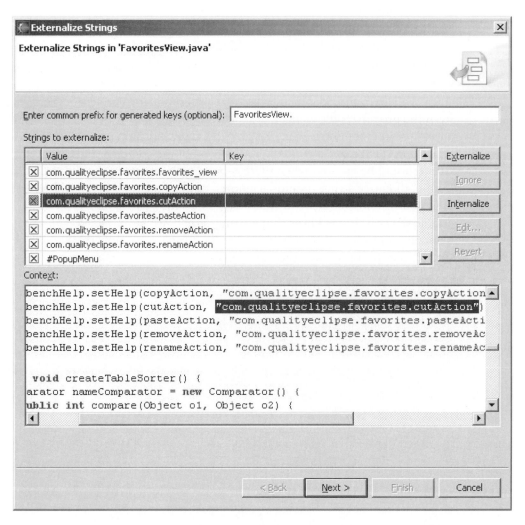

Figure 16–4 Externalize Strings wizard with strings marked as "Never Translate."

Clicking the **Next** button will take you to a page where you can specify where the strings will be externalized and how they will be accessed (see Figure 16–5). The **Package** field specifies the location where the property file will be created, and the **Property file name** field specifies the name of the property file that will be created. It will default to <short package name>.properties (in this case, view.properties). Unless you have a reason to do otherwise, you should simply accept the defaults.

By default, a resource bundle accessor class will be created with the name <short package name>Messages. This class will include code to load the matching properties file and access the strings via their unique keys. If you don't want to have this class created, blank the **class name** field. If you do that—possibly because you want to use an alternative mechanism—you might also want to specify an alternative **string substitution pattern** (the default pattern is designed to match the accessor class that the wizard would create).

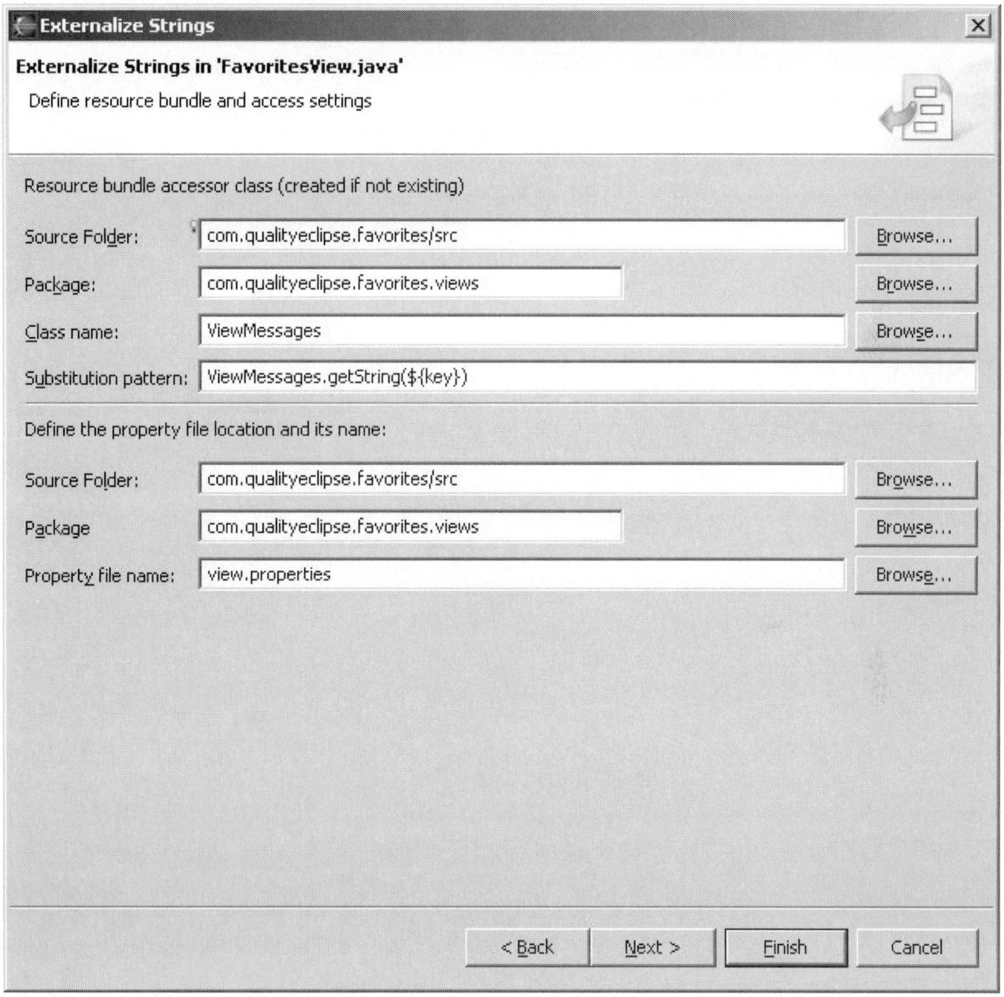

Figure 16–5 Define resource bundle and access settings.

Since the **Externalize Strings** wizard is actually built using the Eclipse refactoring framework, the next two pages are common to all refactoring wizards. The first of these pages (see Figure 16–6) will show any errors or informational messages. The only message you should see at this point is a notification that the properties file does not exist and needs to be created. Click the **Next** button to continue.

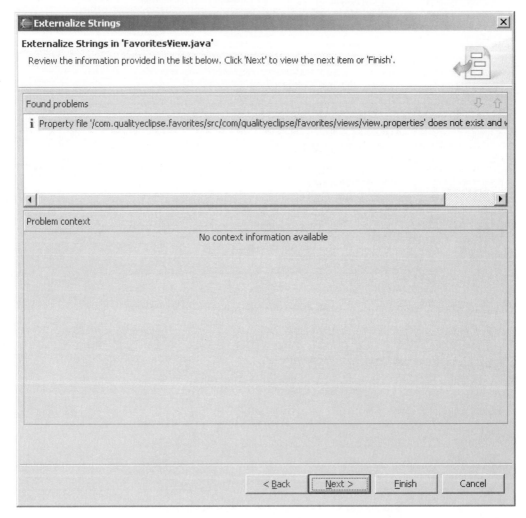

Figure 16–6   The view.properties file needs to be created.

The final page of the wizard will present a list of all the proposed changes that the wizard wants to make (see Figure 16–7). First, you will see all the string substitutions that will be made to the `FavoritesView` class. After that, you will see the contents of the properties file and the resource bundle accessor class.

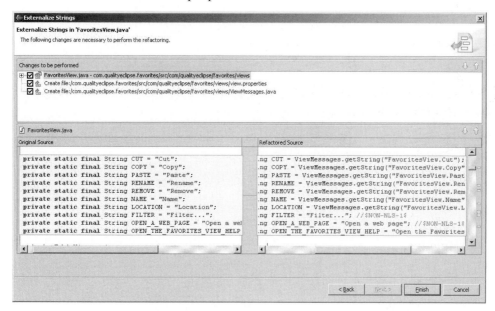

Figure 16–7 Review the proposed changes.

Clicking the **Finish** button will implement all the proposed changes. The original lines from the `FavoritesView` that we concentrated on earlier will be replaced by the following:

```
private static final String CUT = ViewMessages
    .getString("FavoritesView.Cut"); //$NON-NLS-1$
private static final String COPY = ViewMessages
    .getString("FavoritesView.Copy"); //$NON-NLS-1$
private static final String PASTE = ViewMessages
    .getString("FavoritesView.Paste"); //$NON-NLS-1$
private static final String RENAME = ViewMessages
    .getString("FavoritesView.Rename"); //$NON-NLS-1$
private static final String REMOVE = ViewMessages
    .getString("FavoritesView.Remove"); //$NON-NLS-1$
private static final String NAME = ViewMessages
    .getString("FavoritesView.Name"); //$NON-NLS-1$
private static final String LOCATION = ViewMessages
    .getString("FavoritesView.Location"); //$NON-NLS-1$
```

Each string literal is replaced by a static method call to the resource bundle accessor class with the string's key as the argument. Of course, the keys are also string literals, so they have automatically been marked with the //$NON-NLS-1$ tag, which will prevent them from being extracted in the future.

The code for the resource bundle accessor class will look something like this:

```
package com.qualityeclipse.favorites.views;

import java.util.*;

public class ViewMessages {
    private static final String BUNDLE_NAME =
        "com.qualityeclipse.favorites.views.view";
            //$NON-NLS-1$
    private static final ResourceBundle RESOURCE_BUNDLE =
        ResourceBundle.getBundle(BUNDLE_NAME);
    private ViewMessages() {}
    public static String getString(String key) {
        try {
            return RESOURCE_BUNDLE.getString(key).trim();
        } catch (MissingResourceException e) {
            return '!' + key + '!';
        }
    }
}
```

Finally, the `view.properties` file will look like this:

```
FavoritesView.Cut=Cut
FavoritesView.Copy=Copy
FavoritesView.Paste=Paste
FavoritesView.Rename=Rename
FavoritesView.Remove=Remove
FavoritesView.Name=Name
FavoritesView.Location=Location
```

As with the `plugin.properties` file, the translated properties files for each targeted language should be named <basename>_<language>_<country>.properties, where <language> and <country> represent the two-letter codes used to signify the language and country, and <basename> is the name of the original properties file.

> Tip: To make sure that you have externalized all your plug-in's strings (or marked them as non-translatable), consider changing the Usage of non-externalized strings option from "Ignore" to "Warning". This option can be found on the Advanced tab of the Java > Compiler preferences. Alternatively, CodePro includes a String Literals code audit rule that will flag hard-coded string literals (with options to ignore single-character strings, strings containing only whitespace or digits, static final field initializers, strings matching certain patterns, etc.).

While externalizing strings, we have found the following suggestions to be helpful:

- Remove any punctuation characters such as "&" that appear in the key. If you want to separate words within your keys, standardize on a specific character like a period, dash, or underscore.

- Edit the properties file and keep the entries sorted. Sort the entries first based on the file they apply to, and then sort them alphabetically within the file.

- Factor out any common values and create a common key. Move all common keys to their own section of the file. We prefix our common keys with "common." and move them to the top of the file. This reduces the number of translations and removes the possibility of variation in translations.

- When you edit the keys, strive to keep them as close to the original language strings, since this will make the Java code and XML easier to read for the native developer. If you decide to do this, strive to rename the keys when the original language strings are changed, otherwise this might lead to confusion. Of course, numeric keys don't have this problem.

- When the original string contains a colon, such as "Name:", the generated key will contain double underscores. We never define keys such as this, but rather go back to the original string and change "Name:" to "Name"+':'. This not only keeps the keys simple, but it ensures that the colon does not get dropped during translation. The only issue here is whether you truly want to respect local punctuation rules, but that can be fairly tricky.

- You should always consider including an error number with internationalized error messages, so that an error displayed in one language could be addressed by others.

- In the generated static `getString(String key)` method, edit the catch clause to include the following line that will log any missing resource keys to the console. This is much easier than looking for "! <key> !" in your application.

  ```
  System.err.println(e.getMessage());
  ```

16.3   Using Fragments

All the translated properties files could be included in the main plug-in, but this is less than ideal in a situation where the translations will be delivered later than the product itself. If all the translated files need to be included with the main plug-in, you would either need to delay the release of the main plug-in or re-release it when the translations are available. Fortunately, Eclipse includes a mechanism called a *plug-in fragment* that provides an elegant solution to this problem.

Fragments are used to extend the functionality of another plug-in. Fragments are typically used to supply alternative language packs, maintenance updates, and platform-specific implementation classes. When a fragment is loaded, its features and capabilities are merged with those of the base plug-in such that they appear to have come from the base plug-in itself. The developer does not need to know whether the plug-in or one of its fragments contributes a specific resource because the plug-in class loader handles this transparently. This makes it easy to deliver translated versions of plug-in files (e.g., HTML, XML, INI, and properties files) independently of the main plug-in.

The properties files follow the resource bundle-naming rules (as we saw earlier) and are packaged into JAR files. Other resources such as HTML, XML, and INI files are placed into `nl/<language>` or `nl/<language>/<country>` directories, where `<language>` and `<country>` represent the two-letter codes used to signify the language and country (this directory structure was first introduced in Section 15.2.3, "Table of contents (toc) files").

> Tip: Fragments can also be used for smoothing out differences between different versions of Eclipse (see Section 19.2.6.4, "Fragments") and for accessing internal classes and methods (see Section 20.2.6, "Using Fragments").

16.3.1   New fragment project wizard

Creating a new fragment is easy using the **New Fragment Project** wizard. From the **File** menu, select **New > Project** to launch the new project wizard (see Figure 16–8). On this first page of the wizard, select **Plug-in Development > Fragment Project**, followed by the **Next** button.

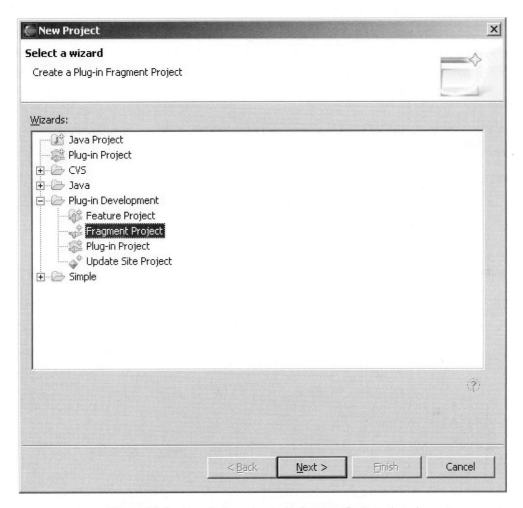

Figure 16–8 New Project wizard with Fragment Project selected.

On the next page of the wizard (see Figure 16–9), enter the name of the project; in this case, it should be "`com.qualityeclipse.favorites.nl1`", which is the same as the plug-in fragment identifier. The Eclipse convention is to name a plug-in fragment project that contributes national language support to a base plug-in with the same name as the base plug-in plus the suffix ".nl1". Click the **Next** button.

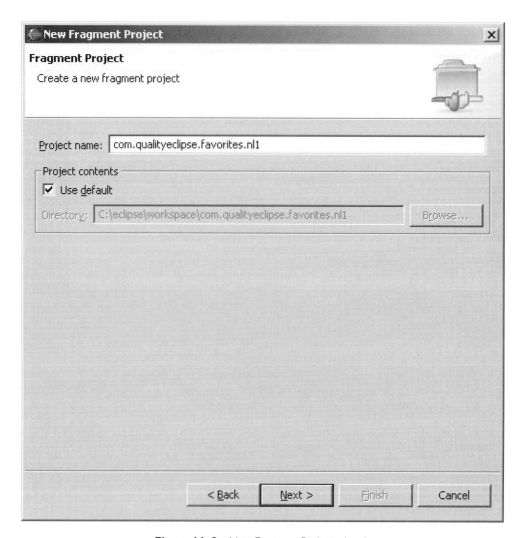

Figure 16–9   New Fragment Project wizard.

The next page of the wizard (see Figure 16–10) provides fields for specifying the Java project information. The default values provided by the wizard are correct in this case, so click the **Next** button.

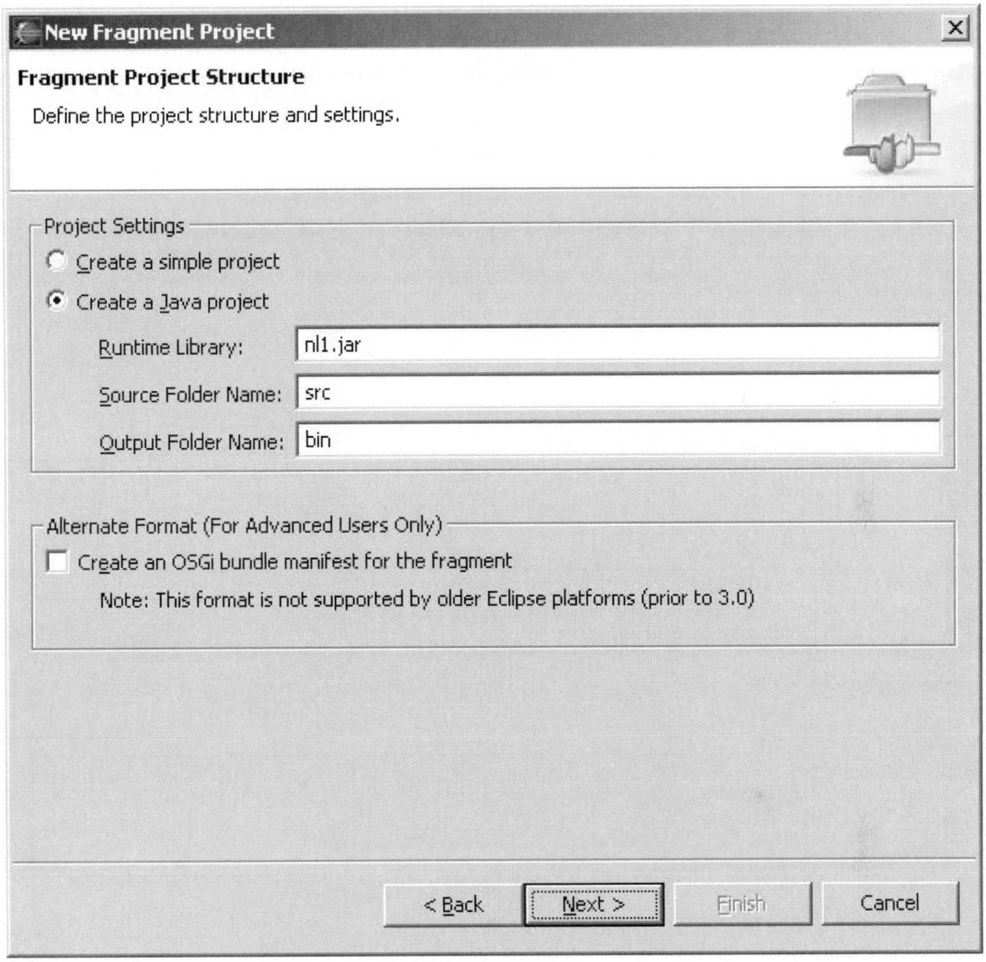

Figure 16–10   Defining the fragment structure.

The **Fragment Content** page (see Figure 16–11) provides fields to name the fragment, set its ID and version number, and identify the plug-in ID and version that it extends. Use the **Browse** button to select the plug-in, if necessary. In this case, we want to extend the existing com.qualityeclipse.favorites plug-in.

The choices available in the **Match Rule** field control the versions of the associated plug-in that can be extended.

- **Perfect** means that the base plug-in exactly matches the supplied version number.

- **Equivalent** means that the version may differ at the service or qualifier level.

- **Compatible** means that plug-in may have a newer minor version number.

- **Greater or Equal** means that the plug-in may have any newer version number. This is the option you should normally choose.

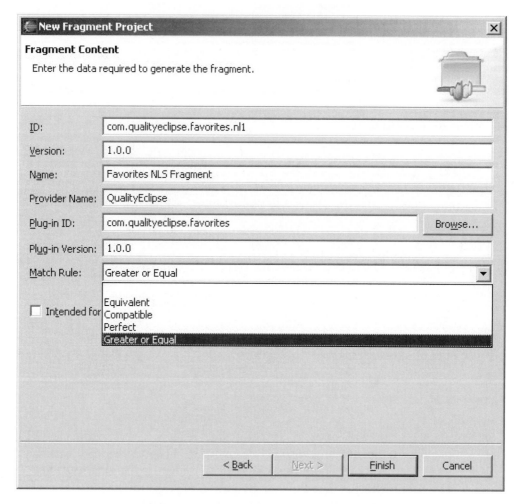

Figure 16–11   Required data for initial fragment files.

Click the **Finish** button to complete the wizard and generate the fragment manifest file.

16.3.2   Fragment manifest file

Double-clicking in the fragment manifest file, fragment.xml, will open the fragment manifest editor (see Figure 16–12). The editor looks very similar to the plug-in manifest editor with **Overview, Dependencies, Runtime, Extension Points,** and **Source** pages.

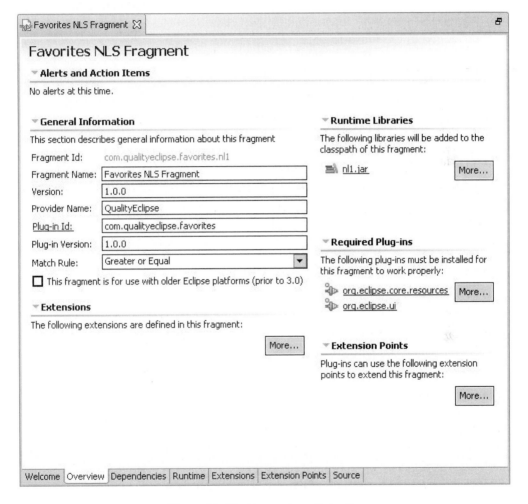

Figure 16–12   Fragment manifest editor.

If you switch to the **Run-time Information** page (see Figure 16–13), you will see that the nl1.jar file is already included in the run-time classpath for the fragment. Any alternative resource bundle files (view_de.properties, for example) will be contained in this JAR file.

Other files, such as translated HTML, XML, and INI files, are located in specially named subdirectories based on the associated locale (language and country combination). To get those directories to show up in the run-time classpath, click the **Add** button to add a "New Library" entry to the list. Right-click on that entry and **Rename** it to "nl/". This is special syntax that will cause the system to substitute the correct classpath entry at run-time based on the current locale. If the locale is set to Germany, for example, "nl" would be substituted by "de", and the "de/" subdirectory would be added to the run-time path.

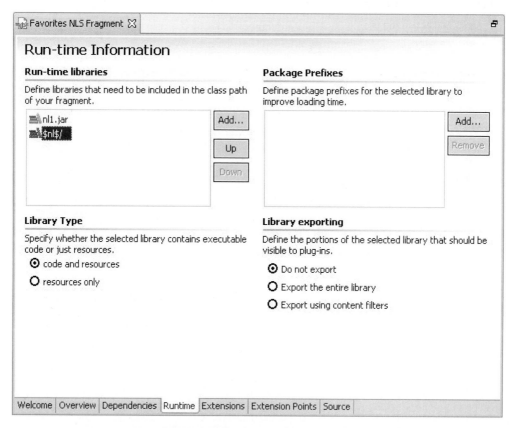

Figure 16–13   Fragment Run-time Information page.

Next, let's switch to the **Source** page and take a look at the generated XML:

```
<?xml version="1.0" encoding="UTF-8"?>
<?eclipse version="3.0"?>
<fragment
    id="com.qualityeclipse.favorites.nl1"
    name="Favorites NLS Fragment"
    version="1.0.0"
    provider-name="QUALITYECLIPSE"
    plugin-id="com.qualityeclipse.favorites"
    plugin-version="1.0.0"
    match="greaterOrEqual">
    <runtime>
        <library name="nl1.jar"/>
        <library name="$nl$/"/>
    </runtime>
</fragment>
```

This source is very similar to what you would expect to see for a plug-in. The first major difference is that fragments don't have their own plug-in life-cycle (they conform to the lifecycle of their associated plug-in), and thus, they don't need their own `class` attribute. The second difference is that the fragment does not declare any of its own dependencies (again, they are inherited from the associated plug-in).

The interesting attributes relative to those found in full plug-ins are the **plugin-id, plugin-version,** and **match** attributes. The **plugin-id** identifies the plug-in that this fragment will extend. The **plugin-version** specifies the version of the target plug-in that this fragment expects to extend. The **match** attribute, as discussed earlier, controls which plug-in versions are viable targets for this fragment.

> Tip: The `runtime` section of the file contains the entries added to the run-time path. If the JAR file contributed by the fragment only contains resources (and no classes), a further optimization is possible by adding a type attribute with a value of "resource". For example:
>
> `<library name="nl1.jar" type="resource"/>`
>
> This will cause the plug-in class loader to only look for resources and not bother trying to load any classes.

16.3.3 Fragment project contents

The last thing we need to do is add all of the translated files to the appropriate directories within the fragment project folder (see Figure 16–14). Assuming that we want to supply German and French translations of various files, the project would contain nl/de and nl/fr directories to contain any translated HTML, XML, and INI files (like those mentioned in Section 15.2.3).

The translated versions of the `plugin.properties` files are placed in the src directory of the project, and the translated versions of the `view.properties` files are placed in the `com.qualityeclipse.favorites.views` directory. All the properties files are then built into the `nl1.jar` file, located at the root of the fragment.

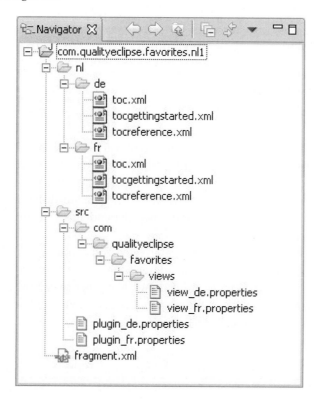

Figure 16–14 Fragment project contents.

16.4 Summary

To make your plug-in accessible to a worldwide audience, it should be internationalized. Extracting the plug-in's human-readable strings into a format that can be easily translated is the most important step. As presented in this chapter, Eclipse provides a number of tools to facilitate this. The **Externalize Strings** wizard makes it easy to extract the strings from your Java code, while fragments provide a convenient packaging mechanism for delivering translated content independent of your main plug-ins.

References

Java internationalization tutorial (*java.sun.com/docs/books/tutorial/i18n/ intro/index.html*).

Kehn, Dan, Scott Fairbrother, and Cam-Thu Le, "How to Internationalize your Eclipse Plug-in," August 23, 2002 (*eclipse.org/articles/Article-Internationalization/how2I18n.html*).

Kehn, Dan, "How to Test Your Internationalized Eclipse Plug-in," August 23, 2002 (*eclipse.org/articles/Article-TVT/how2TestI18n.html*).

ISO 639 language codes (*www.unicode.org/onlinedat/languages.html*).

ISO 3166 country codes (*www.unicode.org/onlinedat/countries.html*).

Eclipse Help: **Java Development User Guide > Tasks > Externalizing Strings**

CHAPTER 17

Creating New Extension Points

Eclipse facilitates enhancements by defining *extension points*, but that technique is not reserved only for Eclipse itself. Each plug-in can define its own extension points that can be used either internally as part of a disciplined and flexible programming approach, or externally as a way for third-party plug-ins to enhance an existing plug-in in a controlled yet loosely coupled, flexible manner. We will discuss the API involved and provide examples of creating extension points so that a third party can extend our plug-in's functionality.

17.1 The Extension Point Mechanism

Up to this point, we have been discussing extension points as a consumer; now we need to delve into the mechanism behind the curtain so that ultimately we can produce our own extension points for others to consume. Not only will extension points make our products more flexible, but, by carefully exposing specific aspects of our plug-in, we can make our products more flexible and customizable. Our goal is to empower our customers to take our products and do things that we never envisioned.

Extension points are used throughout Eclipse as a mechanism for loosely coupling chunks of functionality. One plug-in declares an extension point in its plug-in manifest, exposing a minimal set of interfaces and related classes for others to use; other plug-ins declare extensions to that extension point, implementing the appropriate interfaces and referencing or building on the classes provided (see Figure 17–1).

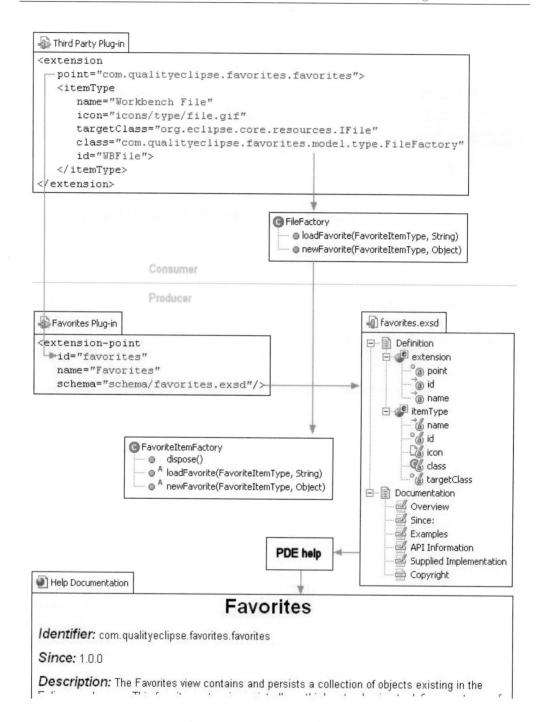

Figure 17–1   Extension point overview.

Each extension point has a unique identifier composed of the plug-in's unique identifier, a period, and a simple identifier containing only alphanumeric characters and underscores. When declaring an extension point (see Section 17.2.1, "Creating an extension point"), only the simple identifier is used. When declaring an extension to an extension point (see Section 17.5, "Using the Extension Point"), the full identifier for the extension point is used.

Each extension point can have a schema defining how the extension point should be used. Although the schema is not necessary for proper extension point usage, the Eclipse PDE can use the schema for basic automated verification of extensions and automatically generated Javadoc-like documentation for the extension point. The schema is an XML formatted file, traditionally having the name `<extension-point-id>.exsd` and located in a schema subdirectory of the plug-in's install directory. For example, the favorites extension point schema discussed later in this chapter will be stored in `<Eclipse_install_dir>/plugins/com.quality-eclipse.favorites_1.0.0/schema/favorites.exsd`.

17.2 Defining an Extension Point

In our **Favorites** product, we would like other plug-ins to extend our product to provide additional types of **Favorites** objects. To accomplish this goal, we will create a new `favorites` extension point and schema plus related infrastructure types that others can extend. As part of this process, we will recast our current **Favorites** objects as extensions to this new extension point to prove to ourselves that the new extension point does indeed work.

17.2.1 Creating an extension point

We begin by opening the **Favorites** plug-in manifest editor and switching to the **Extension Points** page (see Figure 17–2).

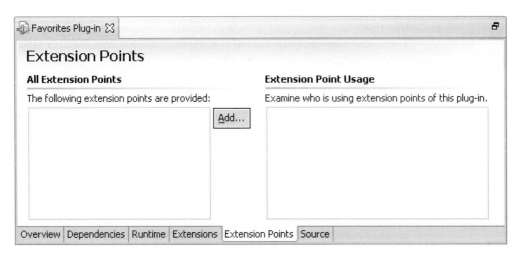

Figure 17–2   The Extension Points page in the plug-in manifest editor.

Click the **Add...** button to open the **New Extension Point** wizard, and
enter "favorites" for the identifier and "Favorites" for the name (see Figure
17–3).

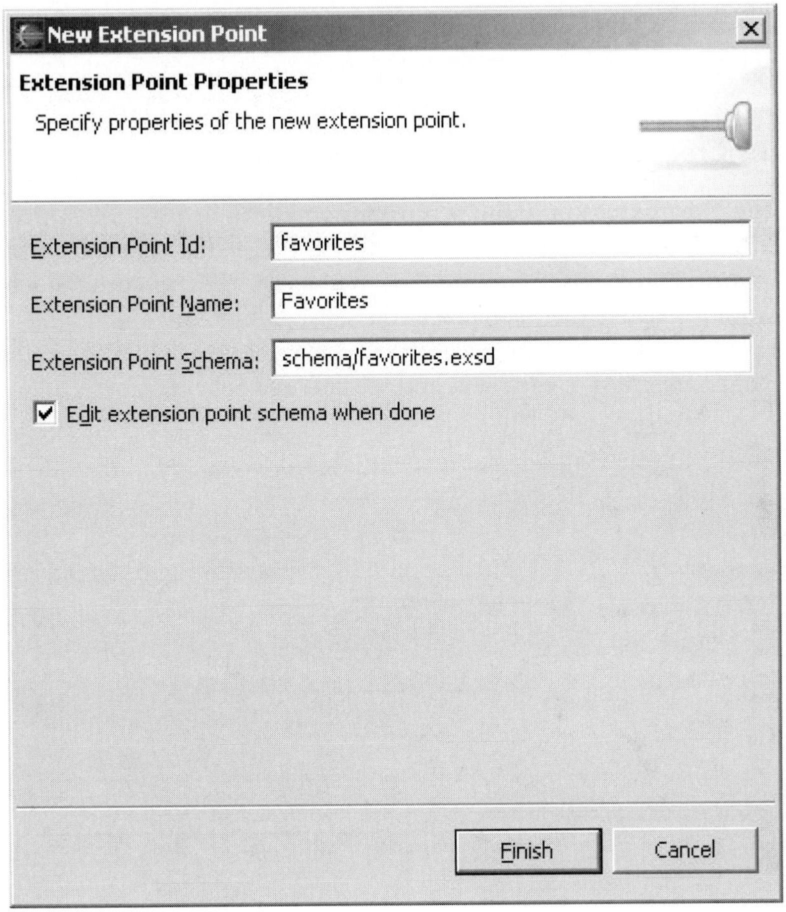

Figure 17–3 The New Extension Point wizard.

Click **Finish** to create the new extension point. Switching to the **Source** page of the plug-in manifest editor reveals a new extension point declaration specifying the identifier, the human-readable name, and the relative location of the schema:

```
<extension-point
   id="favorites"
   name="Favorites"
   schema="schema/favorites.exsd"/>
```

The aforementioned declaration specifies the local identifier of the extension point. The full identifier is the plug-in identifier plus the local identifier; in our case, the full identifier is com.qualityeclipse.favorites.favorites.

17.2.2   Creating an extension point schema

The **New Extension Point** wizard automatically opens the schema editor to edit the newly created favorites.exsd file in the schema directory of the **Favorites** project (see Figure 17–4). If you ever need to open the schema editor again, you can either navigate to the schema directory and double-click on the favorites.exsd file, or select the favorites extension point in the **Favorites** plug-in manifest, right-click, and select **Open Schema**.

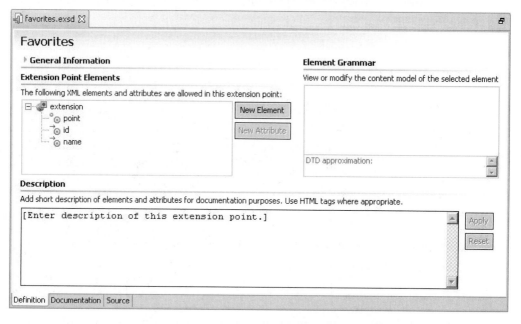

Figure 17–4   Extension point schema editor.

The schema editor has three parts: the **Extension Point Elements** on the left, **Element Grammar** on the right, and documentation composed of the **Description** field at the bottom of the **Definition** page, plus the **Documentation** page itself. The **Extension Point Elements** list contains elements and their associated attributes, which appear in extension to the extension point (see Section 17.2.3, "Extension point elements and attributes"). The **Element Grammar** list contains a description of how the XML elements should appear in the extension (see Section 17.2.4, "Extension point grammar").

To start, let's document our goal so that we have a clear view of what we are trying to accomplish. An extension point schema is used by the PDE to dynamically assemble a help page for the extension point (see Section 17.4, "Extension Point Documentation"). Switch to the **Documentation** page of the schema editor, select **Overview** from the drop-down list, enter the following description, and click the **Apply** button.

```
"The Favorites view contains and persists a collection of objects
existing in the Eclipse workspace. This Favorites extension point
allows third-party plug-ins to define new types of objects for the
Favorites view."
```

Repeat this process by selecting **Example** from the drop-down list to enter the following text (see following). Note the use of the <pre> and </pre> XML tags to denote preformatted text in which whitespace should be preserved; all other whitespace greater than a single space outside those tags is discarded in the automatically generated HTML help text (see Section 17.4).

```
The following is an example
of the Favorites extension point usage:
<p>
<pre>
   <extension point="com.qualityeclipse.favorites.favorites">
      <itemType
         id="com.example.xyz.myNewFavoriteItemId"
         name="New Favorites Item Name"
         class="com.example.xyz.MyFavoriteItem"
         targetClass="com.example.xyz.MyObjectClass"/>
   </extension>
</pre>
</p>
```

And for **API Information,** enter the following:

```
"Plug-ins that want to extend this extension point must subclass
<samp>com.qualityeclipse.favorites.model.FavoriteItemType</samp> and
generate objects that implement the <samp>com.qualityeclipse.favor-
ites.model.IFavoriteItem</samp> interface."
```

> We use the <samp> </samp> XML tags to denote code in a sentence similar to the way that many of the Eclipse plug-ins are documented; the <code> </code> XML tags should work just as well.

17.2.3   Extension point elements and attributes

Extension point elements correspond to XML elements that appear in the extension declaration. Extension point attributes correspond to XML attributes that appear in the extension declaration. For example, in the extension declaration following, itemType is an extension point element, while id, name, class, and targetClass are extension point attributes:

```
<extension point=
   "com.qualityeclipse.favorites.favorites">
   <itemType
      id="com.example.xyz.myNewFavoriteItemId"
      name="New Favorites Item Name"
      class="com.example.xyz.MyFavoriteItem"
      targetClass="com.example.xyz.MyObjectClass"/>
</extension>
```

Extension point attributes have several different properties associated with them. Double-clicking on an attribute in the schema editor opens the **Properties** view and displays the properties (see Figure 17–5). The properties for extension attributes are:

Name—The name of the attribute as it appears in the extension's declaration. For example, in the aforementioned extension declaration, id, name, class, and targetClass are all attribute names.

Type—The type of the attribute: string or Boolean. At this time, these are the only two types recognized by the schema editor and PDE. If your attribute should only be true or false, then select boolean; for all other attributes, select string.

Use—Indicates whether this attribute is required in an extension and thus must be explicitly declared, or whether it is optional, indicating that it may be omitted from an extension declaration. Alternately, the Use may be declared as default, indicating that if it is not explicitly declared, then it defaults to the value specified by the **Value** property listed later.

Kind—If the aforementioned **Type** property is string, then this property indicates how that string should be interpreted: as a java class, as a resource path to an image or the like, or simply as a string for the extension point code to interpret as it likes.

Based On—If the **Kind** is java, then this property indicates the fully qualified name of the class or interface that this attribute must extend or implement.

Restriction—If the **Type** is string and the **Kind** is string, then this property can restrict the value of the attribute to an enumeration or discrete list of valid strings. For example, using this field, you could specify that an attribute could only have the value "one", "two", or "three".

Value—If the **Use** is specified as default, then this property indicates the default value that will be used if this attribute is not explicitly specified in the extension's declaration.

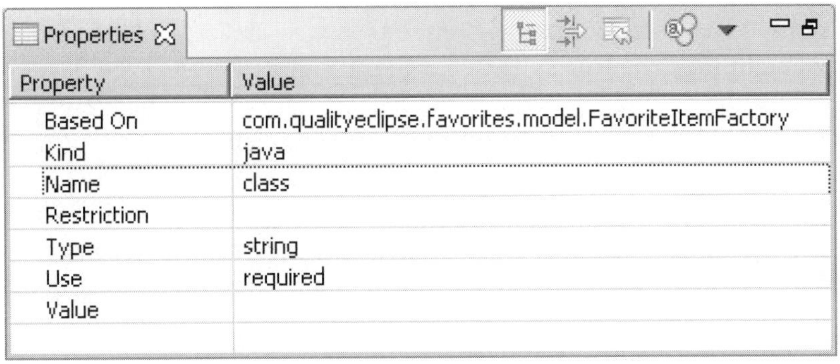

Figure 17–5 Properties view showing attribute property values.

For our **Favorites** product, we want extensions to this extension point to specify information about the type of **Favorites** item being added. The extension point attributes we want to include are:

- **name**—The human-readable name.

- **id**—The unique identifier.

- **icon**—The relative path to an image (optional).

- **class**—The `FavoriteItemType` for creating items of this type.

- **targetClass**—The type of object being wrapped by this type.

> **Tip:** If your extension point is intended for general consumption, then have a plan for lazy extension initialization so that you do not cause more plug-ins than are needed to be loaded, resulting in memory bloat and slowing down the system. For example, in our case, the `targetClass` is used to determine which **Favorites** item type should be used *before* the plug-in that defines it is actually loaded. If we do not have this information specified in the extension, then when a user dragged and dropped a new object onto the **Favorites** view, we would need to load and query each **Favorites** type to determine which type should handle the dropped object. This could potentially pull in many more plug-ins than necessary, bloating and slowing down the workspace. Instead, we pre-screen the types based on the `targetClass` to determine which type may be able to handle the dropped object. If your extension point is intended for use only within your own plug-in, then you do not need the extra complexity and overhead associated with a proxy.

First, we need to add an `itemType` element representing the **Favorites** item type being defined, to which we will add these attributes. To accomplish this, switch back to the **Definition** page, click on the **New Element** button, and double-click on the `new_element1` that was created to open the **Properties** view. In the **Properties** view, change the name to "itemType".

With `itemType` selected in the schema editor, click the **New Attribute** button to add a new attribute to the `itemType` element. In the **Properties** view, change the name to "name". With the `name` attribute selected in the schema editor, enter "A human-readable name for this type of Favorites object." for the description of the name attribute, and click **Apply**. Repeat this process to add four more attributes. When you are done, you should have defined the following attributes for the `itemType` element with the following properties:

- **attribute #1**
  name = "name"
  use = "optional"
  kind = "string"
  description =
      "A human-readable name for this type of Favorites object."

- **attribute #2**
  name = "id"
  use = "required"
  kind = "string"
  description =
      "The unique identifier for this type of Favorites object."

- **attribute #3**
  name = "icon"
  use = "optional"
  kind = "resource"
  description =
      "An option image associated with this type of Favorites object."

- **attribute #4**
  name = "class"
  use = "required"
  kind = "java"
  BasedOn =
      "com.qualityeclipse.favorites.model.FavoriteItemType"
  description =
      "The fully qualified name of the class that extends
      <samp>com.qualityeclipse.favorites
          .model.FavoriteItemType</samp>."

- **attribute #5**
  name = "targetClass"

use = "required"
kind = "string"
description =

"The fully qualified name of the class wrapped by this item
type. This is not the class name for the IFavoriteItem object
returned by either
<samp>FavoriteItemType.loadFavorite(String)</samp> or
<samp>FavoriteItemType.newFavorite(Object)</samp>, but
rather the object wrapped by that IFavoriteItem object that
causes the IFavoriteItem.isFavoriteFor(Object) to return true."

Tip: How should an extension provide behavior for your extension
point? Do you require extensions to implement an interface or instead
extend an abstract base class? If you require extensions to implement an
interface, then you grant more flexibility to the extension writer. On the
downside, any change to that interface will break existing extensions.
Instead, if you require extensions to extend an abstract base class, then
you keep some flexibility while still retaining advantages of loose
coupling. Adding a concrete method to an abstract base class will not
break existing extensions, giving you the opportunity to change the API
in future implementations, all without sacrificing much of the extension
writer's flexibility. If you are *sure* that your API will not change, then an
interface is a great way to go; otherwise, an abstract base class gives you
the flexibility you need to evolve the API.

   If you *need* the flexibility of an interface where an abstract base class
will not do, then consider requiring the interface but providing an
abstract base class that implements that interface for extensions to build
on if they choose. Given this approach, you can change the interface API
and mitigate disruption by adding concrete methods in your abstract base
class that implement any new interface methods. Any extension that uses
the abstract base class will be unperturbed by your interface API changes,
whereas any extension that implements the interface directly must be
modified to fit the new API.

17.2.4   *Extension point element grammar*

After the extension point elements have been defined, we construct the element grammar describing how the elements are assembled in a way that can
be validated by the PDE. When you select an element in the **Extension Point
Elements** list on the left, the grammar associated with the element is displayed
in the **Element Grammar** on the right. The grammar on the right describes the
child elements of the selected element on the left. If you select an element on

the left and no grammar appears on the right, then the selected element on the left cannot have any child elements. Double-clicking on a grammar element on the right opens the **Properties** view and displays the properties associated with the grammar element.

Rather than present all possible grammar elements, we will present several common scenarios and the associated grammar in Table 17–1. The desired XML structure appears on the left. On the right is the grammar used to describe the structure with property values between brackets [ ].

Table 17.1   XML Grammar

XML	Grammar

```<parentElement … >```
    ```<childElement … />```
```</parentElement>```
	+ Sequence
	   childElement

```<parentElement … >```
    ```<childElement … />```
    ```<childElement … />```
    …
```</parentElement>```
	+ Sequence
	   childElement
	     [minOccurs = "0"]
	     [maxOccurs = "unbounded"]

```<parentElement … >```
    ```<childElement1 … />```
    ```<childElement1 … />```
    …
    ```<childElement2 … />```
    ```<childElement2 … />```
    …
```</parentElement>```
	+ Sequence
	   childElement1
	     [minOccurs = "0"]
	     [maxOccurs = "unbounded"]
	   childElement2
	     [minOccurs = "0"]
	     [maxOccurs = "unbounded"]

```<parentElement … >```
    ```<childElement1 … />```
    ```<childElement2 … />```
```</parentElement>```
 - OR -
```<parentElement … >```
    ```<childElement1 … />```
    ```<childElement3 … />```
```</parentElement>```
	+ Sequence
	   childElement1
	  + Choice
	     childElement2
	     childElement3

Whenever anyone extends our extension point, we want there to be one or more `itemType` elements as part of that extension declaration. In the schema editor, select the extension point element `extension` in the **Extension**

Point Elements list, causing Sequence to appear in the **Element Grammar** list on the right. Select Sequence, then right-click and select **New > Reference > itemType**. Expand Sequence so that itemType appears as a child hierarchically under Sequence, and then double-click on itemType to open the **Properties** view. In the **Properties** view select **maxOccurs** and enter "unbounded". After this is complete, you should see itemType (1-*) in the **Element Grammar** list (see Figure 17–6).

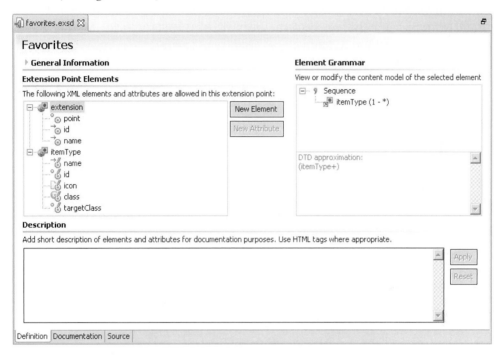

Figure 17–6   The schema editor with the Favorites extension point.

17.3   Code Behind an Extension Point

After the extension point has been defined, we must write the code behind it that builds **Favorites** item types and **Favorites** objects based on the information declared in extensions of the extension point. Following the Eclipse theme of lazy initialization, we want to keep our memory footprint down, so each **Favorites** item type and plug-in containing it must be loaded only if necessary. To achieve this, we refactor portions of FavoriteItemType (see Section 7.2.3) into a new FavoriteItemFactory and then reorganize FavoriteItemType to build types from extension information. This is followed by recasting the **Favorites** item type constants as extensions to the new **Favorites** extension point.

17.3.1   *Parsing extension information*

The first modification to the FavoriteItemType involves building instances of this class from the extension information rather than hard-coding the information in the class as constants. Rename the TYPES array to cachedTypes to more accurately represent the purpose of this static field. Modify the get-Types() method to build a new instance of FavoriteItemType for each extension found.

```
private static final String TAG_ITEMTYPE = "itemType";

private static FavoriteItemType[] cachedTypes;

public static FavoriteItemType[] getTypes() {
   if (cachedTypes != null)
      return cachedTypes;
   IExtension[] extensions =
      FavoritesPlugin
         .getDefault()
         .getDescriptor()
         .getExtensionPoint("favorites")
         .getExtensions();
   List found = new ArrayList(20);
   found.add(UNKNOWN);
   for (int i = 0; i < extensions.length; i++) {
      IConfigurationElement[] configElements =
         extensions[i].getConfigurationElements();
      for (int j = 0; j < configElements.length; j++) {
         FavoriteItemType proxy =
            parseType(configElements[j], found.size());
         if (proxy != null)
            found.add(proxy);
      }
   }
   cachedTypes =
      (FavoriteItemType[]) found.toArray(
         new FavoriteItemType[found.size()]);
   return cachedTypes;
}

private static FavoriteItemType parseType(
   IConfigurationElement configElement,
   int ordinal) {
   if (!configElement.getName().equals(TAG_ITEMTYPE))
      return null;
   try {
      return new FavoriteItemType(configElement, ordinal);
   }
   catch (Exception e) {
```

```
      String name = configElement.getAttribute(ATT_NAME);
      if (name == null)
         name = "[missing name attribute]";
      String msg =
         "Failed to load itemType named "
            + name
            + " in "
            + configElement
               .getDeclaringExtension()
               .getDeclaringPluginDescriptor()
               .getUniqueIdentifier();
      FavoritesLog.logError(msg, e);
      return null;
   }
}
```

> **Tip:** As always, proper exception handling is necessary, especially when handling loosely coupled code via extension points. In this case, the instance creation is wrapped in an exception handler so that an improperly declared extension will not cause this method to fail, but instead will generate a log entry containing enough information for the culprit to be tracked down and corrected.

17.3.2   Constructing proxies

Next, we modify the `FavoriteItemType` constructor to extract the basic information from the extension without loading the plug-in that declared the extension. This instance stands in as a proxy for the factory contained in the declaring plug-in. If a required attribute is missing, then an `IllegalArgumentException` is thrown, to be caught in the exception handler of the `parseType(...)` method described earlier.

```
private static final String ATT_ID = "id";
private static final String ATT_NAME = "name";
private static final String ATT_CLASS = "class";
private static final String ATT_TARGETCLASS = "targetClass";
private static final String ATT_ICON = "icon";

private final IConfigurationElement configElement;
private final int ordinal;
private final String id;
private final String name;
private final String targetClassName;
private FavoriteItemFactory factory;
private ImageDescriptor imageDescriptor;

public FavoriteItemType(
   IConfigurationElement configElem,
   int ordinal) {
```

```
    this.configElement = configElem;
    this.ordinal = ordinal;
    id = getAttribute(configElem, ATT_ID, null);
    name = getAttribute(configElem, ATT_NAME, id);
    targetClassName =
        getAttribute(configElem, ATT_TARGETCLASS, null);

    // Make sure that class is defined,
    // but don't load it.
    getAttribute(configElem, ATT_CLASS, null);
}

private static String getAttribute(
    IConfigurationElement configElem,
    String name,
    String defaultValue) {

    String value = configElem.getAttribute(name);
    if (value != null)
        return value;
    if (defaultValue != null)
        return defaultValue;
    throw new IllegalArgumentException(
        "Missing " + name + " attribute");
}
```

> **Tip:** How do you determine what information to load from an extension immediately versus what should be deferred via lazy initialization to an accessor method? Methods that load extension attribute values, such as `IConfigurationElement.getAttribute (String)`, are very quick to execute because they return already cached information. Other methods, such as `IConfigurationElement.createExecutableExtension(String)`, are quite slow because they will load the declaring plug-in into memory if it has not been loaded already. Our philosophy is to cache and validate attribute values up-front, providing immediate validation and "fast fail" for much of the extension information, but to defer via lazy initialization anything that would cause the declaring plug-in to be loaded.

Potentially, every extension could be invalid and we could end up with no valid instances of `FavoriteItemType` returned by `getTypes()`. To alleviate this problem, we hard-code a single `FavoriteItemType` named `UNKNOWN` and add this as the first object in the collection returned by `getTypes()`:

```
public static final FavoriteItemType UNKNOWN =
   new FavoriteItemType() {
   public IFavoriteItem newFavorite(Object obj) {
      return null;
   }
   public IFavoriteItem loadFavorite(String info) {
      return null;
```

```
      }
};

private FavoriteItemType() {
   this.id = "Unknown";
   this.ordinal = 0;
   this.name = "Unknown";
   this.configElement = null;
   this.targetClassName = "";
}
```

Now, we will revise the accessors for obtaining information about the item type based on our cached extension information. The `icon` attribute is assumed to have a path relative to the declaring plug-in, and the image descriptor is constructed accordingly. Images take precious native resources and load comparatively slowly, thus they are lazily initialized on an as-needed basis. Loaded images are cached so that they can be reused and then properly disposed of when the plug-in is shut down (see Section 7.7, "Image Caching," for `ImageCache` information).

```
private static final ImageCache imageCache =
   new ImageCache();

public String getId() {
   return id;
}

public String getName() {
   return name;
}

public Image getImage() {
   return imageCache.getImage(getImageDescriptor());
}

public ImageDescriptor getImageDescriptor() {
   if (imageDescriptor != null)
      return imageDescriptor;
   String iconName = configElement.getAttribute(ATT_ICON);
   if (iconName == null)
      return null;
   IExtension extension =
      configElement.getDeclaringExtension();
   String extendingPluginId =
      extension
         .getDeclaringPluginDescriptor()
         .getUniqueIdentifier();
   imageDescriptor =
      AbstractUIPlugin.imageDescriptorFromPlugin(
         extendingPluginId,
         iconName);
   return imageDescriptor;
}
```

17.3.3   *Creating executable extensions*

The `loadFavorite(String)` and `newFavorite(Object)` methods are redirected to the `factory` object as specified in the extension. Since instantiating the `factory` object involves loading the plug-in that contains it, this operation is deferred until needed. The `targetClassName` is used by the `newFavorite(Object)` method to determine whether or not the associated `factory` can handle the specified object and thus whether or not the associated `factory` needs to be loaded. The code that instantiates the `factory` object is wrapped in an exception handler so that detailed information can be logged concerning the failure that occurred and which plug-in and extension are involved.

```
public IFavoriteItem newFavorite(Object obj) {
   if (!isTarget(obj))
      return null;
   FavoriteItemFactory factory = getFactory();
   if (factory == null)
      return null;
   return factory.newFavorite(this, obj);
}

private boolean isTarget(Object obj) {
   if (obj == null)
      return false;
   Class clazz = obj.getClass();
   if (clazz.getName().equals(targetClassName))
      return true;
   Class[] interfaces = clazz.getInterfaces();
   for (int i = 0; i < interfaces.length; i++)
      if (interfaces[i].getName()
         .equals(targetClassName))
            return true;
   return false;
}

public IFavoriteItem loadFavorite(String info) {
   FavoriteItemFactory factory = getFactory();
   if (factory == null)
      return null;
   return factory.loadFavorite(this, info);
}

private FavoriteItemFactory getFactory() {
   if (factory != null)
      return factory;
   try {
      factory = (FavoriteItemFactory) configElement
         .createExecutableExtension(ATT_CLASS);
   }
```

```
      catch (Exception e) {
         FavoritesLog.logError(
            "Failed to instantiate factory: "
               + configElement.getAttribute(ATT_CLASS)
               + " in type: "
               + id
               + " in plugin: "
               + configElement
                  .getDeclaringExtension()
                  .getDeclaringPluginDescriptor()
                  .getUniqueIdentifier(),
            e);
      }
      return factory;
}
```

> **Tip:** Whenever instantiating an object specified in an extension, always use the
> `IConfigurationElement.createExecutable(String)` method. The
> `IConfigurationElement.createExecutable(String)` method automatically
> handles references from extensions in one plug-in's manifest to code located in
> another plug-in's run-time library as well as various forms of post-instantiation
> initialization specified in the extension (see Section 20.5, "Types Specified in an
> Extension Point"). If you use `Class.forName(String)`, then you will only be
> able to instantiate objects already known to your plug-in because
> `Class.forName(String)` uses your plug-in's class loader and thus will only
> instantiate objects in your plug-in's classpath (see Section 20.9, "Plug-in Class
> Loaders," for more on class loaders).

The new `factory` type is an abstract base class that must be extended by
other plug-ins providing new types of favorites objects. See the "**Tip**" in Section 17.2.3 for a discussion of interface versus abstract base class. The `fac-
tory` type includes a concrete `dispose` method so that subclasses may perform
cleanup if necessary, but are not required to implement this method if cleanup
is not needed.

```
package com.qualityeclipse.favorites.model;

public abstract class FavoriteItemFactory
{
   public abstract IFavoriteItem newFavorite(
      FavoriteItemType type,
      Object obj);

   public abstract IFavoriteItem loadFavorite(
      FavoriteItemType type,
      String info);

   public void dispose() {
      // Nothing to do... subclasses may override.
   }
}
```

17.3.4   Cleanup

When the plug-in shuts down, we must dispose of all cached images and give each of the `factory` objects an opportunity to clean up. Add the `dispose-Types()` and `dispose()` methods to the `FavoriteItemType` as shown following. Modify the `FavoritesPlugin` `shutdown()` method to call this new `disposeTypes()` method.

```
public static void disposeTypes() {
   if (cachedTypes == null)
      return;
   for (int i = 0; i < cachedTypes.length; i++)
      cachedTypes[i].dispose();
   imageCache.dispose();
   cachedTypes = null;
}

public void dispose() {
   if (factory == null)
      return;
   factory.dispose();
   factory = null;
}
```

17.4   Extension Point Documentation

Now that the extension point and related schema (see Section 17.2, "Defining an Extension Point") have been declared, the PDE will include them in any list of known plug-in extension points. In addition, the documentation snippets added as part of the schema (see Section 17.2.2 and 17.2.3) are dynamically built by the PDE into extension point help pages as requested. Navigate to the plug-in manifest editor's **Extensions** page and click on the **Add...** button. The **New Extensions** wizard now includes the new `favorites` extension point (see Figure 17–7).

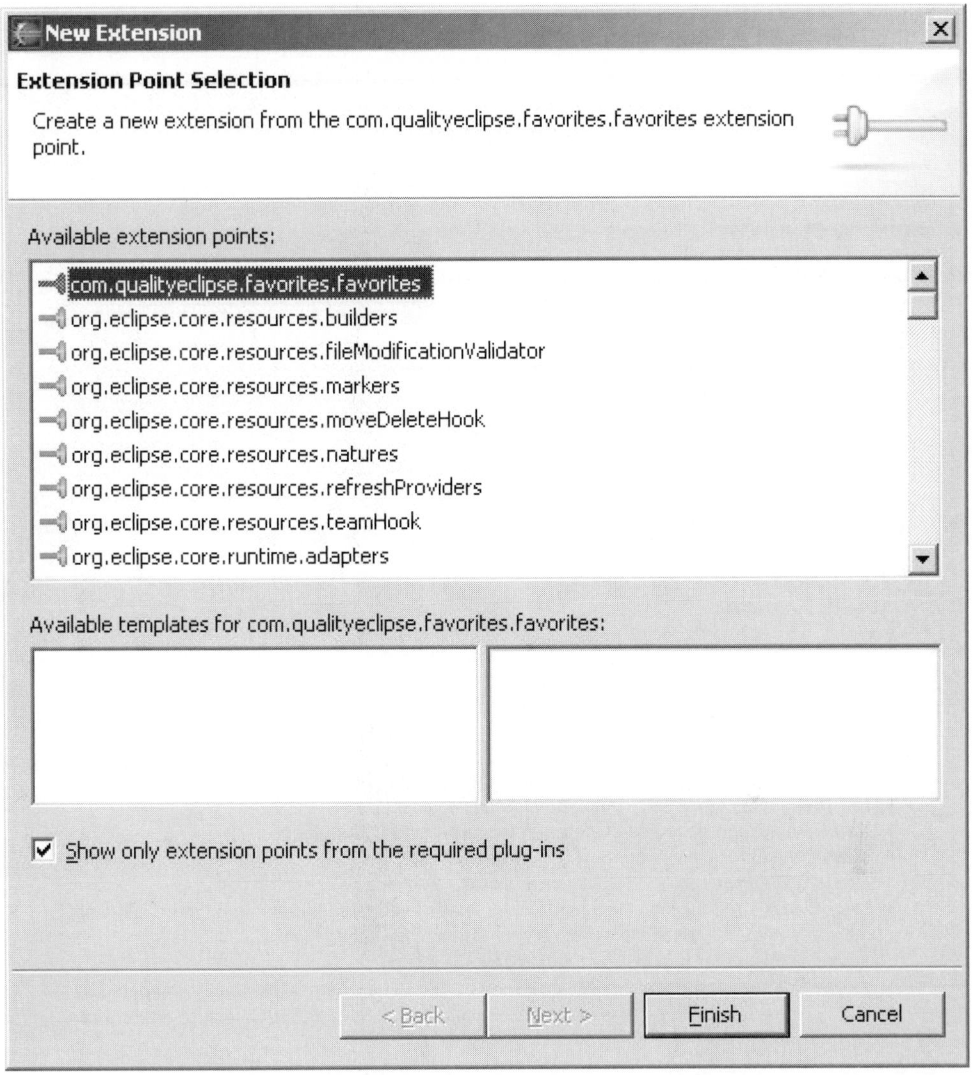

Figure 17–7 New Extension wizard showing Favorites extension point.

To see the dynamically generated help pages, select the favorites extension point and right-click to select the **Details** command. This opens a browser to display the HTML help page for the favorites extension point (see Figure 17–8).

Figure 17–8 Dynamically generated help for the Favorites extension point.

17.5 Using the Extension Point

The FavoriteItemType has been refactored to utilize information from the favorites extension point. So now, the constants in that class must be recast as extensions and associated `factory` classes. This modification will help us test our new extension point.

On the plug-in manifest editor's **Extensions** page, click the **Add...** button to open the **New Extensions** wizard. When the wizard appears, select the new `favorites` extension point (see Figure 17–6) and click **Finish**.

Now that we have created an extension, we need to add a new `itemType` representing the **Workbench File** item type. Right-click on the new favorites extension and select **New > itemType** to add a new **Favorites** item type. Double-click on the new `itemType` to open the **Properties** view and change the properties as follows (see Figure 17–9):

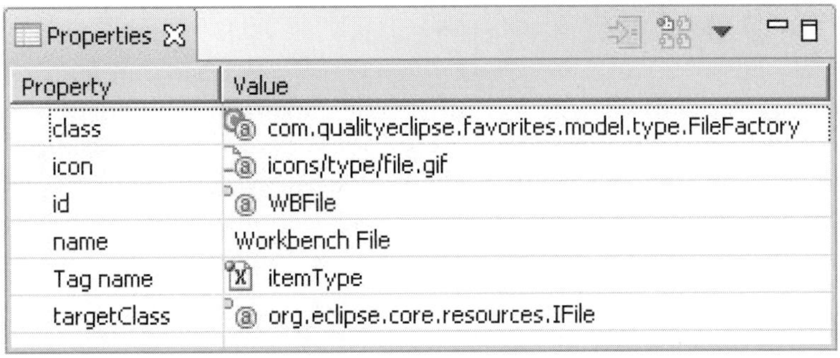

Property	Value
class	com.qualityeclipse.favorites.model.type.FileFactory
icon	icons/type/file.gif
id	WBFile
name	Workbench File
Tag name	itemType
targetClass	org.eclipse.core.resources.IFile

Figure 17–9   Properties view showing Workbench File item type properties.

For the **icon** attribute specified above, we have copied icons from the Eclipse UI and JDT UI plug-ins into our own **Favorites** plug-in. Clicking the "..." button at the right of the **icon** attribute field opens an image selection dialog so that you can select the appropriate image for the item type from images defined in the plug-in.

For the **class** attribute, select the "..." button at the right of the **class** attribute field to open the **Java Attribute Editor** wizard. Enter "com.qualityeclipse.favorites.model.type" as the package name and "FileFactory" as the type name. Click on the **Finish** button to generate the new class. Move the `newFavorite(...)` and `loadFavorite(...)` methods from the WORKBENCH_FILE constant in the `FavoriteItemType` class so that the new `FileFactory` class looks like this:

```
package com.qualityeclipse.favorites.model.type;

import org.eclipse.core.resources.*;
import com.qualityeclipse.favorites.model.*;

public class FileFactory extends FavoriteItemFactory
{
```

```
public IFavoriteItem newFavorite(
   FavoriteItemType type,
   Object obj) {

   if (!(obj instanceof IFile))
      return null;
   return new FavoriteResource(type, (IFile) obj);
}

public IFavoriteItem loadFavorite(
   FavoriteItemType type,
   String info) {

   return FavoriteResource.loadFavorite(type, info);
   }
}
```

Once complete, the first of several **Favorites** item types have been converted from a constant to an extension. Repeat this process multiple times to
recast each constant **Favorites** item type in `FavoriteItemType`, except for the
UNKNOWN item type discussed earlier (see Section 17.3.2).

17.6 RFWS Considerations

The "Extension Point" section of the *RFWS Requirements* includes five
items—three requirements and two best practices—dealing with defining new
extension points.

17.6.1 *Naming conventions*

Requirement #1 states:
  *The rules introduced in "Eclipse Platform Naming Conventions" of the
  Platform Plug-in Developer Guide apply. Specifically: All plug-ins, including
  the ones that are part of the Eclipse platform, must have unique identifiers following the same naming pattern as Java packages. For example, workbench
  plug-ins are named org.eclipse.ui[.*].*

To pass this test, all you need to do is open the Eclipse **Plug-in Registry**
view and show that your extension points conform to the Eclipse standard
naming conventions (see Figure 17–10).

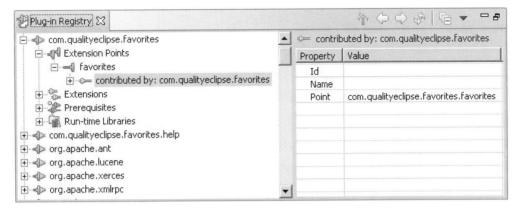

Figure 17–10   Plug-in Registry view showing the Favorites extension point.

17.6.2   Document extension points

Best Practice #2 states:

Documentation on how to use the newly defined extension points must be available for those extension points that are considered public. The necessary documentation of the extension's child tags should be generated as part of the extension point's schema definition. The related interface or class documentation should be generated from the class Javadoc. Documentation should be provided in the plug-in's doc subdirectory.

For this test, show the documentation for your extension points and its associate class or interface. The extension point documentation can be automatically generated from the **Extension** page of the plug-in manifest editor by right-clicking on the extension and selecting **Show Description** (see Figure 17–8).

17.6.3   Interface for executable extensions

Requirement #3 states:

An interface, base class, or abstract class that has methods for expected behavior for those tag attributes that represent executable extensions must be defined.

Show the classes or interfaces that support the executable extensions defined by your extension points. For instance, for the **Favorites** plug-in, we would show the FavoriteItemFactory class.

17.6.4 Treat plug-in registry as read-only

Requirement #4 states:

Plug-ins must not modify or delete the registry elements of other plug-ins. That is, the result returned by Platform.getPluginRegistry() must be treated as read-only.

Before installing your plugin, select the **Help > About... > Configuration Details** command to create a baseline of the current system configuration. After installing your plug-in, select the command again to generate new configuration details and highlight the differences from the original baseline.

17.6.5 Log errors

Best Practice #5 states:

The registry processing code must log any errors that it detects in the plug-in log.

Show that the registry processing code of your plug-in handles any errors in the specification of extensions to your plug-in's extension points. For the **Favorites** extension point, we would create an extension that was missing the name attribute. This would create an entry in the Eclipse **Error Log** view (see Figure 17–11).

Figure 17–11   Error log showing error in extension specification.

17.7   Summary

Extension points are the primary mechanism used to extend Eclipse. Every Eclipse plug-in makes use of dozens of them to contribute new views, actions, editors, and so on. Extension points are not limited, however, to Eclipse itself. Your plug-ins can define extension points either for their internal consumption only or for other third-party plug-ins to use. In this chapter, we demonstrated in detail the process of creating and using a new extension point.

CHAPTER 18

Features and Branding

One or more Eclipse plug-ins can be grouped together into an Eclipse feature so that a user can easily load, manage, and brand those plug-ins as a single unit. This chapter includes an overview of the Eclipse feature framework and shows how to create a simple feature using the built-in feature creation wizard. We will also discuss using features to commercialize or brand a plug-in-based product and will conclude with a description of how to package and deliver features via an update-enabled Web site.

So far, we have created several plug-ins, which have contributed different features to our **Favorites** view. Each plug-in has been loosely coupled to other plug-ins, and collectively have not exhibited any unifying structure or identity. A feature provides this structure and a home for branding elements such as the **About** and **Welcome** pages (see Figure 18–1).

Once packaged as a feature, you will then be able to load and unload your plug-ins as a single unit using the Eclipse **Update Manager.**

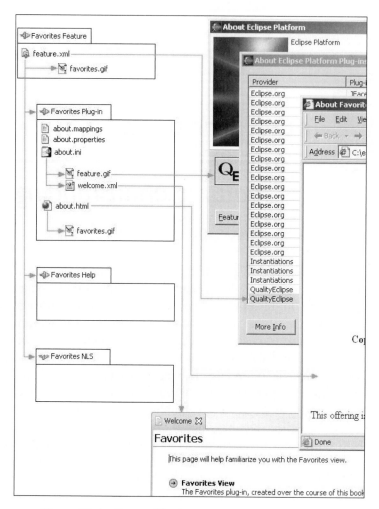

Figure 18–1   Feature file relationships and branding elements.

18.1   Feature Projects

Our **Favorites** example includes three projects—"Favorites Plug-in," "Favorites Help," and "Favorites NLS Fragment"—that we would like to combine together into a single feature.

18.1.1   *Creating a new feature project*

To create our new feature, we will begin by using the **New Project** wizard to create a new **Feature Project** (see Figure 18–2).

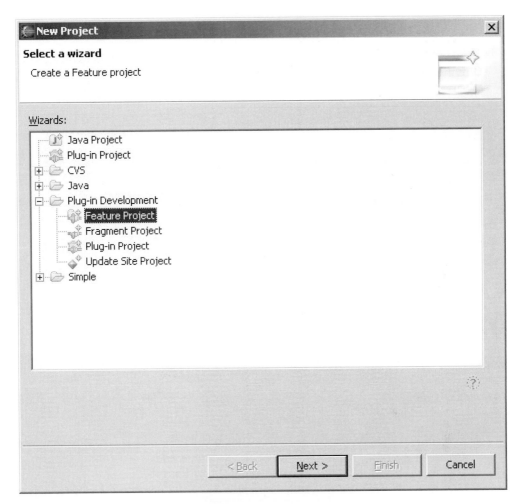

Figure 18–2   The New Project wizard.

On the first page of the **New Feature** wizard (see Figure 18–3), enter "com.qualityeclipse.favorites.feature" as the project name. Click the **Next** button.

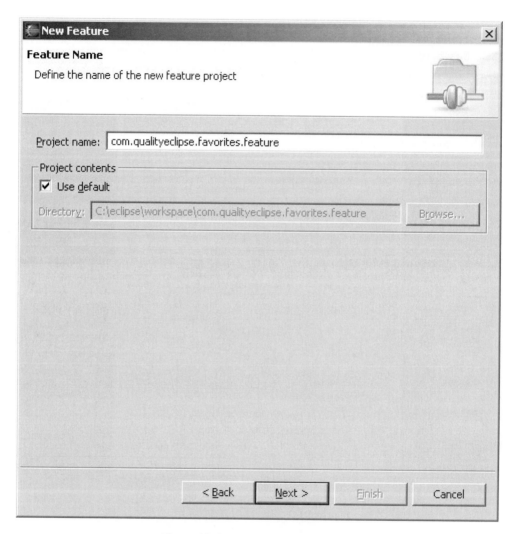

Figure 18–3   The New Feature wizard.

On the second page of the wizard (see Figure 18–4), change the feature ID to "com.qualityeclipse.favorites" so that it matches the ID of our main plug-in. This is important because the generally accepted practice in the Eclipse world is to locate feature branding files (such as about.ini and welcome.xml) in the plug-in with the same ID as the feature (as we will see a bit later, this is not strictly required—see Section 18.1.3, "Feature manifest editor").

A couple of other fields should be filled in on this page as well: Change the **Feature Name** to "Favorites Feature"; leave the **Feature Version** set to "1.0.0"; and set the **Feature Provider** to "QualityEclipse". Click the **Next** button.

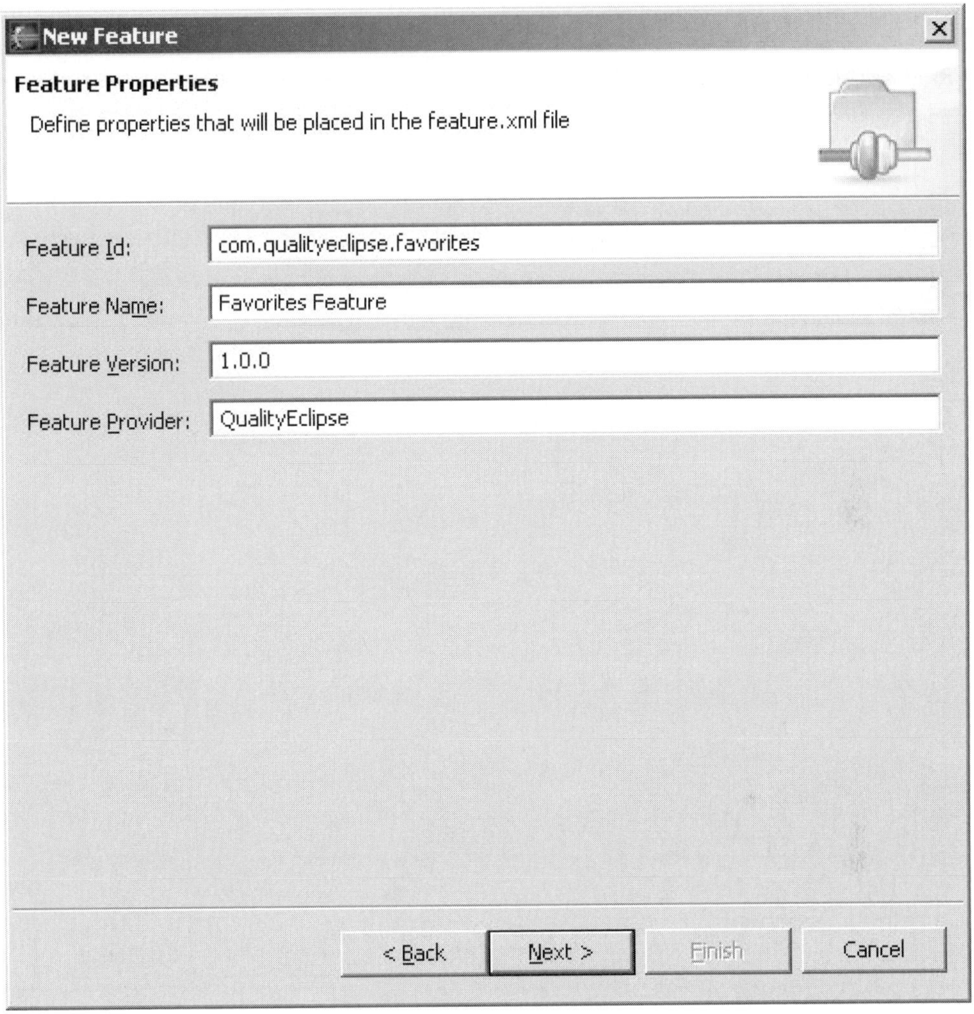

Figure 18–4   Feature properties.

The next page of the wizard (not shown) deals with setting up a custom install handler. This is an advanced feature, which won't be covered in this book. Leave the settings unchanged and click the **Next** button.

On the last page of the wizard (see Figure 18–5), you will see a list of all the loaded plug-ins and fragments defined in your workspace along with their version numbers. In this case, we see the two plug-ins and one fragment that we created earlier in the book. Click the **Select All** button to select them all. Click **Finish** to create the project and generate the feature manifest file.

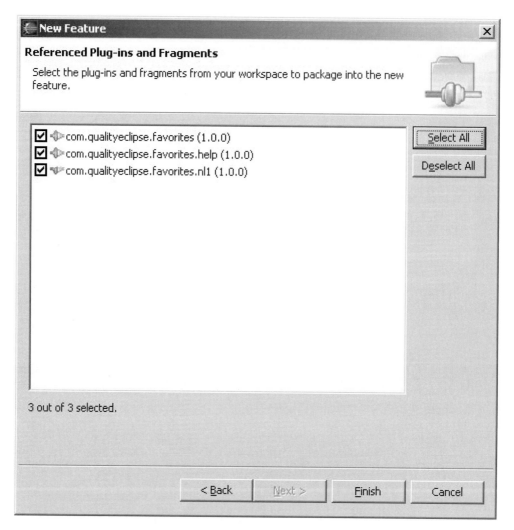

Figure 18–5 Referenced plug-ins and fragments.

18.1.2 Feature manifest files

The wizard created a single file of interest: the feature manifest file. Based on the options selected in the wizard, the feature manifest file (`feature.xml`) will look like this:

```
<?xml version="1.0" encoding="UTF-8"?>
<feature
      id="com.qualityeclipse.favorites"
      label="Favorites Feature"
```

```
        version="1.0.0"
        provider-name="QualityEclipse">

    <requires>
        <import plugin="org.eclipse.ui.ide"/>
        <import plugin="org.eclipse.ui.views"/>
        <import plugin="org.eclipse.jface.text"/>
        <import plugin=
            "org.eclipse.ui.workbench.texteditor"/>
        <import plugin="org.eclipse.ui.editors"/>
        <import plugin="org.eclipse.core.resources"/>
        <import plugin="org.eclipse.ui"/>
        <import plugin="org.eclipse.jdt.core"/>
        <import plugin="org.eclipse.jdt.ui"/>
        <import plugin="org.eclipse.help"/>
    </requires>

    <plugin
        id="com.qualityeclipse.favorites"
        download-size="0"
        install-size="0"
        version="1.0.0"/>

    <plugin
        id="com.qualityeclipse.favorites.help"
        download-size="0"
        install-size="0"
        version="1.0.0"/>

    <plugin
        id="com.qualityeclipse.favorites.nl1"
        download-size="0"
        install-size="0"
        version="1.0.0"
        fragment="true"/>
</feature>
```

The structure is fairly simple. At the beginning of the file, you will find the id, label, version and provider-name attributes. The requires section lists all the plug-ins that this feature needs to have loaded as prerequisites. This list is built automatically by merging the lists of required plug-ins from each of the included plug-ins.

The remainder of the file lists the individual plug-ins and fragments that compose this feature. Each plug-in is identified by its plug-in ID, and the version attribute specifies the specific version of the plug-in that is part of this feature. In general, the version numbers of the included plug-ins should match the version number of the feature. Having the fragment attribute set to true identifies any included fragments.

18.1.3   *Feature manifest editor*

The fragment manifest generated by the wizard contains the barest essential elements needed to define a fragment. Numerous other attributes can be defined to enhance a feature. The feature manifest editor provides a convenient interface for editing the existing attributes of a feature or adding new attributes.

Double-clicking on the feature manifest file, `feature.xml`, will open the feature manifest editor (see Figure 18–6). The editor looks very similar to the plug-in manifest editor with **Overview, Information, Content, Advanced,** and **Source** pages.

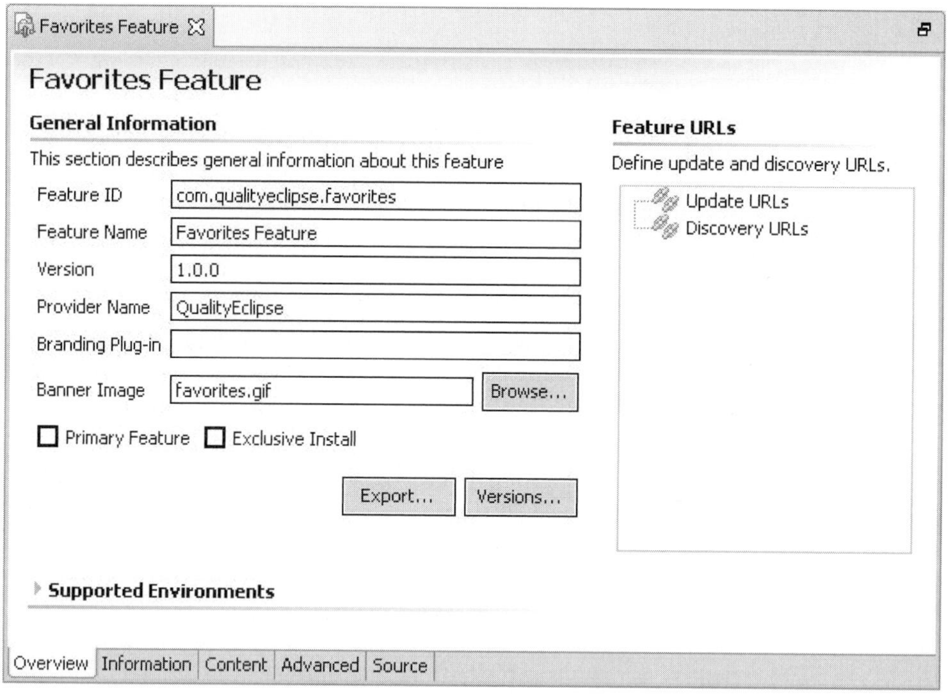

Figure 18–6   Feature manifest editor.

There are a lot of things happening on this page. Initially, the **Feature ID, Feature Name, Version,** and **Provider Name** fields will be filled in based on our inputs to the wizard pages. There are two more fields to make note of here: The **Branding Plug-in** field contains the name of the plug-in that will contain the feature branding files. If this field is left blank (as is the generally accepted practice), the plug-in having the same ID as the feature will automatically be used as the branding plug-in. The **Banner Image** field is used to specify the name of an image file that will be shown when the feature is selected in the Eclipse **Update Manager**.

Below these fields are two checkboxes: The **Primary Feature** option is used to mark this feature as the primary feature defining a product that is built on top of Eclipse. If your feature is meant to plug into an existing Eclipse environment, leave this option unchecked. The **Exclusive Install** option is used to prevent your feature from being installed simultaneously with a number of other features. Unless there is something unique about your feature that prevents it from being installed properly in conjunction with other features, you should leave this option unchecked.

Below the two checkboxes, you will find two buttons: The **Export** button is used to build and deploy the feature. We will ignore this option and will focus on a much more comprehensive build operation in Chapter 19, "Building a Product." The **Versions** button is used to synchronize the version numbers of the included plug-ins and fragments with the version number of the feature. If these version numbers don't match, the **Update Manager** won't be able to install the feature properly. Clicking the button will open the **Version Synchronization** dialog (see Figure 18–7). The dialog contains three options: The first, and most useful option, is **Force feature version into plug-in and fragment manifests**. This will update the manifest files of all included plug-ins and fragments so that their version numbers match the version number of the feature. The second option, **Copy versions from plug-in and fragment manifests,** will copy the individual version numbers from each plug-in and fragment and update the corresponding plug-in entry in the feature manifest file. The final option, **Force versions defined in the feature into plug-in and fragment manifests**, does the reverse and takes the individual version numbers defined for each plug-in in the feature manifest file and updates the manifest files of the corresponding plug-ins and fragments. Select an option and click **Finish** to return to the manifest editor.

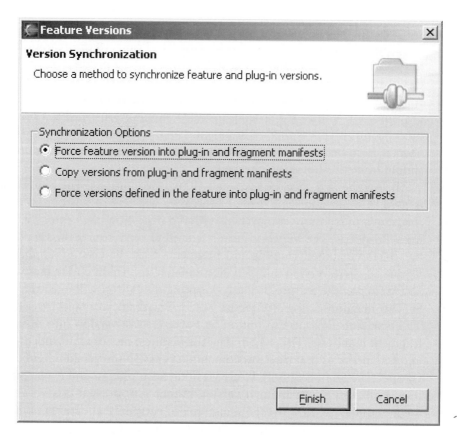

Figure 18–7   The Version Synchronization dialog.

At the right of the manifest editor, there is a tree containing defined **update** and **discovery** URLs. When the **Update Manager** is looking for updates to your plug-in, it will look at the sites defined by your update URLs. The discovery URLs are used to point to other sites of interest to your plug-in. These will be discussed in more detail in Section 18.3, "Update Sites."

For most plug-ins written against the public Eclipse API, portability to different Eclipse platforms won't be a problem. Eclipse does not prevent you, however, from making use of platform-specific functionality (such as ActiveX support under Windows). In situations like that, you need to be able to specify which environments are appropriate for your plug-in. Click the small triangle next to the **Supported Environments** label to expand a previously hidden section (see Figure 18–8). Here, you can supply a comma-separated list of valid values for **Operating Systems, Window Systems, Languages,** and **Architecture.**

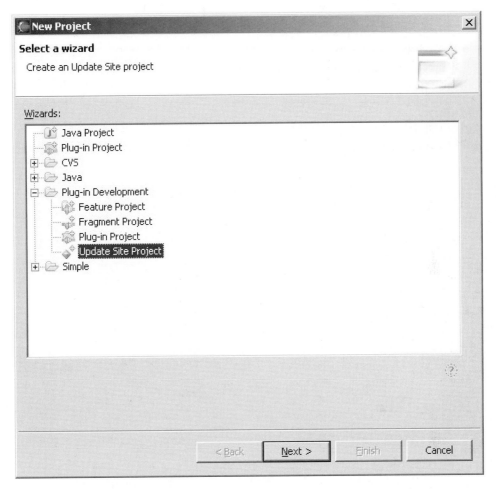

Figure 18–8   Feature manifest editor showing the supported environments.

Clicking on the button to the right of each field will open a selection dialog appropriate to the chosen environment type. For example, the choices available for **Operating Systems** include **aix, hpux, linux, macosx, qnx, solaris,** and **win32** (see Figure 18–9).

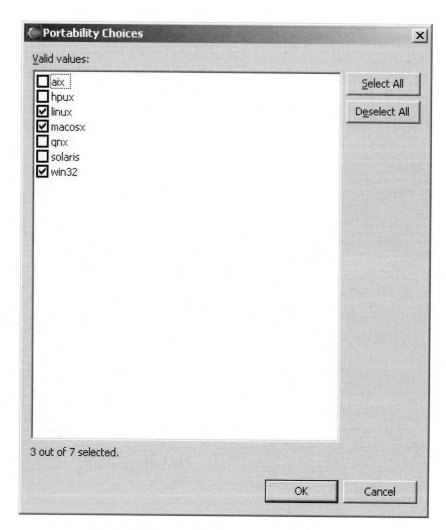

Figure 18–9   Portability choices for operating systems.

The **Section** field on the **Information** page of the editor provides options for specifying description, license, and copyright information about the feature (see Figure 18–10). The feature description will be displayed by the **Update Manager** when the feature is selected. This information, as well as the license and copyright text, is displayed in the **Properties** dialog that appears when the **Show Properties** link is clicked within the **Update Manager**. For each of these items, you can either enter text into the **Text** field or you can specify a URL in the **Optional URL** field. Unless the URL is an absolute reference to a site, the URL is assumed to point to an HTML file that is located relative to the root of the feature.

As you switch between the three **Section** options, make sure to click the **Apply** button after making any changes. If you fail to do so, you will lose your changes. Clicking the **Reset** button will clear your current changes and revert them back to whatever value is contained in the file.

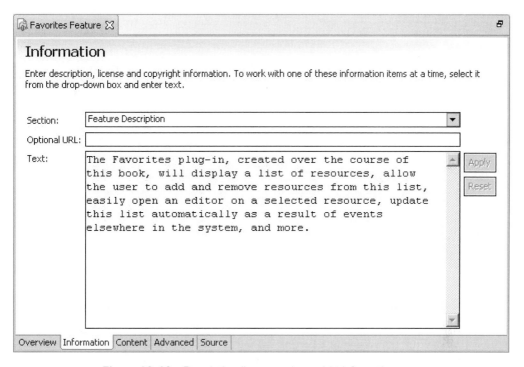

Figure 18–10 Description, license, and copyright information page.

The **Content** page of the editor lists the plug-ins and fragments contained in your feature as well as the list of features and plug-ins required by your feature (see Figure 18–11). In this case, we will see the same three items that we selected when creating the feature originally. Double-clicking on any of these items will open the appropriate manifest editor.

As your project gets more complex, you will find the need to add additional plug-ins or fragments and update the list of required features and plug-ins. Clicking the **Add** button will open a dialog showing a list of all the plug-in and fragment projects available in your workspace. Select one or more and click **Finish** to add them to the list.

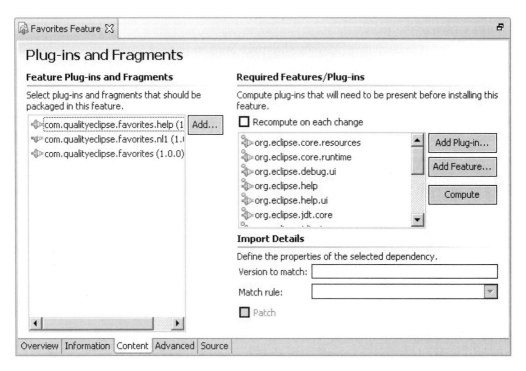

Figure 18–11   Plug-ins and Fragments page.

The **Required Features/Plug-ins** list contains a list of all the features and plug-ins that must be available to install your feature. If any of them is missing, your feature won't be able to load. As stated earlier, the list of required plug-ins was initially computed based on merging the required plug-ins specified by the plug-ins in your feature. You can manually add plug-ins or features to the list by clicking the **Add Plug-in** or **Add Feature** buttons. Clicking the **Compute** button will re-compute the list based on the requirements specified by the plug-ins included in the feature.

For each required plug-in, you can optionally specify a **Version to match** and a **Match rule**. The choices available in the **Match Rule** field control what versions of the plug-in are acceptable prerequisites.

- **Perfect** means that the plug-in must exactly match the supplied version number.

- **Equivalent** means that the version may differ at the service or qualifier level.

- **Compatible** means that the plug-in may have a newer minor version number.

- **Greater or Equal** means that the plug-in may have any newer version number.

If the version number does not match the chosen criteria, that prerequisite will be missing and your feature will not load. In general, you will probably leave these fields blank unless your feature has very specific requirements that will cause it to fail when faced with the wrong version of some expected plug-in (as might be the case if you were using an Eclipse 3.0-specific API that was not available in earlier releases).

The **Patch** option only applies to required features. When this is set, it declares that the feature you are working on is a patch to the selected required feature. This option is rarely used in practice, but if you are interested in finding out more about it, see the **Feature Archives** page in the **Platform Plug-in Developer Guide** contained in the Eclipse online help.

The **Advanced** page of the editor contains a list of subfeatures that are included as part of this feature (see Figure 18–12). Clicking the **Add** button will allow you to select the features that should become children of the current feature.

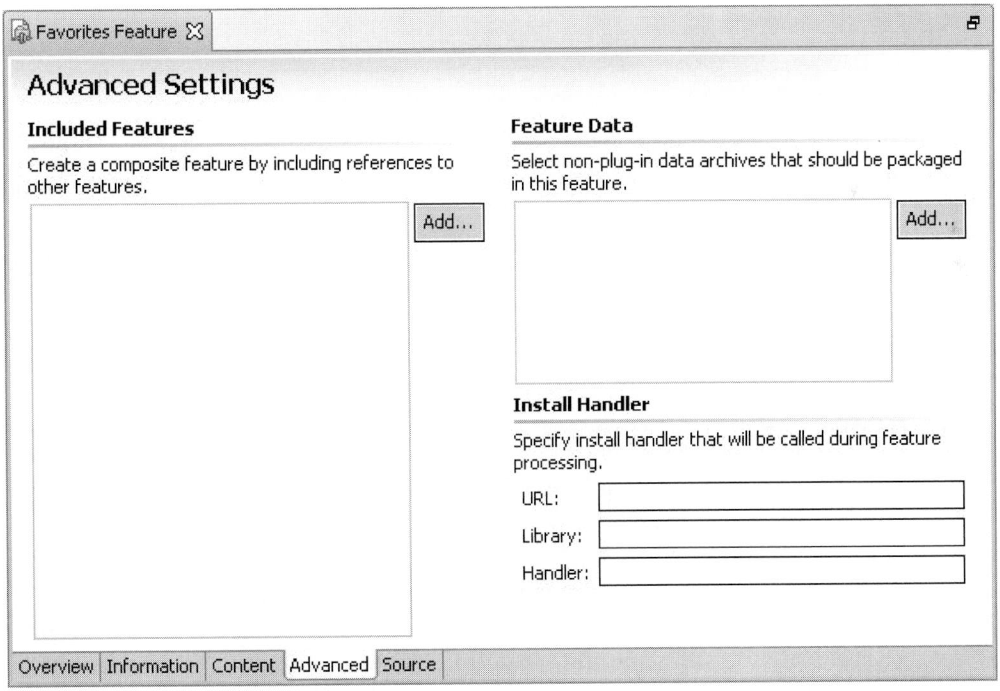

Figure 18–12   Advanced Settings page.

Once you have added a feature, you can right-click on it to see its properties in the **Properties** view (see Figure 18–13). The two required fields are **Id** and **Version**. All the other fields are optional. You can specify a **Match** option (with the same options as were available for required plug-ins and features) that controls whether the inclusion reference is satisfied. If a feature has its **Optional** attribute enabled, it is not required to be present for the parent feature to be successfully loaded (it may be loaded and installed later as necessary). Optional subfeatures may also be enabled or disabled via the **Update Manager** independent of their parent features. The Name attribute is used to supply a name for this feature (for display purpose) in the event that it is missing.

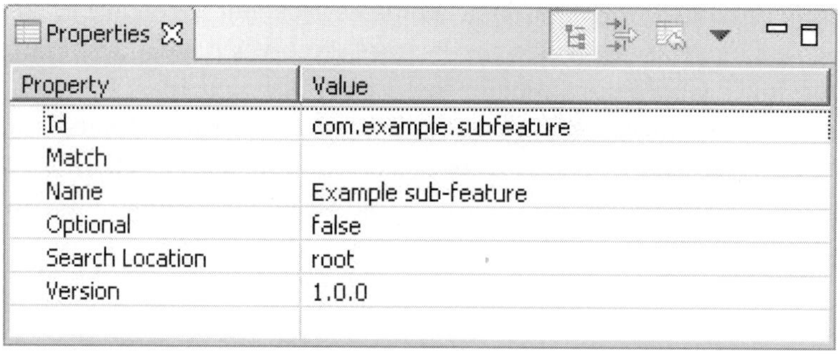

Property	Value
Id	com.example.subfeature
Match	
Name	Example sub-feature
Optional	false
Search Location	root
Version	1.0.0

Figure 18–13   Properties view showing an included feature.

The remaining fields on this page are used for specifying optional non-plug-in items that should be included with this feature as well as advanced installation handlers. These are beyond the scope of this book and won't be discussed further here. For more information, see the **Feature Archives** help page mentioned earlier.

18.2   Branding

In addition to providing structure to your collection of plug-ins and fragments, a feature also provides a single location for all your branding information (e.g., **About** pages, **Welcome** pages, etc.). As stated earlier, the branding elements (such as the banner image shown in the **Update Manager**) are located in the feature project itself; most of the branding elements are located in the feature's associated branding plug-in. This will either be a specific plug-in identified by name or it will be the plug-in with the same name as the feature.

There are quite a few different branding files that come into play at this point. Several of them only apply to primary features while the rest apply to any feature. The files that apply to any type of feature include:

- `about.html`
- `about.ini`
- `about.properties`
- `about.mappings`
- `<feature_image>` (named in the `about.ini` file)
- `welcome.xml`

  The remaining files, which apply only to primary features, include:

- `<about_image>` (named in the `about.ini` file)
- `<window_image>` (named in the `about.ini` file)
- `plugin_customization.ini`
- `plugin_customization.properties`
- `splash.bmp`

18.2.1 The about.html file

Every feature and plug-in should include an `about.html` file. This is a simple HTML file that is displayed when the user opens the Eclipse **About** dialog, opens the **Plug-in Details** dialog, selects a plug-in, and clicks the **More Info** button (see Figure 18–14).

Figure 18–14   Properties view showing an included feature.

Note that to satisfy the RFWS requirements, the about.html must contain the following phrase: "This offering is based on technology from the Eclipse Project". There should also be a link to the Eclipse Web site at *www.eclipse.org.*

18.2.2   The about.ini file

The about.ini file located in the feature's branding plug-in controls most of the feature branding information. It is a standard Java properties file that contains specific keys such as the feature's about text, the name of the image displayed in the Eclipse **About** dialog (see Figure 18–15), the name of the

Welcome page file, and so on. Some of them are required for all features, while others are only needed by primary features.

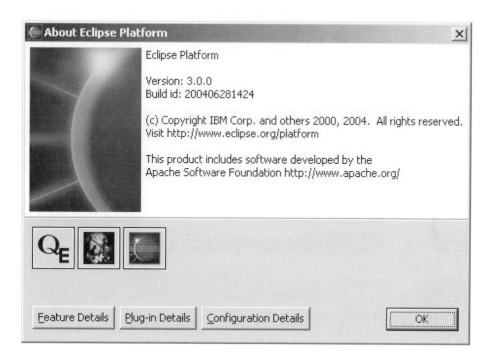

Figure 18–15 The Eclipse About dialog.

Table 18–1 about.ini Keys

Key	Feature Use	Description
aboutText	All	Short multi-line description of the feature
featureImage	All	32x32 pixel image used in **About** dialog
welcomePage	All	File containing **Welcome** page description
welcomePerspective	All	Perspective to show **Welcome** page
tipsAndTricksHref	All	Link to tips and tricks help page
windowImage	Primary Only	16x16 pixel image used in the upper left corner of all workbench windows
aboutImage	Primary Only	Large image used within the **About** dialog
appName	Primary Only	The name of the application

The first key, "aboutText," is a short multi-line description of the feature that should give its name, version number, relevant build information, copyright information, and so on. If the feature is the sole primary feature, this text will be displayed in the Eclipse **About** dialog (see Figure 18–15). If it isn't the primary feature, the text will be visible in the **About Features** dialog (see Figure 18–16), which is accessible by clicking the **Feature Details** button in the **About** dialog.

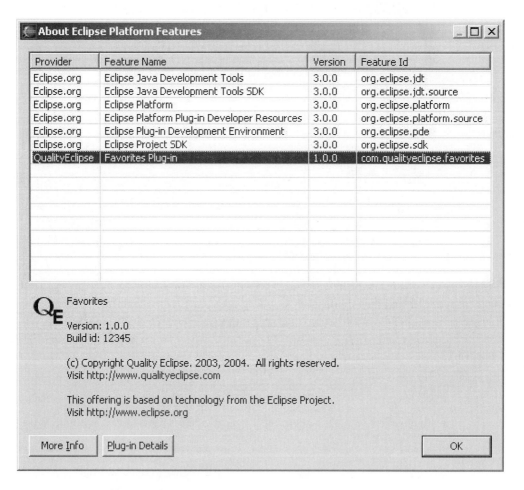

Figure 18–16 The Eclipse About Features dialog.

To localize (translate) this information, the text can be located in an associated about.properties file with a localization key placed in the about.ini file itself. The about text can also be parameterized with values supplied by the about.mappings file. This can be useful encoding information that changes based on the product build (such as a build number) or product install (such as the user's name or license key). For example, the about text might include the phrase "this product is licensed to {0}", where "{0}" represents an argument number that matches a corresponding value in the mappings file, such as "0=Joe User".

The next key in the about.ini file, "featureImage," is used to reference a 32x32 pixel image that will be used to represent the feature in the main **About** dialog (see Figure 18–15) and the **About Features** dialog (see Figure 18–16). If multiple features are installed, multiple feature images will be lined up along the bottom of the **About** dialog.

The "welcomePage" key is used to reference an XML file that contains the feature's **Welcome** page (see Section 18.2.3, "The welcome.xml file"). The **Welcome** page is shown automatically when the feature is first installed and can be accessed at any time via the **Help > Welcome** command. If the welcome page should be shown in a specific perspective, the "welcomePerspective" key can be used to specify the ID of the desired perspective. If your feature does not care which perspective is used, this key should be excluded.

If the feature's documentation includes a "tips and tricks" section, you can reference it with the "tipsAndTricksHref" key. You can access the tips and tricks for any feature that includes them by selecting the **Help > Tips and Tricks** command.

The remainder of the keys supported by the about.ini file only apply to primary features. The "windowImage" key points to a 16x16 pixel image used as the icon in the upper left corner of windows and dialogs in the Eclipse workbench. For the Eclipse workbench itself, this is the ubiquitous Eclipse icon. The "aboutImage" key points to a larger image that is placed next to the about text in the main **About** dialog. If the image is less than 250x330 pixels in size, the image is shown next to the about text. If the image is larger (up to 500x330 pixels in size), the about text will be suppressed. Finally, the key "appName" is used to provide a non-translatable name for the application. For Eclipse, this is just the string "Eclipse".

The about.ini file for the **Favorites** feature should end up looking like this:

```
# about.ini
# contains information about a feature
# java.io.Properties file (ISO 8859-1 with "\" escapes)
# "%key" are externalized strings defined in about.properties
# This file does not need to be translated.

# Property "aboutText" contains blurb for About dialog. (translated)
aboutText=%blurb
```

```
# Property "featureImage" contains path to feature image. (32x32)
featureImage=feature.gif

# Property "welcomePage" contains path to Welcome page.
welcomePage=$nl$/welcome.xml
```

The `about.properties` file contains any translatable strings from the `about.ini` file. For the **Favorites** feature, the file should look like:

```
# about.properties
# contains externalized strings for about.ini
# java.io.Properties file (ISO 8859-1 with "\" escapes)
# fill-ins are supplied by about.mappings
# This file should be translated.

blurb=Favorites\n\
\n\
Version: 1.0.0\n\
Build id: {0}\n\
\n\
(c) Copyright Quality Eclipse. 2003, 2004. All rights reserved.\n\
Visit http://www.qualityeclipse.com\n\
\n\
This offering is based on technology from the Eclipse Project.\n\
Visit http://www.eclipse.org
```

18.2.3   *The welcome.xml file*

The `welcome.xml` file contains the definition of the feature's **Welcome** page (see Figure 18–17). This is distinct from the project's **Welcome** page (see Section 2.2.4, "Project welcome page"), which is displayed when a project is first created. The **Welcome** page is a specially formatted XML file containing the following attributes and tags:

- An optional `title` attribute containing text that will be shown in a large font at the top of the **Welcome** page.

- An optional `format` attribute, which can have values of `wrap` or `nowrap` (the default). If the value is set to `wrap`, the text will be wrapped to fit the size of the editor window. Otherwise, the line breaks will appear as they occur in the text.

- An optional `intro` tag that will contain a block of text that appears at the top of the editor under the title.

- Zero or more `item` tags that will contain blocks of text that will be prefixed by a special bullet point icon.

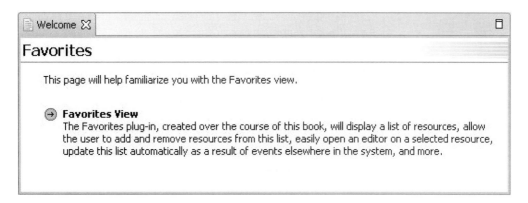

Figure 18–17 The Favorites Welcome page.

The blocks of text contained within the `intro` and `item` tags are displayed in the welcome editor with any line breaks preserved. If the format has been set to `wrap`, the `<p>` tag can be used to indicate where line breaks should occur. Text can be highlighted in bold using the `<b>` tag. Italics are not supported.

Two types of special links can be embedded in the text. The `<action>` tag is used to trigger an Eclipse action (see Chapter 6, "Actions") that performs a variety of tasks, such as opening a view or wizard, or activating an arbitrary command. The `<action>` tag has two required attributes: The `pluginId` attribute points to the plug-in defining the action, and the `class` attribute supplies the fully qualified name of the class implementing the action. For example, to directly open the **Favorites** view from the **Welcome** page, we would write an action class like the following:

```
package com.qualityeclipse.favorites.actions;

import org.eclipse.jface.action.*;
import org.eclipse.ui.*;

import com.qualityeclipse.favorites.FavoritesLog;

public class OpenFavoritesViewAction extends Action {
   /**
    * The unique identifier for the Favorites view.
    */
   private static final String FAVORITES_VIEW_ID =
      "com.qualityeclipse.favorites.views.FavoritesView";

   /**
    * Open the Favorites view.
    */
   public void run() {
```

```
IWorkbenchPage page = PlatformUI
    .getWorkbench()
    .getActiveWorkbenchWindow()
    .getActivePage();
if (page == null)
    return;
try {
    page.showView(FAVORITES_VIEW_ID);
}
catch (PartInitException e) {
    FavoritesLog.logError(
        "Failed to open the Favorites view",
        e);
}
    }
}
```

The second type of link is used to access a help page. The `<topic>` tag contains two attributes: The `id` attribute points to the toc file representing the targeted help book, while the optional `href` attribute provides a path to a specific help page within the help book. For example, to open the **Favorites** help, we would use a topic ID of "/com.qualityeclipse.favorites.help/toc.xml".

The **Favorites** `welcome.xml` file should end up looking like this (note the embedded references to the `OpenFavoriteViewAction` and to the **Favorites** help book):

```
<?xml version="1.0" encoding="UTF-8" ?>
<welcomePage
    title="Favorites"
    format="wrap">
    <intro>This page will help familiarize you with the
    <action pluginId="com.qualityeclipse.favorites"
    class="com.qualityeclipse.favorites.actions.
    OpenFavoritesViewAction">Favorites view</action>.
    </intro>
<item><b>Favorites View</b>
The <topic id="/com.qualityeclipse.favorites.help/toc.xml">
Favorites plug-in</topic>, created over the course of this
book, will display a list of resources, allow the user to
add and remove resources from this list, easily open an
editor on a selected resource, update this list
automatically as a result of events elsewhere in the
system, and more.</item>
</welcomePage>
```

The `QuickStartAction` class provides an easy way to programmatically open the **Welcome** page associated with a feature. Construct a new instance and call `openWelcomePage(...)`, passing the feature identifier as the argument:

```
new OpenWelcomePage().openWelcomePage(featureId);
```

18.2.4   Primary feature file

The remaining branding files are only applicable to primary features. The about and window images files were discussed earlier, which only leaves a couple of additional files to mention.

The `splash.bmp` file (which Eclipse specifically looks for by name) contains the product splash screen. It should be a 24-bit color bitmap, and its size should be approximately 500x330 pixels. If the text in the splash screen needs to be localized, the `splash.bmp` file can be located in a fragment.

If the primary feature needs to change the default preferences of any other installed plug-ins, it can place those new settings in the `plugin_customization.ini` file. Each line in the file should follow the form:

```
<plug-in id>/<preference id>=<value>
```

If any of the values need to be localized, the translated values should be placed in the `plugin_customization.properties` file, which follows the pattern established in Chapter 16, "Internationalization."

18.3   Update Sites

Once you have created a feature and provided a unifying structure and brand identity to your plug-ins, you need to deliver your feature to your users. While you can package a feature as a compressed ZIP file or create your own installer (using InstallShield or something similar), Eclipse provides an attractive Web-based alternative that can manage the delivery, installation, and eventual updating of your feature.

An Eclipse update site is a specially constructed Web site designed to host your features and plug-ins (packaged as JAR files) and describe them with a special site manifest file (the `site.xml` file). The Eclipse **Update Manager** can read this site manifest file and automatically load and install any updates (or new products) that it finds.

18.3.1   Creating an update site project

Just as plug-ins, fragments, and features are represented as projects in your workspace, so too are update sites. To create our update site, we will begin by using the **New Project** wizard to create a new **Update Site Project** (see Figure 18–18).

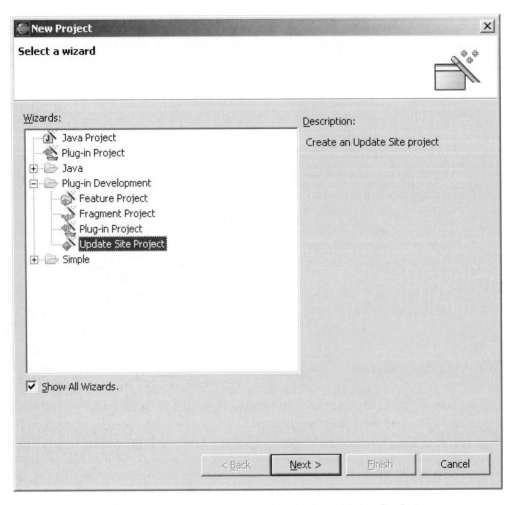

Figure 18–18   The New Project wizard—selecting an Update Site Project.

On the first page of the **New Site** wizard (see Figure 18–19), enter "com.qualityeclipse.favorites.update" as the project name. Click the **Next** button.

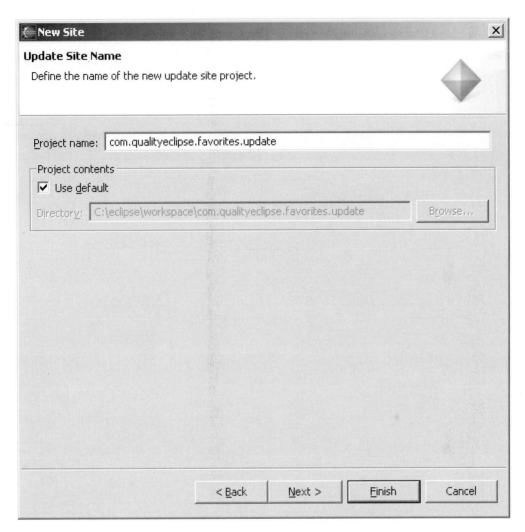

Figure 18–19   The New Site wizard.

On the second page of the **New Site** wizard (see Figure 18–20), we will usually accept the defaults. The options on this page control whether the wizard will generate a default home page for the update site. If a user visits the update site manually, this is the page they will see. Turn on the **Generate a sample web page** checkbox and leave the **Web resources location** field set to "web". Click the **Finish** button to create the project and initial files.

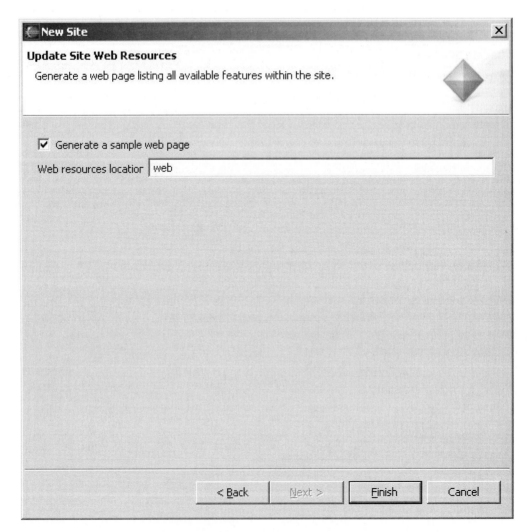

Figure 18–20   Update Site Layout options.

Several files and directories are created by default:

```
/features
/plugins
/web
    site.css
    site.xls
index.html
site.xml
```

The /features and /plugins directories will hold the JAR files containing the feature and plug-in files. When these files are uploaded to the update site, they will be accessible by the **Update Manager**. The /web directory contains the style sheet files used to provide the look of the update site. The index.html file is the main entry Web page for the site. Most of its contents are dynamically constructed based on the contents of the update site.

18.3.2   The site.xml file

The most important file is the site manifest file, site.xml. Initially, it is empty for all practical purposes, so we will need to flesh out its definition. The site manifest editor provides a convenient interface for editing the existing characteristics of the site or adding new attributes.

Double-clicking on the site manifest file will open the site manifest editor (see Figure 18–21). The editor has three pages, **Features, Site Layout,** and **Source.**

Figure 18–21   The site manifest editor.

The **Features to Build** section lists the features that will be built for the update site. Click the **Add** button to see a list of features defined in the workspace. Check the "com.qualityeclipse.favorites" feature and click **Finish** to add the **Favorites** feature to the list. The **Features To Publish** section lists the features that will be published by the update site. To add a feature to the **Features To Publish** list, drag it from the first list and drop it on the second list.

If more than one feature will be made available via the update site, you might want to place them in categories. Click the **Category Add** button to create a new category using the **New Category Definition** dialog (see Figure 18–22). Each category should have a unique **Name**, a **Label**, and a **Description** that will appear in the update site and within the **Update Manager**. Each category that you create is added to the **Features To Publish** list and acts as a drop target. If you want a specific feature to show up in more than one category, drag and drop the feature on each category.

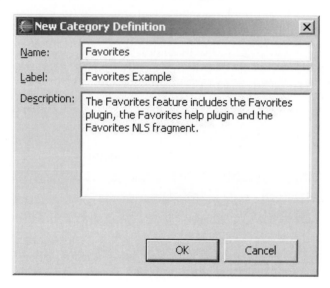

Figure 18–22   The New Category Definition dialog.

Double-clicking on any feature in the **Features To Publish** list opens the **Feature JAR Properties** dialog. In this dialog, you will find one required and a number of optional fields that can be used to provide details about each feature. The required **URL** field is used to specify the location (relative to the site.xml file) on the update site where the **Update Manager** can expect to find the feature's JAR file. For the **Favorites** feature, we will specify "features/com.qualityeclipse.favorites_1.0.0.jar". The **Label** field provides a human-readable label that will be shown on the update site. The **ID** and **Version** fields should correspond to the feature ID and version of the selected feature, respectively.

The remaining fields are optional and used to specify in which environments the selected feature is appropriate. These are very similar to the fields we saw within the feature manifest editor (see Figure 18–8). You will generally leave these fields blank unless your feature has specific run-time requirements.

The **Site Layout** page (Figure 18–23) describes the update site and specifies its Web address and layout. The **Plug-in Location** and **Feature Location** fields contain the values entered in the **New Site** wizard, so we will leave them alone. The **URL** field contains the root Web address of the update site. For our **Favorites** example, we will enter "http://com.qualityeclipse.com/update." Finally, we will enter a description for the site in the **Description** field.

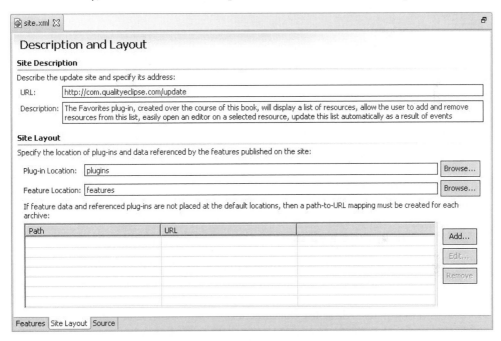

Figure 18–23   The site manifest editor.

At this point, if you switch to the **Source** page of the editor, the source of the site.xml file will look something like this:

```
<?xml version="1.0" encoding="UTF-8"?>
<site>
   <description
      url="http://com.qualityeclipse.com/update">
      The Favorites plug-in, created over the course of this
      book, will display a list of resources, allow the user
      to add and remove resources from this list, easily
      open an editor on a selected resource, update this
      list automatically as a result of events elsewhere in
      the system, and more.
   </description>
   <feature
      url=
         "features/com.qualityeclipse.favorites_1.0.0.jar"
      id="com.qualityeclipse.favorites"
      version="1.0.0"
      label="Favorites Example">
      <category name="Favorites"/>
   </feature>
   <category-def
      name="Favorites"
      label="Favorites Example">
      <description>
         The Favorites feature includes the Favorites
         plugin, the Favorites help plugin and the
         Favorites NLS fragment.
      </description>
   </category-def>
</site>
```

18.3.3   The update web site

Now we are close to seeing what our update site will look like. We will copy the files within the update project to our update Web site, http://com.qual-ityeclipse.com/update in the case of our **Favorites** example. We will also upload a placeholder for the com.qualityeclipse.favorites_1.0.0.jar file we defined earlier (eventually, we would replace it with a JAR file containing the actual files for our feature).

Once the files are uploaded, we can point our Web browser at the update site's URL. The **Favorites** update site will show the description, categories, and features that we defined in the site manifest editor (see Figure 18–24).

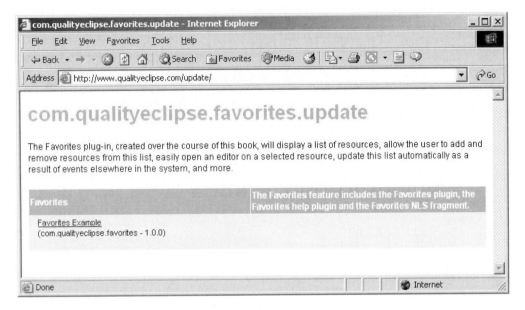

Figure 18–24   The Favorites update site.

18.3.4   *Revisiting the feature manifest*

When we first discussed the feature manifest file earlier in this chapter, we skipped over discussing the **update** and **discovery** URLs. As stated earlier, when the **Update Manager** is looking for updates to your plug-in, it will look at the sites defined by your update URLs.

Re-open the feature manifest editor (see Section 18.1.3) and access the **Overview** page. In the **Feature URLs** section of the editor (see Figure 18–25), right-click on the **Update URLs** category and select the **New > Update URL** command.

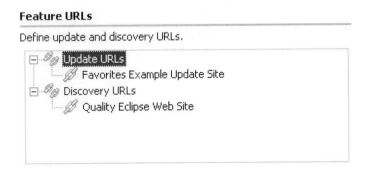

Figure 18–25   Feature URLs within the feature manifest file.

Double-click on the newly created "New update site" entry to open the **Properties** view (see Figure 18–26). Here we will provide a link to our update site. Change the **Label** to "Favorites Example Update Site" and specify the **URL** as "http://www.qualityeclipse.com/update." Any time the **Favorites** feature needs to check for updates, it will search the specified update site.

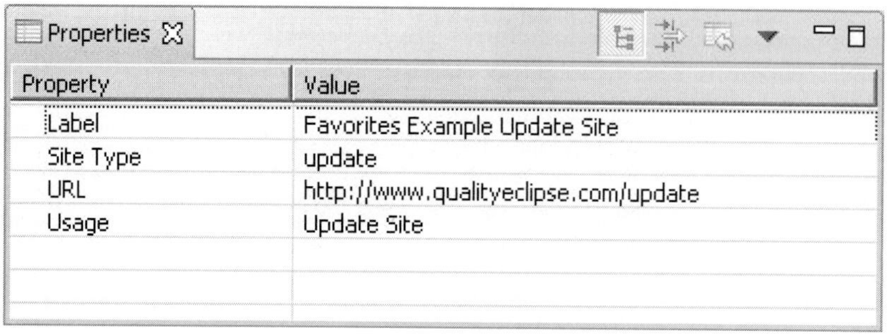

Property	Value
Label	Favorites Example Update Site
Site Type	update
URL	http://www.qualityeclipse.com/update
Usage	Update Site

Figure 18–26   Property view showing the update URL.

While we are at it, we can also add a discovery URL to the feature by right-clicking on the **Discovery URL** category and selecting the **New > Discovery URL** command. In the **Properties** view, enter the **Label** as "Quality Eclipse Web Site" and the **URL** as "http://www.qualityeclipse.com."

18.3.5   *Accessing the update site*

When the update site has been established, it can be accessed using the Eclipse **Update Manager** is a variety of ways.

Selecting the **Help > Software Updates > Manage Configuration** command will open the **Product Configuration** dialog (see Figure 18–27). Expanding the tree on the left will display a list of all of the features loaded in the workspace. Clicking on a feature will show the feature's details on the right.

For each feature, several different tasks are available. The **Disable** task can be used to disable the feature, causing all its contributions to disappear from the workspace. If a feature has been disabled, the **Disable** task will be replaced with a matching **Enable** task. The **Show Properties** task will open a properties dialog showing the version, provider name, license agreement, and so on for the feature.

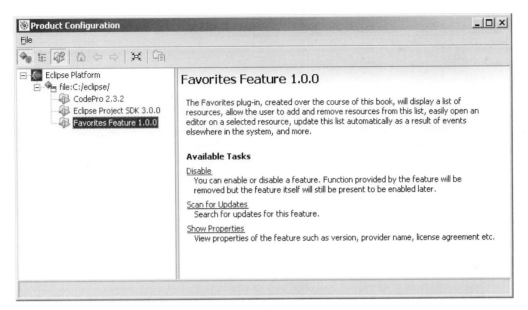

Figure 18–27   The Product Configuration dialog.

Any feature defining an update URL will also show a **Scan for Updates** task. Clicking on that task will cause the **Update Manager** to go to the update site and read the site manifest file. It will then determine whether any newer updates for the feature are available. If any updates are available, they will appear in the **Search Results** wizard (see Figure 18–28). Clicking the **Next** button will switch to the **Feature License** page displaying the feature's license, which must be accepted before the **Finish** button will be enabled. Clicking the **Finish** button will install the update into your workspace.

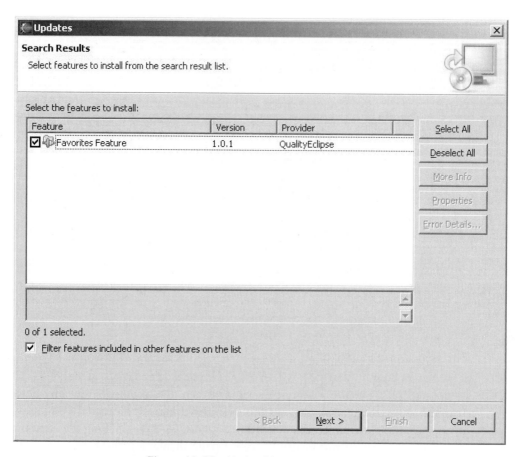

Figure 18-28   Update Manager search results.

In addition to updating via the **Product Configuration** dialog, you can also use the **Feature Updates** wizard, which can be accessed via the **Help > Software Updates > Find and Install** command (see Figure 18–29). Selecting the **Search for updates of the currently installed features** radio button and clicking the **Next** button will cause the **Update Manager** to scan the update sites for all the installed features and display any available updates in the **Search Results** wizard we saw earlier.

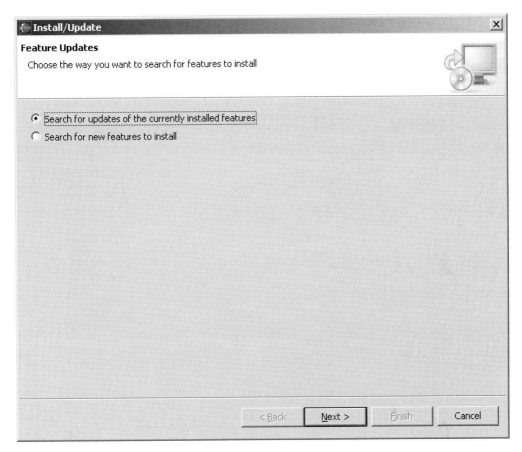

Figure 18–29 The Feature Updates wizard.

If you select the **Search for new features to install** option instead, you will be presented with the option of manually specifying any update sites to search for new features. If we click the **Add Update Site** button and specify a site named "Quality Eclipse" with a URL of "http://www.qualitye-clipse.com/update", the wizard will scan the update site, read the site mani-fest, and automatically discover the "Favorites Example" feature (see Figure 18–30). Clicking **Next,** accepting the license, and then clicking **Finish** will load the feature into your workspace.

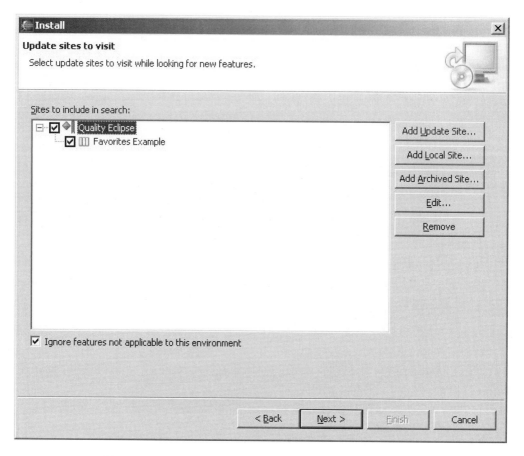

Figure 18–30 Update sites to visit while looking for new features.

18.4   RFWS Considerations

The "Feature Branding" section of the *RFWS Requirements* includes five requirements dealing with branding issues.

18.4.1   Do not override product branding

Requirement #1 states:

> *The ability to provide product branding is limited to product installations. Extension installations should not override the existing product branding either by overwriting the existing product branding feature or by launching using the Eclipse feature option.*

To pass this test, show that your feature does not override any of the existing product branding (either by replacing any files or by using the feature startup option).

18.4.2   Branded feature visibility

Requirement #2 states:

*At least one branded feature must be visible in the **About product** and **About product Features** dialogs.*

Open the Eclipse **About** dialog and show that your feature icon appears above the pushbuttons. Next, open the **About product Features** dialog, select your feature in the list, and show that your feature details are displayed (see Figure 18–15 for an example).

18.4.3   Include attribution information

Requirement #3 states:

*A provider's features and plug-ins must include appropriate attribution information (company name, version ID, name) in the attribution dialogs started using the **Feature Details and Plug-in Details…** buttons found on the **About product** dialog.*

Show that the about text for your feature (see Figure 18–15) includes your company name, the feature version ID, and so on.

18.4.4   about.html file contents

Requirement #4 states:

The plug-in must include an about.html file in the plug-in install directory. At a minimum it must contain:

a. The Eclipse attribution, using the following text and URL:
"This offering is based on technology from the Eclipse Project"
http://www.eclipse.org

b. Any attribution required by any dependent technology used by the plug-in (as defined by the provider of that technology)

c. Any other legal information that the provider is mandated to provide

Show that each of your plug-ins includes an about.html file that properly mentions the use of the Eclipse technology (see Figure 18–13) as well as any other relevant legal information.

18.4.5 Splash screen restrictions

Requirement #5 states:

> *The display of a splash screen for a feature is restricted to when the software is installed in an evaluation or demonstration mode. The splash screen may not interfere with the user or require a special action to disappear. Once a license is purchased, the software must be automatically modified during the application of the license to remove the display of a second-level splash screen.*

For this test, show that your feature either does not have its own splash screen or that it properly deactivates its own splash screen after the evaluation period has expired.

18.5   Summary

Once you have created your product's plug-ins, features provide a mechanism for adding structure and branding. Branding elements such as **About** pages and **Welcome** pages are tied to the feature. The Eclipse **Update Manager** can load and unload a group of plug-ins packaged as a feature and can search Web-based update sites for new versions.

References

Adams, Greg, "Creating product branding," November 27, 2001 (*www.eclipse.org/articles/product-guide/guide.html*).

Glozic, Dejan and Dorian Birsan, "How to Keep Up To Date," August 27, 2003 (*www.eclipse.org/articles/Article-Update/keeping-up-to-date.html*).

Eclipse Help: **PDE Guide > Deploying a plug-in**

CHAPTER 19

Building a Product

As introduced in Section 2.4, "Building a Product," building a commercial product involves packaging up only those elements to be delivered to the customer in a form that the customer can install into his or her environment. Although you can build your product manually, it is better to spend some time constructing an automated build process that is more rigorous and will save time in the long run. In this chapter, we will discuss just such an automated build process for the **Favorites** product and enhance the build script introduced in Section 2.4.2, "Building with apache ant."

19.1 A Brief Introduction to Ant

Ant is a build tool on the Apache Web site (*ant.apache.org/*) that ships as part of Eclipse. It differs from *make* and others of its ilk because Ant is written entirely in Java, can be extended without any native platform-dependent code, and has an XML-based syntax. What follows is a very brief introduction to Ant and its syntax. For more, see the Ant Web site.

19.1.1 Build projects

An Ant build script is XML-based with the following structure:

```
<?xml version="1.0" encoding="UTF-8"?>
<project default="target2" basedir=".">

   <target name="target1">
     <task 1a>
     <task 1b>
     … more tasks here …
   </target>
```

```
<target name="target2" depends="target1">
  <task 2a>
  <task 2b>
  … more tasks here …
</target>

… more targets here …
```

```
</project>
```

Each Ant build script has exactly one project element that has the following attributes:

basedir (optional)—Specifies the working directory to be used while the script is being executed.

default (required)—Specifies the default target that is to be run when the script is run and no targets are specified.

name (optional)—Specifies a human-readable name for the project.

To execute a build script, select the build script in an Eclipse view, such as the **Resource Navigator**, and select the **Run Ant…** command (see Section 2.4.2).

19.1.2   *Build targets*

A project contains one or more internal and external targets. The only thing that differentiates an internal target from an external target is that external targets have a description associated with them while internal targets do not. Each target may have the following attributes:

description (optional)—A description of the task. If this attribute is defined then the target is considered to be external, if not then it is an internal target.

depends (optional)—A comma-delimited list of names of tasks on which this task depends (see discussion later in this section).

name (required)—The name of the task used by other tasks to reference this task.

if (optional)—The name of a property that must be set for this task to be executed. For example, for a task to be executed only if the Ant build script is being launched from Eclipse, then you could use the ${eclipse. running} property (see Section 19.1.4.1, "Predefined properties"):

```
<target name="myTarget" if="${eclipse.running}">
      … do something Eclipse related …
  </target>
```

unless (optional)—The name of a property that must *not* be set for this task to be executed. For example, for a task to be executed only if the Ant build script is *not* being launched from Eclipse, you could use the ${eclipse.running} property (see Section 19.1.4.1):

```
<target name="myTarget" unless="${eclipse.running}">
    … do something non-Eclipse related …
</target>
```

One build target can explicitly call another build target in the same build script using the <antcall> task, or in a different build script using the <ant> task. Alternately, one target can *depend* on another target to achieve a similar effect, *but only within the same build script.* If target A depends on target B, which in turn depends on target C (see Figure 19–1), then if you execute target A, the Ant framework will execute first target C, then target B, and finally target A. This same effect could be achieved by having target A call target B, which in turn calls target C.

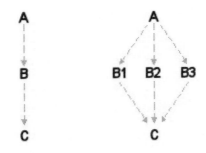

Figure 19–1   Example build target dependencies.

The difference between these two approaches lies in how many times a target is executed. For example, let's assume a more complicated script in which A depends on B1, B2, and B3, and each of these depends on C. In this case, if you execute A then the Ant framework will execute C first, then B1, B2, and B3 in some undetermined order, and finally A. Note that in this case, target C was only executed *once* and not three times as you would expect.

19.1.3   *Build tasks*

Build targets are composed of a sequence of tasks to be executed. There are many different types of Ant tasks, some of which are listed below. Much more complete documentation for Apache Ant tasks can be found on the Apache Ant Web site (*ant.apache.org/*).

ant—Runs Ant on another build file. For example:

```
<ant
        antfile="subproject/subbuild.xml"
        dir="subproject"
        target="compile"/>
```

By default, all the properties in the current build script will be available in the build script being called. Alternatively, you can set the `inheritAll` attribute to "false" and only user properties (i.e., those passed on the command line) will be available to the build script being called. In either case, the set of properties being passed will override any properties with the same name in the build script being called.

```
<ant
        antfile="subproject/subbuild.xml"
        dir="subproject"
        inheritAll="false"
        target="compile"/>
```

antcall—Calls another target within the same build file (see Section 19.1.5, "<antcall> task"). For example:

```
<antcall target="doSomethingElse">
        <param name="foo.name" value="someValue"/>
</antcall>
```

copy—Copies a file or a set of files specified by a `<fileset>` to a new file or directory. By default, files are only copied if the source file is newer than the destination file, or when the destination file does not exist. However, you can explicitly overwrite files with the `overwrite` attribute. For example:

```
<copy file="myfile.txt" todir="../some/other/dir"/>
```
or
```
<copy todir="../new/dir">
    <fileset dir="src_dir" includes="**/*.java"/>
</copy>
```

The `<fileset>` structure in the code above specifies the files to be included in the operation. The two asterisks ("**") indicate that the operation should include files in the directory specified by the `dir` attribute, along with files in any of its subdirectories to an infinite depth.

delete—Deletes a single file, a specified directory and all its files and subdirectories, or a set of files specified by a `<fileset>` (see **copy** above for more information about `<filesets>`). When specifying a set of files, empty directories are not removed by default. To remove empty directories, use the `includeEmptyDirs` attribute. For example:

```
<delete dir="lib"/>
```

or

```
<delete>
    <fileset dir="." includes="**/*.bak"/>
</delete>
```

echo—Echoes a message to the current loggers and listeners, which in our case means the **Console** view. For example:

```
<echo message="Hello, world"/>
<echo level="info">Hello, World</echo>
```

eclipse.convertPath—Converts a filesystem path to a resource path, and vice versa, assigning the result to the specified property (see Section 19.1.6, "Headless ant"). For example:

```
<eclipse.convertPath
        fileSystemPath="${basedir}"
        property="myPath"/>
```

or

```
<eclipse.convertPath
        resourcePath="MyProject/MyFile"
        property="myPath"/>
```

eclipse.refreshLocal—Refreshes the specified resources in the workspace (see Section 19.1.6). For example:

```
<eclipse.refreshLocal
        resource="MyProject/MyFolder"
        depth="infinite"/>
```

where **resource** is a resource path relative to the workspace and **depth** can be one of the following: `zero`, `one`, or `infinite`. This is useful when an Ant build script has created, modified, or deleted a file or folder residing within the Eclipse workspace. Eclipse will not reflect the change in the workspace until after this task executes.

eclipsetools.getclasspath—Resolves a project's classpath and places the result into an Ant property. Optionally, the classpath can be translated from referencing one Eclipse installation to referencing another (see Sections 19.1.6, 19.2.3, "Compiling during the build process," and 19.2.7, "Classpath tools").

eclipsetools.preprocessor—Translates source written for one version of Eclipse into source written for another version of Eclipse prior to compilation (see Sections 19.1.6 and 19.2.6.3, "Preprocessor").

javac—Compiles Java source files into class files (see Section 19.2.3). For example:

```
<javac srcdir="${src}"
    destdir="${build}"
    classpath="xyz.jar"
    debug="on"/>
```

mkdir—Creates a directory, and nonexistent parent directories are created, when necessary. For example:

```
<mkdir dir="${dist}"/>
```

property—Sets a property (by name and value) or set of properties (from file or resource) in the project (see the next section). For example:

```
<property name="foo.dist" value="dist"/>
```

or

```
<property file="foo.properties"/>
```

zip—Creates a ZIP file containing one or more files from a directory, or as specified by a `<zipfileset>` (a `<zipfileset>` is similar to a `<fileset>`; see **copy** above for more information about `<fileset>`). For example:

```
<zip
    destfile="${dist}/manual.zip"
    basedir="htdocs/manual"/>
```

or

```
<zip destfile="${dist}/manual.zip">
    <zipfileset
        dir="htdocs/manual"
        prefix="docs/user-guide"/>
</zip>
```

19.1.4   Build properties

A property is a name/value pair, where the name is case-sensitive. Properties may be used in the value of various task attributes by placing the property name between "${" and "}" in the attribute value.

```
<property name="builddir" value="c:\build"/>
<mkdir dir="${builddir}/temp"/>
```

In this build script, the **builddir** property is assigned the value "build" in the first task, and then this property is resolved in the **dir** attribute of the second task so that the `c:\build\temp` directory is created.

An alternate form of the `property` task uses the `location` attribute:

```
<property name="builddir" location="dir/subdir"/>
```

When specified this way, the value is resolved relative to the ${basedir} before being associated with the **builddir** property. For example, if the ${basedir} is c:\temp, then the statement above would have associated **builddir** with the value c:\temp\dir\subdir. If the property task is modified slightly (notice the slash added before the dir/subdir):

```
<property name="builddir" location="/dir/subdir"/>
```

and ${basedir} is c:\temp, then the statement above would have associated **builddir** with the value c:\dir\subdir. Using the location attribute without a drive letter is more portable; if you specify a drive letter, then your build scripts will only run on a Windows platform.

Unfortunately, a reference to an undefined property will not be reported during Ant execution, but silently ignored. If a property has not been defined, then no string substitution is made. For example, if you reference the **foo** property before it has been defined:

```
<echo message="the foo property is ${foo}"/>
```

then Ant will leave ${foo} unchanged and the message displayed will be:

```
the foo property is ${foo}
```

This makes it more difficult to spot problems, and you might end up with some unusual file or directory names, such as /temp/${plug-in.id}_3.0.0/icons.

19.1.4.1 Predefined properties

Ant provides several predefined properties including all the Java system properties such as ${os.name}, and the built-in properties shown in Table 19–1:

Table 19–1 Predefined Ant Properties

Property	Description
${basedir}	The absolute path of the project's basedir as set with the basedir attribute of the <project> element.
${ant.file}	The absolute path of the build file.
${ant.version}	The version of Ant.
${ant.project.name}	The name of the project that is currently executing as defined by the name attribute of the <project> element.
${ant.java.version}	The JVM version Ant detected, such as "1.1", "1.2", "1.3", or "1.4".

Eclipse provides two additional predefined properties, as shown in Table 19–2:

Table 19–2   Predefined Eclispe Ant Properties

Property	Description
${eclipse.home}	The location of the Eclipse installation directory.
${eclipse.running}	"true" if the Ant build has been launched from Eclipse, else undefined.

19.1.4.2   Property scoping

Properties are global within a build script from the moment they are declared. If one task assigns a value to a property, another task within the same script can then use that property. In the following script, the foo and bar properties are each declared in separate targets and referenced in others:

```
<?xml version="1.0" encoding="UTF-8"?>
<project name="Test" default="test" basedir=".">
    <target name="init">
        <property name="foo" value="xyz"/>
        <echo message="foo=${foo}"/>
    </target>
    <target name="sub1" depends="init">
        <echo message="foo=${foo}"/>
        <property name="bar" value="abc"/>
        <echo message="bar=${bar}"/>
    </target>
    <target name="sub2" depends="init">
        <echo message="foo=${foo}"/>
        <echo message="bar=${bar}"/>
    </target>
    <target name="test" depends="sub1,sub2">
        <echo message="foo=${foo}"/>
        <echo message="bar=${bar}"/>
    </target>
</project>
```

Looking at the output, we can see that the properties foo and bar can be referenced anytime after they are declared:

```
Buildfile: scoping_test_1.xml
init:
     [echo] foo=xyz
sub1:
     [echo] foo=xyz
     [echo] bar=abc
sub2:
     [echo] foo=xyz
     [echo] bar=abc
```

```
test:
     [echo] foo=xyz
     [echo] bar=abc
BUILD SUCCESSFUL
Total time: 234 milliseconds
```

Closer inspection of both the script and the output reveals something disturbing. The `bar` property is declared in target `sub1` and then referenced in target `sub2` even though *sub2 does not depend on sub1*. This is important because **Ant does not guarantee the order in which non-dependent targets will be executed.** In this first case, target `sub1` just happened to be executed before target `sub2`, and thus `sub2` could reference the `bar` property as expected. If we modify the `test` target's `depends` attribute as follows:

```
<target name="test" depends="sub2,sub1">
```

then the `sub2` target will be executed before the `sub1` target, causing the `bar` property to be declared after it is referenced:

```
Buildfile: scoping_test_2.xml
init:
     [echo] foo=xyz
sub2:
     [echo] foo=xyz
     [echo] bar=${bar}
sub1:
     [echo] foo=xyz
     [echo] bar=abc
test:
     [echo] foo=xyz
     [echo] bar=abc
BUILD SUCCESSFUL
Total time: 265 milliseconds
```

In our simple test build script, the problem and solution are obvious, but as your product and thus your build scripts become more complex, this problem could be harder to diagnose. The bottom line is that when task A references a property declared in task B, care must be taken to ensure that task A is directly or indirectly dependent on task B so that the build order is deterministic and the property will be declared before it is referenced.

19.1.4.3 *Property mutability*

Properties are immutable once declared. For example, in the following build script:

```
<?xml version="1.0" encoding="UTF-8"?>
<project name="Test" default="test" basedir=".">
```

```
<target name="init">
   <property name="foo" value="xyz"/>
   <echo message="foo=${foo}"/>
   <property name="foo" value="123"/>
   <echo message="foo=${foo}"/>
</target>
<target name="test" depends="init">
   <echo message="foo=${foo}"/>
   <property name="foo" value="abc"/>
   <echo message="foo=${foo}"/>
</target>
</project>
```

the **foo** property is assigned in the `init` target, and once assigned, it *cannot* be modified (the exception to this rule is the `<antcall>` task—see Section 19.1.5). Unfortunately, multiple assignments are quietly ignored and thus quite a source of confusion.

```
Buildfile: mutability_test_1.xml
init:
     [echo] foo=xyz
     [echo] foo=xyz
test:
     [echo] foo=xyz
     [echo] foo=xyz
BUILD SUCCESSFUL
Total time: 203 milliseconds
```

19.1.4.4 *Properties outside targets*

Properties are special in that they can be declared outside the scope of a target. A property declared in such a manner is defined before any target is executed and is immutable. For example, in the following build script:

```
<project name="Test" default="test" basedir=".">
   <property name="foo" value="xyz"/>
   <target name="test">
      <echo message="foo=${foo}"/>
      <property name="foo" value="abc"/>
      <echo message="foo=${foo}"/>
   </target>
</project>
```

the **foo** property is assigned its value before the **test** target is executed, and its value is *not* changed by the second `property` task within the test target.

```
Buildfile: mutability_test_2.xml
test:
     [echo] foo=xyz
     [echo] foo=xyz
BUILD SUCCESSFUL
Total time: 188 milliseconds
```

19.1.4.5   Properties on the command line

Properties can also be declared outside the build script. A property declared on the command line is defined before the build is launched and is immutable.

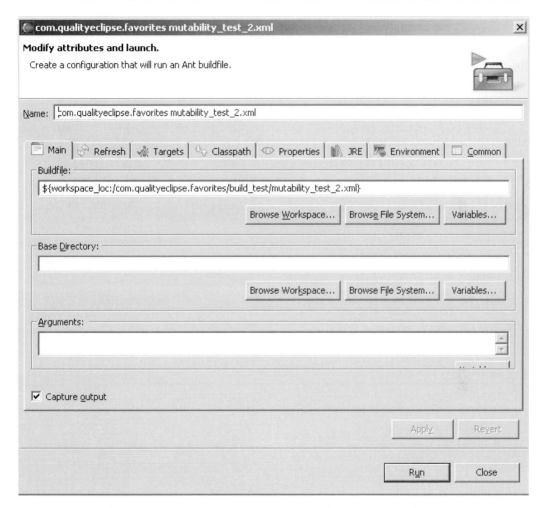

Figure 19–2   Declaring a property as part of the Ant command line.

For example, if we execute the build script described in the previous section using the **Run Ant...** command, switch to the **Main** tab panel (see Figure 19–2), and enter the following in the **Arguments** field:

```
-Dfoo=mop
```

then the **foo** property is assigned its value before the build script is executed, and its value is *not* changed by the property declaration or property task within the build script.

```
Buildfile: mutability_test_2.xml
test:
     [echo] foo=mop
     [echo] foo=mop
BUILD SUCCESSFUL
Total time: 297 milliseconds
```

Alternately, properties can be specified by switching to the **Properties** tab panel (see Figure 19–3) and unchecking the **Use global properties** checkbox. The top part of the page contains individual property declarations, while the bottom part displays a list of files containing property declarations.

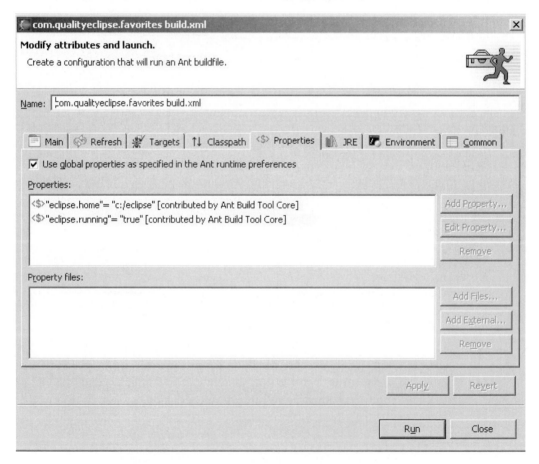

Figure 19–3 Declaring properties and property files applicable to an individual build script.

To specify properties applicable to *all* build scripts in the workspace, open the Eclipse **Preferences** dialog and navigate to the **Ant > Runtime** preference page (see Figure 19–4). Similar to the **Properties** tab panel shown earlier, the top part of the preference page contains individual property declarations, while the bottom part displays a list of files containing property declarations.

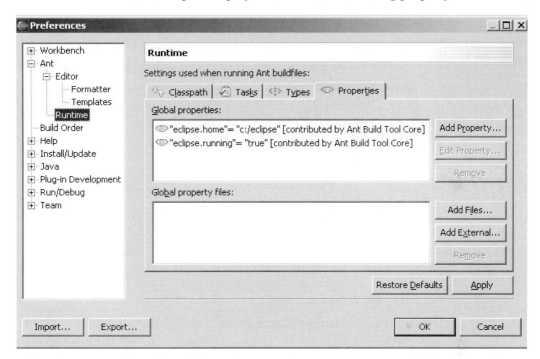

Figure 19–4   Declaring properties and property files applicable to all build scripts in the workspace.

19.1.5   *<antcall> task*

The <antcall> tasks has some unusual aspects worthy of discussion. Parameters specified in an <antcall> task override any properties specified elsewhere. For example, if the following build script is executed:

```
<?xml version="1.0" encoding="UTF-8"?>
<project name="Test" default="test" basedir=".">
   <target name="init">
      <property name="foo" value="xyz"/>
      <echo message="in init, foo=${foo}"/>
      <property name="foo" value="123"/>
      <echo message="in init, foo=${foo}"/>
   </target>
   <target name="test" depends="init">
      <echo message="in test, foo=${foo}"/>
      <antcall target="sub">
```

```
      <param name="foo" value="gob"/>
      </antcall>
      <echo message="in test, foo=${foo}"/>
   </target>
   <target name="sub">
      <echo message="in sub,  foo=${foo}"/>
      <property name="foo" value="abc"/>
      <echo message="in sub,  foo=${foo}"/>
   </target>
</project>
```

the **foo** property is assigned in the init target and should be immutable (see
Section 19.1.4.3, "Property mutability"). However, because **foo** is specified as
a parameter in the <antcall> task, the value *is modified* for the duration of
the <antcall> task; its original value is restored when the <antcall> task
completes.

```
Buildfile: mutability_test_3.xml
init:
      [echo] in init, foo=xyz
      [echo] in init, foo=xyz
test:
      [echo] in test, foo=xyz
sub:
      [echo] in sub,  foo=gob
      [echo] in sub,  foo=gob
      [echo] in test, foo=xyz
BUILD SUCCESSFUL
Total time: 282 milliseconds
```

The <antcall> task resets the depends calculations so that targets may be
executed twice. Consider the previous build script with a slight modification:

```
<?xml version="1.0" encoding="UTF-8"?>
<project name="Test" default="test" basedir=".">
   <target name="init">
      <property name="foo" value="xyz"/>
      <echo message="in init, foo=${foo}"/>
      <property name="foo" value="123"/>
      <echo message="in init, foo=${foo}"/>
   </target>
   <target name="test" depends="init">
      <echo message="in test, foo=${foo}"/>
      <antcall target="sub">
      <param name="foo" value="gob"/>
      </antcall>
      <echo message="in test, foo=${foo}"/>
   </target>
   <target name="sub" depends="init">
      <echo message="in sub,  foo=${foo}"/>
      <property name="foo" value="abc"/>
      <echo message="in sub,  foo=${foo}"/>
   </target>
</project>
```

This modification makes the sub target dependent on the init target. Even though the init target is executed prior to the test target, the init target is executed a second time before the sub target because the sub target was executed using the <antcall> task. In addition, the value for the **foo** property is different the second time the init target is executed, but as discussed above, returns to its original value when the <antcall> task completes.

```
Buildfile: mutability_test_4.xml
init:
     [echo]  in init, foo=xyz
     [echo]  in init, foo=xyz
test:
     [echo]  in test, foo=xyz
init:
     [echo]  in init, foo=gob
     [echo]  in init, foo=gob
sub:
     [echo]  in sub,  foo=gob
     [echo]  in sub,  foo=gob
     [echo]  in test, foo=xyz
BUILD SUCCESSFUL
Total time: 375 milliseconds
```

19.1.6 Headless ant

Running Ant headless (from the command line—without a UI) is well-documented (see *ant.apache.org/*), but using Eclipse-specific Ant tasks will cause the build script to fail; Eclipse-specific Ant tasks need Eclipse to execute properly. Below is a Windows batch file (batch files for other platforms will be similar) used to build the **Favorites** product by launching Eclipse headless and executing the **Favorites** build.xml file (the ==> denotes a continuation of the line above and must not be included):

```
echo off
setlocal

REM **************************************************
set JAVAEXE="C:\j2sdk1.4.2_02\jre\bin\java.exe"
set STARTUPJAR="C:\eclipse_300\startup.jar"
set WORKSPACE="C:\eclipse_300\workspace"
set BUILDFILE=build.xml

REM **************************************************
if not exist %JAVAEXE% echo ERROR:
==>        incorrect java.exe=%JAVAEXE%, edit this file
==>        and correct the JAVAEXE envar
if not exist %JAVAEXE% goto done
if not exist %STARTUPJAR% echo ERROR:
==>        incorrect startup.jar=%STARTUPJAR%, edit this file
==>        and correct the STARTUPJAR envar
```

```
if not exist %STARTUPJAR% goto done

if not exist %WORKSPACE% echo ERROR:
==>       incorrect workspace=%WORKSPACE%, edit this file
==>       and correct the WORKSPACE envar
if not exist %WORKSPACE% goto done

if not exist %BUILDFILE% echo ERROR:
==>       incorrect buildfile=%BUILDFILE%, edit this file
==>       and correct the BUILDFILE envar
if not exist %BUILDFILE% goto done


REM ****************************************************
:run
@echo on
%JAVAEXE% -cp %STARTUPJAR% org.eclipse.core.launcher.Main
==>       -application org.eclipse.ant.core.antRunner
==>       -data %WORKSPACE% -buildfile %BUILDFILE%


REM ****************************************************
:done
pause
```

Copy this batch file into an `external_build.bat` file located in the same directory as the `build.xml` file you want to run, and modify the batch variables shown in Table 19–3 to suit your environment.

Table 19–3   Batch Variables

Script Variable	Description
JAVAEXE	The JRE java.exe to be used when running Ant in a headless Eclipse environment. Typically, this would be the same JRE used to run the Eclipse UI.
STARTUPJAR	The `startup.jar` located in the Eclipse install directory.
WORKSPACE	The workspace directory containing the projects to be built.
BUILDFILE	The relative path from the batch file to the build script used to build the product. Typically, the batch file is located in the same directory as the build script, and so this would specify only the name of the build script.

The first part of the batch file assigns the script variables while the second part validates the existence of files specified by those script variables. The real work is accomplished in the third part, where Eclipse is launched without a UI and the build script is executed.

19.1.7   Ant extensions

Several of the tasks listed above are not part of Ant; some are part of Eclipse and others must be downloaded from the *QualityEclipse* Web site (*www.qualityeclipse.com/*). The additional tasks in Table 19–4 will not work outside of Eclipse:

Table 19–4   Eclipse Ant Task Providers

Ant Task	Provider
eclipse.convertPath	Built into Eclipse as part of the org.eclipse.core.resources plug-in
eclipse.refreshLocal	Built into Eclipse as part of the org.eclipse.core.resources plug-in
eclipsetools.getclasspath	Downloadable from the *QualityEclipse* Web site as part of the com.instantiations.preprocessor plug-in (see Section 19.2.7, "Classpath tools")
eclipsetools.preprocessor	Downloadable from the *QualityEclipse* Web site as part of the com.instantiations.preprocessor plug-in (see Section 19.2.6.3).

By default, Eclipse executes Ant using an alternate JRE. If you are using Eclipse-specific tasks such as those listed above, and you encounter an error similar to the following:

```
Buildfile: com.qualityeclipse.favorites\build.xml
init:
BUILD FAILED: file: com.qualityeclipse.favorites/build.xml:56: Could
not create task or type of type:
eclipsetools_classpath_modifications.

Ant could not find the task or a class this task relies on.

… etc …

Total time: 406 milliseconds
```

then you may need to execute the build script in the same JRE as the workspace. To accomplish this, select the build script, right-click and then select **Run Ant....** In the launch dialog, select the **JRE** tab, select the **Run in the same JRE as the workspace** radio button, and then click the **Update the Ant runtime classpath for the selected JRE – Now** button (see Figure 19–5). This enables the Eclipse-specific Ant tasks to access the underlying Eclipse functionality.

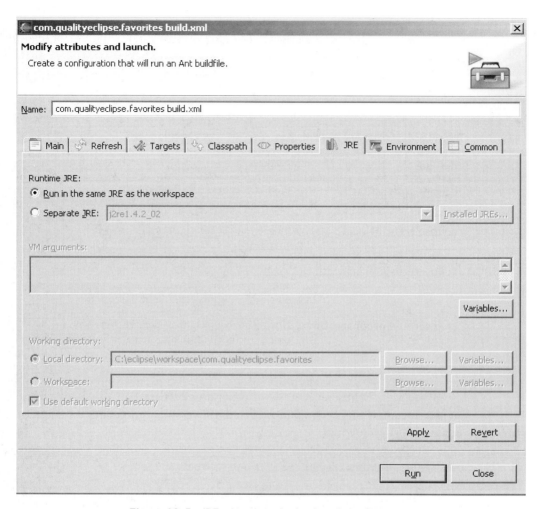

Figure 19–5 JRE tab page in the Ant launch configuration.

19.2   Building the Favorites Product

Now let's revisit the **Favorites** product build script introduced in Section 2.4.2 and compare that with a build script automatically generated by the plug-in development tools. Following that, we will enhance our build script to take into account all of the new bells and whistles we have added since the build script was introduced in Chapter 2, "A Simple Plug-in Example."

19.2.1 Auto-generated build script

The Eclipse plug-in development tools can generate a build.xml file containing a skeleton of a build script. In the **Navigator** view, right-click on the plug-in.xml file and select **PDE Tools > Create Ant Build File**.

```
<project
   name="com.qualityeclipse.favorites"
   default="build.jars"
   basedir=".">

   <property name="bootclasspath" value=""/>
   <property name="basews" value="${ws}"/>
   <property name="baseos" value="${os}"/>
   <property name="basearch" value="${arch}"/>
   <property name="basenl" value="${nl}"/>
   <property name="javacFailOnError" value="false"/>
   <property name="javacDebugInfo" value="on"/>
   <property name="javacVerbose" value="true"/>
   <property name="javacSource" value="1.3"/>
   <property name="javacTarget" value="1.1"/>

   <target name="init" depends="properties">
      <property
         name="temp.folder"
         value="${basedir}/temp.folder"/>
      <property
         name="plugin.destination"
         value="${basedir}"/>
      <property
         name="build.result.folder"
         value="${basedir}"/>
   </target>

   <target name="properties" if="eclipse.running">
      <property
         name="build.compiler"
         value="org.eclipse.jdt.core.JDTCompilerAdapter"/>
   </target>

   <target
      name="build.update.jar"
      depends="init"
      description="Build the plug-in:
         com.qualityeclipse.favorites for an update site.">
      <delete dir="${temp.folder}"/>
      <mkdir dir="${temp.folder}"/>
      <antcall target="build.jars"/>
      <antcall target="gather.bin.parts">
         <param
            name="destination.temp.folder"
            value="${temp.folder}/"/>
      </antcall>
```

```
  <zip
      zipfile="${plugin.destination}
         /com.qualityeclipse.favorites_1.0.0.jar"
      basedir="${temp.folder}
         /com.qualityeclipse.favorites_1.0.0"
      filesonly="false"
      whenempty="skip"/>
    <delete dir="${temp.folder}"/>
</target>

<target
   name="gather.bin.parts"
   depends="init"
   if="destination.temp.folder">
   <mkdir dir="${destination.temp.folder}
      /com.qualityeclipse.favorites_1.0.0"/>
</target>

<target
   name="build.jars"
   depends="init"
   description="Build all the jars for the plug-in:
      com.qualityeclipse.favorites.">
</target>

<target name="build.sources" depends="init">
</target>

<target name="build.zips" depends="init">
</target>

<target
   name="gather.sources"
   depends="init"
   if="destination.temp.folder">
</target>

<target
   name="gather.logs"
   depends="init"
   if="destination.temp.folder">
</target>

<target
   name="clean"
   depends="init"
   description="Clean the plug-in:
      com.qualityeclipse.favorites of all the zips,
      jars and logs created.">
   <delete
      file="${plugin.destination}
         /com.qualityeclipse.favorites_1.0.0.jar"/>
   <delete
      file="${plugin.destination}
         /com.qualityeclipse.favorites_1.0.0.zip"/>
   <delete dir="${temp.folder}"/>
</target>
```

```
<target
   name="refresh"
   depends="init"
   if="eclipse.running"
   description="Refresh this folder.">
   <eclipse.convertPath
      fileSystePath="c:/dev/eclipse_300/workspace
         /com.qualityeclipse.favorites/"
      property="resourcePath"/>
   <eclipse.refreshLocal
      resource="com.qualityeclipse.favorites"
      depth="infinite"/>
</target>

<target
   name="zip.plugin"
   depends="init"
   description="Create a zip containing all the elements
      for the plug-in: com.qualityeclipse.favorites.">
   <delete dir="${temp.folder}"/>
   <mkdir dir="${temp.folder}"/>
   <antcall target="build.jars"/>
   <antcall target="build.sources"/>
   <antcall target="gather.bin.parts">
      <param
         name="destination.temp.folder"
         value="${temp.folder}/"/>
   </antcall>
   <antcall target="gather.sources">
      <param
         name="destination.temp.folder"
         value="${temp.folder}/"/>
   </antcall>
   <delete>
      <fileset
         dir="${temp.folder}"
         includes="**/*.bin.log"/>
   </delete>
   <zip
      zipfile="${plugin.destination}
         /com.qualityeclipse.favorites_1.0.0.zip"
      basedir="${temp.folder}"
      filesonly="true"
      whenempty="skip"/>
   <delete dir="${temp.folder}"/>
</target>

</project>
```

This auto-generated build script is a bit more complicated than our **Favorites** build script, containing five external targets and seven internal targets (see Figure 19–6). The zip.plugin and build.update.jar targets call other targets, and all the targets depend on the init target, which in turn depends on the properties target. If we were to use this script, we would put property assignments into the `properties` target, directory initialization into the `init` target, assemble the product in `build.jars` and `gather.bin.parts`, and finally, assemble the product in `zip.plugin`. This generated build script is certainly one way to organize a build script and its more refactored structure might be better for building a larger product, but we are going to stick with our script and enhance it over the next several sections to perform the tasks we need.

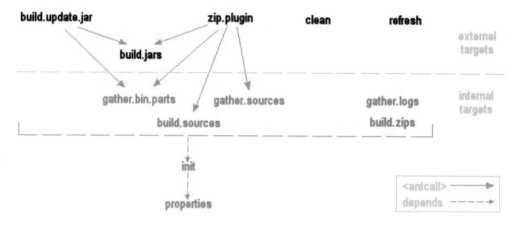

Figure 19–6 The PDE-generated build script.

19.2.2   Refactoring the favorites build script

Before proceeding, we need to review the build script introduced in Section 2.4.2, examining each chunk and refactoring it into a separate target. This new structure will be helpful in building the **Favorites** product for more than just the Eclipse 3.0 platform. To start, gather all the property assignment, directory deletion, and directory creation into a single `init` target. This new `init` target will be responsible for initializing common properties used in building multiple binaries (see Section 19.2.4, "Single versus multiple binaries") and clearing out the temporary directories used during the build process to ensure a clean build.

```
<target name="init">

   <!-- Temporary directory used
      to build the product... will be deleted. -->
   <property
      name="temp_dir"
      location="C:/QualityEclipseTemp"/>

   <!-- Directory where
```

```
            final product will be placed. -->
<property
   name="product_dir"
   location="C:/QualityEclipseProduct"/>

<!-- Directory structure inside zip file
   required to meet RFWS requirements -->
<property
   name="product_prefix"
   value="QualityEclipseTools/eclipse/plugins"/>
<!-- Alternate directory structure inside zip file
   simpler but does not meet RFWS requirments -->
<!-- <property
   name="product_prefix"
   value="plugins"/> -->

<!-- Current product version number. -->
<property
   name="product_version"
   value="1.0.0"/>

<!-- Plug-in's product. -->
<property
   name="main_plugin_id"
   value="com.qualityeclipse.favorites"/>
<property
   name="main_plugin_dirname"
   value="${main_plugin_id}_${product_version}"/>
<property
   name="feature_plugin_id"
   value="com.qualityeclipse.favorites.feature"/>
<property
   name="feature_plugin_dirname"
   value="${feature_plugin_id}_${product_version}"/>
<property
   name="help_plugin_id"
   value="com.qualityeclipse.favorites.help"/>
<property
   name="help_plugin_dirname"
 value="${help_plugin_id}_${product_version}"/>

<!-- Clear out the temp directory. -->
<delete dir="${temp_dir}"/>

</target>
```

Tip: The `product_prefix` property determines the structure of the ZIP file that is created. In the `init` target above, the `product_prefix` property is initialized for product installation in a directory hierarchy separate from the Eclipse install directory as per the RFWS requirements (see Section 3.2.1, "Link files"). For a simpler installation that does not necessitate a link file, change the `product_prefix` property to "plugins" so that the product can be unzipped directly into the Eclipse install directory.

In preparation for building one **Favorites** product binary for each version of Eclipse we plan to support, we refactor the remaining script into several parts: build_common, build_30, and product_30, each of which is dependent on init target. Place the script elements related to building common product elements into a new build_common target, including:

- Icons used by the **Favorites** view and model (see Chapter 7, "Views")

- preferences.ini (see Section 16.2, "Externalizing Plug-in Strings")

- The schema files (see Section 17.2.2, "Creating an extension point")

- The entire feature plug-in and related files (see Chapter 18, "Features and Branding")

- The entire **Favorites** help plug-in (see Chapter 15, "Implementing Help")

In addition, we will zip the help files into a specially named doc.zip file so that they take up less space (see Section 15.2.3, "Table of contents (toc) files"):

```
<target name="build_common" depends="init">

   <!-- Temporary directories used to build
      the common elements... will be deleted. -->
   <property
      name="temp_common"
      value="${temp_dir}/common"/>
   <property
      name="main_plugin_common"
      value="${temp_common}/${main_plugin_dirname}"/>
   <property
      name="feature_plugin_common"
      value="${temp_common}/${feature_plugin_dirname}"/>
   <property
      name="help_plugin_common"
      value="${temp_common}/${help_plugin_dirname}"/>

   <!-- Assemble main plug-in's common elements. -->
   <copy todir="${main_plugin_common}">
      <fileset dir="." includes="schema/**/*.exsd"/>
      <fileset dir="." includes="icons/**/*.gif"/>
      <fileset dir="." includes="*.gif"/>
      <fileset dir="." includes="about.*"/>
      <fileset dir="." includes="welcome.xml"/>
      <fileset dir="." includes="plugin.properties"/>
      <fileset dir="." includes="preferences.ini"/>
   </copy>

   <!-- Assemble feature plug-in elements. -->
   <copy todir="${feature_plugin_common}">
      <fileset
         dir="../com.qualityeclipse.favorites.feature"
         includes="*.xml"/>
      <fileset
         dir="../com.qualityeclipse.favorites.feature"
         includes="*.gif"/>
   </copy>
```

```
<!-- Assemble help plug-in elements. -->
<copy todir="${help_plugin_common}">
   <fileset
       dir="../com.qualityeclipse.favorites.help"
       includes="*.xml"/>
</copy>
<zip zipfile="${help_plugin_common}/doc.zip">
    <zipfileset
       dir="../com.qualityeclipse.favorites.help/html"
       prefix="html"/>
</zip>

</target>
```

Next, place the script elements related to building the Eclipse 3.0-specific elements in a new `build_30` target. Both the `favorites.jar` file and the `plugin.xml` can vary from one version of Eclipse to another, so these are assembled into a temporary directory separate from the common elements. This prepares us for simultaneously building a product for other versions of Eclipse based on the same source.

```
<target name="build_30" depends="init">

   <!-- Temporary directories used to build
      3.0-specific elements... will be deleted. -->
   <property
      name="temp_30"
      value="${temp_dir}/out30"/>
   <property
      name="main_plugin_30"
      value="${temp_30}/${main_plugin_dirname}"/>

   <!-- Assemble main plug-in's 3.0-specific elements. -->
   <copy todir="${main_plugin_30}">
      <fileset dir="." includes="plugin.xml"/>
   </copy>
   <jar jarfile="${main_plugin_30}/favorites.jar">
      <fileset dir="bin"/>
   </jar>

</target>
```

Finally, create a new `product_30` target that assembles the common and Eclipse 3.0-specific elements into a single zip file with the appropriate directory structure for linking to an Eclipse installation (see Section 3.2.1). Add a description to this target to indicate its purpose and make it an external target. In addition, change the build script's default target to be `product_30`, since there is no longer a `product` target.

```
<target
  name="product_30"
  depends="build_common, build_30"
  description="Build the Eclipse 3.0 specific product">

  <!-- Build the product from the temp directory. -->
  <mkdir dir="${product_dir}"/>
  <zip zipfile="${product_dir}/QualityEclipseTools
    _v${product_version}_for_Eclipse3.0.zip">
    <zipfileset
      dir="${temp_common}"
      prefix="${product_prefix}"/>
    <zipfileset
      dir="${temp_30}"
      prefix="${product_prefix}"/>
  </zip>

</target>
```

All this refactoring has resulted in a new and more flexible build structure that can easily be adapted to generate new binaries for other versions of Eclipse (see Figure 19–7). Currently, the product_30 target depends on the build_30 and build_common targets, each of which depend on the init target. This structure scales nicely in that by adding new product_xx and build_xx targets we can easily build additional binaries to support different versions of Eclipse. For example, to support Eclipse 2.1, we would add new product_21 and build_21 targets. Finally, we add a new product target whose sole purpose is to build all the **Favorites** product binaries at once.

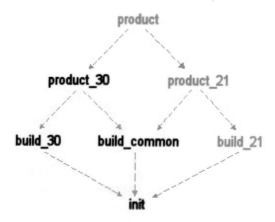

Figure 19–7   Favorites build script structure.

19.2.3   *Compiling during the build process*

The current build script simply copies the Java class files produced by the Eclipse environment into the favorites.jar file. We need to compile the source files during the build process to ensure that we have a full and complete compilation, verifying the work of the Eclipse IDE. In addition, this step will be necessary if we want to produce a binary for each different version of Eclipse we support. Modify the build_30 script to obtain the **Favorites** project's classpath using the eclipsetools.getclasspath task (see Section 19.2.7), compile the source into a temporary bin30 directory, and then produce the favorites.jar file using the newly compiled classes.

```
<target name="build_30" depends="init">

   <!-- Temporary directories used to build
        3.0-specific elements... will be deleted. -->
   <property
      name="bin_30"
      value="${temp_dir}/bin30"/>
   <property
      name="temp_30"
      value="${temp_dir}/out30"/>
   <property
      name="main_plugin_30"
      value="${temp_30}/${main_plugin_dirname}"/>

   <!-- Compile main plug-in's files. -->
   <eclipsetools.getclasspath
      projectName="com.qualityeclipse.favorites"
      propertyName="classpath_30"/>
   <mkdir dir="${bin_30}"/>
   <javac
      classpath="${classpath_30}"
      debug="on"
      destdir="${bin_30}">
      <src path="src"/>
   </javac>

   <!-- Assemble main plug-in's 3.0-specific elements. -->
   <copy todir="${main_plugin_30}">
      <fileset dir="." includes="plugin.xml"/>
   </copy>
   <jar jarfile="${main_plugin_30}/favorites.jar">
    <fileset dir="${bin_30}"/>
      <fileset dir="src" includes="**/*.gif"/>
      <fileset dir="src" includes="**/*.properties"/>
   </jar>

</target>
```

If you get a build error similar to this:

```
BUILD FAILED: file:      .../workspace/com.qualityeclipse.favor-
ites/build.xml:182:
Unable to find a javac compiler;
com.sun.tools.javac.Main is not on the classpath.
Perhaps JAVA_HOME does not point to the JDK
```

you may not have the JDK `tools.jar` file on your Ant classpath. Open the **Ant
> Runtime** preference page (see Figure 19–8) and verify that the `tools.jar` file
appears under **Global Entries**. If it does not, then select **Global Entries**, click
Add External JARS..., navigate to your `<JDK>\lib\tools.jar` file, and click
Open so that the `tools.jar` is added to your Ant classpath.

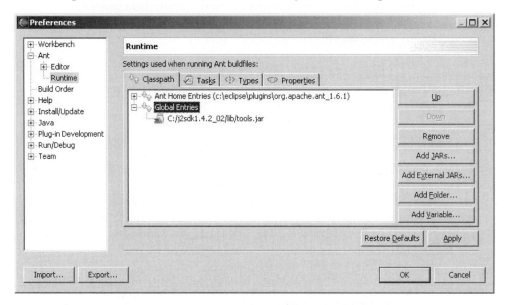

Figure 19–8   The **Ant > Runtime** preference page showing tools.jar.

By default, the `javac` task uses the Java compiler found on the Ant classpath as specified above. To use the Eclipse compiler, set the `build.compiler`
property.

```
<property
   name="build.compiler"
   value="org.eclipse.jdt.core.JDTCompilerAdapter"/>
```

19.2.4   Single versus multiple binaries

What if the public API used by your plug-in has not changed and the code
compiles against each version of Eclipse successfully? Why should you ship a
different binary of your product for each version of Eclipse? Given this sce-

nario, a single binary might run correctly on different versions of Eclipse, *but can you be sure?* There are cases where the same source compiled against two different versions of Eclipse will produce two different binaries, each of which will only execute correctly on one version of Eclipse, not the other. For example, if your code had a method called yourMethod():

```
Your code:
   public void yourMethod() {
      foo(0);
   }

Eclipse 3.0:
   public void foo(int value) {
      ... some operation ...
   }

Eclipse 2.1:
   public void foo(long value) {
      ... some operation ...
   }
```

then yourMethod() method would compile under Eclipse 3.0 and Eclipse 2.1 without any code changes, but would the version compiled under Eclipse 3.0 run in Eclipse 2.1? Things like this make it well worth the up-front time and effort to deliver one binary for each version of Eclipse you intend to support rather than spending that same amount of time and more later on debugging problems in the field.

19.2.5 *Editing the same source with different versions of Eclipse*

Sometimes, different developers using different versions of Eclipse want to work on the same project. If the project in question does not involve any Eclipse plug-ins, then there is no problem. The problem arises when a project uses the ECLIPSE_HOME classpath variable, which is automatically managed by the Eclipse environment to point to the current Eclipse installation. As a result, any project using ECLIPSE_HOME references plug-ins in the current Eclipse installation. For example, a developer using Eclipse 3.0 will have the project compiled against the Eclipse 3.0 plug-ins, whereas someone using WebSphere Application Developer 5.1, which is based on Eclipse 2.1, will have that same project compiled against Eclipse 2.1 plug-ins.

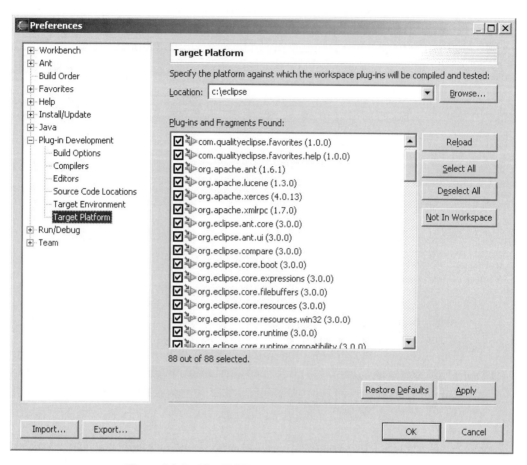

Figure 19–9   The PDE Target Platform preference page.

One solution is to use the PDE **Target Platform** preference page (see Figure 19–9). Using this preference page, you can retarget the ECLIPSE_HOME classpath variable at a different Eclipse installation. The problem with this approach is that it does not address the problem of different projects compiled against different versions of Eclipse. With this solution, you will have all projects compiled against the same Eclipse installation.

Another solution is never using the ECLIPSE_HOME classpath variable at all. Assuming that we want to support Eclipse 2.0, 2.1, and 3.0, we install all three Eclipse versions into separate directories with names like c:\eclipse2.0, c:\eclipse2.1, and c:\eclipse3.0. We then set up three classpath variables named ECLIPSE20_HOME, ECLIPSE21_HOME, and ECLIPSE30_HOME, which point to their respective Eclipse installations. If we have a project compiled against Eclipse 3.0, we would use ECLIPSE30_HOME rather than ECLIPSE_HOME. With this approach, it doesn't matter which version of Eclipse is being used as the code is always compiled against one specific Eclipse version. In addition, this approach lends itself to delivering one binary for each version of Eclipse you support, as shown in the next section.

Given this information, we want to modify the **Favorites** project to use this second approach. Create a new ECLIPSE30_HOME classpath variable and point it at your Eclipse 3.0 installation using the **Java > Classpath Variables** preference page. When the new classpath variable is defined, we could open the **Favorites** project's preference page by right-clicking on the project and selecting **Properties**, and then editing the classpath by selecting **Java Build Path,** but that would be quite time-consuming. Instead, double-click on the **.classpath** file to open it in a standard text editor, then simply perform a find and replace to substitute ECLIPSE30_HOME for ECLIPSE_HOME (by default, files beginning with ".″ are hidden from view via a filter—see the end of Section 1.4.2, ".classpath and .project files").

19.2.6 *Building against different versions of Eclipse*

Many developers, especially tool developers who write code for Eclipse itself, like to use bleeding-edge code, but large IT departments and other paying customers tend to prefer to lag the edge, using older, more established and supported software. This disparity creates a problem because we want to develop plug-ins using the latest and greatest, but our client base, the ones who pay for our development fun, may not have caught up yet. Therefore, we need to ship a product with one binary for each version of Eclipse we support.

To complicate matters, different versions of Eclipse have different public APIs. This means one set of source for each version of Eclipse, or does it? Can we have a single source base that is built into one binary for each version of Eclipse?

19.2.6.1 *Code branches*

One tried and true approach to this problem is to have one code stream or branch in the repository for each version of Eclipse you intend to support (see Figure 19–10). Another is to have separate projects, one per version of Eclipse. Unfortunately, with each of these approaches, there is no single code base, so providing the same new functionality for each version of Eclipse involves merging lots of code from one branch to another.

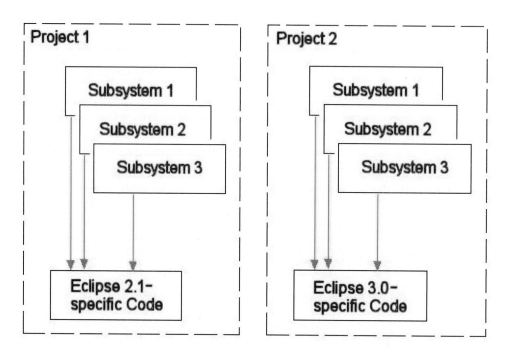

Figure 19–10   Code branches, or multiple projects.

19.2.6.2   Facade pattern

Another approach is a single code base with a facade pattern to handle differences between the versions of Eclipse. One project contains the common code, typically well over 95% of the code, accessing the Eclipse API that has not changed across the versions supported. Additional projects, one for each version of Eclipse, provide glue code for accessing just those public APIs that have changed (see Figure 19–11). This approach could produce a single binary that will provide the same functionality across different versions of Eclipse, but you could have the hidden run-time problems outlined in Section 19.2.4. Another drawback is that related functionality and methods that should be clustered together tend to become spread out across different packages and projects due to the facade pattern being used.

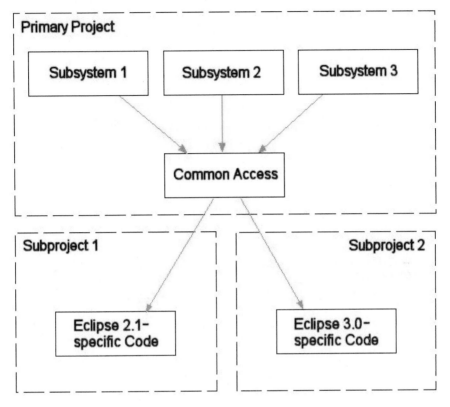

Figure 19–11   Facade pattern.

19.2.6.3 *Preprocessor*

After trying the first two approaches, we settled on using a Java preprocesssor to handle the differences between versions of Eclipse. This way, we have a single code base that is compiled against each different version of Eclipse, verifying that the calls to Eclipse methods match the public APIs available in that version. A build process takes one code base and produces one binary for each version of Eclipse (see Figure 19–12). In contrast to the facade pattern approach, related functionality and methods tend to stay logically clumped together in the same package rather than being spread out across the product, which leads to a more maintainable product.

```
<!-- Identify the version of Eclipse
    against which this source is compiled. -->
<property
    name="preprocessor.version.source"
    value="3.0"/>
```

```
<!-- Identify the versions of Eclipse
    that this source can be compiled against. -->
<property
    name="preprocessor.version.valid"
    value="2.0, 2.1, 3.0"/>

<!-- Translate source in the src directory
    that is compiled against Eclipse 3.0
    into source in the src_21 directory
    that can be compiled against Eclipse 2.1. -->
<eclipsetools.preprocessor
    targetVersion="2.1"
    dir="src"
    todir="src_21"/>
```

Download the Preprocessor   The `<eclipsetools.preprocessor>` task mentioned above is not part of Ant or Eclipse, but an Ant extension that we wrote. We needed it to build our products, and it is freely available for anyone to use at: *www.qualityeclipse.com/ant/preprocessor.*

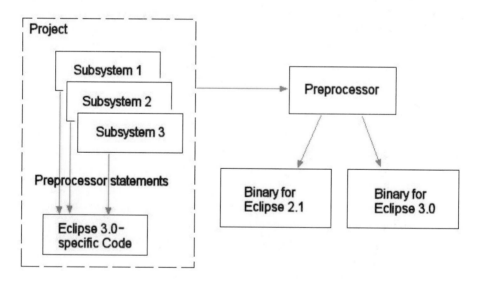

Figure 19–12   Preprocessor approach.

Code to be translated by the preprocessor involves structured Java comments. The preprocessor statements embedded in comments expose the API call for only one version of Eclipse while hiding the different API calls for the other versions. During the build process, the source is parsed and some sections are commented while others are uncommented, all before the source is sent to the

Java compiler (see Figure 19–13). For example, the code below was developed against the Eclipse 3.0 environment, and thus the Eclipse 3.0-specific code is uncommented, while the Eclipse 2.0- and 2.1-specific code is commented.

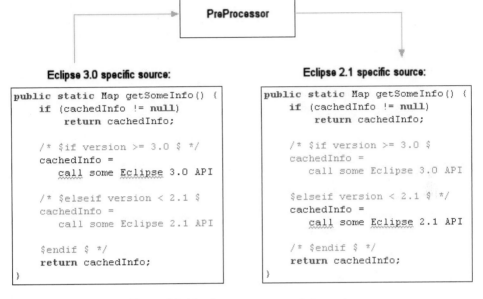

Figure 19–13   Preprocessor translating code.

In addition, differences in the `plugin.xml` can be handled in a similar manner. For example, the `org.eclipse.ui.ide` plug-in only exists in Eclipse 3.0, not in Eclipse 2.1.

```xml
<?xml version="1.0" encoding="UTF-8"?>
<plugin
    id="com.mycompany.myapp"
    name="%pluginName"
    version="1.0.0"
    provider-name="My Company"
    class=" com.mycompany.myapp.MyPlugin">

    <requires>
        <import plugin="org.apache.xerces"/>
        <import plugin="org.eclipse.core.runtime"/>
        <import plugin="org.eclipse.core.resources"/>
        <import plugin="org.eclipse.ui"/>
        <!-- $if version >= 3.0 $ -->
        <import plugin="org.eclipse.ui.ide" optional="true"/>
        <!--$endif $ -->
    </requires>

    … etc …
</plugin>
```

Since we want to support Eclipse 2.1, the next step is to modify the **Favorites** project so that the source correctly compiles against Eclipse 2.1. First, modify the ECLIPSE30_HOME classpath variable so that it points to the Eclipse 2.1 installation and adjust the **Favorites** project classpath. Then, modify the code so that it properly compiles against Eclipse 2.1, placing any Eclipse 3.0-specific code in comments. Finally, revert the classpath variable so that it again points to the Eclipse 3.0 installation, and adjust the preprocessor comments accordingly.

> **Tip:** A tool for automatically adjusting the classpath of a project between versions of Eclipse is available on the *QualityEclipse* Web site (*www.qualityeclipse.com/tools/classpath*).

When preparing the **Favorites** view for Eclipse 2.1, one of the issues encountered is the addHelpButtonToToolBar() method. In this case, the Eclipse 3.0 help public API differs from the Eclipse 2.1 help public API. Because of this, we must adjust the addHelpButtonToToolBar() method in FavoritesView to wrap the Eclipse 3.0-specific code in preprocessor statements and add new Eclipse 2.1-specific code.

```
private void addHelpButtonToToolBar() {
   Action helpAction = new Action() {
      public void run() {

         /* $if version >= 3.0 $ */
         WorkbenchHelp.displayHelpResource(
            "/com.qualityeclipse.favorites.help"
               + "/html/toc.html");

         /* $elseif version < 3.0 $
         IHelp helpSupport = WorkbenchHelp.getHelpSupport();
         if (helpSupport != null)
            helpSupport.displayHelp(
               "/com.qualityeclipse.favorites.help/toc.xml",
               "/com.qualityeclipse.favorites.help"
                  + "/html/toc.html");

         $endif $ */
      }
   };
   … etc …
}
```

   Another difference we encounter is in the **Favorites** plug-in manifest. The manifest references the `org.eclipse.ui.ide` plug-in, which exists in Eclipse 3.0, but not in Eclipse 2.1. Preprocessor statements are added to the plug-in manifest as follows to suppress that requirement in Eclipse 2.1:

```
<?xml version="1.0" encoding="UTF-8"?>
<?eclipse version="3.0"?>
<plugin
    id="com.qualityeclipse.favorites"
    name="Favorites Plug-in"
    version="1.0.0"
    provider-name="QualityEclipse"
    class="com.qualityeclipse.favorites.FavoritesPlugin">

    <runtime>
        <library name="favorites.jar">
            <export name="*"/>
            <packages prefixes="com.qualityeclipse.favorites"/>
        </library>
    </runtime>
    <requires>
        <import plugin="org.eclipse.core.resources"/>
        <import plugin="org.eclipse.core.runtime"/>
        <import plugin="org.eclipse.debug.ui"/>
        <import plugin="org.eclipse.help"/>
        <import plugin="org.eclipse.help.ui"/>
        <import plugin="org.eclipse.jdt.core"/>
        <import plugin="org.eclipse.jdt.ui"/>
        <import plugin="org.eclipse.jface"/>
        <import plugin="org.eclipse.jface.text"/>
        <import plugin="org.eclipse.swt"/>
        <import plugin="org.eclipse.text"/>
        <import plugin="org.eclipse.ui"/>
        <import plugin="org.eclipse.ui.editors"/>
        <import plugin="org.eclipse.ui.views"/>
        <import plugin="org.eclipse.ui.workbench"/>
        <import plugin="org.eclipse.ui.workbench.texteditor"/>
<!-- $if version >= 3.0 $ -->
        <import plugin="org.eclipse.core.runtime.compatibility"/>
        <import plugin="org.eclipse.osgi"/>
        <import plugin="org.eclipse.ui.ide"/>
<!-- $endif $ -->
    </requires>

    … etc …

</plugin>
```

Tip: If you modify the `<requires>` section of the `plugin.xml` without changing the plug-in's version number and then install it overtop of a earlier version of that plug-in, you may need to delete the `<eclipseInstallDir>/configuration` directory because Eclipse caches plug-in dependency information in that directory (see Section 20.10, "OSGi Bundles and the 3.0 Run-time".

This process of switching the classpath variable only needs to be performed once per project to get the code to compile against a different version of Eclipse. To support multiple versions of Eclipse in an ongoing manner, simply code against one version of Eclipse, and then build the product to make sure that it compiles against the others, adding preprocessor statements only as necessary. In practice, this is not a big deal as only a fraction of your code base will include any preprocessor statements (typically less than 1% of the files).

The final step is to run the code through the preprocessor before it is compiled. First, we must add the following declaration to the `init` target so that the preprocessor knows which version of Eclipse the source is coded for and at which versions of Eclipse the source can be targeted:

```
<!-- Preprocessor information. -->
<property
   name="preprocessor.version.source"
   value="3.0"/>
<property
   name="preprocessor.version.valid"
   value="2.1,3.0"/>
```

Next, we modify the `build_30` target to run the source through the preprocessor before it is compiled:

```
<target name="build_30" depends="init">

   <!-- Temporary directories used to build
      the 3.0-specific elements... will be deleted. -->
   <property
      name="src_30"
      value="${temp_dir}/src30"/>
   <property
      name="bin_30"
      value="${temp_dir}/bin30"/>
   <property
      name="temp_30"
      value="${temp_dir}/out30"/>
   <property
      name="main_plugin_30"
      value="${temp_30}/${main_plugin_dirname}"/>

   <!-- Run the source through the preprocessor. -->
   <eclipsetools.preprocessor
      targetVersion="3.0"
      todir="${src_30}">
      <fileset dir="src"/>
   </eclipsetools.preprocessor>

   <!-- Compile the main plug-in's files. -->
   <eclipsetools.getclasspath
      projectName="com.qualityeclipse.favorites"
      propertyName="classpath_30"/>
```

```
<mkdir dir="${bin_30}"/>
<javac
    classpath="${classpath_30}"
    debug="on"
    destdir="${bin_30}">
    <src path="${src_30}"/>
</javac>

<!-- Assemble main plug-in's 3.0-specific elements. -->
<copy todir="${main_plugin_30}">
    <fileset dir="." includes="plugin.xml"/>
</copy>
<jar jarfile="${main_plugin_30}/favorites.jar">
    <fileset dir="${bin_30}"/>
    <fileset dir="${src_30}" includes="**/*.gif"/>
    <fileset dir="${src_30}" includes="**/*.properties"/>
</jar>

</target>
```

19.2.6.4   Fragments

Fragments can be used to smooth out differences between versions of Eclipse (see Sections 16.3 and 20.2.6, both titled "Using Fragments," for more about fragments). If a newer version of Eclipse has an API you want to use but an older version does not, you can use a fragment to insert a helper class into the older version of Eclipse, allowing you access to the necessary internal code. If a class has been added to a newer version of Eclipse that was not present in the older version, then you can backport the entire class to the older version of Eclipse using a fragment. Be aware that your fragment may collide with someone else's fragment doing the same thing; it is safer to add uniquely named helper classes than to backport Eclipse classes.

19.2.7   Classpath tools

The `eclipsetools.getclasspath` task introduced in Section 19.2.3 can modify the classpath for different versions of Eclipse after it retrieves the classpath. Using the `eclipsetools_*` Ant types, we can specify the differences between the Eclipse 2.1 and Eclipse 3.0 classpaths in the `init` target:

```
<eclipsetools_classpath_modifications
    id="classpath_30_to_21">
    <eclipsetools_classpath_modify
        path="ECLIPSE30_HOME/plugins/
            org.eclipse.ui.ide_3.0.0/ide.jar">
        <eclipsetools_classpath_entry
            path="ECLIPSE21_HOME/plugins/
                org.eclipse.ui_2.1.1/ui.jar"/>
```

```
</eclipsetools_classpath_modify>
  <eclipsetools_classpath_variable
    name="ECLIPSE30_HOME"
    path="ECLIPSE21_HOME"/>
</eclipsetools_classpath_modifications>
```

This code defines the modifications necessary to convert the **Favorites** product Eclipse 3.0 classpath to an Eclipse 2.1 classpath. The second line, `id="classpath_30_to_21"`, indicates that the structure being defined can be referenced later in the script using this identifier. The `eclipse-tools_classpath_modify` structure specifies that any occurrence of `org.eclipse.ui.ide` that does not exist in Eclipse 2.1 should be replaced by `org.eclipse.ui`. The `eclipsetools_classpath_variable` structure specifies that any use of the `ECLIPSE30_HOME` classpath variable should be replaced by the `ECLIPSE21_HOME` classpath variable. When we retrieve the **Favorites** project's classpath in the not yet existing build_21 target, we will reference this entire structure using the `"classpath_30_to_21"` identifier to indicate how the classpath should be translated.

> **Download the getclasspath Task** The `<eclipsetools.getclass-path>` task mentioned above is not part of Ant or Eclipse, but an Ant extension we wrote. We needed it to build our products, and it is freely available for anyone to use at: *www.qualityeclipse.com/ant/getclasspath*

19.2.8 Building against Eclipse 2.1

With the preprocessor and classpath tools in place, we are ready to build the **Favorites** project for Eclipse 2.1. Copy the build_30 target into a new build_21 target and replace "30" with "21" and "3.0" with "2.1" so that it looks like this:

```
<target name="build_21" depends="init">

  <!-- Temporary directories used to build
     the 2.1-specific elements... will be deleted. -->
  <property
    name="src_21"
    value="${temp_dir}/src21"/>
  <property
    name="bin_21"
    value="${temp_dir}/bin21"/>
  <property
    name="temp_21"
    value="${temp_dir}/out21"/>
  <property
    name="main_plugin_21"
    value="${temp_21}/${main_plugin_dirname}"/>
```

```
        <!-- Run the source through the preprocessor. -->
        <eclipsetools.preprocessor
            targetVersion="2.1"
            todir="${src_21}">
            <fileset dir="src"/>
        </eclipsetools.preprocessor>

        <!-- Compile the main plug-in's files. -->
        <eclipsetools.getclasspath
            projectName="com.qualityeclipse.favorites"
            propertyName="classpath_21"/>
        <mkdir dir="${bin_21}"/>
        <javac
            classpath="${classpath_21}"
            debug="on"
            destdir="${bin_21}">
            <src path="${src_21}"/>
        </javac>

        <!-- Assemble main plug-in's 2.1-specific elements. -->
        <copy todir="${main_plugin_21}">
            <fileset dir="." includes="plugin.xml"/>
        </copy>
        <jar jarfile="${main_plugin_21}/favorites.jar">
            <fileset dir="${bin_21}"/>
            <fileset dir="${src_21}" includes="**/*.gif"/>
            <fileset dir="${src_21}" includes="**/*.properties"/>
        </jar>

    </target>
```

After that is complete, add a new product_21 build target based on the product_30 target in the same manner:

```
<target
    name="product_21"
    depends="build_common, build_21"
    description="Build the Eclipse 2.1 specific product">

    <!-- Build the product from the temp directory. -->
    <mkdir dir="${product_dir}"/>
    <zip
        zipfile="${product_dir}/QualityEclipseTools
            _v${product_version}_for_Eclipse2.1.zip">
        <zipfileset
            dir="${temp_common}"
            prefix="${product_prefix}"/>
        <zipfileset
            dir="${temp_21}"
            prefix="${product_prefix}"/>
    </zip>

</target>
```

Finally, we can add a new product target that combines the `product_21` and `product_30` build targets. This approach will easily scale to support whatever versions of Eclipse you choose.

```
<target
   name="product"
   depends="product_21, product_30"
   description="Build all versions of the product">
</target>
```

19.2.9   Retargeting source code

Using the preprocessor approach outlined in the previous sections involves source targeted at one version of Eclipse, but generating binaries for other versions of Eclipse. In other words, the code contains some source that is surrounded by preprocessor statements, but uncommented, for the targeted version of Eclipse, while source for the other versions of Eclipse is commented out. At some point, you'll want to change the targeted version of Eclipse from, say, Eclipse 2.1 to Eclipse 3.0. To accomplish this involves using the preprocessor itself to regenerate your source and the introduction of a new classpath tool.

The first step when retargeting the code from Eclipse 2.1 to Eclipse 3.0 involves running the preprocessor over the code to produce revised source that targets the newer version of Eclipse. This is what happens each time the build process runs, only this time, we are taking the result and checking the revised version back into the repository as our basis for new development. Our capability to generate multiple binaries, one for each version of Eclipse, is not lost, only the targeted version of Eclipse has changed.

The second step involves updating the projects' Java build paths by modifying the `.classpath` file (see the end of Section 19.2.5) to use the appropriate classpath variable. For example, if you are moving from development in Eclipse 2.1 to Eclipse 3.0, then replace all occurrences of `ECLIPSE21_HOME` with `ECLIPSE30_HOME`. In addition, you'll need to update the plug-in's directory suffix in the `.classpath` file to match the target version of Eclipse (e.g., `plugins/org.eclipse.swt_2.1.1` changes to `plugins/org.eclipse .swt_3.0.0`).

> **Tip:** A tool for automatically adjusting the classpath of a project between versions of Eclipse is available on the *QualityEclipse* Web site (*www.qualityeclipse.com/tools/classpath*).

19.2.10 *Version checking*

Having one product binary for each version of Eclipse solves one problem while causing another: What if the user installs the wrong binary for the version of Eclipse he or she is using? To solve this, you can add version checking into the plug-in startup method to compare the version of Eclipse for which the binary was produced with the version of Eclipse on which the code is currently executing. If the two versions don't match, then the code immediately informs the user.

```
/**
 * Indicates which IDE the binary expects.
 */
public static final PluginVersionIdentifier IDE_VERSION_EXPECTED =
    /* $if version == 3.0 $ */
        new PluginVersionIdentifier(3, 0, 0);
    /* $elseif version == 2.1 $
        new PluginVersionIdentifier(2, 1, 0);
    $endif $ */

/**
 * Indicates which IDE is being executed.
 */
public static final PluginVersionIdentifier IDE_VERSION_ACTUAL =
    ResourcesPlugin.getPlugin()
        .getDescriptor().getVersionIdentifier();

/**
 * Compares expected IDE version with actual IDE version.
 * @return <code>true</code> if the product is built
 *    to execute in this version of the IDE
 */
public static boolean isValidProductVersionForIDE() {
    return IDE_VERSION_EXPECTED.getMajorComponent()
        == IDE_VERSION_ACTUAL.getMajorComponent()
    && IDE_VERSION_EXPECTED.getMinorComponent()
        == IDE_VERSION_ACTUAL.getMinorComponent();
}
```

This code can be easily added to the FavoritesPlugin class. Once that is in place, you can modify the createPartControl(Composite) method in the FavoritesView, adding the following code to be the beginning of the method:

```
if (!FavoritesPlugin.isValidProductVersionForIDE()) {
    Label label = new Label(parent, SWT.NONE);
    label.setText(
        "This Favorites binary is compiled for "
            + FavoritesPlugin.IDE_VERSION_EXPECTED
            + " but being executed on "
            + FavoritesPlugin.IDE_VERSION_ACTUAL);
    return;
}
```

Now, if the user installs the **Favorites** product binary compiled for Eclipse 3.0 into Eclipse 2.1, he or she will see the following message in the **Favorites** view (see Figure 19–14):

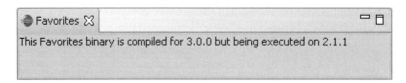

Figure 19–14   The Favorites view containing an IDE version message.

19.2.11   *Building for internationalization*

If you are targeting an international market and have generated a language specific fragment project (see Section 16.3), you need to generate separate deliverables containing language-specific code and resources. For the **Favorites** product, we will generate a new QualityEclipseTools_v1.0.0_nl1.zip file containing the contents of the com.qualityeclipse.favorites.nl1 project. Customers desiring language support for French and German would install this language-specific ZIP file in the same location as the main product. To accomplish all this, we introduce a new product_nl1 Ant build target and then add product_nl1 to the depends attribute of the product target:

```
<target
   name="product_nl1"
   depends="init"
   description="Build language fragment 1">

   <property
      name="nl1_fragment_id"
      value="com.qualityeclipse.favorites.nl1"/>
   <property
      name="nl1_fragment_dirname"
      value="${nl1_fragment_id}_${product_version}"/>

   <!-- Temporary directories used to build
      the nl1 elements... will be deleted. -->
   <property
      name="temp_nl1"
      value="${temp_dir}/nl1"/>
   <property
      name="temp_fragment_nl1"
      value="${temp_nl1}/${nl1_fragment_dirname}"/>

   <!-- Assemble nl1 fragment's elements. -->
   <copy todir="${temp_fragment_nl1}">
      <fileset
         dir="../com.qualityeclipse.favorites.nl1"
         includes="nl/**/*.*"/>
```

```
        <fileset
            dir="../com.qualityeclipse.favorites.nl1"
            includes="fragment.xml"/>
    </copy>
    <jar jarfile="${temp_fragment_nl1}/nl1.jar">
        <fileset
            dir="../com.qualityeclipse
                .favorites.nl1/bin"/>
    </jar>

    <!-- Build the product from the temp directory. -->
    <mkdir dir="${product_dir}"/>
    <zip
        zipfile="${product_dir}/QualityEclipseTools
            _v${product_version}_nl1.zip">
        <zipfileset
            dir="${temp_nl1}"
            prefix="${product_prefix}"/>
    </zip>

</target>
```

19.3 Summary

While you can build your plug-ins manually, this can introduce errors and
subtle differences between builds. Creating a one-click, repeatable build process is essential for delivering (and re-delivering) a commercial Eclipse plug-
in. In this chapter, we introduced Ant and then went into detail about how to
create an Ant-based build process. We then went on to discuss some of the
issues you will face in building and delivering a plug-in for more than one version of Eclipse.

References

The Ant Web site (*ant.apache.org/*).

Loughran, Steve, "Ant in Anger: Using Apache Ant in a Production Development System," Nov. 9, 2002 (*ant.apache.org/ant_in_anger.html*).

The *QualityEclipse* Web site (*www.qualityeclipse.com/ant*).

CHAPTER 20

Advanced Topics

When organizing anything, you more than likely end up with a handful of items that do not fit into any of the existing categories yet are not large or numerous enough to warrant a new category; this book is no exception. This chapter contains miscellaneous topics that bear discussing, but don't really fit anywhere else in the book, including:

- Advanced search—reference projects
- Accessing internal code
- Adapters
- Opening a browser or creating an email
- Types specified in an extension point
- Modifying Eclipse to find part identifiers
- Label decorators
- Background tasks—Jobs API
- Project class loader
- Open Services Gateway initiative (OSGi) bundles and the 3.0 run-time

20.1 Advanced Search—Reference Projects

Eclipse provides an excellent Java search facility for locating source (see Section 1.6.2, "Java search"), yet the scope of any search is limited to the projects loaded in the workspace; if a Java class is located in a plug-in's JAR file, and the plug-in is not on the Java build path of an open project, then the class will not be found. When building Eclipse plug-ins, it is advantageous to include *all* Eclipse plug-ins in the search scope, even those not referenced by any projects under development.

One approach is to load all the plug-in projects from the Eclipse CVS server (see Section 20.6.1, "Modifying the Eclipse base"). Unfortunately, this chews up memory and clutters your workspace with hundreds of additional projects.

Another approach is to create binary projects, one for each Eclipse plug-in. To create one or more binary projects, open the **PDE > Plug-ins** view using the **Show View** dialog (see **Show View** in Section 2.5, "Installing and Running the Product"), select the plug-ins to be imported as projects, then right-click and select **Import > As Binary Project**. Although binary projects take up less memory than source projects, this too will clutter your workspace with hundreds of additional projects.

Our approach, useful for searching and supporting multiple versions of Eclipse at the same time (see Section 19.2.6, "Building against different versions of Eclipse"), is to create one *reference project* for each version of Eclipse to be searched. This project contains no source of its own, but contains all the Eclipse plug-ins on its classpath so that a search can include the entire source for Eclipse. To include or exclude a particular version of Eclipse in your searches, simply open or close the corresponding reference project.

To create a reference project, first create a Java project (see Section 1.4.1, "Using the new java project wizard"), and then add each JAR file in each Eclipse plug-in to the project's Java build path (see Section 1.4.2, ".classpath and .project files"). Adding each plug-in can be a tedious process, so we created a new project wizard to automate this process (see Section 11.2, "Wizards," for information about creating wizards).

> **Tip:** A wizard for creating reference projects is available as part of the QualityEclipse Tools plug-in, downloadable from: *www.qualityeclipse.com/tools.*

20.2 Accessing Internal Code

Eclipse separates classes into two categories: public API and "for internal use only." Any classes located in a package that has "internal" in its name (e.g., `org.eclipse.core.internal.boot`) are internal to the plug-in, should not be referenced by any code outside the plug-in itself, and may change drastically between different versions of Eclipse. All other classes are considered public API, may be called from outside the plug-in, and follow strict Eclipse guidelines for how and when the class and method signatures can change. Needless to say, it is easier to stick to the public API when supporting multiple versions of Eclipse.

During the course of development, you may need to access classes and methods marked internal to a particular Eclipse plug-in. Each time you have such a need, the first thing you should do is double-check that there is not an existing public API that will do the trick instead. If no public API exists, then search the *Eclipse.org* archives or related sites (see Section A.2, "Resources") for a similar problem with a solution you can use. Failing that, post a message on the Eclipse newsgroup describing your situation and asking for suggestions (see the next section). If you don't find a solution, then proceed to file a bug report or feature request in the Eclipse Bugzilla tracking system (see Section 20.2.2, "Bugzilla—Eclipse bug tracking system"). If need be, you can create a fragment (see Section 20.2.6) to access the code necessary until a public API is made available.

20.2.1   Eclipse newsgroup

The Eclipse newsgroup, *www.eclipse.org/newsgroups/index.html*, provides novice and expert alike with an avenue for sharing knowledge. You'll need a username name and password, so if you do not have one, browse *www.eclipse.org/*, then go to **newsgroups > Request a Password**. The more information you provide regarding what you are trying to accomplish and code showing what you have tried so far, the more likely you are to get a response and the information you need. A vague question will likely be ignored or bounced back to you for more information. Do your homework, and above all, don't expect an answer—these are smart folks who will answer depending on their area of expertise, their interest in your question, and their available time—nobody is being paid to help you. The Eclipse newsgroup is open to everyone, so don't be afraid to contribute to the community by offering help to others when you can.

20.2.2   Bugzilla—Eclipse bug tracking system

Once you have double-checked that no public API exists and no one else on the newsgroup has a suggestion as to how your task can be accomplished, submit a bug report or feature request to the Eclipse Bugzilla tracking system:

```
bugs.eclipse.org/bugs/
```

Again, you'll need a username and password, so if you don't have one, browse *www.eclipse.org/*, and then select **bugs > Report a new bug > New Account**. As with the newsgroup, the more information you provide regarding what you are trying to accomplish and code showing what you have tried so far, the more likely the Eclipse team will provide the public API you need in future versions of Eclipse. To increase your odds of success even further, be sure to include details concerning how you think Eclipse should be modified to suit your needs; or better yet, make and submit the modifications yourself (see Section 20.6.1), along with test cases so that the Eclipse development team can simply install your changes, test them, and move on with the rest of their work. Your modifications may involve modifying existing Eclipse code, adding new code, or even adding a new extension point (see Section 17.2, "Defining an extension point"). Be sure to vote for the bugs that you want fixed so that the Eclipse team can get a better feel for what changes are important and which are not. As with the newsgroup, do your homework and don't expect to get everything you want. The Eclipse team is trying to satisfy a diverse community's needs and keep quite busy doing so.

20.2.3   *Options for accessing internal code*

Submitting a request to the Eclipse development team will help with future versions of Eclipse; but, what is to be done to support the current and prior versions? There are several techniques for accessing internal code, including:

- Calling a method directly if it is publicly accessible

- Creating a utility class in the same package

- Copying the code into your own plug-in

- Subclassing

- Manipulating the project's Java build path so that a new version of the class appears earlier, causing the Java VM to use the newer rather than the original version (see Section 20.2.5, "ClassLoader tricks")

- Using plug-in fragments (see Section 20.2.6, "Using fragments")

> If you reference internal code, either directly or indirectly via a fragment, then the onus is on you to change your code if the internal code changes or goes away.

20.2.4   *How Eclipse is different*

Eclipse imposes more restrictions on plug-in interaction than in a typical Java application. Each plug-in has its own ClassLoader, restricting its visibility of the system to code in the plug-ins specified via the plug-in manifest (see Section 2.3.1, "The plug-in manifest"). This means that even though class A in one plug-in resides in a package with the same name as class B in a required plug-in, class A will *not* be able to access the `protected` and default methods in class B. The Eclipse Java development environment will correctly compile the code as if those methods can be accessed, but when the code is executed inside an Eclipse framework, the plug-in ClassLoader will restrict the access, throwing an `IllegalAccessException`. This situation can also arise if the library is not exported by its plug-in manifest (see Section 3.3.2, "Plug-in runtime"), even if the class and methods are all marked as `public`. Since we do not want to modify an existing Eclipse plug-in, we must be a bit more resourceful to work around these restrictions.

> **Tip:** If a third party will be referencing and building on your plug-ins code, then consider exporting all classes in your plug-in as shown in Section 3.3.2. Your classes may be used to build things not originally envisioned by you, and hiding classes prevents others from supporting different versions of Eclipse and your code (see Section 19.2.6). Obviously, wherever you can, provide controlled third-party enhancements through the use of extension points (see Section 17.1, "The Extension Point Mechanism").

20.2.5 *ClassLoader tricks*

Manipulating the ClassLoader in your own plug-in is a seductive approach. When the plug-in starts up, you can forcibly load a particular version of a class into the ClassLoader using the following technique:

```
//Get ClassLoader using a class in plug-in of interest,
//e.g., AST from org.eclipse.jdt.core.dom will do.
PluginClassLoader jdtClassLoader
   = (PluginClassLoader) AST.class.getClassLoader();
URL[] newClasspath = new URL[1];
try {
   newClasspath[0] = new URL(
      "jar:platform:/plugins
      /<myPluginId>_<myVersion>/myCode.jar!/");
   jdtClassLoader.addURLs(
      newClasspath,
      new URLContentFilter[] { new URLContentFilter(true)},
      new URL[] { new URL("file://nowhere")},
      new URLContentFilter[] { new URLContentFilter(false)});

   //Load the class you want to override.
   jdtClassLoader.loadClass(
      "org.eclipse.jdt.core.dom.ASTMatcher");
}
catch (Exception e) {
   // Report and log the exception.
}
```

> **Disclaimer:** We **do not recommend** the ClassLoader technique outlined above and it may not work with the new OSGi run-time structure (see Section 20.10, "OSGi Bundles and the 3.0 Run-time"). We have not tried it and do not use it in our own products. Your experience may vary.

One problem with this approach is that you are effectively replacing code in the Eclipse system rather than augmenting it. Another problem is a class loaded by one ClassLoader is considered different from a class loaded by another ClassLoader, even if it was the same class loaded from the same class library (see Section 20.9, "Plug-in ClassLoaders" for more on ClassLoaders). We keep this approach in our bag of tricks, but have never needed to use it; fragments (see the next section) have proven to be a much better and more stable approach for us.

20.2.6   Using Fragments

A better approach is to work with the Eclipse framework rather than against it by referencing the code directly, if possible, copying the code, if necessary, or by using fragments. Fragments are chunks of code defined in a plug-in-like structure that Eclipse automatically attaches to an existing plug-in (see Section 16.3, "Using Fragments"). As far as the Eclipse system is concerned, code contributed by a fragment is treated exactly the same as code that exists in the target plug-in. Originally, fragments were created to insert different National Language Support (NLS) code into a plug-in based on the intended audience, but we will exploit this mechanism to solve our own problems. Using this technique, we cannot override classes that already exist in the plug-in, but we can insert new utility classes used to access methods that were previously not accessible because they had default or protected visibility.

Fragments have a fragment manifest named `fragment.xml` rather than a plug-in manifest (see Section 16.3.2, "Fragment manifest file"). The structure of the fragment manifest is similar to that of a plug-in manifest:

```
<?xml version="1.0" encoding="UTF-8"?>
<fragment
    id="com.myCompany.myFragment"
    name="My Fragment Name"
    version="2.3.1"
    provider-name="My Company Name"
    plugin-id="org.eclipse.ui.workbench"
    plugin-version="3.0.0"
    match="greaterOrEqual">

    <runtime>
        <library name="MyFragmentCode.jar">
```

```
      <export name="*"/>
    </library>
  </runtime>
</fragment>
```

In this plug-in fragment, we identify the fragment being defined followed by the target plug-in to modify. The `runtime` section at the end identifies the location of the fragment code relative to the fragment installation location. Fragments are installed into the plug-in directory in the same way and with the same restrictions as plug-ins.

20.3 Adapters

Eclipse provides an adapter framework for translating one type of object into a corresponding object of another type. This allows for new types of objects to be systematically translated into existing types of objects already known to Eclipse. When a user selects elements in one view or editor, other views can request adapted objects from those selected objects implementing the `org.eclipse.core.runtime.IAdaptable` interface. This means that items selected in our **Favorites** view can be translated into resources and Java elements as requested by existing Eclipse views without any code modifications to those views (see Section 7.4, "Linking the View").

20.3.1 IAdaptable

For objects to participate in the adapter framework, they must first implement the `IAdaptable` interface, as we have done with `IFavoriteItem` (see Section 7.4.2, "Adaptable objects"). The `IAdaptable` interface contains a single method for translating one type of object into another:

> `getAdapter(Class)`—Returns an object that is an instance of the given class and is associated with this object. Returns `null` if no such object can be provided.

Implementers of the `IAdaptable` interface attempt to provide an object of the specified type. If they cannot translate themselves, then they call the adapter manager to see if a factory exists for translating them into the specified type:

```
private IResource resource;

public Object getAdapter(Class adapter) {
   if (adapter.isInstance(resource))
      return resource;
   return Platform.getAdapterManager()
      .getAdapter(this, adapter);
}
```

20.3.2   Using adapters

Code desiring to translate an object passes the desired type, such as IRe-source.class, into the getAdapter (...) method, and either obtains an instance of IResource corresponding to the original object or null indicating that such a translation is not possible.

```
if (!(object instanceof IAdaptable))
   return;
MyInterface myObject
   = ((IAdaptable) object).getAdapter(MyInterface.class);
if (myObject == null)
return;
… do stuff with myObject …
```

20.3.3   Adapter factory

Implementing the IAdaptable interface allows new types of objects such as our **Favorites** items to be translated into existing types such as IResource, but how are existing types translated into new types? To accomplish this, implement the org.eclipse.core.runtime.IAdapterFactory interface to translate existing types into new types. For example, in our **Favorites** product, we cannot modify the implementers of IResource, but we can implement an adapter factory to translate IResource into IFavoriteItem. The getAdapterList() method returns an array indicating the types to which this factory can translate, while the getAdapter (...) method performs the translation. In our case, the factory can translate IResource and IJavaElement objects into IFavoriteItem objects so our getAdapterList() method returns an array containing IFavoriteItem.class.

```
package com.qualityeclipse.favorites.model;

import org.eclipse.core.runtime.*;

public class FavoriteAdapterFactory
   implements IAdapterFactory
{
   private static Class[] SUPPORTED_TYPES =
      new Class[] { IFavoriteItem.class };

   public Class[] getAdapterList() {
      return SUPPORTED_TYPES;
   }

   public Object getAdapter(Object object, Class key) {
      if (IFavoriteItem.class.equals(key)) {
         FavoritesManager mgr =
            FavoritesManager.getManager();
```

```
        IFavoriteItem item =
            mgr.existingFavoriteFor(object);
        if (item == null)
            item = mgr.newFavoriteFor(object);
        return item;
    }
    return null;
}
}
```

Adapter factories must be registered with the adapter manager before they are used. Typically, a plug-in registers adapters with adapter managers when it starts up and unregisters them when it shuts down. For example, in the **Favorites** product, we add the following field to the FavoritesPlugin class:

```
private FavoriteAdapterFactory favoriteAdapterFactory;
```

The following code, added to the FavoritesPlugin's startup() method, registers the adapter. Our FavoriteAdapterFactory translates IResource and IJavaElement objects into IFavoriteItem objects, so we register the adapter once with IResource.class as the argument and a second time with IJavaElement.class indicating that our adapter factory can translate from these types to others.

```
favoriteAdapterFactory = new FavoriteAdapterFactory();
IAdapterManager mgr = Platform.getAdapterManager();
mgr.registerAdapters(
    favoriteAdapterFactory,
    IResource.class);
mgr.registerAdapters(
    favoriteAdapterFactory,
    IJavaElement.class);
```

In addition, the FavoritesPlugin's shutdown() method must be modified to unregister the adapter:

```
Platform.getAdapterManager().unregisterAdapters(
    favoriteAdapterFactory);
favoriteAdapterFactory = null;
```

The introduction of an adapter factory allows code in the **Favorites** product and any plug-ins that depend on it to be more loosely coupled with the FavoritesManager. For example, rather than directly calling the Favorites-Manager, the FavoritesView.pageSelectionChanged(...) method (see Section 7.4.3, "Selection listener") can be revised to use the adaptable interface:

```
protected void pageSelectionChanged(
   IWorkbenchPart part,
   ISelection selection) {

   if (part == this)
      return;
   if (!(selection instanceof IStructuredSelection))
      return;
   IStructuredSelection sel =
      (IStructuredSelection) selection;

   List items = new ArrayList();
   Iterator iter = sel.iterator();
   while (iter.hasNext()) {
      Object object = iter.next();
      if (!(object instanceof IAdaptable))
         continue;
      IFavoriteItem item =
         (IFavoriteItem)
            ((IAdaptable) object).getAdapter(
            IFavoriteItem.class);
      if (item == null)
         continue;
      items.add(item);
   }

   if (items.size() > 0)
      viewer.setSelection(
         new StructuredSelection(items),
         true);
}
```

Using an adapter factory has a bit more overhead than referencing the FavoritesManager directly. When considering this for your own product, you will need to determine if the advantage of looser coupling outweighs the additional complexity and slightly slower execution time inherent in this approach.

20.3.4   IWorkbenchAdapter

Eclipse uses the IWorkbenchAdapter interface to display information. Many Eclipse views, such as the **Navigator** view, create an instance of WorkbenchLabelProvider. This label provider uses the IAdaptable interface to translate unknown objects into instances of IWorkbenchAdapter, and then queries this translated object for displayable information such as text and images. For your object to be displayed in an Eclipse view such as the **Navigator**, implement the IAdaptable interface and return an object that implements IWorkbenchAdapter or extends the abstract base class WorkbenchAdapter.

20.4   Opening a Browser or Creating an Email

In your product, you may want to provide an easy way for users to reach your Web site or quickly compose an email to your company. Start by creating a button that opens a browser on your product's Web page or creates an email message in the user's default email client when clicked. The simple approach is to use the `launch()` method in the `org.eclipse.swt.program.Program` class (see Section 15.4.2, "Opening a web page"), but unfortunately, that approach does not work with platforms other than Windows. A more comprehensive approach involves platform-specific code.

20.4.1   *OpenBrowserAction*

First, we create an action in which this behavior will reside, including `get` and `set` methods. `setURL(...)` and `newURL(...)` are convenient methods for converting strings to URLs. Since some systems do not support the `mailto:` protocol, we log only the first `mailto:` exception.

```java
package com.qualityeclipse.favorites.util;

import java.io.*;
import java.net.*;
import org.eclipse.jface.action.*;
import org.eclipse.jface.resource.*;
import org.eclipse.swt.*;
import org.eclipse.swt.program.*;
import org.eclipse.swt.widgets.*;
import com.qualityeclipse.favorites.*;
import com.qualityeclipse.favorites.dialogs.*;

public class OpenBrowserAction extends Action
{
    private URL url;

    public URL getURL() {
        return url;
    }

    public void setURL(URL url) {
        this.url = url;
    }

    public void setURL(String href) {
        this.url = newURL(href);
    }

    static boolean mailtoFailed = false;

    public static URL newURL(String href) {
        URL newURL = null;
        try {
            newURL = new URL(href);
        }
```

```
        catch (MalformedURLException e) {
            if (href.startsWith("mailto:")) {
                if (!mailtoFailed) {
                    mailtoFailed = true;
                    FavoritesLog.logError(
                        "mailto protocol is unsupported: ["
                            + href
                            + "] "
                            + e.getMessage(),
                        e);
                }
            }
            else
                FavoritesLog.logError(
                    "Invalid URL spec: " + href, e);
        }
        return newURL;
    }
}
```

Next, add the worker methods to this class that open the browser or create an email message. The browse(...) methods are static and thus can be used by themselves, without creating an instance of OpenBrowserAction. The asyncShowError(...) method ensures that exceptions are logged on the current thread and displayed to the user on the UI thread (see Section 4.2.5.1, "Display," for more on the UI thread).

```
static boolean isBrowserOpen;

public void run() {
    browse(getURL());
}

public static void browse(URL url) {
    if (url != null)
        browse(url.toExternalForm());
}

public static void browse(final String href) {
    if (href == null)
        return;

    // Windows
    if (SWT.getPlatform().equals("win32")) {
        Program.launch(href);
        return;
    }
    // non-Windows
    Thread launcher = new Thread("Browser Launcher") {
        public void run() {
            try {
                if (isBrowserOpen) {
```

```
                  Runtime.getRuntime().exec(
                     "netscape -remote openURL("
                        + href
                        + ")");
               }
               else {
                  Process p =
                     Runtime.getRuntime().exec(
                        "netscape " + href);
                  isBrowserOpen = true;
                  try {
                     if (p != null)
                        p.waitFor();
                  }
                  catch (InterruptedException e) {
                     asyncShowError(
                        "Failed to open browser on " + href,
                        e);
                  }
                  finally {
                     isBrowserOpen = false;
                  }
               }
            }
            catch (IOException e) {
               asyncShowError(
                  "Unable to open browser on " + href,
                  e);
            }
         }
      };
      launcher.start();
   }

   public static void asyncShowError(
      final String msg,
      final Throwable ex) {

      FavoritesLog.logError(msg, ex);
      final String title = FavoritesPlugin.getDefault()
         .getDescriptor().getLabel();
      final Display display = Display.getDefault();
      display.asyncExec(new Runnable() {
         public void run() {
            Shell shell = display.getActiveShell();
            new ExceptionDetailsDialog(
               shell, title, null, msg, ex
            ).open();
         }
      });
   }
```

Tip: The platform-specific code that appears above is inherently more fragile than less specific Java code, so see *www.qualityeclipse.com/util/browser* for the latest notes and code.

This action can now be used in our **Favorites** product, replacing the existing addWebButtonToToolBar() method (see Section 15.4.2) with a revised version that uses OpenBrowserAction:

```
private void addWebButtonToToolBar() {
   OpenBrowserAction helpAction =
      new OpenBrowserAction();
   helpAction.setURL("http://www.qualityeclipse.com");
   helpAction.setToolTipText("Open a Web page");
   helpAction.setImageDescriptor(
      ImageDescriptor.createFromFile(
         FavoritesView.class,
         "web.gif"));
   getViewSite().getActionBars()
      .getToolBarManager().add(helpAction);
}
```

We can also add a toolbar button that creates an email message in the user's default email client. Use "%0A" when specifying the email's content to create separate lines.

```
private void addEmailButtonToToolBar() {
   OpenBrowserAction emailAction =
      new OpenBrowserAction();
   emailAction.setURL(
      "mailto:info@qualityeclipse.com"
         + "?Subject=Question"
         + "&Body=My question is ..."
         + "%0ASecond line"
         + "%0AThird line.");
   emailAction.setToolTipText("Send an email");
   emailAction.setImageDescriptor(
      ImageDescriptor.createFromFile(
         FavoritesView.class,
         "mail.gif"));
   getViewSite().getActionBars()
      .getToolBarManager().add(emailAction);
}
```

This does not send the message, but signals the email client to create the message with the specific information so the user can review and send it. The code above creates an email message that looks something like this:

```
To: info@qualityeclipse.com
Subject: Question
My question is ...
Second line
Third line.
```

> **Tip:** Not all systems or browsers support all `mailto` options. For a complete listing of what can be encoded in a `mailto` request, google "mailto syntax" or see the following: *www.qualityeclipse.com/util/mailtoSyntax.htm*

20.4.2 *LaunchURL*

The `org.eclipse.help.ui.browser.LaunchURL` class provides another mechanism for opening a browser. This action delegate, part of the `org.eclipse.help.ui` plug-in, can be used to add a workbench menu (see Section 6.2.3, "Defining a menu item and toolbar button") that opens a browser on a predefined Web page (reading the code, this action appears to have cross-platform support, but we've only tried this on Windows). For example, in our **Favorites** product, we could add a new action to our top-level **Favorites** menu by adding the following declaration to our plug-in manifest:

```
<extension point="org.eclipse.ui.actionSets">
   <actionSet
      label="Favorites ActionSet"
      visible="true"
      id="com.qualityeclipse.favorites.workbenchActionSet">

      … existing declarations here…

      <action
         label="Open browser on QualityEclipse website"
         class="org.eclipse.help.ui.browser.LaunchURL"
         menubarPath="com.qualityeclipse.favorites
            .workbenchMenu/content"
         id="com.qualityeclipse.favorites.browseWebsite"
         url="http://www.qualityeclipse.com">
      </action>
   </actionSet>
</extension>
```

The `url` attribute in the declaration above specifies the Web page displayed by the `LaunchURL` action delegate. Unfortunately, the plug-in manifest editor does not support the url attribute, so you must switch to the **Source** page to hand-code the attribute.

20.5 Types Specified in an Extension Point

All plug-ins declaring an extension point use the `IConfigurationElement.createExecutable(…)` method to instantiate types specified by other plug-ins (see Section 17.3.3, "Creating executable extensions"). For example, given the following declaration, the `org.eclipse.ui` plug-in will instantiate the `myPackage.MyActionDelegate` class when necessary using the `createExecutable(…)` method:

```
<extension point="org.eclipse.ui.actionSets">
   <action
      label="Open Favorites View"
      icon="icons/sample.gif"
      tooltip="Open the favorites view"
      menubarPath="myMenu/content"
      toolbarPath="Normal/additions"
      id="myProduct.openFavoritesView">
      class="myPackage.MyActionDelegate"
   </action>
</extension>
```

In the declaration above, only the fully qualified class name is specified, but there are a few hidden surprises that we will explore in the following sections.

20.5.1   Parameterized types

Types specified in a plug-in manifest are instantiated using their default no argument constructor, so how can they be parameterized? For example, let's suppose that you have two very similar functions in your menu. How should those functions be implemented? One approach is to have two different action delegates, one for each function, with a shared superclass containing all the common behavior. Another approach is to have a single action delegate, but somehow initialize each instance differently to perform a slightly different operation, but how? It is this second option we are going to explore.

Parameterizing a type—passing additional information to that type during its initialization phase—is accomplished by implementing the org.eclipse.core.runtime.IExecutableExtension interface. If additional information is provided in the plug-in manifest, then Eclipse passes the additional information to the type using the setInitializationData method. The information arrives via the setInitializationData method in different formats depending on how it is structured in the plug-in manifest.

20.5.1.1 *Unstructured parameters*

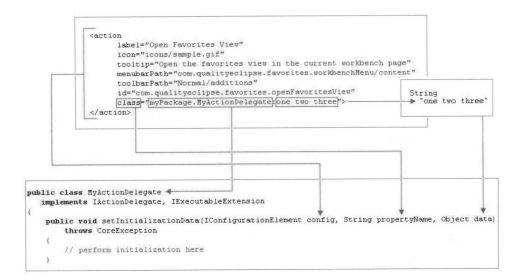

Figure 20–1   IExecutableExtension with unstructured parameters.

One way to parameterize a type is to place a colon at the end of the type's class name followed by a string of information. This string is unstructured and has as much or as little information as desired. Eclipse parses the `class` attribute, using the information before the colon to determine the class to be instantiated, while the information after the colon is passed as a string to the type via the `setInitializationData` method. For example, in the declaration above (see Figure 20–1), the action delegate `myPackage.MyActionDelegate` would be instantiated using its no argument constructor and then the `setInitializationData` method would be called with the string "one two three" as its third argument.

20.5.1.2   Structured parameters

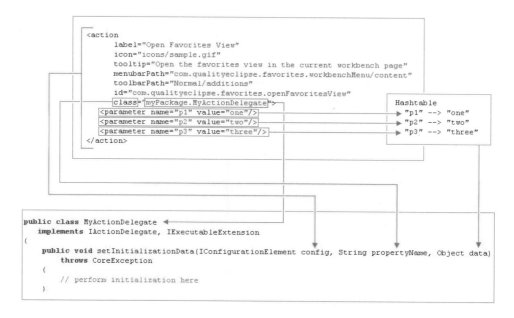

Figure 20–2   IExecutableExtension with structured parameters.

A second more structured approach is to define parameters formally. Rather than all parameters in a single string, each parameter is declared separately as key/value pairs. Each key/value pair is placed into a `java.util.Hashtable` that is passed to the `setInitializationData` method. For example, in the declaration above (see Figure 20–2), the action delegate `myPackage.MyActionDelegate` would be instantiated using its no argument constructor and then the `setInitializationData` method would be called with a `Hashtable` as its third argument. The `Hashtable` would contain the key/value pairs "p1"/"one", "p2"/"two", and "p3"/"three". All other aspects of this second approach are the same as the first.

20.5.2   Referencing a class in a different plug-in

Most of the time, the class being referenced in a plug-in's manifest resides in the same plug-in. But, what if one plug-in manifest references a class that is contained in a JAR file of another plug-in? By default, if the fully qualified class name is specified, then Eclipse makes the assumption that the class resides in the plug-in making the declaration, so it will not find a class that resides in a different plug-in. In this case, precede the class name with the other plug-in's identifier followed by a slash. For example, if "plugin.A" provides an action delegate class that can be parameterized (see Section 20.5.1) and "plugin.B" provides an action that launches a parameterized copy of that class, then the action declaration in "plugin.B" might look something like this:

```
<action
   id="com.qualityeclipse.favorites.showPartInfo"
   label="Show My View Info"
   menubarPath="myMenu/content"
   class="plugin.A/
      plugin.A.actions.ShowPartInfoActionDelegate">
   <parmeter
      name="partClass"
      value="plugin.B.view.myView"/>
</action>
```

20.6 Modifying Eclipse to Find Part Identifiers

Defining new actions using the plug-in manifest editor is a straightforward process, except for finding those pesky identifiers for extending the context menus of specific views and editors (see Sections 6.4, "View Actions," and 6.5, "Editor Actions"). This information is not part of any plug-in manifest and thus must be obtained in some other manner.

One approach is to start with the registerContextMenu method in the org.eclipse.ui.internal.PartSite class and search for references, exploring the code and recording identifiers as you go. This is a viable but time-consuming approach that tends to become out-of-date as new versions of Eclipse arrive.

An alternate approach is a development utility that interrogates the active workbench part, be it an editor or a view, and dumps information about that part, such as the context menu identifiers, to the console. Unfortunately, the API for obtaining this information does not exist (see Section 20.2, "Accessing Internal Code"), so before we create an action delegate, we need to modify the underlying Eclipse system to provide the appropriate accessor methods.

> **Tip:** You can download and install this part information utility from: *www.qualityeclipse.com/util*

20.6.1 Modifying the Eclipse base

To modify the Eclipse base, we first need to check out the appropriate project from the Eclipse repository so that later we can create and submit a CVS patch. Submitting a CVS patch is how such changes are fed back to the Eclipse committers with the hope of getting integrated into the development stream. Connect to the *Eclipse.org* development repository by opening the CVS

Repositories view (see Section 1.8.1, "Getting started with CVS") and selecting **New > Repository Location**. In the **Add CVS Repository** dialog, enter the following values:

Host—"dev.eclipse.org"

Repository Path—"/home/eclipse"

User—"anonymous"

Password—Leave this blank.

Connection Type—"pserver"

Once connected, expand the **HEAD** tree element, locate the org.eclipse.ui.workbench project, and check it out into the workspace (see Section 1.8.2, "Checking out a project from CVS"). Once it is checked out into the workspace, there may be some compile errors in the **Problems** view because the Eclipse being used may be different that the Eclipse against which the plug-in project was compiled. The plug-in project is compiled against the **HEAD** versions of other plug-in projects, but since it cannot locate those other plug-in projects in your workspace, it compiles them against the plug-ins in the current Eclipse installation. There are several different ways to remedy this situation:

- Check out each Eclipse plug-in project on which this plug-in project directly or indirectly depends.

- Download and install (but not launch) the latest Eclipse integration build, then retarget your current Eclipse environment to compile against plug-ins in the integration build using the **Plug-in Development > Target Platform** preference page (see Section 19.2.5, "Editing the same source with different versions of Eclipse"). The disadvantage is that all other plug-in projects in your workspace will also be compiled against this target platform.

- Check out a prior version of the plug-in project that compiles against the plug-ins contained in your Eclipse installation. The disadvantage is that if any of the code you write depends on functionality that has changed between the version you checked out and the **HEAD**, then it may not compile when you submit it back to *Eclipse.org*.

- Do as much as you can using one of the above approaches, then wait until the next Eclipse milestone build is released (they are usually very stable, whereas various integration builds are not). Download, install, and code against the new milestone build and submit your changes as soon as possible back to *Eclipse.org*.

When the `org.eclipse.ui.workbench` project is loaded and its compile errors cleaned up, add the following methods:

org.eclipse.ui.internal.PopupMenuExtender

```
public String getMenuId() {
   return menuID;
}
```

org.eclipse.ui.internal.PartSite

```
public String[] getContextMenuIds() {
   if (menuExtenders == null)
      return new String[0];
   String[] menuIds = new String[menuExtenders.size()];
   int index = 0;
   Iterator iter = menuExtenders.iterator();
   PopupMenuExtender extender;
   while (iter.hasNext()) {
      extender = (PopupMenuExtender) iter.next();
      menuIds[index] = extender.getMenuId();
      index++;
   }
   return menuIds;
}
```

20.6.2   *Creating the global action*

Next, we'll create an action delegate capable of using this newly introduced API. In the plug-in project of your choice (for example, the **Favorites** plug-in project, but not the `org.eclipse.ui.workbench` plug-in project), define a new workbench menu and menu item in the plug-in manifest (see Section 6.2, "Workbench Window Actions"), give it a name similar to "Show Part Info," and associate it with the action delegate shown below. Be sure to modify that plug-in's classpath to reference the `org.eclipse.ui.workbench` project in the workspace rather than the `org.eclipse.ui.workbench` external plug-in, and make sure that `org.eclipse.ui.workbench` is in the required plug-ins list in the plug-in manifest.

```
package com.qualityeclipse.favorites.actions;

import org.eclipse.jface.action.*;
import org.eclipse.jface.viewers.*;
import org.eclipse.ui.*;
import org.eclipse.ui.internal.*;

public class ShowPartInfoActionDelegate
   implements IWorkbenchWindowActionDelegate
{
```

```java
public void init(IWorkbenchWindow window) {
   // ignored
}

public void selectionChanged(
   IAction action,
   ISelection selection) {
   // Ignored.
}

public void run(IAction action) {

   // Determine the active part.
   IWorkbenchPage activePage =
      PlatformUI
         .getWorkbench()
         .getActiveWorkbenchWindow()
         .getActivePage();
   IWorkbenchPart activePart =
      activePage.getActivePart();

   // Search editor references.
   IEditorReference[] editorRefs =
      activePage.getEditorReferences();
   for (int i = 0; i < editorRefs.length; i++) {
      IEditorReference eachRef = editorRefs[i];
      if (eachRef.getEditor(false) == activePart)
         printEditorInfo(
            eachRef,
            (IEditorPart) activePart);
   }

   // Search view references.
   IViewReference[] viewRefs =
      activePage.getViewReferences();
   for (int i = 0; i < viewRefs.length; i++) {
      IViewReference eachRef = viewRefs[i];
      if (eachRef.getView(false) == activePart)
         printViewInfo(eachRef, (IViewPart) activePart);
   }
}

private void printEditorInfo(
   IEditorReference editorRef,
   IEditorPart editor) {

   printPartInfo(editorRef, editor);
}

private void printViewInfo(
   IViewReference viewRef,
   IViewPart view) {

   printPartInfo(viewRef, view);
}
```

```
        private void printPartInfo(
           IWorkbenchPartReference partRef,
           IWorkbenchPart part) {

           println(partRef.getTitle());
           println("  id = " + partRef.getId());
           IWorkbenchPartSite site = part.getSite();
           if (site instanceof PartSite) {
              String[] menuIds =
                 ((PartSite) site).getContextMenuIds();
              if (menuIds != null) {
                 for (int i = 0; i < menuIds.length; i++)
                    println("  menuId = " + menuIds[i]);
              }
           }
        }

        public void println(String line) {
           System.out.println(line);
        }

        public void dispose() {
           // ignored
        }
     }
```

20.6.3 Testing the new utility

Create a new launch configuration (see Section 2.6, "Debugging the Product") and launch a **Runtime Workbench** to test the new utility. Be sure to modify the launch configuration so that it references the `org.eclipse.ui.workbench` project in the workspace rather than the `org.eclipse.ui.workbench` external plug-in. When you activate an editor or view and then select the new global action from the workbench menu bar, you will see the workbench part's information appear in the **Console** view of the **Development Workbench**.

20.6.4 Submitting the change to Eclipse

Once you've created a useful addition to Eclipse and decided that it's of no real commercial value yet it might really help other developers, you can post it to a Web site for others to download and use as they choose, or better still, you can submit it to *Eclipse.org* for inclusion in the Eclipse base via Bugzilla (see Section 20.2.2). For example, if you were to submit these modifications we've made to the Eclipse base (see Section 20.6.1), you would follow these steps:

1. Open a web browser to the Eclipse Bugzilla page (**bugs.eclipse.org/bugs**) and search the submissions to see if someone has already had the same thoughts you have had and already posted a bug or feature request (e.g.,

we've already posted this code to Bug # 39782)

2. If, after a search you've determined that your contribution has not been made by anyone else, then package up your modifications to the Eclipse base code in a CVS *patch*. To create a patch for submission to *Eclipse.org*, select the Eclipse project containing your modifications, right-click and select **Team > Create Patch...** . Note that the patch creation functionality can only be used on a project checked out from a repository such as *dev.eclipse.org* (see Section 20.6.1), and not from imported binary or source plug-in projects.

3. Either create a new bug report and append your patch or append your patch to an existing bug report. Be sure to explain what the patch contains and why you think it should be included in the Eclipse base code.

20.7   Label Decorators

Label decorators visually indicate specific attributes of an object. For example, if a project is stored in a repository, then it has a small cylinder below and to the right of its folder icon in the **Navigator** view. The **Navigator**'s label provider (see Section 7.2.5, "Label provider") returns a folder image, which is then decorated by the repository's label decorator with a small cylinder. The final composite image is then rendered in the **Navigator** view. Label decorators are not restricted to decorating images only; an object's text can be enhanced by adding characters to the beginning or end.

The `org.eclipse.ui.decorators` extension point provides a mechanism for adding new label decorators. Label decorators appear in the **Workbench > Label Decorations** preference page (see Figure 20–3) and can be enabled or disabled by the user. Behavior for a label decorator is supplied by implementing `org.eclipse.jface.viewers.ILabelDecorator`.

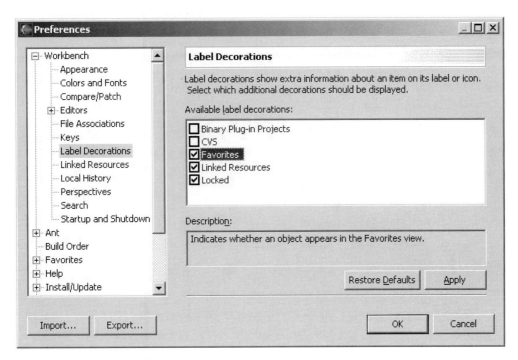

Figure 20–3   The Label Decorations preference page.

20.7.1   *Declaring a label decorator*

In our **Favorites** product, we want to decorate objects in other views that also appear in the **Favorites** view. To accomplish this, we create a new `org.eclipse.ui.decorators` extension (see Section 6.2.1, "Defining a workbench window menu," for an example of creating extensions) with the following values:

adaptable—"true"
A flag that indicates if types that adapt to `IResource` should use this object contribution. This flag is used only if `objectClass` adapts to `IResource`. The default value is `false`.

class—"com.qualityeclipse.favorites.views.FavoritesLightweightDecorator"
A fully qualified name of a class that implements
`org.eclipse.jface.viewers.ILightweightLabelDecorator` (see the next section) or is unspecified if this decorator has only an icon and no behavior (see Section 20.7.3, "Decorative label decorators").

icon—Leave blank.
If the decorator is lightweight and the class is not specified, this is the path to the overlay image to apply (see the next section).

id— "com.qualityeclipse.favorites.favoritesLightweightDecorator"
A unique name that will be used to identify this decorator.

label—"Favorites"
A translatable name that will be used in the **Workbench > Label Decoration** preference page to represent this decorator.

lightweight—"true"
Must be `true`. Heavyweight label decorators are deprecated.

location—"TOP_LEFT"
The location at which to apply the decorator image. Defaults to `BOTTOM_RIGHT`. Valid values include `TOP_LEFT`, `TOP_RIGHT`, `BOTTOM_LEFT`, `BOTTOM_RIGHT`, and `UNDERLAY`.

objectClass—"org.eclipse.core.resources.IResource"
A fully qualified name of a class to which this decorator will be applied. Deprecated in Eclipse 2.1 in favor of the enablement nested element (see Section 6.3.2.5, "The enablement element").

quadrant—Leave blank.
Deprecated in Eclipse 3.0 in favor of **location**.

state—"true"
A flag that indicates if the decorator is on by default. The default value is `false`.

Use the description nested element to provide a brief description of what the label decorator does:

```
<description>
Indicates whether an object appears in the Favorites view.
</description>
```

You can add the `enablement` (see Section 6.3.2.5), the `and`, the `or`, and the `not` subelements (see Section 6.3.2.2, "The visibility element") if you want to more exactly specify when this label decorator is used (see Section 20.7.3 for an example).

20.7.2   ILightweightLabelDecorator

Instances of `ILightweightLabelDecorator` can modify both the image and the text displayed for an object. Create the class that contains the decorative behavior when you specify the `class` attribute by clicking the "..." button at the right of the `class` attribute's value. In the Java Attribute Editor, select **Generate a new Java class**, enter the package name and class name, and click the **Finish** button.

When the initial class has been generated, make sure that the decorator implements ILightweightLabelDecorator and not ILabelDecorator. The decorate(...) method appends "[favorite]" and overlays a small green F to any resource that has been added to the **Favorites** view.

```
package com.qualityeclipse.favorites.views;

import java.util.*;
import org.eclipse.jface.resource.*;
import org.eclipse.jface.viewers.*;
import com.qualityeclipse.favorites.*;
import com.qualityeclipse.favorites.model.*;

public class FavoritesLightweightDecorator
   implements
      ILightweightLabelDecorator,
      FavoritesManagerListener
{
   private static final String SUFFIX = " [favorite]";
   private final ImageDescriptor OVERLAY =
      FavoritesPlugin.imageDescriptorFromPlugin(
         FavoritesPlugin.getDefault()
            .getDescriptor().getUniqueIdentifier(),
         "icons/favorites_overlay.gif");

   public void decorate(
      Object element,
      IDecoration decoration) {

      if (manager.existingFavoriteFor(element) == null)
         return;

      decoration.addOverlay(OVERLAY);
      decoration.addSuffix(SUFFIX);
   }
}
```

The decorator must also notify label listeners when the decoration for an element has changed. In our case, whenever an element has been added to or removed from the **Favorites** view, we notify the listeners that the state of associated resources has changed. This entails registering for change events from the FavoritesManager and then re-broadcasting those events to all registered ILabelProviderListener instances.

```
private final FavoritesManager manager =
   FavoritesManager.getManager();

private final List listenerList = new ArrayList();

public FavoritesLightweightDecorator() {
   // Make sure that the Favorites are loaded.
   manager.getFavorites();
   manager.addFavoritesManagerListener(this);
}
```

```
public void dispose() {
   manager.removeFavoritesManagerListener(this);
}

public void addListener(ILabelProviderListener listener) {
   if (!listenerList.contains(listener))
      listenerList.add(listener);
}

public void removeListener(ILabelProviderListener listener) {
   listenerList.remove(listener);
}

public void favoritesChanged(FavoritesManagerEvent favoritesEvent) {
   Collection elements = new HashSet();
   addResourcesTo(
      favoritesEvent.getItemsAdded(), elements);
   addResourcesTo(
      favoritesEvent.getItemsRemoved(), elements);
   LabelProviderChangedEvent labelEvent =
      new LabelProviderChangedEvent(
         this, elements.toArray());
   Iterator iter = listenerList.iterator();
   while (iter.hasNext())
      ((ILabelProviderListener) iter.next())
         .labelProviderChanged(labelEvent);
}

private void addResourcesTo(
   IFavoriteItem[] items,
   Collection elements) {

   for (int i = 0; i < items.length; i++) {
      IFavoriteItem item = items[i];
      Object res = item.getAdapter(IResource.class);
      if (res != null)
         elements.add(res);
   }
}

public boolean isLabelProperty(
   Object element,
   String property) {

   return false;
}
```

When this behavior is in place, any elements added to the **Favorites** view will have a small "F" overlay and the suffix "[favorite]" in the **Navigator** view (see Figure 20–4).

20.7.3   *Decorative label decorators*

If you simply want to decorate a label by adding a static image in one of the quadrants without any text modifications, then you can specify the `icon` attribute instead of the `class` attribute. If the `class` attribute is not specified, Eclipse places the image specified by the `icon` attribute in the quadrant specified by the `location` attribute. In this case, there is no need to create a class that implements `ILightweightLabelDecorator` because Eclipse provides this behavior for you. A read-only file decorator is one example of a decorative label decorator.

```
<decorator
   lightweight="true"
   location="BOTTOM_LEFT"
   label="Locked"
   icon="icons/locked_overlay.gif"
   state="true"
   id="com.qualityeclipse.favorites.locked">
   <description>
     Indicates whether a file is locked
   </description>
   <enablement>
      <and>
         <objectClass
            name="org.eclipse.core.resources.IResource"/>
         <objectState name="readOnly" value="true"/>
      </and>
   </enablement>
</decorator>
```

With this declaration in the plug-in manifest, a small lock icon appears in the lower left corner of the icon associated with any locked resource (see Figure 20–4).

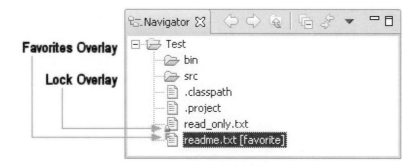

Figure 20–4   Navigator view with Favorites and locked decoration.

20.8   Background Tasks—Jobs API

Long-running operations should be executed in the background so that the UI stays responsive. One solution is to fork a lower priority thread to perform the operation rather than performing the operation in the UI thread. But, how do we keep the user informed as to the progress of the background operation? Eclipse provides a *Jobs API* for creating, managing, and displaying background operations.

In our **Favorites** product, we want to periodically check for the availability of a newer version. Rather than interrupt the user, we want to perform this check in the background and provide the user with non-intrusive progress information as the operation proceeds. To accomplish this, we create NewVersionCheckJob. (Our goal is exercising the Jobs API, not Internet access, so NewVersionCheckJob only simulates a version check.)

```
package com.qualityeclipse.favorites.jobs;

import org.eclipse.core.runtime.*;
import org.eclipse.core.runtime.Preferences.*;
import org.eclipse.core.runtime.jobs.*;
import com.qualityeclipse.favorites.*;
import com.qualityeclipse.favorites.preferences.*;

public class NewVersionCheckJob extends Job
   implements IFavoritesPreferences
{
   private NewVersionCheckJob(String name) {
      super(name);
   }

   protected IStatus run(IProgressMonitor monitor) {

      // Simulate check for new version.
      monitor.beginTask("check for new version", 20);
      for (int i = 20; i > 0; --i) {
         monitor.subTask("seconds left = " + i);
         try {
            Thread.sleep(1000);
         }
         catch (InterruptedException e) {
            // Ignored.
         }
         monitor.worked(1);
      }
      monitor.done();

      // Reschedule job to execute in 2 minutes.
      schedule(120000);

      return Status.OK_STATUS;
   }
}
```

The user will control this operation via a new checkbox on the **Favorites** preference page, so first we add a new constant to the IFavoritesPreferences (see Section 12.2.4, "Favorites preference page"):

```
public static final String
   FAVORITES_NEW_VERSION_CHECK_PREF =
      "favorites.newVersionCheck";
```

Next, we expose this new preference on the **Favorites** preference page by adding a new checkbox. This entails a new field plus additional code at the end of the createFieldEditors() method (see Section 12.2.4).

```
private BooleanFieldEditor newVersionCheckEditor;

public void createFieldEditors() {
   … original code here …
   newVersionCheckEditor =
      new BooleanFieldEditor(
         FAVORITES_NEW_VERSION_CHECK_PREF,
         "Periodically check for new version"
            + " of Favorites product (simulated)",
         getFieldEditorParent());
      addField(newVersionCheckEditor);
}
```

Now we want to tie the new version check job to this preference by adding a preference listener to NewVersionCheckJob. The preference listener either schedules or cancels the job depending on the preference setting as specified by the user.

```
private static final String JOB_NAME =
   "Favorites check for new version";

private static NewVersionCheckJob job = null;

public boolean shouldSchedule() {
   return equals(job);
}

private static final Preferences preferences =
   FavoritesPlugin.getDefault().getPluginPreferences();

private static final Preferences.IPropertyChangeListener
   propertyListener =
   new Preferences.IPropertyChangeListener() {
   public void propertyChange(PropertyChangeEvent event) {
      update();
   }
};
```

```
private static void update() {
   if (preferences.getBoolean(
      FAVORITES_NEW_VERSION_CHECK_PREF)) {
      if (job == null) {
         job = new NewVersionCheckJob(JOB_NAME);
         job.schedule();
      }
   }
   else {
      if (job != null) {
         job.cancel();
         job = null;
      }
   }
}
```

Next, we create additional methods that are called by `FavoritesPlugin` when the plug-in starts up and shuts down:

```
public static void startup() {
   preferences
      .addPropertyChangeListener(propertyListener);
   update();
}

public static void shutdown() {
   preferences
      .removePropertyChangeListener(propertyListener);
}
```

When all of this is in place, selecting the **Periodically check for new version of Favorites product (simulated)** checkbox on the **Favorites** preference page will cause the new version check operation to be periodically performed. Feedback to the user is automatically provided as part of the Jobs API through the **Progress** view (see Figure 20–5). The "**% done**" shown in the **Progress** view is based on the total work specified in the `beginTask(...)` method and the number of units worked is based on calls to the `worked(...)` method. The "seconds left = n" is specified by calling the `subTask(...)` method (see Section 9.4.1, "IProgressMonitor").

Figure 20–5   Progress view for a background operation.

20.9   Plug-in ClassLoaders

Most of the time we can easily ignore ClassLoaders, knowing that as long as our classpath is correct—or in our case, the dependency declaration in the plug-in manifest (see Section 2.3.1)—class loading will happen automatically, without our intervention. But what if we want to load classes that are not known when a plug-in is compiled? Information about code developed by the user in the workspace is accessible via the JDT interfaces such as ICompila-tionUnit, IType, and IMethod, but it is not normally on a plug-in's classpath and thus cannot be executed. Normally, this is a good thing, because code under development can throw exceptions, or under rare circumstances, crash Eclipse without any warning. The Eclipse debugger (see Section 1.10, "Introduction to Debugging") executes user-developed code in a separate VM to avoid these problems, but it is a heavyweight, involving the overhead of launching a separate VM and communicating with it to obtain results. If you need a quick way to execute user-developed code in the same VM as Eclipse and are willing to accept the risks involved in doing so, then you need to write a ClassLoader.

To illustrate and test our ClassLoader, we first declare a new action in the **Favorites** plug-in manifest to appear in the top-level **Favorites** menu (see Section 6.2.3):

```
<extension point="org.eclipse.ui.actionSets">
   <actionSet
      label="Favorites ActionSet"
      visible="true"
      id="com.qualityeclipse.favorites.workbenchActionSet">
      ...
   <action
        class="com.qualityeclipse.favorites.actions
           .ExecuteMethodActionDelegate"
        label="Execute method"
        menubarPath="com.qualityeclipse.favorites
           .workbenchMenu/content"
        id="com.qualityeclipse.favorites.executeMethod"/>
      </actionSet>
   </extension>
```

The ExecuteMethodActionDelegate obtains the selected Java method, loads the type declaring the method, instantiates a new instance of that type, and prints the result of executing the method to the **Console** view. For simplicity, the selected method must be public with no arguments.

```
package com.qualityeclipse.favorites.actions;

import java.lang.reflect.*;
import org.eclipse.jdt.core.*;
```

```java
import org.eclipse.jface.action.*;
import org.eclipse.jface.viewers.*;
import org.eclipse.ui.*;
import com.qualityeclipse.favorites.*;
import com.qualityeclipse.favorites.util.*;

public class ExecuteMethodActionDelegate
    implements IWorkbenchWindowActionDelegate
{
    ISelection selection;

    public void init(IWorkbenchWindow window) {
    }

    public void selectionChanged(
        IAction action,
        ISelection selection) {

        this.selection = selection;
    }

    public void run(IAction action) {
        System.out.println(executeMethod());
    }

    private String executeMethod() {
        if (!(selection instanceof IStructuredSelection))
            return "No Java method selected";
        Object element =
            ((IStructuredSelection) selection)
                .getFirstElement();
        if (!(element instanceof IMethod))
            return "No Java method selected";
        IMethod method = (IMethod) element;
        try {
            if (!Flags.isPublic(method.getFlags()))
                return "Java method must be public";
        }
        catch (JavaModelException e) {
            FavoritesLog.logError(e);
            return "Failed to get method modifiers";
        }
        if (method.getParameterTypes().length != 0)
            return "Java method must have zero arguments";
        IType type = method.getDeclaringType();
        String typeName = type.getFullyQualifiedName();
        ClassLoader loader =
            new ProjectClassLoader(type.getJavaProject());
        Class c;
        try {
            c = loader.loadClass(typeName);
        }
        catch (ClassNotFoundException e) {
            FavoritesLog.logError(e);
            return "Failed to load: " + typeName;
        }
```

```
            Object target;
            try {
                target = c.newInstance();
            }
            catch (Exception e) {
                FavoritesLog.logError(e);
                return "Failed to instantiate: " + typeName;
            }
            Method m;
            try {
                m = c.getMethod(
                    method.getElementName(),
                    new Class[] {});
            }
            catch (Exception e) {
                FavoritesLog.logError(e);
                return "Failed to find method: "
                    + method.getElementName();
            }
            Object result;
            try {
                result = m.invoke(target, new Object[] {
                });
            }
            catch (Exception e) {
                FavoritesLog.logError(e);
                return "Failed to invoke method: "
                    + method.getElementName();
            }
            return "Return value = " + result;
        }

    public void dispose() {
    }
}
```

The ExecuteMethodActionDelegate uses ProjectClassLoader to load the selected class into the **Favorites** plug-in to be executed. This ClassLoader locates the class file using the project's Java build path, reads the class file using standard java.io, and creates the class in memory using the superclass' defineClass(...) method. It is not complete as it only loads source-based classes; loading classes from a JAR file or reference project is left as an exercise for the reader.

```
package com.qualityeclipse.favorites.util;

import java.io.*;
import org.eclipse.core.resources.*;
import org.eclipse.core.runtime.*;
import org.eclipse.jdt.core.*;
import com.qualityeclipse.favorites.*;

public class ProjectClassLoader extends ClassLoader
{
```

```java
private IJavaProject project;

public ProjectClassLoader(IJavaProject project) {
   if (project == null
      || !project.exists()
      || !project.isOpen())
     throw new IllegalArgumentException(
         "Invalid project");
   this.project = project;
}

protected Class findClass(String name)
   throws ClassNotFoundException {

   byte[] buf = readBytes(name);
   if (buf == null)
      throw new ClassNotFoundException(name);
   return defineClass(name, buf, 0, buf.length);
}

private byte[] readBytes(String name) {
   IPath rootLoc = ResourcesPlugin
      .getWorkspace().getRoot().getLocation();
   Path relativePathToClassFile =
      new Path(name.replace('.', '/') + ".class");
   IClasspathEntry[] entries;
   IPath outputLocation;
   try {
      entries = project.getResolvedClasspath(true);
      outputLocation =
         rootLoc.append(project.getOutputLocation());
   }
   catch (JavaModelException e) {
      FavoritesLog.logError(e);
      return null;
   }
   for (int i = 0; i < entries.length; i++) {
      IClasspathEntry entry = entries[i];
      switch (entry.getEntryKind()) {

         case IClasspathEntry.CPE_SOURCE :
            IPath path = entry.getOutputLocation();
            if (path != null)
               path = rootLoc.append(path);
            else
               path = outputLocation;
            path = path.append(relativePathToClassFile);
            byte[] buf = readBytes(path.toFile());
            if (buf != null)
               return buf;
            break;

         case IClasspathEntry.CPE_LIBRARY:
         case IClasspathEntry.CPE_PROJECT:
            // Handle other entry types here.
            break;
```

```
                  default :
                     break;
               }
            }
         return null;
      }

      private static byte[] readBytes(File file) {
         if (file == null || !file.exists())
            return null;
         InputStream stream = null;
         try {
            stream =
               new BufferedInputStream(
                  new FileInputStream(file));
            int size = 0;
            byte[] buf = new byte[10];
            while (true) {
               int count =
                  stream.read(buf, size, buf.length - size);
               if (count < 0)
                  break;
               size += count;
               if (size < buf.length)
                  break;
               byte[] newBuf = new byte[size + 10];
               System.arraycopy(buf, 0, newBuf, 0, size);
               buf = newBuf;
            }
            byte[] result = new byte[size];
            System.arraycopy(buf, 0, result, 0, size);
            return result;
         }
         catch (Exception e) {
            FavoritesLog.logError(e);
            return null;
         }
         finally {
            try {
               if (stream != null)
                  stream.close();
            }
            catch (IOException e) {
               FavoritesLog.logError(e);
               return null;
            }
         }
      }
   }
```

20.10   OSGi Bundles and the 3.0 Run-time

Open Services Gateway initiative (OSGi at *www.osgi.org*) is an independent, non-profit organization with the mission to define a platform for the dynamic delivery of Java software services to networked devices. Eclipse 3.0 has a new run-time layer based on technology from the OSGi. These changes are being implemented as we write this book, so in this section, we will deliver what we know at this point. The follow excerpt from the equinox run-time Web page sheds some light on why this change is occurring (*dev.eclipse.org/ viewcvs/index.cgi/~checkout~/platform-core-home/runtime/index.html*):

"Eclipse originally used a home-grown runtime model. That is, the runtime model/mechanism was designed and implemented specifically for Eclipse. This was good in that it was highly optimized and tailored. It was less than optimal in that there are many issues which are complicated and having a unique runtime mechanism does not allow us to reuse the work done in other areas (e.g., OSGi, Avalon, JMX, ...). To address this, we went looking for a runtime that has a strong specification, a good component model, supports dynamic behaviour, and is reasonably similar to that of Eclipse.

This last point bears some discussion. While we would like to start with a clean slate and adopt/design a runtime which satisfies everyone's wish list, pragmatically, it must still be possible to run old plug-ins on the new runtime with confidence. That is, the new runtime cannot be so completely different so as to make this difficult/totally inefficient/impossible.

To that end, we have implemented a plug-compatible runtime for Eclipse based on the OSGi specification."

In the new Eclipse 3.0 run-time, OSGi *bundles* are synonymous with today's plug-ins. The new structure places a plug-in's dependency and library information in a *manifest.mf* file and a plug-in's extension information remains in the `plugin.xml` file. It appears that this information is cached in the `<eclipseInstallDir>/configuration` directory; if you install a revised plug-in, you may need to delete the `configuration` directory so that the manifest information is re-cached by the Eclipse run-time.

There are no particular benefits of using the `manifest.mf` file over a single `plugin.xml` file, or vice versa. In fact, it appears that only a few of the plug-ins in Eclipse 3.0 use this new structure at this time. That said, the long-term direction is to use this new structure rather than the single `plugin.xml` file, but not for the Eclipse 3.0 release.

The Eclipse 3.0 run-time includes a compatibility layer that is 99% binary compatible with Eclipse 2.1. This means that plug-ins can continue to provide a `plugin.xml` file and the compatibility layer will automatically extract dependency and library information from that file as if it was defined in the `mani-`

`fest.mf` file. There are only a couple of differences that might need to be taken into account:

- Similar to the **Favorites** product discussed in this book, you may need to add both the `org.eclipse.osgi` and `org.eclipse.core.runtime` plug-ins to the list of required plug-ins (see Section 2.3.1, "The plug-in manifest")

- The `org.eclipse.core.runtime.ILibrary` interface is deprecated and will eventually be removed. The corresponding `IPluginDescriptor.getRuntimeLibraries()` method only works for "legacy" plug-ins and not for newer plug-ins.

To create a new bundle project with this new structure, select **File > New > project** to open the **New Project** wizard; in the wizard, select **Plug-in Development > Bundle Project**. Most of the bundle project wizard pages are similar to if not the same as pages in the plug-in project wizard (see Section 2.2, "Creating a Plug-in Project").

For more information about this new OSGi-based run-time layer and porting 2.x plug-ins to 3.0, start at the Eclipse Core home page:

(*www.eclipse.org* > **projects** > **The Eclipse Project** > **Platform** > **Core**) or use the following direct links:

Core—home:
dev.eclipse.org/viewcvs/index.cgi/~checkout~/platform-core-home/main.html

Core—development resources:
dev.eclipse.org/viewcvs/index.cgi/~checkout~/platform-core-home/dev.html

Core—run-time document:
dev.eclipse.org/viewcvs/index.cgi/~checkout~/platform-core-home/runtime/index.html

Core—porting from 2.x to 3.0:
dev.eclipse.org/viewcvs/index.cgi/~checkout~/platform-core-home/runtime/adoption.html

OSGi Alliance—home:
www.osgi.org/

20.11   Conclusion

Throughout this book, we have provided in-depth discussion of the complete process involved in building a commercial-quality Eclipse plug-in. To us, "commercial-quality" means going above and beyond the minimal requirements needed to integrate with Eclipse. To that end, we have tried to present numerous suggestions and examples intended to help you take your plug-in to the next level. If you have followed the guidelines presented in this book, you will also be in a good position to submit your plug-in to IBM for RFWS certification.

We hope that you found this book to be both informative and useful. We also hope that you will use it as a reference to improve the plug-ins that you create, whether they are high-quality, open source, or commercial offerings.

APPENDIX A

Eclipse Plug-ins and Resources

The widespread availability and adoption of Eclipse has spawned an entire cottage industry devoted to adding new features to the environment. As of this writing, there are more than 500 plug-ins available to extend Eclipse in almost any conceivable direction. These range from high-quality, commercial, and open source offerings to not-so-high-quality experiments. In working with Eclipse over the last several years, we have identified (and in some cases, created for ourselves) a number of very useful Eclipse add-ons.

A.1 Plug-ins

The following list of plug-ins—some commercial, some open source, some expensive, some very inexpensive or free—represents our short list of plug-ins that you should seriously take a look at. All of these are very high-quality and very well-respected in the Eclipse community.

A.1.1   CodePro Studio

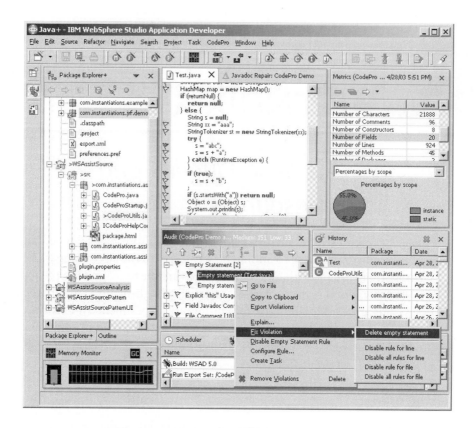

URL: *www.instantiations.com/codepro/*

CodePro Studio (available for $999, with a non-commercial version available
for $99) adds more than 500 enhancements to Eclipse in the areas of best
practices, code quality, developer productivity, and build management. Key
features include code audit, metrics, Javadoc repair, design patterns, dependency analyzer, export sets, Ant integration enhancements, task scheduler, and
team collaboration tools.

* Code audit catches more than 400 audit violations with full support for
  Ant scripts and headless operation. Dynamic code audit mode catches
  errors as they occur, while built-in "quick fix" integration automatically
  fixes most violations. Easily add your own audit rules via an Eclipse
  extension point and exchange audit rule sets with other developers. Generate detailed audit reports in multiple formats.

* Code metrics have drill–down capability and trigger points.

- The project/package dependency analyzer graphically examines cycles and closures. It generates detailed dependency reports and metrics.

- Support for design patterns (all 23 "Gang of Four" plus many others).

- Javadoc repair tool.

- Spell-checker for comments, identifiers, literals, properties, and XML files.

- Enhanced **JUnit Test Case** wizard.

- Color-enhanced Java views.

- Java **History** view.

- Modified **Types** and **Members** views.

- VisualAge Java-style views and perspective.

- Ant script wizard and enhanced Ant tasks.

- Powerful task scheduler for Eclipse scripting.

- Many editor enhancements.

- **Memory Monitor** view.

- Preferences import/export/exchange tool.

- Global workspace administration.

- Inter-workspace messaging.

- Eclipse-based (Koi) collaboration server.

A.1.2   EclipseProfiler

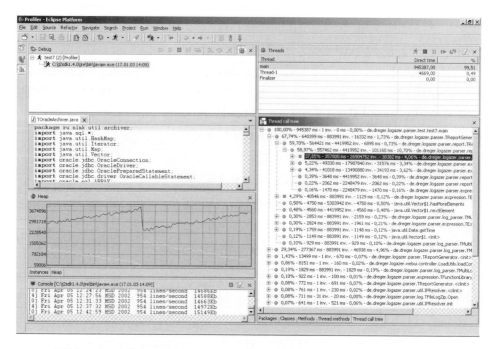

URL: *sourceforge.net/projects/eclipsecolorer/*
This is a free Eclipse plug-in that provides Java profiling tools. It allows a Java developer to tune the performance of his or her Java programs all within the comfort of Eclipse. Key features include:

- Tomcat CPU profiling
- Tomcat heap profiling
- JBoss profiling
- WebLogic profiling
- Resin profiling
- CPU profiling

A.1.3   EclipseUML

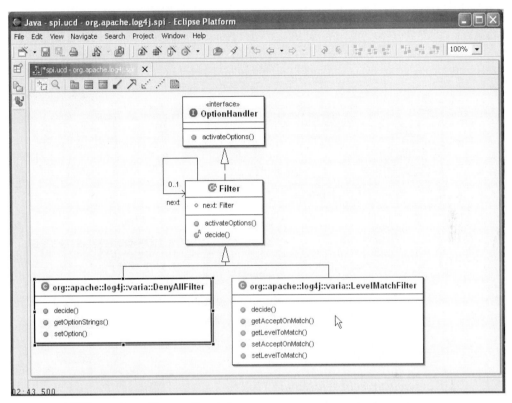

URL: *www.eclipseuml.com/*

EclipseUML is a visual modeling tool, natively integrated with Eclipse and CVS. It is capable of managing hundreds of simultaneous connections and is therefore suitable for large software development projects. Key features of the free edition include:

- Live bi-directional code and model synchronization

- Native Graphical Editor Framework (GEF) integration

- Native Eclipse Modeling Framework (EMF) integration

An Enterprise version (available for $1990) adds the following features:

- Complete Java Version 2 Enterprise Edition (J2EE) lifecycle.

- Complete database modeling lifecycle.

- Open API and UML profiles are being merged and will offer a unique opportunity to fully customize your applications.

A.1.4   MyEclipse Enterprise Workbench

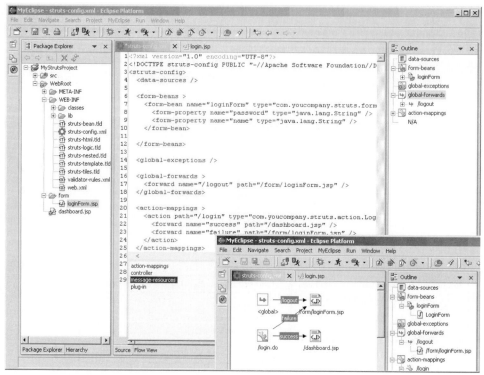

URL: *www.myeclipseide.com/*

MyEclipse Enterprise Workbench (available for $29 via yearly subscription) is a completely integrated product extension for Eclipse and offers a full-featured J2EE IDE based on the Eclipse platform. MyEclipse supports the full development lifecycle (code, deploy, test, and debug) for JavaServer Pages (JSP), Enterprise JavaBeans (EJB), XML, and Struts. Its main features include:

- Smart editors with code completion and syntax coloring for JSP, HTML, Struts, XML, Cascading Style Sheets (CSS), and J2EE deployment descriptors.

- XML editing with smart code completion, DTD caching for offline support, and an outline navigation viewer

- Struts support via a configuration editor with code completion and a layout flow viewer.

- JSP syntax validation and native JSP debugging, plus full support for JSR045.

- Step-through debugging for included JSP files.

- JSP rendering.
- Support for the JSP 2.0 expression language.
- Customizable creation templates for JSPs HTML, XML, servlets, and applets.
- Integrated browser for real-time rendering.
- XDoclet support.
- Creation of Web, EAR, and EJB projects.
- Java project-to-Web project enablements.
- WAR, JAR, and EAR import and export.
- EJB wizards.
- Sync-on-demand, or automated deployment of applications to integrated servers.
- Archive-based deployment (EAR and WAR).
- Over 20 application server connectors, including Bejy Tiger, JBoss, Jetty, Jonas, JRun, Oracle, Orion, Resin, Tomcat, WebLogic, and WebSphere.
- Integrated controls for starting and stopping servers.
- Full hot-swap debugging support for deployed applications.

A.1.5   SWT Designer & Swing Designer

URL: *www.swt-designer.com/*

SWT Designer is a powerful and easy-to-use two-way Java GUI designer based on Eclipse SWT technology. Swing Designer is a companion tool designed to edit Swing applications. Key features of the free version include:

- Implements what you see is what you get (WYSIWYG) GUI editing with native SWT and Swing controls by dragging and dropping composites, layouts, and controls.

- When implemented as a two-way tool, Designer directly generates Java code that can be changed in the graphical editor or directly in source. All changes made directly to the source code will be reflected in the graphical designer.

- Uses only pure SWT and Swing classes, resulting in zero overhead in run-time. There are no special libraries added to projects.

- Contains a handy property editor for easy and intuitive property editing. All changes will be immediately displayed in the code editor and in the graphical designer.

- Displays a component tree, which makes navigation through components much easier.

- Includes SWT applications and JFace dialog creation wizards.

- Fully supports all SWT and Swing controls.

- Fully supports SWT grid, fill, and row layout managers as well as Swing border, flow, grid, card and box layout managers.

- Seamlessly integrates with the Eclipse workbench. Just unpack it and restart Eclipse.

- Allows testing of UIs on-the-fly without compiling by clicking one button.

- Is fully integrated with the Eclipse help system.

The Pro version (available for $199) adds the following features:

- Fully supports all JFace dialogs and viewers.

- Includes JFace applications and JFace viewer creation wizards.

- Has visual menu design support.

- Includes SWT form layout and Swing grid bag layout support with intelligent layout assist and dynamic snap points.

- Supports all Swing layout managers in SWT for easy Swing-to-SWT conversion.

- Allows a user to select and edit multiple widgets simultaneously.

- Creates and embeds custom composites and groups.

- Morph widgets from one type into another.

- Defines custom widget templates.

A.1.6   XMLBuddy

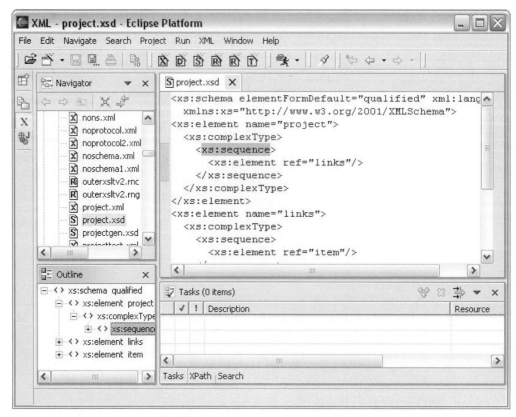

URL: *www.xmlbuddy.com/*

XMLBuddy is the ultimate XML editor for Eclipse supporting XML, DTD, XML schema, RELAX NG, RELAX NG compact syntax, and XSLT. Key features of the free edition include:

- User-configurable syntax coloring for XML and DTD.
- Dynamic code assist for XML driven by DTD or current document contents.
- Dynamically updated outline (tree) view.
- Generates DTD from example XML document.
- Validates XML documents with DTDs or XML schemas.
- Automatically validates XML in background while user edits.
- Formats XML documents, on command or while user edits (auto-flow).

The Pro version (available for $35) adds the following features:

- User-configurable syntax coloring and code assist for XML schema, RELAX NG, RELAX NG compact syntax, and XSLT.

- Dynamic code assist for XML driven by XML schema, RELAX NG, or RELAX NG compact syntax.

- Specialized editors for XML schema, RELAX NG, RELAX NG compact syntax, and XSLT, providing code assist and validation based on built-in schemas.

- Generates XML instance from DTD or XML schema, RELAX NG, or RELAX NG compact syntax schema.

- Converts between DTD, XML schema, RELAX NG, or RELAX NG compact syntax in both directions.

- Applies XSLT transformations.

- Automatically validates DTD, XML schema, RELAX NG, and RELAX NG compact syntax in background while user edits.

- Opens definition in DTDs, XML schemas, or RELAX NG schemas (XML or compact syntax).

A.2   Resources

The following is a short list of Web links for Eclipse-related plug-ins, projects, and information. First, there is the *Eclipse.org* Web site, which should always be your first stop for Eclipse-related information. Following that are a few of the larger sites providing Eclipse-related information and lists of plug-ins. At the end is a smattering of sites containing plug-ins, projects, notes, and information of varying quality that caught our eye.

A.2.1   Eclipse.org

www.eclipse.org/—The place to start concerning Eclipse and Eclipse-related technology for downloads, documentation, articles, mailing lists, and more. There are four main projects at *Eclipse.org* that are further divided into subprojects:

- **The Eclipse Project**—The primary platform and its tools
- Platform—Frameworks and common services
- JDT—Java development tools
- PDE—Plug-in development environment

- **The Eclipse Tools Project**—Secondary tools for Eclipse
- CDT—C/C++ development tools
- COBOL—A fully functional COBOL IDE
- EMF—A Java/XML framework for generating models
- GEF—Graphical editor framework
- Hyades—Framework for automated software quality tools
- UML2—Framework for UML 2.0 modeling tools
- VE—Visual editor; Framework for creating GUI builders
- **The Eclipse Technology Project**—Eclipse-based technology
- AJDT—AspectJ development tools project
- Equinox—Platform run-time configurations for Eclipse
- ECESIS—Eclipse Community Education Project
- Generative Model Transformer—Tools for model-driven software development
- Koi—Fine-grained collaborative services framework
- Stellation—Configuration management system (SCM)
- WSVT—Web service validation tools
- XSD—An XML schema reference library
- **The Eclipse Web Tools Platform Project**—Web tools for Eclipse

The *Eclipse.org* Web site also has a community page (*www.eclipse.org/community/index.html*) that lists upcoming events, courses, and links to related Web sites containing more information on Eclipse.

A.2.2   *Eclipse Plug-in Central*

www.eclipseplugincentral.com—A site dedicated to supporting the growth of the Eclipse community by helping developers locate, evaluate, and acquire plug-ins that can help them deliver their projects faster, better, and cheaper. Eclipse Plug-in Central (EPiC) adds value by offering marketplace updates, reviews, ratings, news, forums, community listings for products and services, and support for the Eclipse Foundation.

A.2.3   *Eclipse plug-in site*

www.eclipse-plugins.info/—A site containing lists of plug-ins sliced and diced by category and hit count (a very rough popularity statistic). Each plug-in has a short description, a place for anyone to comment, statistics, and a link to the plug-in's home page.

A.2.4   Eclipse wiki wiki

eclipsewiki.swiki.net/—A wiki wiki site containing information about Eclipse gleaned from newsgroups, mailing lists, and the like. The availability of this site has been unpredictable, but when available, it contains a wealth of information.

A.2.5   EclipseCon

www.eclipsecon.org/index.htm—The Web site for information about the EclipseCon technical conference.

A.2.6   ANTLR plug-in for Eclipse

antlreclipse.sourceforge.net/—A plug-in providing support for the parser generator ANTLR, including an editor and builder.

A.2.7   Bugzilla plug-in

kered.org/project-eclipse_bugzilla_plugin.html—Proof-of-concept for integrating Bugzilla into Eclipse. Looks promising, but we have not tried it.

A.2.8   Coloring editor

www.gstaff.org/colorEditor/—A free syntax color highlighting editor for Eclipse that uses JEdit's syntax highlighting mode files. There are several other projects and plug-ins on this site, including cSpy and a widget/plug-in inspector.

A.2.9   Eclipse Easter eggs

mmoebius.gmxhome.de/eclipse/eclipse.htm—A list of links and resources for Eclipse, plus a page of Eclipse Easter eggs for fun.

A.2.10   IBM Alphaworks on Eclipse

www.alphaworks.ibm.com/eclipse—A site filled with Eclipse-related technology and articles from the IBM Alphaworks labs.

A.2.11   IBM Eclipse research

www.research.ibm.com/eclipse/—A source of information regarding IBM grants and programs centered on Eclipse-based technology.

A.2.12   PHP plug-in for Eclipse

sourceforge.net/projects/phpeclipse—An open source plug-in providing support for PHP, structured query language (SQL), HTML, and Jtidy. It includes syntax highlighting, command completion, and a preview of pages.

A.2.13   QNX's Momentics

www.qnx.com/products/ps_momentics/—An IDE build on Eclipse for writing code around a real-time OS. We have never used it, but others have recommended it.

A.2.14   QuickShare: XP programming for Eclipse

www.scs.carleton.ca/~skaegi/cdt/—A lightweight code sharing plug-in for XP-like pair programming in a distributed environment.

A.2.15   Sangam: XP programming for Eclipse

sangam.sourceforge.net/—Another code sharing plug-in for XP-like pair programming in a distributed environment.

A.2.16   Wiki editor for Eclipse

www.teaminabox.co.uk/downloads/wiki/index.html—Build your own local wiki pages using this wiki editor integrated into Eclipse. Provides syntax coloring, link traversal, wiki spaces, and more.

APPENDIX B

The Ready for IBM WebSphere Studio Validation Program

IBM WebSphere Studio is IBM's open, comprehensive, multi-language development environment for WebSphere. There are four main products in the WebSphere Studio family: Site Developer, Application Developer, Application Developer—Integration Edition, and Enterprise Developer. There are also many toolkits that add tools for particular components of WebSphere and other IBM middleware (e.g., Voice Toolkit for WebSphere Studio). Customers use a mix of the core products and toolkits depending on the components of the WebSphere platform and other middleware used in their applications. The products and toolkits are generally supported on both Microsoft Windows and Linux systems.

WebSphere Studio is built on the open source Eclipse tools platform, which provides a complete extensibility architecture. Eclipse plug-in tools products from IBM Business Partners can thus integrate tightly to WebSphere Studio and extend WebSphere Studio with the Business Partner tool's unique capabilities. To assist Business Partners in integrating their plug-ins, IBM offers the WebSphere Studio Workbench, a package of the Eclipse platform and additional Eclipse and IBM components used to build WebSphere Studio products. The WebSphere Studio Workbench is available as a free download (*www.developer.ibm.com/websphere/workbench.html*) for any IBM Partner-World for Developers (PWD) member. The WebSphere Studio Workbench may also be redistributed with Business Partners' plug-in products under the included WebSphere Studio Workbench license agreement.

However, for customers to obtain value from a Business Partner plug-in, the plug-in must install safely into WebSphere Studio and interoperate well

793

with the Eclipse platform and other plug-ins. The plug-in must also support the common Eclipse/WebSphere Studio UI and common Eclipse/WebSphere Studio behaviors.

The RFWS software validation program defines integration criteria for plug-ins integrating to WebSphere Studio via the Eclipse platform and components. Compliance with these criteria can help assure your customers that your plug-in product meets WebSphere Studio standards for installation, interoperation, and UI.

The RFWS software validation program is part of IBM's family of "Ready for" technical validation programs (*www.developer.ibm.com/tech/validation*). Any IBM Business Partner that is a member of PWD may validate their plug-in products to the RFWS criteria and join the RFWS program. Business Partners may then use the "Ready for IBM WebSphere Studio" mark with any validated product as visible confirmation of the product's validation to the integration criteria. Use of the mark enables Business Partners to differentiate their RFWS-validated offerings from their competition and enables a shorter sales cycle through increased customer confidence and reduced customer evaluation time.

RFWS is also the gateway to a variety of incremental co-marketing resources to help program members extend their marketing reach. These benefits include RFWS presence at trade shows and IBM road shows, a listing of validated products on the *RFWS Plug-in Central* Web site (*www-106.ibm .com/developerworks/websphere/downloads/plugin/*), and Business Partner content in newsletters and IBM sales flashes.

Trademarks

The following terms are registered trademarks of International Business Machines Corporation in the United States, other countries, or both:

IBM

PartnerWorld

WebSphere

Microsoft and Windows are trademarks of Microsoft Corporation in the United States, other countries, or both.

Other company, product, and service names may be trademarks or service marks of others.

INDEX